EXERCISE PSYCHOLOGY

Janet Buckworth, PhD

The Ohio State University

Rod K. Dishman, PhD

The University of Georgia

Human Kinetics

Library of Congress Cataloging-in-Publication Data

Buckworth, Janet, 1953-
   Exercise psychology / Janet Buckworth, Rod K. Dishman.
     p. cm.
   Includes bibliographical references and index.
   ISBN 0-7360-0078-X
    1. Exercise--Psychological aspects. 2. Physical fitness--Psychological aspects. I.
Dishman, Rod K. II. Title.

   RA781 .B83 2001
   613.7'1--dc21

                           2001039262

ISBN-10: 0-7360-0078-X
ISBN-13: 978-0-7360-0078-9

Acquisitions Editor: Michael S. Bahrke, PhD; **Developmental Editors:** Jennifer Clark and Melissa Feld; **Assistant Editors:** Susan C. Hagan and Laurie Stokoe; **Copyeditor:** Joyce Sexton; **Proofreader:** Sarah Wiseman; **Indexer:** Gerry Lynn Messner; **Permission Manager:** Dalene Reeder; **Graphic Designer:** Fred Starbird; **Graphic Artist:** Denise Lowry; **Photo Manager:** Leslie A. Woodrum; **Cover Designer:** Andrea Souflée; **Photographers:** Leslie A. Woodrum unless otherwise noted, Tom Roberts (pp. 12; 121; 139, left; and 235), Charles E. Moody (p. 330, top), Marlee Stewart (p. 330, bottom); **Art Managers:** Carl D. Johnson and Craig Newsom; **Illustrator:** International Composition Corporation; **Printer:** Edwards Brothers

Printed in the United States of America   10 9 8 7 6 5 4 3

The paper in this book is certified under a sustainable forestry program.

Human Kinetics
Web site: www.HumanKinetics.com

United States: Human Kinetics, P.O. Box 5076, Champaign, IL 61825-5076
800-747-4457
email: humank@hkusa.com

Canada: Human Kinetics, 475 Devonshire Road Unit 100, Windsor, ON N8Y 2L5
800-465-7301 (in Canada only)
email: info@hkcanada.com

Europe: Human Kinetics, 107 Bradford Road, Stanningley, Leeds LS28 6 AT, United Kingdom
+44 (0) 113 255 5665
email: hk@hkeurope.com

Australia: Human Kinetics, 57A Price Avenue, Lower Mitcham, South Australia 5062
08 8372 0999
e-mail: info@hkaustralia.com

New Zealand: Human Kinetics, P.O. Box 80, Torrens Park, South Australia 5062
0800 222 062
e-mail: info@hknewzealand.com

information 01603 773114
email: tis@ccn.ac.uk

21 DAY LOAN ITEM

Please return <u>on or before</u> the last date stamped above

A fine will be charged for overdue items

 CITY COLLEGE NORWICH

To my husband, Chuck Moody, for his encouragement, support, and love; to the memory of my parents, Sigmund and Lois Buckworth, for nurturing my curiosity and faith; and to Lucy and Springer, the dogs, for their infectious enthusiasm for exercise and for making me laugh.

Janet Buckworth

To serious students.

There is nothing so fatiguing as the eternal hanging on of an uncompleted task.

—William James in Henry James (Ed.) 1926.
The Letters of William James.
Boston: Little Brown, p. 249.

Rod K. Dishman

Contents

Preface   ix
Acknowledgments   xiii

Part I   Introduction and Basic Concepts   1

Chapter 1   Foundations of Exercise Psychology   3

Dualism Versus Monism   4
Biological Foundations   6
Cognitive Foundations   7
Behavioral and Social Foundations   8
Subdiscipline or a Field of Study?   9
Contemporary Exercise Psychology   10
An Overview of Physical Activity and Mental Health   11
An Overview of Physical Activity Behavior   14
Summary   15
Suggested Readings   15
Web Sites   15

Chapter 2   Basic Concepts in Exercise Psychology   17

General Concepts   17
Psychological Constructs   18
Multidimensional Scales   22
Covariance Modeling   25
Defining Physical Activity and Fitness   28
Measuring Physical Activity   30
Research Issues   34
Summary   38
Suggested Readings   39
Web Sites   39

Chapter 3 Behavioral Neuroscience 41

Section 1: The Neural Network 42
Section 2: Neurotransmitters 53
Section 3: Brain Cellular and Molecular Biology 58
Section 4: Animal Behavior Models 63
Section 5: Measuring Brain Activity 64
Summary 72
Suggested Readings 72
Web Sites 72

Part II Exercise and Mental Health 73

Chapter 4 Stress 75

Background and Definitions 75
Does Exercise Reduce Stress? 79
Physiological Mechanisms of the Stress Response 80
Contemporary Views: Exercise Research 86
Summary 89
Suggested Readings 89
Web Sites 89

Chapter 5 Affect, Mood, and Emotion 91

Definitions of Terms 92
A Short History of Emotion 96
Contemporary Views of Affect and Emotion 98
Neuroanatomy of Affect and Emotion 99
Factors Influencing the Effects of Exercise on Affect 102
Research on Exercise and Affect 104
Psychophysiological and Behavioral Assessment of Affect, Mood, and Emotion 107
Mechanisms 112
Hazards of Exercise? 113
Summary 114
Suggested Readings 114
Web Sites 114

Chapter 6 Anxiety 115

Prevalence and Social Impact 115
Definitions 116
Types of Common Anxiety Disorders 116
Effects of Exercise 118
Mechanisms 124

Summary   129
Suggested Readings   130
Web Sites   130

Chapter 7   Depression   131

Prevalence and Social Impact   131
Clinical Description   132
Effects of Exercise   133
Mechanisms   144
Summary   152
Suggested Readings   152
Web Sites   153

Chapter 8   Self-Esteem   155

The Self-System   155
Theories and Models   157
Factors Influencing Self-Esteem   158
Measurement   162
Exercise and Self-Esteem   166
Mechanisms   171
Distorted Body Image and Exercise   172
Summary   174
Suggested Readings   175
Web Sites   175

Chapter 9   Sleep   177

Prevalence and Impact of Sleep Disturbances   177
Brief History of Sleep Research   178
Definitions: What Is Sleep?   179
Measuring Sleep   181
Research on Exercise and Sleep   181
Mechanisms   186
Summary   188
Suggested Readings   188
Web Sites   188

Part III   The Psychology of Physical Activity Behavior   189

Chapter 10   Determinants of Exercise and Physical Activity   191

Classification of Determinants   192
Issues in Research   208

Summary   209
Suggested Readings   209
Web Sites   209

Chapter 11   Theories of Behavior Change   211

Behaviorism   213
Cognitive Behaviorism   215
Social Cognitive Theory   216
Bandura's Self-Efficacy Theory   218
Stage Theories   219
Other Theories Applied to Exercise and Physical Activity   223
Issues in Application of Theories of Exercise Behavior   225
Summary   226
Suggested Readings   227
Web Sites   227

Chapter 12   Interventions to Change Physical Activity Behavior   229

Overview   229
Intervention Context   230
Specific Strategies   239
Why Can't We Keep People Active? Mediators and Intervention Effectiveness   251
Summary   253
Suggested Readings   253
Web Sites   253

Chapter 13   Perceived Exertion   255

History   256
Psychophysics and Perceived Exertion   257
Comparing People   262
Signals to Perceived Exertion   265
The Sensory Nervous System   265
Physiological Mediators   268
Psychological and Social-Cultural Influences   273
Perceived Exertion: The Final Common Pathway   276
Practical Use of Ratings of Perceived Exertion   277
Summary   283
Suggested Readings   283
Web Sites   284

Glossary   285
Bibliography   298
Index   320
About the Authors   330

Preface

Exercise psychology is the study of the brain and behavior in physical activity and exercise settings. It is a new field, but it is based on old ideas. The ancient Greek physician Hippocrates, considered the father of medicine, recommended physical activity for the treatment of mental illness. William James, the father of American psychology, stated in 1899 that ". . . muscular vigor will . . . always be needed to furnish the background of sanity, serenity, and cheerfulness to life, to give moral elasticity to our disposition, to round off the wiry edge of our fretfulness, and make us good-humored and easy of approach."

However, it was not until the late 1960s and early 1970s that a systematic body of research related to exercise psychology began to accumulate. The key progenitor of that research was William P. Morgan, who established the ergopsychology (i.e., work psychology) laboratory at the University of Wisconsin in 1970. This was nearly 100 years after William James began conducting experiments at Harvard University in 1875 and Wilhelm Wundt, the father of psychology, established the first psychology laboratory at the University of Leipzig in 1879. Morgan later founded and served as the first president of Division 47, Exercise and Sport Psychology, of the American Psychological Association (APA) in 1986, nearly 100 years after Wundt's student Stanley Hall founded the APA in 1892.

Though subjective experience is the defining feature of psychology that distinguishes it from other disciplines such as physiology and sociology, areas of modern psychology vary in their emphasis on physiological, behavioral, cognitive, or social questions and methods. Hence, several subdisciplines exist in psychology. Notable among these are biological psychology, behavioral neuroscience and comparative psychology, behaviorism, and social psychology. Because exercise psychology uses the traditions of each of these subdisciplines to study physical activity, it is an interdisciplinary field of study rather than a subdiscipline of psychology. Moreover, exercise psychology has roots in exercise science, which itself is an interdisciplinary field of study. Because exercise psychology is concerned with mental health and health-related behaviors within both clinical settings and population bases, it also encompasses approaches from the fields of psychiatry, clinical and counseling psychology, health promotion, and epidemiology.

A unique feature of this text is its presentation of the biological foundations of exercise psychology within the broader contexts of cognitive, social, and environmental influences. In our view, social psychology has dominated the early years of exercise psychology. Though the social agency and impact of exercise are important, the biological basis of brain and behavior is equally important but has been neglected by most researchers in exercise psychology and by most textbooks that have been used in the field. This has been unfortunate given the indisputable fact that physical activity and exercise are uniquely biological in nature; no other behaviors occur for prolonged periods at a metabolic cost several times that of rest. Also, it is instructive to remember that Wilhelm Wundt was trained in physiology and medicine before he established the field of experimental psychology.

The U.S. Congress designated the 1990s as the Decade of the Brain. For the new millennium, the American Psychological Association has initiated the Decade of Behavior, an interdisciplinary effort to promote the importance of behavioral and social science research modeled after the Decade of the Brain. We have strived in this book to balance the biological foundations of brain and behavior with theory and knowledge derived from the behavioristic, cognitive, and social approaches used to study key topics in the field of exercise psychology.

The social significance of exercise and other forms of physical activity in developed nations has never been greater. Sedentary lifestyles are a burden to the public's health in the United States, accounting for an estimated 200,000 deaths annually from coronary heart disease, type II diabetes mellitus, and colon cancer. The combined effect of physical inactivity and excess caloric intake accounts for an estimated 300,000 deaths each year and is a key contributor to the 50% increase in obesity prevalence among U.S. adults during the past decade. Growing evidence also supports that physical inactivity is a risk factor for poor mental health, especially depression, which the World Health Organization has projected will be second only to cardiovascular disease as the world's leading cause of death and disability by the year 2020.

The promotion of leisure-time physical activity has emerged as an important initiative for public health and quality of living in many economically developed nations. The 1996 U.S. Surgeon General's report on physical activity and health provides a consensus on the benefits of physical activity for chronic diseases and mental well-being, and the subsequent 1999 Surgeon General's report on mental health acknowledged a role for physical activity as part of mental hygiene. *Healthy People 2010*, the national health goals of the U.S. Department of Health and Human Services, includes several objectives that collectively call for increasing physical activity in all segments of the U.S. population. Similar policy statements about physical activity's importance in maintaining health have been issued during the decade in Australia, Canada, and Europe.

Nonetheless, leisure-time physical activity levels have remained below recommendations in nations that keep population statistics about physical activity. In the United States, insufficient levels of leisure-time physical activity have not changed appreciably during the past decade. Despite widespread attempts to increase physical activity in the general population, 30% to 40% of U.S. adults aged 18 years or older do not participate in leisure-time physical activity. Only 25% participate at a level sufficient to reduce premature mortality or maintain cardiorespiratory fitness. Less than two-thirds of American youth participate in vigorous physical activity three or more days a week.

This book is dedicated to understanding how leisure-time physical activity can enhance the quality of people's lives. It contains 13 chapters (a baker's dozen), which are organized around key topics that relate to the mental health benefits of physical activity and how to promote them. Part I contains 3 chapters that provide an introduction to the field of exercise psychology and its basic concepts. Chapter 1 includes a historical account of physical activity in the development of the field of psychology since antiquity; a description of the biological, cognitive, behavioral, and social foundations of modern-day exercise psychology; and a brief overview of the social significance of the promotion of physical activity for mental well-being. Chapter 2 defines basic concepts and approaches used to measure psychological variables, physical activity, and physical fitness. Chapter 3 provides a rudimentary discussion of behavioral neuroscience. That chapter should be especially helpful to students who have not yet been exposed to the biological bases of psychology. It will provide important background information for a fuller understanding of the topics in part II, which covers exercise and mental health by presenting 6 separate chapters devoted to the topics of stress; affect, mood, and emotion; anxiety; depression; self-esteem; and sleep. Common themes covered for each topic are clinical features and treatment; public health burden; descriptive and experimental evidence that physical activity is of benefit; and discussion of plausible explanations for that benefit, including possible biological mechanisms. Part III deals with important aspects of understanding the determinants of physical activity behavior, theories of behavior change, interventions that can be used to increase leisure-time physical activity, and perceived exertion.

Exercise Psychology is intended to be used as the first textbook for upper-level undergraduates as well as graduate students who are studying exercise psychology for the first time. We also hope that it is effective as a companion text in broader-based sport psychology courses that include exercise psychology topics.

A textbook's worth is judged by how well it serves teaching. A good introductory textbook should raise many questions and be able to answer most of them. It should also instruct beginning students that knowledge is a growing, evolving process. We think that key ingredients to effective teaching are common to an effective text: up-to-date, logically sequenced content illustrated by clear examples.

Keeping those ingredients in mind, we have strived to avoid merely presenting annotated outlines of the hot, trendy topics found in research journals or reviews of research literature rendered uninformative after being watered down for non-researchers' comprehension. We have selected classical and contemporary topics that have a sufficient body of research to justify inclusion in a textbook, and we feel capable of presenting these topics with a degree of authority. Other topics, such as pain and cognitive function, would be of interest to many people, but we do not include them in this edition because they are either emerging areas of study or we do not feel qualified to address them yet. Perhaps we will have the good fortune to include those and other emerging topics in a subsequent edition of the book. Our guiding motive has been to provide a text that has fidelity with the science but translates that science in ways that will engage, inform, and challenge serious students.

Acknowledgments

We must accept the blame when a book falls short of its goals. When a book succeeds, credit should be shared with the many people who offered material for the book, ideas about what that material should be or how it would be best presented, and an environment that permitted the book to become a reality. Those people include our mentors, including former and present students, who impart to us questions and tactics for attacking them; colleagues, who motivate us to raise the standard of excellence; and our families, who nurture us and sustain our pursuit of that excellence. Special thanks go to Patrick O'Connor, Shawn Youngstedt, Dane Cook, J.B. Crabbe, Rob Motl, Heather O'Neal, Erica Jackson, Carson Smith, and Jacquie D. Van Hoomissen for enhancing the book's scholarship.

We also gratefully acknowledge the helpful advice given by peer reviewers and the people of Human Kinetics, including Mike Bahrke, acquisitions editor; Jenn Clark and Melissa Feld, developmental editors; Susan C. Hagan, assistant editor; Dalene Reeder, permission manager; as well as Joyce Sexton, the copyeditor who valiantly aided our pursuit of the English language.

I

Introduction and Basic Concepts

The psychology of exercise and the psychology of sport both involve examining the relationships between physical movement and beliefs and emotions. However, a primary purpose of sport psychology is to examine the effects of such variables in order to enhance performance or satisfaction in competitive sport. Exercise psychology examines beliefs and emotions, but a primary purpose is to enhance the adoption and maintenance of regular exercise and its effects on psychological well-being. The psychological and biological consequences of physical activity are studied to determine the effects of exercise on mental health. In this part of the book, we place contemporary exercise psychology in perspective with a brief history highlighting notable personalities and studies that made critical linkages between exercise physiology and psychological variables. We discuss tools for a better understanding of exercise psychology research and of subsequent chapters—describing, for example, how psychological variables are measured and analyzed. Definitions and concepts that illustrate the scope and potential of exercise psychology are also presented, and the distinction between physical activity and exercise is discussed. This treatment of exercise psychology differs from others in its emphasis on the biological basis of behavior. A chapter on the physiological structures and functions that link exercise and mental health supports a clearer understanding of subsequent sections on physiological mechanisms, and highlights the importance of biological contributions to behavior and mood.

1

Foundations of Exercise Psychology

Exercise psychology has emerged as a field of study on the basis of a steadily building wave of research conducted during the past 20 years. The ideas underlying the field, however, have been around much longer. Throughout recorded history, philosophers and physicians have written about the connection between mental health and exercise. The relationship between exercise and psychological well-being was recognized as early as the fourth century B.C. Herodicus, an early Greek physician who practiced gymnastic medicine (one of the branches of ancient Greek medicine that relied on exercise) based his therapies on vigorous exercise (Kollesch 1989; Phillips 1994). Hippocrates, considered the father of medicine, acknowledged the value of exercise for both physical and mental illness, though he was initially critical of Herodicus for relying on exercise as a treatment (Littre 1842). Benefits of exercise were noted by early Jewish religious writers. Writings in the old testament of the Holy Bible encouraged purposeful physical activity: "She girdeth her loins with strength, and strengtheneth her arms. She perceiveth that her gain is good. Strength and honour are her clothing; and she shall rejoice in time to come" (Prv. 31: 17-18, 25). "The desire of the slothful killeth him; for his hands refuse to labour" (Prv. 21: 25). "A slothful man is compared to a filthy stone, and every one will hiss him out to his disgrace" (Apocrypha 22: 1). Rabbi Moses ben Maimun (also known as Maimonides), the Jewish philosopher of the 12th century and physician to Saladin, the Sultan of Egypt, provided a strong recommendation for physical activity when he wrote in the Mishneh Torah, "Anyone who lives a sedentary life and does not exercise . . . even if he eats good foods and takes care of himself according to proper medical principles—all his days will be painful ones and his strength will wane" (Maimonides [1199] 1990). Maimonides also recognized the psychological benefits of physical activity. "The most beneficial of all types of exercise is physical gymnastics to the point that the soul rejoices" (Maimonides [1199] 1990).

Robert Burton, the British theologian and scholar, warned about the risks of a sedentary lifestyle in *The Anatomy of Melancholy*, "Opposite to Exercise is Idleness or want of exercise, the bane of body and minde, . . . one of the seven deadly sinnes, and a sole cause of Melancholy" (1632). Those early ideas extended into the 20th century. For example, the effects of exercise on depression were reported in 1905 (Franz and Hamilton 1905); and during the 1930s, exercise was included in recreational therapy for psychiatric patients (Campbell and Davis 1939-1940). A psychobiological perspective on mechanisms to explain the effect of exercise was proposed in 1926, when it was suggested that exercise benefits individuals who are depressed by stimulating nerves and increasing glandular secretion (Vaux 1926).

The ancient Greeks enjoyed and valued physical activity.

Philosophers and physicians have acknowledged the connection between mental health and exercise throughout recorded history.

Dualism Versus Monism

Exercise psychology is defined in part by contemporary questions and approaches toward answering them that have roots in the centuries-old effort by philosophers and early psychologists to explain the nature of the link between mind and body. **Dualism** held that humans have physical bodies and nonphysical souls. Body and mind were viewed as separate, requiring different principles to explain their separate functions. The Greek philosopher Plato was a dualist, asserting a clear distinction between the material world and the soul. The French philosopher, mathematician, and physiologist René Descartes (1596-1650), shown in figure 1.1, also thought that humans were composed of body and soul, but he held that the two components interacted. In *De homine* (i.e., *Treatise of Man*) (Descartes 1972), the first full essay on physiological psychology, completed about 1633, Descartes tried to explain how the soul controlled the body. He believed that the body was a hydraulic machine controlled by a soul that got information from the senses, made decisions, and directed the body by using the brain. To explain reflexive behavior, Descartes proposed that the material body was controlled by the flow of animal spirits from the brain to muscles through hollow tubes (the nerves). The nonmaterial soul

Figure 1.1   Philosopher René Descartes (17th century) conceptualized the human body as a hydraulic machine controlled by a soul.

Provided by the National Library of Medicine.

controlled the body by governing the pineal gland in the brain, which in turn regulated the flow of animal spirits. Descartes' view did not address how a nonmaterial soul could control a material body, or whether the body could affect the soul.

Later, the German philosopher Gottfried von Leibniz (1646-1716) proposed that the body and soul were separate and parallel in function, not interactive. His views laid the philosophical foundation for the emergence of experimental psychology during the mid-to-late 19th century when physicians such as Gustav Fechner (1801-1887), Hermann von

Helmholtz (1821-1894), Wilhelm Max Wundt (1832-1920), and William James (1842-1910) broke from the traditions of medicine and physiology to begin the field of experimental psychology. Fechner, shown in figure 1.2, established the basis for the field of psychophysics in 1850 when he reported that one could scientifically study the link between mind and body by comparing changes in the strength of a physical stimulus, such as light, with changes in the subjective experience of the stimulus, such as the sensation of brightness. Helmholtz, pictured in figure 1.3, pioneered the field of physiological psychology by his research on the perception of sound. He was also the first to measure the speed of nerve conduction. Wundt, once an assistant to Helmholtz, is generally considered the founder of scientific psychology as a discipline separate from medicine and physiology. James is acknowledged as the father of American psychology.

Figure 1.3 German physiologist Hermann von Helmholtz (19th century) pioneered the field of physiological psychology.

Provided by the National Library of Medicine.

Figure 1.2 Gustav Fechner described research methods for studying the connection between mind and body, providing the foundation for the field of psychophysics in 1850.

Psychology Archives—The University of Akron.

Developing about the same time as dualism was the monistic view that a single material principle is adequate to explain reality—that mind and body are the same. **Monism** assumes that the mind exists only by the function of the body and its interaction with the environment. Though Plato's student Aristotle was a dualist, his doctrine of "natural" dualism held that all matter has form, that the soul and the body

constitute a single interdependent entity. The English philosopher Thomas Hobbes (1588-1679), a contemporary of Descartes, extended that view and stated, "all that exists is matter; all that occurs is motion." According to Hobbes, activity of the mind was motion within the nerves and thus would follow the same principles of motion that applied to other matter. Those ideas laid the foundation for regarding mind and body as the same, to be distinguished from the metaphysical soul.

The father of American psychiatry, Benjamin Rush (1746-1813), a signer of the Declaration of Independence, was a monist. He distinguished between moral action (the mind) and moral opinion or conscience; he argued that physical causes, such as size of the brain, heredity, disease, fever, climate, diet, drink, and medicines among other factors, could affect the mind. In 1772, Rush delivered a "Sermon on Exercise" in which he recommended many types of sports and exercises, including dancing, for the young and old to improve the body's strength and health. It is not clear, though, that Rush appreciated a role for exercise in mental health. Indeed, his "relaxation chair" (see figure 1.4) suggests a rather restrained view of physical activity.

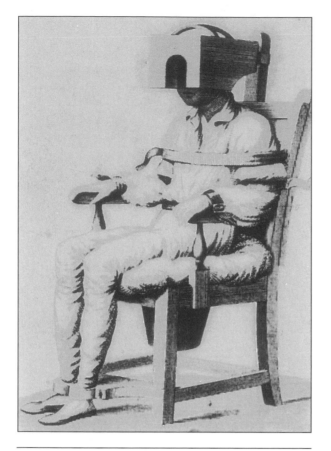

Figure 1.4   Benjamin Rush's relaxation chair.

Provided by the National Library of Medicine.

The brain, and the brain alone, is the source of our pleasures, joys, laughter, and amusement, as well as our sorrow, pain, grief, and tears. It is especially the organ we use to . . . distinguish . . . the bad from the good, and the pleasant from the unpleasant. The brain is also the seat of madness and delirium, of the fears and terrors that assail by night or by day, of sleeplessness . . . of pointless anxieties. (Hippocrates in *Regimen*)

Biological Foundations

The study of exercise has a base in physiology, but it may be surprising for beginning students of exercise psychology to discover that the field of psychology also had its origins in physiology. Wundt, the father of psychology, was trained in medicine and physiology before he established the first psychology laboratory at the University of Leipzig in 1879 (see figure 1.5, a and b). Before that, in 1875, William James

a

Figure 1.5   Wilhelm Max Wundt, known as the father of psychology *(a)*; Wundt in his Leipzig laboratory *(b)*.

Part a: Provided by the National Library of Medicine; part b: Psychology Archives—The University of Akron.

b

was already conducting psychological experiments at Harvard. The **James-Lange theory** of emotion (co-named for a contemporary Danish physiologist) proposed that bodily responses during emotion are the source of the emotional response. Though unsupported by later research, this theory stemmed from a monistic view and stimulated an empirical debate about the biological basis of emotion that continues today, even in exercise psychology.

Wundt's contemporaries were Emil Kraepelin, Sigmund Freud, and Adolf Meyer, leading psychiatrists who supported the application of neuropathology to advance psychiatry, as research in organic pathology contributed to gains in general medicine (Whybrow, Akiskal, and McKinney 1984). In the early 20th century, mainstream psychiatry shifted away from a neurophysiological orientation, although Kraepelin continued to pursue the empirical classification of mental diseases based on pathophysiology. Freud and Meyer shifted toward human experience and introspection to explain and treat psychopathology. However, Meyer later criticized Freud for ignoring the biology of mental disease and introduced the concept of psychobiology to the American Medical Association in 1915 (Winters 1951).

*E*xercise psychology has roots in physiology through its foundation in exercise science and in psychology.

Cognitive Foundations

Wundt was the first scientist to be recognized as a psychologist, probably because he advocated the use of introspection as his primary method of inquiry in the study of perception and elements of the mind. Among his 500 published works was *Principles of Physiological Psychology* (2 vols., 1873-1874). He also founded the first psychological journal, *Philosophische Studien (Studies in Philosophy)*, in 1881. Wundt's ideas were brought to America by an English scientist, E.B. Titchener (1867-1927), who came to Cornell University in 1892. However, it was William James (figure 1.6) who welded the study of consciousness to experimental physiology by expanding the psychophysical methods of Helmholtz and Wundt to link the physiology of perception to symbolic meaning. In 1890, James published the landmark

two-volume text *Principles of Psychology*, which advocated that psychology develop as a cognitive study of consciousness. In his doctrine of relations, James stated that a legitimate scientific psychology must account for both the stream of thought and feeling.

Figure 1.6 William James linked the physiology of perception to symbolic meaning.

Provided by the National Library of Medicine.

Figure 1.7 Charles Darwin, best known for having developed the principle of natural selection, also wrote about the biological basis of emotional expression.

Psychology Archives—The University of Akron.

The writings of Charles Darwin (1809-1882), the English naturalist who formulated the principle of natural selection (figure 1.7), facilitated the monistic view of mind and body unity in modern psychology in two ways. First, Darwin's writings emphasized that all of an organism's features have function; and secondly, his book *The Expression of the Emotions in Man and Animals*, published in 1872, provided a biological view of the basis of emotional expression. Darwin's ideas had a strong impact on the thinking of William James.

Behavioral and Social Foundations

James later focused on the role of attitudes and values in health and disease, and between 1893 and 1896 he taught an advanced graduate seminar on psychopathology at Harvard that influenced the development of scientific psychotherapy. James saw a role for exercise in mental hygiene. In chapter 1, "The Gospel of Relaxation," of his *Talks to Teachers on Psychology: and to Students on Some of Life's Ideals*, he stated the following:

I wish in the following hour to take certain psychological doctrines and show their practical applications to mental hygiene. . . . Consider, for example, the effects of a well-toned *motor-apparatus*, nervous and muscular, on our general personal self-consciousness, the sense of elasticity and efficiency that results. They tell us that in Norway the life of the women has lately been entirely revolutionized by the new order of muscular feelings with which the use of the ski, or long snow-shoes, as a sport for both sexes, has made the women acquainted. Fifteen years ago the Norwegian women were even more than the women of other lands votaries of the old-fashioned ideal of femininity, "the domestic angel," the "gentle and refining influence" sort of thing. Now these sedentary fireside tabby-cats of Norway have been trained, they say, by the snow-shoes into lithe and audacious creatures, for whom no night is too dark or height too giddy, and who are not only saying good-bye to the traditional feminine pallor and delicacy of constitution, but actually taking the lead in every educational and social reform. I cannot but think that the tennis and tramping and

skating habits and the bicycle-craze which are so rapidly extending among our dear sisters and daughters in this country are going also to lead to a sounder and heartier moral tone, which will send its tonic breath through all our American life. I hope that here in America more and more the ideal of the well-trained and vigorous body will be maintained neck by neck with that of the well-trained and vigorous mind as the two coequal halves of the higher education for men and women alike. (James 1899, pp. 199–205)

An influential turn-of-the-century force for social psychological thought was Herbert Spencer, who in 1874 extended Darwin's notions from the biological realm into the social. (It was Spencer, not Darwin, who coined the phrase "survival of the fittest.") Social Darwinism influenced the thinking of many early American psychologists, including William James. It is generally agreed that the first experiment in social psychology was reported in 1897 by American psychologist Norman Triplett, who examined social influences on performance in competitive bicycle racing. Though *Introduction to Social Psychology* by British psychologist William McDougall was published in 1908, it wasn't until the 1924 publication of the text *Social Psychology* by Floyd Allport and the *Handbook of Social Psychology* by Carl Murchison in the 1930s that social psychology was distinguished as an experimental discipline separate from the more naturalistic observational techniques used in sociology. Since German-American psychologist Kurt Lewin popularized the idea in the 1930s that behavior is the product of the interaction between a person and the environment, the studies of attitude measurement and change, group dynamics, social learning and personality, social cognition, aggression, and self-perception have been mainstays of social psychology.

By the early- to mid-20th century, psychoanalysis was the predominant treatment used in psychol-

---

Behaviorism, also known as learning theory or stimulus-response theory, developed empirical principles of behavior by observing consequences of environmental manipulation. Later, cognitive-behaviorism recognized that people's thoughts and feelings can mediate behavior.

ogy and psychiatry, but other perspectives began to take hold. The conditioned reflex studies by the Russian physiologist Pavlov and by American psychologist John Watson and his colleagues, Robert Yerkes and Karl Lashley, followed by the operant conditioning research of Harvard behaviorist B.F. Skinner, laid a foundation for the emergence of "behavior therapy" in the late 1950s. The development of social learning theory (Bandura 1977, 1986) and cognitive behaviorism (Meichenbaum 1977) followed. Biological psychology became mainly limited to research using animals to model the links between brain and behavior, building on Lashley's pioneering work in neuropsychology. Behaviorism fell out of favor in many sectors of psychology, especially Gestalt psychology, because it emphasized behavior and the stimulus-response link to the neglect of the study of consciousness and adaptations by the organism.

The 1960s were dominated by various approaches to psychotherapy that included distinct **models** and techniques. The integration of biological, psychological, and social factors in understanding health and disease was introduced by George L. Engel in his seminal work published in 1977. The modern view of multicausal factors in health and disease has been attributed to Engel's **biopsychosocial model of disease.** This perspective benefited mental health research during the 1990s, which was designated by the U.S. Congress as the "Decade of the Brain." Such an integrated approach is also reflected in *Mental Health: A Report of the Surgeon General*, published in 2000 (United States Department of Health and Human Services), which acknowledged a role for physical activity as part of mental hygiene.

For the new millennium, the American Psychological Association—with endorsement from 50 societies representing the behavioral and social sciences—initiated the "Decade of Behavior," an interdisciplinary effort to promote the importance of behavioral and social science research modeled after the 1990s' "Decade of the Brain." Health is included as one of the five themes of the initiative.

We need to understand the physiological correlates of behavioral responses to exercise.

Today, theoretical advances around the world have led to a rudimentary understanding of how the brain controls thoughts, emotions, and behaviors within different social and environmental settings. Advances in statistical modeling of relationships among social factors and people's introspections have permitted us to form the ideas of the early psychologists into precise social psychology theories useful for understanding and promoting health. Similarly, technological advances in neuroscience, such as the use of microneurography, electrophysiology, microdialysis, nuclear brain imaging, and molecular biology, now permit closer examination of the biological mechanisms of mind and behavior. Thus, the goal of this text is to illustrate the biological foundations of exercise psychology in the study of psychological and behavioral responses to exercise, and to do so within the broader contexts of cognitive, social, and environmental influences.

Social psychology is the study of interpersonal relationships and processes. It deals with the ways in which individuals affect and are affected by other people and by their social and physical environments.

Subdiscipline or a Field of Study?

The term *psychology* was apparently first used around 1530 by a German scholar, Phillip Melanchton. Its original meaning, taken from the Greek *psyche* (soul) and *logos* (study), was the "study of the soul." Later *psyche* was translated as "mind" rather than "soul." To William James, psychology was the "science of mental life," the description and explanation of states of consciousness . . . such "feelings, desires,

---

Biological psychology is the study of brain and behavior using methods of natural science. Physiology, anatomy, genetics, endocrinology, immunology, pharmacology, and molecular biology are applied toward understanding behavior. Responses observed at molecular, synaptic, and neural systems levels of observation are related to integrated behavior (Davis et al. 1988).

cognitions, reasonings, decisions . . . perceptions, emotions" (1890 p. 1). During the past 100 years, **psychology** has evolved as a scientific discipline encompassing the study and application of principles of behavior and mental processes. A **discipline** is defined by unique questions and methods. Hence, though psychology addresses physiological and social aspects of behavior, its central focus on introspection and the individual distinguishes it from the disciplines of physiology and sociology.

> **Health psychology** concerns the scientific understanding of how behavioral principles relate to physical health and illness.

Areas of modern psychology vary in their relative emphasis on physiological, behavioral, cognitive, and social questions and methods. Hence several subdisciplines exist. Notable among these are biological psychology, behavioral neuroscience and comparative psychology, behaviorism, and social psychology. Because exercise psychology uses the traditions of each of these subdisciplines to study physical activity, it may be more properly regarded as an interdisciplinary field of study rather than a subdiscipline of psychology. This view of exercise psychology is also consistent with its roots in exercise science, which itself is an interdisciplinary field that applies the methods and traditions of other disciplines including physiology, medicine, and psychology. Moreover, exercise psychology is concerned with mental health and health behaviors within clinical settings and population bases. Thus it has commonly used approaches from clinical psychology and psychiatry, health promotion, and epidemiology.

> **Behavioral neuroscience** and **comparative psychology** entail the subdisciplines of perception and learning, neuroscience, cognitive psychology, and comparative psychology.

Contemporary Exercise Psychology

Contemporary exercise psychology emerged as a viable field of study over 50 years ago with the publication of the first modern reviews on exercise and mental health topics by Emma McCloy Layman, who was chief psychologist in the Department of Psychiatry at Children's Hospital in Washington, D.C. (e.g., Layman 1960). The past 10 years have witnessed tremendous growth in the number of scientists studying the various areas of exercise psychology. Their roots are in psychology, physical education, and sports medicine, but many are second- and even third-generation descendants of the 1960s-era sport psychologists. A notable "parent" of exercise psychology is William P. Morgan of the University of Wisconsin (figure 1.8), who expanded the application of psychology to physical performance beyond the study of athletes. The foundation for exercise psychology in the 21st century was laid by Dr. Morgan with seminal studies and writings from 1969 to 1979 on depression (Morgan 1969, 1970; Morgan et al. 1970), anxiety (Morgan, Roberts, and Feinerman 1971), hypnosis and perceived exertion (Morgan et al. 1976), exercise adherence (Morgan 1977), and exercise addiction (Morgan 1979b). In addition to establishing psychology as a viable topic in exercise science and physical education, Dr. Morgan promoted exercise psychology within mainstream psychology in the United States. In 1986, he founded and served as the first president of Division 47, Exercise and Sport Psychology, of the American Psychological Association, nearly 100 years after the founding of the association by G. Stanley Hall in 1892.

Figure 1.8   Dr. William P. Morgan.
Provided by Dr. William P. Morgan, the Exercise Psychology Laboratory, University of Wisconsin.

Certainly, other key individuals have been invaluable in the development of the field of exercise psychology. Their contributions are evident throughout this text. Among the early contributors were A.H. Ismail of Purdue University; Herb deVries of the University of Southern California; Robert J. Sonstroem of the University of Rhode Island; Dorothy Harris of Pennsylvania State University; and Daniel M. Landers of Arizona State University, the inaugural editor of *Journal of Sport and Exercise Psychology*. Especially noteworthy are the seminal contributions of Swedish psychophysicist Gunnar Borg, shown in figure 1.9, who pioneered the study of perceived exertion.

Figure 1.9 Dr. Gunnar Borg.
Provided by Dr. Gunnar Borg, Department of Psychology, Stockholm University.

The embryonic development of exercise psychology was captured within the inaugural newsletter of Division 47, Exercise and Sport Psychology, of the American Psychological Association. In describing the goals and purposes of the Division, Founding President William P. Morgan wrote:

Division 47 represents an exciting and quickly developing specialization that cuts across psychology and the sport sciences. Through the Division, scientists and practitioners with a common interest have the opportunity to interact and to further their personal and professional capabilities. . . . The focus of professionals and students in this field of specialization is quite diverse, and scientific inquiry, as well as clinical applications have

historically cut across the interest of many existing divisions. Individuals working in this area come from subspecialties within psychology such as developmental, educational, clinical, counseling, industrial, comparative, physiological, social, personality, hypnosis, motivation, human factors, ergonomics, and health psychology. Although professionals and students in this area represent numerous specialties within psychology, they are bonded together by a common interest in sport and exercise. . . . The term sport can be used as a noun, a verb, or an adjective. For this division, it is used as a noun. This decision follows the European lead where sport can be viewed as competitive athletics; a source of diversion; recreation; or physical activity engaged in for play. In other words, sport involves much more than competitive athletics, and this is the reason why the terms exercise and sport are both included in the Division's title. The terms exercise and sport are intended to broaden the Division's scope. (Morgan 1986, pp. 1–2)

An Overview of Physical Activity and Mental Health

Physical activity can have potent effects on mental health as a function of the exposure (i.e., acute vs. chronic exercise) and the presence and degree of clinical symptoms (i.e., normal psychological health vs. biologically based mood disorders). However, contemporary views of the relationship between physical activity and mental health have been mixed. In 1984, a report from a National Institute of Mental Health panel indicated that there were positive effects from acute and chronic exercise on anxiety and depression (Morgan and Goldston 1987). Even so, five years later, the U.S. Preventive Services Task Force of the U.S. Office of Disease Prevention and Health Promotion concluded that the quality of the available evidence linking exercise with anxiety and depression was poor and that the role of exercise in the primary prevention of mental health problems was poorly understood (Harris et al. 1989). The 1994 *Physical Activity, Fitness, and Health* international consensus text edited by Bouchard, Shephard, and Stephens gives more support to the link between mental health and physical activity. However, the controversy over the strength of the scientific basis for the role of exercise in mental health is illustrated by the omission of any reference to physical activity or exercise in *Practice Guidelines for the Treatment of Patients with Major Depressive Disorders (Revision)* (American Psychiatric Association 2000), although many physicians recommend exercise for their depressed and anxious patients, and by the public health view that the strongest evidence on exercise comes from studies of self-esteem.

Acute and Chronic Exercise: Definitions

Acute exercise is a single, relatively short-lived bout of exercise, such as jogging three miles.

Chronic exercise is exercise carried out repeatedly over time, usually thought of as "regular exercise" or "exercise training" and defined by type of activity, intensity, duration, frequency per week, and the period of time over which activity occurs (i.e., weeks, months).

The U.S. Surgeon General's report on physical activity and health (1996) concluded that regular physical activity reduces feelings of depression and anxiety and promotes psychological well-being.

The long-awaited Surgeon General's report on physical activity and health (1996) provided a consensus on the benefits of physical activity for chronic diseases, such as coronary heart disease and diabetes, but also included statements about the effects of physical activity on mental health. See figure 1.10 for summary statements from this report. Widely distributed research findings from exercise science, exercise psychology, clinical and counseling psychology, and medicine were reviewed to support the conclusions that regular physical activity reduces feelings of depression and anxiety and promotes psychological well-being. In addition to evidence for the prevention and reduction of mild and moderate depression, several longitudinal studies have indicated that a sedentary lifestyle is also a risk factor for depression. It is not clear whether exercise has an effect for individuals who are already in good mental health, but there are general reports of improved sense of well-being. Chronic exercise has been found to improve self-concept and self-esteem, with better improvements in self-esteem for those whose self-esteem is initially low and who value fitness.

The position from the Surgeon General's report supports the use of physical activity as an adjunct treatment for mental health problems. Psychotherapy is expensive and time consuming, and can carry a social stigma in some cultures. Drug treatments are also expensive and can have undesirable aftereffects and side effects. Physical activity as an alternative form of prevention and treatment does not have the complications associated with

© Mark E. Gibson/The Image Finders

Different types of physical activity can provide psychological and physical benefits.

Major Conclusions From the Surgeon General's Report on Physical Activity and Health

- People of all ages, both male and female, benefit from regular physical activity.

- Significant health benefits can be obtained by including a moderate amount of physical activity (e.g., 30 minutes of brisk walking or raking leaves, 15 minutes of running, or 45 minutes of playing volleyball) on most, if not all, days of the week. Through a modest increase in daily activity, most Americans can improve their health and quality of life.

- Additional health benefits can be gained through greater amounts of physical activity. People who can maintain a regular regimen of activity that is of longer duration or of more vigorous intensity are likely to derive greater benefit.

- Physical activity reduces the risk of premature mortality in general, and of coronary heart disease, hypertension, colon cancer, and diabetes mellitus in particular. Physical activity also improves mental health and is important for the health of muscles, bones, and joints.

- More than 60 percent of American adults are not regularly physically active. In fact, 25 percent of all adults are not active at all.

- Nearly half of American youths 12-21 years of age are not vigorously active on a regular basis. Moreover, physical activity declines dramatically during adolescence.

- Daily enrollment in physical education classes has declined among high school students from 42 percent in 1991 to 25 percent in 1995.

- Research on understanding and promoting physical activity is at an early stage, but some interventions to promote physical activity through schools, worksites, and health care settings have been evaluated and found to be successful.

Figure 1.10 The full report can be downloaded from **www.cdc.gov/nccdphp/sgr/pdf/sgrfull.pdf**.

From U.S. Department of Health and Human Services. 1996. *Physical activity and health: A report of the Surgeon General.* Atlanta: U.S. Department of Health and Human Services, Centers for Disease Control and Prevention, National Center for Chronic Disease Prevention and Health Promotion.

psychotherapy or drug treatments, and also offers decreased risk of physical health concerns.

In 1995, the Centers for Disease Control and Prevention and the American College of Sports Medicine issued revised guidelines for level of physical activity to promote health and prevention of disease: at least 30 min of moderate-intensity physical activity accumulated in bouts of 10 min or more on most days of the week (Pate, Pratt, et al. 1995). This recommendation was based on several large-scale, long-term epidemiological studies that showed significant health benefits from moderate amounts of exercise compared to inactivity. There is some concern that this dosage, although suited for currently sedentary individuals, is not a panacea for all medical concerns linked to physical inactivity. Different intensities and modes may be more effective for the prevention and treatment of specific diseases and

Benefits of Physical Activity As a Treatment for Mental Health Problems

1. Self-administration
2. Convenience
3. Low cost
4. Minimal side effects
5. Social acceptability
6. Ancillary physical benefits: increased aerobic endurance, altered body composition, increased muscle tone
7. Decreased risk of physical health concerns: coronary heart disease, colon cancer, type II diabetes mellitus, hypertension, and osteoporosis

disorders, such as obesity and osteoporosis. Physical activity guidelines have not been developed for the promotion of mental health; and although appealing in their simplicity, general recommendations like those that have been applied to physical health will also be shadowed by the issue of dosage specificity. For example, few researchers have attempted to quantify the exercise stimulus necessary to find statistically or clinically significant changes in symptoms of depression. The relationship between exercise dosage and mental health may also vary based on characteristics of the individual and the application of exercise for promotion, prevention, or treatment.

Most Americans do not exercise enough to reap the benefits.

An Overview of Physical Activity Behavior

The established link between physical and mental health and level of physical activity has important implications for public health. The realization of this impact, however, hinges on individuals' adopting and maintaining regular physical activity. Most Americans do not exercise enough to reap the benefits from exercise, and about one-third are sedentary, a proportion that is similar in other industrialized countries. Once people have begun an exercise program, the odds are against their maintaining an active lifestyle. Typically, about 50% of individuals who begin an exercise program drop out within the first six months. Although numerous studies have been conducted to discover interventions that will enhance exercise adherence, this average dropout rate has persisted over the past 20 years. Thus, exercise psychology also encompasses the study of physical activity behavior. Like psychological benefits of exercise, the problem of motivating people to be physically active is not new.

Near the turn of the 20th century, Robert J. Roberts, director of physical education at the YMCA in Springfield, Massachusetts, from 1887 to 1889, said, ". . . I noticed that when I taught . . . more advanced work in gymnastics, athletics, etc., that I would have a very large membership at the first of the year, but that they would soon drop out" (Leonard and Affleck 1947).

In "The Gospel of Relaxation," William James recognized physical inactivity as a challenge to mental hygiene:

I recollect, years ago, reading a certain work by an American doctor on hygiene and the laws of life and the type of future humanity . . . I remember well an awful prophecy that it contained about the future of our muscular system. Human perfection, the writer said, means ability to cope with the environment; but the environment will more and more require mental power from us, and less and less will ask for bare brute strength. Wars will cease, machines will do all our heavy work, man will become more and more a mere director of nature's energies, and less and less an exerter of energy on his own account. So that, if the *homo sapiens* of the future can only digest his food and think, what need will he have of well-developed muscles at all? . . . I cannot believe that our muscular vigor will ever be a superfluity. Even if the day ever dawns in which it will not be needed for fighting the old heavy battles against Nature, it will still always be needed to furnish the background of sanity, serenity, and cheerfulness to life, to give moral elasticity to our disposition, to round off the wiry edge of our fretfulness, and make us good-humored and easy of approach. (James 1899, pp. 205–207)

The ability to change exercise behavior depends on the identification of factors that mediate or influence level of activity, assuming that changing characteristics associated with physical activity will cause corresponding changes in behavior. Knowledge of factors associated with physical *inactivity* can also help to identify high-risk segments of the population and to guide allocation of resources earmarked to increase **exercise adoption** and adherence. Expanding our knowledge of characteristics that influence physical activity in specific populations can support the development of personalized interventions, which can address an emerging trend in consumer behavior—people's desire to be treated as individuals (Miller 1999). Thus, research in exercise behavior must include the identification of exercise determinants as well as the development of interventions to foster adoption and **maintenance.**

Summary

Exercise psychology is an emerging field of study that has a solid foundation in the psychological and biological sciences. Two broad areas of study comprise the psychological effects of acute and chronic exercise and the behavioral dynamics of exercise adoption and maintenance. Physical activity has been shown to affect both physical and mental health, and mechanisms for these psychological effects are likely an interaction among social, psychological, and biological variables. The examination of exercise behavior, and insight into how individuals adopt and maintain regular physical activity in their leisure time, have been grounded in psychological theories of behavior change. The potential impact of exercise interventions on public health is great, considering the low level of activity in most segments of the population and the established links between physical activity and health. While acknowledging the importance of social and environmental context on psychological antecedents and consequences of physical activity, a unique focus of the chapters to follow is the inclusion of perspectives from biological psychology on this uniquely biological behavior commonly known as exercise.

Suggested Readings

Davis, H.P., M.R. Rosenzweig, L.A. Becker, and K.J. Sather. 1988. Biological psychology's relationships to psychology and neuroscience. *American Psychologist* 43: 359–371.

Dishman, R.K. 1986. Exercise compliance: A new view for public health. *Physician and Sportsmedicine* 14 (5): 127–145.

Dishman, R.K. 1998. Physical activity and mental health. In *Encyclopedia of mental health*, ed. H.S. Friedman. Vol. 3. San Diego: Academic Press.

Dishman, R.K. 2000. Introduction. *International Journal of Sport Psychology* 31: 103–109.

Morgan, W.P. 1994a. 40 years of progress: Sport psychology in exercise science and sports medicine. In *40th anniversary lectures.* Indianapolis: American College of Sports Medicine.

Pate, R.R., M. Pratt, S.N. Blair, W.L. Haskell, C.A. Macera, C. Bouchard, D. Buchner, W. Ettinger, G. Heath, A.C. King, A.M. Kriska, A.S. Leon, B.H. Marcus, J. Morris, Jr., R.S. Paffenbarger, K. Patrick, M.L. Pollock, J.M. Rippe, J.F. Sallis, and J.H. Wilmore. 1995. Physical activity and public health: A recommendation from the Centers for Disease Control and Prevention and the American College of Sports Medicine. *Journal of the American Medical Association* 273 (5): 402–407.

Seraganian, P. (Ed.) 1993. *Exercise psychology: The influence of physical exercise on psychological processes.* New York: Wiley.

United States Department of Health and Human Services. 1996. *Physical activity and health: A report of the surgeon general.* Report DHHS publication no. (PHS) 017-023-00196-5. Atlanta: U.S. Department of Health and Human Services, Centers for Disease Control and Prevention, National Center for Chronic Disease Prevention and Health Promotion.

Wozniak, R.H. 1992. *Mind and body: René Descartes to William James.* Bethesda, MD, and Washington, DC: National Library of Medicine and American Psychological Association.

Web Sites

http://serendip.brynmawr.edu/Mind

www.sccu.edu/faculty/ddegelman/amoebaweb/index.cfm?doc_id=862

2

Basic Concepts in Exercise Psychology

One of the easiest ways to inject confusion into a conversation is to use terms that mean different things to each person. For example, "exercise" and "physical activity" are often used interchangeably, but their differences have important implications for understanding exercise psychology. Similarly, the term *stress* is one that most people understand, if vaguely, but it often defies a specific definition. Even among psychologists and psychiatrists, there is confusion about the differences in terms such as *mood, affect,* and *emotion.* We will consider those concepts in detail in later chapters. The purpose of this chapter is to clarify some of the common terms and concepts most relevant to exercise psychology. We pay special attention to the measurement of psychological variables, physical activity, exercise, and fitness. The main goal of the chapter is to aid your understanding, as you read subsequent chapters, of concepts that are abstract to many people. Definition and clarity of terms will also help illustrate some of the challenges of conducting high-quality research on the psychology of exercise. To that end, we introduce general issues about research designs and methodology as a foundation for understanding some of the research discussed in the chapters that follow.

General Concepts

Exercise psychology is the study of the brain and behavior in physical activity and exercise settings. Its main focus has been the psychobiological, behavioral, and social cognitive antecedents and consequences of acute and chronic exercise. It encompasses an analysis of changes in affect, emotions, and moods like anxiety and depression after a single bout of exercise, as well as the assessment of long-term psychological consequences of regular exercise. Exercise psychology also entails the study of the behavior of physical activity, including the psychological, biological, and environmental variables that determine the quality, quantity, and temporal patterns of physical activity.

Exercise psychology includes the study of the psychobiological, behavioral, and social cognitive antecedents and consequences of acute and chronic exercise.

There is extensive empirical evidence that changes in the brain, including the expression of genes, produce changes in behavior and that changes in behavior in turn produce changes in the brain, illustrated in figure 2.1 (Kandel 1998). Thus, an understanding of exercise psychology would be incomplete without an examination of neurobiological systems along with self-reports of subjective experiences and objective descriptions of observable acts. Physical activity, and especially exercise, are biologically based behaviors and thus are well suited for study using a psychobiological model. Psychobiology encompasses the strengths of cognitive and behavioral psychology and a perspective grounded in neuroscience to provide a model for the biological basis of cognition, mood, and behavior.

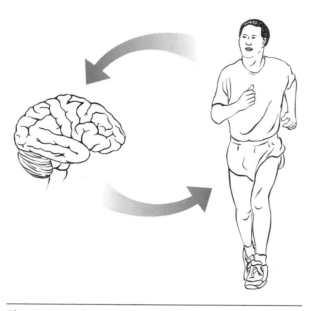

Figure 2.1   The reciprocal relationship between behavior and neurophysiology.

Changes in the brain produce changes in the body, and changes in the body in turn produce changes in the brain.

Nonetheless, a cornerstone of exercise psychology, as for psychology in general, is subjective human experience. So, this chapter begins with a discussion of the definition and measurement of subjective psychological variables, followed by a similar discussion of the measurement of physical activity and fitness. The next chapter will deal with such issues in behavioral neuroscience.

Psychological Constructs

Since its founding by Wundt, Fechner, James, and their contemporaries, psychology has been distinguished from physiology by the measurement of consciousness, for example, of thoughts, judgments, and feelings. Social psychology includes the measurement of judgments people make about themselves and other people. Psychophysics involves measuring judgments people make about their physical environment. Though modern-day psychophysicists have become more interested in comparing people's judgments, the classical approach taken in psychophysics was, and mainly still is, to scale things, not people. This means that the scale of measurement is applied to the thing being judged, not to the person making the judgment; for example, one would measure how foods differ in bitterness and sweetness, not whether people differ in their taste. According to classical psychophysics, differences among people's judgments were error, random fluctuations in sensation. Around the 1920s, psychologists L.L. Thurstone of the University of Chicago and Edward L. Thorndike of Columbia University expanded the use of psychophysical methods to measure social judgments—for example, attitudes—and mental aptitude. They began scaling people. Differences among people were viewed not as error but as real. Concepts such as attitude, personality, and mood were used to describe those differences.

In contrast to psychophysics, which measured consciousness by comparing people's judgments of the characteristic of an object that could also be measured directly (e.g., perceived heaviness vs. weight), this new approach, **psychometrics,** was based on the assumption that unobservable (i.e., latent) psychological variables could be measured indirectly by inference. That inference, though, must be constructed by a logical pattern of associations of **phenomenology** (i.e., people's expression of their experiences) with behaviors, physiological responses, and the social/environmental context in which they occur. For example, a scale or test used to measure depressed mood should include a representative sample of the adjectives in a language that people commonly use to connote varying degrees of hopelessness and despair. Psychometrics is based on a process called **construct** validation, whereby such patterns are established through comparison of different constructs or "traits," using multiple methods of measuring each one (Campbell and Fiske 1959; Cronbach and Meehl 1955; Messick 1989).

Construct Validity

The key steps to measurement of a psychological construct involve demonstrating six principal types of validity: content, factorial, concurrent, criterion, logical, and convergent/discriminant.

▼ Content: The items that compose the test should be representative of the entire known universe of possible items. This ensures that some features of the construct are not omitted and that items better related to other constructs are not included. Researchers usually ensure completeness of content by canvassing experts on the construct and by using focus groups consisting of the types of people who will be taking the test. Content validity is sometimes confused with **face validity,** which implies that a test is valid because it appears valid on its face to most people. The appearance of validity is an important part of acceptance of a test by professionals and the public, but it is a weak scientific standard. Nonetheless, in order for items to have clear meaning they must be chosen so that they match the experiences of the people who will be taking the test.

▼ Factorial: Items that correlate more closely with each other than with other items are identified by a statistical technique known as **factor analysis,** which can be used to determine whether the structure of a test seems consistent with the construct it purports to measure. Exploratory factor analysis (EFA) is strictly empirical; it describes the patterns of correlated responses to items on a test. Confirmatory factor analysis (CFA) ascertains how well the observed pattern of correlated responses fits a predetermined pattern that is based on a theory about what and how many factors are needed to describe the construct. Techniques used to demonstrate factorial validity are discussed later in this chapter because they are a staple of measurement in exercise psychology.

▼ Concurrent: The test scores should be strongly related to other available measures that estimate the construct. For example, rankings of people who complete two tests purportedly measuring anxiety should agree.

▼ Criterion: A person judged to exhibit the key features of a construct according to standardized, expert agreement should score high on a test presumed to measure that construct. For example, someone diagnosed as having a depressive disorder should score higher on a depression scale than a person without a depressive disorder.

▼ Logical: Scores on the test of the construct should change in response to events believed to be causes of change in the construct. For example, a measure of anger should yield higher scores for most people when they are forced to endure frustration, pain, or insults. Likewise, scores on the anger test should be unchanged by situations known to be joyous.

▼ Convergent/Discriminant: Scores on the measure of the construct should be strongly related to behaviors, contexts, and biological responses theorized to be unique components or elicitors of the construct. For example, convergent evidence for the validity of a test of anger would be shown by correspondence with aggressive behavior, menacing facial expression, and increased blood pressure, especially if they occurred in a combative social confrontation. In contrast, scores on a test of anger would not be expected to correlate highly with scores on valid tests of other emotions or with behaviors and biological responses unique to those emotions. Indicators that scores on the test are specific to the construct being measured provide discriminant evidence for construct validity.

Scaling

The Harvard psychophysicist S.S. Stevens defined **scaling** as the assignment of objects to numbers according to a rule. In most psychometric scaling, the objects are text statements, usually statements of attitude, belief, mood, or emotion. A response scale is the method used to obtain responses from people on an instrument. Common approaches include dichotomous scales such as Agree/Disagree, True/False, or Yes/No or ordinal/interval scales ranging, for example, from 1 to 4 or from 1 to 7. However, merely assigning objects or statements to a response scale isn't scaling. Scaling is the development of the measurement instrument. Separately, a response scale is the manner in which responses to each part of the instrument are obtained from respondents.

A controversy that surrounded the emergence of psychometric from classical psychophysical measurement concerned the question whether subjective judgments can be measured as categories, ranks, intervals, or ratios. This issue is discussed in more detail in chapter 13 as it applies to perceived exertion. For now, it is sufficient to consider whether an unobservable, latent construct based on people's self-ratings can be assumed to exist along some continuum or whether it is possible only to place people's judgments into categories that are qualitatively different but not quantifiable.

Quantification requires that subjective judgments can at least be ranked according to frequency, size, strength, and so on. If such rankings are equally distant, they can be measured as intervals. If each interval represents the same proportion of the full range of the measurement scale, the scale measures ratios. If it is possible only to categorize judgments, one could determine that four people held different opinions, but not which person had the strongest or which the weakest. At least, quantification would permit the people to be ranked 1, 2, 3, 4 according to the strength of their opinions. However, ranking would not tell us whether person 4 differed from person 3 as much as person 2 differed from person 1. Interval measurement establishes equal differences, but it does not ensure equal proportions unless the scale has a true zero starting point. The feasibility of a true ratio scale that measures attitudes hinges on the plausibility of someone actually having no opinion (true zero starting point) when he or she says so.

Thorndike, the father of educational measurement, made the following observation in 1904:

If one attempts to measure even so simple a thing as spelling, one is hampered by the fact that there exist no units in which to measure. One may arbitrarily make up a list of words and observe ability by the number spelled correctly. But if one examines such a list one is struck by the inequality of the units. All results based on the equality of any one word with any other are necessarily inaccurate. (Thorndike 1904, p. 7)

Thurstone Scaling

This conundrum of "inequality of the units" was solved, for most practical purposes, by an electrical engineer and psychologist at the University of Chicago named Louis L. Thurstone. He rejected the stimulus-oriented psychology favored by psychophysics and behaviorism and argued for an approach centered on the person. He believed that the focus of psychology should turn from people's judgments of the features of stimuli to the "satisfaction" that people strive for.

Between 1925 and 1932, Thurstone published 24 articles and a book about solutions to the inequality-of-units problem. He showed that scales for measuring subjective variables, such as attitudes, could be constructed from patterns of variations in people's scores according to the normal distribution (Thurstone 1927)—the very thing that psychophysicists had viewed as error! He devised several methods for developing a unidimensional scale, but the method of equal-appearing intervals was the most practical and influential. Based on people's ratings of separate attitude statements, the approach was to order those items according to their scale values, from highest agreement to highest disagreement, and then select items for the final scale that had equal intervals between their response scale values. These were Thurstone's requirements for useful measures:

Unidimensionality—The measurement of any object or entity describes only one attribute of the object measured. This is a universal characteristic of all measurement (Thurstone 1931, p. 257).

Linearity—The very idea of measurement implies a linear continuum of some sort, such as length, price, volume, weight, age. When the idea of measurement is applied to scholastic achievement, for example, it is necessary to force the qualitative variations into a scholastic linear scale of some kind (Thurstone and Chave 1929, p. 11).

Abstraction—The linear continuum which is implied in all measurement is always an abstraction. "...There is a popular fallacy that a unit of measurement is a thing—such as a piece of yardstick. This is not so. ..." (Thurstone 1931, p. 257).

Invariance—"A unit of measurement is always a process of some kind which can be repeated without modification in the different parts of the measurement continuum" (Thurstone 1931, p. 257).

Sample-free calibration—The scale must generalize beyond the group measured. "A measuring instrument must not be seriously affected in its measuring function by the object of measurement. . . . Within the range of objects . . . intended, its function must be independent of the object of measurement" (Thurstone 1928, p. 547).

Test-free measurement—It should be possible to omit several test questions at different levels of the scale without affecting the individual score (measure). ". . .It should not be required to submit every subject to the whole range of the scale. The starting point and the terminal point . . . should not directly affect the individual score (measure)" (Thurstone 1926, p. 446).

Likert, or Summated, Scaling

Likert scaling was developed in the early 1930s by Rensis Likert (pronounced "lickert"), an industrial/

organizational psychologist at the University of Michigan. Like Thurstone scaling, it is a unidimensional scaling method. Each respondent is asked to rate each item on a response scale. For instance, respondents could rate each item on a 1-to-5 response scale like this:

1 = strongly disagree

2 = disagree

3 = undecided

4 = agree

5 = strongly agree

Likert's research examined how many ordinal categories are needed to estimate or predict a single underlying variable believed to be continuous and normally distributed. Just adding a response scale like the one shown to a set of items is not Likert scaling. Items must be selected that will yield a normally distributed response (i.e., a mean of zero with a standard deviation of 1 when the raw scores for each item are converted to a standard normal score).

Likert did not consider the number of choices an important issue (Likert 1932), rather if five alternatives are used, it is necessary to assign values from 1 to 5 with the 3 assigned to the undecided option. There are several other possible response scales (1 to 7; 1 to 9; 0 to 4). All have a middle value that is usually labeled Neutral or Undecided. This helps to approximate a normal distribution of responses. Some response scales use a forced-choice format with an even number of responses and no middle neutral or undecided choice. That forces the respondent to choose between the agree end and the disagree end of the scale for each item. The final score for the respondent on the scale is the sum of his or her ratings for all of the items: a summated scale.

There is no consensus about how many rating categories are best for the scaling of psychological constructs. If there are too few, a test item won't have enough sensitivity to discriminate subtle differences in true levels of the variable being measured. If there are too many, responding can become overly complex and burdensome. The optimal number would be the number that has good sensitivity, is practical, and approximates a normal distribution of responses. One view has been that rating scales are best when they have about five to nine categories. That view was popularized by Harvard psychologist George Miller in the 1950s (Miller 1956). Miller observed that people's abilities to accurately judge physical stimuli and remember information without errors seemed to be constrained to about seven categories, plus or minus about two categories. He used binary decisions to illustrate. One bit of information is the amount of information needed to make a decision between two equally likely alternatives. Two bits are needed to decide among four equally likely alternatives. Three bits permit a choice among eight equally likely alternatives. Four bits of information decide among 16 alternatives, and so on. Hence, another bit of information is added each time the number of alternative choices is increased by a factor of two.

Miller reported that people's accuracy at judging tones, taste, colors, and points on a line typically ranged from about 2 to 3 bits, or four to eight categories. He next observed that people's short-term memory capacity averaged about 23 bits. For example, most people can recall about seven decimal digits, approximating 3.3 bits each for a total of 23 bits. On this basis, Miller proposed a theory about how the span of immediate memory should vary as a function of the amount of information per item on a test. That was Miller's number: 7 ± 2. Most of us recognize the increasing challenge of remembering a new telephone number when it includes the area code (10 digits), or a zip code when the plus-four digits are added at the end (9 digits). Today, most psychometric tests offer four to seven response categories, at least in part because of the influence of Miller's ideas.

Miller's Number: 7 ± 2

"And finally, what about the magical number seven? What about the seven wonders of the world, the seven seas, the seven deadly sins, the seven daughters of Atlas in the Pleiades, the seven ages of man, the seven levels of hell, the seven primary colors, the seven notes of the musical scale, and the seven days of the week? What about the seven-point rating scale, the seven categories for absolute judgment, the seven objects in the span of attention, and the seven digits in the span of immediate memory? Perhaps there is something deep and profound behind all these sevens, something just calling out for us to discover it. But I suspect that it is only a pernicious, Pythagorean coincidence" (Miller 1956, p. 95).

Guttman or Cumulative Scaling

In 1950, sociologist Louis Guttman argued that the meaning of any score from Thurstone or Likert scales was ambiguous unless it was followed by a hierarchical pattern of endorsement among its items:

> If a person endorses a more extreme statement, he should endorse all less extreme statements if the statements are to be considered a scale. . . . We shall call a set of items of common content a scale if a person with a higher rank than another person is just as high or higher on every item than the other person. (Guttman 1950, p. 62)

Guttman scaling is also known as cumulative scaling. The purpose is to establish a one-dimensional continuum for the underlying construct to be measured. This means that a person who agrees with any question on the test should also agree with all the questions that preceded it. Said another way, on a 10-item cumulative scale, a score of 5 would indicate that the respondent agreed with the first five items. A score of 7 would indicate agreement on the first seven questions, and so on. The object is to find a set of items that perfectly matches this pattern. That doesn't happen often, but the degree to which it does is an example of the internal consistency of a scale or test, a form of **reliability.**

Reliability

As is the case for all measures, tests of psychological constructs must be reliable; they must be precise, accurate, and stable across the time period that defines their nature. A valid test must first be reliable, though a reliable test is not necessarily valid. Precision means that a test, or its subscales, is internally consistent; the average correlation among the items is high relative to the variation in people's responses to each item. Accuracy means that the test does not overestimate or underestimate the true value of the construct. Stability means that scores on the test do not fluctuate widely without an explainable cause. Reliability of psychological constructs is usually computed using a statistic called intraclass correlation (R_I). A common index of R_I used to estimate internal consistency is the coefficient α, which is computed as:

$$\alpha = \frac{k\bar{r}}{1 + (k-1)\bar{r}}$$

where k is the number of items on the test and $\bar{r}$ is the mean correlation between items. Hence, including more items and including correlated items each increase reliability.

Multidimensional Scales

The scales that we have considered up to now are designed to measure a single dimension, like the length of a line. That's usually sufficient for many constructs, but what about a concept like self-esteem? Chapter 8 presents overall self-esteem as a concept that is unidimensional but that comprises several dimensions in a hierarchical structure. In chapter 5 we will consider various types of moods and emotions. Psychologists who study emotions mostly agree that there are six basic emotions that are experienced in virtually all cultures (love, joy, surprise, anger, sadness, and fear). Moreover, each type of emotional response can be described by an affective dimension (e.g., pleasant vs. unpleasant) and an arousal dimension (e.g., low vs. high). Separate scales are required to measure these different dimensions.

Semantic Differential

In the late 1950s, social psychologist Charles E. Osgood and his colleagues, George Suci and Percy Tannenbaum, developed a method to graph the differences between individuals' connotations for words and thus measure the "psychological distance" between words (Osgood, Suci, and Tannenbaum 1957). Their method is called the semantic differential. That method advanced the idea of multidimensional scales through the authors' theory that the connotative meaning of any object or term could be essentially described in three dimensions. Osgood and his colleagues named the three dimensions activity, evaluation, and potency. For example, think of the idea of "gymnastics." If you like gymnastics, you would probably rate it high on activity, good on evaluation, and powerful on potency. Other adjectives and dimensions can be used to describe the connotative meaning of things to people; but the scaling of several dimensions through the use of antonyms to describe opposite ends of a continuum was the key, and provides an example of what are known as bipolar scales.

> **Three Dimensions of Connotative Meaning: Osgood and Tannenbaum**
>
> **Evaluative**
>
> Good __:__:__:__:__:__:__ Bad
>
> **Potency**
>
> Powerful __:__:__:__:__:__:__ Weak
>
> **Activity**
>
> Active __:__:__:__:__:__:__ Passive

Scales or Measures?

Scores derived directly from a response scale cannot be used as measures of psychological constructs because they will not perfectly fit the true distribution of the variable being scaled. Contrary to the assumptions of a linear normal distribution characterized by Thurstone and Likert scaling, response scores commonly are nonlinear and are peculiar to the group of people sampled. For example, in 1953 a Danish mathematician, Georg Rasch (1960), found that the only way he could compare past performances on different tests of oral reading was to statistically adjust data (i.e., apply the exponential additivity of Poisson's 1837 distribution) that were produced by a new sample of students responding to both tests (Tenenbaum 1999). Nonetheless, it is common to construct measures using factor analysis, which is described next, to determine whether the scale has multiple dimensions.

Exploratory Factor Analysis

A key statistical tool used to help determine whether measures of psychological constructs should be unidimensional or multidimensional is factor analysis. Researchers use factor analysis to identify patterns of correlations among items on a test by transforming the correlation matrix of items into a smaller number of dimensions, or factors. Factor analysis is used to estimate the number and nature of factors that may underlie the pattern of correlations among a larger group of variables. Technically, it is used to extract common factor variances from sets of measures. A factor is viewed as a construct that is assumed to explain relations in items and scales. Factor analysis yields variables that are inferred rather than measured directly, so it is just one step in the development of valid measures of psychological constructs.

Factor analysis was developed 100 years ago by psychologist Charles Spearman, who thought that all tests of mental abilities such as verbal, mathematical, and analytical skills, were explainable by a single underlying factor of intelligence that he called "g."[1] Spearman was wrong, but the technique with which he tested his ideas has become one of the fundamental tools used to describe psychological constructs and develop rating scales for their measurement.

The major steps in exploratory factor analysis include (1) selecting a set of variables, (2) generating a correlation matrix from the selected variables, (3) extracting factors from the correlation matrix, (4) rotating the factors to increase clarity, and (5) interpreting the meaning of the factors. An example will help clarify the major steps of exploratory factor analysis.

Suppose a researcher has selected six variables labeled A through F to measure verbal and mathematical ability in a sample of college students. The researcher generates a matrix (i.e., a square array of numbers) containing correlations among scores from the six variables, as shown in figure 2.2. The values, or elements, along the diagonal are 1.0 because any variable is perfectly correlated with itself. The values above and below the diagonals are the same because the matrix is symmetrical. The off-diagonal values indicate the correlations among the six variables, which can range between –1.00 and +1.00. The circled areas in figure 2.2 indicate that two distinct patterns may exist among the correlations. Therefore, the pattern of correlations in the matrix suggests that two dimensions or factors underlie the six variables.

The next step is to extract factors from the correlation matrix to determine whether two factors really underlie the relationship among the six variables. The most common method of extraction, labeled principal-axis-factor extraction, utilizes squared multiple correlations as an initial estimate of the variable communalities. Communalities are the common factor variances of each variable (i.e., the portion of the variable's total variance accounted for by the common factors), and estimates of communalities are a necessary starting point for factor extraction. Exploratory factor analysis extracts n (n = number of variables) minus the number of factors (one or a specified number of factors) from the

---

1. Purportedly "g" measured a factor Spearman called "education," which involves making connections among items and their interrelation.

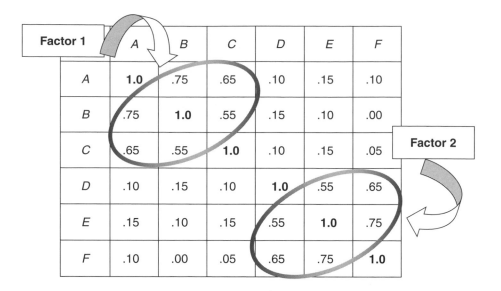

Figure 2.2 Example of a correlation matrix used in exploratory factor analysis.

correlation matrix utilizing an iterative approach such that the first factor accounts for the greatest amount of variance among the items and subsequent factors account for a smaller portion of the variance. The researcher then examines the solution and utilizes criteria (e.g., amount of variance explained by the factors or the extent to which the factors reproduce the original correlation matrix) to determine whether the correct number of factors has been extracted. Two factors were extracted from the correlation matrix in the present example.

The extraction of factors yields the factor matrix in table 2.1. The first two columns contain factor loadings, which are weights that express the degrees of relationships between the original six variables and the two factors. Similar to correlation coefficients, the weights range between –1.00 and +1.00. Inspection of the weights indicates that variables *A*, *B*, and *C* load strongly on the first factor, but weakly on the second factor. Conversely, variables *D*, *E*, and *F* load on the second factor, but not the first factor. The values in the third column are the communalities for the variables, which are computed by summing the square of the factor loadings. The communality of variable *A* is $(.85)^2 + (.05)^2$ = .7250.

The aim in factor analysis is to express each item or scale as the sum of common and unique portions. The common portions of all the variables are by definition fully explained by the common factors, and the unique portions are ideally perfectly uncorrelated with each other. Thus, com-

Table 2.1			
Factors			
Variable	**1**	**2**	**h²**
A	.85	.05	.7250
B	.75	.10	.5725
C	.65	.10	.4325
D	.10	.65	.4325
E	.10	.75	.5725
F	.05	.85	.7250

mon factors are linear combinations of the common parts of the original variables. Factor analysis describes components of the common-factor variance. The total variance of a test item includes three parts: (1) common-factor variance (variance attributable to the common factors), or h^2; (2) specific variance (variance not shared with the common factors); and (3) error variance (1.0 minus reliability). Thus, total variance = 1.0 = h^2 + specific variance + error. The sum of a test item's communality plus its specific variance is its reliability. If we use item *A* to illustrate and assume it has a reliability of .80, its error variance is .20 (.20 = 1.0 – .80), and its specific variance is .075 (1.0 = .7250 + .075 + .20).

Sometimes the matrix of factor loadings is not as clear as depicted in table 2.1, and it must be rotated. Rotation is a method of reorienting the pattern of factor loadings to a more simplistic or interpretable form. Similar to adjusting the magnification lens of a microscope to clarify the view of the contents of a slide, rotation involves adjusting the pattern of factor loadings to clarify the contents within the factor matrix. The adjustment brings clarity to the factor loadings in the factor matrix. Rotation can be either orthogonal (i.e., independent factors) or oblique (i.e., correlated factors). In our example of two factors, visualize the factors as lines or vectors that intersect. An **orthogonal** rotation would determine factor loadings with the two lines at a right angle to each other. An oblique rotation would reduce that angle to determine whether the pattern of the loadings would become more distinct.

The final step involves interpreting the meaning of the factors in table 2.1. The interpretation depends on the size and pattern of the factor loadings for the variables. Variables *A*, *B*, and *C* load strongly on the first factor, but weakly on the second factor. Inspection of the variable content indicates the common element of the variables and the construct underlying the correlations among the variables (e.g., verbal ability). Variables *D*, *E*, and *F* load on the second factor, but not the first factor. The common element of the variables and the construct underlying the correlations among the variables may be mathematical ability.

Exploratory factor analysis is a statistical method used to develop rating scales for the measurement of psychological constructs; correlations between variables are used to extract factors or strongly related groups of variables that represent a distinct construct.

In areas of study where little is known, exploratory factor analysis can be valuable for its ability to suggest patterns underlying the correlations among variables. Unfortunately, the number of factors in the solution is unknown before the exploratory factor analysis, and all of the factors typically influence all of the variables, as shown in figure 2.3. There also is no direct test of the accuracy of the

final factor solution (i.e., indeterminacy) or the relationships of items to a specific factor (i.e., factorial validity). Newer techniques that use covariance modeling are more suited for testing hypotheses about the structure underlying the relationships among variables.

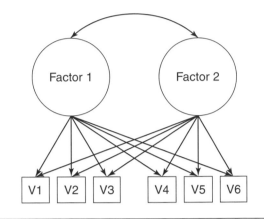

Figure 2.3   Exploratory factor analysis is used to suggest patterns underlying the correlation among variables.

Covariance Modeling

Spearman based factor analysis on methods similar to linear regression, whereby regression coefficients and the estimates of error are found by a statistical solution that minimizes the sum of square differences between a predicted score and an observed score for each person tested. A newer approach called covariance modeling is based on covariances, not each person's scores. Rather than striving to minimize differences between predicted and observed scores, the goal of covariance is to minimize the difference between the covariances observed in a sample of people and covariances predicted by some theoretical model (Bollen 1989).

Covariance modeling represents a powerful class of analytic tools for directly testing the fit of theoretical models to a variance-covariance matrix underlying a set of variables. Two of the main types of analyses that use covariance modeling are confirmatory factor analysis and structural equation modeling. Confirmatory factor analysis is similar to exploratory factor analysis, but it directly tests the fit of a theoretically derived measurement model to a variance-covariance matrix underlying a set of variables. Structural equation modeling involves testing the fit of a theoretically derived model that describes the measurement of and structural relationships among many latent variables or constructs.

C*ovariance modeling uses observed and predicted covariances to determine the fit of theoretical models to a set of variables. Examples include confirmatory factor analysis and structural equation modeling.*

Confirmatory Factor Analysis

The major steps in confirmatory factor analysis (CFA) include (1) selecting a set of variables, (2) generating a variance-covariance matrix from the selected variables, (3) pre-specifying a theoretically based measurement model that explicitly defines the relationship of each variable to a factor, (4) estimating the model parameters, and (5) testing the adequacy of the model using fit indices.

The first two steps are very similar to steps in exploratory factor analysis. The researcher selects a set of variables, collects responses from a sample, and then generates a matrix describing the relationships among the variables. The matrix in confirmatory factor analysis, however, involves variances and covariances rather than correlation coefficients.

The next step, performed after the variance-covariance matrix is generated, illustrates a fundamental difference between exploratory and confirmatory factor analysis. The researcher specifies in advance the measurement model based on theory that explicitly defines the relationship of each variable to a factor, such as the two-factor, correlated model depicted in figure 2.4. The measurement model defines the number of factors, the relationship between factors, the relationship between factors and variables, and the error terms associated with the measured variables.

The next steps involve estimating the modeled parameters and then determining the degree of fit of the model to the data. Various methods of estimation, such as maximum likelihood (i.e., the "best bet" estimate of a population value based on the prior probability of an observed value occurring in the population), attempt to minimize the discrepancy between the sample variance-covariance matrix and the variance-covariance matrix reproduced by the modeled parameters. The minimization process is iterative, and the final model converges when there is not an appreciable reduction in the discrep-

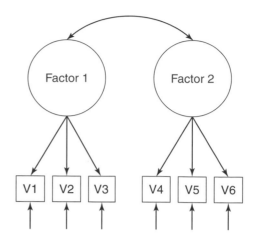

Figure 2.4   A two-factor, correlated model used in confirmatory factor analysis.

ancy between the sample variance-covariance matrix and the variance-covariance matrix reproduced by the modeled parameters.

The model then must be judged for its accuracy, which is based on a number of fit indices. Most fit indices are used to judge either the absolute or the relative fit of the model to the sample variance-covariance matrix. Some indices of fit such as the χ-square statistic (computed as the squared difference between the diagonal and off-diagonal elements of the sample and the reproduced variance-covariance matrices, multiplied by the sample size minus 1) and the goodness-of-fit index (a measure of relative amounts of variances and covariances in the sample matrix predicted by the model) test absolute fit of the model. Relative or incremental fit indices (e.g., non-normed fit index, which is a ratio of the χ-squares for the null and the hypothesized models, corrected for the number of parameters in the models) and the root mean square error of approximation (computed as $[(T - d)/d \times n]^{1/2}$, where $T = \chi$-square from maximum likelihood estimation, $d =$ degrees of freedom in the model, $n = N - 1$) compare the fit of the specified model to a baseline, or null, model, which hypothesizes no relationships among the observed variables. Values of .08, .05, and 0 indicate reasonable, close, and exact fit, respectively. Advantages of CFA include the following:

▼ A direct test of the goodness of fit of an a priori measurement model that is based on theory.

▼ Estimation of correlations among error terms. Ideally errors are independent, but there are instances when adjusting for correlated errors is justifiable and informative.

▼ Tests of the accuracy of the model and its parameters across distinct groups, such as males and females, or across time. If the factor structure underlying a construct is different between groups or times, the summated scores cannot be directly compared; they mean different things, so it is important to demonstrate invariance across groups and time.

▼ Comparisons of latent means that are constructed from raw scores of the factors not summated.

Structural Equation Modeling

Many researchers are interested in examining whether theoretical models can accurately describe the exact relationships among multiple latent or hypothetical constructs. In chapter 11, we will describe theories of physical activity behavior change. Structural equation modeling (SEM), which is an extension of confirmatory factor analysis, can be used to develop and test those theories. For example, a researcher may want to test whether the theory of reasoned action, which postulates that behavior is predicted by intention and that intention is predicted by attitude and societal norms, is a reasonable description of the variables associated with physical activity. Structural equation modeling can determine whether the pattern of relationships among the variables conforms to the theorized pattern.

Structural equation modeling entails several steps. The first step is to select a theoretical model to test—for example, the theory of reasoned action—in order to understand factors associated with physical cal activity. An investigator then operationalizes the constructs within the theory utilizing multiple variables or indicators of each hypothetical variable, collects responses from a sample, and generates a variance-covariance matrix.

Next, the researcher specifies in advance the theoretical model to be tested. The model contains two parts: measurement models and a structural model. Figure 2.5 contains the measurement models and a structural model for a hypothetical test of the theory of reasoned action. Measurement models are specified for each latent variable. Similar to what occurs in confirmatory factor analysis, the measurement models define the number of factors, the relationship between factors, the relationship between factors and variables, and the error term associated with each measured variable. One factor is specified for the measurement models for each latent variable in figure 2.5. The structural model specifies the nature of the relationship or paths among the latent variables. For example, the structural model specifies paths from social norms and attitude to intention and from intention to physical activity.

The next steps are to estimate the modeled parameters and then determine the degree of fit of the model to the data. The purpose of the method of estimation is to minimize the discrepancy between the sample variance-covariance matrix and the variance-covariance matrix reproduced by the modeled parameters. Similar to this step in confirmatory factor analysis, the minimization process is iterative, and the model finally converges when there is not a significant reduction in the discrepancy between the sample variance-covariance

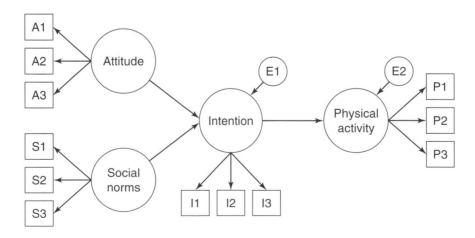

Figure 2.5 Structural model for testing the theory of reasoned action using SEM.

Adapted, by permission, from R.W. Motl, R.K. Dishman, R. Saunders, M. Dowda, G. Felton, D. Ward, and R.R. Pate, 2002, "Examining social-cognitive determinants of intention and physical activity in adolescent girls using structural equation modeling," *Health Psychology* 21, 459-467.

matrix and the variance-covariance matrix reproduced by the modeled parameters.

The model then must be judged for its accuracy based on the fit indices as in confirmatory factor analysis. Therefore, an investigator can specify in advance a theoretically derived model and then test the goodness of fit of the model directly using structural equation modeling. The following are some benefits of structural equation modeling:

▼ Establishment of measurement models that partition true and error score variance among the indicators of each latent variable

▼ Simultaneous estimation of hypothetical paths among multiple latent variables

▼ Unbiased estimates of the relationships or paths between latent variables

▼ Tests of the accuracy of the model and its parameters across distinct groups, such as males and females, as well as across time, and analyses of the effect of experimental interventions on variables (e.g., goals, confidence, mood) that presumably mediate the effects of the intervention on behavior

Defining Physical Activity and Fitness

Physical activity is "any bodily movement produced by skeletal muscles that results in energy expenditure," and is usually measured in kilocalories (kcal) per unit of time (Caspersen, Powell, and Christenson 1985). Categories of physical activity include sleep, occupation, transportation, and leisure. Types of leisure-time physical activity are household activities, other chores, recreation/sports, and conditioning activities (i.e., exercise). **Exercise,** a subset of physical activity, is planned, structured, repetitive bodily movements that someone engages in for the purpose of improving or maintaining one or more components of physical fitness or health. Exercise can be acute or chronic. **Acute exercise** is a single, relatively short bout of exercise; **chronic exercise** is exercise carried out repeatedly over time, usually several times each week for various durations. Depending on its intensity, frequency, and duration, physical activity can increase physical fitness.

Physical Activity Features

Physical activity occurs at varying intensities spanning a range of energy expenditures from rest to multiples of resting metabolic rate (METs). Intensity of physical activity can be about 10 to 15 times resting MET in average people or as high as 20 to 25 times resting MET among the very highly fit. It is important to measure the types, intensities, and durations of physical activity that people engage in because those factors determine physiological responses during exertion that may directly or indirectly influence psychological responses during or after physical activity. It is not yet known how these features of physical activity affect psychological responses, but, as an example, it is possible that pain occurring at high exercise intensities (e.g., above 60% of aerobic capacity in sedentary people) might negatively influence mood and deter future physical activity. Also, muscle fiber recruitment and other physiological responses, such as body temperature, breathing rate and depth, hydrogen ions, and hormones (such as catecholamines, cortisol, and beta-endorphin) increase linearly or exponentially during moderate to heavy intensities of exercise. Any or all of those responses might influence psychological factors indirectly by influencing perceptions of exertion or brain responses (e.g., regional brain blood flow or metabolism). Some of those possibilities are discussed in some detail in chapters 4 through 6 and chapter 13.

This text focuses on exercise because most of the available literature has used a measure of physical activity that fits the definition of exercise. For example, anxiety usually has been examined before and after 20 to 30 min of aerobic exercise (e.g., jogging, cycling, or swimming) at intensities fixed by the investigators, commonly in laboratory conditions. The control of such features of physical exertion is necessary to define precisely whether a "dose response" exists between exercise and psychological outcomes. However, it is equally or more important to determine whether factors such as choice of activity type or intensity (e.g., level of preferred exertion, discussed in chapter 13) or the setting where exercise occurs (e.g., indoors or outdoors, on a track or in a park, in solitude or with others) influence the psychological consequences of physical activity. Virtually no population-based epidemiological studies of physical activity and anxiety have been published to show for whom and in what circumstances the anti-anxiety effects of physical activity occur. Such questions require precise definitions and measures of physical activity and exercise. In contrast, about 25 population-based studies have linked lower levels of physical activity with depression symptoms, and even more studies have shown that individuals in exercise training programs (e.g., 45-60 min of brisk walking 3-5 days per week) had fewer depression symptoms compared to those in placebo control groups after several weeks or months.

Up to now, behavior change interventions directed toward increasing exercise adoption (strategies to recruit new participants) and maintenance (follow-ups to sustain participation) have had better results when the target of the intervention was relatively low-intensity physical activities (e.g., walking) carried out as part of a person's daily lifestyle compared to heavy exercise in a supervised program (Dishman and Buckworth 1996b). Recent interventions have targeted physical activity, as in programs to promote active lifestyles (Project Active: Dunn et al. 1999) or to develop environments that offer opportunities to be more physically active (such as bike paths and attractive, accessible stairs).

Physical activity and exercise are behaviors, and the issues in measuring these behaviors are discussed later. Physical fitness is more straightforward to measure (see next section) and is often used as a behavioral surrogate, under the assumption that level of physical activity is positively associated with fitness. Changes in fitness may also influence some psychological outcomes of physical activity (e.g., physical self-esteem). Some other positive outcomes of physical activity, such as reduced depression, do not appear to depend on increased fitness. Also, it is possible that different components of fitness may be specifically more relevant for different psychological or behavioral outcomes of physical activity. To find out, fitness components must be defined and measured.

Physical Fitness

Physical fitness is the capacity to meet successfully the present and potential physical challenges of life; it is a set of attributes that people have or achieve that relates to the ability to perform physical activity. **Health-related physical fitness** includes the components of cardiorespiratory endurance, muscular strength and endurance, flexibility, and body composition (see table 2.2). The concept of health-related fitness has been expanded by some to include metabolic indexes, such as plasma lipids and glucose tolerance. **Skill-related physical fitness** components are agility, balance, coordination, speed, power, and reaction time.

Aerobic (i.e., cardiorespiratory) **fitness** refers to the maximal capacity of the cardiorespiratory sys-

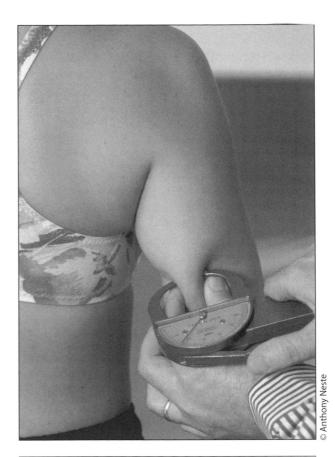

© Anthony Neste

Measures of subcutaneous fat from several sites are used to estimate total percentage body fat.

tem to take up and use oxygen (i.e., $\dot{V}O_2$max) and is typically expressed in milliliters of oxygen per minute adjusted for total body mass or fat-free mass expressed in kilograms. The use of aerobic fitness to represent physical activity has limitations because 25% to 40% of aerobic capacity is genetically determined and the rate of cardiovascular adaptations to increased activity varies between individuals, even among monozygotic (i.e., identical) twins (Wilmore et al. 1997). It may happen that two people who begin a training program with the same aerobic capacity will achieve the same level of physical activity after a specific period of time, but the individual who adapts more rapidly will show a greater increase in aerobic fitness. Nonetheless, it is important to measure fitness in order to determine the *relative* strain a person experiences during moderate to heavy exertion (i.e., the exertion during standard physical activities expressed as a portion of the person's capacity). Levels of, or changes in, other physical fitness measures, such as muscular strength or endurance, body mass or percentage body fat, and flexibility are important to measure

Table 2.2

Health-Related Physical Fitness

Fitness component	Type of measure		
	Laboratory	Epidemiologic	Self-assessment
Cardiorespiratory	Maximal oxygen uptake	Treadmill time Cycling PWC	12 min run/walk Canada Home Fitness Test
Body composition	Underwater weight; DXA	BMI, BIA, skinfolds	BMI, skinfolds
Muscular strength	Limb/trunk dynamometer	Handgrip dynamometer	Trunk/limb lifts
Flexibility	Goniometer	Goniometer	Sit-and-reach
Muscular endurance	Limb/trunk dynamometer	Isokinetic machines	Pull-ups; sit-ups modified

BMI is body mass index (weight in kg/[height in meters])^2; BIA is bioelectrical impedance analysis; a goniometer measures joint angles; a dynamometer measures force and rate of force; PWC is physical working capacity measured as peak power output during an incremental test; treadmill time is duration of a grade-incremented test.

Adapted, by permission, from C.J. Caspersen, K.E. Powell, and G.M. Christenson, 1985, "Physical activities, exercise, and physical fitness: Definitions and distinctions for health-related research," *Public Health Reports* 100: 126–131.

because they might influence psychological effects or determinants of physical activity. For example, perceptions of increased muscularity that can result from resistance exercise training may contribute positively to physical self-esteem. Changes in fitness also can be used to help document adherence to an exercise program.

Adherence

Adherence means conforming faithfully to a standard of behavior that has been set as part of a negotiated agreement. Research on exercise behavior change has typically defined exercise adherence on the basis of attendance or a specified minimal percentage of attendance, such as 60% to 80%. Though arbitrary, the most widely agreed-upon definition of maintenance of an exercise program is adherence for at least six months. That is so partly because the typical exercise program has about a 50% dropout rate during the first six months. Of course, successful programs exceed that average, and six months of maintenance does not ensure against dropping out later. However, these definitions assume equality among all types of nonattendance, do not take into account the level of participation, and usually consider only the number of sessions, which precludes consideration of intensity or duration.

Exercise **compliance** also refers to how well someone follows an exercise program, but this term

is used more often in a medical setting in reference to behaviors related to immediate- and short-term health advice to alleviate symptoms; it has a more authoritative or coercive connotation than does adherence, which is a preferred term because of its emphasis on personal control by the participant.

*E*xercise is a behavior, and fitness is an attribute. There are issues in valid measurement of both exercise and fitness that affect the quality of exercise psychology research.

Measuring Physical Activity

The measurement of exercise behavior and level of physical activity is fundamental to studying exercise and mental health and in testing interventions aimed at changing exercise behavior. This presents a considerable challenge because there is no single standard for measuring physical activity (Montoye et al. 1996; Paffenbarger et al. 1993), and physical activity can be quantified in different ways, such as total time active; hours spent at different intensities expressed in **METs** (multiples of resting metabolic rate per kilogram body mass) or as increased heart rate; units of movement (e.g., count of number of steps); or energy expenditure expressed in kcal. More than a dozen types of methods for measuring physical activity are characterized in table 2.3 according to costs to the study groups; extent of interference with usual activity level; acceptability by people; and the ability of the method to provide specific information about the type, frequency, duration, and intensity of physical activity (LaPorte, Montoye, and Caspersen 1985). The methods generally can be categorized according to whether they measure a direct or indirect observation of physical activity, motion, a physiological response during physical activity, energy expenditure, or a physiological adaptation to physical activity. Four measurable dimensions of physical activity are type, duration, frequency (e.g., days per week), and **intensity** (rate of energy expenditure), although most methods do not assess all four.

There are more than 30 different methods for measuring physical activity, and the selection of method hinges on appropriateness for the target population and the level of sensitivity and specificity necessary to answer the research question.

Table 2.3

Free-Living Physical Activity Assessment

	Study costs			Acceptability		
Assessment procedure	Time	Effort	Interference	Person	Social	Activity specifics
Calorimetry						
Direct	VH	VH	H-VH	No	No	Yes
Indirect	H-VH	VH	H-VH	No	No	Yes
Surveys						
Task-specific diary	L-M	L-M	VH	?	Yes	Yes
Recall questionnaire	L-M	L-M	L	Yes	Yes	Yes
Quantitative history	L-M	L-M	L	Yes	Yes	Yes
Physiologic markers						
Cardiorespiratory fitness	M-VH	M-H	L	?	?	No
Doubly-labeled water	H-VH	M-VH	L-H	Yes	Yes	No
Mechanical and electronic monitors						
Heart rate	H-VH	M-VH	L-M	Yes	Yes	No
Pedometers	L-M	L	L-M	Yes	Yes	No
Accelerometers	L-H	L-M	L-M	Yes	Yes	No
Observation	*H-VH*	*H-VH*	*L-VH*	*?*	*?*	*Yes*

L = low; M = medium; H = high; VH = very high.

Data from LaPorte, Montoye, and Caspersen 1985.

Energy Expended for Various Activities

Activity	Energy Expended (METs*)/h
Sitting and talking	1.5
Driving automobile	2.0
Brisk walk (at 4 mph [6.4 km/h])	4.0
Low-impact aerobic dance	5.0
Weightlifting (vigorous)	6.0
Jogging (general)	7.0
Bicycling (12-13.9 mph [19.3-22.4 km/h])	8.0
Swimming laps (freestyle, vigorous)	10.0
Running (8 min per mile)	12.5

* 1 MET = 1.0 kcal/kg body weight.

Data from Ainsworth et al. 1993.

the research question. For example, a short, self-report questionnaire to estimate overall level of activity might be appropriate for classifying a large sample into low-, moderate-, and high-active groups in a descriptive analysis, but more precise and reliable method(s) should be used in an intervention study designed to measure adherence to a strength-training program.

Occupational work potentially accounts for much of someone's total physical activity, and job classification is one method that has been used to categorize people into activity groups. This method is nonreactive and quick and can be used to classify large groups. However, there can be considerable within-job variability, potential misclassification of intensity, seasonal and secular changes in job requirements, and selection bias. Grouping individuals into activity categories based on job excludes the contribution of leisure and nonoccupational physical activity; and because people have become less active at work, leisure-time physical activity is generally considered more representative of physical activity in a population (Kriska and Caspersen 1997).

Desirable features of physical activity instruments are validity, reliability, practicality (i.e., study costs and acceptability to the target population), nonreactivity or interference (i.e., the method must not alter the population or the behavior it seeks to measure), and specificity (i.e., features of type, intensity, and time are measured). Validation of instruments is a dilemma, and many self-report instruments have not been held to validation through concurrent administration with measures of energy expenditure such as doubly labeled water,[2] assessment of metabolism in a respiratory chamber, heart rate, or motion counters and accelerometers that estimate the force of motion. And there are limitations in using these methods for validation because they either do not tell us the type of activity or do not tell us its intensity.

Understandably, there are strengths and weaknesses for all methods that have been used to measure physical activity and exercise, and different methods will be more or less appropriate based on

A single job classification can have widely different levels of physical activity.

© Bruce Leighty

---

2. A person initially drinks a measured amount of water that has been labeled with a stable isotope ($^2H^1H^{18}O$). The $H_2^{18}O$ is eliminated from the body as both H_2O and CO_2 and thus is a measure of H_2O and CO_2 flux. The $^2H^1HO$ is eliminated only as H_2O and thus is a measure of H_2O flux. The difference between these elimination rates is an estimate of CO_2 flux. Through indirect calorimetric equations, energy expenditure (EE) can then be derived.

© PHOTOPHILE

Although some physical activity is routine, accuracy of recall is still influenced by age, time frame, and other factors.

One of the more frequently used methods for assessing physical activity is the survey recall, although surveys fail to explain more than 45% of variance in direct and indirect measures of physical activity (Durante and Ainsworth 1996). Individuals are asked to report various aspects of their physical activity, such as type and duration, for spans of time ranging from one day to a year or even over their lifetime. The reliability and validity of self-reports of physical activity depend on the respondent's ability to remember, the interviewer/administrator and respondent bias, the day of the week (i.e., weekdays vs. weekend), sequencing of administration of the questionnaire, saliency of the activity recalled, the social desirability of the response, sociodemographic issues, culture, age, gender, obesity, and educational level (Kriska and Caspersen 1997; Durante and Ainsworth 1996). The time frame examined affects the quality of the data such that shorter recall periods are less subject to recall bias and easier to validate, but results are less likely to reflect usual behavior.

More objective measures of physical activity are motion sensors or **accelerometers,** which record force of movement of body or limb mass in the ver-

tical plane or the vertical and horizontal planes. Those data can then be translated into caloric expenditure or quantity of movement, such as number of steps over a period of time. Accelerometers have been validated against a variety of physiological measures, such as graded treadmill maximal workload, treadmill time, submaximal exercise heart rate, body fatness, lung function, and doubly labeled water. Motion sensors can give us information about total activity for a specified period, but do not tell us about type or intensity and are unable to measure movement in activities such as cycling or swimming.

Considering that there are more than 30 different methods to measure physical activity in adults and youths (LaPorte, Montoye, and Caspersen 1985; Sallis et al. 1992), the difficulty in comparing results across studies without uniform assessment methods is obvious. In addition, the fact that physical activity has several definitions as an outcome variable, such as days active per week or total energy expenditure, also makes comparing studies difficult. A collection of popular physical activity questionnaires for different populations, along with descriptions of their use and information about reliability and validity, has been published by the American College of Sports Medicine (Kriska and Caspersen 1997). We can hope that this publication has supported more appropriate and consistent measurement of physical activity and limited additional research with unvalidated questionnaires. Efforts to improve the quality of physical activity measurement were also addressed at the 9th Measurement and Evaluation Symposium of the Measurement and Evaluation Council of the American Association of Active Lifestyle and Fitness (Research Quarterly for Exercise and Sport 2000).

Issues about specific measures of the components of physical activity or physical fitness have largely been ignored by researchers in exercise psychology (Rejeski 1994). This is unfortunate, because it is plausible—as for other health-related outcomes of physical activity (see table 2.4)—that psychological outcomes from physical activity may depend, at least partly, on the physical stimulus of exertion, which can differ according to type and intensity of activity.

How exercise is implemented as an intervention is another issue in exercise psychology research. Very different types and amounts of activity have been employed as the exercise stimulus for very different types of subjects. Researchers testing the effects of acute exercise on psychological variables

Table 2.4

Markers of Physical Activity

Dimension	Mechanism	Criterion	Disease outcome
Calories	Energy cost	Doubly-labeled H_2O	CHD, NIDDM, obesity, cancer
Aerobic intensity	Cardiac function	Oxygen uptake	CHD, NIDDM
Weight bearing	Gravity	Motion sensor	Osteoporosis
Flexibility	ROM	Goniometer	Disability
Muscular strength	Force	Strength	Disability

Reprinted, by permission, from C.J. Caspersen, 1989, "Physical activity epidemiology: Concepts, methods, and applications to exercise science," *Exercise and Sport Sciences Reviews* 17:439.

need to consider the novelty, the controllability (i.e., forced vs. voluntary, programmed vs. spontaneous), and the social/environmental context (e.g., solitary or group, competitive or recreational, indoors on a track vs. outdoors in a park) of the exercise. Physical activity history must also be considered in administering an acute bout of exercise, as well as in determining the effects of an intervention on exercise adherence. Standardizing exercise intensity based on percentage of maximal aerobic capacity is probably not adequate unless the researcher controls the effects of other psychobiological variables (e.g., stress hormones, such as catecholamines and β-endorphin) or sensations of force or pain possibly relevant to the mental health variable in question.

Research Issues

Research in exercise psychology is characterized by many of the issues common to research in cognitive and behavioral psychology, neuroscience, and exercise physiology. The following sections provide definitions of common terms in research, descriptions of research designs that have been used to gain insight into exercise behavior and its consequences, and explanations of experimental artifacts that can confound any scientific study. These topics provide a basis for understanding the discussions of research in subsequent chapters.

Common Terms in Research

Exercise psychology draws from several disciplines, such as epidemiology and clinical medicine; and readers may be unfamiliar with some terms used to describe research in these areas. This section presents selected definitions.

bias—The systematic departure of results from the correct values as a consequence of errors in design or investigational technique.

confounder—An extraneous factor that is not a consequence of exposure or the experimental manipulation. A confounding variable exerts an effect on the outcome such that there is a distortion in a study's effects. Confounders are determinants or correlates of the outcome under study and are unequally distributed among the exposed and unexposed individuals.

effect size—The magnitude of the outcome of an experimental manipulation, usually expressed as a standard score (e.g., [(experimental mean – control mean)/standard deviation]) (see figure 2.6). Effect size can be thought of as how much of a

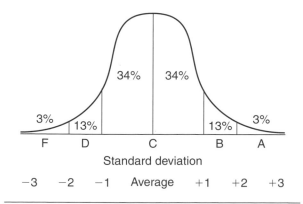

Figure 2.6 Effect size represents the amount of change from the average, or the distance from the mean in a normal curve.

change there is from the average, as in the distance from the mean in a normal curve. For example, one standard-deviation effect is the same as raising a letter grade in a course by one letter (from a *C* to a *B*) based on a bell-shaped, or normal, grading curve.

effectiveness—The ability of an intervention or method to work in other settings, or its level of ecological validity. Can it be practically applied outside of a laboratory setting? Does it work?

efficacy—The ability of an intervention or method to do what it is intended to do. Can it work?

epidemiology—The study of the distribution and determinants of health-related states and events (disease, injury, health behaviors) in a population and the application of this study to the control of health problems. Physical activity epidemiology includes studies of (a) the association of physical activity, as a health-related behavior, with diseases and other health outcomes; (b) the distribution and determinants of physical activity behaviors; (c) the interrelationships of physical activity with other behaviors; and (d) the application of this knowledge to the prevention and control of disease and the promotion of health.

prevalence—The number of existing cases of a disease or condition divided by the total population at a point in time. Prevalence is used to measure the burden of the disease and to plan for the implementation of services.

incidence—The number of new cases of a disease or condition divided by the exposed population over a specified time frame. Incidence is used to measure the effectiveness of treatments or interventions. For example, if there are 150 new cases of depression in a population of 2000 sedentary postmenopausal women over five years, the incidence of depression over five years is 7.5%.

mediator—A variable that is responsible for (mediates) the effects of the predictor on the outcome. For example, many believe that confidence in one's ability to exercise (exercise self-efficacy) mediates the effects of an intervention on exercise participation. Therefore, people adhere after an intervention because of the intervention's effects on self-efficacy.

meta-analysis, or **quantitative review**—A method of synthesizing research literature by cumulating effect sizes or relative risks. This differs from a narrative critique of each study's results based on statistical hypothesis testing, which depends on sample size. A narrative critique of research articles is prone to bias from the subjective perspective of the author. A meta-analysis produces a statistical synthesis with less subjective bias, but it can be biased by the statistical methodology used and the quality of the studies included.

moderator—A variable that influences how an intervention or a mediator affects the outcome and results in an interaction. For example, age would moderate the effects of rock and roll music on enjoyment in an exercise class if the only participants who liked this music were the middle-aged baby boomers.

relative risk—The ratio of the two rates (i.e., proportions) of the occurrence of disease in two groups. If the disease rates are 20% among an inactive group and 10% in an active group, the relative risk for inactivity is 2.0; or conversely, the relative risk for activity is 0.50.

sensitivity—The ability of a test to detect a disease or attribute. For example, a test that is sensitive for depression will have few false-negatives; it will not miss cases of depression when they truly exist.

specificity—The ability of a test to discriminate. For example, a test that is specific for depression will detect only symptoms of depression; it will indicate few false-positives.

Sensitivity and Specificity

Imagine that your goal is to discover the prevalence of employees at a local manufacturing plant who are highly physically active in their leisure time. You administer a scale designed to measure level of physical activity. The scale's sensitivity is its ability to identify those who are highly active. With use of this scale, very few employees who are truly active at high levels are classified as having a low level of physical activity. The scale's specificity is its ability to correctly define those who are not highly active. Very few low-active or moderately active employees are misclassified as highly active. A scale having high sensitivity and specificity will have high predictive validity.

Research Design

Much research in sport psychology has been plagued by studies designed and conducted by psychologists who were unfamiliar with sports medicine, and by exercise physiologists who had a limited background in psychology. The quality of the research in exercise psychology has also been shadowed by this problem. Few researchers have dual degrees in exercise physiology and psychology, and the corresponding gaps in knowledge and experience are reflected in problems in **experimental design** and measurement.

Much of the research has not been based on theory, or has not matched the research to the theoretical model of the psychological construct. For example, theoretically, trait anxiety is stable so there is no need to measure trait anxiety both before and after acute exercise. Some of the research that has used theoretical models has applied them only in part, limiting the ability to explain lack of significant effects. Most applications of social cog-

nitive theories to understanding physical activity typically have not included measures of personal biologic influences on physical activity. Only a few studies applying the transtheoretical model to exercise behavior have included all the model's components.

Several issues relate specifically to research design. Most studies in which the aim is to relate exercise and mental health have been cross-sectional (e.g., screening, correlational) or predictive, and therefore cannot provide information about cause and effect.

In **cross-sectional designs,** subjects are identified and classified as to exposure and outcome at the same point in time. These types of studies are also called prevalence studies. Cross-sectional designs are good for general description and for the identification of trends, but there are problems associated with selective survival and with subject recall when questionnaire data are used.

A **case-control design** is a retrospective design commonly used in epidemiology to "reconstruct"

Scientific Criteria for Causality

A situation or condition can be considered as causing an event if it is a temporal antecedent to the event and if the event would not have occurred had the situation or condition not been present. There are scientific standards to identify something as a cause. Selected criteria used in epidemiology (Mausner and Kramer 1985) to judge the strength of causal evidence linking exercise with mental health benefits are as follows:

1. Strength of association: The lower the disease rate among active people relative to inactive people, the more likely physical activity protects against disease; a halving of the rate of disease is an acceptable standard.

2. Temporal sequence: The measurement of physical activity must precede the onset of disease with sufficient time for healthful biological adaptations.

3. Consistency: The association of increased activity with reduced disease should appear in different regions and in different types of people, using different methods of study.

4. Independence: The association of reduced disease among physically active people is not explained by disproportionately higher occurrence of other causes of the disease among the physically inactive (e.g., age, smoking, poor social support).

5. Dose-response gradient: Increasing levels of physical activity should correspond with decreased levels of disease in a linear or curvilinear manner.

6. Plausibility: Explanations for reduced disease with increased physical activity are coherent with existing theory or knowledge about the etiology of the disease and about biological adaptations that occur with physical activity.

7. Experimental confirmation: Controlled experiments confirm that increasing physical activity prevents or reduces the disease occurrence.

the likely causes of health-related events after they have occurred. Ideally, a representative group of healthy controls are matched with cases (e.g., sick people) on age, gender, and race and are often recruited from the same setting as the cases. Then, a comparison of the two groups is made on the frequency of past exposure to potential risk factors for the disease. Risk factor information is typically obtained by personal interview or from a review of medical records. Disadvantages of the case-control design include difficulty in obtaining a truly representative control group, the inability to study more than one disease outcome at a time, and the potential for recall bias. Case-control studies are useful for the initial development and testing of hypotheses to determine whether there is justification for moving forward to conduct a more time-consuming and expensive cohort study or randomized trial.

Predictive designs and prospective or cohort studies group disease-free subjects according to exposure and then evaluate them over time to determine the disease occurrence in exposed and unexposed groups. The measure of association is expressed as a relative risk. Prospective studies have provided important evidence for the effects of exercise on mental health and have directed attention to potential mediating variables for inclusion in exercise interventions.

Randomized controlled trials are used to determine whether or not associations uncovered in epidemiologic observations or in small laboratory experiments represent cause-and-effect relations that apply to large numbers of people, usually diagnosed with a disease. The validity of the trial depends on having a representative population sample and on similarity between treatment and control groups with respect to characteristics thought to affect outcome. The random assignment of subjects to treatment or control group is essential in order to equally distribute known and unknown confounding variables between groups. **Control groups** should experience all things in common with the treatment group except the critical treatment factor. Some researchers wishing to evaluate the effects of exercise on psychological variables have had the control group sit in a quiet room, attend a lecture, or even receive instructions to imagine exercising. In a clinical population, the effects of exercise on mental health should be compared to a traditional treatment rather than to a no-treatment control.

Control groups should experience all things in common with the treatment group except the critical treatment factor.

Many studies in exercise psychology have used convenient samples and volunteers. This introduces the problem of self-selection of motivated individuals into the study. People who volunteer to be in an intervention study are probably already more likely to adhere to a regular exercise program or believe they will benefit. Anxious individuals are unlikely to volunteer for a study on anxiety and exercise. Many studies of exercise and mental health have thus tested normal subjects, for whom there is little room for improvement regardless of the efficacy of the intervention. Sample size is also an issue in that a large sample may result in a statistically significant effect that has little clinical significance. Likewise, it can happen that the effects from a small sample are clinically important, but a lack of power precludes statistically meaningful differences.

The outcome of interest in mental health research is typically psychological and/or psychobiological constructs, and the experimental, or independent, variable is exercise behavior. Exercise adoption and adherence research uses interventions and psychosocial variables as experimental, or predictor, variables with level of physical activity as the dependent, or outcome, variable. Regardless of the focus, there are inconsistencies and limitations in the measurement of the dependent and independent variables in exercise psychology. Often, there is a lack of clarity in the definition of the psychological constructs being tested, as well as an abundance of different instruments that purport to measure the same construct. Sometimes the researcher develops instruments to measure psychological variables but does not report reliability and validity. Psychological measures of mental health are often inadequate. For example, one should not use self-report alone to assess depression and anxiety; measurements of physiological changes coincident with psychological changes are also needed. Studies in which biological variables are measured can have methodological limitations that restrict the ability to isolate specific mechanisms of action. For example, urinary and plasma levels of metabolites of neurotransmitters involved in mood disorders may be measured in conjunction with acute and chronic exercise. However, absolute levels and increases or decreases cannot be used to estimate adaptations in the central nervous system.

*A*pplication of theory, research design, subjects, and measurement of independent and dependent variables are issues in exercise psychology research.

Experimental Artifacts

Most often, self-report is used to assess psychological constructs that are treated as outcome variables or as mediators of behavior change. Several behavioral artifacts are known to influence research dealing with psychological outcomes (Morgan 1997), and research in exercise psychology is not immune to these effects. Such effects generally involve an alteration of true responses because of factors related to expectations by the participants (e.g., people respond in a way that they think the researcher wants them to), expectations by the experimenter (e.g., a subjective rating is biased), or experimenter effects on the participant (e.g., an investigator knowingly or unknowingly tips off the participant about the purpose of the study). Examples of experimental artifacts include the following:

▼ The **halo effect** is an experimenter expectancy effect in which certain characteristics are ascribed to a subject based on other known characteristics. A tester might assume that someone who scores low on trait anxiety would not be anxious about participating in a graded maximal exercise test, and thus incorrectly interpret signs of anxiety as indications of low fitness, for example, high heart rate and high perceived exertion.

▼ Participants' expectations also influence their responses. Someone who already believes that physical activity helps people sleep better might unwittingly inflate self-reports of how much his or her sleep has been improved after an exercise study.

▼ Demand characteristics include subtle messages about the experimental hypothesis that permit a motivated participant to guess the hypothesis of the study and strive to confirm or, conversely, sabotage the purpose of the study.

▼ **Rosenthal effect,** or the self-fulfilling prophecy, is also known as the Pygmalion effect. This occurs when the participant is motivated to meet the expectations that the investigator has communicated about the participant's attributes or abilities.

▼ **Hawthorne effect** is the tendency of the participants to improve following the manipulation of the independent variable simply because of the attention associated with the treatment. This influence is particularly critical to consider in the design of studies on exercise and mental health. Beneficial psychological changes cannot be fully ascribed to exercise when exercise is compared to a no-treatment condition, because anything might be better than nothing. The researcher should take the Hawthorne effect into account by demonstrating that exercise is better than a placebo treatment condition and that it is as effective as, or more effective than, other traditional treatments.

▼ **Social desirability responding** and **motivated response distortion** must be taken into account because people have a tendency to respond in ways they perceive to conform to socially desirable images of themselves. People can be consciously motivated to distort answers (i.e., lie) on a test in order to present a good impression. They also can unconsciously deceive themselves by distorting reality in order to enhance self-esteem, personal efficacy, and optimism (i.e., self-deception enhancement; Paulhus 1984). This tendency toward socially desirable responses especially threatens the accuracy of scales measuring self-perception constructs that are valued in society, such as self-esteem. People also may overestimate behaviors that are socially valued (e.g., physical activity) or underreport symptoms of disorders that carry a social stigma (e.g., depression).

Summary

The purpose of this chapter was to provide definitions and introduce perspectives on research in exercise psychology. Because an aim of this text is to be accessible to readers with a range of backgrounds, terms familiar to some readers—such as exercise, physical activity, and fitness—were defined and discussed. Other aspects critical to the definition and measurement of psychological constructs, such as scaling and statistical methods, may be less familiar; these were presented in more depth to help make subsequent discussions clearer and to help the reader become a more critical consumer of research. Issues in research were introduced as a basis for understanding the discussions on methodology included in subsequent chapters.

Suggested Readings

Caspersen, C.J., K.E. Powell, and G.M. Christenson. 1985. Physical activity, exercise, and physical fitness: Definitions and distinctions for health-related research. *Public Health Reports* 100: 126–131.

Kerlinger, F.N. 1973. *Foundations of behavioral research*. 2nd ed. New York: Holt, Rinehart & Winston.

Kriska, A.M., and C. Caspersen. 1997. Introduction to a collection of physical activity questionnaires. *Medicine and Science in Sports and Exercise* 29 (S6): S5-S9.

Montoye, H.J., H.C.G. Kemper, W.H.M. Saris, and R.A. Washburn. 1996. *Measuring physical activity and energy expenditure*. Champaign, IL: Human Kinetics.

Morgan, W.P. 1997. Methodological considerations. In *Physical activity and mental health*, ed. W.P. Morgan. *The series in psychology and behavioral medicine*. Washington, DC: Taylor & Francis.

Nunnally, J.C., and I.H. Bernstein. 1994. *Psychometric theory*. 3rd ed. New York: McGraw-Hill.

Web Sites

www.rasch.org/memos.htm (see memo #62)

http://davidmlane.com/hyperstat/index.html

3

Behavioral Neuroscience

Examining the relationship between exercise and changes in social cognitive variables, such as attitudes and self-esteem, contributes to our understanding of how exercise can affect mental health and how to increase exercise adherence. However, behavior and brain function are also determined by biological factors. Though modern-day muscle biologists may not agree, William James remarked in 1899, "it is pretty well understood now that the result of physical training is to train the nervous centers more than the muscles." Thus, readers will need a basic understanding of the central nervous system, the autonomic nervous system, key neurotransmitters, and the *cellular* and *molecular biology* of the brain in order to fully understand subsequent chapters on stress; anxiety; depression; affect, mood, and emotion; and sleep.

This chapter provides a basic overview of **behavioral neuroscience,** which is the measurement of neural events applied to the study of brain and behavior. The goal is not to review neuroanatomy and **neurobiology** in depth, but rather to provide a primer for subsequent discussions on physiological mechanisms for effects of exercise on aspects of mental health. For example, when improvements in depression are suggested in light of the relationship between exercise and galanin or neuropeptide

Y (NPY) inhibition of the locus coeruleus or reduced density of β_1 receptors in the brain cortex, the reader will be able to refer back to this chapter. Section 1 presents the basic anatomy of the central nervous system, the autonomic nervous system, and the hypothalamic-pituitary-adrenal axis. Major functions critical to mood and behavior are included. The measurement and interpretation of *heart rate variability* are also discussed to illustrate the use of noninvasive methods of psychophysiology for understanding how the autonomic nervous system regulates the cardiovascular system during stress or in patients with anxiety disorders. Section 2 reviews the mood-influencing neurotransmitters in terms of their actions in the nervous system. Section 3 presents some basic concepts and techniques used in brain cellular and molecular biology to measure gene expression, including *in situ hybridization histochemistry* and *immunocytochemistry*. The use of animal models of human disease is discussed in section 4. Finally, in section 5, the methods of *electrophysiology, microdialysis, electroencephalography,* and *neuroimaging* are described as they are applied to measure brain activity during behavior and emotional responses. Most of the material covered in later chapters can be generally understood without this chapter, but the content is designed to help students more fully appreciate these complex phenomena and techniques.

Section 1: The Neural Network

The anatomical basis for information processing is the extensive network of neural pathways and circuits that serve to connect the individual with his or her internal world (e.g., memories, tightness in a muscle, hunger) and the external world (see figure 3.1). The neural network is divided into the central nervous system and the peripheral nervous system, shown in figure 3.2. The peripheral nervous system is organized into two components: the somatic nervous system[1] (the cranial and spinal nerves) and the autonomic nervous system. Because of their roles in mental health and behavior, the central nervous system and the autonomic nervous system are described in more detail later.

The central nervous system connects the individual with his or her internal and external world.

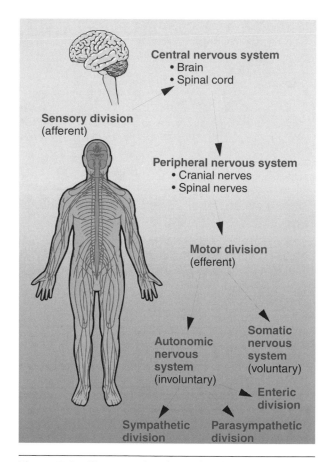

Figure 3.2 The central and peripheral nervous systems in the human body.

Reprinted, by permission, from J.H. Wilmore and D.L. Costill, 1999, *Physiology of sport and exercise,* 2nd ed., (Champaign, IL: Human Kinetics), 64.

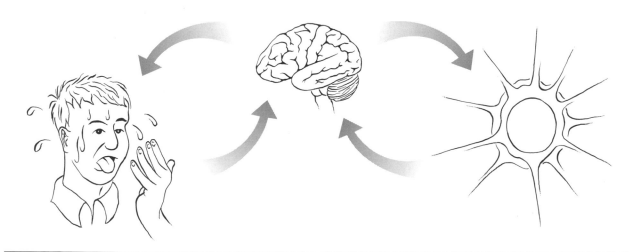

Figure 3.1 The central nervous system processes sensations of heat and light from the environment and orchestrates our physiological, psychological, and behavioral responses.

---

1. The somatic nervous system receives sensory information and controls skeletal muscle movement.

The Somatic Nervous System

The **cranial nerves,** connected directly to the brain, include bundles of axons that form 12 pairs. Cranial nerves are sensory (transmit sensory information to the brain, e.g., olfactory, optic), motor (innervate specific muscles, e.g., hypoglossal—moves the tongue), or both sensory and motor (e.g., vagus) (see figure 3.3).

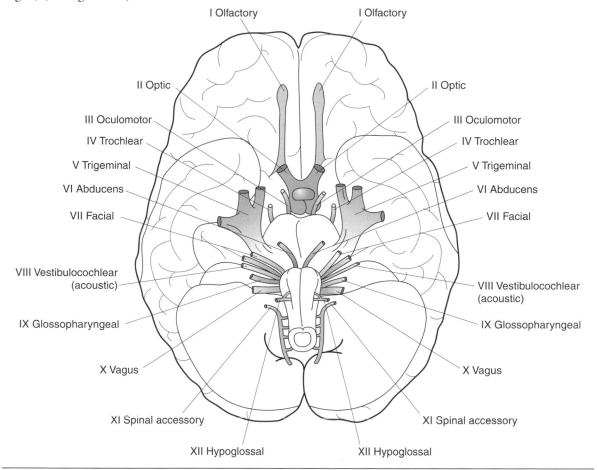

Figure 3.3 Some cranial nerves send sensory information to the brain; some innervate specific muscles; and some do both.

Reprinted, by permission, from S.J. Shultz, P.A. Houglum, and D.H. Perrin, 2000, Assessment of athletic injuries (Champaign, IL: Human Kinetics), 348.

There are 31 pairs of **spinal nerves** that join the spinal cord at regularly spaced intervals and are named according to the segment of the spinal cord to which they are attached (i.e., cervical, thoracic, lumbar, or sacral). Each spinal nerve consists of sensory pathways from the periphery to the spinal cord, as well as motor pathways from the spinal cord to the muscles.

Central Nervous System

The central nervous system is one of the most intricate and complicated systems in the body (see figure 3.4). It is responsible for sensing, screening, processing, storing, and responding to millions of bits of information 24 hours a day, seven days a week. This is a dynamic system that has a reciprocal relationship with the rest of the body and the external world. Every time you learn something new, the chemistry of your brain (often including the transcription of genes encoding brain proteins that regulate neural activity) is altered by that process. A biological framework for the etiology of mental disorders that describes the interaction between structure and function was proposed by psychiatrist Eric Kandel (1998). This framework includes five principles:

1. Actions at the brain level are responsible for all mental and psychological processes.
2. Brain functioning is controlled by genes.
3. Social, developmental, and environmental factors can produce alterations in gene expression.
4. Alterations in gene expression induce changes in brain functioning.
5. Treatments for mental illness exert their effect by producing alterations in gene expression resulting in beneficial changes in brain function.

Thus, within this framework, depression and other mood disorders result from disturbances in brain processes; and treatments such as psychotherapy, medication, or exercise produce changes in brain function at a genetic level that result in alleviation of symptoms. How all this happens is not fully understood, but significant progress is being made in describing the structure and function of the nervous system and its interrelationships with behavior and mood.

The structure of the central nervous system consists of the spinal cord, the brainstem, and the brain (forebrain). The **spinal cord** contains neural circuits that control a variety of reflexive functions; it provides the pathway for bringing sensory input from the periphery to the brain and carrying messages or motor signals from the brain to the periphery. The **afferent,** or sensory, signals travel to the brain via the dorsal horn of the spinal cord to send information about internal organs, muscles, body position, and other peripheral sensations. The **efferent,** or motor, neurons travel down the ventral horn to form the motor portion of the spinal nerves and to innervate muscles. Spinal nerves are not like cables that merely conduct a signal. Considerable processing of neural signals occurs in the spinal cord; this can dramatically alter the signal as it passes between organs and the central nervous system. Dorsal (sensory) and ventral (motor) roots from the spinal cord are fused to form the right and left sides of each of the 31 spinal nerve pairs. Figure 3.5 shows a cross section of a spinal cord with the dorsal and ventral horns labeled. Type III and type IV afferent neural fibers, which primarily transmit nociceptive (pain) signals, innervate mainly both the dorsal and ventral horns of the spinal cord.

Both sensory and motor neurons from the periphery and the brain pass through the brainstem.

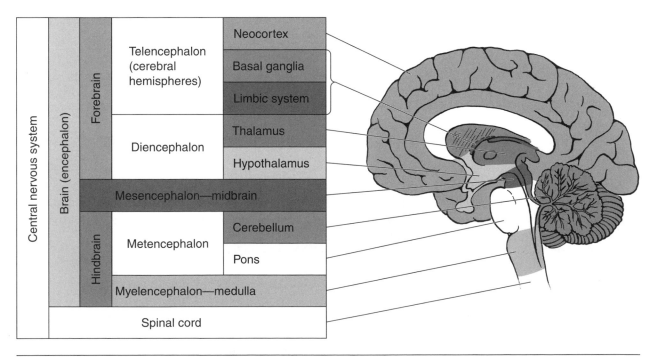

Figure 3.4 The organization of the central nervous system, including the spinal cord and three brain regions (forebrain, midbrain, and hindbrain).

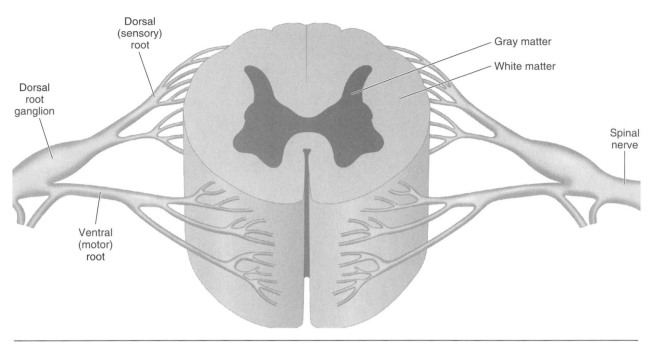

Figure 3.5 Cross section of the spinal cord.

Reprinted, by permission, from J.H. Wilmore and D.L. Costill, 1999, *Physiology of sport and exercise,* 2nd ed., (Champaign, IL: Human Kinetics), 67.

The **brainstem** is a continuous extension of the spinal cord upward into the cranial cavity; it consists of the **medulla** (mylencephalon), **pons** (metencephalon), and **midbrain** (mesencephalon) (see figure 3.6). Far from being a simple conduit, the brainstem contains several neural centers critical to behavior and mood, in addition to controlling functions basic to life, such as arterial blood pressure and respiration.

The medulla marks the transition from the spinal cord to the brainstem. It contributes to the regulation of cardiorespiratory functions and contains the end of the **reticular formation,** which extends up into the midbrain. The major **nuclei** for serotonin (also known as 5-HT) are the **raphe nuclei,** located mainly in the center line of the brainstem near the locus coeruleus. The raphe cells send projections to

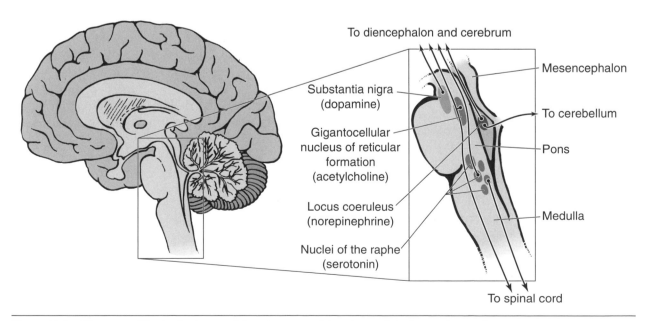

Figure 3.6 Diagram of the brainstem and its primary nuclei and associated neurotransmitters.

parts of the brain that control emotion and behavior (e.g., amygdala, hippocampus, hypothalamus, ventral tegmental area, and frontal cortex), locomotion (e.g., the **striatum** and **cerebellum**), blood pressure (e.g., the area postrema in the brainstem just outside the blood-brain barrier, which is sensitive to changes in concentrations of chemicals in the blood), and the processing of other peripheral signals such as pain (spinal cord). Serotonin is a critical neurotransmitter in anxiety and depression and also functions in the regulation of sleep and eating.

The medulla contains the raphe nucleus, the major nucleus in the brain for the production of the neurotransmitter serotonin.

The pons wraps around the base of the cerebellum and contains nuclei involved in motor control and sensory analysis. The cerebellum is located dorsal to the pons and is a critical component of the motor system, integrating sensory information with information about muscle movement to coordinate movement. The pons contains the **locus coeruleus** (LC), identified as a bluish area just below the fourth ventricle of the brain ("locus coeruleus" comes from the Latin word *caeruleus*, meaning "blue"). The overall role of the LC is to inhibit spontaneous firing in the areas it innervates, which include the cerebellum, hippocampus, amygdala, thalamic and hypothalamic nuclei, cerebral cortex, mesencephalon (midbrain), and spinal cord. The LC is also involved in rapid eye movement (REM) sleep and reward, and it is the major nucleus for **norepinephrine (NE)**, a neurotransmitter important in brain activation and mood regulation. About half the cells that make NE in the brain are located in the LC.

The locus coeruleus, which is the primary site for the production of the neurotransmitter norepinephrine in the brain, is located in the pons.

The midbrain, or mesencephalon, forms the top of the brainstem. It includes portions of the reticular formation, the substantia nigra, the central gray, and the ventral tegmental area. The *reticular formation* is a network of neurons running from the upper spinal cord through the medulla, pons, and midbrain to the ventral diencephalon, where we find the reticular nucleus. The reticular activating system is a structure of many diffuse, interconnected networks of nuclei. It plays a role in the sleep-wake cycle, forebrain arousal, attention, temperature regulation, and motor control. The *substantia nigra* is a major center for the neurotransmitter dopamine and an important **ganglion** (collection of neurons) in motor control. The *central gray* (periaque-ductal gray) is a region tightly packed with neural bodies in the center of the brainstem around the aqueduct that connects the third and fourth ventricles. Some of the functions of the central gray are emotional arousal, fighting, mating, and pain. When opioid **receptors** on neurons in the central gray are stimulated by opiates (e.g., morphine) or opioid peptides (e.g., enkephalins), sensitivity to pain decreases. The *ventral tegmental area* (VTA) is the underside of an area at the top of the brainstem located between the pons and the fourth ventrical of the brain containing neurons that secrete dopamine and project to the nucleus accumbens and the frontal cortex. Activation of the VTA results in pleasure and increased seeking behavior.

Every organ in the body is connected to the brain, which weighs only 1400 g, or 2% of your body weight (about the weight of this textbook!) (Rosenzweig, Leiman, and Breedlove 1999a). The *forebrain* is responsible for your ability to read this book, ride your bicycle, and decide whether you are going to enroll in a strength-training class. The forebrain, which is the most rostral (anterior) portion of the brain, is divided into the **diencephalon** and the **telencephalon.** The most important structures in the diencephalon are the thalamus and the hypothalamus. The **thalamus** has bidirectional connections with many areas in the cerebral cortex. It is the pathway for all sensory systems except the olfactory. The dorsal thalamus processes, integrates, and relays sensory input into the telencephalon. When you step outside for a walk, the sensations of ambient temperature, light, sound, and feedback from your muscles are all processed in the thalamus before they are received in your higher brain for use in making decisions and taking action. The anterior thalamus projects into the limbic system and is involved in motivation and emotion. The medial and lateral nuclei of the thalamus are involved in the mediation of pain.

The **hypothalamus** projects downward to the brain stem; upward to other areas of the diencephalon, cerebrum, anterior thalamus, and limbic cortex; and into the infundibulum to control secretory functions of the pituitary gland, a critical gland in the control of almost all hormone secretion. The hypothalamus controls vegetative functions, like cardiovascular activity, feeding, sleep, and temperature regulation. It also regulates hormonal balance and plays a major role in many aspects of emotional behavior. The hypothalamus is part of the triumvirate of the hypothalamic-pituitary-adrenal axis, which is central in responding to mental and physical stress, as discussed later in this chapter and in chapter 4.

The telencephalon is composed of the neocortex (cerebral cortex), the basal ganglia, and the limbic system. The **neocortex** surrounds the cerebral hemispheres and is characterized by an elaborate folding of tissue, with small grooves (sulci), large grooves (fissures), and large ridges of tissue (gyri) that triple the area of the neocortex; about two-thirds of the surface is hidden in the depths of these folds. The neocortex is the center of higher brain functions, such as problem solving, creativity, and judgment. Areas of the neocortex, such as the primary visual cortex and the primary motor cortex, have been charted according to their input and function. For example, the medial prefrontal cortex serves to shift affective states on the basis of internal and external stimuli, and is the only cortical region that sends direct projections into the hypothalamus. The **basal ganglia** are a collection of subcortical nuclei in the forebrain that includes the corpus striatum (consisting of the caudate and lentiform nuclei) and cell groups associated with the corpus striatum, such as the subthalamic nucleus and substantia nigra. The basal ganglia are critical in the control of movement. The substantia nigra, shown in perspective to the other basal ganglia in figure 3.7, is a major source of dopa-mine in the brain. Dopamine plays a critical role in motor functions, but it is also associated with motivation and mood, as will be discussed later and in chapter 7.

The **limbic system** is a widespread collection of nuclei that completely surrounds the diencephalon.

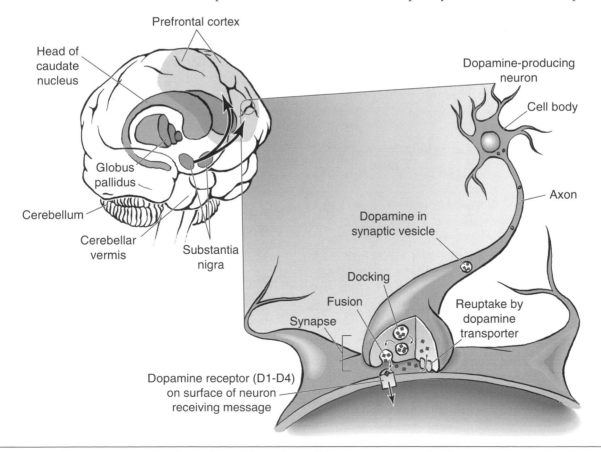

Figure 3.7   Structures of the basal ganglia and the actions of dopamine from production to post-synaptic activation.

Adapted from R.A. Barkley, 1998, "Attention-deficit hyperactivity disorder," *Scientific American* 279(3): 66-71.

It has two-way linkages with the neocortex and elicits behavioral functions that are mediated through the reticular nuclei of the brainstem. The limbic system is considered the seat of emotional behavior and motivational drives and has a role in learning. It is involved in the expression of instinct and mood, self-preservation, and the establishment of memory patterns. Thus, the limbic system controls a variety of functions that are of interest if we want to examine the psychobiology of exercise. Parts of the limbic system that are important in exercise and mental health are the amygdala (Latin for its shape, like that of an almond) and the hippocampus (Latin for its seahorse shape), shown in figure 3.8 in respect to other areas of the limbic system. The **amygdala** is a portion of the limbic system that controls appropriate behavior for social situations and is linked to emotional memory as well as the generation of anger and fear. Its significance in exercise and affect is discussed in chapter 5. The **hippocampus** functions in labeling changes in the environment as threatening and in declarative memory storage. The hippocampus transfers input that is appraised as important into the cerebral cortex. When the hippocampus is stimulated, the individual becomes hypervigilant and apprehensive. Receptors for cortisol on the hippocampus implicate it in physiological responses to depression (chapter 7) and chronic mental stress (chapter 4).

The limbic system is the area of the central nervous system that is the center of emotional behavior and motivation drives.

Autonomic Nervous System

The **autonomic nervous system** (ANS) is a branch of the peripheral nervous system that spans the central and peripheral nervous systems. It was named autonomic (independent, self-governing) because early anatomists discovered its ganglia outside of the central nervous system. The autonomic nervous system regulates the viscera, some glands, smooth muscle, and cardiac muscle primarily by the activity of cranial nerves 3, 7, 9, and 10 and other sympathetic nerves. It is made up of three branches—the *sympathetic*, *parasympathetic*, and *enteric* nervous systems—that send messages via neurotransmitters (NT) from the central nervous system to the ganglia. All pre-ganglionic NT receptors are nicotinic cholinergic (activated by the NT acetylcholine), while the post-ganglionic NT vary as a function of their receptors. Beta- and α-adrenoreceptors are activated by NE and epinephrine, and muscarinic cholinergic receptors are activated by acetylcholine. Figure 3.9 shows autonomic nerves and the organs they innervate. Generally, the sympathetic nervous

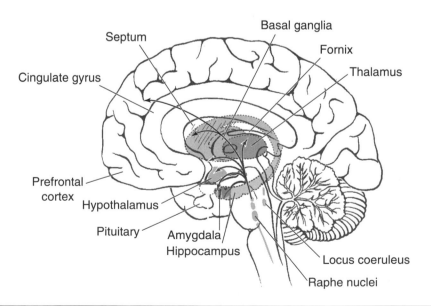

Figure 3.8 Cross section of the central nervous system showing limbic structures (hippocampus, amygdala, cingulate gyrus, fornix). Arrows show the pathways from the raphe nuclei to the central structures.

From C.B. Nemeroff, 1998, "The neurobiology of depression," *Scientific American* 278 (6): 42–47.

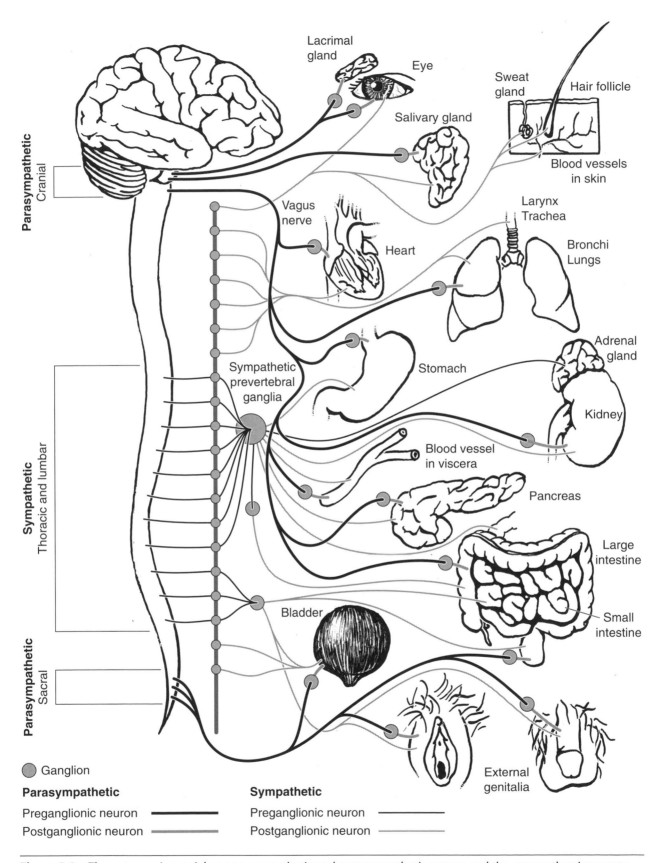

Figure 3.9 The autonomic cranial nerves, sympathetic and parasympathetic nerves, and the organs they innervate.

From Neil R. Carlson, *Physiology of behavior*, 6e. Copyright 1998 by Allyn & Bacon. Adapted by permission.

system is involved in energy expenditure, and the parasympathetic is involved in energy conservation. The *enteric system* controls the intestines.

The continuously active basal rates of sympathetic and parasympathetic nerve discharge are known as sympathetic tone and parasympathetic tone. Effects on an organ can be the result of either an increase or a decrease in sympathetic or parasympathetic activation. At one time the accepted view was that these two systems had a linear reciprocal relationship with tightly coupled reciprocal control. However, Berntson, Cacioppo, and Quigley (1991, 1993) provided compelling arguments and experimental evidence for a broader, two-dimensional model of autonomic control. In their doctrine of autonomic space, activation of the two branches may be coupled or uncoupled. Coupled responses in which both systems are activated simultaneously may be reciprocal or nonreciprocal, the latter entailing concurrent increases or decreases in both parasympathetic and sympathetic activation. For example, an exaggerated stress-related increase in heart rate could be from elevated sympathetic activation alone (uncoupled), potent parasympathetic withdrawal (uncoupled), or both (coupled reciprocal) (Berntson et al. 1993). The absence of a change in heart rate in response to mental stress does not mean there is no autonomic response, but instead can result from an increase in parasympathetic activity that cancels out sympathetic activation (coupled nonreciprocal). The possibility of a physiological response that is not manifest in end-organ activity is important to keep in mind when we are considering the limitations of research on exercise and stress reactivity in chapter 4.

The autonomic nervous system has two branches that control energy expenditure (sympathetic) and energy conservation (parasympathetic). They can act alone, or together with one increasing and the other decreasing activation, or together with both increasing or decreasing activation.

Sympathetic Nervous System

The **sympathetic nervous system** (SNS) is involved in arousal and activities that require energy expenditure, such as exercise. Simply put, the SNS prepares the body for action (such as when you are waiting for the start of a road race) or for the "fight-or-flight" response to perceived threat (such as that posed by a large, snarling dog). Preparing the body for action in the face of mental stress when there is no opportunity for physical action is part of the stress response that may contribute to several stress-related illnesses, such as hypertension.

The SNS consists of 22 pairs of ganglia strung together on either side of the spinal cord, connected to each other and to the spinal cord. The pre-ganglionic neurons connected to the spinal cord are short, while the post-ganglionic neurons are long; the latter connect to the effector organs, such as the heart and sweat glands (see figure 3.9). The post-ganglionic neurons are adrenergic, releasing NE to α- and β-adrenergic receptors on the effector organs to produce a host of effects. The effect from activation and deactivation of the SNS is analogous to turning an electrical current on and off, respectively, to rooms in a house or to the whole house. Depending on the type or severity of circumstances, responses can be specific to a single organ, a few organs, or all the organs innervated by the SNS. Your heart rate increases, you begin to sweat, your eyes dilate, your mouth becomes dry, and other less obvious effects of SNS activation occur together.

The Parasympathetic Nervous System

The **parasympathetic nervous system** (PNS) is involved in the conservation of energy, such as the slowing of heart rate and stimulation of digestion. The PNS has long pre-ganglionic neurons that originate in the head and sacral regions (see figure 3.9). The post-ganglionic neurons are short and are adjacent to the organs they innervate. The NT released post-ganglionically is **acetylcholine,** and the post-synaptic receptors are muscarinic cholinergic. Activation of the PNS is specific, analogous to turning on a lamp in a house, and offers better voluntary control than the SNS. You can salivate at the sight of a hot piece of pie without a corresponding decrease in heart rate.

The sympathetic nervous system is responsible for energy expenditure, and the parasympathetic nervous system contributes to energy conservation.

Autonomic Balance and the Cardiovascular System: Heart Rate Variability

Heart rate variability (HRV) provides information about modulation of heart rate by the autonomic nervous system in a variety of dynamic circumstances (Task Force of the European Society of Cardiology and the North American Society of Pacing and Electrophysiology 1996), including the experience of emotions and during exercise. Heart rate variability is commonly described by the standard deviation of intervals between successive R waves of the cardiac cycle. Short-term variation (e.g., measured during periods of several minutes) can be decomposed mathematically into components of the frequency spectrum that estimate autonomic modulation of heart rate. The high-frequency (HF) component (.15-.5 Hz; a Hz is one complete cycle or period of oscillation per second) is believed to correspond to modulation of HRV by the vagus nerve during breathing and is also called respiratory sinus arrhythmia (see figure 3.10). These relatively fast fluctuations correspond to the changes in heart rate measured when the vagus nerve is electrically stimulated in animals, and reflect the rapid action of acetylcholine in inhibiting heart cells by directly opening ion channels.

The low-frequency (LF) spectrum (.05-.15 Hz) corresponds to baroreflex control of heart rate (i.e., in response to changes in blood pressure) and reflects mixed sympathetic and parasympathetic modulation of HRV in most circumstances. These slower fluctuations of heart rate result from a slower response by the heart to sympathetic modulation than to vagal modulation, mainly because the action of NE on heart cells depends on a second-messenger system to open ion channels rather than a direct action like that of acetylcholine. More about the second-messenger system follows later in this chapter (see figure 3.17). Activity in the very low frequency (VLF) spectrum (.0033-.05 Hz) can provide another index of sympathetic influence on heart rate. To estimate autonomic balance during short-term fluctuations in heart rate, the HF and LF components commonly are normalized to their total power (e.g., [HF/(HF + LF) × 100]) in order to remove influences of VLF. Long-term (e.g., 24 h) monitoring of HRV permits assessment of the ultra-low-frequency spectrum (<.0033 Hz), which is strongly correlated with total HRV (i.e., the standard deviation of the RR interval across the 24 h period).

Low HRV (especially the high-frequency component) is associated with perceived stress and with cardiac arrhythmia, cardiac mortality, and all cause mortality after myocardial infarction. Low HRV has been reported in people with clinical anxiety disorders, including panic, posttraumatic stress, and generalized anxiety disorder. Because perceived stress is a predictor of transient myocardial ischemia, HRV may be a population risk factor for cardiac events (Tsuji et al. 1996). Several studies have shown that people who have high cardiorespiratory fitness have higher HRV, especially in the high-frequency range. Whether fitness can buffer the effects of stress on

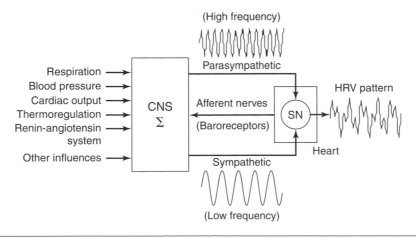

Figure 3.10 The high-frequency parasympathetic and the low-frequency sympathetic contributions to pattern of heart rate variability.

Reprinted, by permission, from R. McCraty and A. Watkins, 1996, *Autonomic assessment report: A comprehensive heart rate variability analysis. Interpretation guide and instructions* (Boulder Creek, CA: HeartMath Research Center), 7.

HRV is not yet known, but a recent study found that middle-aged adults who report persistent emotional stress have less high-frequency HRV (Dishman, Nakamura, et al. 2000), regardless of their age, gender, or level of physical fitness.

Measures of heart rate variability provide information about modulation of heart rate by the autonomic nervous system and can tell us about the sympathetic and parasympathetic contributions to responses in different situations.

Endocrine System

There is a rich, dynamic interaction between the central nervous system and the autonomic nervous system, illustrated by the sympathetic medullary system and the hypothalamic-pituitary-adrenal axis (HPA), which are both activated by the hypothalamus.

The **sympathetic medullary system** includes the SNS and the **adrenal medulla,** which is activated by the posterior hypothalamus through a direct neural pathway. Norepinephrine is synthesized by the chromaffin cells of the adrenal medulla, and NE and epinephrine (Epi) are secreted by the adrenal medulla as hormones into the bloodstream in a ratio of 1 (NE) to 4 (Epi). The actions of NE and Epi are sympathomimetic; that is, they mimic the effects of SNS activation. However, the effects last 5 to 10 times longer than direct SNS stimulation (1-2 min after the stimulus is over) because of the slow removal of these neurohormones from the blood. The primary effect of plasma NE is to increase blood pressure by increasing peripheral resistance. Epinephrine produces more general sympathetic effects, such as increased heart rate and enhanced cellular metabolism.

The **hypothalamic-pituitary-adrenal axis** includes the *hypothalamus*, the *pituitary*, and the *adrenal cortex* (see figure 3.11). The pituitary gland, which is connected directly to the hypothalamus by the pituitary stalk, consists of two main parts (anterior, or adenohypophysis, and posterior, or neurohypophysis) that are separate in function. The adrenal cortex is the outer covering of the adrenal gland.

The *anterior hypothalamus* releases two potent hormones (thyroid-stimulating hormone and corticotropin-releasing hormone) that are involved in the

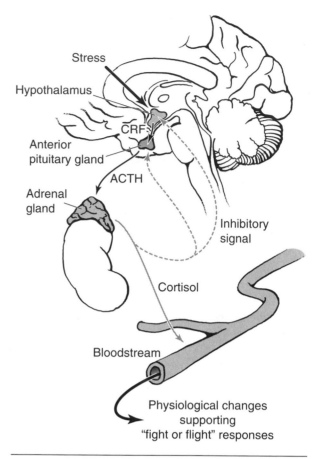

Figure 3.11   Activation of the hypothalamus, pituitary, and adrenal cortex (HPA) in response to stress.

Reprinted from C.B. Nemeroff, 1998, "The neurobiology of depression," *Scientific American* 278 (6): 42–47.

response to physical and mental stress. **Thyroid-stimulating hormone** causes the *anterior pituitary* to release thyrotropic hormone, which stimulates the thyroid gland to release thyroxin. Thyroxin stimulates carbohydrate and fat metabolism and increases metabolic rate. **Corticotropin-releasing hormone** (CRH) is released by the anterior hypothalamus (parvicellular [i.e., small cell] area of the paraventricular nucleus that lies on each side of the third ventricle of the brain) as part of circadian rhythms and in response to physical and mental stress.

Corticotropin-releasing hormone stimulates the *posterior pituitary* to release vasopressin (antidiuretic hormone); it also stimulates the *anterior pituitary* to release prolactin and the co-secretion of **adrenocorticotropic hormone** (ACTH) and β-endorphin into circulation. Adrenocorticotropic hormone activates the **adrenal cortex** to secrete aldosterone and cortisol. It also enhances the response of the adrenal cortex to subsequent stimulation; enhances attention, motivation, learning, and memory retention; and acts as an opiate antagonist. **Cortisol,** the major glucocorticoid secreted by the adrenal cortex, plays a role in the stress response and depression. Major effects of cortisol include control over metabolism, such as stimulation of gluconeogenesis (i.e., synthesis of new sugars from fat or protein) and mobilization of fatty acids for fuel during exercise, and the suppression of the immune response. Release of cortisol is controlled by ACTH, but there are receptors for cortisol on the hypothalamus and anterior pituitary that provide feedback to control the secretion of CRH and ACTH, respectively, and thus provide feedback regulation of cortisol secretion.

Cortisol has a role in the response to physical stress (i.e., exercise) and mental stress, as well as in central nervous system dysregulation associated with mood disorders.

Section 2: Neurotransmitters

The primary way that messages are transmitted throughout the nervous system is in the form of nerve impulses carried from one neuron to another (presynaptic to postsynaptic) through interneuronal junctions called synapses (see figure 3.12). Two basic types of synapses are electrical and chemical, but almost all the synapses in the CNS are chemical. The actions on neurons can be excitatory and inhibitory; these actions are produced in the brain primarily through two transmitter substances: glutamate (excitatory) and γ-aminobutyric acid (GABA; inhibitory). Other neurotransmitters (NT) do not have the information-transmitting effects of glutamate and GABA but produce their effects on the central nervous system by modulating circuits of neurons involved in specific brain functions. They interact with signaling proteins, called *G-proteins*, that are found in the cell membrane. Brain activity is thus influenced by other NT that alter the way in which neurons can process signals from glutamate and GABA. The basic information provided by the

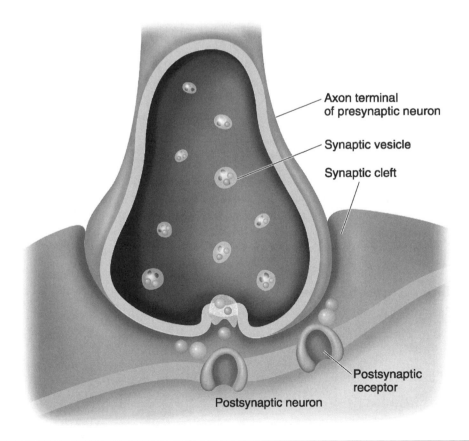

Figure 3.12 A chemical synapse between two neurons.

Reprinted, by permission, from J.H. Wilmore and D.L. Costill, 1999, *Physiology of sport and exercise,* 2nd ed. (Champaign, IL: Human Kinetics), 60.

actions of glutamate and GABA is thus modulated by a number of NT so that the outcome has emotional characteristics or significance. These NT, discussed in the sections that follow, have been studied in attempts to uncover biological mechanisms for the effects of exercise on mood, sleep, and pain perception.

Biogenic Amines

There are two classes of biogenic amines, catecholamines and indolamines, which are collectively known as monoamines.

Catecholamines

Catecholamines include the neurotransmitters *dopamine*, *norepinephrine*, and *epinephrine*. They are involved in sleep, reward, feeding, and drinking, as well as in functional illnesses (schizophrenia and depression) and organic diseases (Parkinson's disease, cardiovascular hypertension, paroxysmal tachycardia). Tyrosine is the amino acid precursor of the catecholamines, and tyrosine hydroxylase is the rate-limiting enzyme under basal conditions. Tyrosine is converted into dopamine via an intermediary step. Dopamine may then be converted into NE or can serve as an NT itself. Norepinephrine may be converted into epinephrine, as shown in figure 3.13.

The **dopamine** (DA) system plays a critical role in motivation and motor functions. It is the key NT in the ventral tegmental area, an area of the brain surrounding the hypothalamus that is involved in pleasure. Increase in extracellular DA in the nucleus accumbens (located near the striatum, part of the basal ganglia; see figure 3.14) is an important brain mechanism involved in natural rewards experienced from behaviors such as eating and physical movement. It has been established that a brain circuit in humans involving the orbitofrontal region of the prefrontal cortex, the thalamus, and the striatum is pivotally involved in the maintenance of survival behaviors that require a repetitive pattern, such as eating, moving, and sex.

*I*mportant neurotransmitters in mental health and exercise are the biogenic amines, such as norepinephrine and serotonin.

Norepinephrine was the first substance identified (in 1901) as a mediator of peripheral nerve cell activity. Norepinephrine makes up 1% of the brain's NT and is relatively slow acting (seconds) compared to classical NT like acetylcholine and GABA, which act in milliseconds. Thus, it is frequently regarded as a neuromodulator; its slower action helps modulate the rapid actions of other NT on neurons. Norepinephrine is distributed topographically (i.e.,

---

Neurotransmitters

Chemical substances that function as synaptic transmitters are called **neurotransmitters** (NT). Neurotransmitters are released directly to an adjacent nerve (postsynaptic), which becomes excited, inhibited, or modified in response to the attachment of the NT to specific receptor proteins in the membrane. An NT in the blood is called a neurohormone.

There are a number of influences on the release of presynaptic NT:

▼ Amount of transmitter available (depends on availability of substrates and enzymes; NT reserves)

▼ Activity of the presynaptic neuron (e.g., chronic activation can deplete presynaptic NT release)

▼ Activation of receptors on the presynaptic nerve by the NT to inhibit the further release (presynaptic inhibition)

These are influences on the effects of NT on the postsynaptic neuron:

▼ Type and amount of NT

▼ Type, density, and sensitivity of the receptor

▼ Presence of other enhancing or inhibiting chemical substances

▼ pH of the surrounding interstitial fluids

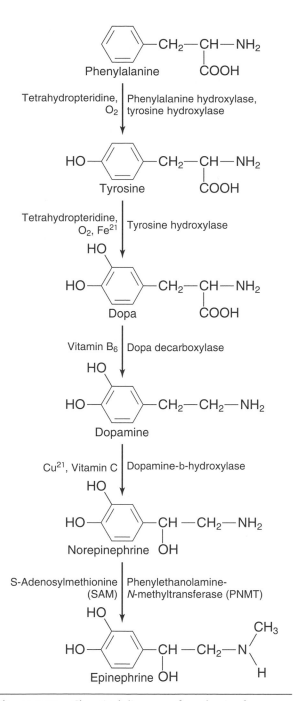

Figure 3.13 Chemical diagram of synthesis of catecholamines.

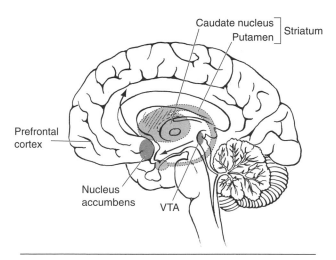

Figure 3.14 The VTA, a major site of brain DA, is shown in respect to the basal ganglia (caudate nucleus, putamen, and nucleus accumbens). Reward pathway from the ventral tegmental area (VTA) to the nucleus accumbens to the prefrontal cortex.

in a distinct pattern) in the brain, rather than diffusely. This permits NE to affect a wide range of functions in the central nervous system, including behavior during threat, pituitary hormonal release, cardiovascular function, sleep, and analgesic responses.

Norepinephrine is synthesized in neurons from the amino acid tyrosine taken up from blood. The primary central site for synthesis of NE in the brain

is cell bodies in the LC. Axons from the LC project into the periaqueductal gray, thalamic nuclei, and hypothalamus. The LC is the sole source of NE provided to the amygdala, hippocampus, all the frontal cortex, and the cerebellum. The LC is a major regulatory site for limbic dysfunction characteristic of both anxiety and depression. It integrates external and internal stimuli in order to regulate autonomic arousal, attention-vigilance, and neuroendocrine responses to behavioral stress. Norepinephrine hyperpolarizes neurons in the LC, enhancing responsiveness to signals from other neurons. A large number of brain NE neurons also lie outside the LC and are located throughout the lateral ventral tegmental fields. Fibers from these neurons intermingle with the LC neurons.

Norepinephrine is also the main nerve chemical of the SNS. Peripherally, it is manufactured in ganglia of the spinal cord and in chromaffin cells of the adrenal medulla, but the major source of NE in the autonomic nervous system is SNS free nerve endings. The rate of NE synthesis varies with the degree of sympathetic nerve activity and associated changes in the activity of tyrosine hydroxylase, the rate-limiting enzyme in the conversion of tyrosine to DOPA, and hence DA and NE synthesis. If NE is not taken back into the presynaptic neuron or is taken back into the presynaptic neuron and is not bound in storage vesicles, it is metabolized by the enzymes monoamine oxidase (MAO) and catecholo-methyltransferase (COMT). The major metabolites of NE are 3,4-dihydroxyphenylglycol

(DOPEG), inside the neuron, and 3-methoxy-4-hydroxyphenylglycol (MHPG) outside the neuron. Levels of NE have been estimated by measuring serum levels of these metabolites, but there are limitations with this method. An increase in serum MHPG, for example, does not indicate whether the rise is due to increased release or decreased reuptake of NE.

Norepinephrine is an important neuromodulator in the central nervous system and in the autonomic nervous system.

In the adrenal medulla, heart, and some brain regions, NE is further metabolized by the enzyme phenylethanolamine-N-methyltransferase to form the hormone **epinephrine** (Epi), which is also known by the Latin name *adrenaline* (see figure 3.13). The neurohormone was named **adrenaline** because it was thought that the substance was produced solely by the adrenal gland; and indeed, in the adrenal medulla, about 80% of the NE formed is converted into Epi. The adrenal gland is located above the kidney, hence the alternate name of epinephrine, which is derived from the Greek *epi nephro* ("upon the kidney"). The primary effect of Epi is cardiac stimulation, but it also serves as a minor transmitter in the brain. Functions of NE and Epi vary depending on the receptors (see figure 3.15).

Indolamines

The **indolamines** compose the second class of biogenic amines and include melatonin and serotonin. **Melatonin,** secreted by the pineal gland, influences circadian phases, such as the sleep-wake cycle. **Serotonin,** or 5-hydroxytryptamine (5-HT), is secreted peripherally by the digestive system and red blood cells and in the brain by the raphe nuclei, which have axon projections into the telencephalon, diencephalon, midbrain, and spinal cord. The primary effect of 5-HT is inhibition of spontaneous activity. It is a general suppressor of neural gain used to re-establish homeostasis (physiological equilibrium). Serotonin influences sleep and mood and has been the target of numerous antidepressant and anxiolytic drugs. Serotonin is also involved in pain, fatigue, appetitive behavior, periodicity of sleep, blood pres-

Adrenergic receptors

The effects of neurotransmitters are dependent on the type of receptors. The actions of norepinephrine (NE) and epinephrine (Epi) are mediated by two types of adrenergic receptors, α-receptors and β-receptors, which are further subdivided into α_1 and α_2 and β_1 and β_2. Generally, NE excites mainly α-receptors and to some extent β-receptors (expecially β_1 in the brain), whereas for the most part, Epi excites α-receptors and β-receptors equally.

α_1: Activates second-messenger phosphoinositide system. The phosphorylation of regulatory proteins that control ion channels and neural conductance/resistance consequent to receptor–second-messenger coupling plays a major role in brain NE activity. When α_1 receptors are bound with NE, physiologic effects also include vasoconstriction and increased peripheral vascular resistance to blood flow, which increases blood pressure.

α_2: Presynaptic autoreceptors. The binding of presynaptic α_2 receptors with NE is associated with an inhibition of NE release through decreases in both NE neuron activity and in the synthesis of NE by a G-protein inhibition of tyrosine hydroxylase. If NE in the locus coeruleus is depleted, the normal inhibition of NE by the α_2 receptors will be reduced, and thus there will be increased release of NE.

β_1: Activates a rise in levels of 3'5'-cyclic adenosine monophosphate (cAMP), which is a second messenger for neural transmissions.

β_2: Presynaptic receptors that enhance NE release. They have a higher affinity for Epi in brain. *When β-adrenergic receptors bind with NE or Epi, physiologic effects include increased heart rate or stroke volume.*

Figure 3.15   The actions of norepinephrine and epinephrine vary depending on the type of receptor.

sure, and corticosteroid activity. Projections from the raphe nuclei into the spinal cord have the ability to regulate pain by triggering the release of enkephalin, which is an **endogenous** opiate.

Synthesis of 5-HT in the brain depends on the neural concentrations of its precursor, tryptophan, which is an essential amino acid. Neural concentrations hinge on levels of free tryptophan in the blood and on transport through the blood-brain barrier. Blood tryptophan is either bound to albumin or in a "free" form. Higher concentrations of free fatty acids result in more free tryptophan because free fatty acids compete for chemical binding to albumin. Levels of free tryptophan also depend on the activity of tryptophan pyrrolase (enzyme in the liver that metabolizes tryptophan), which is activated by glucocorticoids. Transport through the blood-brain barrier is affected by the competition between free tryptophan and large neutral amino acids (aromatic amino acids and branched-chain amino acids) at the transporter level. If levels of these amino acids decrease, which can occur during very prolonged exercise, the amount of tryptophan that can get into the brain increases.

*L*evels of serotonin in the brain are dependent on the neural concentrations of its precursor, tryptophan.

There are more than a dozen receptors for 5-HT in the brain (commonly enumerated as 5-HT1 through 5-HT7 and further designated by subclassifications A-D) that mediate a variety of functions related to mood and behavior. For example, postsynaptic 5-HT1A receptors, located primarily in the limbic region, mediate neural inhibition. Presynaptic 5-HT1A autoreceptors in raphe nuclei are desensitized with repeated stimulation, leading to less inhibition and therefore increased serotonergic release, which has an antidepressant effect. Postsynaptic 5-HT2A receptors, highly concentrated in the frontal cortex, mediate neural excitation. Stimulation of these receptors results in activation of the SNS. Stimulation of 5-HT2C postsynaptic receptors in the choroid plexus[2] results in anxiety, hypophagia, hypolocomotion, and activation of the HPA. In addition, other substances, such as glucocorticoids, can bind to 5-HT receptors and produce effects independently of 5-HT levels.

Other Neurohormones and Neuropeptides

Some of the other key substances that function as neurotransmitters include glutamate, GABA, endorphins, galanin, and NPY.

Glutamate or glutamic acid (an amino acid) is a small-molecule, rapidly acting NT that is the major excitatory transmitter in the brain. It is a product of cell metabolism. For example, people who have allergic reactions to monosodium glutamate are responding to the by-product glutamic acid. Glutamate has three groups of ligand gated ion channels (ionotropic receptors) and three groups of G-protein coupled (metabotropic receptors). The metabotropic receptors have multiple roles in synaptic plasticity. The ionotropic receptors are named after the synthetic **ligands** that bind with them. The slowest and more general receptor is NMDA (N-methyl-D-aspartate); it controls a calcium channel, as well as a magnesium channel, and is involved with seizures, learning, and brain damage after anoxia. Another ionotropic receptor is AMPA (α-amino-3-hydroxy-5-methyl-4-isoxazole proprionic acid), which allows sodium and potassium ions, but not calcium, to pass through the channel leading to very quick excitatory signals. The receptor kainate was named for a nerve poison extracted from seaweed and has a role in the regulation of glutamate release and in excitatory/inhibitory synaptic transmission in the hippocampus.

Gamma-aminobutyric acid (GABA) is an amino acid that is produced from glutamate by the enzyme glutamic acid decarboxylase (GAD). It is the major inhibitory transmitter in the nervous system (see p. 53). GABA acts as a presynaptic inhibitory transmitter in many cases. It is secreted by nerve terminals in the cerebral cortex, as well as in the spinal cord, cerebellum, and basal ganglia. The two receptors for GABA are rather complex. For example, the key receptor type in the brain, the GABA$_A$ receptor, has five binding sites. Besides a site for GABA binding, there is a site that binds with benzodiazepines, a class of tranquilizers used to reduce anxiety, promote sleep, reduce seizure activity, and promote muscle relaxation. Another GABA$_A$ receptor site binds with barbiturates. Receptors for GABA$_A$ control a chloride channel, and GABA$_B$ receptors control a potassium channel (see figure 6.9 on p. 129).

2. The choroid plexus is a highly vascular region of the lining of the cerebral ventricles that secretes cerebrospinal fluid.

Endorphins and **enkephalins** are endogenous opioid peptides whose biochemical properties are identical to exogenous opiates such as heroin and morphine. Beta-endorphins can act as NT, neuromodulators, and hormones. Endogenous opiates are involved in addiction, cardiovascular regulation, respiration, appetite and thirst, gastrointestinal activity, renal function, temperature regulation, metabolism, hormonal secretion, reproduction, immunity, learning, and memory. Beta-endorphins are found in the central nervous system in the arcuate nucleus with extensive projections throughout the brain (i.e., hypothalamus, limbic, periaqueductal gray, brainstem) and in the nucleus tractus solitarius with projections to the ventrolateral medulla. Beta-endorphins also have the capacity to activate the brain's DA centers by inhibiting factors that inhibit those centers. Beta-endorphin binds with the most affinity to μ receptors to produce analgesia (pain relief), respiratory depression, bradycardia, contraction of the pupil, hypothermia, and behavioral indifference and dependence.

Peripherally, β-endorphin is secreted into the blood from the anterior and intermediate pituitary during vigorous exercise, depending on the intensity of the exercise, and secretion is usually accompanied by increases in ACTH. Hence, peripheral levels of β-endorphin are best viewed as an indication of the stress response to exercise.

Peripheral levels of β-endorphin are best viewed as an indication of the stress response to exercise.

Met-enkephalin and leu-enkephalin are pentapeptide endorphins that are widely distributed throughout the CNS. They are co-stored with catecholamines in the adrenal medulla, where they are released with the catecholamines into the gastrointestinal tract, heart, and blood vessels. Beta-endorphin, met-enkephalin, and leu-enkephalin bind with opiate receptors in afferent nerves and spinal neurons to produce analgesia. They also bind to opioid receptors in the brain to help regulate behavior. Endorphins play a role in inhibiting tonic inhibition of DA release in parts of the brain involved with pleasure.

These effects, plus increases in plasma levels with exercise, have led the general public to make the link between enhanced mood with exercise (i.e., "runner's high") and endorphins, even attributing exercise addiction to these endogenous opiates. However, as you will find in subsequent chapters, the evidence for endorphins as a cause of improved mood from exercise is weak. Nonetheless, because endorphins participate in removing tonic inhibition of DA release in parts of the brain involved with pleasure, they could indirectly influence positive moods.

Neuropeptide Y (NPY) is a 36-amino acid peptide colocalized with NE in around 40% of LC neurons (Holets et al. 1988). Neuropeptide Y inhibits LC firing **in vitro.** Thus, one of its functions may be to provide feedback inhibition to LC neurons. Most NPY cell bodies in the LC project to the hypothalamus and thus may be important in helping regulate endocrine responses during stress.

Galanin (GAL) is a 29-amino acid peptide NT that coexists with NE in approximately 80% of LC neurons. Like NPY, galanin hyperpolarizes noradrenergic neurons and inhibits LC firing in vitro. Thus, a possible function of galanin is to provide feedback inhibition to LC neurons. Alterations in gene transcription for tyrosine hydroxylase and/or galanin represent plausible mechanisms for noradrenergic adaptations to stress. A recent study showed that chronic activity-wheel running blunted release of NE in the brain cortex during stress and was accompanied by higher GAL **messenger ribonucleic acid (mRNA)** levels in the LC compared to those in control animals (Soares et al. 1999). Those findings and a related report of increased GAL mRNA in the LC after treadmill exercise training suggest a neuromodulatory role of GAL in brain noradrenergic adaptation to exercise (O'Neal et al. 2001).

Section 3: Brain Cellular and Molecular Biology

In order to accurately characterize the changes in specific brain regions after acute and chronic physical activity, one must be familiar with some concepts and techniques of cellular and molecular biology. Key concepts are (1) signal transmission by receptor binding and second-messenger regulation and (2) gene transcription and translation. Some fundamental techniques include **in situ hybridization histochemistry** and immunocytochemistry.

Understanding of changes in specific brain regions after acute and chronic exercise can be enabled by techniques to measure receptor binding, second-messenger regulation, and gene transcription and translation.

Receptor-Effectors and Second Messengers

The neurotransmitters discussed previously in this chapter cannot directly transmit a chemical signal between neurons. The chemical signal (the first messenger) must be transduced. In transduction, a receptor-effector system activates a second-messenger system that regulates postsynaptic cellular responses. Receptors are cellular proteins that bind endogenous ligands (e.g., neurotransmitters such as NE) and transmit a signal into the cell through the plasma membrane, which results in a structural or metabolic change in an effector cell by the process of *phosphorylation*. Receptors move from the cytosol (interior of cell) and are embedded in the surface membrane of a cell. Figure 3.16 shows a β-adrenoreceptor for NE that has a ser-

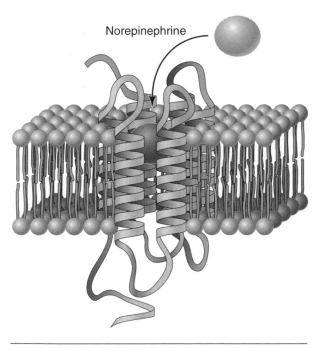

Figure 3.16 Beta-adrenoreceptor for norepinephrine.

pentine shape and crosses the cell membrane seven times.

Binding causes a receptor like a β-adrenergic receptor molecule to change its three-dimensional shape; its loops protrude into the cytoplasm of the cell. This is called endocytosis. Endocytosis activates another protein known as a G-protein. The 1994 Nobel Prize in Physiology or Medicine was awarded jointly to Americans Alfred G. Gilman and Martin Rodbell for their discovery of "G-proteins and their role in signal transduction in cells." A G-protein is formed from three distinct protein subunits, termed α, β, and γ. Whether a G-protein is switched on or off depends on whether it binds with guanosine diphosphate (GDP; off) or guanosine triphosphate (GTP; on). In a few seconds or less, the G-protein will then hydrolyze its own GTP down to GDP, which terminates its activity by a down-regulating **negative feedback** system.

A signal cascade is triggered by the active G-protein. When the β-adrenergic receptor activates the G-protein, the α subunit releases GDP, binds GTP, and falls away from the β and γ subunits. The GTP-bound α subunit breaks away from the receptor and activates an enzyme called *adenylate cyclase*, which promotes the conversion of adenosine triphosphate (ATP) into 3'5'-cyclic adenosine monophosphate (cAMP); cAMP is the second messenger. Figure 3.17 shows the actions of a receptor that open an ion channel in the cell membrane directly (figure 3.17a) and indirectly by a second messenger (figure 3.17b).

High levels of cAMP enable protein kinase A to phosphorylate intracellular proteins that regulate changes in cell structure (e.g., by activating gene expression and protein synthesis) and activity (e.g., by opening ion channels that depolarize cell membrane potentials). Figure 3.18 shows cAMP acting on a calcium channel. A single NE molecule can activate dozens of α subunits of proteins. Each of these will activate the synthesis of an adenylate cyclase, which in turn will synthesize hundreds of cAMP molecules.

Gene Transcription and Translation

The example of the receptor-effector system illustrates the importance of changes in cellular protein levels and function in neural transmission. So, it is important for you to have some understanding of

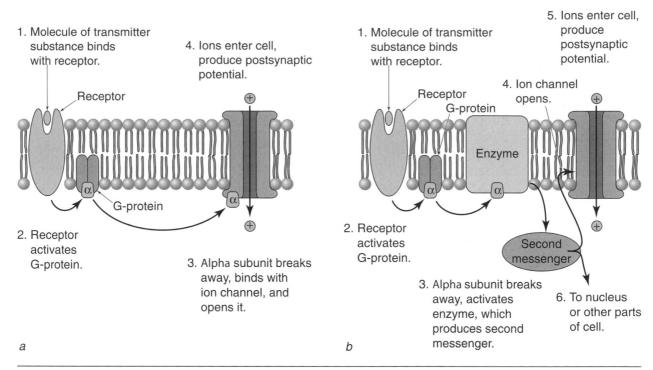

Figure 3.17   Receptors can open an ion channel directly *(a)* or indirectly by a second messenger *(b)*.

From Neil R. Carlson, *Physiology of behavior,* 5e. Copyright 1994 by Allyn & Bacon. Adapted by permission.

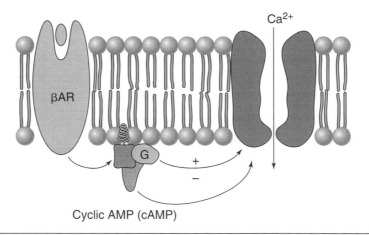

Figure 3.18   Regulation of a calcium channel by the cAMP second messenger.

the role played by gene transcription and translation in the synthesis of proteins.

The central or fundamental genetic dogma of molecular biology explains the difference, and the linkage, between DNA (deoxyribonucleic acid) and proteins. It states that genes, encoded in our DNA, are transcribed into **RNA** (ribonucleic acid) and translated into proteins that execute the functions of a living cell. Deoxyribonucleic acid consists of deoxyribose sugar, phosphoric acid, and four nitrog-

enous bases. The bases can be divided into purines (adenine and guanine) and pyrimidines (cytosine and thymine) based on their chemical structure. These components form what is referred to as a nucleotide. A series of nucleotides joined together creates a single strand of DNA that pairs with a complementary strand (series of nucleotides) to produce the double-stranded helical formation of DNA. The specific sequence of the nitrogenous bases (A, G, C, T) on these strands creates a gene, the information needed to synthesize proteins and other molecules, which ultimately influences the physical and functional characteristics of an organism.

The cascade of information from gene to protein begins with transcription and ends with translation. During **transcription,** one strand of the DNA—called the template or antisense strand—is read by the protein RNA polymerase; an RNA molecule that is complementary to the template strand is synthesized. Ribonucleic acid has four characteristics that distinguish it from DNA: (1) it is single stranded; (2) it contains the sugar ribose instead of deoxyribose; (3) it is smaller; and (4) it contains the nitrogenous base uracil instead of thymine. The remaining strand of DNA that is not read is called the coding strand or sense strand and is considered identical in sequence to the RNA molecule, except for the presence of uracil. The synthesis of RNA, therefore, allows for the transfer of genetic information to a different molecule.

Translation is the process by which the RNA strand is used to create a series of amino acids linked together by peptide bonds. This series of amino acids creates a polypeptide chain that may go through a series of modifications, such as combination with other polypeptide chains or addition of carbohydrate groups, lipids, cofactors, and coenzymes to form a functional protein.

Every cell in the human body contains an identical set of genes, yet each type of cell has a different protein expression profile, suggesting that transcription of the various genes is regulated at the cellular level. Regulation of the level of transcription from a gene occurs through the interaction of proteins (transcription factors) and DNA sequences located near the gene (promoters and *cis*-elements). The binding of transcription factors to the promoter region is important for the recognition of a gene, but the interaction between these factors and other factors bound to *cis*-elements represents one level of transcription control. For example, some steroid hormones cross the cell's plasma membrane and bind to steroid protein receptors located in the cytoplasm. The bound receptor then enters the nucleus and binds to a region of DNA called the hormone response element. Once bound to the DNA, the steroid and receptor may interact with additional transcription factors located at other regions of the DNA. The interaction of the steroid, receptor, hormone response element, and other

transcription factors alters the level of transcription of several genes, thereby influencing gene expression.

Gene regulation allows a cell to respond to the changing environment around it in order to maintain homeostasis.

Gene regulation is an important phenomenon because it allows a cell to respond to the changing environment around it in order to maintain homeostasis. Thus, altering the **in vitro** or **in vivo** environment of a cell makes it possible to observe changes in the level of gene transcription and protein production. Techniques designed to measure these changes, such as in situ hybridization histochemistry and immunocytochemistry, provide insight into the mechanism of action of specific biological functions and experimental conditions.

In Situ Hybridization Histochemistry

In situ hybridization histochemistry is a technique designed to examine steady-state levels of mRNA inside a cell that is located in its original, natural setting. Other techniques that measure mRNA require removal of the nucleic acid from the cell and immobilization on a nitrocellulose or nylon membrane. The advantage of in situ hybridization histochemistry is that by taking thin sections of tissue and hybridizing them to a labeled probe (single-stranded complementary nucleic acid), we can examine mRNA without removing it from the cell (figure 3.19). Therefore we can gain information about the localization of mRNA within specific regions of the tissue or within specific cells within a region. O'Neal et al. (2001) utilized this technique to observe changes in prepro-galanin neuropeptide in the LC (see figure 3.20) after treadmill training in rats. As mentioned previously, galanin is colocalized in 80% of the LC neurons and has been shown to hyperpolarize noradrenergic neurons of the LC. The increase in galanin after treadmill training (see figure 3.21) may provide a plausible mechanism to explain changes in the function of LC neurons after chronic stress.

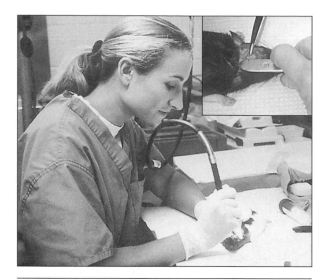

Figure 3.19   Brain surgery conducted on an anesthetized rat.

Provided by the Exercise Psychology Laboratory, Department of Exercise Science, and Department of Psychology, The University of Georgia.

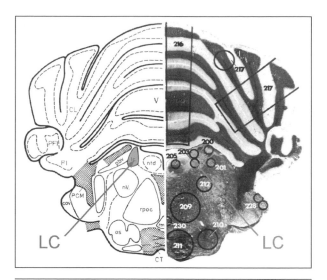

Figure 3.20   Coronal slice through the locus coeruleus.

Adapted, by permission, from M. Palkovitz and M.J. Brownstein, 1988, *Maps and guide to microdissection of the rat brain* (New York: Elsevier), 175.

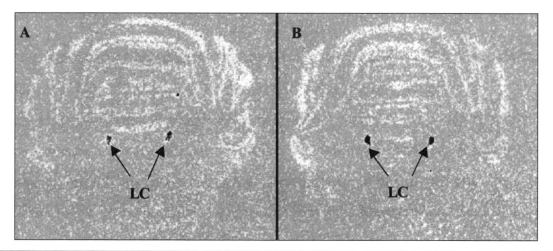

Figure 3.21   Audioradiogram indicating galanin neuropeptide messenger ribonucleic acid in the locus coeruleus after treadmill exercise training in rats (B) compared to sedentary rats (A).

Provided by Dr. Heather O'Neal, the Exercise Psychology Laboratory, Department of Exercise Science, and Department of Psychology, The University of Georgia.

Immunocytochemistry

Measurement of mRNA can help provide information about the level of gene expression, but ultimately it is the level of functional protein that is of interest. **Immunocytochemistry,** a technique designed to measure protein expression, is similar to in situ hybridization histochemistry in that it is conducted in the cell, permitting us to gain information about the localization of protein. Instead of using labeled complementary strands of nucleic acid to visualize RNA, immunocytochemistry utilizes antibodies to visualize protein. Antibodies are proteins that recognize regions, or domains, of other proteins called antigens. The binding of the primary antibody to the antigen identifies specific proteins present in a tissue. Additional antibodies that bind to the primary antibody are needed, however, to visualize the protein using chemical reactions. Often, in situ hybridization histochemistry and immunocytochemistry are used in conjunction to confirm that changes in mRNA level translate into changes in protein expression.

Early Gene Responses

Specific protein expression among different types of cells can vary, making up what is referred to as the cell's proteome, or the collection of proteins expressed in a cell. However, some proteins are ubiquitous, and the level of expression of these proteins is often used to measure cellular activity. One family of proteins that is often examined after application of various stimuli is the Fos family of transcription factors, which dimerize (a dimer is a compound of two like molecules) with members of the Jun family to alter transcription of specific genes. The major members of the Fos family include c-Fos, FosB, Fra-1, and Fra-2; but c-Fos induction is most often examined because it occurs in low levels at baseline and is inducible after a variety of stimuli. In addition, c-Fos is considered an immediate early gene because of the rapidity of induction following stimuli. A recent exercise psychology study that examined c-Fos showed that regular physical activity in wheel running did not alter c-Fos expression in response to foot-shock stress in rats (Soares et al. 1999). Levels of c-Fos are often used as an index of cell activity in response to a stimulus. However, c-Fos responses can be **down-regulated** (decrease in ligand/receptor interactions) after repeated or usual stimulation of the cell, so cells can be activated in the absence of changes in c-Fos (Kovacs 1998).

Posttranslational Regulation

Not only must changes in gene expression be considered, changes in protein level as well as posttranslational alterations of protein function are also important. Knowing that the level of gene expression can be tied to protein expression, and that various proteins interact to affect the functional properties of many cellular events, makes exercise a unique and sometimes difficult stimulus to study in the lab. Unlike other experimental conditions, like those in pharmacological investigations, the "active ingredient" of exercise is difficult to determine and may change depending on a host of factors, including mode, intensity, duration, frequency, and timing of physical activity. For example, with pharmacological investigation, one can begin by examining the receptors that bind to the drug. With exercise, the

point at which to begin characterization can be varied depending on the scientific question of interest. Nonetheless, the use of techniques borrowed from molecular biology to study the effects of exercise on brain function is one of the new frontiers of exercise psychology. Recent advances in neuroimaging techniques that permit application of molecular biology to the real-time study of the human brain are discussed at the end of this chapter. They are just beginning to be applied during exercise. Molecular biology application to exercising animals has been taking place for several years.

Section 4: Animal Behavior Models

Animal models permit the experimental manipulation of brain or behavior within a model of a human disease or behavior to help determine whether biological, anatomical, or pharmacological factors can explain some of the psychological effects or determinants of regular physical activity in humans (McCabe et al. 2000). Among humans, however, social determinants of stress interact with differences among people in how they appraise the meaning of events and how they cope with this appraisal or its consequences. In that way, animal models are inherently limited for drawing inferences about human experience; an animal model is just that, a model. It can guide human studies, but direct inferences about the "human" meaning of animal behaviors are probably more in the "eye of the beholder than in the brain of the animal." As Freud is credited with saying, "Sometimes a cigar is just a cigar."

Nonetheless, most researchers in exercise psychology have exclusively used social cognitive models of stress, limiting our understanding of the biology of behavior in physical activity settings and justifying the use of animal models. So, it is important to consider how animals can be used as models to guide human research. Similarities between validating animal models and the validation of psychological constructs based on human self-reports (outlined early in chapter 2) should be apparent.

A commonly used scheme in pharmacology to judge whether animal models that use stressor tasks are predictive, isomorphic, or homologous is helpful if one wants to evaluate the validity of such models for human depression and anxiety. **Predictive models** typically include specific signs or behaviors that can be reliably changed by drugs known to have clinical efficacy in humans. Predictive models must be based on species or strains that respond to drugs in the same ways as humans do. An **isomorphic model** evokes the same features as in the human disease, which abate after administration of drugs that are clinically useful in humans; but the features generated may not have the same etiology (i.e., course of development) as in the human disease. A **homologous model** meets the standards of predictive validity and isomorphism, and it also has the same etiology as does the human disease. When a homologous model is specific for a single disease, it has construct validity, which is the gold standard, or the ideal test, of validity.

Depression

The escape-deficit model after uncontrollable foot shock is the most highly elaborated animal model of depression, first reported by McCulloch and Bruner (1939) over 60 years ago. The hallmark response to uncontrollable, inescapable foot shock is increased latency to escape from controllable shock administered 24 to 72 h later, presumably resulting from depletion of NE in the LC. A single session of high-intensity uncontrollable foot shock leads to a large decrease in brain NE with less reliable decreases in levels of brain serotonin and DA, perhaps due to slower resynthesis of NE. The escape-deficit model is an attempt to simulate the so-called learned helplessness, or behavioral despair, common in human depression. The animal gives up in its attempts to escape stressors, such as foot shock, forced swimming, or restraint. The escape-deficit model is mostly isomorphic with human depression, featuring weight loss, reduced sex behavior, sleep disturbances (decreased REM sleep latency), and anhedonia (i.e., loss of pleasure). However, such a model is not homologous with human depression. Though self-reward tasks such as sucrose preference and intracranial self-stimulation are used as surrogate measures in the rat for the phenomenological construct of pleasure experienced by humans, it is not possible to determine whether or not a rat feels helpless or hopeless.

Some types of depression and anxiety in humans appear to be endogenous; they cannot be attributed to an uncontrollable stressor. Relatively new models of endogenous depression in the rat involve injecting neonatal pups with clomipramine, a serotonin reuptake inhibitor, leading to decreased REM sleep latency and other key behavioral signs of depression as the rat reaches adulthood. Another endogenous model disturbs brain NT systems, including NE and serotonin, by surgically removing the olfactory bulbs located below the brain frontal cortex. These models each are isomorphic with human depression, and they are responsive to pharmacotherapy. Because their endogenous etiology differs from other animal models based on exogenous stress, the clomipramine and the olfactory bulbectomy models have potential for use in examining the role that physical activity plays in preventing depression not arising from chronic stress.

Anxiety

An increase in locomotion usually reflects an adaptive motivational state in rats, indicating reduced behavioral inhibition (e.g., less freezing). An increase in open-field locomotion has been reported in rats following forced-exercise swimming and after motorized-treadmill running. Locomotion by the rat in an open field is associated inversely with observer ratings of anxiety when the locomotion appears purposeful and the animal exhibits other exploratory behaviors such as rearing or approaching the center of the open field. In contrast, low levels of locomotion, few approaches to the center of the open field, freezing, defecation, urination, and shivering are conventionally regarded as isomorphic with the hypervigilance, hesitancy, fear, and autonomic activation common in human anxiety. Under certain circumstances of threat, increased locomotion seems to indicate panic (i.e., the flight response to a predator). Such a dichotomous interpretation of increased locomotion during open-field testing illustrates the importance of environmental context when one is inferring anxiety from locomotion by rats.

Section 5: Measuring Brain Activity

To determine whether behavior or emotions can be explained by neural activity in the brain, measurement must take place during behavior or emotional responses. For example, Wang et al. (2000) examined the striatum DA release using positron emission tomography scanning before and after a graded maximal treadmill test in human volunteers. Brain imaging techniques have been applied rarely in the field of exercise psychology, however; neural activity has been mainly estimated by measures of brain electrocortical activity by electroencephalography (EEG). The goal of the following sections is to introduce some of the key techniques in neuroscience that can be used to measure neural activity in the brain of humans and other animals.

Electrophysiology

Electrophysiology uses electrodes positioned in the brain cortex or in specific regions of brain neurons to record electrical potentials during behavior or in response to stress in order to determine whether those areas play a role in regulating physiology and behavior. Microelectrodes are constructed of metal wires, usually tungsten or stainless steel, or fine glass tubes filled with a conducting electrolyte fluid (e.g., potassium chloride) that can detect the discharge rate of a single neuron. Macroelectrodes, which are bigger, record the activity of thousands of neurons, or more. They can be implanted in the brain or attached to the surface of the brain cortex, or attached as discs to the scalp. The changing electrical potentials (neural discharge rate) are then amplified, displayed, and recorded on an oscilloscope or ink-writing oscillograph or are digitized for computer display and storage. Similar electrodes can also be used to stimulate brain neurons. Electrophysiology has rarely been used to learn about the brain's response to exercise. Two examples are recordings of discharge rates in the LC (Rasmussen, Morilak, and Jacobs 1986) and the raphe nuclei during walking (Veasey et al. 1995) in cats. Investigators at the University of South Carolina also used electrophysiology for the purpose of intracranial self-stimulation: stimulating electrodes were placed in the ventral tegmentum, a pleasure center that surrounds the hypothalamus, and used to operantly reinforce treadmill running by rats (Burgess et al. 1991).

Microdialysis

Though neurons can discharge without a subsequent release of NT (e.g., when NT synthesis has not kept pace with the discharge rate), the normal response to depolarization of a neuron includes a calcium-regulated migration of vesicles containing stored NT to the cell membrane at the terminal end of an axon, exocytosis of the vesicle (i.e., protrusion into the synapse), and release of the NT into the extracellular, synaptic space between neurons. Other factors can explain increases in the extracellular levels of NT, but under most circumstances NT level is a very good indicator of NT release. Levels of extracellular NT can be measured by **microdialysis.** Dialysis separates molecules of different sizes through use of an artificial membrane that is permeable to only some molecules. A microdialysis probe is made of a small metal tube containing inner and outer compartments, or cannulas, that is implanted into the brain through a guide cannula fixed to the skull using dental cement (see figure 3.22). The inner cannula of the probe serves as an inlet through which artificial cerebrospinal fluid can be pumped into the brain at a rate that permits diffusion of NT molecules from the extracellular brain fluid across the dialysis membrane and into the outer cannula, where it is collected at an outlet (figure 3.23). The retrieved fluid is then analyzed for the concentration of NT by a chemical analysis called high-performance liquid chromatography with electrochemical detection. That technique is based on differing oxidation rates of the proteins that constitute the NT.

As with electrophysiology, microdialysis has been employed rarely in exercise psychology, but it has

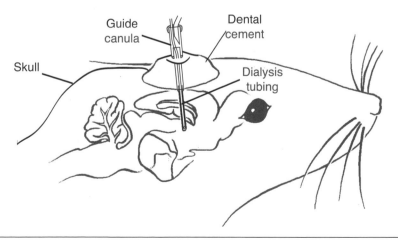

Figure 3.22 Surgically implanted guide cannula for microdialysis of brain neurotransmitters.

Provided by the Exercise Psychology Laboratory, The University of Georgia.

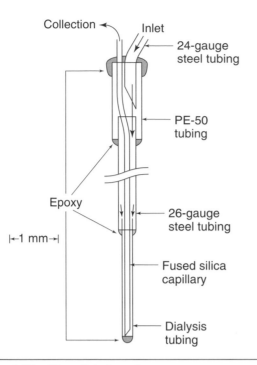

Figure 3.23   Microdialysis probe.

been used to show that brain serotonin (Wilson et al. 1986), NE (Pagliari and Peyrin 1995), and DA (Meeusen et al. 1997) levels are increased during treadmill running in rats. Another study using microdialysis showed that rats that had run for several weeks in activity wheels had a blunted release of NE in the frontal cortex when they were stressed by electric foot shock (shown in figure 3.24; Soares et al. 1999).

Electroencephalography

In humans, the main methods of measuring brain activity have been **electroencephalography (EEG)** and neuroimaging. Several studies of psychophysiological responses to acute exercise have reported the measurement of real-time brain electrical activity via electroencephalographic recording. We will look at these applications in some detail in chapter 5, "Affect, Mood, and Emotion;" chapter 6, "Anxiety;" and chapter 9, "Sleep." Electrodes are placed on the scalp in standardized locations, and recordings are made of the electrical potentials, or brain waves. The most common locations are based on the international 10-20 system, in which placements are in 10% or 20% increments according to head circumference and the distance from the inion (occipital protuberance, i.e., the bump at the base of skull) to the nasion (bridge of the nose; see figure 3.25).

The amplitude of brain waves can reach up to 200 µV, and frequency can range from once every few seconds to 50+ waves per second (Hz). The frequency spectrum is commonly decomposed into ranges, or bandwidths.

In 1875, Richard Caton described brain waves measured directly from the exposed brains of rabbits and monkeys. However, German neurophysiologist Hans Berger is credited with the discovery that electrical potentials could be measured through the scalp. In his 1929 paper, "über das Elektronzephalogramm des Menschen" ("On the Encephalogram of Man"), Berger designated a large regu-

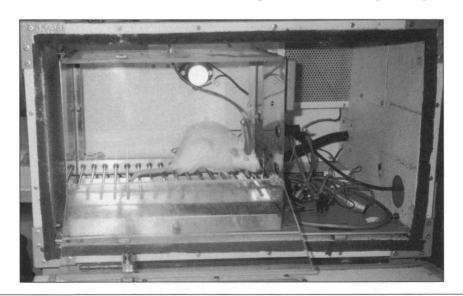

Figure 3.24   Microdialysis during foot-shock stress.

Provided by the Exercise Psychology Laboratory, Department of Exercise Science, The University of Georgia.

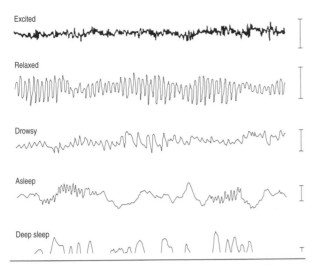

Electroencephalography Frequency Bands

δ (delta)	0.5 to 3.5 Hz	20 to 200 μV
θ (theta)	4 to 7 Hz	20 to 100 μV
α (alpha)	8 to 12 Hz	20 to 60 μV
β (beta)	13 to 30 Hz	2 to 20 μV
γ (gamma)	40 to 50 Hz	2 to 10 μV

Figure 3.25   Electrode sites and nomenclature for the extended 10-20 system used in electroencephalography.

Adapted from *Electroencephalography and Clinical Neurophysiology (Suppl.)* 52, G.H. Klem, H.O. Luders, H.H. Jasper, and C. Elger, "The end-twenty electrode system of the International Federation," p. 6, copyright 1999, with permission from Elsevier Science.

lar wave that cycled about 10 times each second as α and smaller, irregular waves that cycled 20 to 30

times each second as β. Later, H.H. Jasper and H.L. Andrews used γ to designate frequencies above 30 to 35 Hz. W.G. Walter used the term δ for all frequencies below the α band, but later designated the 4 to 7.5 Hz range as the θ band because he thought these brain waves were generated by the thalamus.

Brain activation has classically been assumed to be related to the frequency of EEG activity (e.g., δ waves predominate in deep sleep; θ waves are common in drowsiness; α waves reflect relaxed wakefulness; β waves reflect information processing; figure 3.26). However, some research has shown that

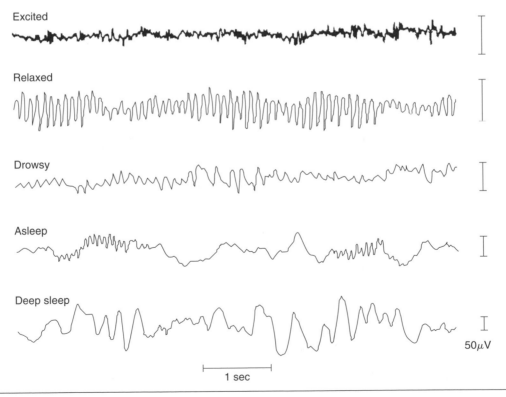

Figure 3.26   EEG recordings for different mental states.

Reprinted from *Electroencephalography and Clinical Neurophysiology* 4, D.B. Lindsley, "Psychological phenomena and the electroencephalogram," pp. 443–456, copyright 1952, with permission from Elsevier Science.

α waves are most related to attention and that β waves are more active during emotion. Paradoxically, barbiturate sedatives have been shown to increase β waves. Brain wave patterns are reliably associated with neural activity, such as specific phases of sleep (chapter 9) and epileptic seizures, and EEG readings have also been found to be associated with emotional states in various circumstances (chapters 4 and 5). However, there is very little agreement among psychophysiologists about the meaning of the various bandwidths for the processing of emotions. The character of the waves depends on the activity of the cerebral cortex, but increased electrical activity at one particular EEG electrode site does not necessarily translate to increased neural transmission from immediately underlying neurons or indicate that brain systems immediately below that particular site are metabolically active.

Neuroimaging

More sophisticated methods for measuring brain activity in areas other than the cortex have been developed with advances in X-ray techniques and computer technology, such as seen in figure 3.27.

Computerized axial tomograms (CATs), or **CT** (computerized tomogram) **scans,** use X rays to enhance small differences in brain density. An X-ray source is moved repeatedly in an arc around the subject's head; and the amount of radiation that is absorbed within the brain, which depends on density, is analyzed at each position. The end product

is two-dimensional pictures of the skull and its contents. Since different substances absorb different amounts of radiation, it is possible with this technology to identify specific structures of the brain.

The interaction of radio waves and a strong magnetic field is used to produce a more detailed picture of the interior of a living brain. **Magnetic resonance imaging (MRI)** provides an image that has more precise resolution than CT. It involves passing a strong magnetic wave through a subject's head. In the presence of a strong magnetic field, the nuclei of some atoms in molecules in the body spin with a particular orientation (Carlson 1998). These nuclei emit radio waves when a radio-frequency wave is passed through the body. Different frequencies are emitted by different molecules, and the MRI scanner is tuned to pick up those from hydrogen molecules and produce pictures of the brain based on the known concentration of hydrogen in specific tissues. Changes as small as the loss of myelin around a group of axons can be detected with an MRI scan.

CT scans and MRI scans provide useful but static images of the brain. We can view the dynamic activity of the brain using **positron emission tomography (PET),** which can reveal glucose uptake of specific nuclei. Radioactive chemicals, most often radioactive glucose, are injected into the blood vessels, and the subject is placed into a device similar to that for an MRI scan. The device detects the positrons emitted by the radioactive glucose in the brain and can provide a picture showing the meta-

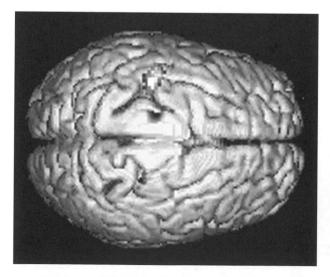
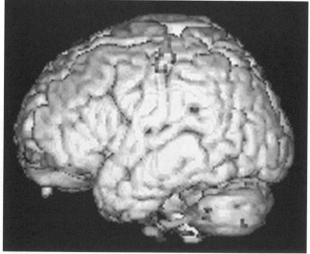

Figure 3.27   Computerized three-dimensional reconstruction of activation of the motor cortex measured by fMRI.
Provided by Dr. Dane Cook, Department of Radiology, New Jersey Medical School.

bolic activity of various brain regions. The high operating costs of the PET scan are a disadvantage; but newer technology has enabled a modification of the less expensive MRI **(functional MRI: fMRI)** that acquires images rapidly enough to provide measurement of brain activity, such as oxygen consumption by active brain regions. In the brain, blood perfusion is presumably related to neural activity, so fMRI, like other imaging techniques such as PET, makes it possible to find out what the brain is doing when subjects perform specific tasks or are exposed to specific stimuli.

*A*dvances in scanning technology have enabled scientists to monitor real-time functioning of specific areas of the brain.

Neuroimaging Techniques

Magnetic Resonance Imaging (MRI): The principles of nuclear magnetic resonance, developed in the 1940s, are based on variations among atomic nuclei in the radio frequencies to which their spinning axis will respond, that is, resonate. All atomic nuclei spin on their axes because they have a positive electronic charge and act as a magnet with north and south poles along the axis of spin. When an object is put in an external magnetic field, the spin axes of all the nuclei in the object line up with the field. Next a signal with a radio frequency (RF) is broadcast at the object in a line perpendicular to the field, causing the spin axes of the nuclei to tilt from the magnetic field by an angle that is unique to the object and the RF to which it will resonate. Within about 20 to 300 ms after the RF signal, the spin axis gradually returns to its position parallel with the external magnetic field. This is called the T2 relaxation time or "spin relaxation time." As it relaxes, each nucleus transmits a radio signal. MRI studies of the brain use hydrogen nuclei, which have different T2 relaxation times in fat and water. Hydrogen nuclei in fats transmit at different frequencies than in water, so tissues having different water-to-fat ratios transmit unique radio signals. Those unique radio transmissions are used to form MRI images of the brain's shape and its chemical properties (Horowitz 1995).

Functional Magnetic Resonance Imaging (fMRI): This method applies the magnetic resonance principle for the purpose of determining which parts of the brain are activated by different types of physical sensation or motor activity, as shown in figure 3.28. It has better resolution of both space and time

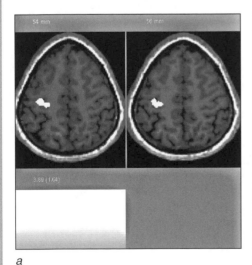

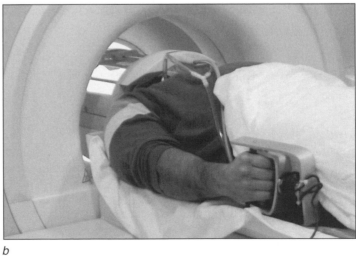

a

b

Figure 3.28 Neuroimage of activation of the motor cortex in the left hemisphere (light area) measured by fMRI *(a)* during handgrip exercise using the right arm *(b)*.

Provided by Dr. Dane Cook, Department of Radiology, New Jersey Medical School.

(continued)

than PET (Cohen and Bookheimer 1994). Special software permits an MRI scanner to detect increased blood flow in areas of the brain that have been activated. Oxygenated arterial blood has a small magnetic effect. However, deoxygenation of hemoglobin has a magnetic effect resulting from the four unpaired iron electrons. This disturbs the local magnetic field in parts of the brain where increased blood flow or increased metabolism occurs. Blood flow is always increased to a greater extent with activation than oxygen extraction is. As a result, the proportion of oxygenated hemoglobin in the red blood cells increases in that region, leading to a longer proton relaxation time that can be visualized as a change in fMRI intensity of about 1% to 10%.

Positron Emission Tomography (PET): Positrons are positively charged electrons. Molecules such as oxygen[15] and carbon[11] emit positrons as they decay. When a positron collides with an electron, the annihilation produces two gamma rays that travel in opposite directions. A special 360° camera (shown in figure 3.29) can detect those reflected rays and thus determine their position in the brain by their intersecting point of origin. PET can assess glucose uptake, blood flow, and pH in the brain by detecting the point of accumulation of a positron-emitting isotope tracer tagged to a biologically active molecule. If multiple annihilations occur, the point of accumulation of the tracer can be located. For example, deoxyglucose is trapped in brain cells after phosphorylation, so tagging it with carbon[11] permits PET to detect its accumulation during increased brain metabolism. The main advantage of PET is that it images metabolic events, not brain structures, as shown in figure 3.30. However, PET can resolve objects about 1 cm apart, whereas fMRI can resolve images in 1 mm range.

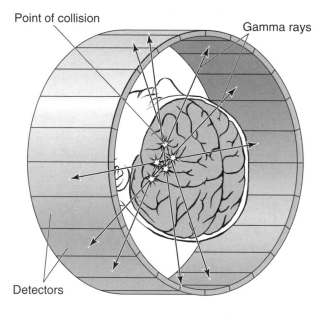

Point of collision

Gamma rays

Detectors

Figure 3.29 Positron emission tomography uses the detection of gamma rays emitted from the collision of positron and electrons to provide an image of metabolic activity in the brain.

Single-Photon Emission Computed Tomography (SPECT): When radiolabeled compounds are injected in tracer amounts, their photon emissions can be detected much like X rays in computerized tomography. The images that are made represent the accumulation of the labeled compound. The compound may reflect, for example, blood flow, oxygen or glucose metabolism, or DA transporter concentration. Often these images are shown with a color scale. Figure 3.31 is a SPECT image that shows low blood perfusion of the frontal lobes (indicated in shades of black) of the brain in a depressed patient.

Near-Infrared Optical Image Scanning (iOIS): Brain tissue is opaque; it does not strongly absorb visible light. However, light does not travel in a straight line through brain tissue, because photons scatter through brain tissue until they pass through or are absorbed. Within the near-infrared light spectrum of about 700 nm to 900 nm, the absorption of light by blood and water is small, but the scatter is large.

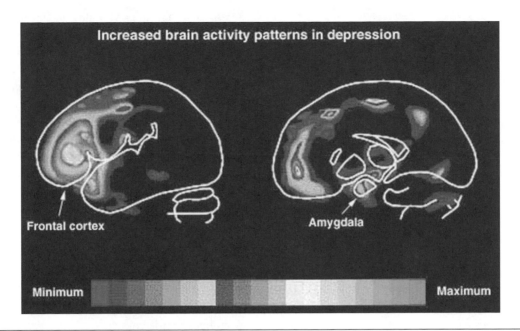

Figure 3.30 PET neuroimage of brain activity in a depressed patient.

Reprinted, by permission, from "Atlas of Brain Perfusion SPECT" at http://brighamrad, harvard, edu, the offical Web site of the Department of Radiology, Brigham and Women's Hospital, Harvard Medical School, Boston. Copyright Brigham and Women's Hospital, Harvard Medical School.

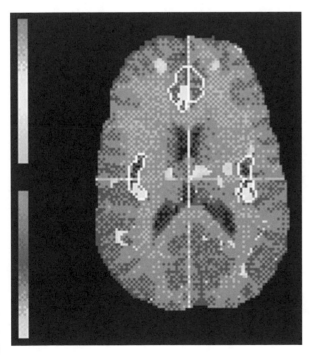

Figure 3.31 Transaxial neuroimage of activation of the anterior cingulate cortex and insular cortex (outlined in white) in both hemispheres measured by SPECT during cycling exercise.

Provided by Dr. Jon Williamson, Department of Physical Therapy, Southwestern Medical Center, University of Texas, Dallas.

Thus, the transport of near-infrared photons in the brain is very diffuse. Local variations in this diffusion are measured by tissue optical absorption using near-infrared spectroscopy. This technique has high sensitivity to the cerebral oxy- and deoxyhemoglobin concentrations; it can resolve changes in brain blood flow and oxygenation within ms.

Summary

Social and cognitive factors, and the methods used to measure and manipulate them, are the cornerstone of exercise psychology, so chapter 2 provides quite a bit of detail on these topics. Nonetheless, neurobiological factors and the methods of behavioral neuroscience are equally important to understanding exercise psychology. Though it has not yet been used much by exercise psychologists, behavioral neuroscience represents a new frontier of the field of exercise psychology. Thus this chapter has introduced its key concepts and techniques. Not only is it important that new students be exposed to this area, but also a rudimentary understanding of this chapter is necessary for a full comprehension of some of the material in later chapters on stress, emotion, anxiety, depression, and sleep. Readers can grasp much of what those chapters cover without having read this chapter. But physical activity, especially exercise, is a family of biologically based behaviors, so any serious student of exercise psychology simply must tackle biological aspects of brain and behavior—challenging as this may be at times.

Suggested Readings

Carlson, N.R. 2001. *Physiology of behavior.* 7th ed. Boston: Allyn and Bacon.

Hatfield, B.D., and D.M. Landers. 1987. Psychophysiology in exercise and sport research: An overview. *Exercise and Sport Sciences Review* 15: 351–387.

Kandel, E.R. 1998. A new intellectual framework for psychiatry. *American Journal of Psychiatry* 155: 457–469.

Rosenzweig, M.R., A.L. Leiman, and S.M. Breedlove. 1999b. Emotions, aggression, and stress. In *Biological psychology: An introduction to behavioral, cognitive, and clinical neuroscience*, ed. M.R. Rosenzweig, A.L. Leiman, and S.M. Breedlove. 2nd ed. Sunderland, MA: Sinauer Associates.

Web Sites

www.loni.ucla.edu/SVG/index.html

www.neuroguide.com/index.html

www.neuroguide.com/neuroimg.html

www.nimh.nih.gov

www.med.harvard.edu/AANLIB/home.html

www.nlm.nih.gov/research/visible/visible_human.html

http://web.indstate.edu/thcme/mwking/nerves.html

www.genome.ad.jp/kegg/catalog/cpd_amine.html

www.iacr.bbsrc.ac.uk/notebook/courses/guide

II

Exercise and Mental Health

The first U.S. Surgeon General's report on mental health was published in 2000, bringing attention to the extent to which mental illness impacts health and the quality of life in this country. Mental health is also a serious public health issue on a global level. The "Global Burden of Disease" study, commissioned by the World Health Organization and the World Bank, indicated that 4 of the 10 leading causes of disability for persons aged 5 and older are mental disorders (World Health Organization 1999). Among developed nations, the leading cause of disability is depression, with manic-depressive disorder, schizophrenia, and obsessive-compulsive disorder ranking near the top. Indeed, the World Health Organization has estimated that by the year 2020, depression will surpass cancer as the second leading worldwide cause of disability and death, behind cardiovascular disease. The prevalence of affective disorders is high in most nations, although the rates vary among countries (Weissman et al. 1996, 1997). In the United States, up to 24% of adults have experienced a mental disorder during the preceding year (Centers for Disease Control and Prevention 1998). In 1996, 31.8 million annual office visits to physicians were for mental disorders; 4.7 million were for depression, and 4.3 million were for anxiety (Schappert 1998). The human suffering is considerable, and the financial costs for mental illnesses are substantial. In the United States, the estimated cost for treatment, social services, disability payments, lost productivity, and premature mortality exceeded $150 billion in 1997 alone (Rice and Miller 1998). The annual cost of each of the two most common disorders, anxiety and depression, is about $45 billion (DuPont et al. 1996; Greenberg et al. 1993). Those costs rival those for other major health problems, such as coronary heart disease ($43 billion), AIDS ($66 billion), and cancer ($104 billion). The prevalence and costs of mental illnesses aside, addressing potential beneficial effects of exercise on the risk and severity of affective disorders is warranted because anxiety and depression are risk factors for other chronic diseases, including coronary heart disease, asthma, ulcers, rheumatoid arthritis, and headaches (Friedman and Booth-Kewley 1987).

There is ample anecdotal support for improvements in mood with exercise. Good experimental evidence also indicates that physical activity can decrease anxiety, prevent and reduce the incidence of mild and moderate depression, and improve self-esteem. Indeed, many clinical psychologists and psychiatrists view exercise as a viable adjunct therapy. The following chapters provide specific information about several mental health concerns and the effects of acute and chronic exercise on their etiology and persistence. Each mental health issue is described from a psychobiological perspective.

Suggested Readings

United States Department of Health and Human Services. 2000. *Mental health: A report of the surgeon general.* (Report DHHS publication no. [PHS] 017-024-01653-5). Atlanta: U.S. Department of Health and Human Services, Centers for Disease Control and Prevention, National Center for Chronic Disease Prevention and Health Promotion.

Murray, C.L., and Lopez, A.D. 1996. *The global burden of disease. A comprehensive assessment of mortality and disability from diseases, injuries, and risk factors in 1990 and projected to 2020.* World Health Organization, World Bank, Harvard University.

CHAPTER

4

Stress

The idea that exercise reduces stress has become a part of folk wisdom, much like views that exercise improves mood, self-esteem, and sleep— topics of later chapters. The benefits of enhanced ability to cope with chronic stress are significant, considering the evidence for the role of mental stress in disease risk and recovery. For example, stress is linked to leading causes of death, such as heart disease, cancer, accidents, and suicide. This chapter discusses whether the scientific evidence supports the idea that exercise alters physiological responses during stress. Because other chapters deal with the effects of physical activity on stress emotions related to anxiety and depressive disorders, this chapter emphasizes whether physical activity or physical fitness blunts physiological responses during types of stress other than exercise.

Background and Definitions

The term *stress* appeared in the English language in the 17th century, borrowed from the French words *destresse* and *estrece*, which meant "hardship" and "oppression." The origin is the Latin word *strictia*, from a verb meaning "to draw tight." Since 1660, when the British scientist Robert Hooke reported his law of elasticity (the tension exerted by a stretched string is proportional to the extension), stress has been viewed by engineers as the way that load (i.e., external force) impinges on a physical object. Stress is distinguished from **strain,** which is the deformation, distortion, or tension in the object that results from stress.

In the life sciences, stress is viewed as an imbalance in physiological systems that activates both physiological and behavioral responses to restore balance. In this way, a stressor is like load, a force that acts on a biological system. Because it is easy to see the analogy between objects resisting or breaking under strain and human tolerance for the burdens of living, it is commonly accepted that stress (imbalance) leads to strain (distortion, tension) in animals as it does in physical objects.

Stress is an imbalance in physiological systems that activates physiological and behavioral responses to restore balance. *Stressors* are the forces that act on a biological system to cause stress.

A Brief History of Stress

In the mid-1800s, the French physiologist Claude Bernard (1867) proposed that life depended on maintaining the *"milieu interieur"* (i.e., internal environment) in a constant state during changes in the external environment. It is now accepted that mammalian cells can exist only when certain ranges of temperature and acid-base balance are maintained and when water, nutrients, and oxygen are available. Systems of cells also depend on such balances. In the 1920s, Harvard physician-scientist Walter Cannon extended Bernard's views through his research on the roles of adrenaline (i.e., epinephrine) and the autonomic nervous system in regulating and maintaining physiological balance during rage and fear. Cannon (1929) introduced the term **homeostasis** to describe this balance, or harmony, of physiological systems. In the early 1930s, Hartman, Brownell, and Lockwood (1932) added to Cannon's ideas by proposing a general tissue hormone theory, which stated that steroids secreted by the cortex of the adrenal gland (e.g., cortisol) are needed by all cells for resisting infection and muscular and nervous fatigue, and for regulating body temperature and body water. Each of these events was credited by the Swiss physician Hans

Selye in forming his theory of a **general adaptation syndrome (GAS)** and the diseases of adaptation, based on activation of the adrenal cortex in response to stress (Selye 1936, 1950).

Homeostasis is the balance or harmony of physiological systems.

To Selye, altered homeostasis was not merely a passing response to changes in the environment. He believed that an animal's physiological systems could learn and maintain adaptive defenses against future exposure to stress. Hence, Selye theorized that many diseases result from maladaptations to the environment that are either insufficient, exces-

Good and Bad Stress

If chronic stress can increase your risk of conditions such as heart disease, high blood pressure, a suppressed immune system, eating disorders, headaches, sleep disorders, and ulcers, you might be wondering if you should attempt to remove *all* stress from your life. The answer is no. A certain amount of stress is needed for optimum health and performance—life without stress would be very boring! Stress researcher Hans Selye clearly distinguished between *distress* ("bad stress") and *eustress* ("good stress"). Some level of stress (eustress) is desirable for optimal performance and well-being; however, all of us can reach a point where stress can become too much (distress) and it starts to inhibit our mental, emotional, and physiological abilities to function effectively (see figure 4.1).

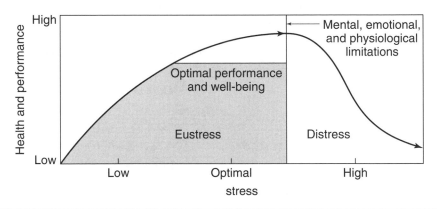

Figure 4.1 A certain amount of stress enhances performance and well-being, but excessive stress can impair mental, emotional, and physiological abilities.

Excessive stress can blunt positive emotions, such as love, joy, and surprise, and exaggerate negative emotions, such as anger, sadness, and fear. Exercise can contribute to your levels of good stress when it is enjoyable and isn't so intense that it causes strain or so frequent that you don't recuperate. Moderate exercise performed regularly can offset negative stress emotions and possibly enhance positive stress emotions.

sive, or poorly regulated (Selye 1950). He proposed that "conditioning factors," such as prior exposure and controllability of a stressor, could alter the GAS. Also, Selye believed that stressors, including muscular exercise, might lead to cross-stressor adaptations that would enhance resistance to psychosomatic and neurotic diseases. His research provided a scientific basis for the development of the **cross-stressor adaptation hypothesis** of exercise, which states that exercise training or increased levels of fitness are associated with an attenuation of stress responses in non-exercise situations (Michael 1957; Sothmann et al. 1996).

Recently, Bruce S. McEwen (1998), a neuroscientist at Rockefeller University, has used the term **allostatic load** to describe the long-term effects of physiological response to stress (including activation of the autonomic nervous system; the hypothalamic-pituitary-adrenal axis; and the metabolic, cardiovascular, and immune systems). **Allostasis** is a term derived from Greek and means the ability to achieve stability through change (i.e., adaptation) (see figure 4.2). Like Selye, McEwen believes that the price paid for such adaptation to stress is allostatic load, the strain that results from overactivity or underactivity of these allostatic systems.

Some people develop a *hypo*activity or *hyper*activity of the normal stress response. It appears that *too small* a stress response can be just as harmful as *too much* of a response, because it may result in other

A *balanced response to stress is optimal: overresponding or underresponding can be dangerous.*

responses that compensate. For example, cortisol stimulates blood glucose for energy, but it also keeps the immune system in check by inhibiting inflammation. If cortisol does not rise during stress, inflammation can result even though there is no infection. On the other hand, too much cortisol can make a person susceptible to infection by overly suppressing the inflammation response; and it can lead to bone loss, muscle atrophy, and elevated insulin levels.

For unknown reasons, the stress response does not subside in some people after a stressful event has ended. For example, public speaking activates the hypothalamic-pituitary-adrenal (HPA) axis and increases blood cortisol in most people, but that response goes away after the person has gained experience. However, about 1 in 10 people will continue to have a cortisol response when they speak in public, regardless of their experience. Likewise, it is not understood why some people lose their ability to mount a stress response after chronic exposure to stressful events. Many researchers are convinced that regular exercise of moderate

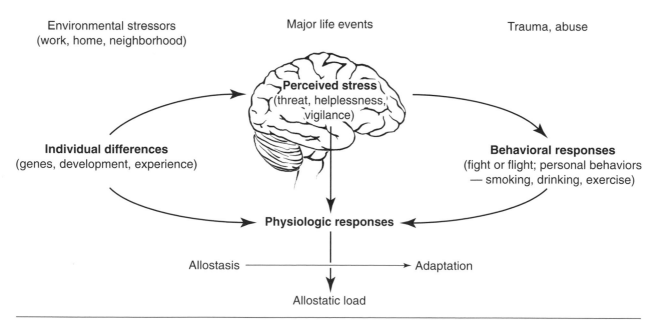

Figure 4.2 Allostasis: the ability to achieve stability through adaptation to stress.

intensity is one of the best ways to offset the allostatic load of chronic stress. That makes sense because we know, for example, that exercise reduces insulin levels that can be raised by high cortisol, and that exercise training lowers blood pressure and resting heart rate. Before considering evidence for a relationship between exercise and the stress response, it is necessary to define the conditions that elicit stress and the main responses during stress.

Defining Stress

Stress can lead to painful *physical symptoms*, such as muscle tension, headache, and stomach upset; *physiological signs*, such as a racing heart, high blood pressure, sweating, flushing, and dry mouth; and *behaviors* ranging from aggression to hyperactivity to withdrawal. Those signs and symptoms can occur independently or together with stress emotions, which include the physiological and behavior responses that are experienced subjectively by the person (e.g., fear, anxiety, anger, despair). Scientists have identified key physiological responses during stress and their patterns of occurrence.

Early studies of humans during the 1950s and 1960s showed that responses by the adrenal glands are largest when stressful tasks are complex and require rapid decision making, or when people are responsible for the welfare of others and/or have little control over the outcomes of critical events. During the late 1960s and early 1970s, Marianne Frankenhaeuser of the University of Stockholm demonstrated that in novel, unpredictable, and threatening circumstances, levels of epinephrine and its related hormone norepinephrine were increased during muscular exertion or mental challenge in proportion to people's perception of stress. However, the increases, particularly in epinephrine, were blunted as people became familiar with the challenge (Frankenhaeuser 1971). A later study showed that cortisol responded the same way (Mason et al. 1976). Those findings led to additional definitions of stress according to how people appraise (i.e., define and evaluate) events as threatening and how they cope with the stress (respond mentally or by their behavior) (Lazarus 1993). People can cope with stress *actively* by striving to overcome the source of the stress or by trying to avoid it (**active coping**), or *passively* by taking it without resistance. Events that result in stress can be described in terms of several other dimensions that are related to the nature of the response (see table 4.1).

Stress can occur during a crisis of high impact and for either a short or long duration, or during the smaller, brief but nagging, hassles of daily living. Positive life events or daily uplifts in spirit can

---

Table 4.1

Dimensions of Events That Can Elicit a Stress Response

Dimensions of stressors can interact. For example, frequent daily hassles over which we have no control that continue for months may have more cumulative ill effects than one short-lived major life event that we are able to resolve ourselves.

Quality	Familiarity	Source
Eustress (positive)	Familiar	Mental (i.e., negative thoughts)
Distress (negative)	Novel	Physiological (e.g., virus) Environmental (social, physical)
Quantity	**Coping response**	**Threat level**
Duration	Active	No threat
Frequency	Passive	Life threatening
Intensity	**Sensory focus**	**Types (perceived)**
Minor hassle	Rejection	Challenge (demands person perceives he or she is confident in overcoming)
Major life event	Intake Intake/rejection	Threat (anticipation of harm) Harm (experienced damage)

An external stressor provokes psychological and physiological responses.

Responses to stress can be active (resistance or avoidance) or passive (taking it without resistance).

Stress Management: Controlling Emotion by Maintaining Rational Thinking

▼ Avoid fatalistic thinking *(No matter what I do, I will never be any stronger than I am now).*

▼ Avoid all-or-none thinking *(I must get an A in this class, or it will be a waste of my time; I can't have any chocolate or I will blow my whole diet).*

▼ Avoid catastrophic thinking, that is, making mountains out of molehills *(I couldn't keep up on the runs this week—I must have a metabolic disease that keeps me from adapting to exercise training).*

Candidates for Chronic Stress

People may be at risk for chronic stress if they

▼ feel overwhelmed by responsibilities,

▼ think they have too much to do in too little time, or

▼ feel uncertain about important consequences that seem out of personal control.

also be stressful, but in a good way, because they reduce boredom and offset negative emotions. Though it is true that some people simply are exposed to more events that cause stress or strain (e.g., family conflicts, money problems, loss of a loved one, too many hard exams), it is also true that personality and coping skills can lessen one's vulnerability to stress. About 50% of a person's temperament—whether it is usually calm or is nervous or fiery—is explained by heredity and early childhood learning. Nonetheless, people can improve their ability to deal with stress by learning skills to reduce exposure to stressful events or by changing their outlook on life. People who view change as a challenge or an opportunity for success, who feel in control, and who have a strong commitment to a purpose in their life (e.g., career, other people, spirituality) seem to deal better with misfortune than people whose outlook interprets change as a threat, who feel out of control, and who lack a guiding purpose in their lives.

Does Exercise Reduce Stress?

Most researchers in exercise psychology who have studied stress have looked at whether exercise affects perceived stress. And many studies have confirmed that people generally report reduced or fewer symptoms of stress when they have been physically active. It appears that aerobic types of exercise lasting up to about 30 min generally are associated with the largest reductions in perceived stress. Aerobic exercise programs lasting at least a few months seem best for reducing reports of chronic stress. Though exercise usually won't eliminate the source of stress, exercise could help reduce stress temporarily by providing a short-term distraction from a problem. An exercise program might increase feelings of control or commitment (e.g., success in doing something important for yourself), which could buffer the impact of stressful events.

Relying on people's self-ratings of stress has problems, however. Using self-reports of reduced stress makes it difficult to disentangle the contribution of exercise to stress reduction from a placebo effect. As in research on anxiety and depression, many participants enter the testing environment with expectations that exercise will decrease tension and improve mood. In addition, a self-rating of perceived stress does not adequately determine whether becoming physically active or physically fit indeed reduces behavioral or physiological responses during stressful events.

*A*cute exercise decreases behavioral and physiological manifestations of the stress response.

Studies that used objective measures of stress seem to confirm the self-reports, though. A few studies have shown that a single exercise session can reduce tension in muscles of the face, arms, and legs, as measured by **electromyography (EMG)** after exercise (deVries and Adams 1972; Smith et al. 2001). Other studies have shown that a single session of exercise can increase electrical brain waves (measured from the scalp by electroencephalography; see chapter 3) in the α frequency band (i.e., 8-12 cycles per second) by a half standard deviation when measured during and after exercise (Crabbe and Dishman 2001). Alpha waves are usually believed to reflect a mental state of relaxed wakefulness. However, exercise also increases smaller, faster β waves (i.e., 13-30 cycles per second) that are increased during brain activation, so it is not yet possible to view the brain wave studies as physiological evidence that exercise reduces stress.

Additionally, these studies did not show that people also *perceived* less tension or stress when the muscle or brain measurements were made. That research is discussed in more detail in chapter 5 on affect, mood, and emotion and in chapter 6 on anxiety. We should note too that most studies of physiological measures related to stress have been in experiments conducted in laboratory conditions and examined whether heart rate and blood pressure during mildly stressful tasks were lower among young and middle-aged adults who were physically active or fit versus people who were more sedentary and less fit, or examined whether those responses were lessened by a single session of exercise (Jackson and Dishman 2002). Some of the limitations of research on exercise and stress are discussed in later sections of this chapter.

Physiological Mechanisms of the Stress Response

Understanding the possible mechanisms for a reduced stress response from exercise requires a basic familiarity with the key physiological responses during stress, how they are controlled by the nervous and **endocrine** systems, and how they differ among types of stressors. (See table 4.2 for types of stressors and associated responses.) Key components of the stress response involve neural and endocrine responses that are regulated by the brain and the autonomic nervous system. They include regions of the brain modulated by the neurotransmitters norepinephrine and serotonin, the sympathetic (including the adrenal medulla) and parasympathetic arms of the autonomic nervous system, and the HPA cortical axis.

Brain Norepinephrine and Serotonin

Norepinephrine and serotonin cells in the brain influence attention and vigilance, pituitary hormone release, and cardiovascular function during stress. They also influence pain, fatigue, and sleep. Neural discharge of the locus coeruleus and the raphe nuclei is increased during arousal, decreased during sleep, and absent during rapid eye movement sleep (when motor activity is inhibited). During stress, cells from the locus coeruleus release norepinephrine, and cells from the raphe nuclei release serotonin into the brain's frontal lobe and into the limbic system, including the hippocampus, amygdala, and hypothalamus (see figure 3.11, p. 52). Norepinephrine regulates other brain cells involved in vigilance against threat, helping to initiate behavioral, cardiovascular, and endocrine responses during stress. Serotonin helps the body return to rest after energy-expending behaviors (e.g., feeling satisfied and full after eating and feeling fatigued after exercise). In these ways, the locus coeruleus and the raphe nuclei operate in the brain similarly to the way the sympathetic and parasympathetic branches of the peripheral autonomic

Table 4.2

Characteristic Features and Physiological Responses to Common Tasks Used in Human Studies of Stress and the Autonomic Nervous System

Task	Coping (active vs. passive)	Sensory focus (intake vs. rejection)	Response pattern	ANS pattern
Mental arithmetic	Active	Rejection	↑HR, ↑SBP, ↑DBP, ↔ SV, ↑CO, ↔ TPR	Strong vagal withdrawal, β-adrenergic
Psychomotor reaction time	Active	Intake/rejection	↑HR, ↑SBP, ↑DBP, ↑SV, ↑CO, ↓TPR	Moderate vagal withdrawal, β-adrenergic
Stroop word-color conflict	Active	Intake/rejection	↑HR, ↑BP, ↑DBP, ↔ SV, ↑CO, ↔ TPR	Moderate vagal withdrawal, β-adrenergic
Forehead cold	Passive	?	↓HR, ↑SBP, ↑DBP, ↓SV, ↔ CO, ↑TPR	Vagal activity, α-adrenergic
Cold pressor	Passive	?	↑HR, ↑SBP, ↑DBP, ↓SV, ↔ CO, ↑TPR	Vagal withdrawal α-adrenergic

ANS = autonomic nervous system; CO = cardiac output; DBP = diastolic blood pressure; HR = heart rate; SBP = systolic blood pressure; SV = stroke volume; TPR = total peripheral resistance; ↑ = increase; ↓ = decrease; ↔ = little change.

Reprinted, by permission, from R.K. Dishman and E.M. Jackson, 2000, "Exercise, fitness, and stress," *International Journal of Sports Physiology* 31:190.

nervous system function to modulate the heart, vessels, and adrenal glands during stress.

During stress, norepinephrine helps to initiate behavioral, cardiovascular, and endocrine responses. Serotonin helps the body return to rest after energy-expending behaviors.

Autonomic Nervous System

Features of the autonomic nervous system (ANS) most relevant for understanding cross-stressor adaptations to regular exercise include (1) innervation of the heart, blood vessels, and the adrenal gland by sympathetic nerves and the vagus nerve and (2) hypothalamic-pituitary hormone responses (see chapter 3, figure 3.13). Though there is great specificity in the ANS in response to different types of stressors, common neuroanatomy in the brain also permits coactivation of ANS responses during intense stress.

Sympathetic and Vagal Effects: Emotional Stress Versus Exercise Stress

Usually when someone experiences stress, activation of the sympathetic nervous system (SNS) increases. Sympathetic nerves from the portions of the spinal cord in the areas of the trunk stimulate organs such as the heart, the adrenal glands, and arteries. Under physical or emotional stress, sympathetic nerves stimulate the heart to beat faster and more forcefully, the adrenal glands to secrete epinephrine and norepinephrine, and the arteries that supply the heart and skeletal muscles to dilate so that blood flow is increased (see figure 4.3). During exercise, these actions help supply the extra blood needed to carry oxygen to the muscles used in locomotion. While the heart is beating, systolic blood pressure rises to help drive blood to muscle. While the heart rests between beats, diastolic pressure remains low, so there is little resistance to the flow of blood to the skeletal muscles (see figure 4.3).

During emotional stress, the same responses occur, though usually to a lesser degree, because the nervous, cardiovascular, and endocrine systems are preparing for a threatening situation, the so-called flight-or-fight response to danger. A major

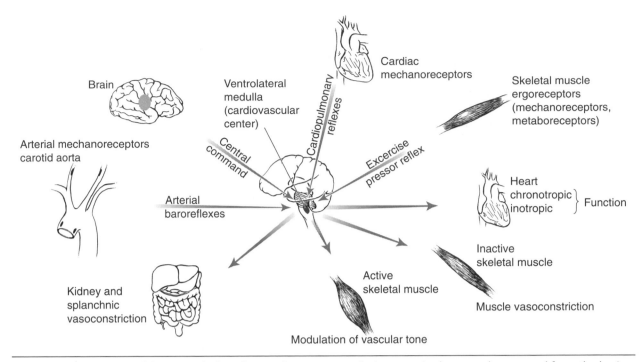

Figure 4.3 Depiction of the control of cardiovascular responses during exercise by central command from the brain and reflexive processing of sensory signals.

Reprinted, by permission, from J.H. Mitchell and P.B. Raven, 1994, Cardiovascular adaptation to physical activity. In *Physical activity, fitness, and health* (Champaign, IL: Human Kinetics), 289.

difference between the two situations, exercise and emotional stress, is that the responses during exercise are necessary for the large increase in body metabolism (i.e., the need for extra energy). Emotional stress usually occurs at near-resting metabolism while people are anticipating a response such as fighting or fleeing from the danger. It is this elevated sympathetic response to perceived, not necessarily real, threat that is common among people with depression or anxiety disorders. Chronic elevations in several of the stress hormones when people feel threatened—but do not physically respond by fighting or fleeing—can make tissues in the brain, heart, and vessels vulnerable to injury or death. The physiological effects of chronically elevated stress hormones can contribute to diseases such as coronary heart disease and suppression of the body's immune system (see figure 4.4).

The main functions of the ANS during exercise are to regulate the increases in heart rate (HR) and blood pressure (BP) needed to increase cardiac output in order to support the increased metabolism of skeletal muscle cells. Secondary functions include the regulation of breathing and temperature. The cardiovascular pressor response, which regulates systolic BP during exercise, is understood to depend on a central command of autonomic efferent

In emotional stress, the ANS prepares the body for the flight-or-fight response to actual and perceived threat; metabolism is at or near rest with anticipation of threat. In exercise stress, the ANS supports increased metabolism of skeletal muscles and regulates breathing and body temperature; metabolism is elevated to perform physical work.

neural activity in the region of the temporal sensory/motor cortex. The centrally controlled pressor response is integrated at the ventrolateral medulla of the spinal cord with a pressor reflex arising from mechanoreceptors (e.g., sensitive to muscle tension) and metaboreceptors (e.g., sensitive to hydrogen ions) in exercising muscle (Mitchell and Raven 1994). Cardiopulmonary and arterial baroreflexes modulate the exercise pressor response, apparently by an upward and parallel resetting of the operating (i.e., set) point of the arterial baroreflexes resulting from central command (Rowell 1993). This means that BP is still regulated

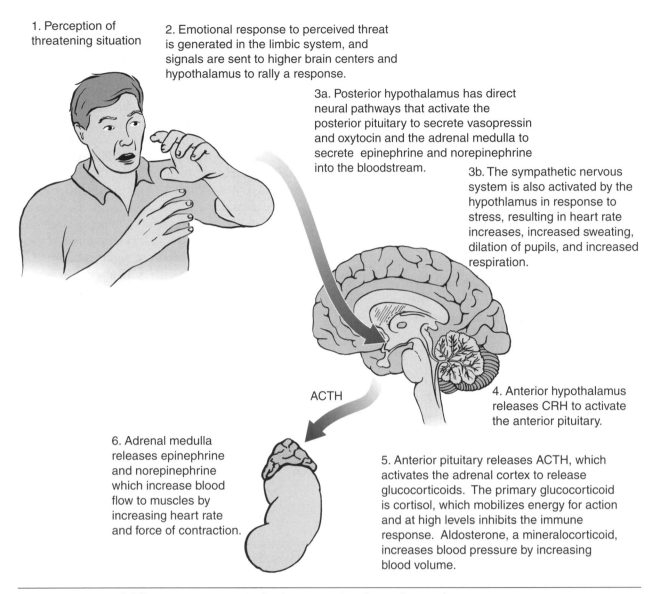

1. Perception of threatening situation

2. Emotional response to perceived threat is generated in the limbic system, and signals are sent to higher brain centers and hypothalamus to rally a response.

3a. Posterior hypothalamus has direct neural pathways that activate the posterior pituitary to secrete vasopressin and oxytocin and the adrenal medulla to secrete epinephrine and norepinephrine into the bloodstream.

3b. The sympathetic nervous system is also activated by the hypothlamus in response to stress, resulting in heart rate increases, increased sweating, dilation of pupils, and increased respiration.

ACTH

4. Anterior hypothalamus releases CRH to activate the anterior pituitary.

6. Adrenal medulla releases epinephrine and norepinephrine which increase blood flow to muscles by increasing heart rate and force of contraction.

5. Anterior pituitary releases ACTH, which activates the adrenal cortex to release glucocorticoids. The primary glucocorticoid is cortisol, which mobilizes energy for action and at high levels inhibits the immune response. Aldosterone, a mineralocorticoid, increases blood pressure by increasing blood volume.

Figure 4.4 Several different systems are involved in supporting the cardiovascular response to stress.

by changes in HR but at much higher levels than at rest. Increased HR during exercise results from an initial withdrawal of cardiac-vagal inhibition of the heart. Vagal withdrawal and subsequent increase in heart rate are followed by increased activation of the heart by sympathetic nerve activity and by hormonal stimulation from catecholamines secreted by the adrenal medulla during intense exercise.

During exercise, the increase in blood levels of norepinephrine comes mainly from sympathetic nerves to the heart, with some of the increase also coming from the exercising skeletal muscles. Some may come from the brain. Exercise training does not usually change levels of norepinephrine in the blood or sympathetic nerve activity to muscles measured while people rest. However, after exercise training, levels of norepinephrine in the blood are lower at a given **absolute intensity** (standard intensity) of exercise (e.g., running a mile in 6 min) and unchanged when that intensity of exercise is expressed as a percentage of **maximal aerobic capacity** (e.g., running a mile at 80% of top speed), but higher than normal at maximal exercise. This means that exercise training seems to increase the capacity of the sympathetic nerves to respond to maximal exercise, but does not change their responses to exercise of the same relative strain as before training. Also, there is no evidence that exercise training leads to a reduced sympathetic response to mental stress, when sympathetic response is measured by epinephrine or norepinephrine in the blood or by activity of sympathetic nerves to muscle.

*E*xercise adaptations for plasma norepinephrine are no change at rest, lower
levels at a given absolute intensity, no
change at the same **relative intensity,**
and increased levels at maximal exercise.

Studies have shown that fitter people, especially women, have lower HR and BP during active mental stress (e.g., mental arithmetic and public speaking) compared to less fit individuals (Spalding et al. 2000); but that is mainly explained by their lower resting HR and BP, common adaptations to regular exercise. In other words, they have lower levels during stress because they have lower levels to start with, not because they have a smaller reaction to the stressors (Buckworth, Dishman, and Cureton 1994; Graham et al. 1996; Jackson and Dishman 2002).

*P*hysically fit people have lower HR and BP
during active mental stress because they
typically have lower HR and BP at rest than
unfit people have.

Lower HR among fit people could result from lower intrinsic rate of the heart (i.e., the rate of the heart's internal pacemaker) or lower activity by sympathetic nerves to the heart, but studies mainly show that it results from increased cardiac-**vagal tone** (see table 4.3 for measurement of ANS activity). The vagus nerve is part of the parasympathetic branch of the ANS. Its neurotransmitter is acetylcholine. Recall that the sympathetic nervous system stimulates energy expenditure and that the parasympathetic nervous system helps store and conserve energy (see chapter 3). The two systems work together to maintain a balance of the body's energy resources both at rest and during stress. For example, the vagus nerve slows the heart's frequency and force of beating and relaxes or dilates arteries that supply blood to skeletal muscle. So, a person who has increased vagal tone after exercise training can better offset the effects of the sympathetic nerves on heart and blood vessels and thus have lower HR and BP at rest and during stress. Increased cardiac-vagal tone also decreases the risk for irregular heartbeats and sudden death in people who have heart disease.

The high metabolism during exercise produces feedback to the brain and central nervous system from peripheral nerves and hormones in the blood; this feedback is used to regulate physiological homeostasis. It is easy to understand why regular exercise and increased fitness would lead to lower HR,

Table 4.3

Measurement of Autonomic Nervous System Activity: Heart Rate Variability

It is not feasible to directly measure the firing rates of the sympathetic and vagus nerves that innervate the heart. Thus, their relative activity is commonly estimated by heart rate variability (HRV).

   Experiments in nonhuman animals have shown that electrical stimulation of the cardiac sympathetic nerves results in fluctuations in heartbeat that are large but slow (LF), whereas stimulation of the vagus nerve results in rapid changes in heart rate (HF).

Term	Definition
Heartbeat	The period of the heart; the time between the R waves in successive QRS complexes
Hertz (Hz)	Frequency, or the number of cycles per second
Low frequency (LF)	.05 to .15 Hz
High frequency (HF)	.15 to .50 Hz
Estimates of autonomic balance during short-term fluctuations in heart rate:	
Cardiac-vagal component:	*HF is normalized to total power:* $[HF/(HF + LF) \times 100]$
Sympatho-vagal component:	*LF is expressed relative to HF:* (LF/HF)

BP, and stress hormones during exercise and to a quicker recovery, because that adaptation would preserve homeostasis and reduce allostatic load. However, it is more difficult to understand why such adaptations to exercise would transfer to other stressors that do not have a high energy cost and do not involve exertion using skeletal muscles. It is not apparent that cardiovascular adaptations to exercise should be expected to generalize to other stressors that do not impose similar psychomotor demands.

In contrast to exercise, most non-exercise stressors elicit little or no sensory afferent activity to regulate cardiovascular responses. Thus, much of any cross-stressor adaptation after exercise must involve central command (i.e., motor nerve discharge to the heart, vessels, or adrenal medulla) or altered responses by organs to central command (e.g., decreased number or sensitivity of receptor cells that bind with epinephrine or norepinephrine). Though such propositions are plausible, the studies done to this point do not support the idea that regular exercise or cardiorespiratory fitness results in a blunted physiological response to stress other than exercise.

*M*uch of any cross-stressor adaptation after exercise must involve central command or altered responses by organs to central command.

On the other hand, studies in rats have shown that voluntary running in activity wheels leads to a blunted stress response during foot-shock stress (as measured by less release of norepinephrine in the brain cortex) (Soares et al. 1999) and a protection against suppression of the innate immune system (Dishman et al. 1995), which appears to be modulated by the sympathetic nervous system during stress (Dishman, Hong, et al. 2000).

Hypothalamic-Pituitary-Adrenal Cortex System: Emotional Stress Versus Exercise Stress

The ANS is activated during stress, but the brain also stimulates energy production by activating endocrine organs, including the pituitary gland and the outer part (cortex) of the adrenal gland (see fig-

ure 4.5). During stress and exercise, the anterior pituitary gland releases adrenocorticotropin (ACTH), which stimulates the adrenal cortex to secrete cortisol. The amount of ACTH available for release is regulated by a gene that is activated by corticotropin-releasing hormone (CRH). This gene is located mainly in the arcuate nucleus of the hypothalamus, which expresses a macromolecule, **proopiomelanocorticotropin (POMC).** ACTH and **beta-endorphin** are cleaved from POMC and are secreted together from the pituitary during stress. Although nerve cells containing CRH are located throughout the brain, most of the CRH that increases ACTH levels comes from the paraventricular nucleus (PVN) of the hypothalamus and is released into the portal blood supply to ACTH-secreting cells in the pituitary. During stress, release of norepinephrine and dopamine in the PVN activates CRH to increase ACTH. Secretion of CRH is inhibited by the hippocampus.

Moderate exercise training results in a diminished HPA response during the same absolute exercise intensity compared to that before training. However, heavy exercise training can be associated with abnormal HPA responses under resting conditions (see chapter 5, p. 113). Generally, fit people have an increased capacity to respond to severe stress. Whether exercise training or aerobic fitness influences HPA responses to milder mental stresses such as daily hassles is not yet known. One study (Sinyor et al. 1983) indicated that trained men had higher levels of cortisol at rest, under mental stress, and during recovery when compared to sedentary men; but the rates of response and recovery were the same for the trained and the untrained men. In other studies, men differing in fitness levels had similar levels of cortisol or ACTH in plasma after mental stress regardless of whether it was novel (Sothmann et al. 1988) or familiar (Blaney et al. 1990). Animal studies have shown no effects of chronic activity-wheel running on plasma levels of ACTH and cortisol after repeated foot-shock in female and male rats (Dishman et al. 1995, 1997).

Exercise studies usually have not measured or controlled reproductive hormones known to influence physiological responses to non-exercise stressors, despite evidence of an interaction between the HPA cortical and the HPA gonadal systems in highly trained women. Treadmill exercise training of female rats treated with estrogen was accompanied by an attenuated ACTH response to familiar treadmill running but a hyperresponsiveness of

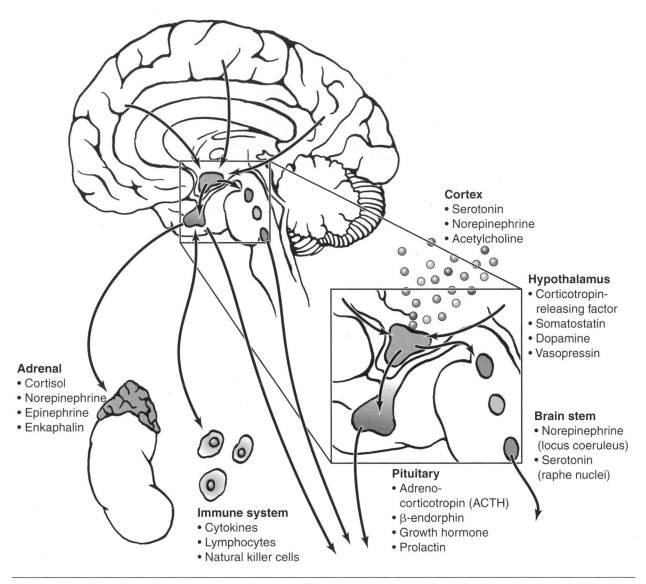

Figure 4.5 Responses of the hypothalamic-pituitary-adrenal cortex system and the sypatho-adrenal medullary system during stress.

Adapted from R.H. Black, 1995, "Psychoneuroimmunology: Brain and immunity," *Scientific American* 2 (6): 17.

ACTH to novel immobilization or foot shock (White-Welkley et al. 1995, 1996). Whether this hyperresponsiveness of ACTH is a healthful adaptation and whether it is due to increased CRH or other factors that release ACTH is not known. The latter seems likely since treadmill exercise training in male rats is accompanied by reduced ACTH after immobilization stress with no change in brain CRH (White-Welkley et al. 1996). Those findings might indicate that the energy and neuromuscular demands of treadmill running lead to an increased potential for HPA responses to novel stressors.

Contemporary Views: Exercise Research

The first review of the cumulative evidence from 25 studies of fitness and physiological stress responses concluded, nearly 15 years ago, that aerobic fitness reduced stress responses by about a half standard deviation, regardless of the type of stressors used or the physiological responses measured (Crews and Landers 1987). Since then, there has not been scientific consensus with that early conclusion (see Dishman and Jackson 2000). This is the case largely because research in exercise psychology has done a poor job in building on what is known about the physiology of stress; especially problematic are the absence of a clear characterization of the features of the stressor used and the lack of any consideration of the regulatory mechanisms that govern physiological stress responses. Specifically, the lack of consensus is explainable primarily by the five factors described in figure 4.6.

Factors limiting past research on exercise and stress reactivity

1. Measurement of fitness and exercise

Early studies did a poor job defining or measuring fitness or exercise. Thus it was hard to determine whether people differed enough to permit a true test of the influence of fitness or exercise habits on stress responses. Also, the use of submaximal heart rate (HR) to estimate peak oxygen uptake ($\dot{V}O_2$peak) confounded the use of HR as both an independent variable (i.e., level of fitness) and dependent variable in several studies. A test-anxious person could show exaggerated HR responses to the exercise test and to the other stressors and be misclassified as unfit because of the emotional elevation in HR during exercise.

2. Measurement of physiological variables

The manner of reporting the methods used to measure physiological variables and to compute their change in response to stressors made it difficult to determine whether the procedures in many studies met international standards for psychophysiological research. The accuracy of the measures was questionable in some studies; the influence of pretest baselines on the stress variables that were measured during stress and recovery was not accounted for in several studies, likely giving a false measure of responsiveness.

3. Research design

About two-thirds of the studies used a cross section of time to compare stress responses among groups classified according to levels of fitness or exercise (rather than comparing responses after a change in fitness or exercise) and did not match the groups on other factors known to influence stress responses, such as temperament, behavior patterns, or reproductive hormone status.

4. Consideration of integrated physiological responses

Investigators gave inadequate consideration to physiological mechanisms that explain variations in integrated responses of variables, such as HR, blood pressure, or circulating stress hormones like norepinephrine, epinephrine, and cortisol. For example, HR responses to a stressor might be similar between people of different fitness levels, but the reasons might be different. A fit person might have less withdrawal of parasympathetic nerve inhibition of the heart despite a similar or greater sympathetic nerve stimulation of the heart. Though the integrated HR response might not differ from that of an unfit person, the different pattern of cardiac sympatho-vagal balance would be important, as it is known to have health consequences.

5. Consideration of characteristics of stressor tasks

Researchers generally failed to compare standardized stressor tasks of equal novelty or difficulty and did not choose tasks according to common or unique features that induce specific or general stress responses (e.g., different sympatho-vagal and sympatho-adrenal medullary responses). Exercise adaptations might extend to certain types or intensities of stressors but not to others.

Figure 4.6 These five factors help to explain why consensus has not been reached in exercise psychology research.

The type of stressor used in research on exercise and stress reactivity is a particularly critical issue (see figure 4.6, factor 5). Unless a stressor is strong enough to engage a general flight-or-fight response (e.g., life or death threat), responses during stress differ widely according to the type of stressor (Allen and Crowell 1989; Dishman, Jackson, and Nakamura 2002) (see table 4.2). Active stressors motivate the person to try to control the challenge (e.g., mental arithmetic, quizzes, reaction-time tasks). Physiological responses include increases in HR, cardiac output, systolic BP, and withdrawal of vagal tone. Passive stressors offer little or no opportunity for the person to control an aversive situation and commonly result in increased HR and increased peripheral resistance to blood flow and diastolic BP. Other responses can also occur such that increased vagal tone results in decreased HR and decreased BP (a so-called playing-dead response). One passive test that elicits a cardiac-vagal response in many people is application of cold to the forehead. Forehead cold can increase BP because of increased resistance to blood flow even though HR is reduced. This response is similar to the mammalian diving reflex, which involves a vagally mediated bradycardia and α-adrenergic vasoconstriction of the skin and viscera.

Generally, BP responses are greater during hand immersion in cold water (cold pressor) than during mental arithmetic, which in turn elicits greater responses than does a psychomotor reaction-time task. In contrast, cardiac output is greater during a reaction-time task or mental arithmetic than during a cold-pressor test. Heart rate increases the most during mental arithmetic compared to the cold-pressor test or reaction-time task. Increased HR during mental arithmetic is explainable by vagal withdrawal, whereas during a reaction-time task it is more influenced by sympathetic innervation of the heart. Blood flow also differs according to type of stressor. Increased cardiac output during a reaction-time task is mainly explained by increased stroke volume, whereas during mental arithmetic it is explained by increased HR. Cardiac output during the cold-pressor test is unchanged because the increased HR is offset by decreased stroke volume (Dishman, Jackson, and Nakamura 2002).

Limitations of past research also make it too early to conclude that regular exercise has no effect on responses during stress that are modulated by the sympathetic nervous system. The reason for the absence of effects in past studies might be the narrow range in the increase of plasma catecholamines evoked by the stressors that researchers have used. Most of the stressors used have been mild, eliciting small increases in a range of about 300 to 500 pg/ml for norepinephrine and 40 to 80 pg/ml for epinephrine. Those levels are below thresholds for norepinephrine (1500-2000 pg/ml) and epinephrine (75-125 pg/ml) that reliably elicit increases in HR and systolic BP (Clutter et al. 1980; Silverberg, Clements, and Fiatarone 1978). A five- to tenfold elevation in norepinephrine and a twofold increase in epinephrine are generally believed necessary for cardiovascular effects, yet the stressors used have seldom resulted in a doubling of catecholamines above basal levels. In contrast, moderate-to-heavy exercise results in a six- to tenfold increase in norepinephrine and a tripling of epinephrine (Clutter et al. 1980).

The types of stressors used in studies of exercise and stress have been milder than many events that are stressful in real life. The experimental stressors usually increase HR by altered sympatho-vagal balance of the ANS's innervation of the heart rather than by hormonal response. For example, during mental arithmetic, heart transplant patients—who have had the autonomic nerves to the heart severed—have an increased BP (Sehested et al. 1995) but not the increase in HR (Sehested et al. 1995; Shapiro et al. 1994) that is observed in people with innervated hearts. Thus, tasks like mental arithmetic do not elicit a stress response by the adrenal gland that is of sufficient magnitude to increase HR.

*E*vidence for modification in the response to mental stress after exercise training is equivocal, but there might be beneficial effects from enhanced vagal tone.

Nonetheless, it remains plausible that increased cardiac-vagal tone after regular exercise might generalize to blunt responses to mild stressors that elicit increases in HR and BP mainly by vagal withdrawal. In contrast, responses by the sympathetic nervous system seem to be unique to different stress organs during mild stressors. Hence, whether altered regulation of the sympathetic nervous system after regular exercise might lead to a generalizable response seems less clear and could depend on the intensity of exercise and other stressors.

Summary

Adults without stress disorders typically say that they feel less stressed after a single exercise session and after a regular exercise program. However, studies have not yet shown convincingly that those findings were uninfluenced by people's expectations of benefits. There has been no research to determine whether exercise reduces stress among people diagnosed with stress disorders. Studies in which physiological responses were measured have shown that cardiorespiratory fitness is associated with a slight blunting of HR and systolic BP reactions during active mental stress, but not during passive stress, such as that caused by placing the hand in ice water. More often, fit people have a lower overall level of HR and, many times, of BP during stress because they have lower resting levels, not because they have a smaller reaction to the stress than do unfit people.

Research has not shown that fitness affects catecholamine responses during stress, but the stressors used have been mild and have not led to responses large enough to adequately test whether fitness really alters the sympathetic response by the adrenal gland. There are not enough studies of other hormone responses, such as cortisol, to permit us to conclude whether exercise and fitness alter other endocrine responses during stress.

There has been very little use of the traditions and methods of biological psychology and neuroscience in the study of exercise, fitness, and stress. Though many people say that exercise helps them cope with stress, we cannot rely solely on social cognitive models of stress that use people's self-rated perceptions to determine whether, or in what circumstances, cardiorespiratory fitness or regular exercise leads to blunted or augmented physiological responses during stress and enhances recovery from stress. Modern students of exercise psychology should learn the basics of neuroanatomy, neurophysiology, and psychopharmacology as well as the techniques of neuroscience to help them conduct sound research on exercise and stress or to collaborate effectively with physiologists or biological psychologists. Nonetheless, the subjective experience of stress remains a cornerstone of inquiry into the nature of stress emotions such as anxiety and depression. Discussions of those topics follow.

Suggested Readings

Dishman, R.K. 1997. Brain monoamines, exercise, and behavioral stress: Animal models. *Medicine and Science in Sports and Exercise* 29 (Jan): 63–74.

Dishman, R.K., and E.M. Jackson. 2000. Exercise, fitness, and stress. *International Journal of Sport Psychology* 31: 175–203.

Sapolsky, R.M. 1994. *Why zebras don't get ulcers—A guide to stress, stress-related diseases, and coping.* New York: Freeman.

Sothmann, M.S., J. Buckworth, R.P. Claytor, R.H. Cox, J.E. White-Welkley, and R.K. Dishman. 1996. Exercise training and the cross-stressor adaptation hypothesis. *Exercise and Sport Sciences Reviews* 24: 267–287.

Web Sites

www.nimh.nih.gov/publicat/index.cfm

www.surgeongeneral.gov/library/mentalhealth/index.html

www.nhlbi.nih.gov/health/index.htm

www.clas.ufl.edu/users/gthursby/stress/

5

Affect, Mood, and Emotion

Most people say they feel better after they exercise. This chapter is about what that means and why it happens. The focus is on the potential that physical activity and exercise have for improving someone's mood and on whether acute exercise alters emotions. The chapter clarifies distinctions between concepts of *affect*, *mood*, and *emotion* and presents the neuroanatomy and theories of affect and emotion. It also presents some key factors that likely influence the effects of exercise on negative and positive moods. In addition, we summarize new studies on emotional response after exercise and address some limitations of the research, including questions about proper measurement.

Positive psychological effects from exercise can moderate and perhaps even mediate the determinants of people's participation in physical activity and exercise. Thus, understanding the relationship between affect and exercise fits with studying exercise and mental health, but also has implications for understanding exercise adherence, a topic covered in the last part of this book. This chapter concludes with a description of the mechanisms that may help explain the relationship between exercise and affect, mood, and emotion. The effects of exercise on specific moods of anxiety and depression are covered in detail in chapters 6 and 7.

James on Exercise

Our muscular vigor will . . . always be needed to furnish the background of sanity, serenity, and cheerfulness to life, to give moral elasticity to our disposition, to round off the wiry edge of our fretfulness, and make us good-humored. . . .

William James (1899, pp. 205–207)

*P*hysical activity behavior can influence affect, but affect can also have an impact on behavior.

William James, the father of American psychology, extolled the benefits of exercise for positive moods, and that common wisdom holds today. Feeling better and reducing tension are among the most common perceived benefits of exercise endorsed by young and middle-aged adults (Steinhardt and Dishman 1989). In a survey of 10 behaviors that people without clinical disorders use to self-manage their moods, exercise was judged to be the overall winner (Thayer, Newman, and McClain 1994). People rated exercise as the best for improving a bad mood, fourth best at raising energy levels, and third to fourth best for reducing tension.

Positive Changes With Exercise

Some positive changes with exercise have been described as

▼ feeling good, relaxed, euphoric, or imaginative;

▼ having a sense of accomplishment;

▼ having improved self-worth;

▼ having a global sense of well-being;

▼ having improved concentration; and

▼ experiencing vivid physical sensations.

Definitions of Terms

The idea that people "feel better" after exercise is commonly accepted, but several different terms are used to describe the psychological response to exercise, and defining them can be difficult. For example, if someone asks you what kind of mood you're in after you have finished a 3-mile jog, you might say that you are in a good mood. If, instead, you are asked how you're feeling, your response would be more specific, such as "relaxed," "carefree," or even "relieved" depending on the circumstances.

Feelings are subjective experiences that can be overt or covert. A **feeling state** refers to bodily sensations, cognitive appraisals, actual or potential instrumental responses, or some combination of these responses (Averill, et al. 1994) (see table 5.1). **Affect** has been defined as the expression of value

given to a feeling state (Batson, Shaw, and Oleson 1992). Wilhelm Wundt, the father of psychology, concluded in 1897 that affect could be described by three dimensions: pleasure-displeasure, excitement-calm, and strain-relaxation. The most widely accepted modern views are: [1] affective experience varies on two primary orthogonal (independent) dimensions (see figure 5.1): (1) valence, or hedonic tone, which can range from attraction/pleasure to avoidance/displeasure; and (2) intensity, or activation, which can range from calm to aroused. [2] specific emotions can be discribed in a circumplex, composed of varying degrees of the primary dimensions of valence and intensity.

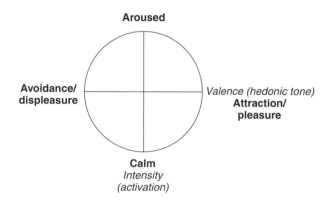

Figure 5.1 A two-dimensional model of affective experience expressed on separate continua of approach-avoidance and level of arousal.

Another popular, but less well supported, view is that there are two dimensions of activation rather than a single continuum (Thayer 1989). From that perspective, the valence of affective experiences depends on the level of activation along two separate dimensions or continuums of (1) energy (i.e., sleepy to energetic) and (2) tension (i.e., calm to tense). Another theoretical model is that arousal is

---

Table 5.1

Categories and Examples of Feeling States

The term "feeling" is used to describe	Example
Bodily reactions and experiences	*Feelings of* pain or fatigue
Cognitive appraisal regarding the value we ascribe to objects or activities	Positive *feelings about* finishing a long jog, or negative *feelings about* the steep hill at the end of a bicycle ride
Actual or potential instrumental responses	*Feel like* getting an ice cream cone, or *feel like* taking a walk

not a separate dimension but is nested *within* positive and negative affect (e.g., sadness has negative valence and low arousal, whereas joy has positive valence and high arousal) (Tellegen 1988).

The latter two views of affective experience are mainly limited to self-report data, and affect is determined using factor analyses of the patterns of people's ratings of adjectives (see chapter 2). Because the models discussed so far are based strictly on people's feelings, they don't consider that biological arousal can vary both on total body metabolism and on neural activity in the brain and autonomic nervous system. At this point, most evidence fits best with the view, depicted in figure 5.1, that the bipolar dimension of valence can be associated with, but is not dependent on, the bipolar dimension of arousal (Davidson 1998a; Lang, Bradley, and Cuthbert 1998). The inclusion of arousal as a separate dimension of affect and emotion is important for studies of exercise because physical exertion is a powerful influence on metabolic arousal. Whether or not physical activity and exercise influence emotional arousal or affective valence has yet to be determined; that question is examined later in this chapter. In all the perspectives mentioned, affective experience is broadly defined and is considered more basic than mood and emotion, although the term has been used synonymously with mood (e.g., Tellegen 1985). As we will see, important aspects of mood and emotion involve biological responses as well.

Temperament refers to a mainly stable, core component of personality that disposes people to emotional responsiveness and changing moods. We commonly describe someone who has periods of emotional ups and downs as moody. Or, we might describe someone who is often angry as having a fiery temperament. Temperament is based on biological (genetic) factors and learned experiences. **Traits** are narrower features of temperament and indicate the tendency to respond to an internal or external event with a particular mood state. For example, someone with high trait anxiety is more likely than others to be anxious while waiting for the results of a job interview. Traits are relatively consistent over time but are easier to change than temperament.

It is not uncommon to say that someone is in a good or bad humor. That has a basis in antiquity. The Greek physician, Galen, believed that humans had four basic temperaments, influenced by the four humors of the body. For example, a *melancholic*, or sad, patient was said to suffer from excess black bile; a *sanguine*, or joyful, person was said to be moved by blood; a *choleric*, or angry, person was said to be

controlled by yellow bile; and a *phlegmatic*, or unflappable, unemotional person was said to be influenced by excess phlegm. Though not biologically true, those ideas still influence us today, as the adjectives remain part of the English language. And joy, anger, and sadness are acknowledged by psychologists, along with love, surprise, and fear, as the key emotions.

*F*eeling, affect, mood, trait, and temperament are different constructs that are related to emotional responses.

Mood is considered a type of affective state that is accompanied by anticipation, even unconscious, of pleasure or pain. Moods can last less than a minute or for days. A particular mood state (e.g., positive) is influenced by overall disposition (temperament and traits) and by brief responses (emotions) composed of feelings, distinct autonomic and somatic activation, and behavior. Conditions leading to moods typically occur over a slow time course, and the effect may accumulate from repeated experiences of an emotion. Events evoking an emotion occur quickly: for example, you might achieve a personal best on a leg press and experience a feeling of elation when you realize how much weight you lifted. Then, if you continue to experience events that evoke positive emotions, such as having a good workout, catching all the green lights on your way home from the gym, and finding your favorite supper waiting for you, you are likely to experience a positive mood. You would anticipate a pleasant evening, and the positive expectation and mood might even be sustained for another day. Moods can also develop spontaneously with no apparent, specific cause.

Moods might alter the way information is processed, which biases cognitions or thoughts (Smith and Crabbe 2000). A sustained positive mood predisposes you to access positive thoughts and feelings. It has been suggested that the biological link for this phenomenon is an enhancement of neural pathways linked to pleasant thoughts and feelings, rendering them more accessible than negative thoughts and feelings. The idea of neural pathway facilitation that favors a certain quality or tone of cognitions has also been used to explain the tendency for depressed individuals to focus on negative thoughts and feelings.

Emotions are brief responses of negative or positive feelings evoked by particular situations; as we just saw, they can contribute to mood. It is also possible that a prevailing mood can prime an emotional response. While mood influences the way information is processed, exerting a bias in valence, emotions influence the activity of the autonomic nervous system. The emotional response consists of behavior and activation of autonomic and hormonal systems (see table 5.2). Thus, there is a physiological component to emotion that is essentially lacking in affect, which is the subjective component of emotion. That is not to say that there is no biological basis to affect. As we will see later in the chapter, there is clearly a neurochemical basis to all subjective experience, including affect, mood, and emotion. Indeed, there is good evidence that the integration of overt behavior, autonomic responses, and hormonal responses is controlled by neural systems that consist of some key brain regions. These are discussed later in the chapter.

The terms "feeling," "affect," "mood," and "temperament" are all emotion-related expressions and describe constructs that differ from emotional responses. An emotion is more narrow in focus than mood and is more short-lived; it is evoked by a specific thought or event, is usually directed toward some goal, and is accompanied by temporary physiological responses. Emotions have been conceptualized as discrete states and paired opposites (see table 5.3). Another view groups emotions into families, which are affective states within a hierarchy from the abstract (basic emotion) to the more concrete. These affective families share common expression, physiological activity, and cognitive appraisals or meaning (Lazarus 1991). There is some evidence of specific patterns of autonomic arousal for different emotions (Cacioppo et al. 1993). Specific emotions can also be described in a circumplex

composed of varying degrees of the primary dimensions of valence and intensity as shown in figure 5.2, a and b.

Emotions sustain activation of systems needed to maintain motivated responses, and the contribution of emotions to behavior has been explored for decades in theory and research. In the late 1800s, Darwin (1872) proposed that emotions are innate and common in lower species and across cultures. The expression of emotions (i.e., "behavior") takes the form of facial expressions that are a species-specific repertoire of muscle movement. The facial expression of emotion is not learned, but inherited,

Table 5.3

Conceptualizations of Emotions

Discrete emotions (Ekman 1992)

Happiness	Surprise	Fear	Anger	Disgust

Paired opposites (Plutchik 1994)

Joy	Sadness
Acceptance	Disgust
Anger	Fear
Expectation	Surprise

Emotion families (Shaver et al. 1987)

Basic emotion	Affective states
Anger	Irritation, annoyance, fury, rage
Fear	Apprehension, anxiety, panic, horror, terror
Love	Affection, attachment, devotion, passion
Joy	Happiness, pleasure, delight, exhilaration
Sadness	Despondency, dejection, depression, grief

Table 5.2

Components of an Emotional Response

Component	Explanation
Behavior	Muscular movements consistent with situation that elicits the emotion (i.e., a smile or scowl)
Autonomic	Responses that facilitate the behavior (i.e., sympathetic activation in fear-provoking situations to facilitate fight-or-flight response)
Hormonal	Reinforcement of the autonomic response (i.e., activation of the hypothalamus-pituitary-adrenal axis to facilitate cardiovascular response and substrate availability)

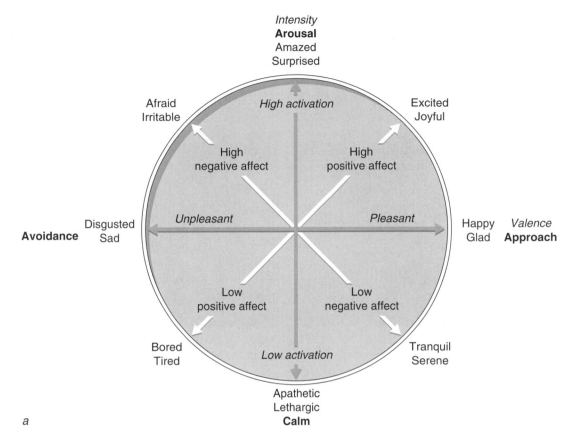

Intensity
Arousal
Amazed
Surprised

High activation

Afraid
Irritable

Excited
Joyful

High
negative affect

High
positive affect

Unpleasant

Pleasant

Avoidance Disgusted
Sad

Happy *Valence*
Glad **Approach**

Low
positive affect

Low
negative affect

Bored
Tired

Low activation

Tranquil
Serene

Apathetic
Lethargic
Calm

a

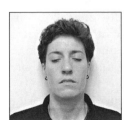

b

Figure 5.2 Watson and Tellegen's (1985) dimensions of positive and negative affect displayed on Russell's (1980) emotional circumplex *(a);* facial expressions that correspond to the primary emotions depicted in part a. Facial expressions for surprise, joy, disgust, anger, and fear are common to virtually all cultures *(b).*

Part b provided by the Exercise Psychology Laboratory, The University of Georgia.

Since Darwin's writings, it has been recognized that humans are not the only animals that use facial expressions and body posture to express basic emotions.

and serves, along with body language, to communicate our emotions to others and to indicate how we are likely to behave. The cross-cultural consistency of specific facial expressions and corresponding emotions has been supported by studies by Ekman and his colleagues (e.g., Ekman and Friesen 1971). Facial expressions for joy, surprise, anger, fear, and disgust are universally recognized in virtually all cultures. This raises the possibility that different brain systems regulate each emotion, not merely positive and negative categories of emotions. If found to be true, that would present a unique challenge for exercise psychology. Why, or perhaps in what circumstances, would exercise be expected to exert an influence on emotions that is independent of the setting where exercise occurs? The biology of exercise mainly depends on the type, intensity, and duration of exertion. To a lesser extent, hostile environmental conditions such as heat or cold, humidity, and altitude affect exercise responses. Is it reasonable that exercise alone would alter specific emotions? Or, might exercise alter some neural system common to positive or negative moods?

A Short History of Emotion

To understand how exercise might alter affect, mood, or emotion, it will be helpful to see how views

on the origins of those concepts have evolved in history. As you'll recall from chapter 1, the James-Lange theory of emotion proposed that bodily responses during emotion are the source of the affective experience. The following excerpts from the article, "What Is an Emotion?" published in the journal *Mind* (James 1884), illustrate the challenge of understanding the precise role of physiological responses in the experience of emotion—a challenge that persists today. James' examples raise the question of whether the modern-day view that physiological and behavioral responses occur only after the person has evaluated events holds true in all circumstances.

Our natural way of thinking about these standard emotions is that the mental perception of some fact excites the mental affection called the emotion, and that this latter state of mind gives rise to the bodily expression. My thesis on the contrary is that the bodily changes follow directly the PERCEPTION of the exciting fact, and that our feeling of the same changes as they occur IS the emotion. Common sense says, we lose our fortune, are sorry and weep; we meet a bear, are frightened and run; we are insulted by a rival, are angry and strike. The hypothesis here to be defended says that this order of sequence is incorrect, that the one mental state is not immediately induced by the other, that the bodily manifestations must first be interposed between, and that the more rational statement is that we feel sorry because we cry, angry because we strike, afraid because we tremble, and not that we cry, strike, or tremble, because we are sorry, angry, or fearful, as the case may be (p. 189).

Without the bodily states following on the perception, the latter would be purely cognitive in form, pale, colourless, destitute of emotional warmth. We might then see the bear, and judge it best to run, receive the insult and deem it right to strike, but we could not actually feel afraid or angry (p. 190).

Is there any evidence, it may be asked, for the assumption that particular perceptions do produce widespread bodily effects by a sort of immediate physical influence, antecedent to the arousal of an emotion or emotional idea? The only possible reply is, that there is most assuredly such evidence. In listening to poetry, drama, or heroic narrative, we are often surprised at the cutaneous shiver which like a sudden wave flows over us, and at the heart-swelling and the lachrymal effusion that unexpectedly catch us at intervals. In listening to music, the same is even more strikingly true. If we abruptly see a dark moving form in the woods, our heart stops beating, and we catch our breath instantly and before any articulate idea of danger can arise. If our friend goes near to the edge of a precipice, we get the well-known feeling of "all-overishness," and we shrink back, although we positively know him to be safe, and have no distinct imagination of his fall. (James 1884, p. 196)

James also used psychiatric cases to make his point, describing especially the symptoms of a panic attack, a modern-day anxiety disorder that is discussed in chapter 6.

In every asylum we find examples of absolutely unmotived fear, anger, melancholy, or conceit; and others of an equally unmotived apathy which persists in spite of the best of outward reasons why it should give way. In the former cases we must suppose the nervous machinery to be so "labile" in some one emotional direction, that almost every stimulus, however inappropriate, will cause it to upset in that way, and as a consequence to engender the particular complex of feelings of which the psychic body of the emotion consists. Thus, to take one special instance, if inability to draw deep breath, fluttering of the heart, and that peculiar epigastric change felt as "precordial anxiety," with an irresistible tendency to take a somewhat crouching attitude and to sit still, and with perhaps other visceral processes not now known, all spontaneously occur together in a certain person; his feeling of their combination is the emotion of dread, and he is the victim of what is known as morbid fear. A friend who has had occasional attacks of this most distressing of all maladies, tells me that in his case the whole drama seems to centre about the region of the heart and respiratory apparatus, that his main effort during the attacks is to get control of his inspirations and to slow his heart, and that the moment he attains to breathing deeply and to holding himself erect, the dread, ipso facto, seems to depart (p. 199).

It must be confessed that a crucial test of the truth of the hypothesis is quite as hard to obtain as its decisive refutation. A case of complete internal and external corporeal anaesthesia, without motor alteration or alteration of intelligence except emotional apathy, would afford, if not a crucial test, at least a strong presumption, in favour of the truth of the view we have set forth; whilst the persistence of strong emotional feeling in such a case would completely overthrow our case. Hysterical anaesthesias seem never to be complete enough to cover the ground. Complete anaesthesias from organic disease, on the other hand, are excessively rare. (James 1884, p. 203)

James next recounts an exchange with a German physician named Strümpell who had published a case study of a 15-year-old shoemaker's apprentice. The boy had lost all sensation except in one eye and one ear. He had reportedly shown shame after soiling his bed and grief at the sight of a favorite food that he knew he could no longer taste. James wrote to Professor Strümpell and asked him whether he was sure that the shame and grief were real feelings in the boy's mind, or only reflexes to perceptions that an observer would interpret as an emotion. This was Dr. Strümpell's response (in translation):

> I think I can decidedly make the statement, that he was by no means completely lacking in emotional affections. In addition to the feelings of grief and shame mentioned in my paper, I recall distinctly that he showed anger, and frequently quarrelled with the hospital attendants. He also manifested fear lest I should punish him. In short, I do not think that my case speaks exactly in favour of your theory. On the other hand, I will not affirm that it positively refutes your theory. For my case was certainly one of a very centrally conditioned anaesthesia (perception-anaesthesia, like that of hysterics) and therefore the conduction of outward impressions may in him have been undisturbed. (James 1884, p. 204)

These passages illustrate the difficulty of uncovering laws that govern human behavior in all settings. The interaction among the stimulus, neural integration of the stimulus, autonomic and hormonal activation, perception and interpretation of the stimulus and physiological response, and subsequent emotional and behavioral responses has been the focus of several theories since the introduction of the James-Lange theory (Carlson 1998; Rosenzweig, Leiman, and Breedlove 1999b).

The **Cannon-Bard theory** proposed a different sequence of events. On the basis of physiological studies of animals during fear and rage conducted around the 1920s, Harvard physician Walter Cannon deduced that the brain decided the appropriate response to a stimulus and that the subsequent physiological response and emotion occurred simultaneously. Social psychologist Stanley Schachter followed in the 1960s with a cognitive theory of emotion in which the emotional response is the result of the interaction between nonspecific physiological reactions (i.e., heart rate increase) and the cognitive interpretation of the arousal. Schachter showed that physiological arousal (induced by injections of adrenaline) was perceived by the person as different emotions depending on the social context. For example, you would interpret an increase in heart rate during walking as "I am afraid" if you had just seen a large, growling dog, but as "I am excited" if an attractive runner had just smiled at you. **Schachter's theory** is based on nonspecific arousal. The level of arousal dictates the intensity of emotion, while the interpretation determines the valence.

However, as already mentioned, there is evidence that different emotions exhibit specific patterns of autonomic arousal; and Clore and colleagues (1994) proposed that appraisal determines not only the valence, but also the intensity of emotions. There is also support for stable individual differences for affect intensity and the ways in which basic emotions are experienced and expressed (Davidson 2000; Gauvin and Spence 1998). Another view is that human emotion is experienced as affect when primitive, reflexive behavioral responses are inhibited (Lang 1995). Contemporary research continues to be influenced by biological-genetic, cognitive, and developmental aspects of emotions (Smith and Crabbe 2000). No single theory has been proven to hold in all circumstances, so it is important to be familiar with the history of the various theories.

The approach-withdrawal model of affect was developed some decades ago when primitive organisms were found to have two primary emotional response dispositions: avoidance and approach. Schneirla (1959) described avoidance as the withdrawal of the organism from noxious stimuli, and approach as attraction and advancement toward appetitive stimuli. This idea was expanded by Konorski (1967) to include the moderating influence of arousal on responses, and by Osgood, Suci, and Tennenbaum (1957) to characterize verbal emotional descriptors in two dimensions: affective valence (aversion to attraction) and biological activation (calm to aroused) (see figure 5.1, p. 92).

Contemporary Views of Affect and Emotion

The current view of emotions is based on these early perspectives. Affective expression is determined by two basic motivational systems linked to anatomical neural circuits that generate appetitive and defensive behavior for the purpose of survival (Davidson 2000; Lang 2000). Motivation has an intrinsic biphasic organization, that is, approach and avoidance-withdrawal. The approach system engages appetitive behavior and generates types of positive affect (e.g., curiosity, enthusiasm, pride, love) consistent with moving toward goals. The avoidance system engages withdrawal from aversive stimuli and generates types of negative affect (e.g., fear and disgust) consistent with protection from harm. Lang (2000) explained the motivational basis of emotions through "natural selective attention," in which attention is primarily determined by the salience of the cue, or its intrinsic motivational significance, and the preexisting drive states. Cues that have appetitive or defensive significance are those cues to which we attend and respond. The intensity of response depends on level of arousal. For example, if a cyclist has been riding all morning and has forgotten her water bottle, her level of arousal will be high as a consequence of thirst. She will attend to cues that have appetitive value for her, such as a water fountain or soda machine. Her response to seeing a lemonade stand on a side street will be a smile (behavior) accompanied by autonomic and hormonal activation to support her appetitive drive to satisfy her thirst.

Affect varies as a function of valance (positive versus negative) and intensity.

Neuroanatomy of Affect and Emotion

The evocation and expression of emotion have a strong biological basis. In 1937, Papez suggested that there is a set of interconnected brain structures responsible for motivation and emotion. Papez's neural circuit proposed that information flowed from the hippocampus via the formix to the mammillary bodies of the hypothalamus, to the anterior thalamus, to the cingulate cortex, and back to the hippocampus (see figure 5.3).

The French anatomist Broca described the limbic lobe (meaning border or fringe) of the brain in 1878. Paul MacLean of the National Institute of Mental Health is credited with expanding the circuit of Papez to a "limbic system" as the seat of emotion to include the prefrontal cortex, the amygdala, and the septum, among others.

Today, cumulative research findings in neuroscience based on lesioning, electrophysiological measures, and **neuroimaging** using positron emission tomography (PET) and functional magnetic resonance imaging (fMRI) have so far identified six key brain regions that seem to be most involved in the expression of human emotion (Davidson and Irwin 1999) (see box on p. 100).

Though these brain regions are believed to operate as systems, not alone, they do appear to have some unique functions:

▼ The *prefrontal cortex* likely works as a memory of affective consequences, permitting an emotion to be sustained long enough to direct behavior toward the goal appropriate for that emotion.

▼ The *hippocampus* appears to process memories of the environment or context in which an emotion occurs. People who have damage to the hippocampus still experience emotion, but often at inappropriate times or places.

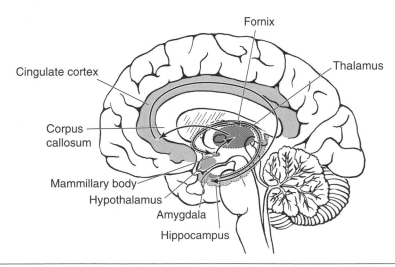

Figure 5.3 Papez (1937) proposed that the experience of emotion was primarily determined by the cingulate cortex, which modulates activity in the hippocampus. The hippocampus projects to the hypothalamus via a bundle of axons named the fornix. Hypothalamic impulses are relayed to the cortex from the anterior thalamus.

Brain Regions Involved in the Expression of Human Emotion

- Three parts of the prefrontal cortex
  1. Dorsolateral (the top, side part of the frontal lobe)
  2. Ventromedial (the middle, bottom part)
  3. Orbitofrontal (the base of the frontal lobe just above the orbits of the eyes)
- Amygdala, especially the central portion
- Hippocampus
- Ventral striatum, especially the nucleus accumbens (below the front of the caudate and putamen)
- Cingulate cortex (a layer of gray matter lying between the cerebrum and the lateral ventricle)
- Insular cortex (an island of involuted cortex near the temporal lobe)

▼ The *ventral striatum*, especially the *nucleus accumbens*, is part of the mesolimbic pathway of dopamine neurons that are key in what is known as reward-motivated behavior. Infusion of cocaine in addicts or nicotine in smokers, as well as the viewing of positive images, activates the accumbens. Thus, it appears to play a role in regulating approach behaviors associated with positive affect.

▼ The anterior *cingulate cortex* is part of the primitive cortex common to species lower in evolution than humans. It seems to help regulate attention during the processing of the valence of an emotion.

▼ The *insular cortex* receives sensory inputs from the autonomic nervous system, especially cardiovascular responses, and sends signals to the central amygdala and the hypothalamus, which each regulate cardiac and endocrine responses during stress.

▼ The *amygdala* plays a key role in integrating overt behavior, autonomic responses, and hormonal responses during stress and emotion. Also, its tonic level of activity is sensitive to negative mood. For example, activity in the amygdala is elevated among patients diagnosed with depression and anxiety disorders. Patients with phobias show increased activity in the amygdala during fear elicited by a phobic object. Even seeing a fearful expression increases blood flow and metabolism in the amygdala. Re-

ceptors on the amygdala are also largely responsible for the anxiety-reducing effects of benzodiazepines and opiates (Carlson 1998).

The amygdala is especially important for processing neural events associated with the experience of learned fear and anxiety. Lesion studies have shown that the emotion of fear is a primitive, hard-wired reaction to immediate danger, but that learned fear and anxiety also depend on the amygdala (LeDoux 1994). A useful probe for studying brain activity linked with fear, anxiety, and other negative or positive emotional states in humans is the acoustic startle eye-blink response or ASER (Lang 1995; Lang, Bradley, and Cuthbert 1998). The ASER is elicited by an abrupt noise (e.g., similar to the sound of a starter's pistol), which is processed as an obligatory reflex from the auditory nerve by ventral cochlear root neurons projecting to the nucleus reticularis pontis caudalis and on to the facial nerve innervating the orbicularis occuli (the muscle that blinks the eye) (Davis 1997; Lee et al. 1996). The ASER is measured by placing surface electrodes beneath and beside the eye to record an integrated electromyographic signal of activity in the orbicularis occuli as the eye blinks. Figure 5.4 shows placement of the electrodes. A typical electromyographic (EMG) response is shown in figure 5.5.

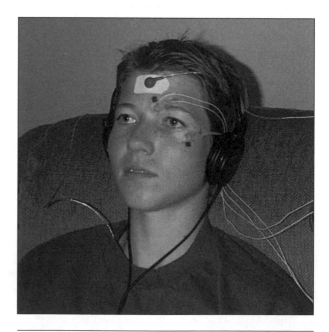

Figure 5.4 Electrode placement for the measurement of the acoustic startle eye-blink response using electromyography.

Provided by the Exercise Psychology Laboratory, Department of Exercise Science, The University of Georgia.

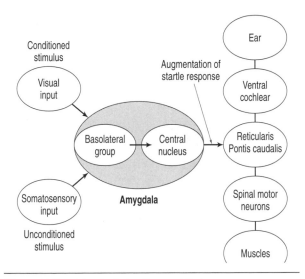

Figure 5.5 A typical startle eye-blink response as measured by electromyography.

Provided by the Exercise Psychology Laboratory, The University of Georgia.

The nucleus reticularis pontis caudalis is innervated by neurons of the amygdala and the periaqueductal gray (PAG) matter, which provide a neuroanatomy enabling the amygdala to modulate the ASER during emotion (see figure 5.6). In humans, the amplitude of the ASER is increased by anticipation of electric shock and by images that evoke fear or are otherwise aversive to the person (Lang 1995). Anti-anxiety drugs such as benzodiazepines reduce the ASER.

Psychophysiologist Peter Lang and his colleagues at the University of Florida believe that the ASER is a defensive reflex elicited mainly in aversive circumstances when the prevailing affect is negative and the motivational state is one of avoidance or withdrawal. By having people view a standard set of pictures that differ in content from highly pleasant to highly unpleasant, these researchers have shown that the ASER is increased in conditions that elicit attention, aversion, and high emotional arousal (Cuthbert, Bradley, and Lang 1996; Lang 1995; Lang et al. 1998). The ASER tends to be reduced when the emotional content of the pictures is rated by the participant as positive or pleasant.

Hemispheric Asymmetry

The function of the neural circuits of affect can differ between the left and right hemispheres. This difference is called **hemispheric asymmetry.** For example, people who have lesion damage to the prefrontal cortex, especially the left dorsolateral area, have increased risk of developing depression (Davidson and Irwin 1999). This is not actually a new finding. The first modern theory of frontal lobe function, proposed by David Ferrier in the 1870s, was in part based on the case of Phineas Gage, who survived massive damage to his left frontal cortex and suffered irreparable loss of mental function. Gage was the foreman of a railway construction gang working for the Rutland and

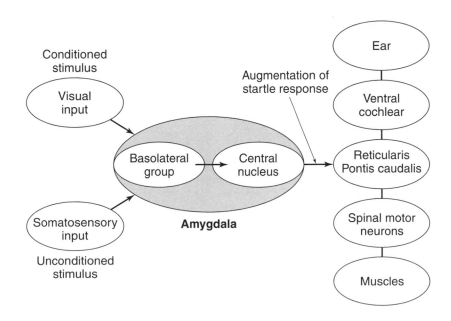

Figure 5.6 Flow diagram of the neurocircuitry of the startle response.

Burlington Rail Road near Cavendish, Vermont. In September 1848, an accidental explosion of a charge he had set blew a 3.5 ft, 13 lb (1 m, 6 kg) tamping iron point first through his left cheekbone and eye and then completely out of the top of his head, virtually destroying his left frontal cortex (figure 5.7). He survived, and in the middle of 1849 he went back to work, but his personality had changed dramatically. Before the accident he had been a capable and efficient foreman with a well-balanced mind. Afterwards, he was judged as "fitful, impatient and obstinate, yet capricious and vacillating, unable to settle on any of the plans he devised for future action." His friends said he was "no longer Gage." His physician, Dr. John Harlow, reported Gage's case and gave the skull and tamping iron to Harvard Medical School, where they are now displayed at the Countway Library of Medicine (Macmillan 2000b). Modern reconstruction of the brain damage based on measurements

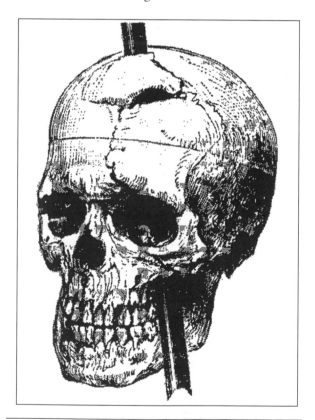

Figure 5.7 Image of a wooden reconstruction from Gage's exhumed skull that appeared in an 1868 report on his case by the attending physician, Dr. Harlow (Harlow 1868). The heavy line approximates the path and thickness of the tamping rod.

Provided by Malcolm Macmillan, School of Psychology, Deakin University, Victoria, Australia.

of Gage's skull and on neuroimaging data indicate that brain damage occurred in both the left and right prefrontal regions involved with **cognition** and emotion—consistent with reports of Gage's altered personality and temperament (Damasio et al. 1994).

Affective Style

Asymmetry in activation of the hemispheres of the frontal cortex in people without clinical disorders has been measured by electroencephalography (EEG) during exposure to pictures that elicit positive or negative affect. Not only is left hemisphere activity higher during viewing of positive images and right hemisphere activity higher during viewing of negative images; but also some people seem to have what is called an affective style, or disposition, to respond to emotional events in a more positive or negative way. Those who have a characteristically dominant activation of the left frontal cortex tend to view emotional events more positively, whereas those having dominant right frontal activation experience events more negatively. Some recent studies even suggest that people's affective styles also influence how quickly they recover from negative emotions or how long they can savor positive emotions (Davidson 2000).

When negative emotions have been evoked in anxiety disorder patients by phobic images (e.g., snakes or spiders), PET and fMRI images have indicated increased blood flow and metabolism in the right inferior prefrontal cortex. Not much evidence has yet been reported on prefrontal changes during the experience of positive affect.

Factors Influencing the Effects of Exercise on Affect

Understanding variables that can moderate the influence of exercise on affect begins with understanding factors that influence affect. Affect varies in valance/hedonic tone and in intensity, and these two dimensions are influenced by a variety of endogenous and exogenous factors. For example, emotional memory systems contain reciprocal connections such that emotions can activate memories/thoughts about the emotions, and thoughts can activate stored emotional responses (Lang 2000). The key determinants of affect also differ for mood and emotion. Watson and Clark (1994) organize potentially important factors that can influence mood into four broad types: exogenous factors, endogenous rhythms, traits and temperament, and characteristic variability. Exogenous factors can be transient conditions in the environment, such as a series of rainy days or new music in an aerobics class. Endogenous rhythms include innate biological processes that are associated with a natural cyclicity in mood, such as the menstrual cycle. Traits and temperament refer to the general tendency individuals have for experiencing positive or negative mood states of specific levels of intensity, and characteristic variability describes the stable individual differences in the magnitude of mood fluctuations.

Example of the Interaction of Factors Influencing Mood

It rained every day for three weeks when Jill first moved to the city. Although she enjoyed an occasional rainy day, she was unable to run outside. Jill used exercise to manage menstrual pain during her cycle; and without her workout routine, this typically enthusiastic and cheerful young woman was in a depressed mood for almost a month.

Moods can be altered by intense emotion repeated at a high frequency over time, such as when someone is surprised by a phone call from an old college friend and has significant improvements in a negative mood by the end of a long conversation about college football games, parties they attended, and antics of their fraternity brothers. Moods are also altered by physiological changes, such as drug effects, lack of sleep, and exercise (Ekman 1994). For example, physical activity was found to influence **diurnal** variation in feeling states in a field study of women: positive engagement, revitalization, and tranquility were higher following exercise than predicted based on diurnal patterns (Gauvin, Rejeski, and Reboussin 2000). The effects of exercise on mood can be influenced by personal, situational, and task variables, such as exercise mode or intensity.

Affect, emotion, and mood are sensitive to a variety of personal factors, such as health (e.g., negative effects from illness or allergies), hormones, and perceptions. Expectations are personal variables that can influence the effects of exercise training on changes in self-esteem (chapter 8), but it does not

appear that positive changes in mood after acute exercise depend on expectations of benefits (Berger et al. 1998; Tieman et al. 2001). There is some evidence that self-efficacy for exercise moderates the effect of exercise on mood, such that higher self-efficacy is associated with positive mood during and after exercise (Bozoian, Rejeski, and McAuley 1994).

Experience with exercise is another personal variable that has been hypothesized as a moderating factor in the effects of exercise on affect, as well as in the importance of mood regulation as a motivator for exercise. A novice exerciser who experiences muscle soreness after the first day of weight training would have a stronger and more negative affective response than an experienced body builder would. The body builder is accustomed to some soreness with exercise, and might even have a positive emotional response if he or she interprets the soreness as a prelude to strength gains from overload based on past training experiences. We should also consider experience with exercise in understanding the effects of exercise on mood. Experienced exercisers rated mood-related reasons for exercising as more important than did inexperienced exercisers in a cross-sectional study of 168 members of fitness centers (Hsiao and Thayer 1998). Advanced members scored higher than the beginners on exercising to improve mood and higher than the intermediate members and the beginners on exercising for socialization.

Situational factors that influence affect include the physical environment (e.g., weather) and the social environment. Laboratory conditions may contribute situational effects that can confound the influence of exercise on mood through the participant's interpretation of the setting. Social environment can interact with a variety of personal and task variables to influence affective responses and mood. For example, a participant in a beginners' aerobics class had felt upbeat and positive with the progress she had been making and the contact with her classmates. She became discouraged and experienced a negative mood after a change in her work schedule caused her to switch to the advanced class, which had a harder routine and more skilled and fit participants.

Characteristics of exercise experience that can influence affective response include intensity, duration, and mode. Recall that affect has valence and arousal dimensions. Exercise itself increases arousal with increasing levels of intensity, and the resulting affect (valence/hedonic dimension) hinges on the participant's interpretation of that arousal. Duration of the exercise bout may also influence mood, but this has not been systematically investigated (Yeung 1996). Duration effects should be evaluated for different modes, intensities, and populations. Exercise mode is another task variable that can affect mood. Chapters 6 and 7 present some of the evidence for differences in anxiety and depression as a function of type of exercise (i.e., aerobic versus strength training).

Interpretation of Arousal From Exercise Influences Affective Response

Chad and his grandfather Frank, who was recovering from a mild heart attack, both experienced shortness of breath walking up a steep hill together. Frank's emotional reaction was fear, and he was in a depressed mood for the rest of the day. To Chad, the breathlessness was a normal physical response, and it generated minimal emotional response or effect on his mood.

Research on Exercise and Affect

Research on affect and exercise has typically involved the measurement of affect with self-report instruments, although human emotion has been estimated using psychophysiological and observational techniques. This section presents a review of self-report instruments that have been used to measure the effects of exercise on affective states and provides examples of studies on the effects of acute exercise and exercise training on affect and mood.

Self-Report Instruments

The most popular instruments used in exercise and affect research have been adjective checklists, particularly the Profile of Mood States (POMS; McNair, Lorr, and Droppleman 1981). Other instruments developed to measure affect include the Positive Affect and Negative Affect Scales (PANAS; Watson, Clark, and Tellegen 1988) and the Affect Grid (Russell, Weiss, and Mendelsohn 1989). Still other scales have been designed specifically to measure affective responses to exercise. These include

the Feeling Scale (Hardy and Rejeski 1989), the Exercise-Induced Feeling Inventory (Gauvin and Rejeski 1993), and the Subjective Exercise Experiences Scale (McAuley and Courneya 1994). The development of these three scales was based on concerns that existing, validated mood scales either were not sensitive or were not specific enough to detect true changes in mood during or after physical activity (Gauvin and Spence 1998), or that affective response to physical activity is somehow different from that experienced in other settings. Though the first concern is plausible, it would relate as much to the range of the response scale as to the structure of the scale content. The second concern is harder to understand.

Why would there be a special set of moods or emotions unique to the experience of exercise? Were that found to be true, the results would represent a provocative exception to 100 years of research that supports the invariance of the expression of moods and emotions across situations and even cultures. The logical extension of the exercise-specific argument would be that specific scales are needed for each human behavior. Joy or happiness after a tasty meal would be a different joy than that after sex, or after a big pay raise, and so on. Though the strength of the valence and emotional arousal of joy might vary after each of those experiences, the structure of joy as a distinct affective experience would be the same. More about this issue is discussed in chapter 6, "Anxiety."

One approach has been to select items from existing general mood or affect scales that seem more sensitive than others to change in response to exercise and to reconfigure those items into a new, specific scale for exercise. Up to now, evidence of the usefulness of this approach (evidence that it yields valid scales measuring affective responses unique to exercise) has not been compelling when judged by the classical standards of construct validation discussed in chapter 2. Nonetheless, exercise-specific scales are discussed in this chapter because it seems likely that this topic will continue to command the attention of exercise psychology researchers for some time (e.g., Ekkekakis and Petruzzello 2000).

The *unipolar POMS* has 65 items that are rated on a 5-point scale ranging from 0, "Not at all," to 4, "Extremely." It includes six discrete affective states: tension-anxiety, depression-dejection, anger-hostility, vigor, fatigue, and confusion-bewilderment. The respondent is asked to focus on current feelings (i.e., "right now"), but the POMS can also be used to rate daily, weekly, or habitual feelings (i.e., "during the past week, including today"). A shortened 30-item version is also available from the publisher, Educational and Industrial Testing Service in San Diego. The POMS has been used frequently to determine antianxiety and antidepressant effects of acute exercise and in overtraining and staleness studies of endurance athletes. In 1998, LeUnes and Burger published a bibliography of POMS research that included 194 studies using the POMS in exercise or sport since its introduction in 1975. Nonetheless, some investigators have questioned its suitability for use with people without clinical disorders (Gauvin and Spence 1998). The POMS was developed for psychiatric populations for the purpose of detecting ongoing effects of therapy in outpatients. It is sensitive to these changes, as well as to changes induced by laboratory manipulations. Also, normative data are available according to gender, age, and psychiatric status, including normal youth and young adults. At issue is whether its emphasis on negative affect allows it to be sensitive to changes in positive mood among people who experience few negative moods.

The *bipolar POMS* was developed to emphasize positive affect and to be more applicable to people without clinical disorders as well as patients experiencing psychiatric disorders. The bipolar POMS has 72 items that are rated on a 4-point scale from 0, "much unlike this," to 3, "much like this." It includes six bipolar scales: composed-anxious, agreeable-hostile, elated-depressed, confident-unsure, energetic-tired, and clearheaded-confused.

The *PANAS* measures positive and negative affect as two relatively independent dimensions using two 10-item mood scales (Watson, Clark, and Tellegen 1988). The scales have high internal consistency and good stability over a two-month period. The two-factor structure of the PANAS was confirmed in a sample of 645 participants in a sport camp, 10 to 17 years old, immediately after an exercise session; but there were questionable psychometrics with three items from the negative affect scale (irritable, distress, and upset) (Crocker 1997).

The *Affect Grid* is a one-item instrument that is based on valance/hedonic tone and arousal dimensions of affect, defined as pleasure-displeasure and arousal-sleepiness (Russell, Weiss, and Mendelsohn 1989). A circumplex model is applied by placing feeling-related concepts in a circular order in a space formed by the two bipolar dimensions (see figure 5.1, p. 92). The Affect Grid has been used effectively by respondents to describe current mood, the meaning of emotion-related words, and feelings conveyed by facial expressions. It has also been found to be valid across cultures (Russell, Lewicka, and Niit 1989).

The *Feeling Scale* is another one-item instrument that measures the valance/hedonic tone of affect (Hardy and Rejeski 1989). Participants rate their current overall feelings on an 11-point bipolar scale with verbal anchors of "Very good" to "Very bad."

The *Exercise-Induced Feelings Inventory* has 12 adjectives that are rated on a 5-point Likert-type scale ranging from "Do not feel" to "Feel very strongly" (Gauvin and Rejeski 1993). It was designed to measure four feeling states (enthusiasm, energy, fatigue, and calmness) assumed to be elicited by positive engagement, revitalization, physical exhaustion, and tranquility, which are stimulus properties of acute bouts of exercise.

The *Subjective Exercise Experiences Scale* was designed to measure global psychological responses that are sensitive to the stimulus properties of exercise (McAuley and Courneya 1994). Two of the three scale factors correspond to positive and negative poles associated with psychological health, which are Positive Well-Being and Psychological Distress. The third factor, Fatigue, represents subjective feelings of fatigue. The scale includes 12 items that are rated on a Likert-type scale ranging from "Not at all" to "Very much so" in terms of the respondent's current feelings.

Measurement Considerations

Most questionnaires that have been used to assess emotions are arguably measuring mood because of the time it takes to complete them (Smith and Crabbe 2000). For example, a 65-item questionnaire such as the POMS has several scales to measure specific emotions and has the items for each scale scattered throughout the test. The feeling state/emotion of the respondent when he or she answers the first scale item could change before the other items are answered, which hampers the validity of the scale. Single-item measures (e.g., bipolar line scales) might be better for addressing this limitation of assessing emotional state; and these types of instruments are probably less likely to change the variable being measured through the measurement act itself than are longer ones. However, a single-item scale such as the Feeling Scale (Hardy and Rejeski 1989) cannot determine what emotion is being rated, or whether different people are experiencing the same emotion, without anchoring the rating to a specific emotional stimulus (Lang 1995).

Measures of affect and exercise usually assess mood, not transient emotional responses.

Acute Exercise

There is a general consensus in the literature that exercise improves affect, but as already discussed, it is prudent to be cautious about overgeneralizing benefits in mood and emotional states without considering some of the moderating variables, such as health status and task characteristics. Yeung (1996) reviewed studies published from 1976 to 1995 that reported the acute effects of a single bout of exercise on mood; the review included 81 studies, only 23 of which were truly experimental. There was support for alleviation of negative mood states and enhancement of positive moods with acute exercise. Eighty-five percent of the studies indicated at least some degree of improved mood after exercise. There were no differences in benefits as a function of age or gender, and most studies that considered fitness did not show differences in mood changes after acute exercise based on fitness or level of physical activity.

Researchers have found differences in mood changes as a function of type of acute exercise. Rudolph and Kim (1996) measured mood responses to aerobic dance, soccer, tennis, and bowling in a sample of 108 physical education students at a Korean university. The Subjective Exercise Experiences Scale was administered before and after the activity. Positive mood was enhanced in students participating in aerobic dance and soccer. There were no changes in negative mood or in moods of tennis players or bowlers. However, participants self-selected into the various exercise modes, and a randomized trial would provide more clarification for the role of exercise task in affective response. Raglin, Turner, and Eksten (1993) randomly assigned collegiate varsity athletes to

cycling or weight-training conditions. State anxiety and blood pressure were measured before 30 min of exercise, immediately postexercise, and at 20 and 60 min postexercise. There were reductions in state anxiety and systolic blood pressure after the cycling but not the weight-training condition. Increases in positive mood have been found in youth sport participants after a game, but the improved mood seemed to be largely determined by perception of achievement and matching of skills against a realistic challenge (Wankel and Sefton 1989). One study of college-age participants showed that mood changes after running exercise were not influenced by competition (O'Connor, Carda, and Graf 1991).

A recent review of studies that used the POMS concluded that the evidence supports associations between acute physical activity and improved mood among nonclinical populations and between chronic exercise and improved mood among clinical populations (Berger and Motl 2000). The POMS has also been employed to identify social or cognitive explanations for mood alteration after exercise. However, currently there is no conclusive evidence identifying a single explanation or clustering of explanations that consistently mediates or moderates the association between exercise and mood change.

Training Studies

Bryne and Bryne (1993) reviewed 30 studies published since 1975 on the effects of exercise training on mood adjustment, such as depression, anxiety, and other states of disturbed mood. Ten of the studies evaluated mood changes in nonclinical populations and showed significant improvements in mood that were not related to changes in fitness. Overall, 90% of the studies reviewed supported the effects of exercise on improving mood.

More recent training studies have been generally supportive of positive effects of exercise on mood for various populations. For example, Partonen et al. (1998) tested the effects of exercise only, exercise plus bright light exposure (2500-4000 lux), and supervised relaxation training conditions on changes in mood over an eight-week period in participants with or without seasonal affective disorder. Participants were randomized to the different conditions and evaluated at four and eight weeks of training and after four months of follow-up. Both exercise groups decreased typical and atypical depression; but improvements in atypical depression, vitality, and role limitations caused by emotional problems were greater in the exercise group with the bright light than in the exercise group with typical illumination.

Mood was improved in initially sedentary older women after a 12-week strength-training program (Tsutsumi et al. 1998). Both high-intensity and moderate-intensity strength-training groups significantly improved positive mood and demonstrated some decrease in tension and state anxiety, although support for moderate intensity was greater. Men infected with HIV-1 (human immunodeficiency virus-1) demonstrated enhanced perceived physical ability, self-efficacy, global positive mood, and overall life satisfaction after 12 weeks of aerobic training and anaerobic weight training (Lox, McAuley, and Tucker 1995). Significant improvements in motor disability, mood, and subjective well-being were also demonstrated in 16 early- to medium-state Parkinson's disease patients after 14 weeks of exercise training (Reuter et al. 1999).

Compared to a contract control class, vigorous exercise included in a 12-week smoking cessation program improved withdrawal symptoms, cigarette craving, and negative affect among initially sedentary women attempting to quit smoking (Bock et al. 1999). However, two studies have shown no further benefits for mood changes from the addition of walking (Nieman et al. 2000), aerobic training, strength training, or combined training (Wadden et al. 1997) among obese women enrolled in obesity-treatment programs.

Positive changes in mood after exercise training have been found in many but not all sample populations.

Mood was monitored before and after each exercise class over a seven-week exercise program in four self-selected exercise groups (Steinberg et al. 1998). Positive mood increased and negative mood decreased during each class, but favorable mood from exercise diminished by the following week. There seemed to be a persistent, acute effect that has also been demonstrated with some of the positive physiological effects of exercise.

Psychophysiological and Behavioral Assessment of Affect, Mood, and Emotion

The evidence from animal research on neurological contributions to appetitive and avoidance behaviors suggests that it is possible to detect emotion in humans with psychophysiological techniques (see figure 5.8). Autonomic activation can be measured with **galvanic skin response** (skin conductance or its inverse, resistance), changes in skin temperature, and cardiovascular responsiveness (chapter 4). Determining the galvanic skin response involves measuring the autonomic-induced

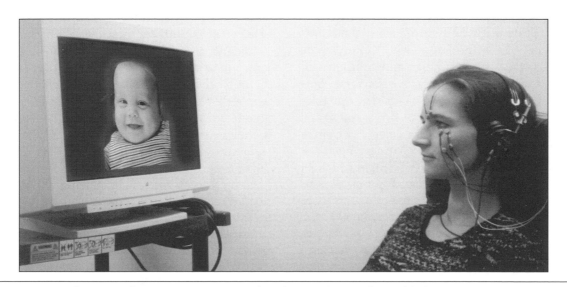

Figure 5.8 Use of emotionally evocative images to elicit the acoustic startle eye-blink response.
Provided by Dr. Carson Smith, Center for the Study of Emotion and Attention, The University of Florida.

changes in the electrical resistance of the tissue path between two electrodes applied to the skin. Emotional arousal has been associated with these changes; skin conductance has been shown to increase with negative emotions and decrease with positive emotions (e.g., Hughes, Uhlmann, and Pennebaker 1994). Changes in skin temperature indicate reflex vasoconstriction and vasodilation from sympathetic activation of the vasculature associated with the stress response. Changes in heart rate and blood pressure in the absence of motor activation are also associated with the stress response and concomitant affect. Limitations of these methods include the lack of specificity to particular emotions. For example, heart rate and blood pressure increase both during the stress of reading a letter from the Internal Revenue Service announcing an audit of your tax returns and while reading a letter from a television producer inviting you to be a contestant on a game show. The physiological responses per se do not indicate the different emotional responses to these situations. There are also concerns regarding the consistent application of recommended psychophysiological measurement protocols to assess autonomic activation (Smith and Crabbe 2000).

The contraction of muscles involves muscle fiber-generated electrical potentials that can be detected with needle electrodes placed in a muscle or patch electrodes placed on the skin superior to the muscle of interest. Electromyographic measures of distinctive facial muscle activation have been associated with various emotional responses (Cacioppo et al. 1986). For example, zygomatic (smile) muscle activity and corrugator (frown) muscle activity differentiate pleasant and unpleasant emotions (Greenwald, Cook, and Lang 1989). Considerable work has been done by Ekman and colleagues to document facial expressions as a behavioral component of emotions, and it appears that the associations between specific emotions and facial expressions are similar across cultures (Ekman 1989). Ekman and Friesen (1976) developed the Facial Action Coding System (FACS), in which 44 distinct, visually observable, facial muscle actions are scored for duration and frequency of activity in response to emotional stimuli. The original FACS and the updated FACS computer image analysis software have measured facial expressions that have been shown to reliably reflect subjectively felt emotion (Bartlett et al. 1999; Ekman, Davidson, and Friesen 1990).

Methods Used in Exercise Studies

Exercise studies have mainly examined tonic (i.e., unperturbed) or reactive (i.e., in response to a stimulus) neuromuscular activity, including the ASER, skeletal and facial muscle activity, and brain electrocortical activity. These methods are described in the following sections along with examples of related research.

Electromyography

The effects of physical exertion, which increases metabolic arousal, on the ASER has not been studied much, but there is reason to think that exertion might directly affect brain biochemistry in a way that could alter the startle response. Though different neurotransmitters have a different effect on the startle response depending on brain region (Davis 1997; Davis et al. 1993), norepinephrine and serotonin generally inhibit startle. Agonists of dopamine D_2 receptors also attenuate the startle response, whereas augmentation of the startle by a D_1 agonist is partly dependent on coactivation of D_2 receptors (Meloni and Davis 1999).

Regional effects have not been determined, but studies of rats have shown that brain concentrations of norepinephrine, serotonin, and dopamine (DA) are elevated during running on a treadmill or activity wheel. Treadmill running also increases the turnover of DA (i.e., replacement of used DA with newly synthesized DA) and increases the number of D_2 receptors in the striatum. Chronic activity-wheel running has been reported to increase dopamine levels and decrease D_2 binding in the whole brain (see Tieman et al. 2001 for a review). Thus, in addition to the increase in metabolic arousal during physical exertion, exercise could alter dynamic features of brain biochemistry in ways that plausibly could affect either the reflexive (obligatory) or emotional (modulatory) components of ASER neurocircuitry. Other neurotransmitters (e.g., GABA/benzodiazepines, corticotropin-releasing factor, and cholecystokinin) can alter the startle response depending on their presence in different brain regions (Davis 1997), so the nature of brain responses by those neurotransmitters after exercise needs to be studied.

To date, only three studies have addressed the effects of acute exercise on the ASER. Changes in ASER amplitude and latency were examined in 26 healthy young men after 20 min of cycling at light and hard intensities (40% and 75% $\dot{V}O_2$peak) and after 20 min of quiet rest (Tieman et al. 2001). Neither intensity of exercise affected ASER amplitude or latency in either sedentary or active participants. These findings indicate that we should not expect possible effects of acute exercise on potentiated startle (or startle responses elicited by positive or negative foreground stimuli) to be confounded by an altered baseline ASER when measured in young healthy men having average physical fitness, regardless of their physical activity habits.

Despite that absence of an effect of exercise in healthy young men, it is possible that basal startle responses might be affected among people having disorders that involve altered neurological responses (e.g., anxiety disorders, attention-deficit hyperactivity disorder [ADHD]). For example, research suggests that brain dopamine systems are disturbed in children who have ADHD. Regional cerebral blood flow studies indicate that children with ADHD have hypoperfusion to the caudate in the striatum, which is largely dopaminergic; and methylphenidate (i.e., Ritalin), the drug of choice for treating ADHD, is a dopamine agonist (Barkley 1998).

The effects of maximal and submaximal treadmill walking (65-75% $\dot{V}O_2$peak) on the ASER were studied in 18 boys and girls diagnosed with ADHD and 25 control children equated on several key variables that might affect the startle response (Tantillo et al. 2002). The main findings were decreased latency of ASER and increased spontaneous eyeblinks in boys with ADHD after maximal exercise, and decreased latency of ASER after the submaximal exercise condition in the girls with ADHD. Eyeblinks by children without a diagnosis of ADHD were not affected by exercise. The third study (Smith et al. 2002) used the ASER to examine whether exercise alters emotional response.

Measurement of Emotion

Very few studies have examined the effect of sustained exercise (i.e., more than a minute) on emotion. Fillingim, Roth, and Cook (1992) found that self-reports of, and corrugator EMG responses to, sadness and anger imagery were not different 8 min after 15 min of very low-intensity cycle ergometry (50 W) compared to 15 min of rest. However, these researchers utilized emotional recall (i.e., internally generated imagery), making it difficult to confirm whether an emotion was actually elicited (see emotion research desiderata in Davidson et al. 1990). Also, they did not consider precondition responses

in their analyses, nor did they quantify the exercise stimulus relative to an individual's maximal capacity.

In what appears to be the first exercise study to examine emotional responses after exercise according to a contemporary theory of emotion (Lang 1995), the influence of low- and moderate-intensity exercise on self-rated anxiety, ASER amplitude and corrugator muscle activity, and state anxiety was examined in 24 healthy college females who either cycled at low or moderate intensities or rested quietly for 25 min (Smith et al. 2002). Acoustic startle eye-blink and corrugator responses, as well as basal, tonic corrugator EMG activity, were measured immediately prior to and 20 min after each condition while participants viewed pleasant, neutral, and unpleasant slides. State anxiety was significantly reduced 20 min after each condition, as was startle amplitude to each type of slide. Baseline corrugator EMG activity did not change after seated rest, but decreased after cycling in direct proportion to exercise intensity. The decreases in startle amplitude were correlated with decreases in state anxiety ($r = .44$). Corrugator EMG responses during the slides were not different between or after the conditions. The findings suggest that anxiolytic conditions of low- and moderate-intensity cycling and seated rest are related to decreased startle amplitude but do not lead to changes in appetitive or defensive responses to affective stimuli.

The possible interaction of innate or learned startle reflexes with other spinal reflexes (e.g., myotendinous responses) that are influenced by arousal and emotional stimuli (e.g., Bonnet et al. 1995) might also be interesting. In a series of studies by deVries (deVries et al. 1981; deVries et al. 1982) and others (Bulbulian and Darabos 1986), the spinal H-reflex was reduced after exercise. The H-reflex is a monosynaptic reflex at the level of the S1-S2 sacral spinal roots elicited by electrical stimulation of the mixed tibial nerve at the popliteal space behind the knee and measured by EMG calf twitch (see figures 5.9 and 5.10). Though the H-reflex is mainly viewed as an index of the excitability of the alpha motor neuron, ascending and descending supraspinal tracts exist that would permit it to be modulated by the central nervous system. Whether the H-reflex is related to mood or emotion after exercise has not been determined.

Electroencephalography

Several exercise studies have examined EEG-measured brain asymmetry in activation based on reported emotions (e.g., Petruzzello and Tate 1997),

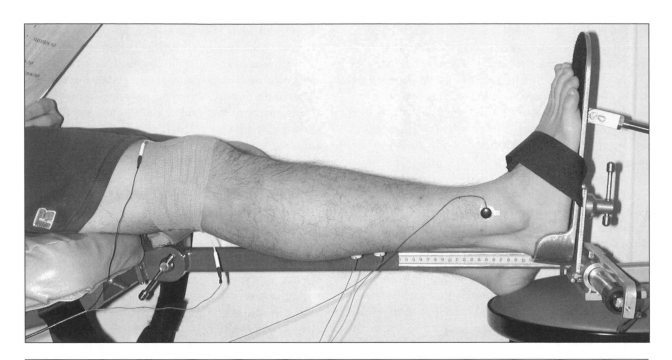

Figure 5.9   Electrode placement for the measurement of the H-reflex in the soleus muscle using electromyography.

Provided by the Exercise Psychology Laboratory, Department of Exercise Science, The University of Georgia.

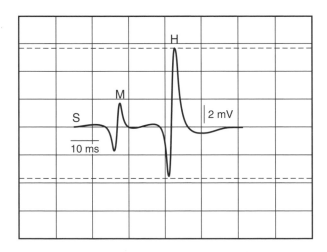

Figure 5.10   An oscillographic record of the H-reflex measured by electromyography.

Provided by the Exercise Psychology Laboratory, The University of Georgia.

but not on stimulus-elicited emotional responses during or after exercise. Subjective appraisal of affective valance has been associated with the frontal region, and level of arousal has been detected in EEG changes in the parietotemporal area (Smith and Crabbe 2000).

Although the effect of physical activity on mood has been examined extensively, little is known about the effect of altered mood on emotional responsiveness (Ekman 1994) or about whether exercise might modulate such an effect (Smith and Crabbe 2000). Frontal cortical asymmetry, as indexed by EEG, has been shown to be a correlate of emotional responsiveness (Davidson 1998b). There also is evidence that frontal EEG asymmetry may be related to phasic shifts in mood. Petruzzello and colleagues (Petruzzello and Landers 1994; Petruzzello and Tate 1997) showed that resting levels of frontal asymmetry were moderately associated with pre- to postexercise changes in moods such as anxiety and energetic arousal. Their 1994 study also showed that changes in anxiety were related to changes in asymmetry from before to after exercise. It is not known to what extent emotional responsiveness may be altered by phasic mood shifts. Mood is improved after exercise, but emotional responsiveness after exercise has received little attention.

A recent study of young men and women having moderate levels of cardiorespiratory fitness looked at the effect of 30 min of cycling exercise at 50% peak aerobic power, compared to 30 min of rest, on change in emotional responses to standardized slides having negative, neutral, and positive valence (Crabbe, Smith, and Dishman 2001). Emotional re-by α asymmetry at rest. However, despite a decrease in state anxiety, the cycling exercise condition did not alter emotional responses or positive and negative affect in response to negative, neutral, and positive slides. Also, though arousal ratings were elevated during exercise, negative or positive affect as measured by the PANAS was not altered by exercise. Hence, the findings did not indicate that moderate-intensity cycling exercise is an emotion-eliciting stimulus or that it affects emotional response by altering mood.

Electroencephalography measures relatively few neurons that are superficial. Surface activation does not ensure that underlying brain regions are correspondingly activated. The brain imaging techniques discussed in chapter 3 have enabled researchers to estimate the rate of cellular metabolism in subcortical areas of the brain (e.g., amygdala) during the experience of different emotions; these techniques hold great promise for exploring the relationship between exercise and affect (Irwin et al. 1996; LaBar et al. 1998). To date, neuroimaging studies of affective or emotional responses to acute exercise, or after exercise training, have not been reported.

Limitations in Research

Acute studies of the effects of exercise on affect share problems with research on emotions and mood in general, such as validity and appropriateness of measurement methods as well as the possibility of unknown but critical moderating and confounding variables. Unfortunately, most research done in the laboratory to study the effects of a single bout of exercise on mood has limited generalizability (poor **ecological validity**). Although many people choose to exercise in closed environments much like those in laboratories (e.g., walking or running on a treadmill or cycling on a stationary machine), many

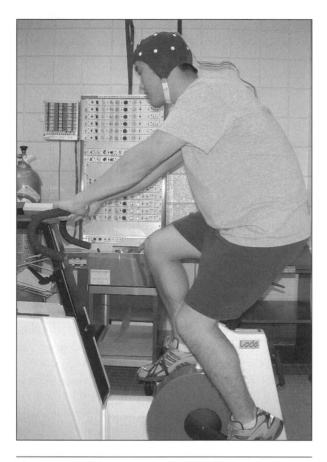

Electroencephalography during exercise.

Provided by the Exercise Psychology Laboratory, Department of Exercise Science, The University of Georgia.

sponses were measured by frontal brain electrocortical asymmetry and self-ratings of valence and arousal using a bipolar rating scale called the Self Assessment Manikin (SAM), shown in figure 5.11.

Consistent with theory (Davidson 2000), frontal brain asymmetry in the α (8-12 Hz) frequency and valence ratings in response to slides were predicted

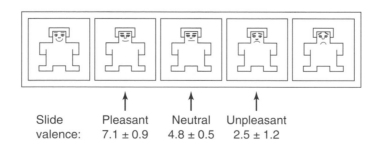

Slide valence:	Pleasant 7.1 ± 0.9	Neutral 4.8 ± 0.5	Unpleasant 2.5 ± 1.2	

Figure 5.11 Self-Assessment Manikin pleasantness ratings.

Adapted, by permission, from P.J. Lang, M.M. Bradley, and B.N. Cuthbert, 1999, *International affective pictures system (IAPSI): Instruction manual and affective ratings*. Technical Report A-4, The Center for Research in Psychophysiology, University of Florida.

studies conducted in natural physical activity settings have shown a positive influence on mood.

It is also hard to blind participants to the purpose of the study when they are asked to complete mood questionnaires before and after an exercise bout. Additionally, there has been a failure to standardize the exercise stimulus, which, considering the potential unpleasantness associated with exercising at high intensities (e.g., well above the lactate or ventilatory thresholds), can confound effects on mood. Many studies have not used nonexercise control conditions. The variability in psychophysiological responses between people and within one person over time makes it difficult to gauge the direction and magnitude of change. For example, the use of baseline values for comparison is confounded by the transient nature of feelings, emotions, and mood. The laboratory situation itself could elevate the affect scores at baseline and exaggerate the decrease after acute exercise. On the other hand, research with people without clinical disorders may show no effect from exercise because of ceiling and floor effects (i.e., the range of scores possible on the test doesn't match the full range of the affective experience of the person), or as a consequence of use of mood instruments designed for clinical populations that may not be sensitive enough to detect changes in people without clinical disorders.

Training studies have been limited by the use of convenience samples, a deficiency in follow-up data, and a lack of replication of findings (Bryne and Bryne 1993). Comparisons between exercise and other treatment conditions are often tentative because the conditions have not been equal in terms of exposure so that effects from amount of attention can be ruled out, and groups have not been randomized. Initial fitness level or physical activity history has often not been considered, and methodologies for measuring fitness and exercise history have been weak. Researchers have analyzed absolute changes before and after acute and chronic exercise, and they have examined the pattern of values over time and

The differences between affective style, or temperament, and feelings, affect, mood, or emotion should be considered in research on exercise and affect.

compared the change with exercise to these typical patterns (e.g., Gauvin, Rejeski, and Reboussin 2000). Despite these scientific weaknesses, the bulk of the evidence supports the idea that physical activity and exercise have a positive influence on mood for most people in many circumstances.

Mechanisms

Berger and colleagues have proposed that to optimize mood enhancement after physical activity, the activity should be enjoyable, aerobic, and noncompetitive and should be performed regularly in a closed environment that is predictable in place and time, at moderate intensities for at least 20 to 30 min (Berger and Motl 2000). However, very few studies of humans have manipulated social, psychological, or biological factors so as to determine mechanisms that might explain the mood-altering effects of physical activity or exercise. Most of the human studies, as well as those conducted on nonhuman animals designed to test plausible mechanisms, have been directed toward understanding effects on the specific moods of anxiety and depression. Those moods and mechanisms are discussed in detail in chapters 6 and 7, but they are introduced here.

Biological

The **endorphin hypothesis** continues to percolate through the lay population. Because plasma endorphins, which are natural opioids, increase with exercise, they are thought of as the "cause" of the enhanced mood and euphoria accompanying exercise. However, there has been little success in finding associations between mood changes and levels of endorphins in well-controlled empirical studies (e.g., Hatfield et al. 1987; see "Other Biologically Based Hypotheses" in chapter 7, pp. 151–152). The **thermogenic hypothesis** proposes that increased body temperature is responsible for positive changes in mood with exercise, but the effects are mixed, and there is little support for this as a valid mechanism (e.g., Youngstedt et al. 1993).

Psychosocial

Although more support exists for psychosocial explanations for mood enhancement from exercise, the effects are likely generated by an interaction among physiological and psychological influences on mood that are altered with exercise.

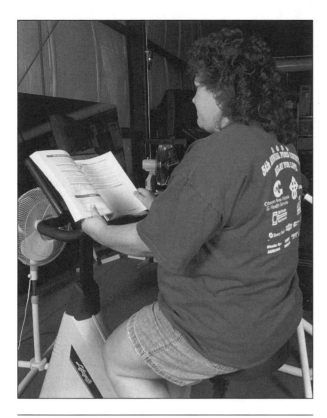

If exercise helps improve mood by distracting from stressors, working while exercising might not provide the same benefits as exercise alone would.

Psychological Benefits From Exercise That May Be Related to Enhanced Mood

▼ Improved emotional stability, self-sufficiency, and conscientiousness from intense, persistent involvement in meaningful activity

▼ Heightened sense of well-being, euphoric high, enhanced sense of self, greater appreciation of the surrounding world

▼ Decreased awareness of feelings of fear, tension, irritability

▼ Distraction from worry and dejection

▼ A countering effect on inertia, fatigue, depression, and confusion

Adapted from Casper 1993.

According to the **mastery hypothesis,** mood is improved after completion of an important and effortful task. Self-efficacy may interact to influence

the effects of exercise on mood such that higher efficacy is associated with more positive effects on mood, as found in the study by Bozoian, Rejeski, and McAuley (1994).

The *distraction hypothesis* proposes that the time out from worrisome thoughts and daily stressors during exercise produces the mood-enhancing effects. The increasing trend of "multitasking," in which individuals negotiate business transactions and organize reports on treadmills and stair climbers, may counter the psychological benefits of exercise if distraction is the primary mechanism for effects. In fact, increases in vigor measured by the POMS were correlated with the tendency to engage in nonassociative thought in 150 experienced runners who completed the POMS before and after a typical run (Goode and Roth 1993). Thoughts about interpersonal relationships as measured by the Thoughts During Exercise Scale were also associated with decreases in tension and anxiety.

Hazards of Exercise?

This chapter has focused on positive affect and mood enhancement with exercise. An exception to the benefits of physical activity is the risk of disturbed mood sometimes seen among highly trained endurance athletes who have become stale as a result of overtraining (i.e., exceeding a physical and psychological optimal volume and intensity over time) (Morgan et al. 1987). Staleness is a syndrome typically characterized by increased tension and depression, chronic fatigue, appetite loss, insomnia, decreased libido, decreased functional capacity or performance, and endocrine abnormalities and suppression of the immune system (Dishman 1992).

Excessive exercise that is problematic has also been observed in non-athletes (Morgan 1979b). "Compulsive exercise," "compulsive athleticism," and "exercise dependence" are some of the terms that have been used in connection with an exercise routine that takes on greater priority than work, family, friends, and social functions. The person continues exercise despite serious injury, and experiences symptoms of withdrawal, such as mood disturbances, anxiety, guilt, and depression, when prevented from exercising (Mondin et al. 1996; Cockerill, and Riddington 1996).

Some studies have indicated that the rate of staleness among non-elite runners and age-group swimmers is about 33% (Raglin and Moger 1999; Raglin and Wilson 2000). However, no epidemiological studies have been done to identify the prevalence or risk factors associated with athletic staleness or abusive exercise in the population. At this time, it appears that each represents a clinical medicine problem among select groups of athletes and fitness fanatics, but neither seems to be a problem for public health. As will be seen in the last part of the book, very few adults in developed nations are physically active at a level whereby they might be at risk for overtraining or exercise abuse (Dishman 1985). This topic is addressed in more detail in "Exercise Abuse" in chapter 8 as it pertains to problems of emotional adjustment and an imbalanced self-concept.

Summary

Affect is typically measured with self-report via paper-and-pencil instruments, but other ways to measure feeling states, affect, mood, and emotions include techniques that measure physiological indicators (such as skin conductance, EMG, EEG, and neuroimaging) and behavioral indicators, like facial expressions. Up to now, the research evidence, though not all scientifically strong, supports the folk wisdom from antiquity that exercise enhances mood. Social, cognitive, and biological explanations for that observation have not yet been identified, but attributing the positive effects of exercise on mood merely to people's self-fulfilling expectations of benefits appears inadequate. Very few studies of physical activity and exercise have examined mood or emotion within a contemporary theory of affect. Also, studies have yet to show that acute exercise of the type commonly practiced for leisure or fitness alters emotional responses—but this is a new area of research. Especially interesting is the question of whether reduction in neuromuscular tension after exercise, as reported in a few studies, may play a role in direct effects of exercise on mood or emotional response.

The reasons many people decide to adopt exercise include weight loss and health benefits. Adoption involves considerable time and effort in the short run, and noticeable results do not occur for a long time. Short-term rewards of mood regulation may prove to be more significant in helping people sustain regular exercise. Exercise motivational inventories have included mood as a factor, and mood continues to be conceptually meaningful as a reason people exercise. Positive mood effects from exercise may be subtle, however, and may not readily surface among novices. Mood enhancement from exercise is hypothesized to be more of a motivator for those who have exercised in the past (Hsiao and Thayer 1998). The influence of intrapersonal factors on exercise adoption and maintenance is covered in chapters 10 and 12.

Suggested Readings

Casper, R.C. 1993. Exercise and mood. *World Review of Nutrition and Dietetics* 71: 115–43.

Davidson, J.R., and W. Irwin. 1999. The functional neuroanatomy of emotion and affective style. *Trends in Cognitive Sciences* 3 (1): 11–21.

Ekman, P. 1994. Moods, emotions, and traits. In *Nature of emotion: Fundamental questions*, ed. P. Ekman and J.R. Davidson. New York: Oxford University Press.

LeDoux, J.E. 1994. Emotion, memory, and the brain. *Scientific American* 270 (6): 50–57.

Macmillan, M.B. 2000a. *An odd kind of fame: Stories of Phineus Gage*. Campbridge, MA: MIT Press.

Plutchik, R., 2001. The naure of emotions. *American Scientist*, 89 (4): 344–350.

Smith, J.C., and J.B. Crabbe. 2000. Emotion and exercise. *International Journal of Sport Psychology* 31 (2): 156–174.

Watson, D. 2000. *Mood and temperament*. New York: The Guilford Press.

Yeung, R.R. 1996. The acute effects of exercise on mood state. *Journal of Psychosomatic Research* 40 (Feb): 123–141.

Web Sites

www.hbs.deakin.edu.au/gagepage/pgage.htm

www.personalityresearch.org/basicemotions.html

www.epub.org.br/cm/nos/mente/teorias_i.htm

Anxiety

Many people who exercise for recreation have noticed a calming effect from a hard workout, reporting that they use exercise to "forget worries" or as an outlet for "nervous energy." Others say they feel more relaxed after moderate physical activity like a brisk walk. The research literature supports the ability of exercise to reduce anxiety in nonclinical populations. Recent study suggests that clinical populations also benefit, although there was a time when exercise was believed to *induce* anxiety in patients who have panic disorder. This chapter provides statistics on the social and financial impact of anxiety and gives definitions of anxiety and anxiety disorders. It presents research connections between anxiety and exercise, including a discussion of mechanisms for beneficial effects.

Prevalence and Social Impact

About 17% of adults aged 18 to 54 in the United States—about 16 to 19 million people—experience anxiety disorders each year (Kessler et al. 1994). In fact, anxiety disorders are more prevalent than all other types of mental disorders except substance abuse. Compared to men, women are more likely to have experienced an anxiety disorder in their lifetimes (31% vs. 19%; Kessler et al. 1994). The prevalence of different anxiety disorders over 12 months and over a lifetime are compared for males and females in figure 6.1, a and b.

Anxiety disorders are frequently complicated by depression, eating disorders, or substance abuse, and

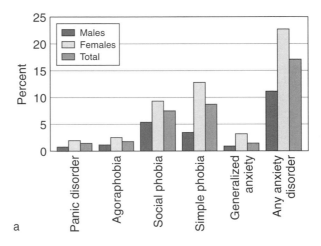

a

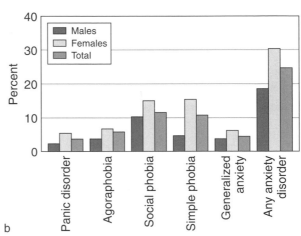

b

Figure 6.1 Twelve-month *(a)* and lifetime *(b)* prevalence of anxiety disorders.

Data from Kessler et al. 1994.

patients with panic disorder are also at greater risk for cardiovascular morbidity (Weissman et al. 1990). Quality of life is impaired in various ways because of anxiety, such as lost productivity at work (Greenberg et al. 1999). In addition to the personal suffering, results from the National Comorbidity Survey indicate that anxiety disorders in the United States cost about $45 billion each year, mainly for health care, drugs, and in lost productivity (DuPont et al. 1996; Greenberg et al. 1999).

Anxiety disorders are more prevalent than any other type of mental disorder except substance abuse.

Definitions

Anxiety is a state of worry, apprehension, or tension that often occurs in the absence of real or obvious danger. Though it is a normal response to real or imagined danger, anxiety is distinguished from fear, which usually is regarded as a brief emotional reaction to a threatening stimulus. Except in the case of most phobias, anxiety is longer lasting and more abstract than is fear. Anxiety is considered a disorder when its symptoms or behaviors are so frequent or severe that they cause pain or impair normal physical or social functioning.

Anxiety is not a new problem. For example, six subtypes of anxiety are found in the writings of the ancient Greeks: death, mutilation, separation, guilt, shame, and diffuse, or nonspecific, anxiety, denoted by words such as "agitated," "danger," "desperate," "frightened," "nervous," "panic," "threatened," "timid," and "troubled" (Newbold 1990). A century ago, Freud noted that chronic, free-floating anxiety occurred frequently in the general population.

Types of Common Anxiety Disorders

There are several different types of anxiety disorders: phobias, panic disorder, obsessive-compulsive disorder, posttraumatic stress disorder, and generalized anxiety disorder. Each type has specific psychological and behavioral characteristics.

▼ The most common type of **anxiety disorder** comprises social and specific **phobias.** *Social phobia,* or social anxiety disorder, is the fear (anxiety) of being judged, criticized, and evaluated by others. People with social phobia have an overwhelming fear of scrutiny and embarrassment in social situations that causes them to avoid many potentially enjoyable and rewarding experiences. Social phobia occurs twice as often in women as in men. *Agoraphobia* translated from Greek means "fear of an open market place," but it refers specifically to fear of being in situations from which escape might be difficult, or avoidance of situations such as being alone outside of the home; traveling in a car, bus, or airplane; or being in a crowded area. People with agoraphobia commonly are afraid to leave their house or a room in the house, and confine themselves in order to reduce their anxiety. *Simple phobia* is the irrational fear and avoidance of specific things (e.g., spiders) or places (e.g., heights). Specific phobias generally do not result from exposure to a single traumatic event (i.e., being bitten by a dog or nearly drowning). These phobias are more likely to run in the family or to be learned vicariously through observation of the experiences of others.

▼ **Panic disorder** is characterized by repeated episodes of intense fear that strike without warning and without an obvious source. Physical symptoms include chest pain, heart palpitations, shortness of breath, dizziness, tingling sensations, chills or blushing and "hot flashes," abdominal distress, and fear of dying or losing control of emotions or behavior. The attack typically has an abrupt onset, building to maximum intensity within 10 to 15 min.

▼ **Obsessive-compulsive disorder** involves repeated, intrusive unwanted thoughts, impulses, or images or compulsive behaviors that seem impossible to stop, and is typified by repetitive acts or rituals to relieve anxiety. Obsessive-compulsive disorder has more of a familial origin than most other anxiety disorders.

▼ **Posttraumatic stress disorder** comprises anxiety and behavioral disturbances that develop within the first month after exposure to an extreme trauma. Such extreme traumatic events commonly include rape or other severe physical assault, near-death experiences in accidents, witnessing a murder, and combat. About 50% of cases of posttraumatic stress disorder improve within six months. For the rest, the disorder typically persists for years and can overwhelm the individual's life.

▼ **Generalized anxiety disorder (GAD)** is defined by excessive or pathologic worry about multiple concerns for at least six months. As already mentioned, Freud noted that chronic, free-floating anxiety occurred frequently in the general population. Generalized anxiety disorder is accompanied by exaggerated vigilance and somatic symptoms of stress and anxiety, such as muscular tension. Among the anxiety disorders, GAD has the highest rate of comorbidity with other disorders (see figure 6.2).

Components of anxiety include cognitions, emotional responses, and physiological changes, such as increased motor tension and autonomic nervous hyperactivity. The cognitive and emotional dimensions distinguish anxiety from **arousal,** which is a nonspecific physiological response characterized by muscle tension, increased heart rate, and heightened alertness. Someone who is highly aroused is not necessarily anxious, but an anxious individual typically demonstrates the physiological characteristics of arousal along with apprehensive expectations, agitation, vigilance for danger signals, and decreases in effective cognitive coping.

Anxiety is commonly described as transient or temporary (state anxiety) and as an expression of personality (trait anxiety). **State anxiety** refers to the immediate psychological and physiological response to a conscious or unconscious perceived threat (i.e., are you anxious now?). State anxiety involves subjective feelings and objective manifestations (e.g., increased heart rate). **Trait anxiety** is a personality characteristic that refers to how prone someone is to appraising events as threatening (i.e., are you an anxious person?). In general, individuals characterized by high trait anxiety perceive a greater number of situations as threatening, more frequently exhibit periods of elevated state anxiety, and have a stronger anxiety reaction to a given situation than people characterized by average or low trait anxiety (Spielberger et al. 1983) (see figure 6.3). Trait anxiety is related to personality, but it is more amenable to change

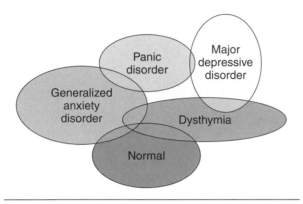

Figure 6.2 Comorbidity of generalized anxiety disorder.

Reprinted with permission from *Medscape Mental Health* (www.medscape.com/medscape/psychiatry/journal/1997/v02.n05/mh3070.woodman/mh3070.woodman.html),©1997, Medscape Inc.

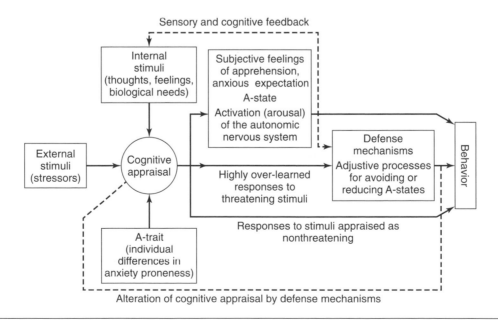

Figure 6.3 A trait-state conception of anxiety.

Reprinted, by permission, from C.D. Spielberger, 1966, Theory and research on anxiety. In *Anxiety and behavior* (New York: Academic Press), 17.

than is a person's core temperament, which is very resistant to change. Although anxiety is a common reaction, a distinction is usually made between normal levels of anxiety and clinical anxiety disorders based on the number and intensity of symptoms, the degree of personal suffering, and the extent to which normal function is impaired (see figure 6.4).

State anxiety is the immediate psychological and physiological response to perceived threat, while trait anxiety is the predisposition to label events as threatening.

Effects of Exercise

The 1996 U.S. Surgeon General's report on physical activity and health (United States Department of Health and Human Services 1996) concluded that regular physical activity reduces feelings of anxiety. However, in the late 1960s and early 1970s, physical activity was thought to be a predicating factor in inducing panic attacks in persons with anxiety neurosis and in some individuals without anxiety neurosis. This negative attitude toward exercise as a potential treatment for anxiety was based on evidence from one study for increased anxiety with infusions of lactate. Pitts and McClure (1967) measured the anxiety response to intravenous infusions

---

Diagnostic and Statistical Manual of Mental Disorders (DSM-IV) criteria for generalized anxiety disorder

A. The person experiences excessive anxiety and worry more days than not for at least six months, about a number of events or activities (such as work or school performance).

B. The person has difficulty controlling the worry.

C. The anxiety and worry are associated with three (or more) of the following six symptoms (with at least some symptoms occurring on more days than not for the past six months). Only one item is required in children.

1. Restlessness or feeling keyed up or on edge

2. Being easily fatigued

3. Difficulty concentrating or mind going blank

4. Irritability

5. Muscle tension

6. Sleep disturbance (difficulty falling asleep or staying asleep or restless, unsatisfying sleep)

D. The anxiety or worry is not confined to the anxiety or worry about having a panic attack (as in panic disorder), being embarrassed in public (as in social phobia), being contaminated (as in obsessive-compulsive disorder), being away from home or close relatives (as in separation-anxiety disorder), gaining weight (as in anorexia nervosa), having multiple physical complaints (as in somatization disorder), or having a serious illness (as in hypochondriasis); and the anxiety and worry do not occur exclusively during posttraumatic stress disorder.

E. The anxiety, worry, or physical symptoms cause clinically significant distress or impairment in social, occupational, or other important areas of functioning.

F. The disturbance is not due to the direct physiological effects of a substance (e.g., abuse of a drug; a medication) or a general medical condition (e.g., hyperthyroidism) and does not occur exclusively during a mood disorder, a psychotic disorder, or a pervasive developmental disorder.

Figure 6.4 Anxiety that many people experience as a normal response to actual and potential stressful situations can be distinguished from clinical anxiety disorders by specific criteria.

Adapted, by permission, from American Psychiatric Association, 2000, *Diagnostic and statistical manual of mental disorders,* 4th ed., text revision 2000 (Washington, DC: American Psychiatric Association).

of lactate, sodium DL-lactate with calcium, and a placebo (glucose) in 10 controls and 14 people with anxiety neurosis at rest. They found increased anxiety in the people with anxiety neurosis after infusion of the sodium DL-lactate that raised blood levels of lactate to about 40 mg/dl. All but one patient experienced an anxiety attack. In some cases, anxiety persisted for two to five days. Pitts and McClure also documented anxiety reactions in some of the control subjects, and concluded that lactate could produce anxiety symptoms. Thus, it appeared that physical activity could cause anxiety symptoms because intense exercise increases muscle and blood lactate; maximal exercise typically increases blood lactate two to three times higher than does sodium DL-lactate infusion.

However, Grosz and Farmer (1972) and Morgan (1979a) presented numerous reasons why infused lactate *would* and increased lactate from exercise *would not* induce anxiety symptoms. For example, infused lactate is quickly converted to bicarbonate and carbon dioxide, which has been shown to be associated with anxiety attacks as a function of the metabolic alkalosis and subsequent hyperventilation (Maddock, Carter, and Gietzen 1991). Exercise-induced elevations in lactate result in metabolic acidosis. Empirical evidence from 15 studies conducted since 1987 also refutes the association between exercise and panic attacks; only five panic attacks were reported during exercise involving 444 exercise bouts performed by 420 panic disorder patients (O'Connor, Smith, and Morgan 2000). Research has also shown that lactate accumulation resulting from exercise is not related to postexercise anxiety in individuals without clinical disorders (e.g., Garvin, Koltyn, and Morgan 1997). Moreover, a small randomized clinical trial recently showed that 10 weeks of aerobic exercise training was effective in reducing symptoms of anxiety among patients with panic disorder and agoraphobia, though not as effective as drug therapy (Broocks et al. 1998).

*E*arly research erroneously attributed panic attacks to participation in vigorous exercise.

The study of physical activity as a treatment for anxiety was impeded in the late 1960s and 1970s by the lactate-anxiety controversy, but the effects of acute and chronic exercise on anxiety have been the topic of numerous studies over the past 30 years. Seminal studies on the effects of acute physical activity on state anxiety conducted by Morgan (1973, 1979a) laid the foundation for a large body of research showing reductions in self-rated anxiety after aerobic exercise. For example, Morgan (1973) measured state anxiety in 40 men before vigorous exercise, shortly after vigorous exercise, and 20 to 30 min after 45 min of vigorous exercise. There was a slight increase in anxiety immediately after exercise, but a significant decrease below pre-exercise anxiety 20 to 30 min later. In a subsequent study, state anxiety reduction after 20 min of exercise at 70% of aerobic capacity was comparable to reductions after meditation or quiet rest in a group of 75 middle-aged men, shown in figure 6.5 (Bahrke and Morgan 1978). That study was especially important because it generated the hypothesis that the key feature common to the conditions was "time-out" or diversion from the source or symptoms of anxiety—and that *distraction* might be a plausible explanation for anxiety reduction after exercise, a view that has been recently supported (Breus and O'Connor 1998).

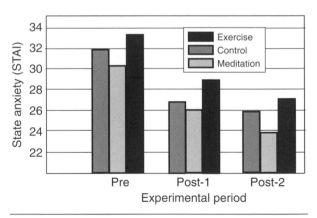

Figure 6.5 State anxiety before and following exercise, meditation, and control treatments.

Data from Bahrke and Morgan 1978.

State Anxiety

A temporary reduction in state anxiety after acute exercise has been reported widely in quantitative (i.e., meta-analysis) reviews of studies conducted on adults without anxiety disorders (e.g., Landers and Petruzzello 1994; Petruzzello et al. 1991). Studies published from 1960 to 1993 indicated an average reduction ranging from 1/4 (McDonald and Hodgdon 1991; Petruzzello et al. 1991) to 1/2 (Landers and Petruzzello 1994) *SD*, with larger changes typically occurring 5 to 30 min after exercise that had lasted about 20 to 30 min. Several studies have suggested that acute exercise is as effective as meditation (Bahrke and Morgan 1978), biofeedback, and drugs (Broocks et al. 1998), but no more effective than quiet rest or distraction in decreasing state anxiety (Bahrke and Morgan 1978; Breus and O'Connor 1998). However, the **anxiolytic** effects of exercise apparently last longer than those of rest or distraction, and short periods of exercise have been associated with decreases in state anxiety that have persisted up to several hours after exercise. For example, Raglin and Wilson (1996) reported that state anxiety was decreased up to 2 h after 20 min of cycling at either 40%, 60%, or 70% of $\dot{V}O_2$peak.

***A**cute exercise can decrease state anxiety as effectively as other traditional treatments, such as meditation.*

Changes in anxiety after exercise reported in studies that were published before 1993 did not differ significantly among exercise intensities expressed as %$\dot{V}O_2$peak (Landers and Petruzzello 1994; Petruzzello et al. 1991), but most of those studies did not quantify relative exercise intensity according to different levels of cardiorespiratory fitness or compare intensities within the same participants. Often, aerobic capacity was estimated based on submaximal fitness tests or heart rate, which can be up to 20% off from actual aerobic capacity. Accurate assessment of exercise intensities is critical for determining the levels of exercise intensity necessary or optimal for reducing anxiety after acute exercise and for prescribing a training program. Studies published since 1993 typically have used standard methods for quantifying exercise intensity. These studies show decreased or unchanged anxiety after intensities ranging from 40% to 70% $\dot{V}O_2$peak (Breus and O'Connor 1998; Dishman, Farquhar, and Cureton 1994; Garvin, Koltyn, and Morgan 1997; Koltyn and Morgan 1992; O'Connor and Davis 1992; Raglin and Wilson 1996) and increased, decreased, or unchanged anxiety after maximal exercise testing with different samples of

participants (Koltyn, Lynch, and Hill 1998; O'Connor et al. 1995).

The fitness levels of participants varied among those studies, but physical activity history was usually described poorly or not measured. A common limitation of the literature on anxiety reduction after acute exercise is the failure of studies to directly compare participants who differ in fitness and physical activity histories. Also, the common approach of expressing relative exercise intensity as %$\dot{V}O_2$peak does not fully equate intensity among people who differ in exercise training. Inactive people experience more metabolic strain than active people when exercising at the same %$\dot{V}O_2$peak (Wilmore and Costill 1994), and this difference could affect anxiety responses after exercise. Moreover, physically active adults, compared with less active adults, have higher expectancies of psychological benefits from exercise (Hsiao and Thayer 1998; Steinhardt and Dishman 1989), and this might bias their self-reports of anxiety reduction after acute exercise.

The bulk of the evidence about anxiety after exercise comes from studies that measured anxiety via self-ratings (Morgan 1997; Petruzzello et al. 1991), which are transparent in their content. Hence, the researchers did not discount the possibility that the reduction in anxiety after exercise was confounded by subject expectancy about the psychological effects of exercise (Morgan 1997). Investigations that addressed an effect of expectancy on reduced anxiety after cycling (Youngstedt et al. 1993) and reduced tension after jogging (Berger et al. 1998) showed mixed evidence of such an effect. A recent study that controlled for physical activity history, fitness, and expectancy of psychological benefits of exercise indicated that young men with low fitness, but not those with high fitness, had reduced state anxiety after 20 min of cycling at a light intensity (40% of $\dot{V}O_2$peak), despite having higher anxiety than the fit men shortly after maximal exercise (Tieman et al. 2002). Thus, in that study, lower fitness and a recent history of physical inactivity did not prevent the young men from experiencing reduced anxiety after submaximal exercise.

Most research on anxiety and exercise has examined the effects of aerobic, low-resistance exercise, such as swimming, cycling, or running, at moderate or high intensities. Anxiety reductions following high-resistance exercise, such as weightlifting, have been examined less frequently. In 1993, Raglin, Turner, and Eksten found no decrease in state anxiety after weight training but significant decreases

Most studies of exercise and anxiety have used aerobic activities.

after leg cycle exercise. Focht and Koltyn (1999) found a reduction in state anxiety after 50% but not 80% of resistance exercise at one-repetition maximum (1-RM), although this effect was delayed by more than 60 min after exercise. In another study, anxiety reductions after resistance exercise were delayed until 1.5 to 2 h after exercise (O'Connor et al. 1993). Bartholomew and Linder (1998) found decreased state anxiety after 20 min of resistance exercise at 40% to 50% of 1-RM, and this effect occurred 15 and 30 min after exercise. They also found that anxiety was increased at 5 and 15 min after 20 min of high-intensity resistance exercise (75-85% of 1-RM).

Trait Anxiety

Unlike the status of research on physical activity and depression, there are virtually no epidemiological studies on the association between physical activity and anxiety, in either patient populations or people without clinical disorders. An exception is the Canada Fitness Survey, in which 22,000 Canadians over age 10 answered questions about anxiety and exercise (Stephens 1988). There were more symptoms of anxiety in those reporting little or no activity compared with those reporting moderate or very active lifestyles.

Petruzzello et al. (1991) concluded from their meta-analysis of exercise and anxiety research that the typical reduction in trait anxiety after exercise training was about 1/3 *SD*, a change of about 3 points on the most common rating scale used in the studies (Spielberger's State-Trait Anxiety Inventory, which ranges from 20 [almost never anxious] to 80 [almost always anxious]). Despite the fact that virtually all the people studied did not have diagnosed anxiety disorders, greater reductions were seen among those people who had higher trait anxiety. Effects for exercise were as good as for other active treatments and better than for control conditions.

It is unlikely that chronic exercise will have a large effect on trait anxiety among people without anxiety disorders, but it can decrease state anxiety in nonpatients who have relatively high trait anxiety.

Exercise Training Among Patients With Anxiety

Few training studies have been conducted with clinical populations, but generally, such individuals show reductions in anxiety regardless of training intensity or changes in aerobic capacity. Martinsen,

Hoffart, and Solberg (1989) examined the effects of aerobic (walking/jogging) and nonaerobic (strength/flexibility/relaxation) exercise on 79 inpatients with various anxiety disorders. Patients, randomly assigned to the groups, exercised for 1 h three days per week. After eight weeks of training, patients in the two groups showed similar and significant reductions in anxiety regardless of changes in aerobic capacity. Benefits of exercise training were also documented in another study of 44 inpatients with a variety of anxiety disorders (Martinsen, Sandvik, and Kolbjornsrud 1989). Inpatients performed 1 h of aerobic exercise five times a week for eight weeks. All exhibited improvements in anxiety symptoms during the study except those diagnosed with social phobia. Patients with GAD and those with agoraphobia without panic attacks maintained their improvements at one-year follow-up. Sexton, Maere, and Dahl (1989) also reported persistence in reduction in anxiety six months after hospitalized patients had participated in eight weeks of moderate- or low-intensity aerobic exercise training. In addition, improvements in psychological symptoms were similar for the two intensities.

In a more recent study, 46 outpatients who had moderate to severe panic disorder with agoraphobia (4 did not have agoraphobia) were randomly assigned to a 10-week treatment protocol of regular aerobic exercise (running), the serotonin reuptake inhibitor clomipramine (112.5 mg/day), or placebo pills (Broocks et al. 1998). The dropout rates were 31% for the exercise group, 27% for the placebo group, and 0% for the clomipramine treatment group. Compared to placebo, both exercise and clomipramine were accompanied by a significant decrease in symptoms, but clomipramine treatment improved anxiety symptoms sooner and more effectively.

Most clinical research on anxiety and exercise has focused on panic disorders (O'Connor, Raglin, and Martinsen 2000). Though some evidence has suggested that individuals with panic disorders are physically inactive and actually avoid exercise (Broocks et al. 1997), there is not a scientific consensus that patients diagnosed with panic disorder avoid physical activity in a phobic way (O'Connor, Raglin, and Martinsen 2000).

Issues in Research

It is important to know whether physical activity and exercise can relax people even though they don't have anxiety disorders. The stress of daily living is routinely accompanied by anxieties that don't lead to a disorder but still negatively impact the quality of the day by causing discomfort or impairing people's work or leisure activities. This is one reason that most studies of exercise and anxiety have involved people who had average or even low levels of anxiety. However, that approach has led to four problems. The first of these is the problem of generalizability. Obviously, the study of people who are not clinically anxious does not tell us whether exercise will be an effective treatment for any of the several anxiety disorders. Considering the high prevalence of the various anxiety disorders, it is important for public health that we learn more about the potential benefits and any hazards of physical activity and exercise among patients diagnosed with anxiety disorders.

The second problem is one of initial levels of low anxiety, which leave little room for anxiety to improve. In other words, exercise would not be expected to make people who aren't anxious less anxious. A few recent researchers studying nonclinical populations were able to examine elevated anxiety by screening large numbers of people to find those who had elevated trait anxiety scores (e.g., Breus and O'Connor 1998), or by provoking higher anxiety pharmacologically by using caffeine (Youngstedt et al. 1998).

The third problem is whether the rating scales used to measure anxiety in most exercise studies have been sensitive enough to detect true reductions in anxiety after exercise. This concern is amplified when the participants are people who have low initial anxiety. Most rating scales that have been used in exercise studies give a single score for anxiety. Some psychologists argue that at the least, worry and physiological symptoms should be measured separately. A special concern has been voiced that the scales used in exercise studies have not been sensitive or specific enough to measure anxiety in response to exercise. Self-report of anxiety usually has been assessed with the State-Trait Anxiety Inventory (STAI; Spielberger et al. 1983), the tension/anxiety scale of the Profile of Mood States (POMS; McNair, Lorr, and Droppleman 1981), or other similar scales that use adjectives to assess an anxious or tense mood. The STAI is the most strongly validated measure of anxiety in the world. However, some researchers have become concerned that the STAI and POMS do not measure anxiety or tension during or after exercise (see Ekkekakis and Petruzzello 1999 for a discussion). One concern is that the questions on the scales might be artificially affected by people's perceptions of physical arousal during exercise. Another is that anxiety during or after exercise is experienced differently than in response to other situations or settings—that the structure of anxiety might be changed by exercise. Some researchers even believe that measures of anxiety designed specifically for exercise are required. Research has yet to show that this is the case. It's hard to imagine why or how anxiety during or after exercise could be a unique phenomenon. Nonetheless, some people experience symptoms related to anxiety, such as muscle tension or pain, without reporting worry. So, it is possible that people having nonclinical anxiety before exercise still might feel calmer and more relaxed after exercise, but that the scales used to measure anxiety don't have enough of the right questions to measure a change in a person's feelings of relaxation. It is an unresolved issue in psychology whether feelings of relaxation are merely the absence of anxiety, whether relaxation and anxiety are opposite extremes of the same feeling (i.e., arousal, activation), or whether they are different feelings.

The fourth problem is the virtual absence of physiological evidence of reduced anxiety. That absence is important for three reasons. The first is related to the problem of sensitivity and specificity of measurement just explained. A few early studies (e.g., deVries, Wiswell, Bulbulian, and Moritani 1981), and a recent one (Smith et al. 2002), have shown that acute and chronic exercise can reduce muscle reflexes and tension. It is not yet clear, though, whether reduced muscle tension after exercise is part of anxiety reduction or is a biological response to exercise that is independent of anxiety. Similarly, moderate to large increases in the α brain wave band frequency measured by electroencephalography (EEG) are common during and after exercise (Crabbe and Dishman 2001; Petruzzello et al. 1991; Kubitz and Mott 1996; see figure 6.6). Increased α activity is traditionally viewed as an index of relaxed wakefulness, but this is not a universal view among EEG experts, and the exercise studies did not show that the increased α activity was caused by the exercise or related to reduced anxiety; other brain wave frequencies presumably unrelated to anxiety also are increased after exercise (Crabbe and Dishman 2001). In addition, reductions in blood pressure after exercise have been interpreted by some investigators as indirect evidence of an anxiolytic effect of exercise (e.g., Petruzzello et al. 1991; Raglin, Turner, and Eksten 1993). However, postexercise hypotension (lowered blood pressure for up to 2 h after exercise) is a well-known physiological phenomenon that occurs even when anxiety is not lowered after exercise (e.g., Youngstedt et al. 1993).

The second reason why physiological measures of anxiety are desirable is the need to corroborate the validity of self-rating of anxiety as a true measure of mood or emotional response. Though physiological measures cannot serve as a substitute for self-report, which is the only way to directly measure a person's feelings, they are more objective than self-reports of anxiety. Hence, they are not as affected by experimental artifacts, such as demand characteristics, experimenter influences on participants' ratings, social desirability, or other participant expectancies about exercise that can artificially bias self-ratings.

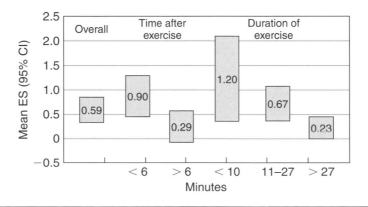

Figure 6.6   Results for encephalogram α brain wave band frequency after exercise.
Data from Crabbe and Dishman 2001.

Finally, and third, the absence of physiological evidence of reduced anxiety is a problem because physiological variables have been a part of most theories of negative emotions, including anxiety, since the time of Hippocrates, thru the era of Charles Darwin and William James, until today (see chapters 1 and 7). Several modern theories propose that electromyographic measures of startle (Lang, Bradley, and Cuthbert 1998) and EEG measures of asymmetry in brain waves (Davidson 1992) provide indexes of people's predisposition to interpret environmental events as negative or threatening. Recently, asymmetry as indicated by EEG (Petruzzello and Landers 1994; Petruzzello and Tate 1997) and an elecromyogram measure of startle (Smith et al. 2002) have been shown to be related to self-ratings of anxiety, but not to overall emotional responses (Crabbe, Smith, and Dishman 2001; Smith et al. 2002).

A final concern is that the influence of the setting in which physical activity occurs is poorly understood. Thayer and coworkers (1987) reported that 10 to 15 min of walking outdoors reduced self-rated tension, but earlier research showed no effect on anxiety following acute treadmill walking (Morgan 1973). McAuley, Mihalko, and Bane (1996) found a reduction in anxiety after exercise of self-selected intensity, despite small increases during exercise, in either a laboratory or a natural setting.

Mechanisms

It is important to determine whether reduced anxiety after acute exercise or an exercise training program can be explained by a direct effect of exercise or merely by other aspects of the exercise setting. It is unlikely that exercise would directly decrease the occurrence of some forms of anxiety, but it might help a person cope with the experience of anxiety. For example, there is no reason to expect that exercise would reduce simple phobias. An individual afraid of spiders will experience anxiety when exposed to a spider whether the person is active and fit or sedentary.

Similarly, people who have social phobias usually recognize that their anxiety is irrational, but their self-consciousness and fear of judgement in social situations persist. As a result, they try to avoid people in social situations as much as possible. There is no reason to expect that physically active people would somehow be protected against developing social anxiety disorder, since it is mainly a learned response. Indeed, cognitive-behavioral therapy has proven the most effective treatment for social phobia. In a cognitive-behavioral group, patients might work on their anxieties in a progressive hierarchy, learning to engage in social introductions, small talk with others, presentations to the group, mock job interviews, sitting in front of the stare of others, performing drama with others, and so on. The idea is to desensitize their anxiety in social situations through experience of social evaluation without negative consequences. Exercise could not do that directly. Indeed, social phobia could well keep someone from exercising in public. However, cognitive-behavioral therapy could be carried out in a group exercise setting, such as in a fitness club. In that case, though exercise would not be the treatment, a person with social phobia might find exercise a way to reduce the symptoms of anxiety caused by a social encounter. A few case studies have even indicated that exercise could help patients who have situational phobia, perhaps by helping them learn to cope with feelings of arousal such as those produced by heavy exertion (e.g., Orwin 1974).

On the other hand, exercise might hold more promise for helping people cope with the symptoms of GAD. If shown to be effective, exercise could offer an important public health benefit for people with GAD, as one survey has indicated that only about 25% of people with GAD ever receive treatment (Uhlenhuth et al. 1983).

Clarifying the exercise intensity, mode, and duration that make the greatest impact on anxiety symptoms, and identifying the resulting effects on psychological and physiological markers of anxiety, can provide insight into mechanisms for the anxiolytic effects of exercise. There is consensus that exercise reduces anxiety, but there is no consensus on how this happens. The first step in understanding the relationship between exercise and anxiety reduction is to understand something about the etiology of anxiety. There is evidence for a moderate genetic contribution to an individual's susceptibility to developing an anxiety disorder, but the genesis of anxiety disorders is likely a function of biological, behavioral, and environmental factors (O'Connor, Raglin, and Martinsen 2000). Theories that have been used to explain the genesis of anxiety disorders include genetic, as well as cognitive-behavioral, psychodynamic, sociogenic, and neurobiological theories. No single theory can adequately explain the etiology of anxiety, and the effects of exercise on anxiety are likely also multifaceted. The most active areas of research have been in cognitive and neurobiological aspects of anxiety (O'Connor, Raglin, and Martinsen 2000).

Cognitive Theories

Cognitive theories, as noted in chapter 11, explain behavior and feelings by focusing on cognition. For example, the development of trait anxiety is characterized as cognitively learned through personal or observed exposures to physical threats or negative evaluations of failures. From this perspective, pathological anxiety develops as a result of cognitive appraisals, such as overestimating the intensity of a feared event, underestimating one's ability to cope, or catastrophically misinterpreting physiological symptoms associated with anxiety (e.g., interpreting an increased heart rate as a possible heart attack) (O'Connor, Raglin, and Martinsen 2000). Support for a cognitive component in anxiety disorders is provided by McNally, Foa, and Donnell (1989), who found that patients with anxiety disorders exhibited a recall bias for anxiety-

related information compared to nonclinical controls. The patients with anxiety were more likely to attend to and remember stimuli that were either threatening or perceived as threatening.

Cognitive explanations for effects of exercise on anxiety have also been proposed. Physiological sensations from exercise can help redefine the subjective meaning of arousal and can compete with the perception of anxiety symptoms. Sensations of the heart pounding during exercise can be "reframed" from a symptom of anxiety to a sign of a good workout. Exercise can also distract attention from anxiety-provoking thoughts and produces a "time-out" from cares and worries **(distraction hypothesis).** Breus and O'Connor (1998) tested the time-out, or distraction, hypothesis (Bahrke and Morgan 1978) by measuring state anxiety (STAI) in 18 high trait-anxious college females before and after exercise at moderate (40% of aerobic capacity) intensity, exercise while studying, studying only, and quiet rest. There was no change in anxiety after exercise while studying, studying only, or quiet rest. There was a significant decrease in anxiety after the exercise-only condition, which indicates

Exercise can be used as a distraction from anxiety about impending exams.

that the anxiolytic effect of exercise (exercise as time-out from worries and concerns) was blocked by studying.

The time-out hypothesis states that exercise distracts attention from anxiety-provoking thoughts and produces a time-out from cares and worries.

Neurobiological Theories

Neurobiological explanations of the etiology and manifestation of anxiety have been enhanced by increased sophistication of measurement in human research, such as brain imaging technology. Neurobiological theories on the development of anxiety have been intertwined with those for depression since there is evidence that anxiety and depression are linked to dysregulation of some of the same neural systems (e.g., noradrenergic and serotonergic systems). Patients with major affective disorders usually have anxiety as a prominent symptom, and many anxious patients have a history of depression.

A neurobiological perspective on anxiety supports the integration of cognitive and neurological theories. For example, neural circuits involved in anxiety must include afferent nerve fibers that allow potentially threatening stimuli to be sensed so they can be interpreted as threatening by higher brain areas. These brain areas must appraise the input and integrate it with relevant memories. If the stimuli are then interpreted as representing a threat, the response depends on efferent nerves that generate a coordinated endocrine, autonomic, and muscular response. The effects of these different neural systems are dependent on several neurotransmitters, which have been targets for the pharmacological treatment of anxiety disorders.

There is evidence from human and animal research that the amygdala, locus coeruleus (LC), midbrain, thalamus, right hippocampus, anterior cingulate cortex, insular cortex, and right prefrontal cortex are involved in the genesis and expression of anxiety (Goddard and Charney 1997; Reiman 1997). The amygdala seems to be the critical central neural structure involved in the psy-chophysiological components of fear and anxiety responses (see chapter 3) (Goddard and Charney 1997). The amygdala receives input from the thalamus and LC and from sensations that have been integrated with higher cortical areas. Anxiety from direct experiences (state anxiety when a dog growls), unconscious processing (spontaneous panic attack), and prior experiences (posttraumatic stress) can thus be mediated through the amygdala. Efferent projections to a variety of centers controlling cognitive, affective, neuroendocrine, cardiorespiratory, and musculoskeletal functions allow the amygdala to play a key role in the manifestation of anxiety symptoms (Goddard and Charney 1997). For example, the amygdala and the LC have projections into the hypothalamus, which contributes to activation of the sympathetic nervous system.

Much of our understanding of neurobiological mechanisms involved in anxiety has built upon studies of animal behavior. For example, as noted in chapter 3, increased locomotion in the rat usually reflects an adaptive motivational state of low behavioral inhibition (e.g., less freezing), especially when the locomotion appears purposeful and the animal exhibits other exploratory behaviors such as rearing or approaching the center of the open field. In contrast, low levels of locomotion, few approaches to the center of the open field, freezing, defecation, urination, and shivering in rats are conventionally regarded as indexes of hypervigilance, hesitancy, fear, and autonomic activation, which are responses that are common in human anxiety. Under some circumstances of threat, increased locomotion in rats indicates panic (i.e., the flight response to a predator).

Neurobiological mechanisms for the anti-anxiety effects of exercise have not been well studied with an established animal model of anxiety. The limbic-motor integration model of anxiety elaborated by Mogenson (1987) is relevant for the study of physical activity and anxiety behaviors in the rat. In this model, fearful locomotion is controlled by the limbic system's modulation of the tegmental pedunculopontine nucleus of the mesencephalic locomotor system by reciprocal inhibition between γ-aminobutyric acid (GABA) and dopamine transmission within the **corpus striatum**. GABA efferents from the nucleus accumbens to the ventral pallidum apparently inhibit locomotion.

Important inputs to the amygdala, which coordinates freezing or flight behaviors during perceived threat, come from the hippocampus, which helps regulate checking of the environment against memories of danger; the ventral tegmentum (VTA), a pleasure center that surrounds the hypothalamus and helps regulate approach behaviors (see figure 6.7); and the periaqueductal gray (PAG), a pain-processing area that surrounds the duct between the third and fourth brain ventricles, as well as the dorsal raphe nuclei, which each influence locomotion during threat (see figure 6.8).

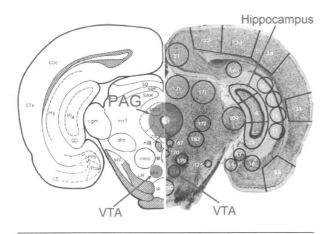

Figure 6.7 Anxiety-associated locomotion; periaqueductal gray matter (PAG) surrounding the aqueduct between the third and fourth brain ventricles, the hippocampus, and the ventral tegmental area (VTA) surrounding the hypothalamus regulate fear behaviors during threat in the rat.

Adapted, by permission, from M. Palkovits and M.J. Brownstein, 1988, *Maps and guide to microdissection of the rat brain* (New York: Elsevier Science), 152.

Insight into the mechanisms for anxiety disorders and potential explanations for effects of exercise come from the psychopharmacology literature, studies on the effects of drugs on neurotransmitter systems, and research on the effects of exercise on these systems. The serotonergic and noradrenergic systems have been implicated in anxiety, and there is good evidence for contributions from specific neurotransmitters, such as GABA.

Serotonin

Numerous antidepressant and anxiolytic drugs affect serotonergic systems, for example by blocking

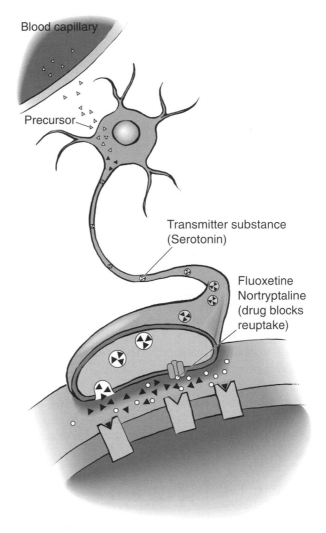

Figure 6.8 Serotonin reuptake inhibition at the level of the receptor.

serotonin reuptake (see figure 6.8) or acting on serotonergic receptors as agonists/antagonists. The serotonin reuptake-inhibiting drugs, such as clomipramine and fluoxetine, are often used to treat several anxiety disorders (Goddard and Charney 1998). Anxiety can be induced in a majority of panic patients, but in a minority of controls, through blocking of the binding of serotonin at the receptor level with serotonin receptor agonists, such as the nonselective serotonin agonist m-chlorophenylpiperazine (Charney et al. 1987), which implies a dysregulation in the serotonergic system in these patients.

Exercise and serotonergic system. Animal studies have shown increased activity of the raphe nuclei and serotonin synthesis with exercise training (Dishman 1998). There is also indirect evidence for effects from exercise on central serotonergic systems based on measures of tryptophan disposition in the blood and concentrations of **5-HIAA** (serotonin [5-HT] metabolite) in cerebrospinal fluid (Chaouloff 1997). Mechanisms for increased brain levels of serotonin with exercise involve the effects of exercise on the substrate tryptophan (see chapter 3). Exercise induces increased lipolysis, or the breakdown of triglycerides into free fatty acids, which are used to fuel increased levels of muscular contraction. Increased serum levels of free fatty acids compete with tryptophan for binding with albumin, leading to increases in free tryptophan. This increase in free tryptophan stimulates an influx of tryptophan into the brain, and thus the potential for increased synthesis of serotonin. The increase in free fatty acids has the best support as a mechanism for increased serotonin with exercise (Chaouloff 1997). Exercise also may result in decreased levels of large neutral amino acids (aromatic amino acids and branched-chain amino acids), which compete with free tryptophan at the transporter level of the blood-brain barrier. However, there is mixed evidence for changes in branched-chain amino acids with acute exercise (Chaouloff 1997).

*E*xercise may affect anxiety by altering substrate utilization that facilitates uptake of tryptophan into the brain and subsequent increased synthesis of serotonin.

Norepinephrine

Several lines of evidence implicate the noradrenergic system in anxiety (O'Connor, Raglin, and Martinsen 2000). Suppressing effects of norepinephrine (NE) with β-adrenergic blockers, which downregulate the NE receptor-effector system, have shown efficacy in the treatment of social phobia (Gorman and Gorman 1987). The function of the LC and the release of NE have also been implicated in anxiety disorders. There is a general association between spontaneous LC activity and vigilance and arousal. The LC increases the signal-to-noise ratio by decreasing the background rate of spontaneous firing in the hippocampus, thalamic, and cortical areas and enhancing evoked responses in the lateral geniculate nucleus and visual cortex. It has been hypothesized that patients with panic disorder have an abnormally regulated α-2 noradrenergic receptor system, which is involved in the regulation of NE release from the LC. Panic patients have been found to exhibit both a blunted growth hormone response to the α-2 receptor agonist clonidine (Tancer, Stein, and Uhde 1993), and an exaggerated anxiety and physiological response to the α-2 receptor antagonist, yohimbine (Charney et al. 1992). Alpha-2 receptor agonists, such as clonidine, decrease LC activity (i.e., decrease NE release); and antagonists, such as yohimbine, increase LC activity. In animals, stimulation of the LC results in anxiety-like behaviors and produces behavioral and physiological changes commonly associated with anxiety. Ablation of the LC eliminates these anxiety responses.

Exercise and noradrenergic system. Diffferences in adrenergic receptors can serve as an indication of SNS and NE or EPI activity. Researchers interested in the effects of exercise on these systems have examined adrenergic receptor density in humans. Endurance-trained athletes have higher-than-normal β-adrenoreceptor density on lymphocytes (a type of white blood cell), and a session of prolonged physical activity at high intensity is accompanied by increased β-adrenoreceptor density on lymphocytes. However, lymphocyte adrenoreceptors are $β_2$ types with high affinity for epinephrine, like those found in skeletal and smooth muscle, the liver, and peripheral sympathetic tissue. It is unclear whether they provide an index of peripheral SNS receptors, but they do not provide a measure of brain NE activity (Dishman 1998).

*E*ffects of exercise on NE to benefit individuals with anxiety disorders may be at the level of the LC, but research with humans to prove this has been limited.

In rats, exercise training has been found to increase levels of NE in the LC, amygdala, hippocampus, and hypothalamus (Dishman, Hong, et al.) and to decrease release of NE in the brain frontal cortex (Soares et al. 1999) after stress. In humans, changes in brain NE activity after acute physical activity have been estimated via measurement of 3-methoxy-4-hydroxyphenylglycol (**MHPG;** NE metabolite) levels in urine, plasma, or cerebral spinal fluid. Studies of urinary MHPG after a single session of physical activity showed increased MHPG excretion or no change. At rest, 20% to 60% of MHPG in peripheral blood or urine comes from metabolism of brain NE. However, the increase in blood levels of NE during exercise comes mainly from sympathetic nerves innervating the heart, with some coming from the exercising skeletal muscles; thus the relevance for anxiety of increased MHPG in blood after acute exercise is unclear (Dishman 1998).

Gamma-Aminobutyric Acid

The function of GABA as the major neural inhibitory neurotransmitter implies a role in moderating arousal level, and a substantial body of evidence implicates GABA in anxiety disorders. Gamma-aminobutyric acid neurons and receptors are widely distributed in brain areas thought to be important for the expression of anxiety, including the hypothalamus, periaqueductal gray, septum, hippocampus, and amygdala (Menard and Treit 1999). Gamma-aminobutyric acid and benzodiazepines, such as diazepam or Valium, will bind to the $GABA_A$ receptor and inhibit activity of neurons in the brain by opening a chloride channel and hyperpolarizing the cell (see figure 6.9). The benzodiazepines are effective in treating GAD, and the benzodiazepine receptor inverse agonists (e.g., the β-carbolines) produce strong anxiety reactions (Dorow 1987).

A recently proposed hypothesis has linked biological and cognitive processes characterizing anxiety (Sarter and Bruno 1999). Benzodiazepines inhibit cholinergic neurons originating in the basal forebrain. These basal forebrain neurons innervate all cortical areas and are known to be involved in modulating cortical information processing. Basal forebrain neurons also receive **afferent** input from the LC and amygdala. Sarter and Bruno (1999) hypothesized that increases in the excitability of cortical cholinergic inputs from the basal forebrain play a role in the cognitive aspects of anxiety and promote an increased processing of anxiety-related stimuli. The inhibition of these cholinergic neurons by benzodiazepine would be a mechanism for decreasing cognitive processing of stimuli that promote anxiety.

Exercise and GABA. Dishman et al. (1998) studied the effects of chronic activity-wheel running and treadmill exercise training on central nervous system neurotransmitter systems in rats. They found increased levels of GABA and a decreased number of $GABA_A$ receptors in the corpus striatum and increased open-field locomotion among the activity-wheel runners, consistent with an anxiolytic effect according to the limbic-motor integration model of Mogenson (1987). The explanation for an anxiolytic effect of exercise based on GABA may be through exercise effects on central cholinergic function, which is inhibited by benzodiazepine receptor agonists. Exercise training can induce alterations in peripheral cholinergic function (Zhao et al. 1997), which presents the possibility that improvements in anxiety following exercise training may accrue as a result of adaptations in central nervous system cholinergic neural circuits (see O'Connor, Raglin, and Martinsen 2000 for a discussion).

Improvements in anxiety following exercise training may be through adaptations in central nervous system cholinergic or GABAergic neural circuits.

Summary

Anxiety is a response to a real or perceived threat that has cognitive, behavioral, emotional, and physiological components. Acute anxiety is experienced by most people at some time or another with minor effects, but an anxiety disorder can be incapacitating. Several million people have anxiety disorders, and the financial and emotional costs are considerable. Pharmacological treatment has some risks and disadvantages, and the potential use of exercise as a

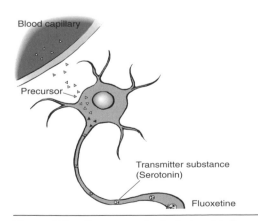

Figure 6.9 Gamma-aminobutyric acid$_A$/benzodiazepine ionophore.

means of prevention and treatment is appealing in view of its additional health benefits.

Little research has been conducted with clinical populations besides individuals with panic disorder, and most studies have tested participants with nonclinical initial levels of anxiety. However, anxiety reductions following acute exercise have been consistently observed in individuals with nonclinical levels of anxiety, even with little room for anxiety scores to improve, and the bulk of the initial research on effects of exercise training with clinical populations has been promising. Aerobic exercise seems to decrease acute anxiety, but the effects of intensity and duration need more study. There are also mixed results on the effects of resistance exercise on acute anxiety.

Several plausible mechanisms have been examined in attempts to explain how acute and chronic exercise might bring about reductions in anxiety. Plausible mechanisms linking anxiety improvements with exercise are being developed with an increased understanding of relevant neurobiology. This mechanistic work needs to be conducted in patients who have clinical anxiety disorders and in individuals without a clinical anxiety disorder who are experiencing above-average anxiety. Multiple approaches are recommended, including the use of noninvasive brain imaging, neurotransmitter-blocking agents, and psychophysiological methods (e.g., correlating brain cortical EEG with self-reported anxiety responses to exercise). Animal models of anxiety also have a potentially important role to play in generating useful new knowledge about neurobiological mechanisms that might explain anxiety reduction after exercise and physical activity.

Suggested Readings

Morgan, W.P. 1979a. Anxiety reduction following acute physical activity. *Psychiatric Annals* 9 (3): 36–45.

O'Connor, P.J., J.S. Raglin, and E.W. Martinsen. 2000. Physical activity, anxiety and anxiety disorders. *International Journal of Sport Psychology* 31 (2): 136–0155.

Petruzzello, S.J., D.M. Landers, B.D. Hatfield, K.A. Kubitz, and W. Salazar. 1991. A meta-analysis on the anxiety-reducing effects of acute and chronic exercise. Outcomes and mechanisms. *Sports Medicine* 11 (Mar): 143–182.

Raglin, J.S. 1997. Anxiolytic effects of physical activity. In *Physical activity and mental health*, ed. W.P. Morgan. Washington, DC: Taylor & Francis.

Web Sites

www.nimh.nih.gov/anxiety/

www.mentalhealth.com/p.html

www.medscape.com/Home/Topics/psychiatry/psychiatry.html

7

Depression

Most people have experienced transient feelings of sadness or depressed mood. The depression passes after minutes or hours, but we remember how much effort routine activities, even doing the laundry, seemed to require. Many people report that periods of physical inactivity make them vulnerable to feeling depressed whereas exercise seems to lighten their mood. However, the relationship between exercise and depression is like the chicken-and-egg dilemma: are people depressed because they are sedentary, or are they sedentary because they are depressed? Longitudinal studies have offered some evidence that physical inactivity increases the risk of depression, and exercise training studies with clinically depressed patients have demonstrated improvements in depressive symptoms. We may find an explanation for this by examining the extensive research on the psychobiological mechanisms of depression. This chapter provides a foundation for understanding the relationship between exercise and depression by reviewing the scope of the problem; offering clinical definitions; describing the research literature on exercise and depression; and explaining the current social, cognitive, and psychobiological mechanisms for effects.

Prevalence and Social Impact

At least one-third of all individuals are expected to experience at least one bout of depression in their lifetimes (Ernst, Rand, and Stevinson 1998). In 1996, 12.6 million of the annual office visits to physicians were for major depression or other types of depressive disorders (Schappert 1998), and depression is one of the most common complaints of all adults who seek psychotherapy. Feeling depressed, however, is only part of clinical depression, which is a severe condition with persistent emotional, physiological, and cognitive components. Estimates from epidemiological research in England, Finland, Australia, and the United States suggest that 8% of women and 4% of men have some form of clinical depression at any point in time (Lehtinen and Joukamaa 1994). In the United States, 4.5% to 9.3% of all women and 2.3% to 3.2% of all men have a major depressive disorder. As shown in figure 7.1b, the National Comorbidity Survey indicated a lifetime rate of 17% for major depression (21% among women and 13% among men) and a rate of 10% when people were asked whether they had been depressed in the previous 12 months (Kessler et al. 1994). With the exception of manic episodes in bipolar disorder, women have about twice the rate of depression that men do.

Only 30% of people with depression seek the help of a professional (Shapiro et al. 1984), and according to the National Depressive and Manic-Depressive Association, only 10% of depressed individuals receive adequate treatment (Hirschfeld et al. 1997). So, it is important to determine whether physical activity can help prevent and treat depression.

Clinical depression has high personal, social, and economic costs. Individuals with depression experience loss of pleasure, feelings of hopelessness, and

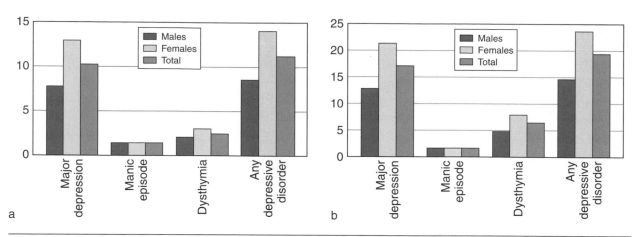

Figure 7.1   Twelve-month *(a)* and lifetime *(b)* prevalence of depression.

Data from Kessler et al. 1994.

difficulty with interpersonal relationships. Some-one who is depressed has an increased risk of sui-cide. Clinical depression is the strongest mental disorder risk factor for suicide in youth and adults (Petronis et al. 1990). Suicide rates are highest in older adults, and depression is also a significant risk factor in this population (United States Department of Health and Human Services 2000). In 1990, an estimated 15,000 men and 3400 women in the United States committed suicide as a result of de-pression (Greenberg et al. 1993). There is evidence for some long-term physical consequences of de-pression, such as decreases in bone mineral density and increased rates of coronary disease and hyper-tension (Gold and Chrousos 1999; Jonas, Franks, and Ingram 1997). Depression accounts for 20% of all health care costs, which include direct costs for treatment and indirect costs due to premature death, absenteeism from work, and reduced pro-ductivity (Greenberg et al. 1993).

***A**lthough 8% of women and 4% of men have clinical depression at any point in time, only 30% of people with depression seek professional help and just 10% get adequate treatment.*

Clinical Description

Defining depression can be difficult because it in-cludes several types of mood disorders with oppo-site symptoms (e.g., increase *or* decrease in sleep; increase *or* decrease in appetite) (see table 7.1). *Di-agnostic and Statistical Manual of Mental Disorders* (American Psychiatric Association 2000) places mood disorders into four categories: (1) depression, (2) bipolar, or manic-depressive, disorder, (3) mood disorders due to a medical condition, and (4) substance-induced mood disorders. The first cat-egory includes **major depression** (figure 7.2) and the milder chronic form, **dysthymia.** The two prin-cipal subtypes of major depression are melancholic and atypical depression, although 53% of patients who meet the criteria for major depression do not meet the criteria for either subtype. The second category, bipolar, or **manic-depressive, disorder,** is characterized by periods of depression alternat-ing with periods of elevated, expansive, or irritable mood; exaggerated self-confidence; risky or asocial behavior; or even paranoia.

Manic-Depressive Disorders

▼ Bipolar I: Major depression alternates with mania, or uncontrollable elation.

▼ Bipolar II: Major depression alternates with hypomania, a milder form of elation.

▼ Cyclothymia: Milder depression alternates with hypomania.

Twice as many women than men are depressed. Reasons for this difference are unknown, but they likely relate to genetics, endocrine effects, and so-cial learning. For example, risk factors for bipolar

Table 7.1

Subtypes of Unipolar Affective Disorder (Major Depression)

Melancholia	Atypical depression
Physiological hyperarousal	Physiological hypoarousal
Insomnia	Hypersomnia
Loss of appetite	Increased appetite
Early-morning awakening	Fatigue
Profound sense of unworthiness	Blunted affect
Diminished libido	Diminished libido
Endocrine dysregulation	Endocrine dysregulation
Pessimism	Profound inertia
Loss of pleasure	
Decreased slow-wave sleep	
Fear	
Preferential access to painful memories	

depression include being female, especially aged 35 to 45, having a family history of depression or alcoholism, parturition in previous six months, recent negative life events, lack of a confiding relationship, and having a negative home environment. The etiology of depression in general involves stress emotions linked by neurobiological processes. Depression can be caused by catastrophic events, such as death of a loved one, loss of self-esteem (e.g., feeling unworthy because a valued goal was not met), or chronic anxiety or stress, or can occur for no apparent reason.

Effects of Exercise

Physical activity has been recommended by physicians since ancient times to combat depression. About 2500 years ago, Hippocrates prescribed exercise for his patients who experienced *melancholia*—a term still used today by psychiatrists to describe deep depression. A report from the beginning of the 20th century appears to have been the first modern study of exercise and depressed patients. The mood and reaction times of two

Diagnostic and Statistical Manual of Mental Disorders (DSM-IV) Criteria for Major Depression

At least five of the following symptoms are present during the same 2-week period, one of which must be either depressed mood or loss of interest or pleasure:

1. Depressed mood most of the day, nearly every day (can be irritable mood in adolescents or children)
2. Markedly diminished interest or pleasure in all, or almost all, activities most of the day, nearly every day
3. Significant weight loss or gain without dieting
4. Insomnia or hypersomnia
5. Psychomotor agitation or retardation
6. Fatigue or loss of energy
7. Feelings of lethargy or restlessness
8. Feelings of worthlessness or excessive guilt
9. Impaired concentration or indecisiveness
10. Recurrent thoughts of death or suicide

To be diagnosed as major depression, the symptoms should not meet criteria for mania, should not be due to direct physiological effects of a substance (e.g., alcohol) or to a general medical condition (e.g., hypothyroidism), and cannot be better accounted for by bereavement.

Figure 7.2 Many people report experiencing depression at some point in their lives, but major depression is a serious mood disorder with specific diagnostic criteria.

Adapted, by permission, from American Psychiatric Association, 2000, *Diagnostic and Statistical Manual of Mental Disorders*, 4th ed., text revision 2000 (Washington, DC: American Psychiatric Association).

depressed males were improved on days when they exercised for about 2 h compared to days when they rested (Franz and Hamilton 1905). About 65 years later, the first experimental study showed that self-ratings of depressive symptoms could be reduced in men after an exercise training program (Morgan et al. 1970). That finding was extended to a small randomized clinical trial of psychiatric outpatients showing that the reduction in depressive symptoms after 12 weeks of running therapy was equivalent to or greater than that after two forms of group psychotherapy (Greist et al. 1979). Moreover, 9 of the 10 patients treated with running therapy were still running and not depressed nine months later, while depressive symptoms had returned in the other patients.

Since those early studies, there have been more than 1000 correlational, quasi-experimental, and experimental research trials related to depression and exercise (Ernst, Rand, and Stevinson 1998). In 1984, the National Institute of Mental Health Workshop on Exercise and Mental Health concluded that exercise was associated with a decreased level of mild to moderate depression (Morgan and Goldston 1987). That conclusion was upheld at the Second International Consensus Symposium on Physical Activity, Fitness, and Health held in Toronto in 1992 (Bouchard, Shephard, and Stephens 1994) and by the 1996 U.S. Surgeon General's report, *Physical Activity and Health*. The documentation of an association between exercise and the reduction in symptoms of mild to moderate depression has come from population studies, narrative and quantitative reviews (i.e., meta-analyses) of the research literature, and exercise training studies conducted with clinical and nonclinical populations.

Most studies of exercise and depression have involved young to middle-aged adults. Too few studies have been done with children to permit a conclusion. Among people over age 65 (O'Connor, Aenchbacher, and Dishman 1993; O'Neal and Dishman 2002), the evidence suggests that the benefits of exercise for *reducing* symptoms of depression may diminish as people age; however, despite more age-related symptoms of depression among older people (e.g., sleep and cognitive disorders), older adults have a lower prevalence of clinically diagnosed depression than young and middle-aged adults. The benefits of physical activity for helping *prevent* depression usually occur regardless of people's age, gender, race, or socioeconomic status.

*T*he benefits of physical activity for helping prevent depression apparently occur regardless of people's age, gender, race, or socioeconomic status.

Preventing Depression: Population Studies

Among 25 population-based studies that have been reported around the world since the first one in 1988, 22 reported an inverse relationship between physical activity and depression according to at least one analysis (O'Neal and Dishman 2002). Figure 7.3 illustrates relative risks and 95% confi-

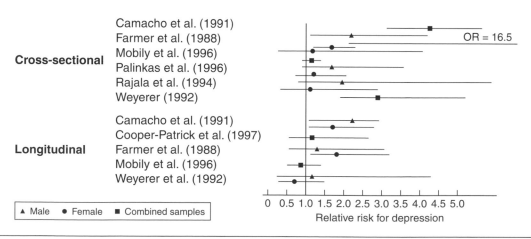

Figure 7.3 Results on the relationship between physical activity and depression from selected population-based studies.

Data from O'Neal and Dishman 2002.

dence intervals (odds-ratios in the cross-sectional studies) from selected studies. Nearly all of the studies have shown that symptoms of depression are more likely to occur among people who report little or no leisure-time physical activity, but about half the results didn't reach a high level of statistical significance, often because the sample sizes were too small given relatively small and variable reductions in risk.

Three important early studies and their findings were as follows:

1. The National Health and Nutrition Examination Survey I (NHANES I), a 1975 survey of nearly 7000 Americans aged 25 to 74, found that people who said they got little or no exercise in their leisure time also reported more symptoms of depression (Stephens 1988).

2. The Canada Fitness Survey of 22,000 Canadians aged 10 years and older yielded similar findings (Stephens 1988). In this 1981 survey, inactive people reported more symptoms related to negative moods in comparison to people who said they were moderately or very active in their leisure time.

3. A study conducted in Upper Bavaria, Germany, between 1975 and 1984, of 1500 people aged 15 and older, noted the prevalence of several types of depressive disorders for those who stated that they currently did not exercise for sports, as compared with those who stated that they did regularly exercise for sports (Weyerer 1992).

In all three studies, higher rates of depression occurred among inactive people regardless of physical illness, gender, age, and social class. However, the studies presented only cross-sectional comparisons of active and inactive people; that is, the studies merely took a "snapshot" of physical activity and health measured at the same time. They didn't determine whether it was inactivity or depression that occurred first. It's possible that people became less active after becoming depressed, rather than becoming depressed as a consequence of inactivity. As shown in figure 7.4, physical inactivity did not predict higher depression five years later in the Upper Bavaria study.

Results from the NHANES study were more encouraging. About 1500 of the people originally interviewed in NHANES I were interviewed again eight years later (Farmer et al. 1988). That follow-up survey first measured physical activity and then

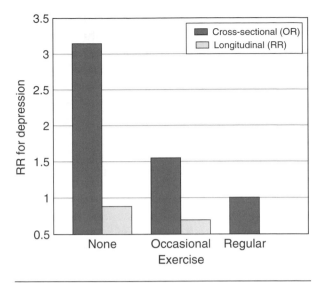

Figure 7.4 The Upper Bavarian field study measured level of physical activity and assessed depression by clinical interview in 1536 community residents. The odds ration (OR) for depression for inactive people was 3.15, but physical inactivity did not significantly increase risk of depression at five-year follow-up.

Data from Weyerer 1992.

looked for the later occurrence of the symptoms of depression. Among the findings of the NHANES I follow-up were these:

▼ The rate of depression among sedentary Caucasian women who were *not* depressed in 1975 and who remained inactive was twice that of women who said they participated in a moderate amount of physical activity and who remained active over the eight years.

▼ Caucasian men who were depressed and inactive in 1975 and who remained inactive were 12 times more likely to be depressed after eight years than those who were initially depressed but who had become physically active.

Again, these findings were observed regardless of age, education level, and socioeconomic status.

Two other important prospective studies followed depression over time and compared people's risk according to their physical activity:

▼ In the Alameda County Study conducted near Oakland, California, about 5000 nondepressed adult men and women completed surveys on physical activity and depression in 1965, 1974, and 1983 (Camacho et al. 1991). Participants were classified as low active, medium active, and high active based on frequency and intensity of self-reported physical activity. Inactive people who were not depressed in 1965 had a 70% increase in risk of depression in 1974 compared to those who were initially highly active. Associations between changes in activity from 1965 to 1983 and symptoms of depression in 1983 suggested that the risk of depression was alterable by increasing exercise, but this association was not independent of the other risk factors for depression.

▼ In a study of about 10,000 Harvard male alumni from the mid-1960s through 1977, physical activity was shown to reduce the likelihood of developing physician-diagnosed depression (Paffenbarger, Lee, and Leung 1994). Men who expended 1000 to 2500 kcal per week by walking, climbing stairs, or playing sports had 17% less risk of developing depression than their less active peers. Those who expended more than 2500 kcal per week had a 28% lower risk.

Other Risk Factors for Depression Often Controlled Statistically in Population Studies

- ▼ Age
- ▼ Education
- ▼ Chronic conditions
- ▼ Social isolation
- ▼ Perceived health
- ▼ Physical disability
- ▼ Physical symptoms
- ▼ Autonomy
- ▼ Stressful life events: moving, job loss, separation or divorce, death of spouse, and financial difficulties

Treating Depression: Experimental Studies

Most of the experimental research showing that exercise improves self-ratings of depressive mood has been done with mentally and physically healthy people, but some experiments involving people diagnosed with mild to moderate unipolar depression have shown improvements in mood after several weeks of moderately intense exercise. When the exercise program lasted several months, the improvements in people's self-ratings of depression

were as large as those usually seen after psychotherapy. The best results for fighting depression occurred when outpatients were in an exercise program and also received psychotherapy. A few studies of exercise programs lasting four to six months showed improvements comparable to those typically seen after drug treatment. Though exercise appears comparable to drug therapy for treating mild to moderate depression, its clinical effects on reducing symptoms occur later than they do with drug therapy. The minimal or optimal type or amount of exercise for reducing depression is not yet known; but it appears that an increase in physical fitness is not required, and resistance exercise has been effective in a few studies.

© Photo Network

Various types of physical activity can help alleviate and reduce the risk for depression.

Reviews and Meta-Analyses

Several reviews and meta-analyses of exercise and depression research support the notion that exercise reduces the risk of depression and has a beneficial effect for those who are depressed (see table 7.2 and figure 7.5 for summaries of results). Evi-

Table 7.2

Exercise and Depression: Reviews

Gleser and Mendelberg (1990): 13 training studies

Evidence for fitness effects on depression was mixed.

Sport and exercise were as effective as traditional treatments.

One-year follow-up results indicated sustained effects of exercise on depression.

Bryne and Bryne (1993): 10 mixed studies

90% found exercise to be as effective as an antidepressant.

Martinsen (1990, 1993, 1994): Three reviews of studies of clinically anxious and depressed individuals with at least quasi-experimental design

Exercise is more effective than no treatment and as effective as traditional treatments (group psychotherapy, individual therapy, and meditative relaxation).

Changes in aerobic fitness are not necessary to achieve psychological benefits.

The clinically depressed have lower fitness than nondepressed people.

Exercise adherence rates for inpatient and outpatient depressed individuals are similar to those in the general population.

Exercise can be a useful adjunct to traditional therapies.

dence for improvements from acute exercise and at follow-up in training studies suggests that the antidepressant effects of exercise are both immediate and long-term. Exercise also compares well with traditional forms of treatment in these studies.

Exercise Training Studies

Most studies involving chronic exercise and depression have used an aerobic exercise intervention such as walking and/or jogging. However, the types of people studied, degree of initial depression, use of comparison groups, and implementation of the exercise program have varied among studies.

***B**oth aerobic exercise training and resistance exercise training have a positive effect on patients with clinical depression.*

Martinsen, Medhus, and Sandvik (1985) and Martinsen, Hoffart, and Solberg (1989) examined the effects of exercise training on depression in hospitalized psychiatric patients diagnosed with major depression. In the first study, 43 patients

were randomly assigned to either exercise or an occupational therapy control group in addition to their standard treatment, which included psychotherapy and medication. After nine weeks of training, patients in the exercise group exhibited significantly larger reductions in self-reported symptoms of depression relative to the control group. In the second study, 99 inpatients diagnosed with unipolar depressive disorders (major depression, dysthymic disorder, and atypical depression) were randomly assigned to either aerobic or nonaerobic exercise. Following eight weeks of training, both groups exhibited significant reductions in depression scores as shown in figure 7.6a. However, the change in depression scores did not differ between the two conditions, although the aerobic group exhibited significant increases in maximal oxygen uptake ($\dot{V}O_2$max) compared to no change in $\dot{V}O_2$max for the nonaerobic group (figure 7.6b). Thus, both forms of exercise were effective in reducing depressive symptoms.

Doyne et al. (1987) compared the effectiveness of aerobic exercise and resistance exercise in decreasing depression. Forty females aged 18 to 35 years who were diagnosed according to Research Diagnostic Criteria for depression were assigned

North, McCullagh, and Tran (1990): 80 cross-sectional or longitudinal, published or unpublished studies

▼ Exercise groups decreased depression scores 0.53 standard deviation *(SD)* more than comparison groups (overall effect size [ES] –0.53 ± 0.85).

▼ There were significant effects for all forms of depression, aerobic and anaerobic exercise, and exercise programs of varying length.

▼ Acute and chronic exercise significantly decreased depression.

▼ Subject characteristics

– Health accounted for more variance than most of the other variables coded.

– Effects were greatest for those initially most physically and psychologically unhealthy (ES of –0.94 ± 1.16).

– Middle-aged (25-64) group showed the largest decrease in depression compared to other age groups (ES of –0.74 ± 0.95).

▼ Program characteristics

– Longer programs had larger effects (ES of –2.93 for 21-24 weeks and ES of –0.11 for less than 4 weeks).

– Both aerobic and anaerobic exercises had significant effects on depression.

▼ Exercise had better antidepressant effects than relaxation and enjoyable activities.

▼ Exercise was as effective as psychotherapy, but exercise and psychotherapy together were better than exercise alone.

Craft and Landers (1998): 30 studies of chronic exercise with clinically depressed subjects

▼ Exercise groups were 3/4 *SD* less depressed than comparison groups (overall ES of –0.72 ± 0.10 standard error).

▼ Subjects who were moderately to severely depressed showed a greater decrease in depression than those who were mildly to moderately depressed.

▼ There were no differences for age, sex, intensity, duration, frequency, or change in fitness.

▼ Exercise was not different from other types of treatments.

▼ The longer-duration training programs had larger effects than the shorter ones.

Lawlor and Hopker (2001): 14 randomized controlled trials of chronic exercise with people diagnosed as having depression.

▼ Exercises had a 1.1 *SD* (95% CI: –1.5 to –0.6) reduction in depression symptoms, usually measured by the Beck Depression Inventory (a 7-point scale reduction; 95% CI: –10 to –4.6), when compared to people who received no treatment.

▼ Exercise effects were similar to the effects of cognitive therapy.

▼ The studies had important methodology weaknesses (e.g., use of volunteers, use of symptom ratings rather than clinical diagnosis as the outcome measure, failure to conceal group assignment, exclusion of drop-outs from the analysis) that clouded a clear determination about the independent effectiveness of exercise for treating depression.

Figure 7.5 Summary of results on exercise and depression from meta-analyses.

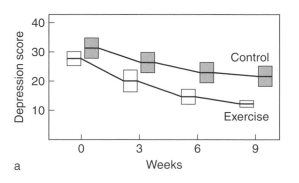
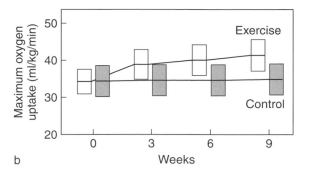

Figure 7.6 Depression decreased after eight weeks of exercise *(a)*, regardless of whether maximal aerobic fitness increased *(b)*.

Adapted, by permission, from E.W. Martinsen, A. Medhus, and L. Sandvik, 1985, "Effects of aerobic exercise on depression: A controlled study," *British Medical Journal* (Clinical Research Edition) 291 (July 13): 109. Copyright 1985 by BMJ Publishing Group.

Depression has decreased after both strength training and endurance exercise training.

to aerobic exercise (running) or weightlifting groups. After eight weeks of exercise training, both exercise groups exhibited significant reductions in depression scores while the waiting list control group exhibited no changes. The reduction in depression scores was similar for the two forms of exercise. Results from these two studies imply that changes in aerobic capacity are not necessary for antidepressant effects of physical activity.

Singh, Clements, and Fiatarone (1997) conducted a 10-week progressive resistance exercise training study among elderly subjects who met *DSM-IV* criteria for major or minor depression or dysthymia.

Compared to a health education comparison group, the resistance exercisers had larger reductions (about 4-5 *SD*) in depressive symptoms on both Beck Depression Inventory self-ratings and diagnostic interview ratings by clinicians.

Fremont and Craighead (1987) compared aerobic exercise to traditional psychotherapy for depression in a sample of 49 men and women 19 to 62 years of age with self-reported symptoms of mild-to-moderate depression. Participants were randomly assigned to a supervised running group, individual cognitive psychotherapy, or combined running and psychotherapy. After 10 weeks of treatment, all groups exhibited significant reductions in depression scores, but there were no differences among the groups (see figure 7.7). Thus, exercise was found to be as effective as traditional psychotherapy, but there was no additional benefit when exercise was added to psychotherapy.

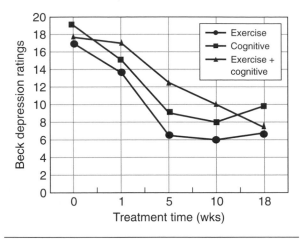

Figure 7.7 Changes in self-reported symptoms of depression for men and women randomly assigned to supervised running, individual cognitive psychotherapy, or running plus psychotherapy.

Data from Fremont and Craighead 1987.

Aerobic exercise was compared to standard medication in a training study of 156 older men and women who were clinically diagnosed with major depressive disorder (Blumenthal et al. 1999). Par-

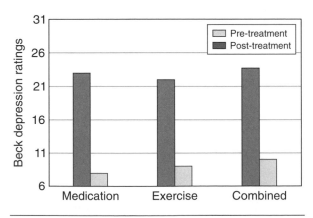

Figure 7.8 Decreases in depression after 16 weeks for groups of older men and women clinically diagnosed with major depressive disorder randomly assigned to groups receiving antidepressant medication, aerobic exercise, or aerobic exercise plus medication.

Data from Blumenthal et al. 1999.

ticipants were randomly assigned to aerobic exercise, antidepressants, or combined exercise and medication. After the 16-week program, all three groups demonstrated similar decreases in depression that were statistically and clinically significant (see figure 7.8). The medication-only group exhibited the fastest initial response; but by the end of the program, the exercise treatment was equally effective in reducing depression in this older sample. It is worth noting that a follow-up study of these older men and women reported that patients in the exercise group were more likely to be fully recovered and less likely to have relapsed into depression six months after treatment than the drug treatment patients (see figure 7.9) (Babyak et al. 2000).

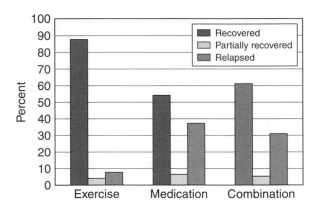

Figure 7.9 Extent of recovery and relapse among men and women with major depressive order six months after treatment. Groups were exercise, medication, and medication plus exercise.

Reprinted, by permission, from M. Babyak, J.A. Blumenthal, S. Herman, P. Khatri, M. Doraiswamy, K. Moore, W.E. Craighead, T.T. Baldewicz, and K.R. Krishnan, 2000, "Exercise treatment for major depression: Maintenance of therapeutic benefit at 10 months," *Psychosomatic Medicine* 62 (5): 633–638.

Exercise Can Benefit Depression During Recovery From Physical Illness

About a dozen experiments have shown that patients recovering from a heart attack report a moderate reduction in self-rated depression (about 1/2 *SD*) when they participate in a cardiac rehabilitation exercise program (Kugler, Seelbach, and Kruskemper 1994). Improvements in symptoms of depression have also been reported among breast cancer survivors who exercised (Segar et al. 1998).

How Much Is Enough?

It is important to learn how much physical activity is minimally or optimally needed to help protect against or treat depression. At present, there does not seem to be a clear dose response between the intensity or total amount of daily physical activity and depression. On balance, though, it appears that being sedentary increases risk for depression but that high levels of exercise may not be more protective against depression than lower levels.

In the Canada Fitness Survey (Stephens 1988), people were seemingly protected from symptoms of depression if their daily leisure energy expenditure was at least 1 kcal/kg body weight per day, which is a low level of activity (e.g., about 20 min of walking). Risk of depression was not further reduced when the energy expenditure was raised to 2 to 5 kcal/kg body weight per day.

Data from the Harvard alumni study (Paffenbarger, Lee, and Leung 1994) did suggest a dose-dependent reduction in depression with increased exercise; this occurred after more than 3 h of vigorous sports or 2500 kcal of expenditure per week (figure 7.10). However, the significance of those findings is limited, because fewer than 1 in 10 adults in America expend this much energy in leisure-time physical activity.

The effects of setting and exercise intensity on depressive mood were examined in a study of 357 healthy older adults without clinical depression

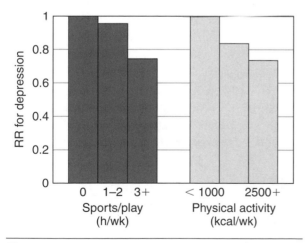

Figure 7.10 The analysis of activity habits from 1962 through 1966 and incidence of depression during 23- to 27-year follow-up among Harvard alumni (*N* = 10,201 males) shows that Relative Risk (RR) for depression was improved with some regular activity.

Data from Paffenbarger, Lee, and Leung 1994.

(King, Taylor, and Haskell 1993). Sedentary men and women between the ages of 50 and 65 were randomly assigned to one of three exercise training programs (i.e., high-intensity group exercise, high-intensity home exercise, and low-intensity home exercise). After 12 months, no significant differences between groups were observed. However, subsequent data analysis revealed an inverse relationship between level of exercise participation and depression scores independent of exercise format and intensity.

*E*xcessive exercise training in athletics (i.e., overtraining) can induce depressive states in some athletes (Morgan 1994b). A majority of youth and adults are sedentary, though, so depression resulting from overtraining is not a concern for the general population.

Though a few studies have tested the effects of resistance or flexibility exercise on depression, most have used jogging as the mode of activity; a few used cycling. Exercise training usually was prescribed based on the guidelines of the American College of Sports Medicine for the types and amounts of exercise recommended for cardiorespiratory fitness in otherwise healthy people (see table 12.4 on p. 239). Because no adverse effects were reported in these studies, the following exercise guidelines should be appropriate for people with depression who are otherwise healthy:

▼ Three to five days a week

▼ 20 to 60 min each session

▼ 55% to 90% of maximal heart rate

People beginning an exercise program should always increase the intensity and length of their workouts gradually, but gradual progress is especially important for someone who is depressed. Gradual progress helps to maximize feelings of success, as well as to control and minimize potential feelings of failure that can arise if the person can't sustain the program because it called for too quick a progression. It is important to remember that continued participation is more important for reducing depression than increasing fitness is. Figure 7.11 illustrates how sustaining an exercise program fits into the broader scheme of reducing relapse during the treatment of depression.

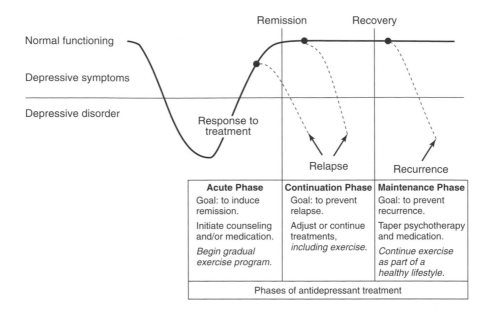

Figure 7.11 Exercise in relation to relapse during treatment for depression.

Reprinted, by permission, from H.A. O'Neal, A.L. Dunn, and E.W. Martinsen, 2000, "Depression and Exercise," *International Journal of Sport Psychology* 31 (2): 110–135. Adapted from D.J. Kupfer, "Long-term treatment of depression," *The Journal of Clinical Psychiatry* 52 (5 suppl.): 28–34. 1991. Copyright 1991, Physicians Postgraduate Press. Reprinted by permission.

Recommendations for Supervising Exercise Training of Persons With Depression

▼ *Be familiar with the symptoms and basic treatment of mental disorders and have referral sources on hand.* If someone expresses emotional or psychological problems that seem to be beyond normal adjustment issues, you may want to express concern and have available some names and numbers of local resources to let the person know that professional help is available. Be tactful! It is important for all health care providers to be knowledgeable about how to recognize and respond to suicidal ideation. Familiarize yourself with commonly prescribed medications for depression. People may feel more comfortable reporting information about medications rather than providing a psychiatric diagnosis on the intake. Also, some medications may have side effects, such as weight gain or fatigue, that may influence a person's motivation to exercise.

▼ *Avoid minimizing the person's feelings or concerns.* Most people prefer someone who simply listens and exhibits compassion rather than someone who attempts to soothe or give advice. For person-centered psychotherapy, the core conditions for change are genuineness, empathy, and warmth. Avoid making your regard for the patient dependent upon the person's meeting your standards for exercise participation.

▼ *Establish boundaries in your relationships with your patients.* As you develop a rapport with your patients, it is likely that you will encounter someone who begins to think of you as a counselor. Be supportive and encouraging while avoiding fostering dependence. For most people you work with, this will not be a problem. However, a person with a mental disorder may latch onto the first individual who seems to take a sincere interest in his or her life, and boundaries may be difficult to establish. It is your responsibility to set the limits of your relationship with patients according to professional ethics and what is comfortable for you.

▼ *Assess current physical activity habits and fitness.* Because individuals with depression have difficulty managing time and accomplishing daily tasks, they may overestimate the amount and intensity of physical activity. Any activity may seem like a tremendous burden. For individuals who exhibit motor retardation and hypersomnia, daily activity may be reduced beyond that of a typical sedentary person and consequently their fitness may be low. People in this situation may question their ability to perform *any* exercise and should be reassured that the program will be designed specifically for them.

▼ *Determine the person's motivation for exercise.* What by-product of exercise has meaning for this person? Is the motivation internal or external? Are there specific goals the person wants to accomplish? Are these goals realistic? It is important to consider the individual's motivation in the context of his or her mental state in order to establish goals, prescribe the appropriate exercise, promote adherence, and help the person develop a positive perception of exercise and self.

▼ *Make the exercise enjoyable and nonthreatening.* Since low motivation, fatigue, and reduced pleasure are core symptoms of depression, it is important to make the activity as pleasurable as possible. One way to do this is to find out what activities the individual has enjoyed in the past and create an environment that reflects his or her interests. Identify and minimize the features of exercise that the person finds intimidating. One individual may enjoy the social aspect of group aerobics while another finds a group atmosphere threatening. And although you want to avoid making the exercise too hard, it is also important to avoid making the exercise so easy that it seems like a waste of time or a "non-accomplishment."

▼ *Make the exercise accessible.* Getting the person to the exercise session may be the biggest hurdle. Discuss and develop plans for overcoming the barriers that could prevent the individual from attending an exercise session (time, transportation, work and family conflicts, etc). This step may require you to help the individual problem solve at the most basic level. For example, you may have to help work out an alternative plan if the person's spouse has to use the car at the scheduled exercise time.

▼ *Encourage personal responsibility by including the person in the planning of the exercise program.* The degree of control that the patient is willing or able to handle will vary with the individual. Avoid overwhelming people by giving them too much responsibility, but at the same time try to promote a sense of independence and accomplishment. Watch for cues that will let you know what is right for each person, and be ready to give or take more control as needed. Don't let the individual give you the credit for his or her success. Encourage the person to take pride in his or her accomplishments, no matter how small.

▼ *Be prepared for nonadherence and excuses.* It is important to be nonjudgmental. Avoid blaming, and try to minimize the opportunity for guilt and self-blame. Don't allow the individual to magnify a lapse into a total sense of failure. Plan for lapses and trouble situations, and problem solve in advance with the patient's input. Don't accept vague excuses; instead, identify a concrete, modifiable cause for the lapse and develop strategies to overcome the barrier. View lapses as a learning process, and establish an opportunity for success as soon as possible after a lapse.

▼ *Encourage the person to increase physical activity outside the established exercise sessions.* Set small, readily attainable activity goals (established by joint agreement) that the person can accomplish between sessions. Have the person keep a record of his or her activity habits, barriers/setbacks, exercise accomplishments, and so on to use as a tool for future problem-solving sessions. For example, use of step counters is a simple and inexpensive way to encourage self-monitoring and goal setting.

▼ *Watch for sabotage.* Habits, whether psychological or exercise-related, become comfortable, and any departure from that "comfort zone" may be resisted by the patient or by significant others who depend on that person to behave in a certain way. Thus, there may be subtle attempts by the patient or others to discourage change, and these potential deterrents of change should be identified and addressed directly.

▼ *Be aware of what behavior is being reinforced.* For many people, negative attention is better than no attention. If you always express concern for missed sessions or are more attentive when people appear anxious/depressed, then that behavior may increase. Positively reinforce the desired behavior in a way that is meaningful for the individual. Remember that what is reinforcing for one person may not be reinforcing for another.

Reprinted, by permission, from H.A. O'Neal, A.L. Dunn, and E.W. Martinsen, 2000, "Depression and exercise," *International Journal of Sport Psychology* 31 (2): 133–135.

*B*eing sedentary increases the risk for depression, but high levels of physical activity may not be any more protective than moderate amounts of physical activity.

*W*eaknesses in research on exercise and depression include using subjects who were not depressed, measuring depression only with self-report, not including a placebo control group, and inadequately documenting the exercise stimulus used in the training protocol.

Mechanisms

There is ample evidence that exercise is associated with decreases in depression, but we are still discovering the underlying reasons for these antidepressant effects. Explanations for this association are based on social, cognitive, and biological mechanisms. Possible social cognitive explanations for antidepressant effects associated with exercise programs include subjective expectations, diversion from stressful stimuli, attention, improved self-image, feelings of control, social interaction, and social support (see figure 7.12) (Ernst, Rand, and Stevinson 1998). Although plausible, these explanations have not been empirically tested in well-designed studies (O'Neal, Dunn, and Martinsen 2000). Also, even if shown to be true, they would not provide an explanation of a direct effect of physical activity independent of the setting in which the physical activity occurred. For example, in one study, 30 mildly depressed elderly men and women were randomly assigned to either 20 min of outdoor walking with a student or 20 min of social contact with a student twice weekly for six weeks or to a waiting-list control group (McNeil, LeBlanc, and Joyner 1991). As figure 7.13 shows, the reductions in depression after walking were the same as after merely meeting weekly with a student. Hence, it is possible that the social contact with the student was responsible for the depression reduc-

tion in both conditions. Walking might have been superfluous to the antidepressant effect.

Biological mechanisms offer more potential for establishing a direct, causal relationship. However, even biological explanations might not directly support an independent effect of exercise on reducing depression. For example, bright light treatment is effective for some depression; thus, exercising in bright sunlight might reduce depression more because of the light exposure than because of the exercise. Nonetheless, to support biological plausibility, explanations for reductions in depression with increased physical activity should be consistent with what is known about the etiology of depression and about biological adaptations that occur with physical activity.

*E*xercise may decrease depression because of psychosocial benefits, such as enhanced self-esteem or increased social support.

Neurobiology of Depression

Some background on the etiology of depression can help in making the link between changes in symptoms of depression and exercise adaptations. The two most prominent neurobiological models of depression are the monoamine hypothesis and the hypothalamus-pituitary-adrenal (HPA) axis model.

*T*he biological basis of depression is centered in dysregulation of the monoamine system and the HPA axis.

Monoamine Hypothesis

Critical insight into the neurobiology of depression began to develop in the 1950s when unexpected psychological side effects were noted from medications prescribed for physical illnesses. Depressive symptoms were found in 15% of hypertensive patients treated with reserpine. Reserpine controls blood pressure by inactivating storage

Proposed Psychosocial Mechanisms for Effects of Exercise on Depression

Subjective expectations: Prevailing folk wisdom is that exercise makes you feel better, so individuals might begin exercise with the expectation that their moods will improve (placebo effect).

Diversion from stressful stimuli: Decreases in anxiety and depression may be explained by a "time-out," or distraction, from worries and concerns during an exercise session. The psychological respite from stress emotions may have residual effects that are strengthened with each exercise session, and the mood improvement can reinforce repeated bouts of activity.

Attention: Individuals involved in exercise programs typically have one-on-one contact with fitness professionals and other participants. The positive attention from others may foster a sense of value and self-worth in that the attention implies that the depressed individual is important to others.

Improved self-image: Physical adaptations to regular exercise include some cosmetic benefits, such as increased muscle tone, in addition to improved exercise tolerance. Physical self-concept can be enhanced, and along with it self-esteem, which is a critical psychological variable in mental health.

Feelings of control: Feelings of helplessness and hopelessness are core in depression. Participation in exercise enables the depressed individual to exert control over one aspect of his or her life. Re-establishing a sense of power in one area may transfer to perceptions of control in other areas of life and increase a sense of hope.

Social interaction: Social isolation can be a contributing and sustaining factor in depression, and participating in exercise programs in a hospital, community center, or commercial fitness center can provide personal contact that may decrease a sense of isolation.

Social support: Exercising with others can offer the depressed person opportunities for tangible and intangible validation that he or she is important to others, as well as instilling a sense of being part of a community.

Figure 7.12   Although these mechanisms are plausible, a direct, causal relationship between physical activity and depression has not yet been empirically tested.

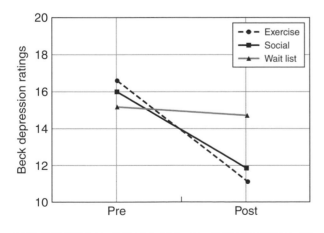

Figure 7.13   Reduction of depression after an exercise program (walking) versus regularly scheduled social contact with another person.

Data from McNeil, LeBlanc, and Joyner 1991.

granules containing norepinephrine (NE) and serotonin (5-HT) in peripheral nerves, thus depleting NE and serotonin intracellularly. Because it is an alkaloid, reserpine can cross the blood-brain barrier. Hence, a side effect appeared to be depletion of NE and serotonin in the brain, contributing to depressed mood in some people. About the same time, improved mood was observed as a side effect of treating tuberculosis with iproniazid, which inhibits monoamine oxidase (MAO), an enzyme that degrades NE and 5-HT. Studies conducted in the 1960s and 1970s showed reduced levels of metabolites of NE (i.e., MHPG, see chapter 3) and metabolites of serotonin (i.e., 5-HIAA) in some depressed populations compared to people without clinical disorders. In addition, patients who had bipolar depression secreted low levels of MHPG (NE metabolite) when depressed and

Social contact during physical activity might be a mechanism for the antidepressive effects of exercise.

Provided by CRIS Senior Service.

Table 7.3	
Functions of Norepinephrine and Serotonin in the Central Nervous System	
Norepinephrine	**Serotonin**
Hormonal release	Sensory perception
Cardiovascular functioning	Regulation of pain
Rapid eye movement sleep	Fatigue
Analgesic responses	Appetitive behavior
Arousal	Periodicity of sleep
Reward	Temperature regulation
Sexual behavior	Corticosteroid activity
Vigilance	Dreams
Regulation of mood	

above-normal levels when manic. The evidence for a relationship between levels of NE and/or serotonin and depression led to the **monoamine depletion hypothesis** of depression.

According to the **depletion hypothesis,** depression is caused by a deficiency of NE at central **adrenergic** receptors and/or a deficiency of serotonin, and mania results from excessive NE. Norepinephrine and serotonin, as discussed previously, are major neurotransmitters whose functions in modulating most brain areas involved in stress and mood make them prime candidates in the etiology of depression (see table 7.3 and chapter 3, pp. 54–57). In addition, there is a structural and functional relationship between **noradrenergic** and serotonergic systems. For example, there are projections from the locus coeruleus (LC), the main NE-producing cell in the brainstem, to the raphe nuclei that synthesize brain serotonin, as well as to serotonin-producing cells surrounding the LC.

In support of the depletion hypothesis, the primary action of several antidepressant medications is to increase levels of NE and/or serotonin. Most common antidepressant drugs up-regulate central nervous system α-adrenergic and serotonergic receptors, down-regulate postsynaptic β-adrenergic receptors (or inhibit the second messenger, adenylate cyclase) or prevent the metabolism of neurotransmitters after they are released (see table 7.4). Antidepressants are significantly more effective than placebo for treating depressive disorders (Williams et al. 2000). Drug treatment alters the levels of NE and serotonin within hours—but, importantly, changes in symptoms do not occur for about two to three weeks.

The delay in symptom reduction when levels of neurotransmitters were increased challenged the depletion hypothesis. The etiology and maintenance of depression are not as simple as a deficiency of NE or serotonin, and ensuing studies have not supported depletion of neurotransmitters as a cause of depression. For example, some depressed patients have high or normal levels of MHPG, and lower levels of MHPG in the cerebral spinal fluid (CSF) have not been verified. Two effective treatments for depression, electroconvulsive shock treatment and the drug iprindole, do not affect monoamine levels (Maas 1979).

The monoamine model was modified to describe depression as a function of **dysregulation** of the noradrenergic and serotonergic systems rather than only a matter of decreased transmitter levels. Depression is thought to result from a disruption in these neurotransmitter systems' self-regulating abilities and from overstimulation of neural centers such as the prefrontal cortex, amygdala, hippocampus, and periventricular gray. A major proposed site of dysregulation is the LC.

A key response to low levels of NE is up-regulation (i.e., an increase in the number or sensi-

Table 7.4	
Classes of Antidepressant Drugs	
Drug class	**Actions**
Tricyclics (TCAs)	Alter the brain's responses to the neurotransmitters norepinephrine (NE) and serotonin (i.e., prevent reuptake of NE and serotonin by blocking presynaptic receptors) *Monoaminergic agonists—keep neurotransmitters in contact with postsynaptic receptors, which prolongs the effects*
Monoamine oxidase inhibitors (MAOIs)	Block the action of an enzyme (MAO) that breaks down the transmitters NE, dopamine, and serotonin within the neuron *Increase the release of these neurotransmitters*
Selective serotonin reuptake inhibitors (SSRIs)	Target the serotonergic system and enhance the activity of serotonin by preventing its reuptake by the neuron after release into the synapse

tivity) of postsynaptic β_1 receptors for NE. That response can then lead to a hyperresponsiveness of neurons to NE when it is released into the synapse. A hallmark feature of therapeutic response to antidepressant drugs is a down-regulation of β_1 receptors and a return to normal sensitivity to NE. An intact brain serotonergic system is needed for that response.

In addition, presynaptic α_2 autoreceptors are normally involved in negative feedback to control the release of NE. With decreased levels of NE, there is decreased self-inhibition of the LC by its α_2 autoreceptors. Negative feedback is removed, leading to excessive release of NE from LC neurons. That response can lead to temporary depletion of NE in the brain because of excessive firing of NE cells during stress. Because the main action of NE is to modulate the firing rates of other cells in the brain by inhibition, the end result can be hyperactivity of neural centers that regulate negative moods such as depression.

Much of the physiological research on depression has focused on the brain monoaminergic systems, particularly noradrenergic and serotonergic systems. However, the monoamine dopamine (DA) should also be considered in the etiology of depression (O'Neal, Dunn, and Martinsen 2000). A main area of DA-producing cells in the brain is the ventral tegmental area (VTA), a horseshoe-shaped area surrounding the hypothalamus. Electrical stimulation of the VTA produces pleasure. Though NE is not a major neurotransmitter in the VTA, depletion of brain NE appears to indirectly suppress normal activity of DA in the VTA. The

DA system plays a critical role in reward, motivation, and motor functions. For example, natural rewards and reinforcement involve the release of DA in the nucleus accumbens (see chapter 3).

Thus, dysregulation of this system may contribute to the anhedonia (i.e., loss of pleasure) and psychomotor disturbances that are observed in depression. For example, disturbances in dopaminergic projections to limbic structures have been shown in response to prolonged elevations in corticotropin-releasing hormone (CRH) and cortisol with chronic stress (Chrousos 1998), and certain antidepressant drugs influence dopaminergic activity by targeting DA receptors or altering DA metabolism (Willner 1995).

Hypothalamus-Pituitary-Adrenal Axis Model

The integration of neurobiological systems (i.e., HPA axis and monoamine) in depression is illustrated by the need for adequate concentrations of **glucocorticoids** for normal NE function (Gold and Chrousos 1999). There is considerable evidence that the HPA axis plays an integral role in the etiology of depression. For example, symptoms of depression, such as weight loss and sleep disturbances, can be directly linked to disruptions in the HPA axis.

The HPA axis plays a major role in the stress response (see chapter 4), and a dysregulation in the stress response has been implicated in the etiology of depression. When a real or imagined threat is perceived, the paraventricular nucleus (PVN) of the hypothalamus releases CRH into the median eminence of the anterior pituitary. Corticotropin-releasing hormone acts on the pituitary to signal the release of adrenocorticotropic hormone (ACTH) and β-endorphin from the precursor molecule, proopiomelanocorticotropin. Adrenocorticotropic hormone then exerts its effect on the adrenal gland to stimulate increased synthesis and release of cortisol from the adrenal cortex. The integrated function of this system is to prepare the body for fight or flight. (Please refer to chapter 3 and see chapter 4 for a more detailed description of the physiological response to stress.)

Functions of the Hypothalamus-Pituitary-Adrenal Axis

- ▼ Regulation of hunger and satiety
- ▼ Sexual behavior
- ▼ Sleep
- ▼ Growth
- ▼ Hormonal secretions
- ▼ Regulation of the physiological response to stress

Though activation of this system is critical for an appropriate stress response, excess activation of the HPA axis may play a role in the development of depression. In fact, symptoms of melancholia resemble a state of profound stress and can be precipitated by stress (Gold and Chrousos 1999). Hippocampal cells contain glucocorticoid receptors that mediate the suppression of the CRH neuron in the hypothalamus (see figure 7.14). Normally, when high levels of cortisol feed back to glucocorticoid receptors at the level of the hippocampus and hypothalamus, there is a subsequent *reduction* in the production of CRH and corticosteroid secretions (i.e., negative feedback—output inhibits the activity of the initial input). However, hypercortisolism can damage hippocampal glucocorticoid receptors that produce feedback inhibition of the HPA axis, down-regulating the hippocampal receptors and leading to overactivation of the HPA axis. Hypercortisolism may also result in abnormally high levels of cortisol and ACTH by altering the brainstem monoaminergic system or other neural systems that regulate HPA function, such as the amygdala and prefrontal cortex (Gold and Chrousos 1999). Indeed, hypercortisolism is found in about

50% of depressed patients. With depression, there is also an overall increase in ACTH, a loss of sensitivity in steroid-negative feedback, and an increased sensitivity to all doses of CRH. Because CRH and glucocorticoids influence limbic structures important in emotional responding, including the nucleus accumbens, amygdala, and hippocampus, elevated levels of CRH and cortisol under conditions of chronic stress may disrupt functioning in brain regions that regulate emotion (Gold and Chrousos 1999).

Evidence for Biological Plausibility of Exercise Affecting Depression

There are virtually no studies examining the biological mechanisms that could explain the antidepressant effects of physical activity and exercise among humans. However, several encouraging lines of research using the methods of neuroscience and animal models of stress and depression have emerged in exercise psychology during the past decade.

Monoamine Dysregulation Hypothesis

According to the **monoamine dysregulation hypothesis,** depression is the result of a dysregulation in the biogenic monoamine system. Thus, exercise may decrease depression by exerting a regulatory influence on this neurotransmitter system. For example, there is some evidence that chronic exercise affects NE and 5-HT receptors on the brainstem, and brainstem NE neurons project to the ventral tegmentum, a major reward center. Exercise adaptations, such as increased synthesis of monoamines, could affect limbic structures through a connection with motor neurons; and sensory afferents from muscles could stimulate higher brain centers by way of the thalamus.

*E*xercise may decrease depression through adaptations such as increased synthesis of NE and serotonin in the central nervous system.

The aim of a number of human and animal studies has been to describe the effects of exercise on

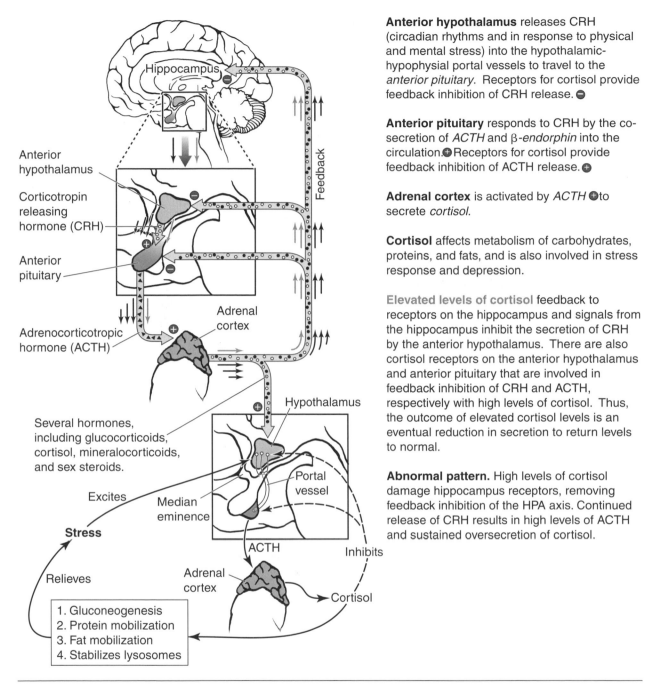

Anterior hypothalamus releases CRH (circadian rhythms and in response to physical and mental stress) into the hypothalamic-hypophysial portal vessels to travel to the *anterior pituitary*. Receptors for cortisol provide feedback inhibition of CRH release. ⊖

Anterior pituitary responds to CRH by the co-secretion of *ACTH* and β-*endorphin* into the circulation.⊕Receptors for cortisol provide feedback inhibition of ACTH release. ⊕

Adrenal cortex is activated by *ACTH* ⊕to secrete *cortisol*.

Cortisol affects metabolism of carbohydrates, proteins, and fats, and is also involved in stress response and depression.

Elevated levels of cortisol feedback to receptors on the hippocampus and signals from the hippocampus inhibit the secretion of CRH by the anterior hypothalamus. There are also cortisol receptors on the anterior hypothalamus and anterior pituitary that are involved in feedback inhibition of CRH and ACTH, respectively with high levels of cortisol. Thus, the outcome of elevated cortisol levels is an eventual reduction in secretion to return levels to normal.

Abnormal pattern. High levels of cortisol damage hippocampus receptors, removing feedback inhibition of the HPA axis. Continued release of CRH results in high levels of ACTH and sustained oversecretion of cortisol.

Figure 7.14 Actions and effects of corticotropin-releasing hormone on the hypothalamus-pituitary-adrenal (HPA) axis (normal and abnormal patterns).

Redrawn, by permission, from M.R. Rosenzweig, A.L. Leiman, and S.M. Breedlove, 1999, *Biological psychology: An introduction to behaviorial, cognitive, and clinical neuroscience*, 2nd ed. (Sunderland, MA: Sinauer Associates), 125.

NE and its synthesis and metabolism. In humans, changes in brain NE activity after acute physical activity have been estimated by measuring levels of MHPG (the primary NE metabolite) in urine, plasma, or (rarely) cerebral spinal fluid. Studies with depressed and nondepressed subjects have found either an increase or no change in levels of urinary MHPG after acute exercise. The meaning of these studies for understanding exercise and depression is unclear, though. For example, at rest only about one-third of the MHPG in peripheral blood or urine comes from metabolism of brain NE. In acute exercise that is light to moderate intensity, NE levels have been shown to increase two-to sixfold, but most of this increase comes not from the brain but from sympathetic post-ganglionic nerve endings innervating the heart, with some coming from the exercising skeletal muscles. This increase in NE is related to biological adjustments to meet the strain of exercise. Levels and changes in NE or serotonin in specific brain regions must be assessed to determine central effects of exercise training. But this is understandably difficult in human research, and the use of brain imaging methods to study the effects of exercise on depression has not yet been reported.

Animal research has provided better evidence for a mediating effect of exercise on monoaminergic systems implicated in depression. Studies have shown changes in brain NE and 5-HT levels with acute and chronic exercise in rats (Dishman, Renner, et al. 2000; Dunn and Dishman 1991; Dunn, Reigle et al. 1996). Also, chronic exercise of moderate intensity has been accompanied by reduced release of NE in the brain cortex (Pagliari and Peyrin 1995b), shown in figure 7.15, and down-regulation of β-adrenergic receptors in the brain cortex (Yoo et al. 2000; Yoo et al. 1999), comparable to the effects of antidepressant drug treatment. A key action of antidepressant drugs known as selective serotonin reuptake inhibitors (SSRIs) is inhibition of the serotonin transporter (SERT), a protein that transports serotonin molecules back into the serotonin cell after release. This blocks reuptake, leaving serotonin in the synapse longer and presumably providing more molecules for binding with 5-HT receptors postsynaptically (see figure 7.16).

Though chronic exercise has been shown to increase levels of brain 5-HT, a recent study showed no effect of chronic treadmill running on messenger RNA (ribonucleic acid) for SERT in the dorsal raphe nucleus (Van Hoomissen et al. 2002).

Researchers treated neonate male rats with clomipramine, a serotonin reuptake inhibitor that causes long-term depletion of brain NE and adult-onset depression in the rat. After reaching maturity, the rats that had exercised for 12 weeks by running either in activity wheels or on a treadmill had increased levels of NE in the brain frontal cortex compared to the sedentary controls (Yoo et al. 2000). Both exercise groups had increased levels of NE, while the activity-wheel runners had a therapeutic decrease in β-adrenergic receptors that was equal to the effect of an antidepressant drug and had improved sexual performance, a behavioral sign of an antidepressant effect.

A common model of human depression in animal studies is repeated exposure to uncontrollable, inescapable stress that results in depletion of brain NE or 5-HT and subsequent deficits in the animals' behavior to escape the stress when escape becomes possible. The first study to use that model after chronic exercise showed that sedentary rats had lower NE and 5-HIAA levels in LC, hippocampus, and amygdala after exposure to uncontrollable, inescapable foot shock when compared to rats that had been permitted to run on activity wheels for six weeks (Dishman et al. 1997). The sedentary animals also exhibited 28% higher 5-HT in the amygdala following foot shock. The activity-wheel

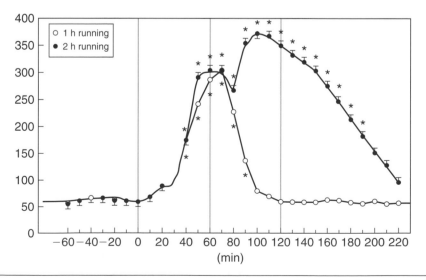

Figure 7.15 Changes in norepinephrine levels during treadmill running after treadmill exercise training.
Data from Pagliari and Peyrin 1995b.

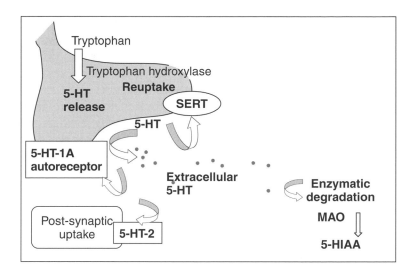

Figure 7.16 Diagram of a serotonin synapse that shows the possible fates of serotonin after it is released by the pre-synaptic neuron: post-synaptic uptake, binding with pre-synaptic autoreceptors, reuptake into pre-synaptic neuron via actions of SERT (serotonin transporter).

runners subsequently exhibited a quicker escape from controllable foot shock than sedentary animals, indicative of an antidepressant effect of the wheel running.

There is evidence that either acute or chronic exercise in animals influences dopaminergic activity, and changes in density and affinity of DA receptors have been shown following chronic training in animals (see Dishman et al. 1998 for a review). Those changes have been reported to occur in parts of the striatum, which regulates locomotion, rather than the VTA or nucleus accumbens. So, it is not known whether exercise affects DA in brain regions most involved with regulating moods like depression.

Hypothalamic-Pituitary-Adrenal Cortical Axis Hypothesis

Chronic exercise training results in a diminished endocrine response during standard exercise (Richter and Sutton 1994). Thus, effects of physical activity on the regulation of the HPA axis may be another means by which exercise affects depression. Animal studies provide some support for exercise-induced effects on the HPA axis that could be related to antidepressant effects. For example, treadmill-trained female rats had attenuated ACTH and corticosterone responses to treadmill running but a hyperresponsiveness of ACTH to immobilization stress (White-Welkley et al. 1995) and foot shock (White-Welkley et al.). Whether this hyperrespon-siveness of ACTH is a healthful adaptation and whether it is attributable to increased

CRH or other factors that affect CRH release are not known. Altered CRH activity with exercise would be particularly relevant for depression, since CRH increases activity of the brainstem LC. Recall that the LC plays a key regulatory role in modulating brain and peripheral sympathetic nervous system responses to appetitive and aversive behaviors that are central to depression.

*A*daptations in the HPA axis from exercise training may help to re-regulate disruptions that have fostered biological contributions to depression, but research on this issue is limited.

Other Biologically Based Hypotheses

The hypothesis that *increased brain blood flow* during acute exercise can explain changes in mood has not been developed in a way consistent with current evidence. Brain blood flow and metabolism are increased by various stressors in humans and rats (Bryan 1990), but the effects of exercise are unclear. Both animal and human studies using indirect estimates of blood flow (e.g., xenon clearance) suggest that cerebral flow is increased during acute exercise (e.g., Thomas et al. 1989). However, changes in regional distribution consistent with altered metabolism in brain areas most associated with emotion, such as the frontal cortex or limbic areas, have not been shown. Studies of dogs and miniature pigs have used radio-labeled microspheres that lodge in the microvasculature to measure brain blood flow during exercise. These studies suggest that increased flow to the cerebellum, motor-sensory cortex, and spinal cord (e.g., Gross, Marcus, and Heistad 1980), presumably due to locomotory demand, accounts for the increased brain blood flow during exercise. One nuclear imaging study showed increased glucose uptake (which is directly linked with blood flow) in the visual cortex of migraine patients after acute exercise (Hollmann et al. 1994); but at this point, brain imaging has not been used to study anxiety or depression after exercise.

The popular hypothesis that endorphins are responsible for changes in mood or anxiety following exercise remains plausible, but it has been perpetuated without much consideration of available evidence. Plasma β-endorphin is reliably elevated after release from the pituitary gland during intense exercise. A plausible link between peripheral β-endorphin or enkephalins and mood or analgesic responses to acute exercise has not been established. The bulk of the research has shown that opioid antagonists do not block mood changes after exercise. The ability of increased β-endorphin in the blood to have an influence on the brain is blocked by the blood-brain barrier to peptides at the body temperatures characteristic of typical exercise. There is no consensus on brain changes in opioid activity following exercise. While opioid-mediated analgesia could indirectly influence mood, exercise-induced analgesia has not yet been shown to explain improved mood in humans (Cook and Koltyn 2000). Peripheral opioid responses to acute exercise apparently inhibit catecholamine influences on cardiovascular, respiratory, and endocrine responses during exercise.

Summary

Major depression is a common mental health disorder that can have serious effects; it is characterized by significant distress or impairment in social or occupational functioning or both. Traditional treatments for depression are time consuming, costly, and often ineffective. Side effects of pharmacological interventions may include fatigue, cardiovascular complications, and possible addiction. Thus, exercise may be a desirable alternative or adjunct treatment. Overall, the literature supports some effect of exercise on reducing the primary risk of depression and alleviating symptoms in individuals diagnosed as having mild to moderate depression. In some studies, reductions in depression after exercise training have been as great as those seen after psychotherapy or drug therapy.

However, specific parameters of exercise type, frequency, and intensity necessary for optimizing positive effects are not yet established. Well-controlled studies that encompass a range of demographic groups and fully consider subject characteristics still are needed to determine whether the apparently protective effect of exercise against the risk of developing depression is an independent one and is consistent across gender, age, race/ethnicity, education, socioeconomic level, and mental status. Individuals with depression typically possess reduced levels of muscular endurance (Morgan 1968), physical working capacity (Morgan 1969), and cardiorespiratory fitness (O'Neal, Dunn, and Martinsen 2000; Martinsen, Strand, et al. 1989) compared to mentally healthy individuals. But it is possible to implement a carefully graduated exercise program successfully with proper attention to unique problems of treatment adherence. Though recent randomized controlled trials have added credence to the view that moderately intense exercise is an effective approach to reducing symptoms of mild to moderate depression, exercise is not yet medically recognized as a treatment for depression (American Psychiatric Association 2000). Understanding the mechanisms, especially neurobiological mechanisms, whereby exercise directly and independently reduces depression is one of the next frontiers of exercise psychology.

Suggested Readings

Drevets, W.C. 1998. Functional neuroimaging studies of depression: The anatomy of melancholia. *Annual Review of Medicine* 49: 341–361.

Ernst, E., J.I. Rand, and C. Stevinson. 1998. Complementary therapies for depression: An overview. *Archives of General Psychiatry* 55 (Nov): 1026–1032.

Gold, P.W., and G.P. Chrousos. 1999. The endocrinology of melancholic and atypical depression: Relation to neurocircuitry and somatic consequences. *Proceedings of the Association of American Physicians* 111 (1): 22–34.

Leibenluft, E. 1998. Why are so many women depressed? *Scientific American Presents* 9 (2): 52–60.

Nemeroff, C.B. 1998. The neurobiology of depression. *Scientific American* 278 (6): 42–47.

O'Neal, H.A., A.L. Dunn, and E.W. Martinsen. 2000. Depression and exercise. *International Journal of Sport Psychology* 31 (2): 110–135.

Web Sites

www.hopkinsmedicine.org/drada/
www.ndmda.org/
www.psychologyinfo.com/depression/
www.nimh.nih.gov/publicat/depression.cfm
www.nimh.nih.gov/publicat/resfacts.cfm

8

Self-Esteem

Exercise can have its effect on mental health through multiple social and psychobiological mechanisms; but regardless of how the change comes about, the outcome is manifest, at least partly, in attitudes, beliefs, or feelings about the self. Exercise has great potential for changing self-perceptions, and anecdotal accounts of why people exercise often include reports of improvements in self-concept and self-esteem. However, experimental evidence for increases in self-esteem that can be directly attributed to an independent effect from exercise is limited. This chapter delineates the relationship between how people feel about themselves and their levels of physical activity. Theories and models of self-concept and self-esteem are presented to lay the foundation for understanding the interaction between exercise behavior and self-perceptions. The measurement of physical self-concept and self-esteem is described in some detail to help the reader appreciate some of the issues in conceptualizing and measuring **attitudes** and **beliefs** about the self. The ways in which self-esteem is defined and assessed with respect to exercise has affected the scope and quality of research in this area. This chapter reviews the literature examining the relationship between self-perceptions and exercise behavior to summarize what we know and to illustrate issues in studying exercise and self-esteem.

Self-esteem is one of the key indicators of good mental health and a significant correlate of life adjustment.

Effects of Positive and Negative Self-Esteem

A positive assessment of oneself can enhance mood and support healthy behaviors, while negative self-esteem can lead to depressed mood and disadvantageous behaviors.

▼ High self-esteem is associated with independence, leadership, adaptability, and resilience to stress (Wylie 1989).

▼ Low self-esteem is associated with depression, anxiety, and phobias (Baumeister 1993).

▼ Self-esteem may moderate the stress-illness relationship by influencing the appraisal of stress and subsequent physiological responsivity (Rector and Roger 1997).

The Self-System

The self is a complex system of constructs that has been organized by theorists into a directing/organizing self and a composite of attributes and characteristics that make up the self in action (Harter 1996). The *directing self* organizes the *self in action* into a coherent structure, which is commonly termed *self-concept* by social psychologists or *identity* by clinical psychologists and psychiatrists (Fox 2000). **Self-concept** is an organized configuration of perceptions of the self that are within conscious awareness. It is multidimensional, and it includes many subcomponents, or domains, such as the academic self, the social self, the spiritual self, and the physical self. Self-concept is a critical factor in mental health. A stable and coherent framework of self is necessary for making sense of the world.

The concept of a unidimensional core identity has expanded to intuitively appealing and practical multidimensional models of the self (e.g., Shavelson, Hubner, and Stanton 1976; Marsh 1997). Figure 8.1 presents an example of a multidimensional hierarchical model. Imagine the self-concept system as a pyramid, with global self-concept at the apex and general constructs at the next-lower level. Specificity increases downward, with the most situation-specific self-perceptions at the base. Higher-order constructs are dependent on lower-order components. For example, how you define yourself socially depends on relationships with family, coworkers, and friends. Changes in specific components (i.e., communications with siblings) affect these more general constructs and influence global self-concept. Self-esteem in this model is a result of the personal assessment of how one is doing with respect to the constructs that are highly valued and considered important.

The **self-schemata** is a cognitive structure that represents individuals' knowledge of themselves and their attributes, and is thought by some theorists to guide how people retrieve, select, and store information about themselves. Kendzierski (1994), applying the self-schemata concept to exercise, proposed three types of individuals. *Exerciser schematics* describe themselves as exercisers and hold physical self-constructs as important to their self-image. *Nonexerciser schematics* do not see themselves

as active, but they value physical self-constructs. *Aschematics* do not see themselves as active, and they do not value physical self-constructs. Experience is part of schemata development, but the development of the exercise schemata depends on events and activities including but beyond exercise experiences.

A common understanding of **self-esteem** is that it refers to how much one likes or values oneself, and there is an intuitive association between positive self-esteem and good mental health. In the social sciences, self-esteem, a hypothetical construct, is the *evaluation* of the self-concept and includes feelings associated with that evaluation. It is the summary judgment of how well the self is doing in specific areas and overall based on one's personal value system and standards. Self-esteem can thus be quantified as the sum of evaluations of different attributes of one's self. Other terms used to describe self-esteem are *self-worth*, *self-regard*, *self-respect*, and *self-acceptance* (Blascovich and Tomaka 1991).

Self-esteem was initially conceived as a global construct, but the conceptualization has expanded into one that is more multidimensional. Facets of self-esteem (e.g., judgment of physical capabilities) contribute to global self-esteem to the extent that those attributes are important to a sense of self (see figure 8.2). Thus, to understand self-esteem we must consider the dominant culture and the individual's internalization of the culture's values and ideals. For example, if the cultural ideals include a lean body and an individual has a high percentage body fat, physical self-esteem will be low to the extent that the person values physical self-concept and accepts cultural ideals. If the dominant culture elevates family and social relationships above physical appearance and other subcomponents of physical

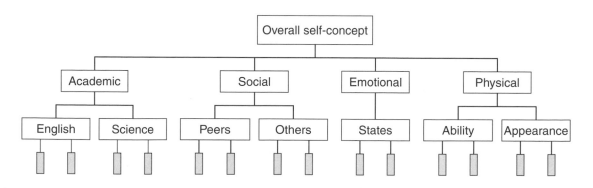

Figure 8.1   A multidimensional hierarchical model of the self; specificity increases from the apex (overall self-concept) to the base.

Reprinted, by permission, from R.J. Shavelson, J.J. Hubner, and G.C. Stanton, 1976, "Self-concept: Validation of construct interpretations," *Review of Educational Research* 46 (3): 407–441.

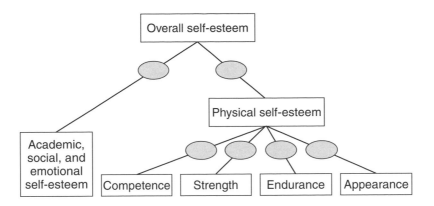

Figure 8.2 Different people emphasize different facets of themselves in forming their self-esteem. Based on Fox and Corbin 1989.

self-concept, body size will have less influence on self-esteem.

While some researchers distinguish between self-concept and self-esteem, others (e.g., Sonstroem 1998) consider facets of self-concept to be components of global self-esteem. This integration is based on the idea that we cannot describe the self without some evaluation and an affective response. For example, in the Exercise and Self-Esteem Model (Sonstroem and Morgan 1989), one of the domains of global self-esteem is physical self-worth. Physical self-worth is influenced by physical competence and physical self-acceptance in several subdomains, such as strength and aerobic endurance. Physical competence is what you think you can do and is similar to self-concept. Self-acceptance is what you feel about what you can do, and indicates how satisfied you are with your level of competence. This level of satisfaction represents a component of general self-esteem.

Self-concept is an objective accounting of who we are. Self-esteem is how we feel about who we are.

Self-esteem has a clear link to psychological well-being, but it also serves to direct behavior. This motivational feature of self-esteem guides behavior through the desire for self-enhancement. The **self-enhancement hypothesis** is based on the premise that people do things that they expect will result in positive feelings of competence and esteem (Biddle 1997). They act as they perceive themselves to be, and engage in behaviors they think will lead to success and enhancement of the self. Thus, behavioral choices are influenced by the need to increase or sustain positive evaluations of self-concept. The concept of self-efficacy is useful in this model in that individuals are more likely to engage in a behavior if they are confident that they will be successful and will thus be able to enhance their sense of self. This model can be used to predict future behavior. For example, if you have high self-efficacy for swimming but little confidence in your ability to roller blade, you are more likely to take a date to a pool than to a roller rink.

Theories and Models

A model that incorporates physical self-concept and self-esteem to explain how exercise might influence global self-esteem is the Exercise and Self-Esteem Model developed by Sonstroem and Morgan (1989) and expanded to include physical self-worth (Sonstroem, Harlow, and Josephs 1994) (see figure 8.3). This model is hierarchical and multidimensional with global self-concept/self-esteem at the apex and psychosocial perceptions progressing down from the general to the specific. Specific physical criteria, such as time to run a mile, interact with specific exercise self-efficacy, which is a component of the subdomain physical condition. Physical self-worth is expected to mediate the effects of physical condition self-concept on self-esteem. This model offers a cognitive link between higher-order constructs of the self and actual behaviors. McAuley, Mihalko, and Bane (1997) tested this model in a 20-week training study with 41 male and 42 female sedentary middle-aged adults. They found significant

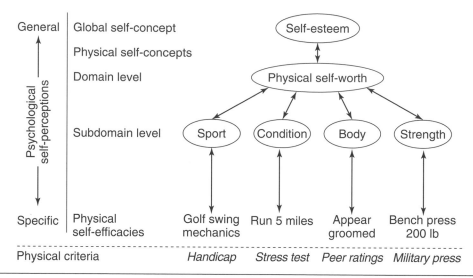

Figure 8.3   Exercise and Self-Esteem Model.

Reprinted, by permission, from R.J. Sonstroem, 1998, "Physical self-concept: Assessment and external validity," *Exercise and Sport Sciences Reviews* 26: 133–164, figure 6.2.

increases in global self-esteem, physical self-worth, and physical condition. There were no changes in global self-esteem when the investigators controlled for physical self-worth, a result that supports this model of exercise and self-esteem.

Self-concept is multidimensional and hierarchical, and self-perceptions can vary from level to level.

Fox and Corbin (1989) presented a conceptual model of the physical self via the development of the Physical Self-Perception Profile shown in figure 8.4. This model also includes physical self-worth, along with sport competence, attractiveness, physical condition, and strength. Since perceptions of the self-concept are influenced by how someone values a particular domain, Fox and Corbin stress the relationship between physical competencies and importance, and include a measure of importance (Perceived Importance Profile) (Fox 1990).

Who individuals think they are affects their self-esteem and guides their behavior. They process information and make decisions via the self-schemata so that behavior and the outcomes of behavior are consistent with goals and a personal theory of the self (Fox 1997). Thus, the self is an active agent in

self-concept development and maintenance, and degree of success is reflected in the self-esteem. In addition to maintaining consistency, the self directs behaviors that will serve to enhance the self. According to the self-enhancement hypothesis, specific activities to enhance the self are directed by a need to feel competent, worthy, and loved by others. People are motivated, then, to act in order to feel connected to others and to experience a sense of self-determination. Fox (1997) describes several self-enhancement strategies that are summarized in table 8.1.

Self-esteem is influenced by demographic characteristics, the physical body, sensory input, psychosocial dynamics, and the social and cultural environment.

Factors Influencing Self-Esteem

Demographic characteristics, such as gender and age, influence self-concept. Numerous studies have found more favorable self-concept and self-esteem scores in males compared to females across age groups. Generally, there is a linear decrease in self-

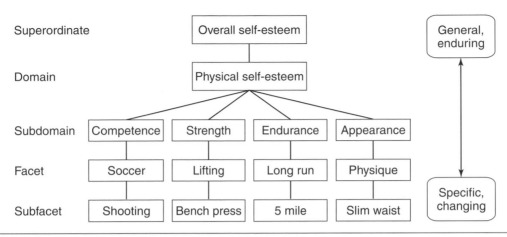

Figure 8.4 Structure of physical self-esteem.

Based on Fox 1990.

Table 8.1

Self-Enhancement Strategies

Behavioral strategy	Example
Choose behaviors that have a high probability of success and positive affect.	George rowed for his college crew team, so he decides to buy a kayak and attend a few roll sessions.
Act in ways to maximize social approval and support.	George gives the novices in his class tips he learned from crew, and they help each other load the kayaks at the end of class.
Withdraw from activities that tend to result in failure, lack of success, and negative affect.	Folks from roll class organize a trip to a bike trail to go in-line skating on Sunday, but George bows out. In high school he fell several times trying to learn how to roller skate and does not want to make a fool of himself in front of his new friends.
Psychological strategy	**Example**
Discount the importance of activities that do not result in success and positive affect.	George thinks that in-line skating is dangerous for other people cycling and running on the bike trails.
Shape attributions for events to present the self-concept in the best light.	George believes he helps the roll class go more smoothly by helping out when the instructor is busy. He thinks they are making faster progress and benefiting from his knowledge and skills.
Engage in self-affirmation and self-verification when the self-concept is threatened.	Some of the folks in the roll class reject George's advice and ignore his comments, saying "This is not the same as crew." George gets a book on kayaking and identifies skills kayaking shares with rowing. He pays attention to the classmates who ask him for help.

Data from Fox 1997.

concept scores with age to the early or middle teen years, at which point self-concept scores level off or increase before rising into adulthood (Sonstroem 1998). Self-concept seems to be stable in adulthood in respect to effects of age. Hirsch and Lykken (1993) looked at self-concept factors in 678 monozygotic and 547 dizygotic twin pairs (aged 27-86 years)

and concluded that self-concept crystallizes early in adulthood and reflects a strong genetic influence. Nonetheless, there are malleable physical, psychological, and social variables that can contribute to the evaluation of self-concept. Changes in the body's structure and function influence self-perceptions. Adolescence, pregnancy, weight loss/gain, injury, menopause, disease, and aging are examples of events that alter the physical self and have an impact on self-perceptions. One way in which physical changes can influence self-esteem is through the modulating effects of sensory input on self-evaluation. The muscle strain experienced in a weightlifting class by someone recovering from an injury, and the joint stiffness an older woman feels getting out of an automobile, are examples of sensations that can contribute to poor physical self-esteem.

The *physical body* provides a substantial interface between the individual and the world and influences self-esteem. Appearance is a means of communication and an expression of status and sexuality. Judgment of the physical self influences global self-esteem, but the importance of the physical self in self-esteem is greater when the other self components are less developed. The lack of a complex sense of self has been presented as one reason that exercise can have a more potent influence on self-esteem in children than on people of other ages.

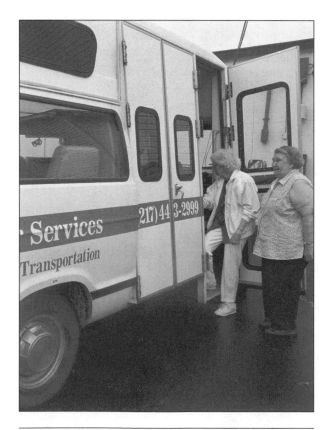

Physical sensations, such as stiffness and pain, during activities of daily living contribute to physical self-concept and self-esteem.

Self-esteem is influenced by characteristics of the physical body and the interaction between self-perceptions and the ideals of popular culture.

The physical body had a significant role in self-identity and self-esteem in 20th-century society, and will likely continue to have a strong influence. Sparks (1997) discussed the concept of the "socially constructed body" and referred to a theme for framing the body based on "the *mechanical body* and the *body beautiful*" (p. 87). Advances in medical technology have made it possible to reshape and rebuild physical attributes. Cosmetic surgery and a range of ergogenic aids have expanded the limits of the possible in physical appearance and performance. The increased perception of control over appearance and function has been supported by the media and by product promotion. The body has been redefined as a symbol of health, success, and wealth. The physical self has become an item of social currency.

The view of the body as malleable also promotes self-regulation and individual responsibility for our health and wellness. However, there can be negative effects on self-esteem when unrealistic cultural ideals for shape and size are adopted and used to judge one's appearance, especially as typical correlations between perceived attractiveness and physical self-worth have been about $r = .70$ (Fox 1997). Self-esteem is threatened when there is a discrepancy between competence and importance, such as when high importance is attached to body image but competence to make necessary changes to fit the ideal is low. For example, consider the effects on self-esteem from an obese teenager's inability to lose weight and keep it off using fad diets. According to cognitive discrepancy models, adopting unrealistic ideals will lead to poor self-concepts even when accomplishments are otherwise good. Marsh (1999) tested this model in a study in which 793 high school students indicated their actual, ideal, future, and potential body images by selecting from 12 silhouettes that varied along an "obese-skinny" continuum. Marsh found support for a cognitive discrepancy model in that more demanding, increasingly slender ideal body images had a significant, negative impact on self-concept. Inasmuch as un-

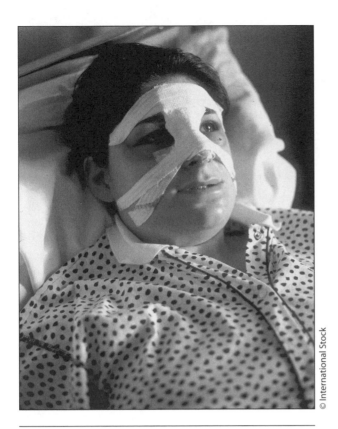

Changing our physical appearance has become easier with advances in medical technology.

self from the environment and others, discovering personal causation, testing the environment, and learning about the self from the responses of others (Sonstroem 1998)—can be viewed from the standpoint of a self-determination model as internal regulation of behavior.

Self concept is developed in part through the establishment of internal standards for the self. Internal standards are established by evaluation of personal behavior (i.e., mastery, degree of improvement, goal achievement, and objective performance). Self-concept, however, develops in a *social environment*, and the influences of society and cultural values are strong. The perspective of a core identity that develops through interactions between the self and society ("socially constructed self;" Sparks 1997) highlights the challenge of maintaining a coherent self-identity in response to changing roles and social expectations. Cross-cultural studies demonstrate the power of society in defining what is acceptable. For example, judgments about physical size and shape are matched against cultural ideals; African American women with lower socioeconomic status who are heavy do not have a poor body image, while Caucasian American women who are heavy aspire to a thin, lean ideal (Davis 1997). Gender also plays a role in the cultural messages about the ideal body. Henriques and Calhoun (1991) measured self-esteem and current body esteem in male and female white and black college students on two occasions one week apart. Blacks and men had higher self-esteem scores, and white women had the lowest scores at both assessments. In addition, changes in weight satisfaction and feelings of sexual attractiveness were more highly correlated with self-esteem for white women than for men and black women.

Social and cultural factors influence self-concept development and evaluation through the application of external standards to the self. External standards include *referred appraisals* and *social comparisons* (Sonstroem 1998). **Referred appraisal** is how we think significant others perceive us. From this perspective, self-concept is formed by our appraisals of what significant others think about us. Most of us are familiar with the idea of a self-fulfilling prophecy, which has been demonstrated countless times in the classroom and on athletic fields when teachers and coaches have high expectations of students who end up meeting those expectations. External standards also influence self-concept development through *social comparison*, which involves observing

realistic ideals for the female body are promoted in the United States and other industrialized societies, the lower physical self-esteem in females across the life span is not surprising.

Psychological dynamics also influence self-esteem. For example, Ryan and Deci's self-determination theory (Deci et al. 1991), which evolved from cognitive evaluation theory (Deci and Ryan 1980) contributes the concepts of contingent versus true self-esteem and self-determination to understanding how self-esteem is influenced. Motivation for behavior exists on a continuum that ranges from *amotivation* through four levels of *extrinsic motivation* to one *true motivation*. Contingent self-esteem is based on meeting external standards; there is no personal control over reinforcement, and behavior is not self-determined. True self-esteem is based on meeting personally defined standards, and behavior is internally regulated. *True* or intrinsic *motivation* is integrated into self-identity, and self-esteem is enhanced through mastery or self-determination, which supports feelings of independence and confidence. Successful resolution of self-identity developmental tasks—which include separating the

Psychosocial Contributions to Self-Esteem

▼ Perceived competence
▼ Self-approval
▼ Perception of power
▼ Self-acceptance
▼ Sense of self-worth

From Fox 1997.

others and comparing ourselves to them. A middle-aged mother of four may acknowledge her physical ability to carry her 3-year-old child around during a day trip to an amusement park (internal standard based on objective performance), but she may not consider herself physically strong if she compares herself to friends who lift weights at a gym (external standard based on social comparison).

The setting and peer group used for social comparisons can have a significant impact on self-evaluations. For example, a recreational weightlifter who identifies himself as the strongest man at the local gym in his small town may discover that he is not as strong as most of the men working out at a gym in Los Angeles. Marsh et al. (1997) demonstrated this "big-fish-little-pond" effect in a study of physical self-concept in 1514 elite athletes and non-elite high school students. Physical self-concepts were higher for the elite than the non-elite groups, as would be expected. However, non-elite athletes in the athletically selective high school whose comparison group was the elite athletes scored *lower* than general students (non-athletes) from a non-sports high school on several physical self-concept variables.

Characteristics of individuals with low self-esteem have been summarized by Fox (1997). For example, individuals with low self-esteem have a less defined sense of self and less self-knowledge. They are thus more susceptible to external cues and events that can threaten self-esteem. Their self-concept is composed of simpler and fewer components, which offer fewer opportunities to self-affirm when self-concept is threatened. There is also a mismatch between level of perceived competence and importance attached to those competencies. For example, someone with low self-esteem may define herself primarily through physical attractiveness and define what is ideal through "infomercials" promot-

ing expensive exercise equipment or dietary supplements. She may be unaware of the realistic limits her stocky body shape places on her. Her ongoing failure to make the desired changes in her body fosters low self-efficacy for achieving a highly valued slim, muscular body and will perpetuate low self-esteem.

Measurement

The nature of self-esteem as a hypothetical construct contributes to issues in measurement because there are no objective criteria to validate measures against. Instead, researchers must use **convergent validation** (strength of association with established scales that measure other similar variables and constructs) and **divergent validation** (lack of association with scales that measure dissimilar constructs) strategies, and/or evaluate the scale's **face validity** (consonance of the scale items with accepted definitions of the concept to be measured).

Self-Esteem as a Hypothetical Construct

Self-esteem is a hypothetical construct that is quantified, for example, as the sum of evaluations across salient attributes of one's self or personality. (Blascovich and Tomaka 1991, p. 115)

*S*elf-esteem and self-concept are multidimensional constructs and are difficult to assess unless instruments are also multidimensional.

Issues in Measurement of Self Variables

The measurement of psychological constructs is discussed in some depth in Chapter 2, and the issues and strategies presented in that chapter also apply to the development of instruments to measure self-perceptions. For example, instruments need to be based on some theory of the self, and the target population should be considered in creating scale items. Fox (1998) described additional issues in self-perception scale development, such as the clarity of the item format.

For example, the Physical Self-Perception Profile uses the structured-alternative format. This format requires that respondents make two choices per scale item. First, the respondents select which one of a pair of contrasting statements is most like them; then they indicate whether the statement is "really true of me" or "sort of true of me." The Likert-type scale is more familiar to most individuals and may reduce potential threats to reliability that may arise from complicated item formats, such as the structured-alternative style.

Subscale content should be based on theory. However, since the theory itself may be incomplete, subscales should also be constructed using input from the target population regarding the target concepts.

The level of subscale specificity is complicated by lack of knowledge about the range of physical activity and sport experience of the population. For example, it is hard for people to rate their confidence in tennis if they have never picked up a racket. Some address this issue by phrasing items so that respondents judge their ability in different sport and exercise areas on their own terms of reference, and researchers also use specific scales for specialized populations. For example, items associated with competence in general skills, such as agility, would allow the respondents to come up with their own frame of reference, like tennis or soccer. However, a scale with items addressing specific tennis competencies could be used to determine differences between males and females who join a tennis club.

Determining reliability of self-perception instruments depends on the theoretical perspective on the stability of the construct. Global self-esteem is viewed by many as trait-like, and thus should demonstrate good test-retest reliability. Constructs closer to the base of a hierarchical model, such as strength self-esteem, are more mutable. Thus, differences in scale values between administrations may be due to actual change, confounding the ability to measure the stability of the instrument over time. Researchers developing instruments to measure physical activity also have a dilemma in determining the temporal stability of a questionnaire (see chapter 10 on determinants).

Social desirability was discussed in Chapter 2 as an experimental artifact. This tendency toward socially desirable responses threatens the accuracy of scales measuring self-perception constructs that are valued in society, such as self-esteem. Sonstroem and Potts (1996) included measures of social desirability in their examination of the association between physical self-concepts and life adjustment variables. Although the associations between self-deceptive enhancement scores and scores on the Physical Self-Perception Profile were in a healthy direction, the authors concluded that physical self-evaluations contain a degree of inaccuracy. Fox (1998) recommended including scales measuring conformity and social desirability in the development of self-perception instruments.

Contemporary self-concept and self-esteem models are hierarchical and multidimensional. Thus, scales developed based on these models must undergo validation of the scale as a whole and of the individual components. External construct validation involves administering the scale in conjunction with established instruments and measuring the degree of association. Marsh (1997) describes a method of external validation called *between network validity*. A measure of self-concept would be compared with other constructs according to a theoretically based, logical pattern of relationships. The scale should be significantly related to some scales and not to others as predicted by theory. There should also be predictable differences between scores from distinct populations. For example, scores on a subscale of aerobic endurance should be higher for runners than for sedentary individuals. Additionally, validation should occur at the theoretical level with the internal structure of the instrument, which Marsh refers to as *within network validity* (1997). Components of a hierarchical multidimensional model at the same level should not be correlated because the model presumes they are independent. A self-concept instrument that is developed based on the Shavelson, Hubner, and Stanton (1976) multidimensional hierarchical model should have distinct, multidimensional components (i.e., academic, social, physical, emotional, spiritual) that are not correlated. Each component should have specific subcomponents (*physical* includes performance and appearance), which can each also have specific components (*performance* includes strength, endurance, coordination, flexibility, etc.). The statistics for determining the within network validity of self-concept instruments include factor analysis and multitrait-multimethod analysis (Marsh 1997) introduced in chapter 2.

Instruments to Measure Self-Perception

Components and relationships associated with the physical self that should be studied for an understanding of human functioning across the life span include physical self-perceptions, the influence of these perceptions on physical activity and other health behaviors, changes in physical self-perceptions from physical activity and other health behaviors, and mechanisms for effects of changes in physical self-perception on self-esteem (Fox 1998). Valid and reliable ways to measure self-perceptions are necessary for understanding the relationship between physical activity behavior and self-concept and self-esteem discussed earlier. Several different instruments have been developed since the 1950s to measure self-perceptions relevant to physical activity and are described in the following sections. Early research in physical self-concept was dominated by studies evaluating body image and its relationship with global self-esteem (Marsh 1997). Thus, because of the historical significance as well as the importance of body image in self-esteem and in exercise motivation, we begin with selected instruments to measure body image.

Body Image

Body image has been assessed using a variety of methods, including distortion techniques, silhouette and photograph rating, computer-generated reproductions of perceived body shape and size, and paper-and-pencil questionnaires (see figure 8.5). One of the first scales to measure body image was

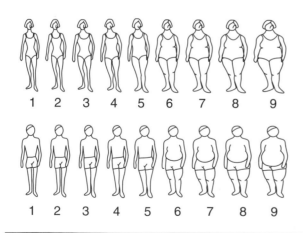

Figure 8.5   Perception of body size can be assessed by asking a respondent to mark which one of the figures shown above is most like him- or herself.

the Body Cathexis Scale, developed by Secord and Jourard in 1953. Body cathexis is defined as "the degree of feeling satisfied or dissatisfied with various parts or processes of the body" (Secord and Jourard 1953, p. 343). The respondent rates 46 body parts and functions on a 5-point scale ranging from "have strong feelings and wish change could somehow be made" to "consider myself fortunate," and the scores are summed. Body image scores are based on affect rather than perception. A limitation of the Body Cathexis Scale is its assessment of body image as a unidimensional concept (i.e., single score derived from sum of responses). The Body Esteem Scale was developed by Franzoi and Shields in 1984 based on the Body Cathexis Scale. This revised scale is divided into three gender-specific factors measured by 32 items. For males, subscales include physical attractiveness, upper body strength, and physical condition. Subscales for females measure sexual attractiveness, weight concern, and physical condition.

Measurement of body image can be unidimensional or multidimensional, but there is general agreement that body image is a multidimensional psychological construct. Although body image has been conceptualized to include several elements, the two constructs that appear consistently in the literature are evaluation or appraisal of the body and expression of satisfaction with the body (Rowe, Benson, and Baumgartner 1999). One of the newer scales with good psychometric properties is the Body Self-Image Questionnaire (BSIQ), which has nine subscales (Rowe, Benson, and Baumgartner 1999). The subscales are Health/Fitness Influence, Investment in Ideals, Attention to Grooming, Height Dissatisfaction, Negative Affective, Social Dependence, and three that incorporate evaluative components (Overall Appearance Evaluation, Health/Fitness Evaluation, and Fatness Evaluation).

Self-Concept

Early scale-development research was guided by a unidimensional conceptualization of self-concept. As with the Body Cathexis Scale, the sum of responses to several items was used to compute a single, global self-concept score. This approach assumes equal weight for items representing different aspects of the self, such as academic and physical self-concepts. Specific scales to measure the physical self were limited by this conceptual framework (e.g., Body Cathexis Scale) until the emergence of multidimensional models (e.g., Shavelson, Hubner, and Stanton 1976) and self-perception profiles (e.g., Harter 1982) in the late 1970s and early 1980s. The inclusion of a hierarchical model provided an organization that fostered scale development research and testable hypotheses, as well as subscales that assessed self-concept in specific domains.

The Tennessee Self-Concept Scale (original: Fitts 1965; Roid and Fitts 1994) was the first multidimensional self-concept scale in which self-concept was composed of general and specific factors. Separate scores are generated for physical self, moral-ethical self, personal self, family self, and social self domains. For each domain, identity (e.g., description of physical self), self-satisfaction (degree of satisfaction with physical self-image), and behavior (participation in physical activities) can be computed (Blascovich and Tomaka 1991). Although designed to measure self-concept, this scale has been used as a general measure of self-esteem in many studies (Blascovich and Tomaka 1991).

The Self-Description Questionnaire (SDQ) (Marsh, Smith, and Barnes 1983) was developed to test the Shavelson, Hubner, and Stanton (1976) model in children younger than adolescence. The SDQ measures self-concept based on a multidimensional *hierarchical* self. It includes measures of general sense of self, more-specific facets, or domain self-concepts, and even more-specific skills and abilities within each domain. The two domains are academic and nonacademic. The nonacademic domain consists of physical abilities, appearance, relationship with peers, and relationship with parents. Marsh also developed two other versions of this scale to use with adolescents (SDQ-II; Marsh, Parker, and Barnes 1985), and late-adolescents/adults (SDQ-III; Marsh and O'Neill 1984).

Physical Self-Concept

The identification of self-concept as multidimensional prompted the development and refinement of more complicated instruments to measure physical self-concept. The two multidimensional physical self-concept scales described next were developed on the basis of a structural model of self-concept. Advances in computers and multivariate statistical techniques have been applied to these newer scales and have enabled researchers to enhance the quality of these physical self-concept assessments.

In the late 1980s, Fox and Corbin (1989) developed the Physical Self-Perception Profile (PSPP) to measure physical self-concepts based on work by Harter (1985, 1986) and the Shavelson, Hubner, and Stanton (1976) model. Content validation was undertaken by extensive reviews of previous research and interviews with college students regarding important components of the physical self. The PSPP has five subscales (see box below). Each scale has items that reflect perception about product (competency/adequacy), process (acquisition/maintenance), and perceived confidence (self-presentation). A global physical self-worth subscale is also included. The format of the items, structured-alternative, was chosen to reduce social desirability responding, but may be confusing. The Perceived Importance Profile (PIP) was developed to accompany the PSPP to measure the importance placed on each subdomain with regard to more global self-worth, but support for its value in models of physical self-concept and esteem is mixed (Fox 1998; Marsh 1997).

Physical Self-Perception Profile Subscales

▼ Sport competence

▼ Physical condition

▼ Body attractiveness

▼ Physical strength

▼ Physical conditioning

From Fox and Corbin 1989.

The Physical Self-Description Questionnaire (PSDQ) was developed based on the Marsh/Shavelson hierarchical model of self-concept (Marsh 1990). Respondents rate each of the 70 statements on a 6-point true-false response scale, and scores for 11 scales are generated from the responses (see box on next page). The process by which the PSDQ was validated is a model for scale construction in the social sciences: using 14 field criteria of physical fitness to establish criterion-related validity (Marsh 1993), establishing convergent and discriminant evidence for construct validity judged against existing instruments (Marsh et al. 1994), and testing the invariance of the scales in four age groups who completed the PSDQ four times during a two-year period (Marsh 1998).

> **Physical Self-Description Questionnaire**
>
> **Global subscales**
> ▼ Physical self-concept
> ▼ Global self-esteem
>
> **Physical self-concept subscales**
> ▼ Body fat
> ▼ Strength
> ▼ Activity
> ▼ Endurance/fitness
> ▼ Sports competence
> ▼ Coordination
> ▼ Health
> ▼ Appearance
> ▼ Flexibility
> ▼ Self-esteem

Self-Esteem

Self-esteem was initially thought to be a global construct. The most frequently used self-esteem scale—and the standard that has been used in subsequent self-esteem scale development—is the Rosenberg Self-Esteem Scale (Rosenberg 1965). It is global and unidimensional, and consists of 10 items that have strong internal consistency and test-retest reliability. The Coopersmith (1967) Self-Esteem Inventory (SEI) is another popular unidimensional measure of self-esteem. It was originally developed for children and has been adapted for adults. Although the revision to this scale (SEI Form B; Coopersmith 1975) was thought to measure positive self-regard unidimensionally, subsequent analyses have found different factor structures, indicating multidimensionality; but no stable interpretable pattern has been determined (Blascovich and Tomaka 1991).

The conceptualization of self-esteem has expanded into one that is more multidimensional through the influence of Shavelson, Hubner, and Stanton (1976). There are facets of self-esteem that contribute to more-global self-esteem. For example, how you judge your ability to run a mile influences the esteem you hold for your physical capabilities. The Janis-Field Feelings of Inadequacy Scale (FIS) (Janis and Field 1959) was adapted by Fleming and Watts (1980) and Fleming and Courtney (1984) to use in a multidimensional fashion. Five factors were found to contribute to global self-esteem: social confidence, academic ability, emotionality, physical appearance, and ability.

The Physical Estimation and Attraction Scales (PEAS; Sonstroem 1978) includes two global components defined as estimation (self-perceptions of physical ability) and attraction (measured interest in physical activity). The PEAS was derived from a forerunner of the Exercise and Self-Esteem Model (Sonstroem and Morgan 1989) to measure estimation and attraction, which were defined as mediating variables in physical ability, physical activity participation, and self-esteem relationships. Use of the PEAS has declined, but it is an example of an early attempt to go beyond unidimensional measurements and to combine instrument development with model building.

Global self-esteem is rather stable, and using it as an outcome variable in exercise research is limited because meaningful changes in self-esteem from physical activity are difficult to detect. Global scales may lack the necessary sensitivity, although researchers persist in using global scales to measure changes after exercise interventions. Targeting self-evaluations of very specific attributes is one way to overcome this problem, and it is an approach that is supported by a hierarchical multidimensional model of self-esteem. Hierarchical models raise the need to address two issues in scale construction (Marsh 1998). First, items should be relevant; that is, they should be applicable to what you are interested in measuring. For example, "I can bench press twice my body weight," would not be as predictive of entering a 5K road race as, "I can exercise for a long time without getting winded." Second, items should be at the same level of specificity as the construct you want to measure. "I am physically fit," would not assess the subdomain of strength self-concept as well as "I am strong," would. Tracking changes in the Fatness Evaluation subscale of the BSIQ over the course of an exercise program targeting fat loss is an example of using a measure that is at the same level of specificity as your intervention. You would be more likely to detect changes in this specific relevant subscale than in a global score derived from the BSIQ.

Exercise and Self-Esteem

The body of research on exercise and self-esteem is not as extensive as that addressing the relationship between exercise and other psychological variables, such as depression and stress responsiveness. The overall evidence for effects of exercise on global self-esteem is mostly positive, but mixed (McAuley 1994; Fox 2000). Ambiguous results may reflect limitations in study design and instrumentation as well as the trait-like nature of self-esteem, which renders it less likely to be changed by interventions. Research that has addressed the relationship between exercise and self-esteem is described in the next section and is organized into summaries of meta-analyses and reviews, examples of correlational and longitudinal studies, and discussion of research with special populations.

Meta-Analyses and Reviews

Compared to the literature dealing with exercise in relation to other mental health areas, there have been few reviews of research on exercise and self-esteem or self-concept. Gruber (1986) surveyed the literature on interventions exploring the relationship between physical activity and self-esteem development in children. He found 84 intervention studies and conducted a meta-analysis with the 27 studies that reported adequate data for the analysis. The average effect size (ES) supporting positive effects of exercise on self-esteem was .41. The development of global self-esteem was influenced by participation in directed play and/or physical education in elementary school children, with more benefits found in children low in self-esteem and in those from special populations (see figure 8.6). Greatest gains from exercise for self-esteem were for children with disabilities, with a .57 ES. Benefits from fitness-type activities (ES = .89) were greater than those from participation in creative activities (ES = .29), sports (ES = .40), and motor skill activities (ES = .32). However, confidence intervals were not provided for these differences, which often were based on very few studies and may not represent true differences in effects.

Also, results from this meta-analysis should not be taken as strong evidence against improvements in children's self-esteem from playing sports. Almost all the studies in Gruber's meta-analysis used global measures of self-esteem, which may not reveal changes in specific physical self-evaluations. Research that has included scales to measure specific subcomponents of self-esteem, such as sport-related self-esteem (e.g., Anshel, Muller, and Owens 1986), has shown increases from sport participation.

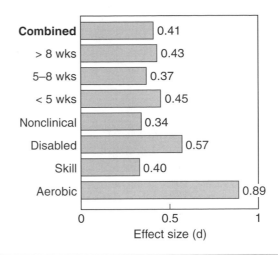

Figure 8.6 Meta-analysis of 27 longitudinal studies in children. There was no effect for length of training; effects were larger for children who were disabled and from aerobic activities.

Data from Gruber 1986.

Lirgg (1991) conducted a meta-analysis of 35 studies to examine the magnitude of gender differences in self-confidence in physical activity. There was a significant effect such that males were more confident than females, although all but one of the tasks were "masculine" (i.e., strength-focused, competitive) or gender neutral. Females were significantly more confident than males in the one study that used a "feminine task" (i.e., expressive, graceful). The magnitude of the gender differences was not affected by level of competitiveness of the task situation.

Fox (2000) conducted a qualitative review of 37 randomized and 42 nonrandomized controlled exercise intervention studies that measured the effects of exercise on self-esteem and physical self-perceptions. The description of the studies sheds light on the difficulty in producing an organized review of the literature. Outcome variables were a variety of constructs measured with several different instruments. Only a few of the more recent studies were based on theoretical models and used instruments with sound psychometrics and subscales to measure multidimensional physical self-concepts. General conclusions, even considering the weakness and scarcity of the research, are positive. Almost 80% of the studies indicated significant changes in physical self-worth and other physical self-perceptions after exercise training, but only half of the results were significant for positive changes in self-esteem. Positive effects were found for men and women, but greater benefits were measured in those initially lower in self-esteem. Both aerobic and weight training positively influenced self-esteem, but there was some indication that the short-term effect is greater for weight training.

Two general reviews are also worth noting. McAuley wrote a chapter in *Physical Activity, Fitness, and Health: International Proceedings and Consensus Statement* (Bouchard, Shephard, and Stephens, 1994) on the psychosocial benefits and outcomes of physical activity. Among the articles on physical activity and self-esteem that he reviewed, 60% reported positive associations. However, most of the studies were cross-sectional, and there was an over-reliance on global self-esteem measures. Few studies addressed the relationship between changes at the domain level, such as physical self-worth, and changes in global self-esteem. In another more general review of physical self-concept, Sonstroem (1998) presented the conceptualization of physical self-concept and measurement issues along with critiques and summaries of skill development and self-enhancement research. Although most evidence points to changes in self-esteem with participation in exercise programs, the studies Sonstroem evaluated lacked control for confounding variables, such as perceived task demands, response distortion, and expectancy for self-esteem changes.

Positive associations between exercise and self-esteem have been found, but effects are stronger for individuals initially lower in self-esteem.

Correlational Evidence

Correlational evidence for a positive relationship between physical activity and physical self-concept has been found in several studies in adolescents and adults (e.g., Anderson and Cychosz 1995; Beckett and Hodgdon 1991; Marsh and Peart 1988). Research also supports a relationship between aspects of physical self-concept and positive emotions and attitudes in several age groups (e.g., Ehrenberg, Cox, and Koopman 1991; Kavussanu and McAuley 1995; McAuley, Mihalko, and Bane 1997; Sonstroem 1998). For example, among 260 adults, physical self-esteem scores (PSPP) were higher

among exercisers than non-exercisers, and self-reported physical activity was strongly correlated with self-esteem ($r = .89$) (Sonstroem, Speliotis, and Fava 1992). Physical self-concept and physical self-esteem were related to physical activity in a study of 89 male and 94 female college students, with higher levels of physical self-perceptions reported by males than by females (Hayes, Crocker, and Kowalski 1999). Davis, Claridge, and Brewer (1996) examined the personality dynamics of body esteem in women who engaged in high-level exercise ($n = 84$) and non-exercising women ($n = 81$). Exercisers had significantly higher body esteem and lower neuroticism and body mass index than non-exercisers.

Physical self-concept is influenced by level of physical activity and has consistently shown moderately strong correlations with global self-esteem across the life span (Fox 2000), although more so with physical self-esteem (see figure 8.7). Thus, correlational evidence suggests that participation in physical activity and exercise could play a meaningful role in physical self-esteem through effects on physical self-concept.

Exercise has more potent effects on physical self-concept and self-esteem than on general self-perceptions.

	Correlations	
	Overall self-esteem	Physical self-esteem
Physical self-esteem	.62	
Sport competence	.32	.49
Condition	.33	.65
Body appearance	.48	.72
Strength	.24	.43

Figure 8.7 Evaluations of one's appearance and physical function are more strongly related to physical self-esteem than to overall self-esteem. $N = 1191$ college females and males.

Data from Fox and Corbin 1989.

Longitudinal Studies

Several studies have documented favorable changes in self-concept and self-esteem after participation in aerobic and strength conditioning programs. As shown in correlational studies, there is stronger evidence for changes in physical self-worth and other physical self-perceptions than for global self-esteem (Fox 2000; Sonstroem 1998).

Most studies of children that have been conducted since Gruber's 1986 meta-analysis have continued to find positive effects of exercise on changes in self-esteem (e.g., Boyd and Hrycaiko 1997), and effects have been found in children as young as 3 to 5 years old (Alpert et al. 1990). However, not all of the more recent studies of exercise training and self-esteem in children have demonstrated significant effects. Faigenbaum et al. (1997) did not find differences in self-concept or self-efficacy after an 8-week strength-training program implemented with 15 children aged 7 to 12 years, although there were significant changes in physical strength measures. Effects on self-perceptions after a 13-week aerobics training program were also not demonstrated in 67 children in grades three through five (Walters and Martin 2000). Discussions in both studies suggest that ceiling effects for the self-perception measures contributed to the lack of significant findings. High initial scores left little room for improvement after exercise.

Self-esteem is closely tied to body esteem in females, particularly white females (Calhoun 1999). Females are at greater risk of developing eating disorders, and the precipitating and escalating distortions in body image and negative effects on self-esteem have likely contributed to the interest in potential benefits of exercise training on self-perceptions in women. There is evidence that participating in regular exercise has positive effects on body esteem in women. Bartlewski, Van Raalte, and Brewer (1996) examined the effects of aerobic exercise on body image concerns of female college women. Significant increases in body esteem and decreases in physique anxiety were found for female students in an aerobics class, but not for those in a comparison academic class, from the beginning to the end of an academic term. Positive effects of exercise on body perceptions were also found for older women in a study by McAuley et al. (1995). Physique anxiety was prevalent in a cross-sectional sample of middle-aged and older women, but participation in a 20-week aerobic exercise program resulted in a decrease in physique anxiety for those middle-aged women who also had a favorable change in body composition.

Improvements in self-esteem among females have been demonstrated for various exercise modes, such as walking (e.g., Palmer 1995), strength training (Brown and Harrison 1986), and strength training and aerobic exercise (Aşçii 2002; Caruso and Gill 1992). Significant improvements in physical self-concept have also been demonstrated in college males after strength-training classes (Tucker 1983), as well as in male and female college students after strength-training classes compared to the aerobic exercise of swimming and a no-exercise control condition (Stein and Motta 1992).

Studies with middle-aged males and females have shown effects for changes in self-perception with physical activity, as well. For example, McAuley, Mihalko, and Bane (1997) measured changes in domain and global levels of self-esteem after a 20-week walking exercise program in sedentary middle-aged male and female adults. The participants showed significant increases in global self-esteem, physical self-worth, and physical condition. There is also some evidence that positive changes in self-perceptions after an aerobic training program are maintained after the program is over. DiLorenzo et al. (1999) measured changes in psychological and physiological variables in males and females aged 18 to 39 after a 12-week aerobic program and found significant improvements at posttest (see figure 8.8). At the one-year follow-up, physiological and psychological benefits remained significantly improved from baseline.

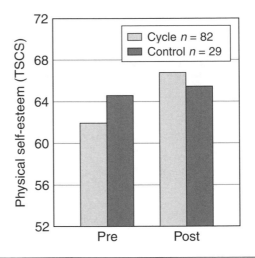

Figure 8.8 Exercise training is associated with increased self-esteem. The increase in physical self-esteem after training ($d = .57$) was larger than the increase in overall self-esteem ($d = .35$, raw data not graphed). $N = 82$; 30 min of cycle ergometry, four times per week for 12 weeks at 70% to 85% capacity.

Data from DiLorenzo et al. 1999.

Special Populations

The strongest effects for the influence of exercise on self-esteem are for those initially lower in self-esteem (see figure 8.9; McAuley 1994). It follows that individuals who have experienced threats to their self-esteem could benefit from improvements in physical self-concept. We look now at research on exercise and self-esteem in a number of diverse special populations, from women during pregnancy to individuals with developmental disabilities to persons diagnosed with cancer, among others.

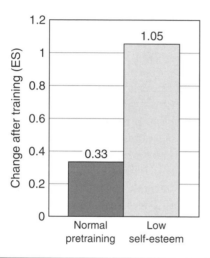

Figure 8.9   Self-esteem appears to increase the most after exercise training among those with low versus higher self-esteem. Change in self-esteem after two separate eight-week aerobic exercise training programs (effect size) is shown.

Normal: data from Wilfley and Kunce 1986; Low: data from Ossip-Klein et al. 1989.

Exercise can have specific beneficial effects for self-esteem in women during and after pregnancy through an impact on body image and through improved endurance and other physiological adaptations. Evidence from some studies indicates that exercise can help with premenstrual syndrome and dysmenorrhea and that physically active women have better moods across the menstrual cycle than sedentary women (Mutrie 1997). Exercise can also help maintain or enhance self-esteem during menopause, although little specific research has been conducted in this area.

It is well established that physiological adaptations from exercise training contribute to significant improvements in activities of daily living in older adults (American College of Sports Medicine Position Stand, "Exercise and Physical Activity for Older Adults" 1998). There is growing evidence for psychological benefits of regular exercise, such as alleviation of depression symptoms and an improved sense of personal control and self-efficacy. For example, low-income older adults who participated in physical activity as part of the Community Healthy Activities Model Program for Seniors (CHAMPS) program improved self-esteem, and individuals who adopted and maintained physical activity over the six-month intervention period improved scores for anxiety, depression, and overall psychological well-being (Stewart et al. 1997).

Exercise and sport have positive effects on self-esteem and other psychological variables in children, adolescents, and adults with developmental disabilities (Dykens, Rosner, and Butterbaugh 1998). Participation in exercise and sport is associated with reduced maladaptive behavior, along with improved physical fitness, self-esteem, and social competence in this population. Participation in Special Olympics has resulted in higher social competence and more positive self-perceptions compared with those of individuals similar in age and IQ who do not participate (Dykens and Cohen 1996). Individuals with physical disabilities are likely to experience psychological gains from exercise, such as an increase in self-esteem, although large-scale longitudinal studies are needed to determine the optimal programs for specific benefits (Shephard 1991). Courneya and Friedenreich (1999) reviewed the literature on physical exercise and quality of life following cancer diagnosis, and found consistent positive effects from exercise on physical and functional well-being, as well as beneficial effects on psychological functioning, including improved self-esteem.

The physical self plays a role in the development of the whole self, but the level and impact of physical activity and concomitant physical changes on self-esteem depend on a variety of factors, such as the value the individual places on aspects of physical self-concept and initial self-perceptions. Detecting effects from exercise on self-perceptions depends on the quality of the measurement instruments, the sample population, and the ability to measure level and type of exercise during the observation period. Based on the conceptual examination of self-esteem and self-concept, it is not surprising when studies that use global measures of self-esteem, such as the Tennessee Self-Concept Scale and the Rosenberg Self-Esteem Scale, do not show effects from exercise training programs. Many studies examining the effects of exercise on self-concept and self-esteem have also been limited in design by the self-selection of subjects to different exercise modes. Controlled research designs and the application of psychometrically sound instruments based on a multidimensional and hierarchical model of self-concept will certainly make meaningful contributions to what we know about the effects of exercise on self-esteem in various populations.

Mechanisms

Mechanisms for changes in anxiety and depression from exercise training have been the topic of numerous studies, with some support for psychobiological effects. There has been considerably less research to determine how exercise may change self-esteem. The relatively stable nature of self-esteem, particularly in adults, obviously makes detection of changes more difficult; and the lack of clinical criteria for self-esteem instruments prevents identification of a practical amount of change. Though alterations in fitness are readily perceived by people and provide a concrete, tangible basis for self-evaluation, self-concept changes in adults after aerobic or strength-training programs often do not track closely with changes in fitness variables (see figure 8.10). Thus, biological mechanisms for changes in self-perceptions do not easily come to mind.

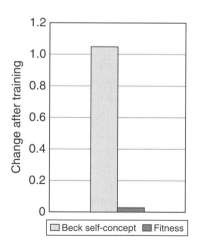

Figure 8.10 Changes in self-esteem are not necessarily dependent on changes in fitness. Change after training (effect size): self-esteem increased 1.05 (*SD*), but fitness (estimated from submaximal exercise test) did not change after eight weeks of jogging in 40 mildly depressed college women.

Data from Ossip-Klein et al. 1989.

Identifying mechanisms is also complicated by influences of possible mediating factors, such as group dynamics, situation factors, exercise history, personality characteristics, self-efficacy, and health status. However, several psychologically based mechanisms have been proposed.

> **Psychosocial Factors Influencing Self-Concept and Self-Esteem After Exercise**
>
> ▼ Exercise-induced improvements in perceptions of competence or appearance
> ▼ Improved sense of autonomy and control over the body
> ▼ Improved sense of self-acceptance
> ▼ Sense of well-being
> ▼ Sense of belonging and significance through social contact from exercise in a group or the social setting

The positive effects on self-esteem from exercise are likely due to psychosocial rather than biological mechanisms.

Other factors related to social influence or personal expectancies might artificially influence a person's rating of self-esteem. Desharnais et al. (1993) approached the question of mechanism from a rather novel perspective. They hypothesized that motivated individuals in an exercise program would have psychological benefits simply because they expect that they will. In other words, Desharnais et al. proposed a strong **placebo effect.** In the study, male and female adults were randomized to an experimental and a control exercise class. The two classes received the same training and both groups had increased fitness, but the participants in the experimental class were told initially and throughout the training program that it was designed to improve physical and psychological well-being. Self-esteem as measured by the Rosenberg Self-Esteem Scale increased significantly for the treatment but not the control class, supporting the presence of a placebo effect for improvements in self-esteem from exercise training (see figure 8.11). This study is also interesting because of the significant differences in global self-esteem.

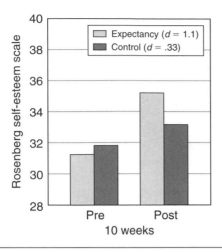

Figure 8.11 Participants in one group (expectancy) were told that training would "improve their psychological well-being," whereas those in the control group (Control) were not explicitly told to expect this. The greater increase in self-esteem after 10 weeks of training illustrates a placebo effect.

Data from Desharnais et al. 1993.

What Is a Placebo?

In research, a **placebo** is any treatment given to a control group that is meant to have no effect and is used in comparison to the treatment that is being tested. In therapy, it is a treatment that is deliberately used for non-specific, psychological, or psychophysiological effect on the assumption that there is no specific activity for the condition being treated.

Distorted Body Image and Exercise

In addition to evidence that physical activity and exercise can have a positive influence on physical self-esteem, there is evidence from clinical studies that some people who are highly physically active also have psychiatric disturbances that are associated with distorted body image (Davis 2000). That has led to some concern among health professionals that exercise training might carry some risk for psychopathologies related to eating disorders, substance abuse, and social adjustment problems. The epidemiological experiments and controlled clinical trials have not been conducted that are necessary to determine the prevalence of these disorders and the extent exercise is an independent, causal risk factor for their development. Nonetheless, it is important to acknowledge that exercise may present such risk and that these topics are worthy of clinical attention and scientific investigation.

Eating Disorders

Results from a clinical study (Yates, Leehey, and Shisslak 1983) suggested that excessive exercisers, particularly runners, present symptoms analogous to anorexia nervosa: a common family history, similar socioeconomic class and pressures; preoccupation with food and leanness; and personality traits of anger suppression, asceticism, denial of medical risk, introversion, and perfectionism. Although exercise is promoted as a healthy alternative to restrictive dieting among weight-conscious females, the possibility that exercise commitment could lead to anorexia or bulimia for some people who have a risky personality or history is a concern.

Though there are undoubtedly anorectics or bulimics who are compulsive exercisers, controlled research (Blumenthall, Rose, and Chang 1985; Dishman 1985) has indicated that in most cases, exercise commitment and anorexia nervosa are separate entities. In fact, there are case reports that describe effective treatment of anorexia using a combination of psychotherapy and running. Although anorectics often boost the impact of food restriction by hyperactivity, their fitness ($\dot{V}O_2$peak) is very low compared to committed exercisers (Einerson, Ward, and Hanson 1988), and stress-hormone profiles differ between the groups. Anorectics often have elevated scores on standard tests of psychopathology, while habitual runners usually score in the normal range of the same tests and show mood profiles that indicate positive mental health (Blumenthal, Rose, and Chang, 1985). Table 8.2 lists shared and unique characteristics of anorexic and athletic females.

Some studies with small samples of elite ballerinas, gymnasts, and wrestlers found higher than expected rates of eating problems. However, it has not been established how long the eating problems persist in these populations, and whether they represent goal-appropriate behaviors for the sport, rather than medical or psychological pathology (Dishman 1985). *Anorexia Athletica* has been pro-

Table 8.2

Anorexic Versus Athletic Female

Shared features

Dietary faddism
Controlled calorie consumption
Specific carbohydrate avoidance
Low body weight
Resting bradycardia and low blood pressure
Increased physical activity
Amenorrhea or oligomenorrhea
Anemia (may or may not be present)

Distinguishing features	
Athlete	**Anorexic**
Purposeful training	Aimless physical activity
Increased exercise tolerance	Poor or decreasing exercise performance
Good muscular development	Poor muscular development
Accurate body image	Flawed body image (patient believes herself to be overweight)
Body-fat level within defined normal range	Body-fat level below normal range
	Biochemical abnormalities if abusing laxatives and/or diuretics

Data from McSherry 1984.

posed as a subclinical syndrome of anorexia nervosa (Sundgot-Borgen 1994), and 22% of a sample of over 500 elite Norwegian female athletes were judged at risk for an eating disorder (Sundgot-Borgen 1994). However, the prevalence of disordered eating and the independent, causal risk of sport and exercise have not yet been established by controlled epidemiological and clinical studies. In most cases, the eating behaviors of athletes do not appear to signal anorexia nervosa or bulimia (O'Connor and Smith 1999).

Muscle Dysmorphia

Harvard affiliated researchers proposed a form of body dysmorphic disorder they have termed **muscle dysmorphia** in which both men and women develop a pathological preoccupation with their muscularity (Phillips, O'Sullivan, and Pope 1997). They presented case studies that supported an association between muscle dysmorphia and severe subjective distress, impaired social and occupational functioning, and abuse of anabolic steroids and other substances (Gruber and Pope 2000; Pope et al. 1997).

Diagnostic Criteria for Body Dysmorphic Disorder

A. Preoccupation with an imagined defect in appearance. If a slight physical anomaly is present, the person's concern is markedly excessive.

B. The preoccupation causes clinically significant distress or impairment in social, occupational, or other important areas of functioning.

C. The preoccupation is not better accounted for by another mental disorder (e.g., dissatisfaction with body shape and size in anorexia nervosa)

Reprinted, by permission, from American Psychiatric Association, 1994, *Diagnostic and Statistical Manual of Mental Disorders*, 4th ed., p. 468.

The investigation of body dysmorphic disorder was continued in a test of the hypothesis that men in Western societies would desire to have a leaner and more muscular body than they had or perceived (Pope et al. 2000). The height, weight, and body fat of college-aged men in Austria ($N = 54$), France ($N = 65$), and the United States ($N = 81$) were measured. Next, the men chose a pictorial body image that they felt represented (1) their own body, (2) the body they ideally would like to have, (3) the body of an average man of their age, and (4) the male body they believed women would prefer. The men's actual fat and muscularity was compared with that of the four images chosen. Despite modest differences between measured body fat and the amount of fat of the images chosen, men from all three countries chose an ideal body that was 28 lb more muscular on average than themselves. The men also estimated that women preferred a male body about 30 lb more muscular than themselves, even though women in fact said they preferred an ordinary male body. The investigators speculated that the wide discrepancy between men's ideal body image and actual muscularity might help explain muscle dysmorphia and some anabolic steroid abuse.

Another study reported comparisons on psychological and behavioral variables between 24 men classified as having muscle dysmorphia and 30 comparison weightlifters without clinical disorders recruited from gymnasiums in the Boston area (Olivardia, Pope, and Hudson 2000). Men with muscle dysmorphia scored higher on body dissatisfaction, risky eating attitudes, prevalence of anabolic steroid use, and lifetime prevalence of *DSM-IV* mood, anxiety, and eating disorders. These men also frequently reported that they experienced shame, embarrassment, and impaired function at work and in social situations. Similarly, several cases of body dysmorphia were also reported among 75 women bodybuilders recruited from Boston-area gymnasiums (Gruber and Pope 2000).

Exercise Abuse

Separate from cases of eating disorders and muscle dysmorphia are case reports of compulsive involvement or dependence with exercise training. Morgan (1979b) described eight cases of "running addiction," defined as when commitment to running exceeded prior commitments to work, family, social relations, and medical advice. Similar cases have been labeled as "positive addiction", "runner's gluttony", "fitness fanaticism", "athlete's neurosis", and "obligatory running" (Dishman 1985; Sacks and Sachs 1981). However, we understand very little about the origins, diagnostic validity or the mental health impact of abusive exercise. For most people, the benefits of exercise exceed the risks of abuse.

However, emotional or social adjustment problems may be present when an individual is unable or unwilling to interrupt or taper an exercise training program, or to replace a preferred form of exercise with an alternative despite a medical exigency, or vocational or social responsibilities. The few studies that show psychopathology in habitual runners also indicate that an exaggerated emphasis on exercise roles or fitness abilities (as can happen for other areas of life) can reflect a pre-existing proneness to problems of an imbalanced and insecure self-concept (Davis 2000; Dishman 1985).

Summary

Self-esteem is an important concept in the social sciences and in everyday life. Self-esteem is determined through a combination of personal convictions and internalized values from the dominant culture and selected subcultures, and consists of the evaluation of the various aspects of self-concept. Most individuals would agree that positive self-esteem is associated with good mental health, so linking exercise with improvements in physical self-concept and thus with better self-esteem offers another reason for adopting and maintaining a physically active lifestyle. Obviously, though, things are not that simple. This chapter included a discussion of how self-esteem and self-concept are related; it also presented models for understanding how exercise can influence our self-perceptions. The physical self, which includes the physical body and the way in which the body is valued and judged, is an important component of self-esteem and seems to be critical in Western societies. Thus, changes in structure, function, and physical self-concept with exercise can have a significant impact on self-worth. Self-esteem also influences behavioral choices as a function of expectations about how the behavioral outcomes will affect self-perceptions. According to self-enhancement theory, people will choose activities in which success is likely over those with the likelihood of failure. And there is good evidence that behavior can affect self-esteem. For example, people make more positive judgments about the self after successfully completing a difficult task (e.g., mastery experiences).

Generally, the effects of exercise on self-esteem are strongest for those lowest in initial self-esteem. Effects from physical activity or exercise are specific; they influence perceptions of physical performance ability, for example, but not academic self-esteem. Careful measurement of self-concept and self-esteem is critical, and the sensitivity gained through use of a multidimensional hierarchical model of the self will benefit the ability to detect and explain effects of exercise on the self in various populations over time. Intuitively, body image influences self-esteem, particularly in societies in which appearance is highly valued, and is a construct that we should measure when exploring the relationship between exercise and self-esteem. Finally, it is also important to consider that there can be risks to mental health or social adjustment associated with extreme dedication to exercise or preoccupation with fitness or physique. Concepts such as anorexia athletica, muscle dysmorphia, and exercise abuse are not recognized as psychiatric diagnoses related to distorted self-image. Nonetheless, their appearance in clinical and scientific literatures illustrate that their measurement, prevalence, health consequences, and relationship with exercise warrant study.

Suggested Readings

Fox, K.R. 1998. Advances in the measurement of the physical self. In *Advances in sport and exercise psychology measurement*, ed. J.L. Duda. Morgantown, WV: Fitness Information Technology.

Gauvin, L., and J.C. Spence. 1998. Measurement of exercise-induced changes in feeling states, affect, mood, and emotions. In *Advances in sport and exercise psychology measurement*, ed. J.L. Duda. Morgantown, WV: Fitness Information Technology.

Marsh, H.W. 1997. The measurement of physical self-concept: A construct validation approach. In *The physical self: From motivation to well-being*, ed. K.R. Fox, 27–58. Champaign, IL: Human Kinetics.

Sonstroem, R.J. 1998. Physical self-concept: assessment and external validity. *Exercise and Sport Sciences Reviews* 26: 133–164.

Web Sites

http://edweb.macarthur.uws.edu.au/self/default.htm

www.self-esteem-nase.org/

www.mentalhelp.net (search word "self-esteem")

One-third of our lives is spent asleep, so understanding ways to improve the quality of sleep is an important area of research. Most people assume that they will sleep well after spending a day doing hard manual labor. That assumption seems to have led to the belief that exercise will also foster a good night's sleep. Although exercise is a habit that can promote sleep, and is recommended by the American Sleep Disorders Association (see box), there is surprisingly little **empirical research** on exercise in relation to disturbed sleep. This chapter provides information about what sleep is, how it is measured, and what factors influence it. We review research on sleep and exercise and address possible mechanisms for the influence of exercise on sleep.

Prevalence and Impact of Sleep Disturbances

The annual prevalence of sleep loss (i.e., insomnia) is nearly one-third of the adult population in the United States and 20% to 40% worldwide (Hetta et al. 1985; Janson et al. 1995; Klink and Quan 1987; Mellinger, Balter, and Uhlenhuth 1985; Ohayon, Caulet, and Guilleminault 1998). Insomnia and sleepiness during the day are both associated with increased risk of accidents and mental health problems and decreased productivity at the workplace. The direct cost of sleep disorders and sleep deprivation in the United States is about $15.9 billion

---

Sleep Hygiene Recommendations to Promote Sleep

▼ Caffeine should not be consumed within 3 to 4 h of bedtime.

▼ Quitting smoking can improve sleep.

▼ Alcoholic beverages should be avoided within 4 to 6 h of bedtime.

▼ Regular exercise promotes sleep, but morning exercise has little effect on sleep, and evening exercise (within 6 h of bedtime) disrupts sleep.

▼ A dark, quiet, comfortable environment is ideal for sleep.

▼ Avoid heavy meals close to bedtime. Light snacks and dairy products may promote sleep.

▼ Sleep only when drowsy.

▼ Maintain a regular arise time.

▼ Use the bedroom only for sleep and sex.

▼ Avoid daytime napping.

Data from American Sleep Disorders Association 1997.

annually, with an estimated indirect cost of $50 to $100 billion when the costs of sleep-related individual accidents are added, including litigation, destruction of property, hospitalization, and death (National Commission on Sleep Disorders Research 1993). The Institute of Circadian Physiology in Boston has estimated that sleeping problems cost companies in the United States about $70 billion annually in lost productivity, medical bills, and industrial accidents.

Insomnia is common in as many as 40% of adults worldwide.

Insomnia and sleepiness contribute to personal stress, increased risk of accidents, and decreased productivity, at an annual direct and indirect cost of $65 to $165 billion in the United States alone.

Only about 5% to 20% of people who experience sleep disturbances will seek help from a primary care physician; about half of those who seek treatment will receive a drug prescription, usually a hypnotic or anxiolytic benzodiazepine. Many who do not seek treatment purchase over-the-counter sleep aids or use caffeine or alcohol, which can worsen the sleep problem in the long term (Kripke et al. 1998). So-called natural sleep-promoting agents have unestablished efficacy and may carry risks to health. For example, melatonin has been promoted as a "miracle" sleep drug, but there is no clear evidence that it promotes sleep. For older adults, whose sleep problems can often be attributed to advanced circadian phase (i.e., early sleep and early awakening), taking melatonin at night could worsen sleep problems by further advancing the circadian phase. Negative side effects of melatonin, including nausea, nightmares, and headaches, may offset its supposed benefits (Guardiola-Lemaitre 1997).

Brief History of Sleep Research

In 1913, French scientist Henri Pieron wrote a book entitled *Le Probleme Physiologique du Sommeil*, the first text to use a physiological approach to describe sleep. Dr. Nathaniel Kleitman, generally acknowledged as the father of American sleep research, began research on the regulation of sleep, wakefulness, and circadian rhythms at the University of Chicago in the 1920s. Kleitman's seminal studies included research on the effects of sleep deprivation. In 1953 he and one of his students, Dr. Eugene Aserinsky, discovered rapid eye movement (REM) during sleep.

Research on sleep began in the 1920s and REM sleep was identified in the early 1950s, but interest in sleep research is in its infancy.

Another of Kleitman's students, Dr. William C. Dement, described the "cyclical" nature of nocturnal sleep in 1955, and in 1957 and 1958 established the relationship between REM sleep and dreaming. There now are over 200 accredited sleep disorders centers and laboratories in the United States alone that are designed to recognize and treat sleep disorders. Against this historical background, scientific interest in the effects of exercise on sleep is in its infancy (Youngstedt 1997, 2000).

Definitions: What Is Sleep?

Sleep is a state of reversible unconsciousness characterized by little movement and reduced responses to external stimuli. All mammals sleep, and it is believed that lowered brain metabolism during slow-wave sleep provides a rest period for the brain. Dreaming occurs during **rapid eye movement (REM) sleep;** and though there is debate over the purpose of dreams, REM sleep appears critical on the basis of a rebound phenomenon that occurs after REM deprivation in which more time than normal is spent in REM sleep. Extensive sleep deprivation has a significant effect on cognitive functions and mood, such as the occurrence of perceptual distortions and hallucinations, but little impact on the ability to perform physical exercise (Carlson 1998).

Stages of sleep are identified by corresponding neural, physiological, and behavioral patterns, although the most familiar to the general public is REM sleep, during which dreaming occurs.

Being asleep is not analogous to putting your body and brain on hold. Sleep consists of different stages with corresponding neural, physiological, and behavioral patterns. On the basis of polysomnographic studies, sleep has been divided into periods of REM sleep and four stages of non-REM (NREM) sleep during which sleep progressively deepens. Stages 3 and 4 combined constitute **slow-wave sleep (SWS),** when people are hardest to awaken. About 75% of the night's sleep is NREM (~5% stage 1, ~50% stage 2, and ~20% stages 3 and 4 [SWS]). During sleep, activity of the brain cortex fluctuates along a continuum from synchronous, low-frequency, high-amplitude activity to asynchronous, high-frequency, low-amplitude activity (see figure 9.1). This continuum can be delineated by corresponding periods of δ (0.5-3 Hz), θ (3.5-7.5 Hz), α (8-12 Hz), and β (13-30 Hz) activity (one wave per second is 1 Hz). **Alpha wave** activity is commonly described as relaxed wakefulness. Sleep progresses from drowsiness to *stage 1*, marked by θ activity, which usually lasts 1 to 7 min. *Stage 2* occurs later, denoted by θ activity, sleep spindles (short bursts of 12-14 Hz), and K complexes (sudden sharp spikes). Spindles occur several times a minute throughout stages 1 to 4, while K complexes occur only in stage 2. *Stage 3* begins later, characterized by δ activity. Increasing δ activity denotes *stage 4*, or deep sleep. Sleep then becomes progressively lighter as the person reenters stage 3 and stage 2 sleep, followed by an episode of REM sleep. Rapid eye movement sleep

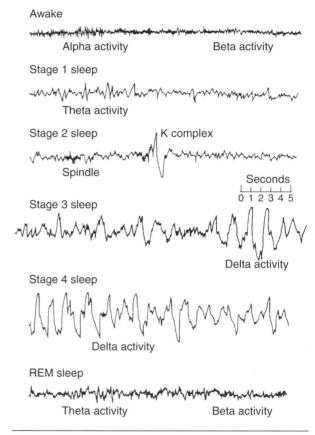

Figure 9.1 Fluctuations in brain activity during various stages of sleep.

Reprinted, by permission of Oxford University Press, from J.A. Horne, 1988, *Why we sleep: The functions of sleep in humans and other mammals* (Oxford, UK: Oxford University Press), ©1988 by James Horne.

typically begins about 45 min after the onset of stage 4 sleep. Beta activity, rapid eye movement, and little skeletal muscle activity occur during REM sleep.

Neurons located in the pons area of the brainstem trigger REM sleep and inhibit spinal cord neurons, leading to temporary muscle paralysis (figure 9.2). Within the pons, the nucleus reticularis pontis oralis/caudalis (RPO/RPC) is the most important site for the production of REM sleep (figure 9.3). Many of these neurons responsible for REM sleep use acetylcholine as the neurotransmitter. Dorsal raphe (serotonin) and locus coeruleus (norepinephrine) neurons help turn off REM sleep. Activation of the *basal forebrain* is a key in starting NREM sleep. It is thought that temperature-sensitive neurons in the *preoptic area of the anterior hypothalamus* that project to the basal forebrain are key in the control of SWS.

During the night (8 h), a sleeper without clinical disorders has four or five sleep cycles. Each lasts about 90 min and contains 20 to 30 min of REM sleep. The length of sleep stages changes throughout the night. The sleep cycle is controlled by centers in the brainstem, probably in the medulla. Slow-wave sleep, which seems to be controlled by the basal forebrain region, predominates during the first third of the night. Rapid eye movement predominates during the last third of the night and is initiated by acetylcholine released in the pons. Actions of the locus coeruleus and raphe nucleus are suppressed during REM sleep.

The most common form of the 84 types of sleep disorders is insomnia, which is defined as the subjective complaint of sleep disruption. Insomnia is characterized by difficulty in initiating and/or maintaining sleep. It is actually a symptom, and not a disorder per se. Common forms of insomnia that might be helped by exercise are defined in figure 9.4.

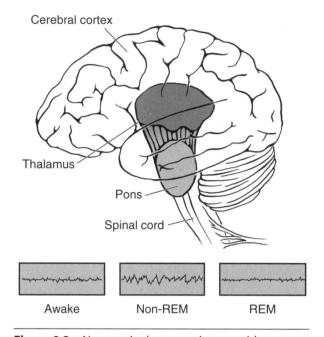

Figure 9.2   Neurons in the pons trigger rapid eye movement sleep and inhibit spinal cord neurons.

Based on Siegel 2000.

Components of Sleep

Sleep is described by the amount of time spent in the following states:

▼ Stage 2
▼ Stages 3 and 4 (stages 3 and 4 combined equal SWS)
▼ REM
▼ REM latency
▼ Wakefulness after sleep onset (WASO)
▼ Sleep onset latency (SOL)
▼ Total sleep time (TST)

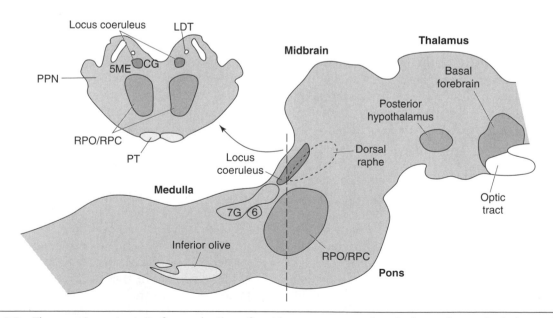

Figure 9.3   The most important site for production of rapid eye movement sleep is the nucleus reticularis pontis oralis/caudalis (RPO/RPC).

From E.R. Kandel, J.H. Schwartz, and T.M. Jessell, 1991, *Principles of neural science,* 3rd ed. (New York: Elsevier). Reprinted with permission of The McGraw-Hill Companies.

Common Types of Insomnia That Exercise Might Help

Sleep onset insomnia (delayed sleep phase syndrome): The major sleep episode is delayed in relation to the desired clock time. This delay results in symptoms of sleep onset insomnia or difficulty in awakening at the desired time.

Psychophysiological insomnia: A disorder of somatized tension (conversion of anxiety into physical symptoms) and learned sleep-preventing association that results in a complaint of insomnia and associated decreased functioning during wakefulness.

Transient insomnia (adjustment sleep disorder): Represents sleep disturbance temporally related to acute stress, conflict, or environmental change causing emotional agitation.

Periodic insomnia (non–24-hour sleep-wake syndrome): Consists of a chronic (lasting a long time), steady pattern comprising 1- to 2-hour delays in sleep onset and wake times in an individual that occur on a daily basis.

Hypnotic-dependency insomnia (hypnotic-dependent sleep disorder): Characterized by insomnia or excessive sleepiness that is associated with tolerance to or withdrawal from hypnotic medications.

Stimulant-dependent sleep disorder: Characterized by a reduction of sleepiness or suppression of sleep by central stimulants, and resultant alterations in wakefulness following drug abstinence.

Alcohol-dependent insomnia (alcohol-dependent sleep disorder): Characterized by the assisted initiation of sleep onset by the sustained ingestion of alcohol that is used for its hypnotic effect.

Figure 9.4 Exercise is believed to help some types of insomnia.

Measuring Sleep

After an individual has approached his or her physician for help with a sleep disturbance and has received treatment, usually pharmacological, the decision to continue sleep treatment depends on subjective ratings of improved sleep. Hence, quality and quantity of sleep is often estimated through the use of questionnaires. However, self-assessments of sleep are often inaccurate. For example, sleep patients frequently exaggerate their loss of sleep, and treatment often involves demonstrating this overestimation to the patient. Conversely, patients who have sleep apnea (cessation of breathing during sleep) often are unaware of their disturbed sleep. Objective measures of sleep provide more accurate information on the amount and staging of sleep, which is necessary for an understanding of the biological mechanisms that govern sleep. Sleep can be estimated using a motion sensor (i.e., an actigraph) that detects movement, especially wrist movement, during sleep. **Actigraphy** of wrist movement can determine whether someone is asleep or awake with accuracy as high as 95%. Though convenient and practical for long-term monitoring in studies of large numbers of people, actigraphy is not as accurate as **polysomnography,** which combines the use

of electroencephalographic (EEG) records of brain waves; electromyographic (EMG) records of eye and chin muscle activity to detect REM sleep; strain gauge sensors on the chest and abdomen for recording respiration; and EMG electrodes on the legs for recording leg movements to determine sleep stages (see figure 9.5).

*S*elf-assessments of quality and quantity of sleep are often inaccurate and cannot provide information about brain waves and REM, which are measured with EEG, EMG, and other objective methods.

Research on Exercise and Sleep

Large-scale studies on exercise and sleep have relied on self-reports of sleep and exercise and their associated limitations. Smaller studies have used more objective measures of sleep that provide better

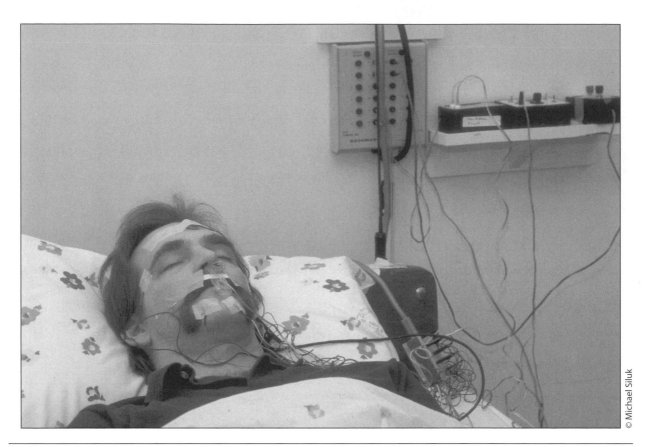

Figure 9.5   Use of polysomnograph to measure aspects of sleep

evidence for effects of exercise on sleep, although the research is limited.

Epidemiological Studies

In a survey of nearly 1200 middle-aged men and women (ages 36-50 years) living in Tampere, Finland (Vuori et al. 1988), people ranked exercise first when asked to, "state, in order of importance, three practices, habits, or actions which you have observed to best promote or improve your falling asleep immediately or your perceived quality of sleep."

A more recent survey of randomly selected women (n = 403) and men (n = 319) living in Tucson, Arizona, indicated that the prevalence of self-reported sleep problems and daytime sleepiness was lower among those who said that they were physically active (even among those exercising just once a week) compared to those who were sedentary (Sherrill et al. 1998; figure 9.6).

Such epidemiologic comparisons of sleep between physically active and inactive individuals cannot establish the direction of causality. An equally plausible hypothesis is that those who sleep better

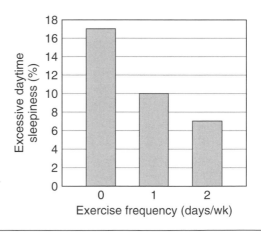

Figure 9.6   Epidemiological evidence for the relationship between exercise and daytime sleepiness.

Data from Sherrill, Kotchou, and Quan 1998.

are less tired during the day and therefore more willing to engage in regular exercise (O'Connor and Youngstedt 1995). Moreover, physically active individuals may be more likely to engage in other healthy habits conducive to sleep, such as limited intake of alcohol and tobacco and greater exposure to bright light, all of which can improve sleep. Another explanation for anecdotal reports of better sleep after exercise might be that people are more likely to exercise when they have more time; hence better sleep might occur on exercise days because they already feel less stressed by other priorities (Driver and Taylor 2000).

In epidemiological studies exercise is associated with better sleep, but the effects may be attributable to other related factors, such as personality or participation in other health habits conducive to sleep.

Subjective ratings of sleep that are obtained in exercise studies might not be valid if participants enter the study expecting to benefit because they already believe that exercise will promote sleep. This is likely because of the folk wisdom, yet to be fully confirmed by science, that exercise helps sleep. According to this belief, the value of sleep is that it conserves or restores energy and that physical fatigue is synonymous with sleepiness.

Meta-Analysis of Exercise and Sleep Research

A quantitative synthesis of the cumulated studies on the effects of an exercise session on sleep showed that acute exercise did not alter the time it took to fall asleep or the amount of wakefulness during the nighttime sleep period (Youngstedt, O'Connor, and Dishman 1997). On average, exercise was followed by increases in total sleep time (10 min), SWS (4 min), and REM latency after sleep onset (13 min) and also a decrease in REM sleep (7 min) (see table 9.1). Those effects ranged from about .2 to .5 *SD*, which are small to moderately large effects statistically but which equate to only a few minutes of sleep in each stage, well within normal night-to-night variation.

Contrary to previous results, exercise that was associated with a high heat load did not increase SWS above the average effect of exercise, but high heat load was associated with increased wakefulness after sleep onset. A long duration of exercise (about 2 h) was associated with larger increases in total sleep time and larger decreases in REM, but this is of

Table 9.1

Acute Effects of Exercise on Sleep

Quantitative synthesis of 34 studies

Variable	Effect size
Slow wave	0.19 (4.2 min)
REM	−0.49 (−7.4 min)
REM onset	0.52 (13.1 min)
TST	0.42 (9.9 min)

REM = rapid eye movement; TST = total sleep time.
Data from Youngstedt, O'Connor, and Dishman 1997.

little practical importance for most people, who typically exercise 20 to 45 min each session.

Exercise can significantly increase sleep time and decrease REM sleep, but meaningful increases in total sleep time require long-duration exercise, of at least 1 h.

The trivial effects of acute exercise on SWS contrast with the assumption that exercise increases SWS. Also, it is not clear that an effect of exercise on SWS means that sleep will be improved. For example, both drug treatment and exercise can increase SWS, but people don't report that they have better sleep or have less daytime sleepiness with these interventions (Landolt et al. 1998; Youngstedt et al. 1999b).

Exercise Training

Several studies have shown that physically active or fit individuals have more SWS and total sleep time. Because the comparisons were made at a cross section of time (i.e., a single point in time), these studies do not demonstrate that the improved sleep was caused by exercise rather than by other differences between the groups (e.g., healthy habits or personality); they also do not address the possibility that people who sleep well are more likely to exercise.

Though an early experimental study indicated that stopping regular exercise led to disrupted sleep (Baekeland 1970), most studies of the effects of chronic exercise on sleep have also been limited by a focus on good sleepers. Nonetheless, moderately large improvements ranging from a half to nearly a full standard deviation have been seen after exercise training: quicker SOL, less REM sleep, more total sleep time, and more SWS (see table 9.2).

Table 9.2

Sleep Variables Most Affected by Chronic Exercise

Variable	Effect size *(SD)*
TST	0.94
REM	−0.57
Sleep onset	0.45
Slow wave	0.43

Results are based on a meta-analysis of 12 experiments with good sleepers. TST = total sleep time; REM = rapid eye movement.

Data from Kubitz et al. 1996.

Encouraging results have been found more recently in randomized, controlled studies with older people who complained of poor sleep. In a study of older depressed patients (mean age ~70 years), Singh, Clements, and Fiatarone (1997) found significantly greater improvement in self-reported sleep quality following 10 weeks of weight training (*n* = 15, three times per week) compared with health education training (see figure 9.7).

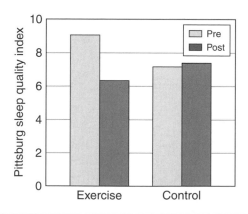

Figure 9.7   Thirty-two depressed older adults (mean age 71) were randomly assigned to a control group or weightlifting exercise (three times per week for 10 weeks). A score greater than 5 indicates sleep problems; lower scores indicate better sleep.

Reprinted, by permission, from N.A. Singh, K.M. Clements, and M.A. Fiatarone, 1997, "A randomized controlled trial of the effect of exercise on sleep," *Sleep* 20: 95–101.

Likewise, King et al. (1997) tested 43 older (ages 50-76 years) adults with moderate sleep complaints and found significantly greater improvements in self-reported sleep quality following 16 weeks of moderate aerobic exercise compared with results in a waiting-list control group (figure 9.8).

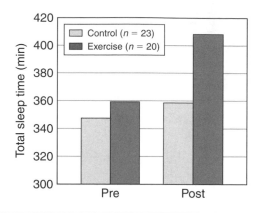

Figure 9.8   Adults aged 50 to 76 with moderate sleep problems completed 30 to 40 min of aerobic exercise four times per week for 16 weeks. The controls maintained their usual activity levels.

Data from King et al. 1997.

Other convincing evidence that chronic exercise promotes sleep was provided by Guilleminault et al. (1995). Thirty individuals (mean age 44 years) with psychophysiologic insomnia were randomly assigned to three different four-week treatments: (a) sleep hygiene education; (b) sleep hygiene combined with exercise (daily walking for 45 min); and (c) sleep hygiene plus bright light (daily 1 h exposure of 3000 lux). Sleep was assessed during the weeks before and after these treatments. Whereas sleep hygiene by itself resulted in a decrease in total sleep time of 3 min, the exercise treatment elicited a chronic increase in total sleep time of 17 min. However, the most impressive result of this study was that the bright light plus exercise condition increased total sleep time by nearly an hour.

*T*here is some evidence that exercise training has a positive impact on sleep in individuals with sleep complaints.

Issues in Sleep and Exercise Research

Several characteristics of the person and of exercise can influence whether, or to what extent, exercise affects sleep. *Level of fitness* is a factor that could influence the effects of exercise on sleep. It is plausible that exercise might promote sleep in physically fit or active persons but be stressful and hinder sleep among unfit and inactive persons. However, experimental evidence indicates that fitness does not moderate the effects of acute exercise on sleep (Youngstedt, O'Connor, and Dishman 1997); this evidence agrees with surveys showing that exercise promotes sleep in the general population, which is largely sedentary (Vuori et al. 1988).

Body heating from exercise as a mechanism is consistent with a proposed sleep hypothesis. The anterior hypothalamus plays an important role in regulating both heat loss and sleep. A popular hypothesis is that sleep, especially increased SWS, is improved when heat-loss mechanisms in the hypothalamus are activated by body heating (McGinty and Szymusiak 1990). Studies in which people have been immersed in hot water have supported this hypothesis by demonstrating increased SWS (Horne and Staff 1983; figure 9.9).

One study of fit women without clinical disorders showed that increased SWS after acute exercise depends upon body heating during exercise. Slow-wave sleep was increased after passive heating of the body to a level similar to that achieved during heavy exercise (Horne and Staff 1983; see figures 9.9 and 9.10). A study by Horne and Moore (1985) showed that

Body heating can promote slow-wave sleep by activating heat-loss mechanisms in the hypothalamus and the brain.

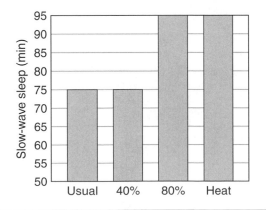

Figure 9.9 Body heating and sleep: immersing people in hot water increased their percentage of slow-wave sleep as much as exercising at 80% of aerobic capacity.

Data from Horne and Staff 1983.

SWS elevations following exercise could be reversed by body cooling. Since that study, sleep researchers and professionals have generally accepted that exercise helps sleep because it increases body temperature. However, a limitation of the Horne and Moore study was that body temperature was not assessed at bedtime or during sleep. Also, the exercise was performed approximately 6 h before bedtime, apparently enough time for body temperature to return to baseline levels. Meta-analysis data showing no positive moderating effects of heat load on sleep further contradict the thermogenic hypothesis (Youngstedt, O'Connor, and Dishman 1997).

Body temperature increases proportionately with exercise intensity, so sleep should be best helped after heavy exercise. Only about 10% of the general population exercise vigorously on a regular basis, so on the basis of the body temperature hypothesis, exercise should not be expected to help the sleep of most people. However, if less intense exercise is just as helpful for sleep, as evidence suggests (Youngstedt, O'Connor, and Dishman 1997), then more people may improve their sleep with exercise.

Characteristics of exercise behavior that have been examined with respect to sleep are *duration of exercise*

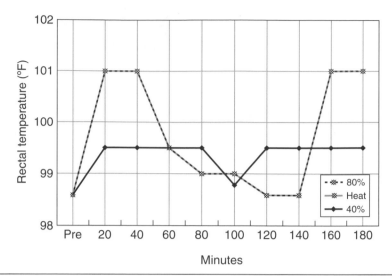

Figure 9.10 Conditions of heavy exercise (80% capacity) and passive heat produced the same body temperature. This permitted a test of whether sleep would be affected by increased body temperature during exercise.

Data from Horne and Staff 1983.

and *how long before bedtime the exercise occurs.* The cumulative evidence from sleep studies indicates that as exercise duration is increased beyond 1 h, total sleep time increases substantially (Youngstedt, O'Connor, and Dishman 1997). That observation raises questions about the practical usefulness of exercise. Most people are unlikely to exercise for the 1 h per day found necessary to reliably improve sleep.

A common opinion of the public and of health professionals is that vigorous exercise close to bedtime will disturb sleep. Two recent studies have clearly contradicted that viewpoint. O'Connor, Breus, and Youngstedt (1998) found no detrimental effect on sleep of 1 h of exercise at an intensity of 60% of aerobic capacity 30 to 90 min before typical bedtime. Also, Youngstedt et al. (2000) found no effect on sleep of very exhaustive exercise consisting of 3 h of cycling at 70% aerobic capacity that was completed just 30 min before bedtime. Moreover, a random population-based survey of Finnish adults (*n* = 1190) showed that most who exercised vigorously in the evening (after 8 P.M.) reported mainly positive effects on sleep (Vuori et al. 1988). Nighttime is a practical time to exercise for many people, so unsubstantiated claims that nighttime exercise disturbs sleep might be a false barrier to exercise among people who can't find the time to exercise during the day.

E*xercising close to bedtime will not disrupt sleep in most people.*

Mechanisms

Understanding how exercise might influence sleep may not only have significance for clinical applications, but may also reveal important information about sleep function. However, the question of mechanisms whereby exercise may facilitate sleep remains unresolved. Body heating, discussed earlier, is one mechanism with equivocal support. Other possible but unconfirmed explanations include body restitution, energy conservation, and

© International Stock

Substantial increases in total sleep time have been found with exercise bouts lasting longer than one hour.

increased secretion of melatonin, which helps regulate circadian sleep. This section outlines some of what we know about the mechanisms of light exposure, anti-anxiety and antidepressant effects, circadian phase-shifting, and biochemical effects.

Light Exposure

Low levels of illumination in the natural environment are significantly associated with depression and sleep disturbance, and bright light treatments are effective in reducing some types of depression and in enhancing sleep. The average adult receives about 20 min of daily exposure to bright light (i.e., more than 2500 lux) (Espiritu et al. 1994), but many people who exercise outdoors in the middle of the day (1 h at 10,000 lux) can get 10 times that much. Studies of acute exercise have not provided information about illumination during the exercise or throughout the day. The discrepancy between experimental evidence and anecdotal reports about exercise might be explained by the fact that many studies have been conducted inside laboratories, whereas most people who exercise do so outdoors as part of their daily routines, where light can be thousands of times brighter than normal indoor lighting. Even if bright light exposure does not mediate the effects of exercise on sleep, exposure to bright light might augment the sleep-promoting effects of exercise. Additive effects of exercise and bright light for reducing depression have been reported (Partonen et al. 1998).

Anti-Anxiety and Antidepressant Effects

Anxiety disrupts sleep, and exercise can reduce anxiety for several hours in some circumstances (see chapter 6). Therefore, it is plausible that exercise might promote sleep by reducing anxiety. The one study that has explored this mechanism (Youngstedt et al. 2000) was inconclusive. Although participants who exercised had significant reductions in anxiety 20 min after exercise compared with a sedentary control condition, there was no difference in anxiety between conditions at bedtime, which occurred 4 to 6 h after the exercise, and there was no association between sleep and anxiety level at bedtime. Regular exercise also has antidepressant effects, so it could promote sleep indirectly by alleviating symptoms of depression, which include disordered sleep (Singh, Clements, and Fiatarone 1997).

*P*otential mechanisms for effects of exercise on sleep include an indirect effect through light exposure during exercise outdoors, decreased anxiety/depression, circadian phase-shifting effects, and biochemical effects from exercise.

Circadian Phase-Shifting Effects

Sleep can be disrupted when there is a desynchronization between a person's circadian pacemaker—which largely regulates sleep and wakefulness—and the sleep-wake schedule. Examples include shift work (i.e., when people work and sleep at odd hours) or jet travel across several time zones. About one-third of people aged 60 years or older experience a chronic state of circadian

© AFP/Corbis

Many athletes who traveled to the 2000 Summer Olympic Games in Sydney, Australia, had shifts in their sleep-wake cycles from crossing several time zones.

malsynchronization that impairs sleep as much as other mechanisms underlying aging sleep patterns, such as sleep apnea and periodic limb movements during sleep. Correcting circadian phase can elicit dramatic improvements in sleep in older individuals. Evidence now suggests that exercise can elicit substantial circadian phase-shifting effects, comparable to those that occur in response to bright light (Van Reeth et al. 1994).

Biochemical Effects

Adenosine increases in muscles and interstitial fluids during exercise, and it is thought to facilitate dilation of blood vessels when low levels of fuel and oxygen are detected (Radegran and Hellsten 2000). Adenosine is also believed to play an important role in the regulation of sleep (Porkka-Heiskanen et al. 1997). Youngstedt, Kripke, and Elliott (1999) found that increases in SWS after exercise were nearly three times greater after a placebo treatment compared with consumption of caffeine, which blocks adenosine neurotransmission.

An explanation for delayed effects of exercise on sleep might be prolonged elevation in blood levels of chemicals that affect sleep. One plausible sleep factor might be **prostaglandins.** Horne and Shackell (1987) found that elevations in body temperature (2 °C) and SWS after passive body heating 2 h before bedtime were reversed by aspirin, a prostaglandin inhibitor.

Summary

Acute exercise leads to a moderate delay in the onset of REM sleep, a small decrease in the amount of REM sleep, and a small increase in SWS and total sleep time—among good sleepers. The biggest limitation of studies of the effects of exercise on sleep has been a focus on good sleepers. Convincing studies using polysomnographic measures of sleep after chronic exercise, among initially sedentary people who are poor sleepers, have not been conducted. The small number of studies on chronic

physical activity in sleepers without clinical disorders indicates small-to-moderate effects of increased SWS and TST, with decreased SOL, WASO, and REM sleep. Larger effects might be observed in individuals with sleep problems (Youngstedt, O'Connor, and Dishman 1997; 2000). Until there is more research on individuals with disturbed sleep or on experimentally induced sleep disruption (Youngstedt et al. 1999b), we will not understand the potential of exercise for promoting sleep. We still have an incomplete understanding of potential benefits of exercise on the sleep of people who have insomnia or other sleep disorders. However, we are more confident that the risks of exercise disturbing sleep are minimal; there currently is no evidence to indicate that moderate-to-vigorous leisure-time physical activity, including exercise that causes delayed-onset muscle pain (Breus, O'Connor, and Ragan 2000), will harm most people's sleep.

Suggested Readings

Carskadon, M.A., and W.C. Dement. 1989. Normal human sleep: An overview. In *Principles and practice of sleep medicine*, ed. M.H. Kryger, T. Roth, and W.C. Dement. Philadelphia: Saunders.

Driver, H.S., and S.R. Taylor. 2000. Exercise and sleep. *Sleep Medicine Reviews* 4: 387–402.

O'Connor, P.J., and S.D. Youngstedt. 1995. Influence of exercise on human sleep. *Exercise and Sport Sciences Reviews* 23: 105–134.

Youngstedt, S.D. 1997. Does exercise truly enhance sleep? *Physician and Sportsmedicine* 25 (10): 73–82.

Youngstedt, S.D., P.J. O'Connor, and R.K. Dishman. 1997. The effects of acute exercise on sleep: A quantitative synthesis. *Sleep* 20 (Mar): 203–214.

Web Sites

www.sleepquest.com/
www.med.stanford.edu/school/psychiatry/coe/
www.npi.ucla.edu/sleepresearch/linkscss.htm

PART

III

The Psychology of Physical Activity Behavior

The previous chapters have focused on the psychological benefits of exercise and increased levels of physical activity. Given the evidence for improved mood as well as the public perspective that "exercise is good for you," the low rates of participation in leisure physical activity in developed nations with market economics (Caspersen, Merritt, and Stephens 1994) are perplexing. Interventions to promote long-term increases in leisure physical activity have also had modest, though encouraging, effects (Dishman and Buckworth 1996; Dishman et al. 1998). Apparently, there are considerable impediments to enhancing physical and mental health through the promotion of physical activity. This problem, like other contemporary concerns of exercise psychology, is not new. English-born Robert Jeffries Roberts, director of physical education in the late 1880s at the Young Men's Christian Association in Springfield, Massachusetts, stated, "I noticed when I taught slow, heavy, fancy, and more advanced work in acrobatics, gymnastics, athletics, etc., that I would have a very large membership at the first of the year, but that they would soon drop out" (Leonard and Affleck 1947).

This part of the book explores the dynamics of exercise behavior that are relevant for addressing the problems of inactivity and nonadherence. The next three chapters present the evidence about likely determinants of exercise, theories of behavior change, and interventions designed to increase exercise adoption and adherence in order to offer insight into why people do or do not participate in regular physical activity in their leisure time. A final chapter on perceived exertion brings home our perspective that exercise is a behavior with intrinsic physiological characteristics. The perception of the immediate physiological sensations from physical activity is an important part of the way someone thinks about his or her identity with respect to exercise, and these perceptions can influence subsequent behavioral choices.

Descriptive research that identifies correlates of physical activity behavior and exercise is useful for characterizing groups, tracking trends in the relationships among variables, and stimulating further research. However, application of theoretical models is necessary for explaining and predicting behavior, as well as for creating viable hypotheses and developing interventions. In most cases, research using interventions to increase physical activity has done a poor job of verifying that the intervention changed theoretical mediators of physical activity (Baranowski, Anderson, and Carmack 1998; Dishman 1991); but this could be a result of inadequate application of theory to research, or of problems in measuring behavioral outcomes and psychosocial variables. The following chapters present summaries of what we know about exercise behavior. We also provide critiques of the research on determinants of exercise and physical activity, on the application of theories, on interventions to change physical activity behavior, and on perceived exertion.

10

Determinants of Exercise and Physical Activity

Considerable research has been conducted to identify factors that increase or decrease the likelihood that someone will adopt and maintain an active lifestyle. Most of these studies have been cross-sectional or prospective. Few controlled studies have involved experimental manipulation of variables presumed to operate as determinants, and it is likely that multiple factors interact together to "cause" exercise adoption and maintenance. Therefore, throughout this chapter we use the term "determinant" to refer to variables for which there are established reproducible associations or predictive relationships, rather than cause-and-effect connections.

The term "determinants" is used not to imply a cause-and-effect relationship, but to refer to established reproducible associations that are potentially causal.

There are several practical implications for knowing the determinants of exercise and physical activity. Theories guide research, but evidence from well-designed studies can be used to support or refute the application of specific theories to exercise behavior. Many theories of behavior have been applied to exercise promotion, as you will see in chapter 11, and they have yielded mixed results in describing and predicting physical activity behavior. Thus, identifying determinants of physical activity can promote revisions and improvements in theoretical models used in exercise research and interventions. For example, there is no consistent association between physical activity behavior and perceived social pressure to exercise (i.e., subjective norm). This weak relationship presents a challenge to the application of the theory of reasoned action to physical activity because subjective norm (i.e., normative beliefs) is one of the key variables this theory proposes for understanding and predicting behavior. On the other hand, there have been consistent significant differences in exercise self-efficacy (i.e., confidence in one's ability to engage successfully in a specific behavior) among sedentary individuals, individuals interested in beginning regular exercise, novice exercisers, and individuals who have maintained regular exercise. This relationship between exercise self-efficacy and levels of physical activity and motivation to exercise strengthens the application of a stage model that includes self-efficacy, such as the transtheoretical model of behavior change.

> ## Benefits From Studying Exercise Determinants
>
> ▼ Defining determinants promotes the design and application of better theoretical models.
>
> ▼ Inactive segments of the population can be identified and resources for promoting exercise adoption and maintenance can be properly allocated.
>
> ▼ Discovering modifiable variables that influence behavior change will foster increased efficacy of interventions that target those variables.
>
> ▼ Identifying determinants in special populations will enable more personalized interventions.

Knowing determinants of exercise and physical activity can also help to identify inactive segments of the population and guide allocation of resources earmarked to increase exercise adoption and adherence in these high-risk groups. In the United States, the degree of urbanization is associated with level of physical activity. The highest prevalence of physical inactivity is found in the rural South. Given that gender (female) and income are other established determinants of physical inactivity, the funding of intervention programs targeting low-income southern females who live outside of urban centers would be warranted.

Determining malleable variables that influence behavior change can direct interventions to target those variables and increase the efficacy of the intervention. Modifiable variables consistently associated with physical activity include social support, self-efficacy, perceived barriers, perceived benefits, enjoyment of activity, processes of change, intention to exercise, and lower intensity of exercise. These are examples of variables that should be tested in intervention research to see if changes in them will result in changes in behavior—rather than investing time and money on variables that are inconsistently or weakly related to physical activity, such as exercise knowledge.

Finally, expanding our understanding of characteristics that influence physical activity in specific populations will foster personalized interventions more likely to meet the needs of the target group, and thus increase the probability of maintaining the

behavior change. Although some variables, such as self-efficacy, social support, and perceived barriers, operate across a range of populations, the strength of specific determinants probably varies among different population subgroups. For example, social support may influence exercise behavior more in women than in men, and the type of social support for exercise (e.g., from family or friends) may vary in importance as a function of gender. Increasing the availability of personalized interventions can also address an emerging trend in consumer behavior in which people want to be treated as individuals, and not just as an "urban female, aged 25-35," for example (Miller 1999).

Classification of Determinants

The social cognitive theory provides a convenient framework for organizing the myriad variables that have been studied along with level of physical activity. One useful aspect of the social cognitive theory is a dynamic interacting structure that organizes determinants into characteristics of the person, the environment, and the target behavior. In this chapter, determinants of exercise and physical activity are organized and described under three general categories: past and present characteristics of the person, past and present environments, and aspects of exercise and physical activity. See table 10.1 for a summary of determinants and their association with physical activity.

Identifying determinants that reside in the person is of practical importance because this allows us to distinguish population segments that are responsive or resistant to physical activity interventions. For example, cigarette smoking and low income can be markers of underlying habits and circumstances that reinforce sedentary behavior. Identifying environmental influences can give insight into real and perceived barriers to exercise adoption and maintenance. Addressing determinants at the environmental level also demonstrates the need to implement interventions beyond the individual and small group to include facility and policy planning at the community and national levels. More efforts are being made to evaluate the effects of the constructed environment on behavior, such as studies to determine the influence of the layout of roads in neighborhoods (i.e., community structure) on walking patterns of residents (figure 10.1, p. 195). Aspects of physical

Table 10.1

Associations of Determinants With Physical Activity in Adults

Determinant	Associations with activity in supervised program	Associations with overall physical activity
Demographic and biological factors		
Age	0 0	– –
Blue-collar occupation	– –	–
Education	+	+ +
Sex (male)		+ +
Genetic influences		+ +
High risk for heart disease	0	–
Income/socioeconomic status		+ +
Overweight/obesity	0	0 0
Race/ethnicity (nonwhite)		– –
Psychological factors		
Attitudes	0	0
Perceived barriers to exercise	–	– –
Enjoyment of exercise	+	+ +
Outcome expectancy values (expect benefits)	+	+ +
Health locus of control	0	0
Intention to exercise	+	+ +
Knowledge of health and exercise	0	0 0
Perceived lack of time	– –	–
Mood disturbance	–	– –
Normative beliefs	0	0 0
Self-efficacy	+ +	+ +
Self-motivation	+ +	+ +
Self-schemata for exercise (self-image as an exerciser)		+ +
Behavioral attributes and skills		
Activity history during childhood/youth		+
Activity history during adulthood	+ +	+ +
Dietary habits (quality)	0 0	+ +
Past exercise program	+ +	+
Processes of change		+
School sports	0	0 0

(continued)

Table 10.1

(continued)

Determinant	Associations with activity in supervised program	Associations with overall physical activity
Behavioral attributes and skills (continued)		
Skills for coping with barriers		+
Smoking	– –	0 0
Decision balance sheet	+	+
Social and cultural factors		
Class size	–	
Exercise models		0
Group cohesion	+	
Past family influences		0
Physician influence		+ +
Social support from friends/peers	+	+ +
Social support from spouse/family	+ +	+ +
Social support from staff/instructor	+	
Physical environment factors		
Access to facilities: actual	+	+
Climate/season	–	– –
Access to facilities: perceived	+	0 0
Cost of program	0	0
Disruptions in routine	–	
Home equipment	+	0
Physical activity characteristics		
Intensity	– –	–
Perceived exertion	– –	– –

Key: + + = repeatedly documented positive associations with physical activity

+ = weak or mixed evidence of positive association with physical activity

0 0 = repeatedly documented lack of association with physical activity

0 = weak or mixed evidence of no association with physical activity

– – = repeatedly documented negative associations with physical activity

– = weak or mixed evidence of negative association with physical activity

Blank spaces indicate no data available.

Adapted from R.K. Dishman, J.F. Sallis, and D.R. Orenstein, 1985, "The determinants of physical activity and exercise," *Public Health Reports* 100(2): 161.

Figure 10.1 Researchers are making more efforts to evaluate how elements of the constructed environment influence patterns of physical activity.

activity itself, such as intensity and mode, can have significant effects on adoption and maintenance. For example, a sedentary individual would be more likely to join a walking program than a high-intensity aerobics dance class; and adherence to low-intensity, leisure physical activity is better than adherence to more vigorous exercise (Dishman and Buckworth 1996b). There are also differences in determinants of level of physical activity and exercise behavior, as well as of participation in supervised and unsupervised programs (Dishman, Sallis, and Orenstein 1985).

a practical slant on studying determinants. Reciprocal determinism describes a mutually influencing relationship among two or more factors (figure 10.2; see also figure 11.3, p. 217). Thus, determinants of physical activity are not isolated variables. They interact dynamically to influence behavior, and the pattern of this interaction among variables will change over time; the types of determinants and the strength of their influence will change over the course of the behavior (i.e., adoption, early adherence, long-term maintenance) and developmental stage of the individual.

No single variable explains and predicts physical activity and exercise.

There is no single variable that explains and predicts physical activity and exercise behavior. The significance of specific determinants must be considered in the context of other personal, environmental, and behavioral factors and from the perspective of **reciprocal determinism,** which is a component of social cognitive theory that provides

Example of Interaction Between Exercise History and Environment

Someone who has just started exercising might be motivated to walk when the weather is nice regardless of whether he or she is alone, but walk when it is cold only if friends come along. After regular exercise has become an established behavior, external support becomes less important and walking does not depend on the company of others regardless of the weather.

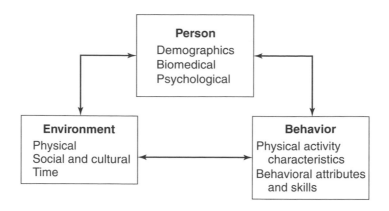

Figure 10.2 Determinants of exercise behavior.

Age, fitness, and exercise history can influence the choice of exercise mode and location —*and* how much the weather will be a barrier to participation.

Characteristics of the Person

Important factors that influence decisions and actions reside or originate within the individual. Many individual variables, such as decision-making skills or perceptions of exercise benefits and barriers, are targets of behavior change interventions. Other characteristics of the person related to level of physical activity are not amenable to change (e.g., age and gender), but must be identified and considered in the design of exercise promotion programs and interventions. The characteristics of the person that have been considered in determinants research have been organized into demographic and biological factors; psychological, cognitive, and emotional factors; and behavioral attributes and skills.

Demographic and Biological Factors

Demographic variables that are consistent correlates of physical activity are gender, age, ethnicity, education, income, and occupation. Males are more likely to be active than females. The *gender difference* in exercise and level of physical activity is consistent among various racial/ethnic groups. Higher levels of physical activity in male children may be related to differential development of motor skills, differences in body composition, and gender socialization toward sport and physical activity (Kohl and Hobbs 1998). In adolescents and adults, gender differences in level of physical activity vary based on exercise mode and physical activity intensity. Data from the National Health Interview Survey, the 1992 Youth Risk Behavior Survey, and the 1991 Health Promotion/Disease Prevention supplement for adults were analyzed to determine gender-specific, age-related changes in physical activity patterns (Caspersen, Pereira, and Curran 2000). Prevalence of physical inactivity was not different for adolescent males and females except

at age 17, when a greater proportion of females were physically inactive. Male adolescents reported moderately greater prevalence of regular sustained activity, but there were large differences for regular vigorous activity and very large differences for strengthening activity. For adults, differences between males and females were moderate for physical inactivity (more females) and regular sustained activity (more males), but large for strengthening activity (more males). Participation in regular vigorous activity was not different between adult males and females until they reached the 65 to 74 age group and beyond, when higher levels were found for males.

Overall participation in physical activity decreases with increasing age, although age has less of an impact on moderate-intensity activity (figure 10.3). Middle adulthood (30-64 years) is associated with lower levels of regular vigorous activity and strengthening activities, but the pattern of activity is relatively stable until retirement, when there is some improvement until the final period of life (Caspersen, Pereira, and Curran 2000).

Level of physical activity declines with age during adolescence, but the age at which the decline begins and the pattern of decline are not clear (Stone et al. 1998). Sallis (1993) reported a decline in

© Anthony Neste

Vigorous physical activity is more likely to decrease for girls than for boys as they age.

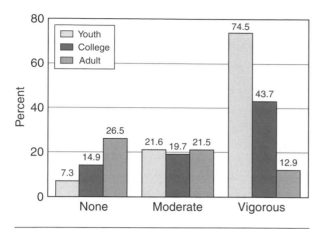

Figure 10.3 Participation in physical activity among males.

Data from Behavioral Risk Factor Surveillance 1992, College Health Risk Behavior Survey 1995, Youth Risk Behavior Surveillance System 1995.

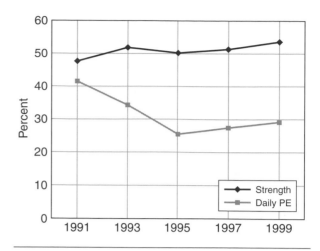

Figure 10.5 Trends in physical activity: controlling for grade in school, sex, and race.

Data from Kann et al. 2000.

physical activity between 1.8% and 2.7% per year in boys between 10 and 17 years of age. Physical activity in girls decreased between 2.6% and 7.4% per year between ages 10 and 17. Results from the 1999 Youth Risk Behavior Surveillance System (Kann et al. 2000) indicate that vigorous physical activity decreased significantly from grades 9 to 12, more so for females. Lower levels of moderate-intensity activity were reported, but the declines were not as great as for vigorous activity (figure 10.4). Although participation in daily physical education declined from 1991 to 1999, there was a significant positive linear trend for participation in strengthening exercises (figure 10.5).

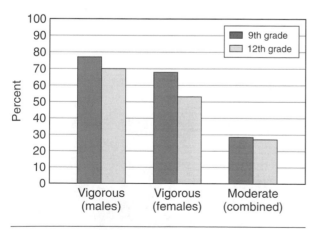

Figure 10.4 Participation in vigorous and moderate physical activity: male and female adolescents.

Data from Youth Risk Behavior Surveillance System 1999.

Several studies have examined determinants of physical activity in younger age groups. Sallis, Prochaska, and Taylor (2000) reviewed 108 studies published between 1970 and 1999 on determinants of physical activity in children (ages 3 to 12) and adolescents (ages 13 to 18). For children, positive associations were found for gender (male), healthy diet, physical activity preferences, intentions to be active, previous physical activity, access to program or facilities, and time spent outdoors. Negative associations were found for general barriers to exercise. Variables positively associated with physical activity in adolescents were sex (male), ethnicity (European American), achievement orientation, intention, perceived competence, community sports, sensation seeking, sibling's participation in physical activity, previous physical activity, parental support, support from significant others, and opportunities to exercise. Negative associations for adolescents were age, depression, and being sedentary after school and on weekends. Other reviews have indicated that exercise self-efficacy is a significant factor in level of physical activity for both children and adolescents (e.g., Sallis and Owen 1999), although the Sallis, Prochaska, and Taylor (2000) review showed inconclusive evidence for self-efficacy. There are also mixed associations between parents' activity levels and the activity levels of their children. The relationship is stronger for females but less significant for adolescents in general (Kohl and Hobbs 1998). For adolescents, peer pressure is a stronger social determinant of physical activity level than family support, although in youth (Sallis et al. 1992) and college students (Wallace et al. 2000), family support for exercise is more important for females and peer support is more important for males.

In terms of *ethnic influence*, non-Hispanic whites are generally more active than other racial/ethnic groups regardless of age. Results from the 1997 Youth Risk Behavior Survey showed that non-Hispanic white students (66.8%) were more likely to participate in vigorous physical activity than Hispanic (60.4%) and African American students (53.9%) (Kann et al. 1998). The effects of ethnicity were different for moderate-intensity activity. More African American (28.3%) and Hispanic (26.7%) youth participated in moderate-intensity activity than non-Hispanic whites (16.8%).

Compliance with the public health recommendation for adolescents and youth to engage in at least 3 h of moderate to vigorous activity per week was examined by ethnicity in the National Longitudinal Study of Adolescent Health, a nationally representative, school-based sample of adolescents in grades 7 to 12 in the United States (Gordon-Larson, McMurray, and Popkin 1999). Non-Hispanic whites were more likely to meet the physical activity recommendations, with the greatest proportion of African Americans (36.7%) less active than recommended. Lower levels of physical activity in females compared to males were also found in this sample. Almost 50% of African American females, 44% of Asian females, 41.6% of Hispanic females, and 37.2% of non-Hispanic white females reported zero to two sessions of moderate to vigorous physical activity per week. For males, low participation ranged from 26.8% for Hispanic adolescents to 23.1% for Asian adolescents.

Although there is an association between exercise and ethnicity, evidence that this relationship is independent of social class is inconclusive. Crespo et al. (2000) analyzed physical inactivity and indicators of social class (i.e., education, family income, occupation, employment, poverty, and marital status) among Caucasians, African Americans, and Mexican Americans completing the Third National Health and Nutrition Examination Survey between 1988 and 1994. The authors found that in each category of social class, women and minorities showed a higher prevalence of leisure-time inactivity than Caucasian men.

Income is a component of *socioeconomic status* (SES), which has a strong inverse relationship with sedentary lifestyle for both sexes and every race and ethnic group (United States Department of Health and Human Services 1996). For example, African American males in poverty are three times as likely to be sedentary as African American males with a high family income. Socioeconomic status is also positively associated with physical activity in children and adolescents. For children and adolescents, higher SES means more access to physical activity programs in and out of school. Transportation to facilities and events influences accessibility and represents an important form of direct support from parents and responsible adults that can influence exercise participation.

Longitudinal population studies that evaluate concurrent changes in physical activity and changes in purported determinants can provide stronger evidence for the role of specific personal variables in exercise adoption and adherence. *Education* and *income* are positively associated with physical activity and have been associated with increased activity in prospective studies. For example, individuals with similar aerobic capacities in high school had significantly higher aerobic capacities eight years later if they were civil servants, white-collar workers, or students compared to those who were in blue-collar jobs or unemployed (Anderson 1996). Adoption of vigorous physical activity by sedentary individuals has been predicted by age (inverse), self-efficacy, and neighborhood environment for males and by education, self-efficacy, friend social support, and family social support for females (Sallis et al. 1992). Other prospective studies have shown associations between declines in physical activity in adults and social isolation, lower education, low income, blue-collar occupation, marital status (unmarried), depression, low levels of life satisfaction, and less-than-excellent perceived health (Kaplan et al. 1996; Schmitz, French, and Jeffery 1997).

A variety of factors have been correlated with lack of adherence to structured exercise programs (Franklin 1988). Personal factors include smoking, blue-collar occupation, low self-esteem, depression, anxiety, and low ego strength. Characteristics of the program that are related to dropping out are excessive cost, inconvenient time/location, lack of exercise variety, exercising alone, lack of positive feedback or reinforcement, and poor leadership. Other factors related to nonadherence are lack of spousal support, inclement weather, excessive job travel, injury, medical problems, and job change or move.

*A*ge, ethnicity, education, income, occupation, and biology are personal characteristics that influence exercise behavior and level of physical activity.

Most of the research on determinants of physical activity has focused on cognitive, social, and environmental variables. However, intrinsic *biological influences* may significantly affect level of physical activity. Rowland (1998) proposed an anatomical-physiological entity that regulates the amount of daily physical activity as do analogous brain centers that control behavioral-physiological processes such as hunger and temperature regulation. Biological regulation of physical activity is one of the interacting mechanisms for regulation of energy balance, along with caloric intake and energy expenditure in the form of resting metabolic rate.

Biological influence may also be involved in variations in level of spontaneous activity. Beunen and Thomis (1999) reviewed the literature on genetic determinants of sport participation, daily physical activity, and resting metabolic rate as a temperamental trait. They reported that studies have shown small to moderately high contributions to interindividual variations in daily physical activity, and attributed the range in heritabilities to differing methods and design. However, they did conclude that genetic factors contribute to level of daily physical activity and that activity as a temperament trait is under genetic control. The genetic contributions to exercise adherence warrant closer examination.

Physiological adaptations to exercise training also have a genetic component. There is evidence for high-, low-, and no-responder genotypes in regard to exercise training. Wilmore et al. (1997) described individual responses to training with respect to aerobic capacity, plasma lipoprotein, insulin response, skeletal muscle enzyme activity, and adipose tissue metabolism that ranged from a low of 0% to highs of 50% to 100% of pretraining values. There was significant variation in the response to exercise training with respect to level and rate of change, even considering effects from age, gender, and prior exercise experience. Research is needed to explore the effects of responder **genotype** on psychological variables, such as self-efficacy and self-motivation, that are relevant for exercise adherence.

Other physiological variables can play a critical role in behavior and interact significantly with psychosocial constructs. For example, physical discomfort has been negatively correlated with self-report of physical activity, and those who perceive their health as poor are unlikely to adopt and adhere to an exercise program. It's interesting that there has been no consistent association between obesity or being overweight and exercise or overall physical activity (Dishman and Sallis 1994).

Psychological, Cognitive, and Emotional Factors

Cognitions, such as attitudes, beliefs, and values, are personal characteristics that researchers have studied as potential influences on physical activity behavior. The cognitive variable that has been consistently associated with physical activity in almost every study that included it is **self-efficacy,** which is someone's belief in his or her ability to engage successfully in a specific behavior with a known outcome. Self-efficacy is similar to level of confidence and is based on judgments of capabilities. Self-efficacy is central to Bandura's social cognitive theory, in which it is designated as the most powerful determinant of human behavior. Self-efficacy, by definition, is task and situation specific. For example, a recreational swimmer can be confident that she can easily swim a mile in the 50 m (54.7 yd) indoor pool (high self-efficacy) but have no faith in her ability to water-ski (low self-efficacy). Thus, the more specific the measure of self-efficacy, the better the potential to predict the behavior.

Longitudinal studies with different populations have shown that exercise self-efficacy increases as one moves from an established sedentary lifestyle to long-term maintenance of regular exercise, and that level of self-efficacy predicts subsequent physical activity. Exercise self-efficacy can be both a determinant and a consequence of exercise (figure 10.6; McAuley and Blissmer 2000). Self-efficacy influences the choice of activities, the amount of effort expended, and the degree of persistence. Research on exercise and self-efficacy supports a greater role for self-efficacy in adoption and during the early stages of an exercise program, but it may also be important in maintenance, depending on the type of physical activity (e.g., maintenance of vigorous exercise; Sallis et al. 1986). Significant improvements in exercise self-efficacy after exercise training have been demonstrated in a variety of populations (e.g.,

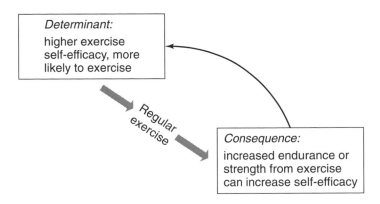

Figure 10.6 Exercise self-efficacy can be both a determinant and a consequence of physical activity.

men infected with HIV-1 [human immunodeficiency virus-1]: Lox, McAuley, and Tucker 1995; older adults: McAuley, Lox, and Duncan 1993), and interventions have been designed to enhance exercise self-efficacy as a strategy to effect behavior change (e.g., McAuley et al. 1994).

The cognitive variable that has the strongest consistent relationship with exercise is self-efficacy.

Another theory-based cognitive variable related to physical activity and exercise is **behavioral intention,** which is the central determinant of voluntary behavior according to the theory of planned behavior. Behavioral intention can provide an indication of motivation, such as how much effort someone is willing to put into a particular activity. Most research that has tested the effects of intention on exercise has found strong relationships between intention and overall physical activity. Godin (1994), examining 12 studies of exercise and intentions, reported correlations between behavioral intention and exercise that ranged from $r = .19$ to $.82$ with a mean of $r = .55$.

Self-motivation is also positively associated with supervised and overall physical activity. Successful endurance athletes have consistently scored high on self-motivation, and self-motivation has discriminated between adherents and dropouts across a wide variety of settings including adult fitness programs, cardiac rehabilitation, commercial spas, corporate fitness programs, and college campuses (Knapp

1988; Sonstroem 1988) and associated with physical activity in adolescent boys (Biddle et al. 1996) and girls (Motl et al. 2002).

Other cognitive variables that have been positively associated with supervised and overall physical activity are *enjoyment of exercise* (Motl et al. 2001), *expectations of benefits* (Motl et al. 2000; Dishman et al. 2002), *self-schemata* (e.g., seeing self as an exerciser; chapter 8), and *exercise stage of change*. For example, lower enjoyment of activity was an independent predictor of insufficient physical activity for both male and female Australian college students, along with lower social support from family and friends (Leslie et al. 1999). Exercise stage of change is a classification based on current and previous exercise behavior and motivational readiness to become and remain physically active. Exercise stage has been positively associated with supervised and overall physical activity, and has been used successfully in several studies to predict adoption and maintenance of regular exercise (Prochaska and Marcus 1994).

Perceived barriers to exercise are negatively associated with supervised and overall physical activity in adults and children. Lack of time has a stronger inverse association with participation in structured programs than with overall physical activity. A perceived lack of time is also the principal and most common reason given for dropping out of supervised clinical and community exercise programs and for inactive lifestyles. For many, however, reporting a lack of time may reflect a lack of interest in or commitment to physical activity—saying there is not enough time to exercise is more socially acceptable. Thus, lack of time may be a true determinant, a perceived determinant, the reflection of poor behavioral skills, such as time management, or a rationalization for a lack of motivation to be active.

Lack of time and caregiving duties were the most frequently reported barriers to physical activity in a sample of 2912 middle-aged and older women in the United States (King et al. 2000). The other most frequently reported barriers to physical activity were lack of energy, being too tired, and lack of a safe place to exercise. When the data were analyzed across racial/ethnic groups, there were differences in barriers that correlated with being sedentary. For example, being tired was strongly associated with less physical activity for Hispanic women, but not other racial/ethnic groups. Caregiving duties were associated with less activity only for African American women. Some of the results from this study do not mirror what we think would support or hinder physical activity, such as the positive association between physical activity and unattended dogs for African American women. This finding may reflect more opportunities to observe dogs in the surrounding neighborhood from being outside walking or working in the yard, for example. This finding may be a marker of getting outside more to observe such events. Another issue is a concern with the validity of traditional instruments for measuring physical activity for minority women. In any case, these results provide important information and illustrate the need for additional research to clarify associations between barriers and physical activity in specific population groups.

Several psychological variables that have weaker relationships with physical activity and exercise are *attitudes*, *control over exercise*, *psychological health*, and *poor body image*. Although some studies have shown weak relationships between exercise and *personality variables*, there is consistent evidence that neuroticism is negatively related and extraversion is positively related to exercise behavior (e.g., Courneya and Hellsten 1998). Research has shown no consistent associations between supervised or overall physical activity and health locus of control, normative beliefs, stress, susceptibility to illness/seriousness of illness, value of exercise outcome, and knowledge of health and exercise. Knowledge alone does not seem to be enough to change behavior, but clear, relevant information about the benefits of physical activity and ways to become more active may be a factor in motivating individuals to consider adopting regular exercise. For example, in a study by Lee (1993), sedentary women who were not interested in starting an exercise program had the lowest scores on knowledge about exercise compared to active women or women who were considering beginning regular exercise.

Personal and Environmental Barriers Associated With Physical Activity in U.S. Middle-Aged and Older-Aged Women

Caucasian: age (–), education (+), lack of energy (–), hills in neighborhood (+)

African American: frequency of seeing others exercise (+), caregiving duties (–), unattended dogs (+)

Hispanic: education (+), hills in neighborhood (+), too tired (–), discouragement from others about exercising (+)

American Indian, Alaskan Native: self-consciousness about physical appearance (+), education (+), poor health (–)

+ = positive association with physical activity; – = negative association with physical activity.

Adapted, by permission, from A.C. King, C. Castro, S. Wilcox, A. A. Eyler, J. F. Sallis, and R. S. Brownson, 2000, "Personal and environmental factors associated with physical inactivity among different racial/ethnic groups of U.S. middle-aged and older-aged women," *Health Psychology* 19: 354–364.

Behavioral Attributes and Skills

Activity history during adulthood and participation in an exercise program in the past are positively associated with supervised and overall physical activity. *Dietary habits* (positive), *processes of change* (transtheoretical model; see chapter 11), and *smoking* (negative) are associated with participation in supervised programs. There is also some evidence for a relationship between physical activity and decisional balance (i.e., the costs vs. the benefits of exercise), skills for coping with barriers, and Type A behavior pattern. Activity history during childhood/youth, alcohol, school sports, and sport media use have had no consistent association with supervised or overall physical activity. The lack of a relationship between physical activity and sport in childhood/youth and adult levels of physical activity is troubling. Many models for physical education in the public schools are based on teaching and fostering sport or activity skills that can be carried over into adulthood. The competitive nature of school sports may overshadow the implementation of this philosophy and confound long-term effects.

Lack of time is one of the most frequently reported reasons for not exercising and for dropping out of an exercise program.

Researchers have investigated associations between level of physical activity and other health behaviors, such as dietary habits and smoking. Pate et al. (1996) examined associations among physical activity and other health behaviors from the 1990 Youth Risk Behavior Survey. Data from over 11,000 youths aged 12 to 18 indicated that little or no involvement in physical activity was associated with cigarette smoking, marijuana use, poor dietary habits, television watching, failure to wear seat belts, and perception of low academic performance. Level of physical activity was not associated with cocaine use, sexual activity, physical fighting, or self-perception of weight. Steptoe et al. (1997) assessed prevalence of physical activity and other health habits over the previous two weeks in 7302 males and 9181 females aged 18 to 30 in a total of 21 European countries. For the whole sample, physical inactivity was significantly associated with smoking, unsatisfactory sleep time, no desire to lose weight, low social support, and depression. Knowledge was not a determinant of physical activity in this population, but there was evidence that knowledge had a positive influence on beliefs in health benefits of physical activity. Relationships between physical activity and alcohol consumption were inconsistent.

Time spent watching television is not related to exercise, and the association between television watching and child and adolescent obesity is mixed (Robinson 1998), although strong positive relationships between hours of television viewing and body mass index have been found in adults (Owen et al. 2000). Television watching and other sedentary behaviors like working on the computer are typically viewed as part of the continuum of physical activity, with MET[1] values between 1 and 1.5 (Owen et al. 2000). Dietz (1996), Owen et al. (2000), and others have proposed an independent and interactive relationship between sedentary be-

haviors and physical activity behaviors, which warrants further examination. High levels of physical activity are not necessarily correlated with low levels of sedentary behaviors. For example, a marathon runner may have a sedentary job and also spend hours each evening using the computer. However, there is some evidence for an association between higher levels of computer use and increased likelihood of physical inactivity in young adults (Fotheringham, Wonnacott, and Owen 2000). Identifying determinants of sedentary behaviors may have practical implications in view of some of the research showing that intervention to decrease participation in sedentary behaviors is efficacious in increasing level of physical activity (e.g., Epstein et al. 1997).

Environmental Determinants

Exercise physiologists have been accused of dealing with the body while ignoring the mind, and psychologists have been charged with treating the mind and disregarding the body. Exercise psychologists should incorporate the strengths of these two disciplines to consider the entire person, but we need to take another step and study the person-environment interaction. (Even the most committed cyclist pauses before she takes her bike out in a snowstorm!) A strength of the social cognitive theory is the inclusion of environmental factors in a model of behavioral influences. Environmental determinants of exercise behavior and physical activity can be divided into the human environment and the physical environment.

Human Environment

Relationships and interactions with others can have a strong impact on behavior. For example, social environment was the strongest independent predictor of being physically active in a cross-sectional study of 3342 adults from six European countries (Ståhl et al. 2001). Social support includes formal or informal comfort, assistance, and/or information from individuals or groups and can vary in frequency, durability, and intensity (Courneya and

---

1. One MET is equal to energy expended for resting metabolism. MET values are assigned to physical activity based on the ratio of the metabolic rate for that activity to resting metabolic rate adjusted for body mass. See chapter 2 for examples of METs for different activities.

McAuley 1995). Social influences in the form of social support and prompting typically have strong positive associations with physical activity, and social isolation has shown negative associations. In a meta-analysis of social influence and exercise, Carron, Hausenblas, and Mack (1996) examined the separate effects of social influence variables on exercise behavior, cognitions, and affect (satisfaction and attitude). Overall effect sizes were small to medium, but effects of .62 to .69 were found for family support and important others on attitudes about exercise, and for family support and task cohesion on exercise behavior. Social support from family and friends is consistently related to physical activity in cross-sectional and prospective studies, and increased group cohesion in exercise classes leads to increased exercise adherence (Estabrooks 2000). Support from a spouse appears also to be reliably correlated with exercise participation, and better exercise adherence has been found for individuals who join fitness centers with their spouses than for married individuals whose spouses do not join.

The impact of social interactions and social influences on exercise appears to be different for males and females. For example, adherence to a structured exercise program was predicted by females' perceptions that they received adequate guidance and reassurance of worth, but social provisions did not predict adherence in men (Duncan, Duncan, and McAuley 1993). In a study of college students, social support for exercise from family was related to level of physical activity for females, but support from friends was more significant for exercise in males (Wallace et al. 2000).

The relationship between social support for exercise and gender may be different over the course of contemplating, adopting, and maintaining exercise. Results from a cross-sectional study of healthy middle-aged adults indicated that perceived expectations to be physically active and motivation to comply with perceived expectations were greater for inactive women than for inactive men (Troped and Saunders 1998). Men and women who were adopting or maintaining exercise were similar on motivation to comply. Thus, social support for exercise may be a more important influence for women in the early stages of exercise adoption and should be considered when interventions that target sedentary women are developed.

Better adherence to regular exercise is found in spouses who exercise together.

Social support is related to physical activity, but this influence is modified by gender.

In general, participation in supervised exercise programs is weakly associated with class size and social support from staff/instructor. No consistent associations have been found for exercise models or past family influence and exercise or physical activity.

Physical Environment

Climate or season is the only characteristic of the natural physical environment that has a strong and consistent association with overall level of physical activity. In children and adolescents, activity levels are lowest in the winter and highest in the summer. Observational studies suggest that time spent outdoors is one of the single best correlates of physical activity in preschool children (Kohl and Hobbs 1998; Sallis and Owen 1999). Opportunities for being physically active outdoors also decrease for adults during the winter, and this can affect physiological markers of physical activity. One study that compared exercise classes conducted in autumn and spring found that six-month follow-up measures of aerobic capacity were significantly lower at the follow-up after winter (autumn class) than after summer (spring class) (Buckworth 2001). In addition, aerobic capacity significantly increased for those retested after summer. However, students who had participated in strength-training classes during the same measurement periods demonstrated no seasonal effects for measures of strength, suggesting that weather is not as great a barrier to participation in strength training as it is to engaging in aerobic activities.

Disruptions in routine have a weak negative association with participation in supervised programs, and costs of programs and home exercise equipment show no consistent associations with supervised or overall physical activity. Access to exercise facilities has been found to influence participation, although the relationship is complicated. Access can be considered in terms of environment (i.e., geography), economics, and safety—for example, running in some New York City neighborhoods is risky because of air pollution and high crime rates. However, access can also be considered in terms of perception. When access to facilities has been measured by objective methods (e.g., distance), access typically has been related to both the adoption and maintenance of supervised and overall physical activity. However, perceived access is associated only with participation in supervised programs.

Season or climate has a strong and consistent association with level of physical activity.

Raynor, Coleman, and Epstein (1998) considered the interaction between accessibility and the reinforcing value of the alternatives in a study of 34 sedentary adult males. Accessibility was operationalized as physical proximity to physically active and sedentary alternatives. Amount of time out of a possible 20 min that participants spent exercising was compared among four conditions that varied as a function of accessibility to both active and sedentary alternatives (figure 10.7). The most time (20 min) was spent exercising when the active alternatives were near (in the same room) and the sedentary alternatives were far (5 min walk away). Regardless of the accessibility of the active alternatives, if the sedentary alternatives were near, less than 1 min on average was spent exercising. Participants were active 42% of the time when both alternatives were less accessible. Raynor, Coleman, and Epstein (1998) concluded that sedentary adult males would be more physically active if the physical activities were more convenient and the sedentary activities were less convenient.

Recent years have seen increased recognition of the importance of the constructed physical environment and the social-political environment in determining level of physical activity (Owen et al. 2000). The nature of the physical environment (e.g., density of population; quality of pedestrian environment; composition of the neighborhood with respect to retail, service, and community facilities) influences commuting behavior and incidental physical activity (see figure 10.1, p. 195). For example, in a sample of 449 Australian adults aged 60 and older, environmental factors that were significantly associated with being physically active were finding footpaths safe for walking and access

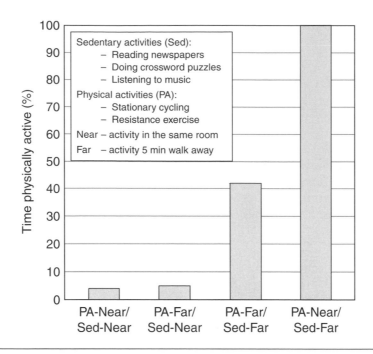

Figure 10.7 Participation in physical activity as a function of accessibility and behavioral alternatives.

Adapted, by permission, from D.A. Raynor, K.J. Coleman, and L.H. Epstein, 1998, "Effects of proximity on the choice to be physically active or sedentary," *Research Quarterly for Exercise and Sport* 69: 99–103.

to local facilities (Booth et al. 2000). The degree of urbanization and region are environmental characteristics that are also associated with the level of leisure-time physical activity in the United States (see table 10.2). Data from the 1996 Behavioral Risk Factor Surveillance Survey indicate that the overall prevalence of physical inactivity is lowest in central metropolitan areas (27.4%) and in the West (21.1%; Centers for Disease Control and Prevention 1998). Physical inactivity is highest (36.6%) in rural areas, particularly in the southern United States (43.7%). The inverse relationship between degree of urbanization and physical inactivity is relatively consistent when data are stratified by age, gender, level of education, and household income.

Physical Activity Characteristics

Characteristics of exercise (i.e., mode, intensity, duration, and frequency) are possible determinants of physical activity. Results from a meta-analysis of interventions to increase physical activity indicate no significant effects for frequency or duration on exercise adherence. The types of activities with the best adherence (i.e., largest effect sizes) were leisure-time activities and low-intensity activities (Dishman and Buckworth 1996b). Activity characteristics in-

teract with age and gender, such that participation in vigorous and strength-training exercise is greater for adolescent males compared to adolescent females and adults (Caspersen, Pereira, and Curran 2000). Studies that have presented separate analyses for moderate-intensity activities have noted *increased* levels of activity with age.

*L*ow- and moderate-intensity activities generally have better adherence than higher-intensity activities.

Exercise intensity has an inverse relationship with adoption and maintenance of exercise programs (Pollock et al. 1991; Sallis et al. 1986). Although adherence was similar in a one-year randomized exercise trial with middle-aged adults assigned to low or high exercise intensities (King et al. 1991), each group selected intensities during the year that regressed toward a moderate intensity. Basing exercise prescriptions on preferred intensities is a strategy worth examining for increasing adherence to exercise programs.

Table 10.2

Percentage of Adults Reporting No Participation in Leisure-Time Physical Activity, by Degree of Urbanization and Demographic Characteristics—United States, Behavioral Risk Factor Surveillance System 1996

Characteristic	Metro* %	(95% CI++)	Metro+ %	(95% CI)	Urban& %	(95% CI)	Urban@ %	(95% CI)	Rural** %	(95% CI)
Geographic region&&										
Northeast	27.7	(26.6-28.7)	26.8	(25.4-28.1)	27.7	(24.4-31.1)	27.6	(24.5-30.6)	23.3	(15.9-30.7)
Midwest	28.5	(27.2-29.8)	29.0	(27.4-30.5)	34.2	(30.7-37.6)	31.2	(29.4-33.0)	32.0	(29.1-35.0)
South	31.6	(30.3-32.9)	32.2	(31.2-33.2)	36.8	(34.4-39.1)	42.1	(40.4-43.8)	43.7	(40.3-47.2)
West	22.6	(21.3-23.9)	23.3	(21.7-24.9)	23.8	(21.8-25.8)	25.5	(22.8-28.2)	24.6	(19.9-29.3)
Sex										
Men	25.1	(24.2-26.1)	26.8	(25.8-27.8)	29.8	(27.7-31.9)	34.1	(32.5-35.8)	37.1	(33.9-40.3)
Women	29.5	(28.7-30.4)	31.2	(30.4-32.1)	32.7	(30.9-34.5)	36.6	(35.2-38.0)	36.2	(33.4-39.0)
Age group (years)										
18-29	22.2	(20.8-23.5)	22.4	(20.9-23.8)	23.6	(20.4-26.9)	25.0	(22.6-27.3)	29.0	(23.7-34.4)
30-44	25.2	(24.1-26.2)	26.5	(25.4-27.6)	29.1	(26.6-31.6)	32.8	(30.8-34.7)	34.4	(30.7-38.0)
45-64	29.5	(28.3-30.7)	32.0	(30.7-33.3)	34.6	(32.1-37.1)	40.4	(38.4-42.4)	40.4	(36.5-44.3)
65-74	32.0	(30.0-33.9)	34.6	(32.6-36.5)	36.4	(32.5-40.3)	38.7	(35.9-41.5)	37.5	(32.1-42.9)
75	42.2	(39.7-44.7)	43.3							
Education										
< High school	49.1	(46.9-51.4)								
High school	33.0	(31.8-34.2)	34.5	(33.3-35.6)	35.9	(33.5-38.3)	37.7	(36.0-39.3)	39.3	(36.1-42.6)
Some tech. school	23.8	(22.7-25.0)	23.4	(22.3-24.6)	25.5	(23.1-27.9)	28.9	(26.9-31.0)	26.9	(22.9-30.9)
College graduate	16.7	(15.8-17.6)	16.6	(15.6-17.7)	17.2	(14.8-19.5)	20.2	(18.0-22.4)	25.8	(21.1-30.5)
Annual income										
< $10,000	41.2	(37.9-44.5)								
$10,000-$19,999	38.9	(36.8-40.9)	39.7	(37.7-41.7)	37.7	(34.2-41.3)	43.7	(41.0-46.4)	42.6	(37.9-47.4)
$20,000-$34,999	30.9	(29.6-32.3)	30.8	(29.5-32.1)	33.4	(30.8-36.0)	33.9	(32.0-35.8)	36.4	(32.7-40.2)
$35,000-$49,999	23.4	(22.0-24.8)	24.5	(23.0-26.0)	24.7	(21.5-27.8)	30.0	(27.4-32.5)	31.5	(26.3-36.6)
$50,000	7.5	(16.5-18.4)								
Total	27.4	(26.8-28.0)	29.1	(28.4-29.8)	31.3	(29.9-32.7)	34.4	(33.3-35.5)	36.6	(34.5-38.7)

* Population > 999,999

+ Population 50,000-999,999

& Population 20,000-49,999

@ Population 2,500-19,999

** Population < 2,500

++ CI = confidence interval.

&& Northeast = Connecticut, Maine, Massachusetts, New Hampshire, New Jersey, New York, Pennsylvania, Rhode Island, and Vermont; Midwest = Illinois, Indiana, Iowa, Kansas, Michigan, Minnesota, Missouri, Nebraska, North Dakota, Ohio, South Dakota, and Wisconsin; South = Alabama, Arkansas, Delaware, District of Columbia, Florida, Georgia, Kentucky, Louisiana, Maryland, Mississippi, North Carolina, Oklahoma, South Carolina, Tennessee, Texas, Virginia, and West Virginia; and West = Arizona, California, Colorado, Hawaii, Idaho, Montana, Nevada, New Mexico, Oregon, Utah, Washington, and Wyoming.

Reprinted from Centers for Disease Control and Prevention, 1998, "Self-reported physical activity by degree of urbanization—United States, 1996," *Morbidity and Mortality Weekly Report* 47 (50): 1097–1100.

Injury appears to have a strong influence on maintaining or abandoning regular physical activity, and there is a well-documented dose-response relationship between physical activity and orthopedic injuries (Macera et al. 1989). Injuries from high-intensity, high-volume exercise can end an exercise program, but participants' subjective responses to injury can influence the probability that they will adopt an alternative exercise mode when injured.

Characteristics of physical activity influence exercise behavior, but factors moderating adoption and maintenance of different intensities and modes of exercise are probably different. Courneya and McAuley (1994) found differences in determinants of exercise frequency, intensity, and duration based on the theory of planned behavior. For example, behavioral intention was a stronger predictor of duration than of exercise frequency or intensity. However, few studies have examined differences in determinants of the adoption and maintenance of different exercise modes (e.g., walking vs. weight training).

Issues in Research

More than 300 studies of physical activity determinants have been published (Sallis and Owen 1999); these should give some general indication of what is and what is not related to participation in exercise programs and overall level of physical activity. Several variables have already been described that have consistent associations with physical activity (e.g., age and income). However, physical activity behavior is complicated and dynamic, and it is not surprising that no single variable can reliably describe and predict level of physical activity. Indeed, variables are likely different for different people, and the level of influence and specific key factors will change during the natural history of the behavior and as a function of developmental periods. For example, some determinants of physical activity are similar for children and adolescents (e.g., barriers), but many more personal, social, and environmental influences are different (Sallis, Prochaska, and Taylor 2000).

Accurate measurement of suspected determinants is a primary issue in physical activity determinants research. The assessment of some demographic variables, such as gender and age, is fairly consistent across studies. However, several instruments can be used to measure the same psychosocial construct. For example, two studies on the influence of enjoyment on exercise maintenance yielded opposite results, but they used different instruments to measure enjoyment.

Drawing conclusions about the relationship between exercise and purported determinants is complicated by the variety of instruments used to measure the same psychosocial construct and by the specific nature of some psychological variables. For example, there is a general acceptance of exercise self-efficacy as an exercise determinant, but global exercise self-efficacy measures may not present a true picture of the relationship between self-efficacy and exercise. By definition, self-efficacy is situation specific, and measures of self-efficacy should be specific to the study design and hypotheses. Specific self-efficacy scales were developed by Sallis et al. (1988) to measure self-efficacy for making time to exercise and self-efficacy for resisting relapse. Self-efficacy for resisting relapse would be appropriate for an intervention study that includes a follow-up, whereas self-efficacy for making time to exercise would be more useful in discriminating level of physical activity in a cross-sectional design. A global measure of self-efficacy would not be as sensitive as specific measures of exercise self-efficacy would be under these conditions.

There is no consensus for measuring physical activity, and potential psychosocial exercise determinants have been assessed using a variety of instruments.

Research on exercise determinants is also limited by an absence of uniform standards for defining and assessing physical activity. There are considerable challenges in accurately measuring physical activity that can affect our ability to identify exercise determinants (see chapter 2). Self-reports of physical activity are less accurate for people who exercise irregularly. Activities at moderate and low intensities are easily forgotten and difficult to measure, making it hard to discover the factors that control adoption and adherence of these types of physical activity. It is also difficult to get accurate estimates of levels of physical activity in children, and *how* children engage in activity is a further complication. Children may have many short (less than 1 min) bouts of high-intensity exercise throughout the day, making it hard to quantify volume of activity and energy expenditure.

Summary

Determinants of exercise and physical activity are variables that have shown consistent correlations with level of activity. Age, gender, education, income, self-efficacy, perceived barriers, enjoyment, self-schemata, lack of time, exercise history, social support, and season are some of the variables that have shown repeated associations with physical activity and exercise. However, there are complex multiple interactions among exercise determinants that change over time. Making sense of inconsistencies in the research is challenging, but identifying factors that are significantly associated with level of physical activity and the adoption and maintenance of regular exercise is a valuable line of research with practical benefits. Understanding personal and environmental factors that are associated with sedentary lifestyles and low rates of adoption and adherence can help identify high-risk groups to which programs can be directed. Identifying modifiable variables that have strong and consistent associations with adoption and adherence can focus the direction of interventions on multiple levels, including changes in the structured environment. However, too few studies are available on children, persons who are elderly, those who are physically challenged, and ethnic and minority groups; direct comparisons of variables affecting exercise behavior in males and females are limited, as are studies specific to exercise mode. Issues in the measurement of physical activity and purported determinants must be considered in evaluating and designing research in this area.

Suggested Readings

Dietz, W.H. 1996. The role of lifestyle in health: The epidemiology and consequences of inactivity. *Proceedings of the Nutrition Society* 55: 829–840.

Dishman, R.K., and J.F. Sallis. 1994. Determinants and interventions for physical activity and exercise. In *Physical activity, fitness and health: International proceedings and consensus statement*, ed. C. Bouchard and R.J. Shephard. Champaign, IL: Human Kinetics.

Owen, N., E. Leslie, J. Salmon, and M.J. Fotheringham. 2000. Environmental determinants of physical activity and sedentary behavior. *Exercise and Sport Sciences Reviews* 28: 153–158.

Rowland, T.W. 1998. The biological basis of physical activity. *Medicine and Science in Sports and Exercise* 30 (3): 392–399.

Sallis, J.F., and N. Owen. 1999. *Physical activity and behavioral medicine*. Thousand Oaks, CA: Sage.

Web Sites

www.cdc.gov/nccdphp/dnpa/

www.cdc.gov/nccdphp/brfss/

www.cdc.gov/nccdphp/dash/yrbs/

CHAPTER 11

Theories of Behavior Change

Throughout the centuries philosophers, and more recently psychologists, have tried to understand why people behave the way they do. Many attempts have been made to organize information about people and the world around them that can be used to explain and predict human behavior. However, there are countless individual and contextual variables that interact in patterns to influence behavior, and these patterns change over time. This complex abundance of information has been reduced and made more manageable through the application of theories.

Exercise psychology has applied several theories from the social and psychological literature to explain and predict the effects of physical activity on mental health. Various theories have also been applied to explain and predict the adoption and maintenance of an active lifestyle. In chapter 12 on interventions, you will see how different theoretical perspectives that are used to reach the same goal can result in different treatments and different interpretations about what influenced the outcome. In this chapter, we focus on the major theories that have guided exercise psychology research. We discuss basic definitions and core concepts and provide examples of how the theory has been applied.

A theory is a type of model (table 11.1). Models are generalized, simplified representations that are used to organize vast amounts of information. Models guide our thoughts and actions by defining which of myriad variables to focus on and which to ignore in a given situation. They help us to explain and to predict the world around us. Shared models allow us to interpret information in similar ways. Even the novice computer user knows that the small picture of a printer on the computer screen can be used to control the printer's functions. The picture of a printer is an iconic model. **Iconic models** are models with two or three dimensions that look like what they represent but are smaller or larger. **Analogue models,** such as maps, use a set of properties to represent the actual set of properties of the idea or event using transformational rules (e.g., 1 in. = 1.5 miles [2.4 km]).

Theories are symbolic models that are used to guide the design, execution, and interpretation of research. A theory is the formulation of underlying principles of certain observed phenomena that have been verified to some degree. Theories of human behavior provide assumptions about behavior and specify relationships among key variables that are necessary to explain and predict behavior. Theories allow us to predict what will occur beyond empirical

Table 11.1

Types of Models

Model type	Description
Iconic	Two- or three-dimensional model that looks like what it represents, but is larger or smaller. Examples include photographs and sculptures.
Analogue	Actual set of properties of an idea or event represented in two or three dimensions using transformational rules that can represent change or a process. Examples include maps and graphs. *Attendance in an aerobics class over 12 weeks can be presented in a graph, with time in weeks on the x-axis and percentage of participants attending each week on the y-axis* (see figure below).
Symbolic	Intrinsically meaningless symbols that represent ideas, events, or things and are not at all like what they represent. Examples include scripts and mathematical models. Theories are linguistic or mathematical models that guide the design, execution, and interpretation of research. *The exercise and self-esteem model in figure 8.3 (p. 158) has been tested in several research studies.*
Mixed	Combination of models that represent large and complex amounts of information. Examples include Web sites and books. *The 1996 Surgeon General's report on physical activity and health can be viewed on a Web site at* **www.cdc.gov/nccdphp/sgr/pdf/sgrfull.pdf**.

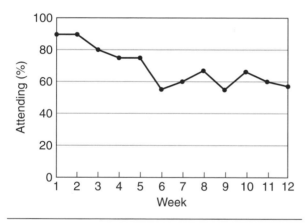

Typical dropout rate in an exercise program.

evidence; they allow us to go beyond what we already know. For example, the theory of behaviorism puts emphasis on antecedents and consequences of a target behavior to predict the frequency of that behavior. If we know that Jeff likes to spend time with Mary, we can predict that he will run more if he runs with Mary, who exercises regularly.

Theories of behavior change are models that represent human behavior. Over the years, several theories have been developed to order all the things that could influence what people do and why they do it. These theories represent different **ontological** assumptions (about what things are made of) and **cosmological** assumptions (about how things are

Theories are principles and assumptions that are used to explain and predict; theories of behavior change are models of human behavior.

organized and how they change). For example, behaviorism is based on a **materialistic** perspective on the nature of reality that reduces the mind to the functioning of the nervous system and biochemical/electrical processes. Behavior is described through linear chains of cause-and-effect relationships in which a stimulus and response are linked together through learning. Cognitive psychologies stem from **idealism,** in which reality is seen as the expression or embodiment of the mind. What we do, how we feel, and how things affect us are presumed to be influenced by learned associations among thoughts, affects, actions, and contexts. Thus, theories influence the ideas we accept and the actions we perform. They enable us to interpret and organize information in a logical and consistent format. Theories also spur research to prove or disprove that a certain theory is the correct way to view behavior.

Behaviorism

In the early part of the 20th century, John B. Watson (1919) wrote *Psychology From the Standpoint of a Behaviorist*, in which he asserted that psychology should be a science of behavior and not of the mind. Watson was followed by B.F. Skinner in the late 1930s, whose first important book, *The Behavior of Organisms*, was published in 1938. Skinner and his colleagues conducted numerous carefully controlled laboratory experiments over the next 40 years in their search for observable facts that affect learning. They developed empirically derived principles of behavior that include a central role for environmental determinants. Behaviorism, also known as learning theory, is based on the assumptions that psychology is about behavior and that a true account of behavior should not consider mental states, which are not open to direct observation and cannot be measured independently. Personality is seen as the sum of an individual's observed responses to the external world. Using behaviorism as a theoretical foundation involves focusing on the quantitative relationships between **independent** (cause, stimulus) and **dependent** (effect, response) **variables.** Key variables and predictions center on the relationships among stimulus, response, and consequences. As already mentioned, the emphasis is on looking at linear chains of cause-and-effect relationships in which the stimulus and response are linked through learning. Empirical research, which assumes that encounters with objects and events yield objective knowledge, provides the foundation for approaching the explanation and prediction of behavior. Change or learning is assumed to work the same way for all people.

Key variables in behaviorism to explain and predict behavior are the observable antecedents and consequences of the behavior.

Classical conditioning and **operant conditioning** provide the framework for understanding and modifying behavior through associative learning. Classical conditioning entails learning to associate two stimuli and is based on the work of Ivan Pavlov, whose ideas played an important role in the development of behaviorism. An **unconditioned** (or reinforcing) **stimulus** that is capable of eliciting a reflexive response is paired with a neutral stimulus. You may be familiar with the example of the pairing of food, which elicits salivation in the dog, with the ringing of a bell (figure 11.1). Eventually, the dog salivates when the bell rings even though no

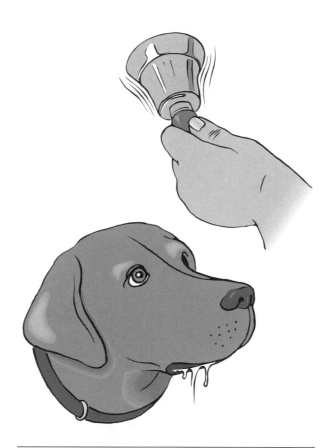

Figure 11.1 Classical conditioning is illustrated by Pavlov's famous experiment in which a dog learned to salivate in response to a ringing bell.

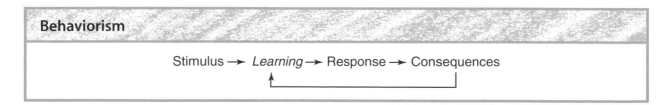

Behaviorism

Stimulus → *Learning* → Response → Consequences

food is present. The bell has become a **conditioned stimulus** and will continue to elicit the salivation in the dog (now a conditioned response) unless the bell is never paired with the food again. In this case, the salivation response will diminish and eventually disappear, a process called extinction.

Operant conditioning involves pairing a reinforcing or punishing event with a voluntary response in order to change the rate of responding. In this case, the respondent learns to associate the stimulus with a response. To enhance the response rate, a **reinforcing stimulus** (reward/reinforcement) should occur in the presence of another stimulus when a specific response occurs. The rat who got a food pellet when it pressed the bar received a reinforcing stimulus (food) when the voluntary behavior of pressing the bar occurred (figure 11.2). Eventually, the response (operant behavior) will occur in the presence of the other stimulus, or in this case, when the rat encounters the bar. A **discriminative stimulus,** or prompt, is an environmental cue about the nature of a behavioral consequence. Cheese bubbling on a pizza (discriminative stimulus) indicates a very good chance that eating the pizza (behavior) will result in a burned mouth (behavioral consequence).

Figure 11.2 Operant conditioning is used to increase the frequency at which a rat presses a bar by rewarding this behavior with food.

Obviously, stimuli and the reinforcing events are critical variables for understanding and predicting behavior when one uses behaviorism as a theoretical foundation. Events and situations coming before (**antecedents,** stimulus, cues) and after (**consequences, reinforcement,** rewards, punishments) a specific behavior are identified to explain the behavior. Consequences that will explain the behavior should be related directly/concretely or symbolically to that behavior. Changes in the consequences will increase or decrease the frequency of the behavior. For example, feeling relaxed and in a good mood after jogging will increase the frequency of this behavior. If jogging, now a conditioned behavior, no longer results in reinforcement (i.e., hot weather makes the jogging stressful), the behavior tends to occur less often and will eventually be extinguished if consequences continue to be unpleasant.

Antecedents and Consequences

Concrete antecedent: dog barks until you take her out for a walk

Concrete consequence: fatigue after a vigorous exercise session

Symbolic antecedent: coupon for a free aerobics class

Symbolic consequence: certificate for completing an exercise program

Behavior theory has been useful in conceptualizing types of antecedents and consequences that can influence exercise adoption and maintenance (table 11.2). **Latency,** the amount of time that passes between the stimulus and the response, can be used to identify antecedents and consequences as **proximal** (close in time to the target behavior) or **distal** (occurring long before or after the target behavior). For example, a notice that the swimming pool will be closed in two weeks is a *distal antecedent* to attending aerobics classes or jogging while the pool is closed. Clear and cool weather when a jogger wakes up can be a proximal antecedent for running that morning. Being late for class after completing an extra two sets of strengthening exercises is a proximal consequence of that exercise session. Losing or maintaining weight is a distal consequence of regular exercise.

Table 11.2

Types of Antecedents and Consequences Predicted to Influence Exercise Behavior

Type	Examples
Environmental	Weather, commercials, media, air quality, access to facilities, safety, time
Social	Modeling (in media and face-to-face), friends, family
Cognitive	Thoughts, attitudes, beliefs, values; emotions; self-efficacy, self-concept; motivation
Physiological	Gender, health, fitness, fatigue, pain, ability
Personal	Exercise history, health history, education, income, personality, states, traits

Many earlier research studies on exercise adherence were based on principles of behaviorism and used reinforcement control and stimulus control to increase physical activity. It was presumed that behavioral patterns are sustained because they are cued and reinforced. Thus, exercise was viewed as a behavior that can be modified (acquired and maintained) by changing the antecedents, the behavior itself (skill development, shaping), and the consequences (rewards, reinforcement) of the behavior. For example, several studies reported using contingency contracting, in which subjects received specific rewards after meeting predetermined criteria for exercise frequency and duration. Little or no attention was given to cognitive processes, affect, or motivation.

Cognitive Behaviorism

The early work of Donald Meichenbaum, one of the founders of the "cognitive revolution" in psychotherapy, laid the groundwork for extending behavior modification to include cognitions and thus for development of cognitive behaviorism. In one study, the behavior of impulsive first- and second-grade children was altered by training them to talk to themselves first overtly and then covertly to increase self-control (Meichenbaum and Goodman 1971). Subsequent research in clinical populations indicated that traditional behavior modification strategies supplemented with self-instructional training resulted in better and more sustained outcomes (Meichenbaum and Cameron 1994). This led to the conclusion that what the individual says to him- or herself, rather than environmental consequences of behavior, is of primary importance in modifying maladaptive behaviors.

Cognitive behaviorism is a theoretical perspective that shares some assumptions with behaviorism. The stimulus and the response are central to explaining behavior, but a significant difference from behaviorism is that cognition is defined as the critical mediating variable. Where behaviorism contends that matter is the only reality and that reality is understood though the physical sciences, cognitive behaviorism is based on an *interactive dualistic* perspective. This perspective in turn is based on the assumption that we are made up of both material and nonmaterial phenomena (dualism). The nonmaterial phenomena include sensations, perceptions, thoughts, and feelings that interact with and influence the material self.

A wide range of dysfunctional or maladaptive behavior results from faulty cognitions and beliefs that have an effect on behavior through the resulting emotional response. Learning or insight can serve to restructure, augment, or replace faulty thoughts with behaviorally effective beliefs and cognitive skills. Simply put, cognitions moderate behavior, and cognitions can be changed. Thus, the key to changing behavior is to change the thoughts. A popular strategy based on this model is **cognitive restructuring.** Cognitions are identified that limit the likelihood of positive action by eliciting a negative emotional response, such as a sense of futility ("I can never stick with an exercise program"). The faulty statement is reframed to be more realistic and supportive of the potential for change ("I have not been able to maintain regular exercise yet"). A number of strategies that have emerged from cognitive behaviorism, such as self-monitoring and goal setting, have been used frequently in exercise behavior change interventions (see chapter 12).

Cognitive behaviorism holds that cognitions determine behavior and that cognitions can be changed.

Social Cognitive Theory

Social cognitive theory evolved from social learning theory, which proposes that the majority of behaviors are learned through social interaction. Social cognitive theory was formalized in the mid-1980s through the work of Albert Bandura. Walter Mischel is a contemporary of Bandura's who emphasized cognitive and situational variables in understanding human behavior, and contended that intra-individual cognition was an important influence on behavior. Bandura built on the idea of intra-individual cognition and extended his own work on observational learning and self-regulation. Bandura's *Social Foundations of Thought and Action: A Social Cognitive Theory* (1986) describes the conceptual framework of this theory.

Social cognitive theory uses cognitions in the context of social interactions and behavior to explain human action, motivation, and emotion. Important concepts in social cognitive theories are described in table 11.3. Basic assumptions of social cognitive theory are that behavior is founded in cognitive activity, is purposeful action, and is under the direct control of the individual—that is, individuals are capable of self-reflection and self-regulation.

Self-reflection refers to an ability to symbolize and thus anticipate and plan for future events. Something that a person anticipates will occur in the future becomes a mental formulation in the present time and can serve to motivate current behavior. Behavior is thus controlled and regulated in anticipation of symbolized future events.

Another assumption within social cognitive theory is that self-regulating processes mediate the effects of most environmental influences. Cognitive mechanisms that support **self-regulation** (e.g., how people modify their own behavior) include personal goal setting, efficacy expectations, outcome expectations, and outcome values. The ability to symbolize and conceptualize a future helps to guide the development of goals, which are devised according to standards whose achievement will elicit positive self-evaluation. Goals are set that represent valued and desired objectives and point out a discrepancy between *actual* behavior and the *target* behavior. The discrepancy provides negative feedback that stimulates the direction and intensity of actions to reduce the incongruity. For example, Joe believes that running a 5K road race (target behavior) will demonstrate that he is a good runner, and he values this self-concept. However, Joe can run only 3 km without stopping (actual behavior). The discrepancy between how far he *wants* to run and how far he *can* run helps to direct his training program. Thus, goals provide direction and motivation in support of self-regulation.

Self-efficacy is the degree to which an individual believes he or she can successfully engage in a specific behavior in a particular situation with known

Table 11.3	
Key Variables in Social Cognitive Theories	
Variable	**Explanation**
Outcome expectancies	Outcomes are what is expected to happen externally and to oneself as the result of a behavior. Benefits (desired outcomes) and costs (undesired outcomes) can have differing influences depending on their relationship to the behavior (proximal or distal) and the individual's perceived vulnerability.
Outcome value	The outcome can have different degrees of reinforcement value or incentive value, and can be something one wishes to obtain or to avoid.
Intention	Intention is simply what one says one will do.
Self-efficacy expectancy	Self-efficacy is a cognition. It is a belief in one's ability to engage successfully in a specific behavior with a known outcome.

Expecting positive, valued outcomes and having high self-efficacy for exercise will increase the chances someone will exercise during lunch.

According to social cognitive theory, behavior is the outcome of social learning, and characteristics of the person, environment, and behavior itself interact to influence behavior.

outcomes. Self-efficacy is a learned belief that is developed through experiences and modeling. It includes three specific domains, which are strength, generality, and level. *Strength* refers to the perceived ability to overcome common barriers to engaging in a behavior *(Can I make time during lunch to go for a walk?)*. *Generality* is the ability to generalize the behavior to other similar behaviors *(If I can play tennis, can I also play racquetball?)*. *Level* is the degree or intensity to which a behavior can be engaged in successfully *(If I can run 3 miles with*

friends, can I run in a 5K race? Can I train for and run in a 10K race?). The significance of self-efficacy in behavior change is further developed in Bandura's self-efficacy theory, which is described on pages 218–219.

Outcome expectation is the perception that a given behavior will lead to a certain outcome. Outcomes are what is expected to happen to oneself and to the external situation as a result of a behavior.

Assumptions of Social Cognitive Theory

1. People have symbolizing capabilities.
2. Behavior is purposive or goal directed and is guided by forethought. This is dependent on the capability to symbolize.
3. People are self-reflective; they can analyze and evaluate their own thoughts and experiences.
4. People are capable of self-regulation; they can alter their own behavior and their environment; they adopt personal standards for their behavior and use those standards to guide behavior and motivate themselves.
5. Environmental events, inner personal factors (cognition, emotion, and biological events), and behavior are mutually interacting influences (triadic reciprocality; figure 11.3).

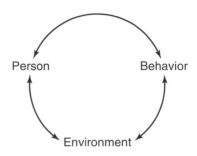

Triadic reciprocality

Person ... Behavior

Environment

Assumption: environmental events, inner personal factors (cognition, emotion, and biological events), and behavior are mutually interacting influences.

Figure 11.3 Triadic reciprocality represents the dynamic interaction among the person, behavior, and environment.

The influence of benefits (desired outcomes) and costs (undesired outcomes) on the behavior depends on a variety of factors, such as whether they are proximal or distal to the behavior. *If Sue walks for an hour after work five days a week, she believes she will lose weight (distal desired outcome), but she will have less time to spend with her family (proximal undesired outcome).*

Outcome value refers to the incentive value or reinforcement value of the outcome. Value is determined in part by the extent to which the outcome will affect the individual's sense of welfare and self-esteem. Thus, the outcome can be something one wants to obtain or avoid, and the strength of the value will influence effort and persistence. *Brad entered a new high school in the fall, and the boys in his class had been lifting weights for several years. Brad started working out with weights every day after school. Increasing muscular strength and size is very important to Brad because he wants to be more like his new friends and fit in.*

A central concept of social cognitive theory is that individuals also influence the environment, and this influence is bidirectional (e.g., reciprocal determinism). It is proposed that behavior change operates through mutually interactive effects among aspects of the person, the environment, and the behavior itself. This dynamic interaction, called **triadic reciprocality,** was used in chapter 10 to frame the relationships among several physical activity determinants. Exercise determinants have been organized into these three categories—that is, person, environment, and behavior—but research to test the dynamic interaction has been limited.

Triadic Reciprocality (Example)

The likelihood that a young female will participate in vigorous exercise depends on what benefits she expects from exercising and the value she places on that outcome (person variables), access to a safe place to exercise and peer influences (environmental variables), and the level of intensity and type of exercise (characteristics of the behavior). *Having a safe place to play basketball could influence perceived benefits in someone who knows she will need an athletic scholarship to attend college, but a peer making fun of the way she dribbles can affect the perception of benefits versus costs and/or the intensity of her practice.*

Bandura's Self-Efficacy Theory

Bandura's self-efficacy theory is a competency-based theory that has been applied to exercise behavior in more than 100 studies (McAuley and Mihalko 1998). An assumption of this theory is that the primary mediator of all behavior change is the cognitive mechanism called self-efficacy, which has been described as an important variable in social cognitive theory and in the transtheoretical model of behavior change (see pp. 220–222). According to Bandura's self-efficacy theory, self-efficacy expectancy, outcome expectancy, and outcome value are three basic cognitive mediating processes that determine behavior (figure 11.4). Adoption and persistence in behaviors are determined by the expectations about one's skills and capabilities to engage successfully in the specific target behavior in particular situations, as well as expectations about the outcomes and the value placed on those outcomes.

Self-Efficacy Expectations (Example)

At his medical exam, Matt weighs 10 lb (4.5 kg) more than his target weight. This information motivates him to seek out strategies to help achieve his goal weight. Self-efficacy expectations will determine choice of specific goals, strategies, effort, persistence, and affective responses he has to his level of performance. If Matt is confident that he can fit a walking program into his schedule but has always had problems sticking with any diet, he will be more likely to control his weight through exercise than by changing his eating habits.

Adoption of a behavior follows from self-initiated reactions that are stimulated by a discrepancy between personal goals or standards and knowledge of personal achievement.

The higher the self-efficacy, the higher the goals one sets and the more persistence one exhibits toward reaching those goals. Individuals dissatisfied with their current exercise or fitness who adopt challenging goals, and are confident (i.e., have high self-efficacy) that they can attain their goals, will presumably have optimal motivation for maintaining exercise (Dzewaltowski 1994). If someone has high self-efficacy and fails, he or she will attribute the

Cognitive Mediating Processes That Determine Behavior

Self-efficacy expectancy: Beliefs and expectations about how capable one is to perform the necessary behaviors to achieve an outcome. Self-efficacy is specific to a situation and behavior, but it can generalize to other similar situations and behavioral demands. High self-efficacy for following an aerobics routine increases the likelihood someone will enroll in an aerobics class, but might not generalize to confidence in beginning weight training.

Outcome expectancy: Estimation of the probability that a behavior will produce a specific outcome or result. Desired outcomes can be extrinsic (tangible) or intrinsic, such as self-respect or self-satisfaction. The outcome expected is related to the efficacy for a specific behavior. For example, one might believe that swimming is one of the best modes for achieving overall fitness but have low confidence about swimming enough on a regular basis to increase fitness.

Outcome value: Reinforcement value or incentive value of the desired outcome. If increased fitness is highly valued, the effort and persistence to follow a fitness regimen are greater than if fitness is not valued.

Figure 11.4   These three cognitive mediating processes are part of Bandura's self-efficacy theory.

failure to insufficient effort and be more likely to persist. Someone with low self-efficacy may attribute failure to low ability, and this person is more likely to give up.

Self-efficacy expectations are developed from performance accomplishments (i.e., mastery experiences), vicarious experiences (i.e., modeling or observing others), verbal persuasion (i.e., encouragement or positive feedback), and interpretation of physiological/psychological arousal (e.g., perceived exertion). Performance accomplishments provide the most potent influence on efficacy expectations. Self-efficacy increases when one masters difficult or previously feared tasks. Skills are developed and refined and coping mechanisms are developed through personal experiences. Vicarious experiences are experiences in which people learn by observing events or people. Observing someone similar to oneself succeeding through effort and being rewarded increases one's efficacy to also perform that specific behavior. Verbal persuasion can take the form of self-talk or encouragement from significant others. High physiological arousal during performance of a task can impair performance and decrease efficacy expectations. Strategies to change behavior based on self-efficacy theory focus on manipulating these sources of efficacy information to increase exercise self-efficacy.

Stage Theories

The general paradigm for predicting behavior in the early development of behavior change theories was based on order, stability, and equilibrium. Theories of causality, such as behaviorism, evolved from a mechanistic view in which fixed sequence pathways link events in patterns of cause-effect relationships. The view was that elements necessary for change and their interactions were not modified by their relationships or history, and change was predictable and controllable. The influence of **field theory** led to a broadening of the concept of change to include the proposition that events are a function of the nature and organization of *all* conditions in which they are embedded. Most of the theories presented so far have conceptualized behavior change as an event that is influenced by a number of different variables in a linear pattern; individuals are placed on a continuum of probability of change according to their scores on multiple predictor variables. Newer models have been influenced formally and informally by quantum theory, nonlinear thermodynamics, and chaos theory to consider the contributions of instability, diversity, nonlinear relationships, and temporality in explaining change. The latter concept—that of a temporal dimension—has been included in some of the newer and more promising stage models of behavior change.

Stage models of behavior reflect the dynamic, nonlinear process of behavior change.

Stage theories assign each individual to one of a limited number of categories, or stages. Individuals in the *same* stage are similar to each other with respect to specific characteristics, such as level of physical activity, and individuals in *different* stages demonstrate substantial differences in these characteristics. Stage theories may also include parameters for how long you stay in a particular stage and for the usual sequence of movement from stage to stage. You would typically spend a certain amount of time and/or accomplish specific tasks in stage A before you are "ready" to move to stage B. However, movement through the stages of health behavior change is not inevitable or progressive. For many people, behavior change does not follow an orderly, predictable pattern. Often, individuals trying to change a health behavior will get "stuck" in a stage or cycle through stages out of sequence or at varied rates of progression. Stage models allow for the process to go forward, go backward, cycle, or stop, providing a context for describing relapse and re-adoption.

In addition to the concept of irregular progression, stage theories define barriers to change that are similar among people in specific stages and are important for progression to the next stage. Because there are different barriers in each stage and specific tasks that must be accomplished to move to the next stage, stage models imply stage-specific interventions.

The stage model that has been most frequently applied to exercise and physical activity is the **transtheoretical model of behavior change,** also known as the stages of change model (see figure 11.5). The transtheoretical model of behavior change is a general model of intentional behavior change that includes a temporal component as a critical factor in describing and predicting behavior. In the late 1970s Prochaska and DiClemente, observing smokers trying to quit without professional intervention, found that these self-changers passed through specific stages as they tried to decrease or eliminate this health-related behavior.

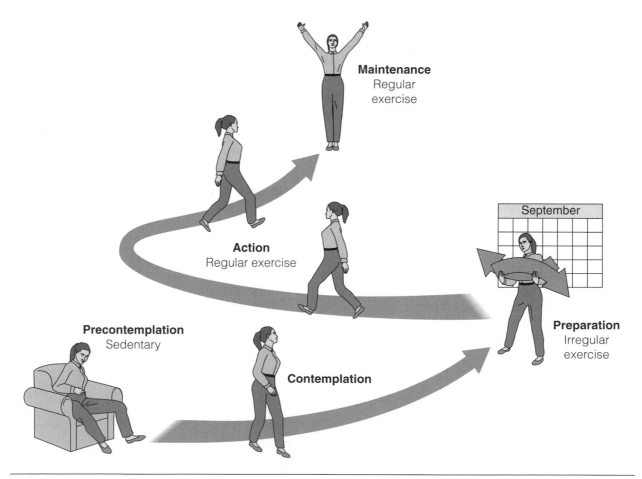

Figure 11.5 The process of adopting and maintaining regular exercise is described through specific stages of behavior change.

Stage Theories: Stages and Possible Patterns of Behavior Change

Stages of Behavior Change

A (not engaging in the target behavior)

B (not engaging in target behavior but having strong intentions)

C (recent adoption of target behavior)

D (established participation in the target behavior)

Examples of Possible Patterns of Change

Progressive order: A → B → C → D

Backwards: A → B → C → B → A

Cycle: A → B → A → B → A

Prochaska and DiClemente developed transtheoretical therapy in the late 1970s and early 1980s based on this research and a transtheoretical analysis of 18 leading systems of psychotherapy (see Prochaska 1979; Prochaska and DiClemente 1982, 1983). The underlying principles and mechanisms of transtheoretical therapy were then used to construct the transtheoretical model of behavior change.

The transtheoretical model describes health behavior adoption and maintenance as a process that occurs through a series of behaviorally and motivationally defined stages (figure 11.5). Although the model was developed to describe changes in addictive behavior, it has expanded to include the adoption of preventive health behaviors and the use of medical services. Dishman in 1982, Sonstroem in 1988, and Sallis and Hovell in 1990 promoted the concept of a dynamic model of exercise behavior. In the early 1990s, Marcus and others applied the transtheoretical model to exercise behavior (e.g., Marcus et al. 1992; Marcus and Simkin 1993).

The transtheoretical model includes three levels: stage of change, constructs hypothesized to influence behavior change, and level of change. Level of change has not been addressed in the exercise literature, and many studies applying and/or testing the transtheoretical model with exercise use only the first level of this model, that is, stage of change. Stage is the temporal dimension in which change unfolds. Empirical analysis has established five distinct stages that are relatively stable but open to change. A six-month time period is typically used to define stages, assuming that six months is about as far in the future as people can anticipate making changes. A sixth stage, *termination*, represents a point at which there is 100% confidence in ability to maintain the behavior change and there is no risk of a relapse to previous stages. Some researchers (e.g., Cardinal 1999) have begun to apply this last stage to exercise.

Number and descriptions of exercise stages of change have been varied. For example, some researchers do not include a time frame for intention to begin exercise (e.g., within 30 days) as a criterion for classification in the preparation stage. Others have divided preparation into two stages, characterized by some exercise but distinguished by intention to adopt regular exercise. *Physical activity* stage of change has also been applied in research studies and interventions that address the Centers for Disease Control and Prevention and the American College of Sports Medicine's recommendations for daily physical activity.

Exercise Stages (Example)

Precontemplation stage: Individuals are inactive and have no intention to start exercising. They are not seriously thinking about changing their level of exercise within the next six months, or they deny the need to change.

Contemplation stage: Individuals are also inactive, but they intend to start regular exercise within the next six months.

Preparation stage: Individuals are active below a criterion level (typically defined as at least three times per week for 20 min or longer), but intend to become more active in the near future (within the next 30 days).

Action stage: Individuals have engaged in regular exercise at the criterion level for less than six months. Motivation and investment in behavior change are sufficient at this stage, and the perceived benefits are greater than the perceived cost. However, this is the least stable stage. Individuals in the action stage are at greatest risk of a relapse.

Maintenance stage: Individuals have been exercising regularly for more than six months. Exercise behavior is more established than in the other stages, and the risk of a relapse is low.

The second level of the transtheoretical model includes three constructs that are hypothesized to influence behavior change. They are self-efficacy, incorporated from the social cognitive theory (see discussion earlier in this chapter); **decisional balance,** which is the evaluation of the pros and cons of the target behavior; and **processes of change,** which are the strategies used for changing behavior. Several studies have examined exercise stage and self-efficacy for exercise; and in general, self-efficacy is lowest in the early stages (e.g., precontemplation) and higher in each adjacent stage, with the highest exercise self-efficacy seen in the maintenance stage. There is some longitudinal evidence that exercise self-efficacy increases as one moves from an established sedentary lifestyle to long-term maintenance of regular exercise (Marcus et al. 1994; Sallis, Hovell, and Hofstetter 1992). However, these data cannot tell us if people are more active because they have higher self-efficacy, or if they have higher self-efficacy because of past success with exercise so that their experience is the true determinant of their current behavior.

Decisional balance is another construct from the transtheoretical model that is believed to influence exercise behavior. Based on the decision theory of Janis and Mann (1977), perceived costs and benefits to oneself and significant others are considered important influences on behavior change. There is good evidence that two constructs (i.e., pros and cons) are adequate for exercise. The relationship between the pros and cons of exercise and exercise stage typically shows that pros increase and cons decrease with movement to each subsequent stage. Most of the evidence for exercise also indicates that the crossover between pros and cons occurs during the contemplation or preparation stage; this is consistent with several other health behaviors (see figure 11.6).

The processes of change are strategies associated with movement along the stages and are divided into cognitive/experiential and behavioral. Cognitive/experiential processes are defined as the set of processes through which an individual gathers relevant information on the basis of his or her own actions or experiences. An example of a cognitive process is self re-evaluation, in which the individual reappraises values regarding inactivity. Behavioral processes are the set of processes in which the information is generated by environmental events and behaviors, such as stimulus control and reinforcement control.

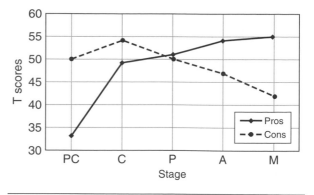

Figure 11.6 Decisional balance: pros and cons by stages of change. PC = precontemplation; C = contemplation; P = preparation; A = action; M = maintenance.

From J.O. Prochaska, W.F. Velicer, J.S. Rossi, M.G. Goldstein, B.H. Marcus, W. Rakowski, C. Fiore, L.L. Harlow, C.A. Redding, D. Rosenblum, and S.R. Rossi, 1994, "Stages of change and decisional balance for 12 problem behaviors," *Health Psychology* 13 (1): 39–46. Copyright © 1994 by the American Psychological Association. Adapted with permission.

The level of change dimension is the context in which the problem behavior occurs. These levels include symptom/situational, maladaptive cognitions, current interpersonal conflicts, family/systems conflicts, and intrapersonal conflicts. Although not typically applied in exercise research, identifying the level of the problem could be used to guide interventions. For example, the level of change for someone who wants to begin strength training but does not have access to a fitness center would be situational. Setting up a home exercise program would have more efficacy for this person than targeting his or her cognitions.

Despite its appeal as a model for exercise behavior change and its application in several intervention studies, some uncertainty remains about whether the transtheoretical model has stages and processes that are applicable to understanding exercise behavior change (Dishman 1991; Rosen 2000; Weinstein et al. 1998). Indeed, Bandura (1997) raised several concerns and criticisms of the transtheoretical model in general, such as a lack of adherence to basic tenants of traditional stage theory (i.e., qualitative transformations across stages and invariant sequence of change). A recent meta-analysis of the transtheoretical model literature included exercise studies in an examination of the sequencing of processes of change across stages for different health behaviors (Rosen 2000). Experiential and behavioral processes of change were applied sequentially across stage transitions for smoking cessation, but were employed concomitantly by people trying to adopt regular exercise, which suggests that readiness for exercise may not be a discrete variable but a continuous variable (Rosen 2000). If so, stage models in general may not have an advantage over continuum models, such as social cognitive theory for conceptualizing exercise behavior change. The usefulness of the transtheoretical model for exercise interventions has also been mixed. Targeting specific processes of change to facilitate progression of exercise behavior across stages is based on the assumption that differences between adjacent stages found in cross-sectional studies point to processes that need to be changed to progress to the next stage. However, the efficacy of targeting specific processes to promote stage progression has yet to be adequately tested; there have been few longitudinal prospective designs and the instruments to measure stage (e.g., Reed, Velicer, Prochaska, Rossi, and Marcus 1997), and processes of change have been poorly validated for exercise (Dishman 1991; Dishman 1994a; Rosen 2000).

Other Theories Applied to Exercise and Physical Activity

The theories reviewed so far are the prominent models in exercise behavior research, but several other models have also been applied to exercise, with varying success.

Theory of Reasoned Action

The theory of reasoned action was developed by Fishbein and Ajzen to explain and predict social behavior in specific contexts (e.g., Ajzen and Fishbein 1974). A basic assumption is that people make rational decisions about their behavior based on information and beliefs about the behavior and its consequences, what they expect, and the value they place on the outcome. However, the most important predictor of behavior is the intention to perform or not perform the behavior. Behavior is thus addressed at the level of individual decision making.

Intention is a function of the attitude toward the behavior and the attitude toward the social norms regarding the behavior. Attitude toward the behavior is a function of beliefs about the consequences of engaging in the behavior and an evaluation of those consequences. Individuals can have many dif-

ferent beliefs about the same behavior and can have evaluations of the consequences related to each belief. For example, Jim may believe that exercise can help him lower his serum cholesterol, but maintaining a regular exercise program will take time away from writing his dissertation. Subjective norms (i.e., attitudes toward social norms regarding the behavior) consist of perceptions of how important others think the behavior is and the individual's motivation to comply with others' expectations.

According to the theory of reasoned action, behavior adoption is not related to personality, education, or cultural background except in their impact on attitudes toward the behavior and subjective norms. This theory has been applied to exercise behavior with some success, with attitudes generally explaining 30% of intentions to exercise. There is less support for the association between subjective norm and exercise intentions (see chapter 10). This model gives a static profile of beliefs and attitudes and does not account for changes in cognitions over time.

Theory of Planned Behavior

According to Ajzen's theory of planned behavior, which is a modification of the theory of reasoned action, attitudes toward exercising and social norms about exercise also influence the intention to exercise, which is the causal mediator of exercise behavior (Ajzen 1988). The theory of planned behavior adds the assessment of **perceived behavioral control** (perception that one possesses the resources and the opportunity to execute the behavior or attain the goal) as a direct determinant of the behavior and an indirect determinant through its influence on intentions. It is assumed that most behaviors are on a continuum from total control to no control. Perceived behavioral control will vary across situations and is influenced by resources, opportunities, and skills. Measurement of perceived behavioral control has varied such that it has been operationalized as perceived barriers to executing the behavior as well as control over goal attainment.

Applications of both the theory of reasoned action and the theory of planned behavior to exercise behavior research have typically involved measures that are specific to the behavior, context, and goal in question (e.g., Hausenblas, Carron, and Mack 1997; Kimiecik 1992). This specificity of measurement is a major strength of these theories given the wide variety of exercise behaviors and settings. These two theories also provide a basis for understanding the factors involved in initiating exercise behavior.

Health Belief Model

The health belief model was developed by Rosenstock and others in the 1950s to explain poor compliance with immunization and tuberculosis screenings. The health belief model explains health behavior at the level of individual decision making regarding the adoption or cessation of behaviors related to risk or control of a disease. The model centers on perceptions of how much of a personal threat the disease is and how effective the behavior change will be in reducing the threat. The likelihood of taking action will be influenced by a cue to action (internal or external) and demographic and sociocultural variables. The readiness to adopt a health behavior depends on motivation, evaluation of the threat of illness resulting from not changing behavior, and perception that the behavior in question will reduce the threat. Modifying factors include demographics, structural factors (cost, complexity), attitudes, interaction factors (between patient and care provider), and enabling factors (social pressure, past experiences). Social support and self-efficacy have been added to the original model, which should enhance its predictive utility. This model appears more useful for preventive health behaviors and compliance with medical regimens, and less successful when applied to exercise. It is, essentially, an *illness avoidance* model. In fact, some studies indicated that perceived susceptibility was *inversely* associated with exercise adherence. It may

be that physical activity and exercise are not perceived as health behaviors. People exercise for social interaction, enjoyment, mastery, and competition, as well as to enhance health; and motivation for exercise can change.

Relapse Prevention

Most of the theories described in this chapter can be applied to the adoption and maintenance of behavior change. The **relapse prevention** model, which was derived from social learning theory, focuses on the maintenance of voluntary self-control efforts. The goal in the application of the model is to help people who are attempting to modify their behavior to cope effectively with situations that could tempt them to return to the old, undesired behavior pattern. Marlatt and Gordon (1985) originally designed the model to enhance maintaining abstinence from a high-frequency, undesired behavior, that is, addictive behavior. Maintenance of behavior change is described in the context of the person's ability to cope with relapses cognitively and behaviorally.

Relapse begins with a **high-risk situation,** which is a situation that challenges one's confidence in adhering to a desired behavior change. An adequate coping response leads to increased self-efficacy and decreased probability of relapse. Inadequate coping or no coping leads to decreased self-efficacy and possibly positive expectations of what will happen if the behavior change program is skipped ("I can go to the football game if I don't go to the gym today"). The more rigid the rule is, the more obvious the slip. For example, if the "rule" is to exercise three days per week at 6:15 A.M. for 35 min, starting 10 min late can be perceived as a slip. Perception of slipping may lead to the abstinence violation effect, or in the case of exercise, the *adherence* violation effect. One of the characteristics of this effect is the experience of cognitive dissonance—an incongruity between thoughts or feelings and behavior. For example, the slip behavior (i.e., missing an exercise class) does not match the self-concept of being in control of exercise behavior. Another cognitive component of the abstinence/adherence violation effect is all-or-nothing thinking, such as defining oneself as either a success or a failure, which is also a risk for increased mental stress (see chapter 4). The emotional components of abstinence/adherence violation include a sense of failure, self-blame, lowered self-esteem, guilt, and perceived loss of control, which can set the stage for relapse.

Health Belief Model: Beliefs That Influence Exercise Behavior

1. Perceived susceptibility to developing health problems because of inactivity (e.g., coronary heart disease, obesity)

2. Perceived impact of the health problems on quality of life (perceived severity)

3. Belief that adopting an active lifestyle will be beneficial

4. Extent to which the benefits of exercising exceed the cost of exercising (perceived cost-benefit ratio)

High-risk situations and rigid rules increase the risk of relapse.

A lifestyle imbalance in which "shoulds" exceed "wants" also predisposes one to relapse. Someone who spends more time doing what "should" be done at the expense of doing what he or she "wants" to do feels deprived, and the desire for indulgence or self-gratification increases. *Bill has been exercising each weekend since his blood pressure was elevated at his last physical. He has missed several fishing trips because of his exercise program, and he feels frustrated and left out when his friends talk about how much fun they had.* Positive expectations of not adhering to the behavior change make relapse more attractive, as well. *If he skipped his workout this weekend, Bill could try out his new fishing rod on a trip to the coast with his friends.*

Conceptually, the relapse prevention model seems useful for exercise adherence, given that 50% of those who begin a regular exercise program will drop out within the first six months, most within the first three months. However, the model was developed for maintaining cessation of high-frequency undesired behaviors, and exercise is a low-frequency, desired behavior. It is clear when someone relapses from smoking cessation, but it is hard to operationalize a slip from regular exercise and define when a slip becomes relapse. It may be difficult to identify an exercise lapse or to deal with a lapse in time to forestall relapse. One component of relapse prevention training that may not be effective with exercise is a planned relapse, in which the individual voluntarily returns to the undesired behavior, in this case inactivity, for a short period of time under controlled conditions. Planned relapse may not be a good strategy for acquisition behaviors in general, particularly in the early stages of behavior change (Marcus and Stanton 1993). Other strategies from relapse prevention, such as identifying high-risk situations and planning for them, and setting flexible goals (rules), have been applied to exercise with some success.

Habit Theory

A habit is defined as a behavior that has been performed repeatedly and has become automatic. It is thus performed without conscious thought or without the benefit of a decision in which at least one other course of action is considered. A habit is a thing done often, and thus, according to habit theory, easily (Ronis, Yates, and Kirscht 1989). Habit theory proposes that automatic cognitive processes are set in motion by situational cues, so conscious thought is not required. Situational consistency contributes to habit formation; therefore, vivid, numerous, and consistent cues support behavior change maintenance. Another supposition of habit theory is that the more simple and discrete the behavior, the more likely it will become habitual and will be elicited by situational cues. Thus, components of an exercise routine can be examined, and parts of the routine can be identified as potential habits. For example, putting running clothes out the night before, driving to the gym after work, or stopping work at noon to walk with friends are behavioral candidates for control by automatic cognitive processes.

Aarts, Paulussen, and Schaalma (1997) developed a model of physical exercise and habit formation to describe the process by which exercise habits are formed. This model contains several of the components of habit formation just discussed. The development of a physical activity habit begins with an initial contemplative decision process in which the need to exercise is evaluated based on perceptions of desirability, social pressure, and behavioral control. A positive evaluation leads to intentions and the actual exercise behavior. If the consequences of the behavior are pleasant, the recurrence of exercise depends on the opportunity to perform the behavior under similar circumstances. Over time, the contemplative decision process becomes less complex. As the behavior is repeated, it will be automatically activated by the situational features that precede exercise. Exercise becomes a habit that no longer needs reasoned consideration. The development of lifelong exercise habits depends on overcoming several obstacles, such as lack of positive immediate consequences and difficulty in repeating the same behavior in similar circumstances (i.e., disruptions in exercise routine from changes in work schedule, social obligations, etc.), which impedes the repetition that is important in habit formation.

Issues in Application of Theories of Exercise Behavior

Just as there is no single determinant of exercise and physical activity, no single theory seems to be adequate for describing and predicting exercise behavior. The theories we have presented are all reasonable models of human behavior and contain many of the variables related to exercise behavior that determinants research has revealed. However, many theories have been applied to exercise incompletely, and few studies have been conducted to empirically test the application of specific theories to exercise behavior. Weinstein, Rothman, and Sutton (1998) address this issue in an article reviewing conceptual and methodological issues in the application of stage theories to health behaviors; they also include strategies to test the validity of stage models that could be applied to exercise stage research.

In a review of exercise behavior change interventions, Baranowski, Anderson, and Carmack (1998) argued that interventions work through mediating variables, but that current theoretical models used to select mediating variables often do not account for substantial amounts of variability in the targeted outcome. The authors recommend more basic behavioral and social science research to understand physical activity behavior, which would include examination of theoretical constructs. Meeting this charge can clarify the role of personal, environmental, and behavioral variables and their relationships in predicting and explaining patterns of physical activity. An example of a study that tested constructs from various theoretical models to magnify determinant-behavior relationships was reported by Courneya and Bobick (2000). The social cognitive constructs from the theory of planned behavior were found to mediate the relationship between the processes of change and stages of change from the transtheoretical model. In chapter 10 we indicated that the evidence for a relationship between social norms (from the theories of reasoned action and planned behavior) and exercise behavior has been inconsistent. Courneya and Bobick also found that social norm was not important for overall changes in exercise stage, but social norm did distinguish the precontemplation stage (inactive and not considering starting exercise) from the contemplation stage (inactive but planning to begin regular exercise). Social norm may be relevant for the decision to consider exercise adoption. The identification of this relationship supports the Baronowski, Anderson, and Carmack (1998) recommendation to integrate constructs from alternative theoretical models in studying exercise behavior.

Certainly, the design, implementation, and interpretation of research on exercise behavior must be based on theory. Many theories of human behavior are available, in addition to those described in this chapter, that can be used to understand and predict exercise behavior. The selection of a theory should be guided by the evidence for its application to the unique characteristics of exercise and the relationships between theoretical constructs and exercise behavior. Some researchers are addressing this issue by attempting to develop theories specific to exercise (e.g., Aarts, Paulussen, and Schaalma 1997), while others advocate integrating theories across multiple domains of the social, behavioral, and biomedical sciences (Epstein 1998). This latter approach may prove more fruitful since few social or behavioral theories of behavior include a biological component, and this aspect of exercise, though often overlooked, can be a potent influence on exercise behavior.

Summary

Behaviorism considers behavior change to be the result of modifications in antecedents and consequences and their cuing and reinforcing strength. Cognitive behaviorism defines intra-individual factors as the key to behavior change. Application of social learning-based theories to exercise behavior involves describing exercise and physical activity as volitional behavior influenced by conscious decision making, and emphasizes the role of self-efficacy, attitudes, beliefs, and intentions to varying degrees. Though attitude models in general account for no more than 35% of the variance in exercise behavior, these models are primarily concerned with decision making, which is a predisposing factor in terms of actual behavior change. Enabling factors (accessibility, availability of resources, environmental factors) and reinforcing factors (rewards and incentives) add to the explanation of exercise adoption and maintenance, and should be considered in a comprehensive model of exercise behavior that includes a biological component. Psychosocial, physiological, and environmental factors change over time, and thus their contributions to exercise behavior are dynamic. The inclusion of a temporal dimension in a model of exercise behavior, such as that described by the transtheoretical and relapse prevention models, expands our ability to understand how people change and has implications for improving the effectiveness of interventions.

Suggested Readings

Bandura, A. 1986. *Social foundations of thought and action.* Englewood Cliffs, NJ: Prentice-Hall.

Baranowski, T., C. Anderson, and C. Carmack. 1998. Mediating variable framework in physical activity interventions: How are we doing? How might we do better? *American Journal of Preventive Medicine* 15 (4): 266–297.

Biddle, S.J.H., and C.R. Nigg. 2000. Theories of exercise behavior. *International Journal of Sport Psychology* 31 (2): 290–304.

Epstein, L.H. 1998. Integrating theoretical approaches to promote physical activity. *American Journal of Preventive Medicine* 15 (4): 257–265.

Ford, D.H., and H.B. Urban. 1998. *Contemporary models of psychotherapy: A comparative analysis.* New York: Wiley.

Godin, G. 1994. Social-cognitive models. In *Advances in exercise adherence*, ed. R.K. Dishman. Champaign, IL: Human Kinetics.

Prochaska, J.O., and B.H. Marcus. 1994. The transtheoretical model: Applications to exercise. In *Advances in exercise adherence*, ed. R.K. Dishman. Champaign, IL: Human Kinetics.

Web Sites

www.bfskinner.org/index.asp

www.nacbt.org/

www.psy.pdx.edu/PsiCafe/KeyTheorists/Bandura.htm

www.uri.edu/research/cprc/transtheoretical.htm

12

Interventions to Change Physical Activity Behavior

Anyone who has tried to change a health-related behavior knows that doing something as simple as drinking more water each day is not easy, even though we know it is good for us and we feel better for doing it. Exercise is good for us, and we feel better when we exercise on a regular basis, but it is not a simple behavior. Without intervention, there is, on average, a 50-50 chance that someone who has started an exercise program will stop within six months. The aim of this chapter is to describe models and strategies used to get people to start and stick with regular exercise; we hope also to offer some insight into why the efforts to keep people physically active have not been successful.

Overview

The primary goals in exercise behavior change research are to get sedentary or irregularly active individuals to adopt regular exercise and to keep physically active individuals exercising on a regular basis. Deciding what needs to be changed and which strategies should be used is based on the procedural model guiding the intervention. Procedural models define what should be done, when, and under what conditions to produce a specific outcome. They are derived from propositional models or theories, such as behaviorism, that were discussed

in chapter 11. For example, if the theoretical foundation of the intervention is behaviorism, then the assumptions about how changes in behavior occur are based on the relationships between antecedents, consequences, and the target behavior. The procedural model derived from behaviorism would involve strategies such as stimulus control (modifying the antecedents) and reinforcement control (modifying the consequences), and the goal would be defined in terms of changing the rate of responding (increase or maintain the frequency of exercise). The choice of specific theory-based variables to target should be based on documented factors that mediate exercise behavior—which is another reason to study **determinants** of physical activity.

The goal of exercise interventions is to increase the number of people who adopt and maintain a physically active lifestyle.

We need to keep several points in mind when considering the various approaches used to promote the adoption and maintenance of a physically active lifestyle. First, changing the level of physical activity is not like changing most other health

Getting family members to the park for recreational activities takes multiple steps and considerable coordination and effort.

behaviors. With physical activity, the goal is to adopt and maintain a positive health behavior, rather than to give up or stop a negative health behavior, such as smoking cigarettes. Second, physical activity is unique in that it is a biologically based behavior. There is an interaction between physiological and psychosocial antecedents and consequences of physical activity. For example, fatigue and soreness, which are possible physiological consequences of a bout of exercise, can be interpreted cognitively as lack of capability and lead to lower self-efficacy. Third, physical activity is a complicated behavior. Walking the dog, attending an aerobics class, and taking the family to the park are all preceded by chains of cognitive, behavioral, and social events with multiple decisions and actions. Some of these activities, like getting the family to the park for a Saturday fitness event, have many links, while taking the stairs instead of the escalator may simply involve noticing a sign promoting physical activity and walking to the stairs. Decisions and subsequent actions are influenced by personal characteristics, physiological responses and adaptations, social factors, and environmental conditions. Fourth, exercise is a dynamic behavior, as illustrated by the application of the stage models to exercise (see chapter 11). Different factors influence adoption, early adherence, long-term maintenance, and resumption of exercise after a period of inactivity. The last point concerns the targeted quality and quantity of physical activity. The type of regimen should match the

objectives of an exercise program; swimming five days a week for an hour each time will facilitate weight loss, but weight-bearing exercise is necessary to prevent osteoporosis.

Characteristics of Exercise as a Target Behavior

- ▼ The goal is to adopt and maintain a positive health behavior.
- ▼ Exercise is a biologically based behavior.
- ▼ Exercise is preceded by chains of psychological, behavioral, and social events that require multiple decisions and actions.
- ▼ Different combinations of factors mediate adoption, early adherence, long-term maintenance, and resumption of exercise after relapse.
- ▼ The quality and quantity of exercise vary as a function of purpose.

Intervention Context

We present the context for describing interventions to change physical activity in terms of characteristics of the person (i.e., target group), the setting, and the level of the intervention. Characteristics of the target group, such as age, living situation, and income, should be considered in selecting interventions. For example, a program for increasing physical activity in overweight middle school children will be very different from strategies designed to increase the number of factory workers who adopt regular exercise. The setting, which can range from a high school physical education class to an urban recreation facility, presents a variety of resources and limitations. Interventions can be applied on an individual, group, community, or societal level, and this will also influence the choice of specific strategies. Numerous approaches have been used to influence physical activity. This chapter provides descriptions of several interventions and their potential for changing physical activity behavior in various populations. We end with a discussion of issues in the development and implementation of exercise behavior change interventions.

A comprehensive model of exercise interventions requires consideration of characteristics of the target group, the intervention setting, and the level of the intervention to guide program goals and selection of strategies.

Characteristics of the Person

It is becoming increasingly evident that interventions applied in general, without consideration of the unique demands of the population, will have limited impact. *One size does not fit all.* Information about the client or target group enables us to select the best strategy, the most appropriate setting in which to implement the strategy, and the level of intervention that will have the greatest impact. Exercise stage, demographic characteristics, and cognitive variables (such as knowledge, attitudes, and beliefs) are some of the personal characteristics that have been considered in the development and implementation of exercise interventions.

Exercise Stage of Change

Determining exercise stage of change as described by the transtheoretical model of behavior change (see chapter 11, p. 220) is useful because different goals and strategies are necessary based on whether someone is currently active or not and on her in-

tentions to begin or maintain regular exercise (table 12.1). For example, cognitive strategies, such as increasing knowledge about personal benefits of physical activity, would be directed toward someone in the precontemplation or contemplation stage. Someone in the preparation or action stage would benefit more from behavioral strategies like reinforcement management and stimulus control.

Traditional strategies will not work with someone who is not ready to change. For example, individuals in the *precontemplation stage* may be resistant to recognizing or modifying a problem. Auweele, Rzewnicki, and Van Mele (1997) examined factors in adoption of exercise in 133 male and 132 female sedentary middle-aged adults in Belgium. They found a significant group of indifferent sedentary adults for whom exercise was irrelevant (60% of total sample). These individuals did not include exercise as part of their lives or self-concepts and did not see exercise as a way to achieve desired goals. The authors proposed that there simply may be individuals who will not be receptive to any intervention.

Contemplators are aware of the problem and are thinking about changing, but they have not made the commitment to change. At this point, the costs are perceived to be greater than the benefits of exercising. Cognitive factors to consider are the perceived barriers to starting an exercise program, outcome expectations, outcome values, and psychosocial variables, such as exercise self-efficacy. Exercise history can affect self-efficacy in that someone who has had a positive experience with exercise will have more confidence in his or her ability to exercise again.

Individuals in the *preparation stage* have already begun to change their behavior. They intend to begin regular exercise within a short period of time and may already be exercising, but below a criterion level. Setting goals that are based on capabilities, values, resources, and needs is important. Accomplishing challenging goals will increase a sense of mastery, which will also enhance exercise self-efficacy.

Most people who start an exercise program drop out within the first six months. Therefore, the first few months after someone has adopted regular exercise *(action stage)* are critical. Establishing a regular exercise routine involves a significant commitment of time and energy. According to habit theory (chapter 11, p. 225), most of the behaviors necessary for engaging in exercise still require conscious consideration and active decision

Table 12.1

Exercise Stage, Goal, and Sample Behavior Change Strategies

Exercise stage	Goal	Strategies
Precontemplation	To begin thinking about changing	Providing information about the role of exercise in good health Strengthening actual and perceived personal benefits of exercise Reducing or countering actual and perceived costs and barriers of exercise Fostering a personal value for exercise
Contemplation	To adopt regular exercise	Marketing and media campaigns with accurate, easy-to-understand guidelines for beginning an exercise program Activities to increase exercise self-efficacy, such as mastery experiences Evaluating pros and cons of exercise
Preparation	To adopt regular exercise at an appropriate target level	A thorough physical and psychosocial assessment (self-monitoring) Establishing realistic and reasonable goals Evaluating environmental and social supports and barriers and modifying barriers accordingly
Action	To establish exercise as a habit	Behavior modification strategies, such as shaping, stimulus control, reinforcement control, and self-monitoring Relapse prevention
Maintenance	To maintain lifelong regular exercise	Re-evaluating exercise goals Introducing variety into the exercise routine Planning ways to cope with potential lapses

making in the early adoption period. Strategies such as those in table 12.1 can support the new behavioral patterns while exercise becomes a more established, automatic routine. Relapse prevention is another important tactic to use with novice exercisers.

Maintaining regular exercise is the goal for novice and long-term exercisers. Individuals who have been regularly active for more than six months *(maintenance stage)* have a decreased risk of relapse. However, permanent maintenance is not guaranteed, and there remains the potential for lapses in an exercise routine due to relocation, family commitments, travel, medical events, or other disruptions.

Demographics

Demographic variables, such as age, gender, ethnicity, and education, are not targets for change. However, demographic variables often function as moderators. You'll recall (chapter 2) that a moderator is a variable that affects the direction and/or strength of the relationship between the independent variable and the outcome variable. Modera-

tors always function as independent variables (Baron and Kenny 1986) and can be represented by an interaction, such as better adherence for males than females to an exercise intervention that promotes competition (figure 12.1).

Demographic characteristics can influence the receptiveness to interventions and exercise behavior itself. Obviously, the presentation of the inter-

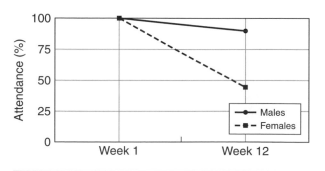

Figure 12.1 *Gender* moderates the effects of the intervention on attendance. Attendance at the beginning and end of a competition-based exercise intervention.

vention and the materials must suit the educational level and developmental stage of the target group. Behavior change strategies and physical activities that will appeal to elementary school children are not the same as those that will motivate college students. Demographic characteristics also yield important information about structuring an intervention so that it is more enticing to participants. For example, older adults as compared to younger people find health and fitness motives more salient for adopting and maintaining an active lifestyle. Females are more likely than males to adopt exercise for weight loss (McAuley et al. 1994), but this may not be the case with African American females (see chapter 8). Social interaction may also be more important in an exercise program for females than for males, who may find competitiveness a greater incentive to exercise (Markland and Hardy 1993).

Cognitive Characteristics

Identifying attitudes and beliefs about physical activity provides important information for designing and implementing behavior change strategies. For example, we would not expect a sedentary middle-aged woman who believes she is active enough in her job to respond to a sign-up sheet for a work site aerobics program, but she may be ready to listen to compelling information in a media campaign about the benefits of physical activity for women like herself. Knowledge is not enough to change behavior, but clear, relevant information about the personal benefits of physical activity and practical suggestions for ways to become more active can influence attitudes, beliefs, and expectations.

Exercise self-efficacy is frequently studied as a determinant of exercise behavior and is a key mediator of behavior change according to several theoretical models. The relationship between self-efficacy and exercise adoption is fairly consistent, but the role of self-efficacy in maintenance is less well established. For example, Oman and King (1998) examined the relationship between self-efficacy and adherence over two years and found that baseline self-efficacy predicted adherence

© Terry Wild Studio

Competition is an important exercise motivator for males, whereas affiliation needs are more likely to get females involved in exercise.

during adoption but not during the early maintenance phase. McAuley et al. (1994) also found a significant relationship between self-efficacy and exercise during the beginning but not the end of a program to enhance exercise self-efficacy. However, Garcia and King (1991), examining the relationship between self-efficacy and exercise adherence in a middle-aged community sample, found a positive correlation between self-efficacy and adherence for months 1 to 6 and months 7 to 12. Cognitive processes may also be more important in establishing a behavior than in regulating it. Several studies have shown that cognitive processes of change are used more in the early stages of behavior change (contemplation and preparation) than after the behavior has been established (action and maintenance).

Cognitive strategies may be effective in establishing a new behavior, but are less influential in regulating a behavior.

Self-motivation is another cognitive characteristic that can affect the utility of interventions. Motivation is influenced differently for people with ego versus task orientations. **Ego orientation** refers to motivation based on winning or being better than someone else, while **task orientation** indicates motivation to persist in order to master the task. The point of reference for someone with a task orientation is not the behavior of someone else (winners and losers) but past personal performance. This person's goal is self-improvement. Some studies indicate that males are more likely than females to have an ego orientation and thus might be more likely to participate in physical activities that provide opportunities for competing against others.

Intervention Settings

Settings in which interventions can take place include the home, medical care facilities, schools, work sites, and the community. Different settings present real and perceived barriers and supports for physical activity depending on the target group.

The setting of the intervention presents specific supports and barriers for different target populations and goals.

Home-Based Programs

Home-based programs can offer accessibility and convenience for someone limited by family commitments, finances, location, or transportation. Implementing a home-based program should include initial instruction in self-management strategies and appropriate exercise prescriptions, particularly for those just beginning to exercise. Support for exercise that can occur in group programs may be lacking in home-based programs, but regular mailings and phone contacts from providers can supply some social support and feedback. Studies that have compared adherence rates for home-based programs to those for programs in traditional exercise facilities have generally indicated positive results for the home-based interventions (e.g., King et al. 1991; Oman and King 1998). Strengths of home-based programs include privacy, low cost for the participant and provider, and the opportunity for participants to personalize the intervention, such as choosing the time to exercise and the type of activity.

Health Care Facilities

Health care facilities have great potential as a setting in which to promote exercise, particularly for women, who are more likely than men to visit their physicians. Time constraints, lack of training in medical school regarding exercise behavior, and lack of reimbursement for preventive services have limited the implementation of exercise promotion programs in hospitals, community clinics, and private practices. However, some programs have addressed these barriers. Project PACE (Physician-Based Assessment and Counseling for Exercise) is an example of a program that has used stage-matched materials with some success in health care settings to increase exercise adoption and adherence (e.g., Calfas et al. 1996). The general format involves administering a brief questionnaire to determine the patient's exercise stage before he or she meets with the physician. The patient receives a stage-matched written program with specific recommendations, which the patient and physician then review. Some type of follow-up, such as booster calls by the health educator or another staff member, is used to monitor progress with the program and answer questions. The need to have materials tailored to patients' exercise stage to promote exercise in this setting has been questioned, though. Bull, Jamrozik, and Blanksby (1998) tested the effects of verbal advice from a physician, combined with standard or stage-matched supportive written material on exercise, in initially sedentary patients at 1, 6, and 12 months after the office visit. Compared to a control group that received no materials or advice, more patients who received an intervention were active 1 and 6 months later, regardless of type of intervention.

Physical education in schools provides opportunities to exercise, but the requirement for physical education classes decreases with increasing grade.

Schools

Schools are a critical setting for the development of health behaviors, but most physical education classes do not teach the cognitive or behavioral skills necessary to increase activity out of class or to maintain exercise upon graduation. Only 26% of states in the United States require lifetime physical activity courses in high school (Pate, Small, et al. 1995). There is some evidence for moderate effects of comprehensive school-based health promotion programs when a randomized design is used, measurements are valid and reliable, and extensive interventions are utilized (Stone et al. 1998). The Child and Adolescent Trial for Cardiovascular Health (CATCH) is an example of a multicenter randomized trial that targeted children in grades 3, 4, and 5 (Luepker et al. 1996). The intervention, which was based on social cognitive theory and organizational change, was implemented in class, with

the family, and through policy changes in schools randomized into experimental (56 schools) and control (40 schools) groups. Participants in the CATCH program increased moderate to vigorous physical activity in class and vigorous activity out of class.

Most of the studies implementing interventions in the schools have targeted upper-elementary-age students; few have been done in high schools. Unfortunately, there is a disturbing national trend toward reduction in required physical education classes with increasing grade, and data indicate that there is no compensatory increase in physical activity out of class. In addition, children are sedentary the majority of the time during physical education classes. Since physical activity significantly declines in adolescents, more community opportunities for recreational activities and sports should be considered. Other directions for interventions through the schools could include curriculums that target behavioral skills necessary for lifelong physical activity, the integration of physical activity into other academic classes (such as having students compute target heart rate zone in math class or write essays in English class on making exercise fun), noncompetitive inclusive after-school recreation programs, and programs that include parental involvement.

Only 46% of the population aged 18 to 35 continue an active lifestyle beyond the school years. Efforts to promote exercise adoption and adherence in college settings could impact this trend (Leslie, Sparling, and Owen 2001). The lifestyle of a college student includes prolonged sedentary activities, such as sitting in a classroom, reading and studying, and doing computer-based work. A pattern of sedentary activity can develop and be reinforced in college that is sustained after graduation. Maintaining a sedentary lifestyle during and after college can have significant health repercussions in view of the heart disease risk factors already present in some college students (Sparling, Snow, and Beavers 1999). And college students make up a large portion of the population. There were 14.6 million students enrolled in colleges and universities in the United States in 1998, and about 44% of the high school graduates in 1998 were enrolled in college in 2000 (Chronicle of Higher Education 2000).

Studies of college alumni have shown that a conceptually based physical education program and more required hours of physical education produced alumni with better attitudes toward exercise who also reported more physical activity (Brynteson and Adams 1993). Additionally, according to these studies, required physical education in college was associated with better health knowledge; more positive attitudes toward exercise, diet, and smoking; and exercise post-graduation (Pearman et al. 1997). However, a survey of four-year institutions conducted in 1998 indicated that only 63% required physical education for graduation, a figure that was down from 67% in 1993 (Hensley 2000). This was the first recorded decline in required collegiate physical education since 1978, and 10% of the schools reported that physical education requirements had been eliminated.

There have been two intervention studies in college settings. An academic class to teach concepts-based physical education and self-management skills was developed for college seniors in Project GRAD (Graduate Ready for Activity Daily; Sallis et al. 1999). Post-graduation self-report of physical activity using the 7-Day Physical Activity Recall phone interview was compared with data for control participants who had taken health education classes their senior year. The authors found no significant immediate effect on physical activity in the males, modest effects for the females, and no effects at the two-year follow-up. In ARTEC (Active Recreation on Tertiary Education Campuses), Australian college students' activity preferences were targeted to promote physical activity in an eight-week intervention, and significant increases were found in the proportion of students on the target campus who reported high levels of physical activity (Leslie et al. 2000).

Work Site

The work site is another setting for exercise interventions with a captive audience for 40 (plus or minus) hours per week. The percentage of work sites that offer physical activity and fitness programs increased from 1985 to 1994 (22% to 42%), but these programs vary widely with respect to facilities available, activities offered, target audiences, costs to employees, and incentives. In general, work site fitness programs have had equivocal success. On-site fitness facilities may be convenient to some; but they may be a barrier to individuals who have work hours that conflict with scheduled programs, who rely on others for transportation home, or who simply do not want to spend more time at the work site. Issues in work site programming include documentation of a favorable cost-benefit ratio for employee fitness programs, selection of goals and a target audience, development of means to institu-

tionalize a fitness program that will sustain corporate culture changes, implementation of rewards and incentives, and participant recruitment and retention. A meta-analysis of 26 studies published between 1972 and 1997 found a small (0.25 SD) effect size for work site interventions increasing level of physical activity (Dishman et al. 1998). Work site programs may provide information and encouragement to get employees to begin exercising, but additional studies using valid research designs and measures are needed.

Communities

The settings for physical activity interventions in communities are diverse (e.g., places of worship, private and nonprofit fitness centers, and city/county recreational departments), and type of intervention can range from exercise classes to mass media campaigns. Programs in places of worship can provide the impetus to begin exercising and the social support and encouragement to stay active, as well as positive role models, peer-led exercise classes, and information about exercise through church channels. For-profit and nonprofit fitness centers, such as the YMCA and the YWCA, have been traditional sites for exercise promotion and fitness programs. Comprehensive facilities, flexible hours of operation, promotion of classes for beginners, and low-cost or complimentary child care are features that have been included to increase accessibility to more people. Many city or county recreational departments have neighborhood recreational centers and area parks. The effectiveness of their physical activity programs depends on a number of factors, such as safety, privacy, hours of operation, transportation, and child care.

Entire communities have been the site of several long-term multi-community interventions targeting a number of different health behaviors. For example, the Stanford Five-City Project targeted smoking, nutrition, weight control, blood pressure, and physical activity using a variety of methods, such as applied social learning theory, diffusion of innovations, community organization, and social marketing. There were only modest changes in level of physical activity after six years, but less emphasis was placed on targeting physical activity than the other health behaviors (Young et al. 1996). Problems in detecting changes from large-scale community interventions that last several years are compounded by changes in societal attitudes and norms regarding physical activity and trends in health practices. For example, the Minnesota Heart Health Project used health professional and community leaders as role models and opinion leaders, as well as personal, intensive, and multicontact programs to promote increases in physical activity. Although participants in the treatment communities reported consistently more physical activity compared to the comparison town, levels of physical activity increased for both groups.

Level of Intervention

Interventions can take place at different levels within each setting. There are one-on-one programs (e.g., Project PACE) and programs for small groups, such as a strength-training class or a walking club. The intervention can also be applied on a broader level—on the community level (e.g., Stanford Five-City Project), in legislation supporting increased physical activity (e.g., requiring the construction of bike paths), or nationwide through federal health promotion agencies. In 1997, the U.S. Centers for Disease Control and Prevention launched a national program to promote moderate physical activity among adults. The "Physical Activity: It's Everywhere You Go" campaign kit was developed for use by health professionals and community leaders across the nation to target sedentary adults who

were thinking about becoming or just starting to become physically active.

With respect to duration, programs can range from one-time events to broad-based interventions spanning several years. Community-based fun runs or walks supporting a local charity may happen only once per year, but they can be opportunities for individuals who primarily want to help the organization to start thinking about exercise for its own sake. How long an intervention should be to increase adherence has not been established. Studies that have measured exercise stage of change imply that those who have been regularly active for more than six months are at reduced risk of relapse. However, results from our meta-analysis of exercise interventions indicate that effects were unrelated to the number of weeks the intervention lasted or the length of the follow-up period (Dishman and Buckworth 1996b).

Interest is growing in interventions at the community or societal level that entail environment engineering, community action, and legislation to support active lifestyles. Local governments and health agencies can develop safe, accessible facilities for exercise with well-equipped buildings and competent staff. Actions can be taken to ensure safe neighborhoods for walking, jogging, and bicycling through improvements in lighting and construction

Many non-profit organizations sponsor road races to raise money and promote their causes; promotion of exercise might be a positive side-effect.

of sidewalks and bike paths. Making the environment more conducive to physical activity is a goal of "Active Community Environments," a program of the U.S. Department of Health and Human Services, Centers for Disease Control and Prevention. Efforts include collaboration with the National Park Service's Rivers, Trails, and Conservation Assistance Program to promote the development of parks and recreational areas close to population concentrations, as well as with public and private agencies to promote National and International Walk-to-School Day.

A multidimensional perspective is necessary for understanding physical activity behavior and guiding intervention development at the level of the environment. Sallis and Owen (1999) proposed an ecological model that uses the "behavioral setting" to explain and predict influences on physical activity. The behavior setting includes intrapersonal, social environmental, and physical environmental factors (see table 12.2). This framework can be used to identify behavior settings in which people are more likely to be physically active, and to determine where more potent interventions can be

---

Characteristics of Communities That Support Physical Activity

▼ Sidewalks

▼ On-street bicycle facilities

▼ Multi-use paths and trails

▼ Parks

▼ Recreational facilities

▼ Mixed-use development and connected grid of streets (allowing homes, workplaces, schools, and stores to be close together and accessible to pedestrians and bicyclists)

---

implemented. For example, bike paths, downtown walkways, and attractive visible stairs are aspects of the constructed environment that should foster increased activity in an urban setting.

Utilization of an ecological model expands our ability to identify barriers to physical activity, which

---

Table 12.2

Factors in the Behavioral Setting That Influence Physical Activity

Factor	Categories	Examples
Intrapersonal	Demographics Biological Cognitive/Affective Behavioral	Age, health status, self-efficacy, self-regulation skills
Social environmental	Supportive behaviors Social climate Culture Policies governing incentives for activity/inactivity Policies governing resources and infrastructures related to activity/inactivity	Recreational habits of friends and family, work site fitness programs, "mall walker" groups

Physical environmental	*Natural*
	  Weather
	  Geography
		Relative humidity and temperature, grade of hills

	Constructed
	  Urban/Suburban
	  Architectural
	  Transportation
	  Entertainment
	  Recreation
		Population density, road maintenance, community budget for street lights, environmental lobbies, high school physical education requirements

Adapted from Sallis and Owen 1999.

Cold weather and snow can be a barrier to physical activity to some people but an opportunity to others.

are also defined on different levels (see table 12.3). Personal barriers can be psychological, such as low exercise self-efficacy or perceived lack of time, and physical, such as past injuries. Barriers can also be interpersonal—for example, peers may provide support and encouragement for sedentary behaviors. Environmental barriers are natural (e.g., inclement weather) and constructed (lack of transportation to an exercise facility; unsafe neighborhoods). A culture that promotes thinness and associates it with fitness fosters another barrier to exercise. Introducing a temporal dimension to this model addresses the impact of life transitions like graduation, marriage, childbirth, or divorce on an established exercise routine, along with seasonal variations in opportunities for physical activity.

Specific Strategies

A quantitative meta-analysis of 127 studies and 14 dissertations published between 1965 and 1995 was conducted to determine the efficacy of interventions to increase exercise adherence and factors that moderate their success (Dishman and Buckworth 1996). Recall that a meta-analysis takes available studies on a specific topic and reduces their findings to a common quantitative metric, expressed as an effect size. The overall effect size weighted by sample size was .75; that is, overall, interventions produced a .75 *SD* increase in exercise adherence. Using the course grade analogy from chapter 2, this is like increasing your grade from a C– to a C+. The effectiveness of interventions was not different

Table 12.3

Barriers to Physical Activity

Factor	Examples
Intrapersonal	Non-exerciser self-schemata, low exercise tolerance, poor time management skills, lack of time, low income
Social environmental	Sedentary peer group, unsafe neighborhood, culture that does not value physical activity
Physical environmental *(Natural and constructed)*	Extended periods of high temperatures and humidity, urban congestion, lack of parks

as a function of age, gender, or race. The most successful interventions applied behavioral modification strategies (e.g., stimulus control, reinforcement control) to healthy subjects in a group setting. Effects were larger for low-intensity leisure activities compared to strength training or aerobic exercise. Adherence was also better in studies using **mediated approaches** (e.g., print mailings, telephone).

In this section we describe specific strategies to increase exercise adoption and adherence. Health education, exercise prescriptions, and behavior and cognitive behavior management are strategies that have been used to change exercise behavior in a variety of settings. Stage-matched interventions have been applied in community and medical settings and hold promise for increasing the success of exercise programs. Aspects of relapse prevention training are important in fostering exercise adherence. Environmental approaches are taking on a more important role as we recognize the impact of situational and social factors on behavior change and maintenance.

Health Education

Interventions described as **health education** generally treat exercise as a disease prevention or health promotion behavior and target changes in cognitive variables. Programs using health education approaches have had little impact on exercise adherence (Dishman and Buckworth 1996b). However, such programs can increase knowledge and influ-

ence attitudes and beliefs about exercise to help inactive individuals consider beginning an exercise program. They can also provide concrete information about exercise classes and programs, which is useful for novice exercisers. Examples of health education applied to exercise include health screenings/health risk appraisals, mass media campaigns, and marketing strategies.

Health Screenings and Health Risk Appraisals

According to social cognitive theory, goals are developed when there is a discrepancy between actual and desired behaviors or characteristics. Health screenings and health risk *appraisals*, by documenting fitness characteristics of an individual in relation to healthy norms, can make information personally relevant and enhance motivation to become more active. However, controlled studies using health risk appraisals and fitness test information as interventions have shown little or no effect on behavior. Attitudes and intentions may be affected, but not behavior. Generally, programs to increase knowledge may have short-term effects, but no lasting change.

Mass Media

Mass media can promote health behavior change by introducing new ideas, reinforcing old messages to maintain behavior change, promoting attention to existing programs, and supplementing community-based interventions (Flora,

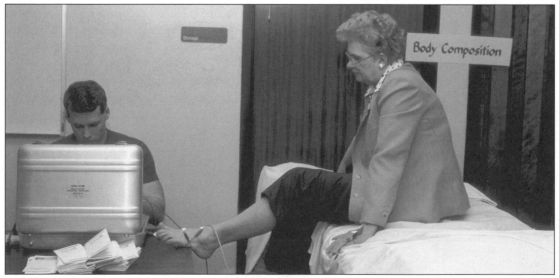

Health screenings of fitness characteristics provide individuals with concrete information about personal health risk.

Maibach, and Maccoby 1989). The success of mass media campaigns in changing exercise behavior was evaluated in a recent review of 28 studies of media-based interventions (Marcus et al. 1998). National and community physical activity campaigns were generally effective in increasing knowledge but not in changing behavior. Short-term behavior change occurred with more direct interventions that used print media or telephone contacts, with better results for more contact and more tailored interventions.

The goals of a media campaign vary according to the individual's behavior and readiness to change. A media campaign directed to individuals in the precontemplation stage should capture people's attention and motivate them to contemplate becoming more active. For those who are already considering participation in an activity program, the desired outcome is to motivate them toward action by increasing the personal relevance of the behavior change and decreasing the perceived barriers to exercise. Mass media are probably most useful in promoting exercise adoption. The usefulness of a media campaign is diminished for individuals who are already exercising. One can expect better results from mass media interventions if they apply concepts from social marketing, such as integrating models of consumer behavior and considering attributes of the target population (e.g., media habits, education) in developing and disseminating intervention materials.

Exercise Prescriptions

Exercise prescriptions have been used to increase exercise adoption and adherence but have not been effective when used as a single strategy. The lack of effects with sedentary individuals may be related to the nature of the traditional prescription, which is to exercise three to five times per week for 15 to 60 min at a defined intensity (table 12.4). The intensity of the exercise and the structure of the regimen are barriers to some sedentary individuals, whose reluctance to become more active may have been tied to a misperception that the traditional prescription was their only option (Pate, Pratt, et al. 1995). Evidence from large-scale studies of physical activity and aerobic fitness was examined in the early 1990s, and research concluded that health benefits can be gained from minimal increases in activity and fitness. These findings and the low prevalence of exercise adherence provoked reconsideration of the traditional exercise prescription, and new recommendations were presented in 1995 (see chapter 1, p. 13). The Centers for Disease Control (CDC)/American College of Sports Medicine (ACSM) active lifestyle recommendation (i.e., accumulate 30 min or more of moderate-intensity physical activity in bouts of at least 8 to 10 min on most days of the week) is for individuals who are sedentary or just beginning an exercise program. It is meant to complement, not replace, traditional prescriptions by offering an *alternative* approach for experiencing the health benefits of exercise.

Table 12.4

American College of Sports Medicine Exercise Prescription Recommendations

	Intensity (%$\dot{V}O_2$max)	Duration (minutes)	Frequency (days/week)	Key points
1990	50-85	20-60	3-5	Stressed developing and maintaining fitness, body composition; recommended guidelines for muscular strength and endurance
1991	40-85	15-60	3-5	Encompassed activities that may enhance health without having major impact on fitness
1995*	Moderate	30 or more; at least 8-10 each bout	Near daily	Emphasized the important health benefits of moderate physical activity

* Centers for Disease Control and American College of Sports Medicine recommendations.
Data from Pate, Pratt, et al. 1995.

Characteristics of Lifestyle Physical Activity

▼ Duration: accumulate at least 30 min

▼ Frequency: most days of the week

▼ Intensity: at least moderate to vigorous

▼ Mode: leisure, occupational, or household

▼ Planned or unplanned

▼ Self-selected activities

Adapted from Dunn, Andersen, and Jakicic 1998.

Lifestyle physical activity has been the target of several interventions. Jakicic et al. (1999) were the first researchers to compare the effects of multiple short-bout exercise and long-bout exercise on change in weight, adherence, and fitness. Women who were overweight were randomized to five days per week of (a) progressive programs of continuous sessions, (b) multiple 10 min bouts at convenient times throughout the day, and (c) multiple 10 min bouts with exercise equipment (e.g., motorized treadmill) provided to their homes. Fitness and leisure-time physical activity improved in all three groups during the 18 months of the intervention, with less decline in adherence in the short-bout group that had the home equipment compared to the short-bout group without equipment.

A group-based lifestyle physical activity program was compared to a traditional structured exercise program in Project Active (Dunn et al. 1997, 1999). The effects of the two six-month intervention programs on modifying risk of cardiovascular heart disease in sedentary individuals were examined in 235 initially sedentary men and women. Physiological variables associated with risk of cardiovascular heart disease, as well as psychosocial variables that are part of the transtheoretical model of behavior change (see chapter 11), were assessed at baseline, 6 months, and 24 months. The structured exercise program prescribed 20 to 60 min sessions of supervised exercise three to five days a week at 50% to 85% of aerobic capacity at a state-of-the-art fitness center. Goal setting, self-monitoring, and verbal reinforcement were part of the traditional intervention. The lifestyle intervention prescribed the CDC/ACSM recommendation to accumulate at least 30 min of moderate-intensity exercise most days of the week. Group meetings were held weekly for the first 16 weeks and biweekly in weeks 17 to

24, during which stage-specific cognitive and behavioral strategies were presented. After 24 months, aerobic capacity was significantly higher than at baseline for both groups. Both groups had significant decreases in blood pressure and percentage body fat, and most subjects in both groups were meeting the CDC/ACSM criteria. The structured group demonstrated significant beneficial changes in total cholesterol, high-density lipoprotein cholesterol, and low-density lipoprotein cholesterol from baseline to 24 months. Dunn et al. (1997) found that participants who increased the use of selected behavioral and cognitive strategies, increased self-efficacy, and increased benefits versus barriers to exercise were more likely to reach the CDC/ACSM criteria.

These and other studies that have targeted lifestyle physical activity support the effectiveness of a lifestyle approach to changing physical activity and health risks. (See Dunn, Andersen, and Jakicic 1998 for a review of lifestyle interventions.) The lifestyle approach to increasing and maintaining level of physical activity increases the options for sedentary individuals less inclined to participate in structured exercise programs. The flexibility of a lifestyle-based approach to physical activity may reduce perceived barriers to participation, such as time and effort, and make regular physical activity more psychologically accessible to the general population. A woman who is sedentary and overweight might not have considered regular exercise when the traditional prescriptions were promoted, but would consider the active lifestyle recommendation, especially if she is already walking at some level. But keep in mind that this recommendation is not the solution for all health concerns. For example, weight loss is fostered by greater caloric expenditure compared to intake, and increasing evidence points to the need to include both aerobic and strength-training activities in physical activity programs. The CDC/ACSM lifestyle recommendation might be just the thing to get someone with a weight-loss goal to start exercising, but other rewards for being more active must be present during early periods of behavior change until noticeable weight loss with this level of activity occurs.

*E*xercise prescriptions must be based on the individual's capabilities and goals.

Behavioral Management

Behavioral management approaches encompass a wide range of strategies typically applied to individuals and small groups. Stimulus control, reinforcement control, and contingency contracting are based on behaviorism. These strategies are rooted in the traditions of behavior modification and cognitive behavior modification therapies and generally target the antecedents (cues) and consequences of exercise behavior. Antecedents and consequences are related directly/concretely (a friend asks you to go roller blading; you have a sharp muscle cramp after a maximal treadmill test) or symbolically (high school bowling trophy; picture of you finishing a swim competition) to the target behavior. Antecedents and consequences are also considered with respect to their temporal association with the target behavior (e.g., proximal [close in time] or distal [occurring long before or after]).

Behavior modification has one of the best track records for increasing exercise adherence. The key is targeting critical antecedents and meaningful consequences.

Stimulus Control

Stimulus control involves manipulating antecedent conditions, or cues, that can prompt behavior *or* the decision to engage in a behavior (seeing the weather report for rain all week is a cue to decide about alternatives to running outside). Antecedents can be cognitive (reading a flyer from a new fitness facility in your neighborhood), physiological (feeling stiff from studying all day), or external (your dog approaches you with the leash in her mouth). Stimulus control can include strengthening cues for the target behavior and minimizing cues for competing behaviors. Competing behaviors are activities that impede engaging in the target behavior. Eating a hamburger and watching television are competing behaviors for jogging in your neighborhood. Keeping the television turned off when you get home can minimize the cue for a sedentary activity that would compete with an afternoon jog. Cues for exercise are strengthened when they are repeatedly linked with the target behavior, for example, exercising at the same time in the same place each day.

Environmental stimuli, such as posters, phone calls, and adhesive notes, can serve as cues to prompt exercise. The effect of prompting frequency and structure on adherence to a walking program was examined by Lombard, Lombard, and Winett (1995). A total of 135 volunteers were placed into one of five prompt-condition groups using stratified random assignment. Groups differed on frequency of prompts (one time per week vs. once every three weeks) and structure of prompts (high structure with feedback and goal setting vs. low structure with just "touching base"). Prompts were delivered over the phone, and behavior was monitored with self-report exercise logs for 24 weeks. Adherence at six months was significantly better for participants in the high-frequency prompt condition, regardless of prompt structure. Forty-six percent of participants who were contacted each week were walking three or more times per week for at least 20 min at six months compared to 13% of those who had less frequent prompts.

Strategy	Definition	Examples
Two Behavioral Management Strategies		
Stimulus control	Modifying conditions or cues that come before the target behavior	Adhesive notes, placement of exercise equipment in visible locations, recruiting social support, telephone prompts, billboards
Reinforcement control	Modifying a desired condition or event during or following the target behavior to increase the frequency of the behavior upon which the reward is contingent	Verbal praise, T-shirts, certificates

Stimulus control is frequently used with individuals and small groups, but can be applied on a community level. "Point-of-decision" informational prompts can serve in a variety of settings to encourage people to walk or bicycle instead of driving and to use the stairs instead of the elevator. A classic study by Brownell, Stunkard, and Albaum (1980), which was replicated by Blamey, Mutrie, and Aitchison in 1995, successfully used a point-of-decision cue to increase physical activity. A poster encouraging people to take the stairs was placed near the escalator and stairs in a public building. During the intervention in both studies, significantly more people used the stairs than before or after the poster was displayed.

Reinforcement Control

Motivation to exercise depends on anticipated future benefits (outcome expectations). However, the more distal the desired outcome is from the behavior, the less power it has as a motivator. More immediate intrinsic and extrinsic rewards must be provided to support the behavior. **Reinforcement control** increases the frequency of a target behavior by presenting something positive (positive reinforcement) or by removing something negative (negative reinforcement) during or following the behavior (table 12.5). Examples of negative reinforcement for exercise are a decrease in psychological stress and an improvement in injury recovery during a rehabilitation program. However, positive reinforcement is used more often with exercise. A positive reinforcement, or reward, can be intrinsic (direct results of the behavior, usually affective or cognitive) or extrinsic (tangible reinforcements for the behavior). Intrinsic rewards can be a sense of satisfaction, achievement, enhanced self-esteem, or muscle relaxation. Examples of extrinsic rewards to increase or maintain regular exercise are certificates, T-shirts, coupons, and items with personal saliency, such as football tickets. Reinforcement can involve providing the reward during or after the target behavior or pairing a low-preference behavior with a high-preference behavior (i.e., contingency reinforcement). An example of contingency reinforcement is setting up an exercise program so that the person must complete an aerobics routine before watching a favorite soap opera.

Reinforcement is crucial in the early stage of exercise adoption because the longer someone has been inactive, the longer it will be before the exercise behavior itself becomes reinforcing. Immediate feedback from exercise for novices can be pain and fatigue, which can be punishing. Immediate, extrinsic, positive rewards can counter this. Reinforcement control can also be used to change the contingencies or consequences that support or maintain a sedentary lifestyle. Some consequences of exercise that encourage inactivity are fatigue, muscle soreness, anxiety about time, perceived negative attention from more fit individuals, and shame or embarrassment about body or performance. Ways to counter these consequences are to set appropriate exercise prescriptions to reduce per-

---

Table 12.5

Reinforcement and Punishment

	Objective	Type	
		Positive	Negative
Reinforcement	*Increase* the frequency of the target behavior	*Add* something positive:	*Remove* something negative:
		Charting number of miles walked on the gym achievement board after each walking class	Stretching after a jog to decrease muscle tightness
Punishment	*Decrease* the frequency of the target behavior	*Add* something negative:	*Remove* something positive:
		Muscle cramps after long walks	Missing supper with family on nights swimming class meets

ceived physical strain and to offer exercise classes exclusively for beginners and less fit individuals.

Contingency Contracts

Contingency contracts (behavioral contracts) use reinforcement strategies to reward a specific behavior. Elements of contracts include objective measures of success, specific consequences of meeting and not meeting mutually agreed-upon objectives, a time frame, and the involvement of at least one other person. Written contracts have several benefits: the individual participates in developing the behavior change plan; the written outline of expected behaviors serves as a reference over time; terms of the contract are incentives to gain rewards or avoid **punishment;** and there is a formal commitment between the participant and another person to make specific changes. An example of a behavioral contract is shown in figure 12.2.

Cognitive Behavior Modification Techniques

Cognitive behavior modification techniques are based on cognitive behavior theory and social cognitive theory. These strategies for initiating and maintaining behavior change focus on the individual and include decision making, self-monitoring, goal setting, self-efficacy enhancement, and relapse prevention training. They incorporate many of the characteristics of reinforcement control and stimulus control, but the targets of the interventions are the cognitive variables assumed to be mediators of behavior. The goal for the cognitively based strategies is to teach participants the cognitive and behavioral skills needed to control the conditions that prompt and reinforce behavior. Client participation in the change process is stressed. For example, self-reinforcement involves the participant's establishing his or her own rewards and the specific criterion level of the target behavior necessary to achieve the rewards. The strategies we consider next, along with self-reinforcement and contingency contracting, are cognitive behavioral approaches.

*T*he focus of cognitive behavior modification is on the individual. The goal is to teach cognitive and behavioral skills so that the individual can modify the conditions that prompt and reinforce behavior.

Decisional Balance

Decision making, or decisional balance from the transtheoretical model, is a behavior change strategy in which the participant writes down all anticipated short- and long-term consequences of the behavior change. Through this process, people become aware of benefits of the new behavior and receive help in finding ways to avoid or cope with anticipated negative consequences. Evaluating the costs and benefits of exercise is an important strategy for individuals contemplating adoption of exercise because the perceived costs, or cons, of exercise likely outweigh the perceived benefits. This strategy can be used to point out benefits of exercise that the individual might not have considered. Decision making can also be effective in identifying potential barriers to behavior change that can then be dealt with proactively. For example, someone who plans to exercise at 6:00 A.M. during the week may not have considered how getting up that early will affect a spouse who works the late shift.

Self-Monitoring

The strategy of **self-monitoring** is used in smoking cessation and other health behavior change programs to identify the cues and consequences of the target health behavior. Thoughts, feelings, and aspects of the situation before and after successful and unsuccessful attempts at the target behavior are recorded and reviewed. Self-monitoring is a practical way to collect information about behavioral patterns that one can use to identify cues and barriers to exercise. Internal and external cues that inhibit and prompt exercise can be determined, and consequences of exercise can be examined in terms of their reinforcing properties. Information from self-monitoring can also help to identify the best times within a person's schedule for an exercise routine and any accommodations that will be necessary, such as having supper an hour later in order to exercise after work. Self-monitoring may be particularly useful for people who have been active in the past as a strategy to identify factors that contributed to their lapse in regular exercise. Electronic notebooks and calendars, computer programs, graphs, and charts can be used to record daily or weekly progress. Periodic evaluation of behavioral records by fitness professionals can provide meaningful positive feedback and help to monitor goals.

Goal Setting

A basic assumption of many cognitively based theories is that motivation is regulated by conscious

Behavioral Contract

Goal

To participate in the Valentine's Day 10K with my boyfriend

Behavioral objective (What I will have to do to reach my goal)

To run 10K without stopping

Time frame

October 1 through February 13

To reach my goal, I will (specific behaviors necessary to reach my goal)

1. Jog at least 20 or more minutes five days a week for the next four weeks

2. Run on the track one day each weekend

If I (insert activity of interest)

run at least five days a week for the next month

then (insert reward)

I will buy a new pair of running shoes.

Goal-supporting activities

1. Train with my boyfriend one day on the weekend

2. Put the Valentine's Day 10K flyer by my running shoes

3. Chart my progress in my date book

Barriers and countermeasures

1. Rain: I will go to the gym and run on the treadmill or go to an aerobics class.

2. Final exams: I will take 10- to 15-minute jogging breaks and run the stairs at the library.

3. December holidays at home: I will take my parents' dog for long walks/runs at least twice.

This contract will be evaluated every (insert time frame)

4 weeks

Date:_____

Signed:_____   Signed:_____

Figure 12.2   Example of a behavioral contract also known as a contingency contract.

goals. **Goal setting** is an effective strategy for supporting exercise behavior change. Functions of goal setting are to provide direction, determine level of effort to be expended, foster persistence, and support the search for strategies. In order for goals to be realistic and achievable, a comprehensive psychological and physiological assessment is necessary. For example, someone who wants to decrease the time it takes for her to jog 3 miles (4.8 km) has to know her present 3-mile jog time. Exercise testing can provide baseline fitness information for designing a safe and personalized exercise program that is less likely to result in punishing physical consequences, such as muscle soreness or injury, and more likely to be the type of routine that will meet the individual's specific goals. Test results can be motivating when the participant compares his or her results to healthy norms or previous results. Repeated testing can also provide feedback for evaluating and revising goals.

A psychosocial assessment yields valuable information about attitudes, beliefs, expectations, and past experiences that can be barriers or supports to goal achievement. Reviewing previous attempts at change can show what worked and what did not, decreasing the likelihood of repeating past mistakes. Identifying psychological barriers, such as low exercise self-efficacy, helps shape goals that can address the needs of the whole person in his or her social context.

A large body of research on goal setting in sport indicates several characteristics of goals that enhance performance (e.g., Kyllo and Landers 1995).

Characteristics of Good Goal Setting

▼ Reasonable
▼ Realistic
▼ Does not depend on someone else
▼ Specific
▼ Measurable
▼ Challenging
▼ Time frame
▼ Flexible
▼ Meaningful
▼ Motivating
▼ Short-term and long-term
▼ Includes rewards

Many of these also enhance exercise behavior. Flexible, specific goals that are consistent with capabilities, values, resources, and needs are more effective than general, nonspecific goals. Short-term and long-term goals are better than long-term goals only. Since self-efficacy increases with mastery experience, initial goals should be challenging but realistic in order to foster confidence.

Examples of Exercise Behavior Goals

General	Behaviorally specific and measurable
To get more fit	To increase by 10% how long I can run for my next graded exercise test
To exercise regularly	To walk four to five days this week for 20 to 30 min each day
To get stronger	To bench press 125% of my body weight by June 5

Self-Efficacy Enhancement

Self-efficacy is one of the most consistent psychosocial determinants of exercise adherence. Belief in your capabilities influences behavior, affect, and cognitions. Acquisition of new behaviors, effort to be expended on a task, the length of time you persist despite obstacles, your emotional reactions, and your thought patterns are affected by self-efficacy. Several studies have implemented interventions specifically designed to *enhance exercise self-efficacy* as a method of promoting behavior change.

As discussed in chapter 11, efficacy expectations are based on mastery accomplishments, social modeling, verbal persuasion, and interpretation of physiological states (table 12.6).

▼ *Mastery experiences* may be the most potent method for increasing self-efficacy; individuals who are successful at meeting challenging tasks acquire and refine skills and develop coping strategies that foster confidence in the ability to repeat the task or similar tasks (generality dimension of self-efficacy). One can facilitate mastering a challenging task by dividing the task into manageable components and arranging them in logical order from easy to hard. Novices who attend an advanced aerobics class can be discouraged by the fast-paced, complicated steps,

Table 12.6

Sources of Self-Efficacy Information

Source	Exercise examples
Mastery accomplishments	Swimming 1/2 mile for the first time; increasing weights in a strength-training program; getting a hole in one after taking golf lessons; learning a new dance step successfully
Social modeling	Disabled individuals attending Special Olympics; adolescent girls watching the U.S. women's soccer team play; a retired physical education teacher taking a group from a senior citizen center on a walk in the park
Verbal persuasion	Jogging partner tells you that you are setting a faster pace than before; spouse tells you that your exercise is paying off in how trim you look; fitness coordinator comments on your good form during a bench press
Interpretation of physiological states	Being able to keep up a conversation after walking up a steep hill; being reminded that sweating a lot after exercising on a hot day is how your body cools you down; identifying how the sensation of muscle strain relates to amount of weight lifted *and* number of repetitions

while those who enroll in a beginners' class can learn the routine "one step at a time" and increase their confidence in their ability to follow more complicated patterns.

***T**he most powerful way to enhance self-efficacy is through mastery experiences.*

▼ *Social modeling* can take the form of mastery models or coping models. In both cases, modeling is more effective if the model is similar to the participant, for example, if an older woman watches other women in her age group successfully lifting weights. Mastery modeling entails watching someone succeed at a task; coping modeling presents someone having difficulty with a task but eventually succeeding. The latter strategy is useful in demonstrating effective problem-solving strategies relevant to the task and the target group. Exercise interventions to enhance self-efficacy have used mastery modeling, for example, having participants watch videos of individuals with similar characteristics engaging in exercise at various levels of progress.

▼ *Verbal persuasion* can enhance self-efficacy through provision of encouragement and support from significant or powerful others. Verbal persua-

sion applies timely and specific feedback about exercise behavior and can be thought of as a form of positive reinforcement. Feedback is more effective if it comes from a credible source and is specific and meaningful. A student volunteer telling a cardiac rehabilitation patient, "You did a good job today," as the patient walks out of the clinic is not as effective as the rehabilitation director telling him, "Congratulations, you were able to walk an additional 1/2 mile today," as he steps off the treadmill. Information from self-monitoring can be used to teach self-persuasion. Negative self-talk surrounding exercise bouts is identified ("I just can't walk more than two miles,") and reframed to encourage positive patterns of cognitions regarding exercise ("Six months ago I couldn't walk around the block. I am making steady progress").

▼ *Interpretations of physiological and emotional responses* can hamper self-efficacy—for example, feeling anxious before a test and interpreting your emotional response as a sign that you are not prepared. Novice exercisers often view the normal physiological responses to exercise (i.e., increased respiration and heart rate, sweating, and muscular sensations) with some anxiety or discomfort. Interventions have addressed this component of self-efficacy by including information for participants about the normal physiological responses to exercise and ways to interpret these responses.

© Aneal T. Vohra/Unicorn Stock Photo

Self-efficacy for exercise is enhanced for older adults when they see people like themselves being physically active.

Relapse Prevention

You'll recall the discussion of relapse prevention as a model of behavior in chapter 11 (see pp. 224–225). Relapse prevention as an intervention was initially implemented with people who had decreased or eliminated an undesired high-frequency behavior, such as smoking. Exercise behavior is a low-frequency, health-promoting/enhancing behavior; nevertheless, applying components of relapse prevention to exercise adherence has proven successful to some extent. Several studies have tested the relapse prevention model with exercise and have found increased adherence when this model was used as part of broader cognitive behavior modification programs.

The basic format for relapse prevention interventions involves the identification of high-risk situations and the development of effective coping strategies. High-risk situations are circumstances that challenge one's confidence in maintaining the desired behavior change. High-risk situations for maintaining regular exercise are events or situations that are incompatible with exercise, such as eating, drinking, overworking, or smoking. Some specific relapse antecedents for exercise are boredom, lack of time, laziness, vacation, and illness (Simkin and Gross 1994).

High-risk situations for exercise relapse are boredom, lack of time, laziness, vacation, and illness.

Knapp (1988) described the application of relapse prevention to exercise in detail. First, participants learn about the processes of relapse. Next, they identify high-risk situations for themselves. Self-monitoring is a useful strategy for obtaining this information. On the basis of identified high-risk situations, participants receive skills training to improve their coping responses. Strategies include assertiveness training, time management, and stress management. Expecting positive outcomes from not exercising (e.g., watching a favorite television show if you skip aerobics class) increases the risk of relapse, so the positive outcome expectations of not exercising are identified and addressed (e.g., taping the television show and watching it as a reward after going to aerobics class). Participants learn how to plan for slips by setting aside backup times for exercise and alternate modes (e.g., walking on a treadmill if the pool is closed) and places to exercise.

Drinking alcohol is incompatible with exercise, and can distinguish a high risk situation for lapsing from regular exercise.

For example, if snow in the forecast puts an evening walking routine at risk, an aerobics tape can offer an alternative way to work out. Flexible goals (walk *or* do aerobics three to four times a week) can provide protection from potential slips and all-or-none thinking that increases risk of relapse. Someone who thinks he or she has "blown it" by missing one exercise session is especially at risk of relapse. Rigid goals that are easily not met ("I will run at 12:10 each day for 45 minutes,") also set someone up for relapse. Another relapse prevention strategy is to correct a lifestyle imbalance in which "shoulds" outweigh "wants." One can reframe exercise into a desired, pleasurable activity instead of an obligation by setting up activities that are fun and by including rewards for exercising.

Community-Based Interventions

There are powerful social and technological inducements to be sedentary, such as television and labor-saving technologies, which have contributed to the disturbing increase in obesity in the United States. Some measures to counter these influences have taken the form of *community-based interventions*. Psychological and behavioral theories have been applied to induce behavior change on a large scale at the organizational (community recreation centers, church-based fitness programs, diffusion strategies through schools), environmental (facility planning, construc-

> ### Examples of Legislation to Promote Physical Activity
>
> ▼ *Alter the environment to encourage physical activity for transportation.* Close streets in city to cars; create convenient bike paths and footpaths.
>
> ▼ *Revise building codes.* Make stairs easy to find, centrally located, attractive, and safe.
>
> ▼ *Fund facilities for recreation.* Create more parks and recreation centers that are safer and more convenient to low-active segments of the population; provide adequate personnel for programs and security.
>
> ▼ *Create tax incentives.* Provide tax incentives for companies with work site fitness programs.
>
> ▼ *Modify health insurance regulation.* Reduce insurance premiums for heath behaviors like regular physical activity.

tion of bike paths), and social (family interventions) levels. Cost-effective or pragmatically convenient avenues, such as mailings, telephone, e-mail, and Internet sites, have been used to reach large numbers of individuals for whom traditional clinically based interventions are not accessible or acceptable.

Convenient and safe bicycle paths make biking a practical and popular form of transportation.

The use of media as a strategy to change physical activity behavior is expanding via the development of information technologies. Many of us think of newspapers, television, and radio as forms of mass media that can be used to promote physical activity. Newer forms of communications technology—such as interactive computer-mediated programs, Web- and e-mail-based interventions, and telephones with interactive personalized protocols—support personalized physical activity interventions on a large scale. A drawback with the use of new media is the more limited ability to reach disadvantaged groups who are likely at greater risk of physical inactivity and may have less access than others to new technology (Marcus et al. 1998).

Why Can't We Keep People Active? Mediators and Intervention Effectiveness

The prevalence of adults in the United States who engaged in recommended levels of activity increased slightly from 24.3% in 1990 to 25.4% in 1998, whereas reports of no physical activity decreased from 30.7% to 28.7% (Centers for Disease Control and Prevention 2001). These small changes are not surprising coupled with the stability of the 50% dropout rate from exercise programs. A wide range of interventions have been implemented over the past 25 years in attempts to increase adoption and adherence to regular exercise, but the impact from a public health standpoint is minor. Physical, social, and political environments are receiving more attention as targets for interventions, and multilevel interventions may prove to be more effective than more traditional approaches.

We attempted to address the questions "What works best, under what conditions, and with whom?" in our meta-analysis of exercise intervention studies, and found the strongest effect for behavior modification strategies (Dishman and Buckworth 1996b). However, only about 20% of the studies reviewed reported a follow-up to the intervention, and those studies typically showed that increases in physical activity or fitness associated with the interventions diminished as time passed after the end of the intervention.

Certainly, we need more long-term intervention studies and repeated follow-up assessments to track the process of adherence and relapse. Changes in the environment that support and promote an active lifestyle may be necessary to sustain behavior change initiated through interventions, as well. However, in order to understand the reasons for our limited success in getting people to adopt and maintain regular physical activity, we also need to take a closer look at *how* interventions have been developed and implemented. Many interventions have been developed without a theoretical model or with only selected components of a model. Without a theoretical framework, the choice of variables cannot be well justified and the ability to interpret results is limited. Even when interventions have been based on theory, the amount of variability in outcome that has been explained has rarely been above 30% (Baranowski, Anderson, and Carmack 1998).

Interventions are typically not tested to see whether they change the variables they are designed to change, or whether the target variables are actually responsible for changes in the outcome variable. Deciding which theories and strategies have the best chance of increasing exercise adherence requires careful analysis of the effects of the intervention on the theoretical mediator variables and the effects of the purported mediators on behavior.

Ideally, exercise interventions should change the variables that are, according to a theory, responsible for changes in the outcome. Testing the intervention to make sure that these key variables are actually changed (i.e., construct validation of the intervention) has not been a matter of course in physical activity interventions. Results from McAuley et al. (1994) illustrate the importance of evaluating the intervention. McAuley et al. implemented an intervention to increase exercise behaviors through self-efficacy enhancement strategies. They found significant treatment effects for changes in behavior, as well as a significant relationship between increases in self-efficacy and behavior. However, the treatment effects were not mediated through self-efficacy.

In chapter 2, we defined *mediator* as the variable that accounts for the relationship between the independent variable and the outcome variable. For example, an intervention (independent variable) to increase exercise adherence (outcome variable) using Bandura's self-efficacy theory would aim to increase exercise self-efficacy (the mediator) (figure 12.3). Baron and Kenny (1986) published a seminal article that distinguished between moderators and mediators of behavior change and social psychological outcomes. Using their model, three conditions must be met for exercise self-efficacy to be a mediator in our example. First, there must be a significant relationship between the intervention and exercise self-efficacy. Second, there must be a significant relationship between exercise self-efficacy and exercise adherence. Simply put, the intervention should increase self-efficacy, and increases in self-efficacy should be related to better adherence. Finally, to support the mediator role of exercise self-efficacy, the effects of the intervention on adherence should not be significant when one controls for the relationship between the intervention and self-efficacy *and* the relationship between self-efficacy and adherence. Thus there is evidence that self-efficacy accounts for the relationship between the intervention and the outcome because removing it weakens or eliminates the intervention's effect.

Mediators that have been tested in the physical activity literature include processes of change, decisional balance, and self-efficacy (Dunn et al. 1997; Pinto et al. 2001); self-efficacy and social support for exercise (Calfas et al. 1997); perceived barriers and enjoyment (Castro et al. 1999); and knowledge, attitudes, and self-efficacy (Young et al. 1996). Results have been mixed. Baranowski, Anderson, and Carmack (1998), in a practical critique of mediating variables in physical activity interventions, in-

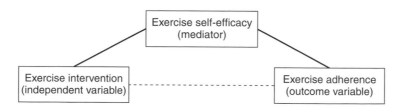

Figure 12.3 Self-efficacy mediates the effects of the intervention on exercise adherence when there are significant relationships between the intervention and self-efficacy, and between self-efficacy and exercise adherence (solid lines). Additionally, the relationship between the intervention and exercise adherence is not significant when the effects of self-efficacy are removed (dotted line).

dicated that the lack of attention to the intervention-mediator and mediator-outcome relationships has left us not knowing why our programs are successful or how to change hypothesized mediator variables consistently with our interventions. An answer—though the complete answer is certainly more complicated—is that the lack of effectiveness of interventions in sustaining exercise behavior is a function of the need for better models of exercise behavior, for better application of what we know about moderator variables, and for basic research on the mediator-intervention-outcome relationship.

Summary

Interventions must be applied based on characteristics of the target group, limitations of the setting, and consideration of potential personal and environmental barriers to participation. There is good evidence for the effectiveness of strategies based on behavior modification. However, there is no consensus on guidelines for interventions to increase and maintain physical activity, and gaps remain in what we know about long-term maintenance of regular exercise. Traditional interventions have not addressed the cyclical or dynamic nature of exercise behavior, and the average dropout rate from structured exercise programs has remained at 50% for the past 25 years. Intervention research has focused on implementing behavior change strategies and measuring the subsequent change in level of physical activity, often with instruments lacking established reliability and validity. Few studies have tested the construct validity of the intervention by determining whether the intervention changed the selected mediators and whether the mediators changed the target behavior. Future research should be directed toward testing the validity of theories for exercise behavior and testing the construct validity of interventions. Controlled longitudinal studies with specific populations are needed to establish what works and with whom. There is also the need to implement interventions at the level of the social and physical environment. Environments that prompt increased activity, offer accessible facilities, remove real and perceived barriers, and reward physical activity are likely prerequisites for adoption and long-term maintenance of an active lifestyle.

Suggested Readings

Baranowski, T., C. Anderson, and C. Carmack. 1998. Mediating variable framework in physical activity interventions: How are we doing? How might we do better? *American Journal of Preventive Medicine* 15: 266–297.

Baron, R.M., and D.A. Kenny. 1986. The moderator-mediator variable distinction in social psychological research: Conceptual, strategic, and statistical considerations. *Journal of Personality & Social Psychology* 51: 1173–1182.

Blair, S.N., M. Booth, I. Gyarfas, H. Iwane, B. Marti, V. Matsudo, M.S. Morrow, T. Noakes, and R. Shephard. 1996. Development of public policy and physical activity initiatives internationally. *Sports Medicine* 21 (3): 157–163.

Dishman, R.K., and J. Buckworth. 1996b. Increasing physical activity: A quantitative synthesis. *Medicine and Science in Sports and Exercise* 28 (6): 706–719.

Dunn, A.L., R.E. Andersen, and J.M. Jakicic. 1998. Lifestyle physical activity interventions. History, short- and long-term effects, and recommendations. *American Journal of Preventive Medicine* 15: 398–412.

Marcus, B.H., N. Owen, L.H. Forsyth, N.A. Cavill, and F. Fridinger. 1998. Physical activity interventions using mass media, print media, and information technology. *American Journal of Preventive Medicine* 15 (Nov): 362–378.

Web Sites

www.cdc.gov/nccdphp/dash/presphysactrpt/

www.bikefed.org/
    cdc_active_community_environments.htm

http://nsc.org/walkable.htm

http://paceproject.org

www.cooperinst.org/

www.ncppa.org/

www.cdc.gov/nccdphp/dnpa/readyset/press.htm

13

Perceived Exertion

Perceived exertion is an individual's subjective judgment of strain, or effort, during physical activity. It results mainly from a perceptual integration of various sensations that arise from physiological and chemical signals associated with muscular force production and increased energy expenditure during exercise. Perceived exertion is a **gestalt**—*gestalt* being a German word that roughly translated into English means a pattern, a segregated whole, or a totality. Thus, a person's overall judgment about exertion represents more than its parts (i.e., specific sensations during exercise; see figure 13.1). Nonetheless, it is important to understand the specific sensations that contribute to the whole perception. Those sensations arise from physiological strain, which differs according to the type and intensity of exercise and someone's level of fitness or training. Examples include sensations of force from contracting muscles during limb movements and during breathing; sensations of

temperature, sweat, and pain or discomfort; and other factors that change in proportion to how energy expenditure varies during heavy exercise.

Because the brain filters sensations, an individual's personality or mood might also affect perceived exertion—directly by influencing the quantity or quality of perceptions, or indirectly by influencing how people report perceived exertion to others. How people rate perceived exertion can be influenced by external cues within the setting where exercise occurs, including distractions or factors that motivate people to consciously or subconsciously raise or lower their ratings reported to others in order to make a good impression on someone else.

Nearly 40 years of research on perceived exertion has led to a large body of information supporting its endorsement by the American College of Sports Medicine (ACSM) as a practically important component of exercise testing and prescription (ACSM 2000). Studies also suggest that perceived

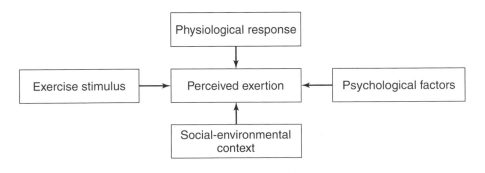

Figure 13.1 Perceived exertion as a gestalt.

exertion is an important factor influencing whether people choose to be physically active and how vigorously they perform physical activity.

History

Debates about the existence of a **"muscle sense"** were common among physiologists and psychologists in Europe during the mid-to-late 19th century. In 1892, American psychologist James McKeen Cattell, a student of Wundt and longtime owner-publisher of the journal *Science*, reported what appears to have been the earliest scientific study of perceived exertion when he and a colleague sought to determine whether men could accurately produce a handgrip force that they perceived to be twice or one-half that of a standard force (Fullerton and Cattell 1892). The next study of perceived handgrip force didn't appear until 1959 (Stevens and Mack 1959), and it was not until the 1960s that the concept of perceived exertion, as we now know it, emerged. Swedish psychophysicist Gunnar Borg became interested in people's perceptions of physical work after being informed by his medical colleagues that some of their patients who complained of having lost capacity for work actually had normal working capacities during cycling exercise. That indicated to Borg that the patients had underestimated their actual level of fitness. Later, Dr. Borg developed the first rating scales that could be used to measure perceived exertion, stimulating the development of perceived exertion as a field of scientific study and application (Borg 1962).

*S*wedish psychophysicist Gunnar Borg developed the first rating scales for the measurement of perceived exertion, and coined the term rating of perceived exertion (RPE).

Perceived exertion is a perception of quantity more than of quality. Observations that people's judgments about the quantity of a physical stimulus might be distorted by their perceptions were first described and organized into lawlike postulates by psychophysicists during the first half of the 20th century. It is now known that judgments by people about the intensity of a physical stimulus do not necessarily grow linearly as the stimulus grows lin-

Types of Perception

Perceptions of physical stimuli can be judged by quality or quantity. According to early Harvard psychophysicists S.S. Stevens and E.H. Galanter, quality, such as the hue or position of a light or the pitch of a sound, exists along a *metathetic* continuum, whereby "discrimination behaves as though based on a substitutive mechanism at the physiological level." In contrast, quantity, such as the brightness of light or the loudness of sound, exists along a *prothetic* continuum, whereby "discrimination appears to be based on an additive mechanism by which excitation is added to excitation at the physiological level" (Stevens and Galanter 1957).

early. Determining the pattern of increase in perceived exertion with increasing intensity or duration of exercise is fundamentally important for prescribing and monitoring exercise among the public. Exercise professionals usually give their clients recommendations about proper amounts of exercise based solely on physiological responses or adaptations to exercise that increase in a mainly linear pattern. If people perceive the amount of exercise in a nonlinear way, or perceive the amount to be less or more than physiological indicators of strain suggest, their comfort, fitness, or health may suffer.

*J*udgments by people about the intensity of a physical stimulus do not necessarily grow linearly as the stimulus grows linearly. Determining how perceived exertion increases with increasing intensity or duration of exercise is fundamentally important for prescribing and monitoring exercise.

This chapter presents the basics of (1) ways in which the methods of psychophysics have been used to determine the growth of perceived exertion during exercise; (2) ways in which exercise professionals without training in psychophysics can use practical rating scales to measure perceived exertion during exercise; (3) the physiological, psychological, and social environmental factors that influence perceived exertion, in addition to the actual physical work being done; and (4) practical applications of perceived exertion for exercise testing, prescription, and monitoring of exertion during exercise.

Psychophysics and Perceived Exertion

Researchers in the field of **psychophysics** study psychological judgments of physical stimuli. Those judgments are based on a *sensation* (a passive process defined as the stimulation of sensory nerve fibers by a stimulus) and a *perception* (an active process defined as the cognitive interpretation of sensations). The study of psychophysics is based on standardized methods of manipulating physical stimuli and measuring the perceptual response to the stimuli. Just as those methods have been used to measure perceptions of specific physical stimuli (e.g., the brightness of light; loudness of sound; and speed, length, or passage of time), they can be used to measure perceived exertion during exercise.

***S**ensation is the stimulation of sensory nerves by a stimulus or signal. Perception is the cognitive interpretation of sensations. Perceived exertion is the rating of such perceptions during exercise.*

Classical Psychophysics

Three common methods employed by classical psychophysicists are the method of limits, the method of adjustment, and the method of constant stimuli. The **method of limits** involves judging the magnitude of stimuli presented in a series across a range of intensities in ascending and descending orders. This method allows one to determine the lower and upper thresholds for perception. The lower threshold is called the *stimulus threshold*, which corresponds to the minimal intensity of the stimulus that someone perceives as *just noticeable*; stimulus intensities below the stimulus threshold are not perceived. The higher threshold is called the *terminal threshold*, which corresponds to the maximal intensity of the stimulus that someone can perceive;

stimulus intensities above the terminal threshold are not perceived.

The **method of adjustment** involves making judgments of equality between two stimuli. A person is presented with a stimulus having a standard, objectively measured intensity and is then asked to adjust a comparison stimulus until he or she perceives it to be of the same magnitude as the standard stimulus. The **method of constant stimuli** also involves the presentation of a standard stimulus and a comparison stimulus. In this case the task for the person judging the two stimuli is to indicate whether or not the comparison stimulus is perceived and/or whether or not it is different from the standard stimulus. The comparison stimulus that is perceived to be different from the standard stimulus 50% of the time is referred to as the **just noticeable difference (j.n.d.).** The j.n.d. represents the smallest amount of change in the intensity of the stimulus required in order for it to be perceived.

***A** just noticeable difference (j.n.d.) is the smallest amount of change in the intensity of the stimulus required in order for it to be perceived.*

Classical psychophysicists were interested in scaling physical stimuli in order to determine the shape of the relationship between the physical growth of a stimulus and perceived growth of the stimulus, averaged across people. Good examples are judgments of sound or the brightness of light. A whisper is easily heard in a quiet room but is inaudible in a cheering crowd. The beam of a car's headlights can be blinding in a rearview mirror but so dim in daylight that it is easy to forget to turn the headlights off. Mathematical laws that describe such perceptions more precisely provide a good start for understanding the growth of perceived exertion.

Common experience can make the mathematical laws of psychophysics easier to understand. For example, when humans hear linear increases in sound pressure level or wattage generated by an electrical amplifier, they do not perceive sound as increasing linearly. Rather the judgment of sound grows mostly as a logarithm of light intensity, such that a 200 W stereo amplifier is not perceived to be twice as loud as a 100 W amplifier, which is not perceived to be twice as loud as a 50 W amplifier.

The first mathematical equation describing the growth of human perception of physical stimuli was proposed by German physiologist Ernst Heinrich Weber. In his 1834 book, *De Tactu (About Touch)*, Weber reported his findings that sensations have stimulus and terminal thresholds and presented his most widely recognized concept, the j.n.d. On the basis of his theoretical work on the perception of weight, temperature, and pressure, Weber proposed that the j.n.d. was a ratio of the magnitude of the stimulus, rather than an absolute amount. For example, a greater weight must be added to 100 lb (45 kg) than to 50 lb (22.7 kg) for a person lifting a weight in order for the person to notice that any weight has been added. Weber's law states that the amount of change in the stimulus necessary to produce a j.n.d. grows at a constant (k) linear percentage of the magnitude of the physical stimulus (S). For example, if the j.n.d. during cycling exercise were 10 W at an exercise stimulus of 100 W, k would be .10 (i.e., 100/10). At 200 W, the j.n.d. should be 20 W (i.e., 200 × .10), and at 300 W it should be 30 W. Thus, according to Weber's law, each stepwise increment in exercise intensity would be perceived to have less quantity than the previous increment because the absolute value of each j.n.d. would increase.

However, Weber's law is not congruent with what humans typically experience during exercise. Perceived exertion during moderate intensities generally increases in proportion to increases in exercise intensity. And, as people approach maximal exertion, the j.n.d. for increased power output becomes smaller, such that increases in intensity are more easily noticed.

The scientist who first determined that Weber's ideas did not hold for all types of perception and sense modalities was one of his students, Gustav Fechner, who studied anatomy under Weber at the University of Leipzig. Fechner is credited with mathematically formalizing Weber's ideas as a law-like relationship between stimulus and perception. Fechner then tested that law in his own studies of the perception of distance, brightness (even going temporarily blind after his constant staring at the sun), and lifted weights. He proposed a modified Fechner-Weber law around 1860 in his book *Elemente der Psychophysik*.

The Fechner-Weber law states that the j.n.d. increases logarithmically with the magnitude of the stimulus. That is, Fechner proposed that the j.n.d. grows to an increasingly greater degree with each linear increment in intensity—not by some constant fraction, as proposed by Weber, but by a common log (i.e., log-base 10) of the fraction. According to the Fechner-Weber law, the j.n.d. would increase as a positively accelerating function of increased exercise intensity.

Hence, the perception of exertion during exercise would increase in a negatively accelerating fashion. Peak perceptions of exertion would approach a plateau as exercise intensity increases toward maximal effort. However, the Fechner-Weber law is also inconsistent with the increase in perceived exertion that humans experience during increasing exercise intensity.

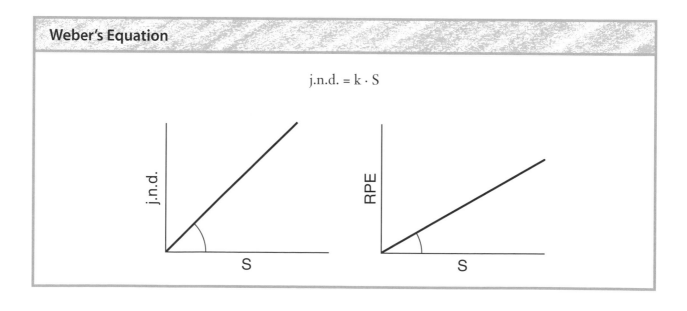

Weber's Equation

$$j.n.d. = k \cdot S$$

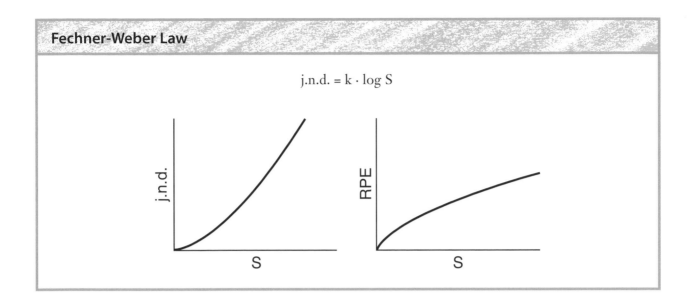

Fechner-Weber Law

$$j.n.d. = k \cdot \log S$$

Modern Psychophysics

In the 1950s, Harvard psychophysicist S.S. Stevens proposed a power law as a replacement for the Fechner-Weber law (Stevens 1957). Whereas Fechner argued that *"equal relative increments of stimuli are proportional to equal increments of sensation,"* Stevens' power law postulated that *"equal stimulus ratios yield equal response ratios."* Computationally, Stevens' law states that the perception or response (R) is proportional to a constant (k) multiplied by the stimulus (S) raised to a power exponent, *n*.

The exponent *n* in Stevens' power law is deter-

mined by first graphically plotting the $\log_{10}$-transformed stimulus values on the *x*-axis and the $\log_{10}$-transformed perception values on the *y*-axis. Then, the best-fitting straight line is drawn (or estimated from statistical software) through all the points on the log-log plot. The slope of this straight line is the exponent *n* in Stevens' power law. If the exponent is 1.0, the function describing the relationship between the stimulus and the perception is linear. If the exponent is less than 1.0, the function is negatively accelerating; if the exponent is greater than 1.0, the function is positively accelerating. Figure 13.2 illustrates these power functions.

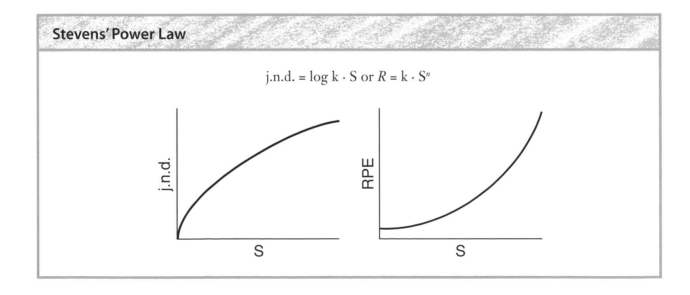

Stevens' Power Law

$$j.n.d. = \log k \cdot S \text{ or } R = k \cdot S^n$$

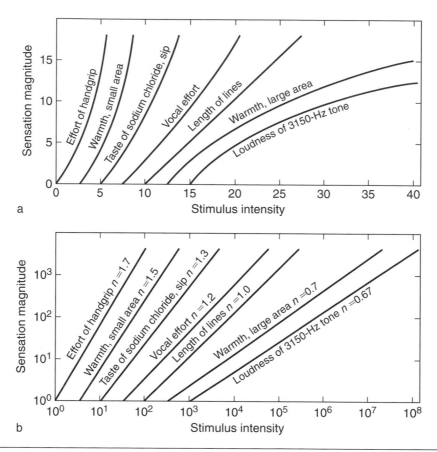

Figure 13.2   Linear *(a)* and log-log *(b)* plots of Stevens' power functions.

Reprinted from S.S. Stevens, 1957, "On the psychophysical law," *Psychological Review* 64: 153–181.

Logarithm or Power Function?

Understanding how logarithms and power functions have been applied to psychophysical relationships is fundamentally important in understanding perceived exertion. The scaling of human perception of sound provides a good example. The perception of sound is measured on a decibel (dB) scale such that each 10 dB increase represents a doubling of the perceived magnitude of the sound. On the decibel scale, a barely audible sound is given the value of 0 dB. The loudest sound that can be tolerated without pain is about 120 dB. The deciBel scale was developed by Bell Laboratories in the early 1900s such that each increment on the scale would represent a doubling of the previous level on the scale. However, while testing the new scale, researchers determined that human perception of sound did not follow a constant fraction of the sound stimulus as initially proposed by Weber. Rather it more closely approximated a logarithm of the j.n.d. in sound.

Later, S.S. Stevens argued that growth of sound perception only appeared to describe a logarithm of the j.n.d. because the scientists had used the classical psychophysical methods of limits, adjustment, and constant stimuli, which only indirectly estimated the real growth in perceived loudness. Stevens used more direct scaling methods, such as asking people to judge when a sound was some ratio (e.g., double or half) of a standard sound. He determined that the perception of loudness did not grow as a logarithm of the j.n.d. in the stimulus as proposed by Fechner, but as a power exponent of the stimulus. The function describing increasing loudness of a 3 kHz tone was determined by raising the increments in sound pressure level by an exponent of 0.67. Hence, perceived loudness grew as a negatively accelerating function.

Stevens' power law had a large impact on the field of psychophysics, as it was able to explain the relation between many different types of sensation and perception, such as brightness, loudness, the pain of electric shock, the length of lines, and the effort of handgrip contractions, showing that perceptions increase exponentially, accelerating positively or negatively, with increases in stimulus intensity.

Stevens' power law explains the relation between many different types of sensation and perception, showing that perceptions increase exponentially, accelerating positively or negatively, with increases in stimulus intensity.

Types of Measurement Scales		
Scale	**Purpose**	**Example**
Nominal	Classify or group	Social security number
Ordinal	Rank	Order of finish (1st, 2nd, 3rd)
Interval	Indicate distance	Fahrenheit thermometer (10 °F vs. 20 °F)
Ratio	Indicate proportion	Kelvin temperature scale (150 °K vs. 300 °K)

Methods of Scaling Perception

Measurement of a psychophysical judgment is accomplished by scaling, which is the assignment of categories or numbers to describe or differentiate perceptual events. Four types of scales are used to assess perception: nominal, ordinal, interval, and ratio. Nominal scales simply name the object or event and thus yield the least amount of information. Ordinal scales not only name the object or event but also rank it, providing a crude index of quantity without specifying how much the ranks differ. Interval scales indicate the magnitude of differences in addition to naming and ranking the object or event. A Fahrenheit thermometer uses an interval scale. It indicates that the difference between 20 °F and 10 °F is the same as the difference between 10 °F and 0 °F. But, 0 °F is not absolute zero on the Fahrenheit scale, so 20 °F is not twice as warm as 10 °F. Ratio scales are the most informative, because they have an absolute zero that permits a measure of proportion in addition to naming, ranking, and quantifying distances. A good example is the Kelvin scale of temperature developed in 1848 by British physicist Sir William Thompson, the Baron Kelvin of Largs, Scotland. This scale has an absolute zero. Thus, a temperature of 300 °K is twice as high as a temperature of 150 °K.

The two most commonly used ratio scaling methods in psychophysics are magnitude estimation and magnitude production. **Magnitude estimation** involves presenting to someone a standard stimulus (called a *modulus)*, such as a 10 kg weight, and asking the person to label his or her perception of heaviness, or force, with any number. Next, differing weights are presented in a random order, and the person making the ratings is asked to assign a numerical value to each weight in reference to the rating assigned to the modulus. This approach is also called free magnitude estimation, as the person is free to choose any number to label the modulus. In some instances the numerical value for the modulus is chosen by the experimenter; individuals are then free to choose any number to rate their perception of force.

Magnitude production involves a similar procedure, but the person making the judgments is asked to produce a response that he or she judges to be proportional to a given magnitude of the stimulus. Both estimation and production tasks involve a process called ratio setting. For example, someone might be asked to estimate when a stimulus is one-half or double the preceding stimulus, or some other percentage of that stimulus.

Common rating methods in psychophysics require people to estimate or to produce a response that is some ratio of the magnitude of a stimulus.

The Power Law and Exercise

Studies using ratio-setting methods during hand-gripping and leg cycling exercise have shown that the growth of perceived exertion during increasing exercise intensities is more consistent with Stevens' power law than with the Fechner-Weber law.

Under most circumstances, the exponent describing the relation between exercise intensity and RPEs from magnitude estimation ranges between 1.5 and 1.7. This means that as exercise intensity increases, the perception of exertion increases in a positively accelerating fashion; or said another way, at low exercise intensities the perceived exertion should increase more slowly, but at higher exercise intensities the perceived exertion should increase more rapidly.

Comparing People

The goal of classical psychophysics was to compare perceptions of different stimuli, not to compare one person's perception of a stimulus with someone else's perception. Indeed, differences among people were considered to be error or noise in the perceptual system. Borg modified Stevens' power law for perceived exertion by including two other terms: perceptual noise (*a*) and stimulus threshold (*b*). Those terms provide the starting point for a graph of the stimulus-response curve for perceived exertion, as shown in figure 13.3. Perceptual noise is a person's perception of exertion at rest, and the stimulus threshold is the work rate that is just noticeable above rest. Adding those terms allows an adjustment for variables that affect a person's level of perceived exertion at rest (e.g., muscle soreness or fatigue).

Borg's Modification of Stevens' Power Law

$$R = a + c\,(S - b)^n$$

Borg's Range Principle

Ratio scaling methods best yield the true growth function of most perceptions. However, their limitation is that no common standard is used that permits a comparison of two people's *level* of perception. Ratio scaling methods can determine whether the rate of growth in the perceived magnitude of a stimulus is twice as great compared to another, but they do not permit a judgment about the absolute level of a perceived magnitude. Ratio scaling of a perception permits each person to choose his or her own starting point for later comparisons. Since

people's starting points are based on personal perceptions, which will surely differ, there is no way to compare the level or absolute magnitude of two people's perceptions. For example, the numbers that one person chooses to represent his or her perceptions (e.g., from 1 to 10) may be different from the numbers another person chooses to represent his or her perceptions (e.g., from 100 to 1000). It is not possible to know that the initial perception rated as 10 was 1/10 the level of another person's initial perception rated as 100.

Borg recognized this limitation of ratio scaling and developed a category rating scale, which performs much like an interval scale, to permit standardized comparisons of perceived exertion. The RPE scales can be used to compare responses across individuals or groups of individuals based on a key assumption known as Borg's range principle (Borg 1961).

Borg's range principle assumes that most people have had similar experiences with physical exertion, retaining memories of past physical exertion levels so that perceptions of "no exertion" and "maximal exertion" have a shared meaning among people. According to the range principle, a judgment of 50% the intensity of maximal exertion would have the same perceptual meaning for two people even if it represented a different absolute exercise intensity for each person. In the example shown in figure 13.3, the exercise intensity (S) perceived as 50% of R_{max} intersects the same position on the R function curve for person 1 and person 2, about 85% of each person's S_{max} (as indicated by the extrapolated dotted lines). Despite the higher S_{max} of person 2, R_{max} is the same for the two people.

Borg's Range Principle

People who have had similar experiences with physical exertion will have the same perceptual range for feelings of exertion despite the fact that their physiological ranges for tolerating the strain of exercise (e.g., as evidenced by a lower or higher physical working capacity, strength, or maximal aerobic capacity) will differ widely. People's perception of maximal exertion provides a common point of reference, permitting comparisons among people at intensities that represent the same proportion of the perceptual range.

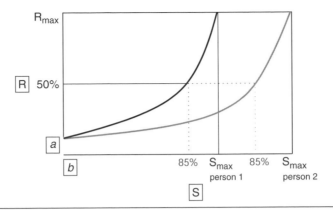

Figure 13.3 This graph illustrates Borg's range principle. The intensity of the response (R), in this case perceived muscular force, is plotted as a function of the intensity of the stimulus (S) (weight lifted) for two people who differ in maximal strength (S_{max}). R_{max} represents the subjective intensity corresponding to S_{max}. R_{max} is assumed to be the same for both people according to the range principle. Coefficient *a* represents perceptual noise (i.e., R in the absence of S). Coefficient *b* represents the stimulus threshold. The horizontal dotted line shows the 50% R_{max}. Note that 50% R_{max} is the same for both people, occuring at 85% of S_{max} despite the higher S_{max} of person 2 (as indicated by the vertical dotted lines).

Quantitative Semantics

Another assumption of Borg's approach to rating scales is that the adjectives people use to describe different levels of exertion convey a meaning of quantity that is commonly understood by most people. That assumption has been verified by a method called *quantitative semantics*, which measures the approximate numerical intervals that separate words according to the quantities they connote to people, on average. So, according to Borg's research, when perceived exertion is rated on an interval scale, shown in figure 13.4, the difference between the adjectives light and hard (heavy) has the same perceptual quantity as does the difference in quantity indicated between the numbers 11 and 15. Hence, the selection and placement of verbal descriptors, or anchors, were intended to help people understand the perceptual meaning of the rating scale.

According to Borg's range principle, RPE during exercise should change in direct proportion to oxygen consumption, expressed not as absolute uptake in L/min but as a percentage of maximum oxygen uptake capacity. One way to test the validity of Borg's assumptions would be to compare RPE with a measure of relative metabolic strain during physical exertion. Indeed, the most consistent finding about perceived exertion is that in many circumstances, RPE is linearly correlated with exercise intensity expressed as the $\%\dot{V}O_2max$.

Figure 13.5 shows that RPEs between about 10 and 16 approximate exercise intensities between 45% and 85% of aerobic capacity. That linear

6	No exertion at all
7	Extremely light
8	
9	Very light
10	
11	Light
12	
13	Somewhat hard
14	
15	Hard (heavy)
16	
17	Very hard
18	
19	Extremely hard
20	Maximal exertion

Figure 13.4 Borg's 6-20 category rating of perceived exertion scale.

Reprinted, by permission, from G. Borg, 1998, *Borg's perceived exertion and pain scales* (Champaign, IL: Human Kinetics), 31.

D*uring aerobic exercise, perceived exertion is directly related to relative exercise intensity expressed as the $\%\dot{V}O_2max$.*

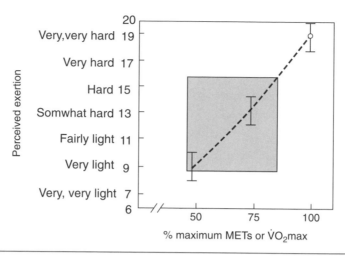

Figure 13.5   Category ratings of perceived exertion are related to percentage maximal oxygen consumption or percentage maximal METS during exercise.

relationship between RPE and %V̇O₂max appears inconsistent with Stevens' power law stating that, *"equal stimulus ratios yield equal response ratios,"* which predicts that the power exponent of exercise intensity will exceed 1. If so, how can RPE be linearly related to increasing %V̇O₂max, % maximal power output, or % maximal force, when each one is a ratio of the stimulus? One possible explanation, which we will address later, is that the power law does not accurately describe the growth of perceived exertion in all circumstances. That could be the case because perceived exertion is a complex integration of several senses, not a single sense.

Another explanation is that Borg's 15-graded, 6 to 20 RPE scale as well as other category scales, such as the University of Pittsburgh's 0 to 10 OMNI scale for children, permits comparisons among people on levels of perceived exertion but gives a distorted picture of the true growth of perceived exertion. The 15-graded RPE scale, shown in figure 13.4, is numbered 6 through 20. As this scale is a category scale, it does not have an absolute zero point; it has an artificial "floor" and may not be sensitive to j.n.d.'s at lower exercise intensity. Also, there is a limit, or ceiling, of 20 to the maximal rating that can be made with the 15-graded RPE scale. Thus, if someone's RPE judgments increase as exercise intensity increases (as is common during most graded exercise tests), then it is possible that the ceiling of the scale is reached prior to his or her actual maximum. From that point on, the person is forced to provide the maximal rating of 20, even though the intensity of exercise, and the perception of exertion, would likely continue to increase

beyond the first rating of 20 given. This effect, common to most category scales, is appropriately termed a *ceiling effect.*

Borg used the principles of ratio setting and quantitative semantics to construct another rating scale with ratio properties, the category-ratio 10-item (CR-10) scale, shown in figure 13.6. It is not influenced by ceiling effects because it has its ratio properties; it has an absolute zero point and does not have a ceiling. The scale is numbered 0 through 10 and includes a maximal point that is used by each individual to rate perceived exertion in relation to a near-maximum rating of 10. For example, if a muscular contraction felt 20% greater than the value judged as 10, the person would respond with a rating of 12; if it felt half-again as forceful as that perceived at a rating of 10, the person would give a rating of 15. The decision to use the 6-20 or the CR-10 scale depends on the research or practical purpose of measuring RPE, which we will discuss in subsequent sections on physiological correlates and exercise testing and prescription. Proper instructions for administration of the scales are very important and can be found elsewhere (Borg 1998, p. 104).

Borg's CR-10 RPE has ratio properties and estimates perceived exertion at low and high exercise intensities better than the original 6-20 category-interval scale does.

0	Nothing at all	"No P"
0.3		
0.5	Extremely weak	Just noticeable
0.7		
1	Very weak	
1.5		
2	Weak	Light
2.5		
3	Moderate	
4		
5	Strong	Heavy
6		
7	Very strong	
8		
9		
10	**Extremely strong**	**"Max P"**
11		
↯		
●	Absolute maximum	Highest possible

Figure 13.6 The category-ratio 10-item scale for rating perceived exertion.

Reprinted, by permission, from G. Borg, 1998, *Borg's perceived exertion and pain scales* (Champaign, IL: Human Kinetics), 50.

Ratings of perceived exertion can be made with both scales for the overall body (sometimes known as global RPE), or ratings can be differentiated to specific body parts (Pandolf 1982). Local or differentiated RPE are ratings obtained for a specific body part or region, such as chest, leg, or arm effort. The decision to assess global and/or local ratings may depend on several factors, including type of exercise, clinical health of the individual, or a particular research question. For example, during cycling exercise, it might be important to obtain perceived exertion about the legs, as well as the overall RPE. When testing a patient with chronic obstructive pulmonary disease, it might be especially important to know about breathing problems that affect RPE, so one would ask for local ratings of chest or breathing effort during exercise.

Signals to Perceived Exertion

In 1830, British physiologist Charles Bell proposed "muscular sense" as a sixth sense, existing on a par

with sight, sound, smell, taste, and touch. He postulated the existence of special peripheral afferent nerves that are activated by changes in posture and locomotion. His view was not widely accepted, and the prevailing view—held by a number of people including Wilhelm Wundt, the father of psychology—was that of a "sensation of innervation," whereby outgoing (efferent) impulses are sent from motor nerve cells to muscle, accounting for the muscular sense without a need to consider peripheral sense organs. That view persisted until late in the 19th century.

The Muscular Sense

Sir Charles Scott Sherrington, the 19th-century British neuroscientist who coined the term *synapse*, argued that both central and peripheral views about muscle sensations were needed to explain that sensations arise from both passive and active movements. He defined *the muscular sense* as "all reactions on sense arising in motor organs and their accessories."

A person's feelings of exertion and the ability to judge the quantity of those sensations depend on the perceptual integration of several sensations arising from different signals from all over the body. Unlike the 5 to 10 traditional senses, the sense of exertion does not have a specific sense organ. Rather, feelings of exertion represent an integration, or *gestalt*, of many signals having different origins. All of these signals are physiological in origin in that they all result in an excitatory or inhibitory postsynaptic electrical potential, consistent with the definition of a prothetic sense by Stevens and Galanter (1957). Nonetheless, it has become common to categorize signals that originate outside of the central nervous system as *physiological mediators* of exertion. Signals that originate within the central nervous system, such as those that activate brain regions regulating such concepts as personality, attention, and past experience (or memory), are termed *psychological mediators* of perceived exertion.

The Sensory Nervous System

How physiological responses provide signals to sensations during exercise and how those sensations are filtered and integrated into perceived exertion ultimately depend on how those responses are processed by the sensory nervous system. All sensory information is transmitted to the spinal cord through type Ia, Ib, II, III, and IV afferent nerve fibers, all of which terminate at the tertiary, primary, or secondary (Brodmann's areas 3, 1, and 2) somatosensory cortexes (figure 13.7). Signals of muscle fiber position and velocity of contraction are transmitted by type I afferent nerve fibers. Sensations of force and stretch in skeletal and respiratory muscles, tendon stretch, and joint position and pressure are transmitted by type II afferent neurons carried through the *dorsal column medial lemniscal system* of the spinal cord, which may also transmit signals related to metabolism. Sensations of pain and temperature are carried by a different bundle of afferent fibers, called the *anterolateral system*, in the spinal cord. Sensory signals sent by noxious chemical stimulation, such as lactate and/or hydrogen ions, are transmitted by type III and IV afferent fibers via the anterolateral system. Figure 13.8 illustrates the medial lemniscus and anterolateral sensory nervous tracts in the spinal cord.

Those two sensory systems (dorsal column medial lemniscal and anterolateral) carry sensory nerve traffic up the spinal cord and provide input into several brain regions located beneath the cortex, which regulate mood. Afferent fibers also travel to the basal ganglia and the cerebellum, areas involved in the initiation and termination of movement patterns (such as walking) and fine motor control. At the same time, signals are being sent farther up into the thalamus and then finally to the primary sensory cortex. Figure 13.9 (p. 268) uses a homunculus (little man) to illustrate the relatively small representation of the skeletal muscles on the brain cortex compared with the large representation of the head, hands, and feet. Normal integration of all of these sensory signals regulates homeostasis of physiological systems during the stress of increased metabolism in exercise and also provides the physiological basis for perceived exertion and subjective fatigue.

Because RPE increases as work load or rate increases, any physiological response that increases with work could be related to RPE. Thus, it is important to distinguish physiological responses providing or modifying a signal that can be sensed during exercise, and therefore mediate RPE, from indexes of the physiological strain of exercise that are merely correlated with perceived exertion. An example of the latter is heart rate (HR), which increases linearly with work rate but is not perceived by most people during exercise. Hence, HR provides an index of strain but not a signal or sensation that is perceived as exertion. The following questions can help distinguish a physiological response as a mediator of RPE.

▼ Is the factor a biologically plausible cause for altering the perception of effort?

▼ Does the relationship between the factor and perceived exertion hold under all conditions?

▼ Can the factor be directly sensed by the individual?

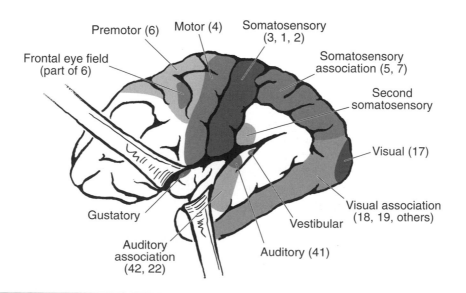

Figure 13.7 Brodmann's areas in the human brain.

Reprinted, by permission, from J. Nolte, 1999, *The human brain: An introduction to its functional anatomy,* 4th ed. (St. Louis: Mosby), 520.

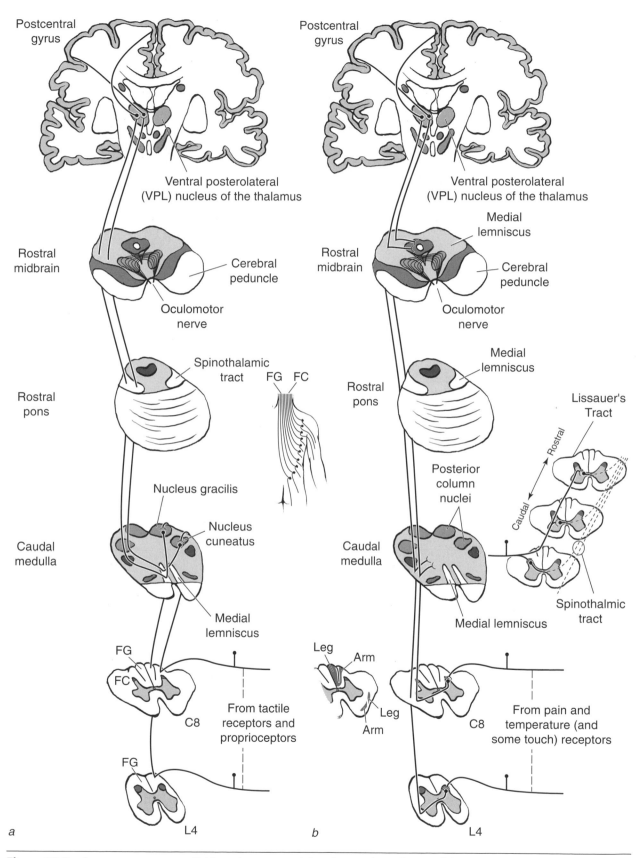

Figure 13.8 Sensory nervous medial lemniscus tracts *(a)* and anterolateral tracts *(b)*.

Reprinted, by permission, from J. Nolte, 1999, *The human brain: An introduction to its functional anatomy,* 4th ed. (St. Louis: Mosby), 232 and 236.

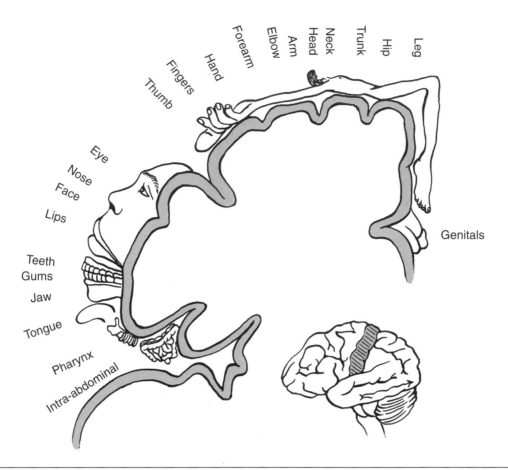

Figure 13.9   Homunculus of sensory nervous system: A homunculus (little man) is used to show that most of the body can be mapped onto the sensory cortex of the brain using electrical stimulation. The distortions illustrate that the portion of the cortex dedicated to each body part is proportional to the amount of precision needed to control it, not its size.

From The Brain: A Scientific American Book by Scientific American © 1979 by Scientific American. Used with the permission of W.H. Freeman and Company.

Heart rate (HR) increases as exercise intensity increases, but it is not perceived by most people during exercise, as sensations of heavy breathing and muscular force are. Thus, HR provides an index of strain but not a signal or sensation that is perceived as exertion.

Physiological Mediators

Physiological mediators of perceived exertion have been categorized as either respiratory-metabolic or peripheral in origin. Respiratory-metabolic signals are a group of physiological responses that influence the rate and depth of breathing (known as $\dot{V}_E$ or minute ventilation) and the relative metabolic strain (i.e., %$\dot{V}O_2$peak) during exercise. Peripheral signals include sensations of force from the working muscles, sensations of pressure or force from joints and tendons, as well as sensations resulting from noxious chemicals that appear in the blood (such as hydrogen ions) during very intense exercise (e.g., above 50-90% of $\dot{V}O_2$peak) and repeated lifts of heavy weights. Rating of perceived exertion is dominated during low-intensity exercise by local factors such as muscle force; but as exercise intensity increases, central factors, including sensations associated with increasing blood lactate and hyperventilation, play a more significant role (see table 13.1). The RPE typically corresponds with

%$\dot{V}O_2$peak at all intensities regardless of the type of exercise mode. However, experimental manipulations of minute ventilation, blood lactate, blood pH, and blood glucose at unchanged levels of power out-put or %$\dot{V}O_2$peak can perturb the association of %$\dot{V}O_2$peak and RPE.

Respiratory-Metabolic Correlates and Mediators of Perceived Exertion

Heart rate, blood pressure, oxygen uptake, and ventilation are respiratory-metabolic responses to increases in exercise intensity that change along with perceptions of exertion. Only ventilation, however, meets the criteria for a sensory mediator of perceived exertion.

Heart Rate and Blood Pressure

Because HR usually increases linearly with increasing exercise intensity, as does RPE, it is not surprising that HR and RPE are correlated with each other during incremental exercise. This happens not because HR is causing RPE to increase, but rather because HR increases to circulate more blood to meet the increasing energy needs of the active muscles. The relationship with HR was used as early evidence that RPE was a valid estimate of exertion. Borg presumably numbered his 15-graded scale from 6 to 20 to correspond with the typical range of HR from rest to maximal exertion, such that multiplying the RPE by 10 would provide a rough estimate of HR (Borg 1970, 1982). However, that relationship holds only under circumstances in which the environment is strictly controlled and exercise intensity is incremented in periods of just a few minutes. In many other circumstances of prolonged exercise, HR and RPE can uncouple. A constant of 20 to 30 beats per minute must be added to the calculation of HR, such that

$$HR = RPE \times 10 \; (+ \; 20 \; to \; 30).$$

Blood pressure (BP) during exercise is not highly related to perceived exertion. Systolic blood pressure (SBP) increases with increases in intensity, though not linearly, and diastolic blood pressure remains stable or decreases slightly during dynamic exercise. The end result of those responses is a moderate increase in mean arterial pressure (MAP). Since MAP does not change appreciably during exercise, it should not be viewed as a mediator of perceived exertion. However, rate-pressure product (i.e., SBP $\times$ HR) is a good estimate of the oxygen demand of the heart during exercise, which is not related to RPE but can be related to ischemia of the heart and ratings of chest pain in people with heart disease.

It is unlikely that HR or BP serve as mediators of perceived exertion. Under certain conditions such as thermal stress or administration of cardiac drugs that alter HR (e.g., propanolol, which blocks β-adrenoreceptors on the heart), perceived exertion is uncoupled from HR. Also, HR can be affected by emotional states; and both humans and monkeys can be taught, using biofeedback of HR, to lower HR during exercise at low intensities. Furthermore, RPE during prolonged exercise at a constant intensity rises with the passage of time

Table 13.1

Physiological Correlates of Rating of Perceived Exertion

Level	Symptoms	Metabolic intensity %$\dot{V}O_2$peak	Relative contribution		
			Respiratory-metabolic $\dot{V}_E$	%$\dot{V}O_2$peak	Peripheral
I	Movement awareness	< 50	Limited	Proportional	Dominant
II	Discomfort tolerance	50-70	Moderate	Proportional	Dominant
III	Noxious pain avoidance	> 70	Significant	Proportional	Dominant

Model of the potentiating relationship between respiratory-metabolic and peripheral signals of exertion at low (level I), moderate (level I), and high (level III) metabolic rates.

Reprinted, by permission, from R.J. Robertson, R.L. Gillespie, J. McCarthy, and K.D. Rose, 1979, "Differentiated perceptions of exertion: Part II. Relationship to local and central physiological responses," *Perceptual and Motor Skills* 49: 691-697.

despite the fact that HR and BP remain essentially unchanged (Jackson et al. 1981). And it is unlikely that most people can accurately sense changes in HR or BP during exercise.

Oxygen Uptake ($\dot{V}O_2$)

The increase in oxygen consumption during exercise, particularly when expressed as relative exercise intensity (i.e., %$\dot{V}O_2$peak), is strongly related to perceived exertion under many circumstances. As with HR, though, the association between RPE and %$\dot{V}O_2$peak can be altered during exercise. Manipulating other factors (e.g., environmental temperature or blood levels of lactic acid) while keeping the relative exercise intensity constant alters RPE. Also, RPE at a given %$\dot{V}O_2$peak becomes lower after exercise training, so other physiological or psychological factors must also be important influences on perceived exertion. It is also unlikely that an individual can directly sense $\dot{V}O_2$. Because the relationship between RPE and $\dot{V}O_2$ can be perturbed and because it seems unlikely that people can actually sense oxygen consumption, %$\dot{V}O_2$peak is probably an index of perceived exertion rather than a signal to sensations underlying perceived exertion.

Ventilation

At low exercise intensities, signals associated with breathing do not appear to influence perceived exertion. But people can sense increases in the rate and effort of breathing as exercise becomes more effortful, and those sensations become an increasingly important influence on perceived exertion as the intensity of exercise increases (Killian 1987). In patients with asthma or other chronic obstructive lung diseases, ratings of breathlessness are the most important contributor to overall RPE (Yorio et al. 1992). Feelings of force or stretch from the inspiratory muscles also contribute to feelings of exertion, as well as the overall breathing rate.

When ventilation is manipulated by changing the content of the oxygen or carbon dioxide in the air, RPE corresponds with the increases and decreases in ventilation, even though the actual intensity of the exercise has not changed. It seems very unlikely that humans can directly perceive the amount of oxygen being consumed or the amount of carbon dioxide being expired. However, the ventilatory equivalent for oxygen ($\dot{V}E/\dot{V}O_2$) and the percentage of maximal oxygen uptake (%$\dot{V}O_2$max) during exercise provide very good indexes of the relative metabolic strain being experienced.

Rating of perceived exertion at the ventilatory threshold, the point where the exponential growth of ventilation during heavy exercise is most pronounced, typically ranges between 12 and 14, which approximates "somewhat hard" on Borg's 6-20 category scale (Hill et al. 1987). Some evidence suggests that when the brain recruits more skeletal muscle fibers to generate more force during heavy exercise, it also stimulates heavier breathing to match the increasing metabolic demand of the exercise. In addition, increases in lactic acid during heavy exercise can contribute to increased ventilation.

Peripheral Correlates and Mediators of Perceived Exertion

Peripheral responses to increases in exercise intensity contribute more to perceptions of exertion than do cardiovascular-metabolic responses. There is evidence that RPE during incremental exercise is mediated by the concomitant accumulation of blood lactic acid (via influences on pain and ventilation), increase in muscle recruitment and contraction, and increase in skin temperature. Although the release of catecholamines and stress hormones is also associated with increases in exercise intensity, the relationship between changes in these substances and RPE is likely not causal. Figure 13.10 presents a useful illustration of the relationship between perceived exertion and perceptions of different physiological responses to increases in power output.

Blood Lactic Acid

At high intensities of exercise, concentrations of lactic acid increase in skeletal muscles and the blood, when muscles' need for oxygen exceeds the ability of the muscles' oxidative enzymes to utilize the oxygen being supplied. The major by-product of this increased anaerobic metabolism is excess production of lactic acid. Borg appears to have been the first to recognize that the blood level of lactic acid during exercise had the same exponential rise as did perceived exertion measured by ratio-setting methods (Borg 1962). Later study confirmed that the lactic acid increases in muscle and in blood during heavy incremental exercise correspond closely with RPE measured by an early version of Borg's 0-10 category-ratio scale (Noble et al. 1983). During incremental exercise, RPE measured by Borg's 6-20 category scale will not correspond well with lactic

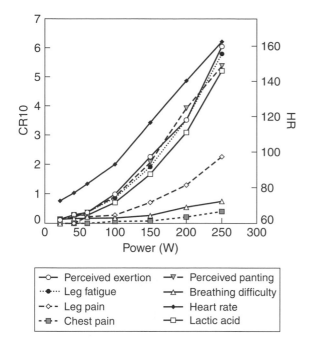

Figure 13.10 The increase of HR, lactic acid, and subjective somatic symptoms (see symbols) according to the Borg CR-10 scale with power (in watts) during bicycling in a strong group of healthy males.

Adapted, by permission, from G. Borg, 1998, *Borg's perceived exertion and pain scales* (Champaign, IL: Human Kinetics), 64.

acid accumulation, because RPE will increase linearly while lactic acid increases curvilinearly.

The accumulation of lactic acid is accompanied by increased hydrogen ions that decrease the pH level of the blood. Though lactic acid is probably not a signal for perceived exertion, it influences at least two physiological changes that contribute to sensations underlying perceived exertion. The first is pain and the second is ventilation.

Nociceptive nerves (nerves that carry pain signals) are sensitive to increased hydrogen ion concentrations, so lactic acid formation can be sensed as painful and the sense of pain could increase perceived exertion (Kostka and Cafarelli 1982; Robertson et al. 1986). However, the exact role of lactic acid in exercise-induced pain is not known, as other noxious chemicals (e.g., substance P or prostaglandins) that may contribute to perceptions of pain, as well as analgesic chemicals (e.g., β-endorphin), can be elevated in the blood at exercise intensities above 50%$\dot{V}O_2$peak.

The acidosis caused by lactic acid is buffered during light to moderately intense exercise by bicarbonates in the blood. The carbonic acid that is formed is dissociated in the lungs to water and

carbon dioxide, which is exhaled and adds to the volume of breathing in proportion to the carbon dioxide formed. At very heavy intensities, the excess carbon dioxide stimulates breathing centers in the brain to further increase ventilation. Because the onset of blood lactate accumulation or the lactate threshold (the point at which the exponential growth of blood lactate levels during exercise is most pronounced) is closely coupled in time with ventilatory threshold and occurs at the same percentage of $\dot{V}O_2$peak, it is not surprising that RPEs of 12 to 14 on Borg's 6-20 category scale also are usually observed at the lactate threshold during graded incremented exercise (e.g., DeMello et al. 1987), though lower ratings occur when lactate threshold is induced using speed-incremented exercise in fit people (e.g., Boutcher et al. 1989).

Muscle Recruitment and Contraction

Neurophysiological signals resulting from muscular contraction during exercise are processed through a feedforward-feedback mechanism (see figure 13.11). A feedforward mechanism occurs when motor (efferent) commands are simultaneously transmitted to the working muscle and the sensory cortex in the brain. A feedback mechanism operates when sensory (afferent) information regarding tension, velocity, and position from peripheral receptors in the muscle (muscle spindles, Golgi tendon organs, and mechanoreceptors) is transmitted to the sensory cortex. The integration of these pathways permits the complex processing of the

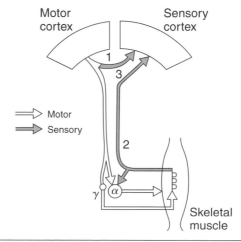

Figure 13.11 The feedforward-feedback mechanism.

Reprinted, by permission, from E. Caffarelli, 1982, "Peripheral contributions to the perception of effort," *Medicine and Science in Sports and Exercise* 14: 384.

physiological signals underlying perceived exertion (Cafarelli and Bigland-Ritchie 1979).

Muscle fiber type may also mediate perceived exertion. The exact differences between the signals sent by slow- and fast-twitch fibers are not fully understood. Lactate production during exercise is positively related to percentage of fast-twitch fibers, suggesting that those people with more fast- than slow-twitch fibers will experience a greater degree of metabolic acidosis. And, as mentioned previously, some evidence suggests that the brain feeds forward motor commands to breathing centers to increase ventilation at the same time motor commands are sent to skeletal muscles to increase force. Experiments using curare (a drug that blocks the chemical signals of acetylcholine at the neuromuscular synapse) to partially paralyze muscles indicate that RPE is increased proportionately to the increase in the central motor command from the brain to recruit more muscle fibers (Gandevia 1982).

Temperature Regulation

Core body temperature (Tc) increases as energy expenditure increases during exercise in proportion to percentage maximal working capacity. Thus, like HR, Tc is an index of relative metabolic strain. During prolonged (e.g., 30 min or longer) exercise under conditions in which the body's heat dissipation is burdened by high air temperature and high humidity, Tc increases more because the radiation gradient from the body to air and evaporation of sweat are lowered. Under these hostile conditions, RPE will increase. However, experiments that have manipulated Tc during constant exercise intensity, under conditions of room temperature and humidity, have failed to show that Tc is an independent signal for RPE (see Robertson and Noble 1997).

Skin temperature, on the other hand, can be perceived as a distinct sensation (compared to Tc) and may contribute to feelings of exertion during very hot and humid conditions. Though people can sense changes in skin temperature, the evaporation of sweat during exercise maintains, or can lower, skin temperature when air temperature remains constant because of heat used to vaporize water on the skin surface and heat transferred to passing air via convection. However, dilation of capillaries near the skin surface may lead to sensations of subcutaneous heat that are independent of skin surface temperature.

Catecholamines and Stress Hormones

Epinephrine and norepinephrine (see chapter 3) are catecholamines released from the adrenal medulla by the sympathetic nervous system in response to the stress of heavy exercise. They act as neurotransmitters or as hormones to stimulate contraction of muscle cells in the heart and to constrict or relax blood vessels that supply skeletal muscles. Similar to what occurs with lactic acid, catecholamines increase exponentially as exercise intensity increases, with the rise in epinephrine occurring later, at higher intensities, than the rise in norepinephrine and lactic acid. Also as with lactic acid, the increases in blood levels of catecholamines during heavy incremental exercise correspond to RPE measured by Borg's 0-10 category-ratio scale of RPE (Skrinar, Ingram, and Pandolf 1983).

Much of the increased norepinephrine comes also from nerves that innervate the heart and those that innervate blood vessels supplying skeletal muscles during exercise, pointing to the role of norepinephrine in increasing circulation and BP to support increased metabolism. The secretion of epinephrine is more closely related to energy metabolism and to the emotional stress of heavy exercise. The roles of catecholamines in the maintenance of blood glucose levels, the regulation of muscle glycogen, and the control of emotional responses are potential mechanisms by which catecholamines could influence perceived exertion. However, like blood lactic acid, catecholamines may better represent an index of metabolic strain than a signal for RPE.

During exercise at intensities above about 60% of $\dot{V}O_2$peak, the anterior pituitary gland secretes adrenocorticotropin (ACTH) and β-endorphin into the bloodstream. The amount secreted is linear with increasing relative intensity. The role of ACTH is to stimulate the release of cortisol from the adrenal cortex to aid glucose metabolism during stress. The role of β-endorphin is mainly to assist catecholamines in the regulation of circulation, breathing, and temperature control during increased metabolism, and in some circumstances analgesia (i.e., pain reduction). Drugs that block sensory nerve traffic from the legs during cycling exercise blunt the secretion of ACTH and β-endorphin without impairing a person's ability to generate power and without lowering RPE. Thus, it is unlikely that ACTH and β-endorphin directly influence perceived exertion. Rather, it is more likely that their increases during exercise result from stress associated with high perceived exertion.

Psychological and Social-Cultural Influences

Though perceived exertion is influenced to a large degree by physiological responses that provide or influence signals underlying sensation, psychological and social-cultural factors also can mediate perceived exertion by (1) filtering sensations at the level of the central nervous system; (2) influencing how sensations, or an integrated perception, are evaluated; and (3) influencing rating behavior (i.e., the act of reporting perceived exertion to another person). Relatively few studies have clearly explained how psychological and social-cultural factors influence RPE. Nonetheless, there are some results that seem plausible, given current understanding about psychological theory and perception.

Psychological and social-cultural factors can alter perceived exertion by influencing how sensations are processed by the nervous system, how perceptions are evaluated, and how RPE is reported to another person.

Augmentation-Reduction

Classical psychophysicists were interested in scaling sensations, that is, comparing the growth functions of perceptions of different physical stimuli. They considered differences among people in their judgments about the same stimulus to be error or "perceptual noise," probably because these scientists' backgrounds were in mathematics, physics, and physiology. In contrast, psychologists who study the ways in which people differ from each other (i.e., study personality) consider variations in psychophysical judgments among people to be indicative of real differences that can be explained by psychological variables. Indeed, most of the major theories of personality include a factor describing how people modulate the intensity of a stimulus. In the 1960s, Harvard medical psychologist Asenath Petrie

had people judge changes in the width of a wooden dowel held between the thumb and forefinger so that she could measure what she termed *kinesthetic figural aftereffect*. Her research showed that some people consistently overestimated psychophysical stimuli while making judgments about size, while others underestimated. She dubbed them **augmenters** and **reducers,** respectively, and proposed that the lower tolerance for pain that she observed among augmenters could be explained by their naturally overstimulated nervous system. In contrast, reducers were believed to be naturally understimulated, so they could tolerate more sensations related to pain.

Petrie's findings were consistent with the earlier research of the famous Russian psychologist Pavlov and British psychologist Hans Eysenck. Pavlov proposed a temperament trait called strength of excitement (SE) that referred to the ability to perform efficiently under levels of high stimulation without showing emotional disturbance. Eysenck later developed two temperament traits, extraversion-introversion and emotional stability-neuroticism, which linked the nervous system with behavior in much the same way as Pavlov's single trait of SE did. An extroverted, stable person would be predicted to judge the intensity of a stimulus as lower than would an introverted, neurotic person. A logical extension of those lines of research is that people characterized as perceptual reducers or as extraverted and emotionally stable would be expected to perceive less exertion when compared with augmenters or introverted neurotics during exercise of the same intensity. Research in the 1970s by Bob Robertson at the University of Pittsburgh on perceptual reducers (Robertson et al. 1977) and by William P. Morgan at the University of Wisconsin on personality and mood (Morgan 1973) suggested that this indeed occurs.

Personality and Mood

Morgan found that people who scored high on self-ratings of anxiety, neuroticism, and/or depression made more errors in rating perceived exertion than people who scored low on those tests. Also, people with a higher degree of somatic perception (i.e., the awareness of bodily sensations during stressful situations) reported higher RPEs than persons less aware of such sensations. Compared to introverts, extraverted individuals perceive a given exercise intensity as less effortful, and persons with higher extroversion scores may prefer to exercise at higher workloads. Other psychological variables that have been shown to influence perceived exertion in some individuals include attentional style (whether someone focuses on body perceptions or dissociates from them during exercise), locus of control (whether people feel they have control over themselves and the environment), and self-efficacy (high confidence in personal abilities about physical exertion; Morgan 1981).

Hypnotic Suggestion

Morgan and colleagues also showed that imagined changes in work rate influence RPE even when the actual work rate is not changed (Morgan et al. 1973). After hypnotic suggestions that the exercise was harder, young men reported higher RPE even though they actually were cycling at a constant power output of 100 W for several minutes. They did not seem to be faking the ratings, as HR and ventilation also increased. The imagined intensity apparently evoked a central command from the brain to the autonomic nervous system to increase heart and breathing rates as though a real increase in the metabolic rate of the exercise were occurring.

Comfort, Fatigue, and Perceived Exertion

The focus of most studies of perceived exertion has been on increasing or decreasing the intensity of exercise across a wide range of intensities with each level lasting a fairly short period of time (e.g., 1-5 min). That is a good approach for studying how people judge intensity, but it does not fully simulate exercise experiences, during which people often spend 20 to 60 min at an intensity that does not fluctuate very much. Common experience informs us that perceived exertion tends to increase over time even when the actual intensity of the exercise does not change. When someone is asked to maintain a constant *force* or workload, perceived exertion will increase with time. In contrast, if a person is asked to maintain a constant *effort*, the amount of force or work that the person produces will decrease because the work will feel harder as the duration of the task increases. Yale researchers observed that the exponent of the power function for perceived effort during cycling exercise doubled when the duration of each increase in power output ranging between 100 to 200 W

increased in duration from 15 s up to 5 min (Cafarelli, Cain, and Stevens 1977). Feelings of fatigue may thus be another factor affecting perceived exertion.

Perceived exertion tends to increase over time, even when the actual intensity of the exercise does not change. Thus feelings of fatigue may affect perceived exertion.

In the 1970s, Michigan State University psychologist S. Howard Bartley, who studied perception and had an interest in the subjective aspects of fatigue, made an important distinction between the *homeostatic* perceptual system (composed of internal receptors responsible for regulating the balance or harmony of physiological systems in order to maintain cellular function) and the *comfort* perceptual system (consisting of the awareness of senses of pain, temperature, movement and position, and touch, including some of the homeostatic signals). Partly on the basis of Bartley's ideas, military physiologists (Weiser, Kinsman, and Stamper 1973) asked young men to ride a cycle ergometer at about 60% of aerobic capacity until they felt too uncomfortable to continue. The average time was about 36 min. Subjective ratings by the men described three main types of related responses: (1) general fatigue (e.g., worn out, tired, weary); (2) leg fatigue (e.g., weak legs, leg cramps), which had a subcomponent of cardiopulmonary symptoms (e.g., shortness of breath, heart pounding); and (3) task aversion (e.g., sweating, uncomfortable, would rather quit) (see figure 13.12). Those findings were the first to suggest that perceived exertion during prolonged exercise could have both comfort and homeostatic dimensions that might affect perceived exertion as well as preferred exertion, the level of exertion that someone is motivated to endure.

Subjective fatigue appears to be composed of both homeostatic, *or general* cardiopulmonary and local muscular *sensations, and* comfort *components.*

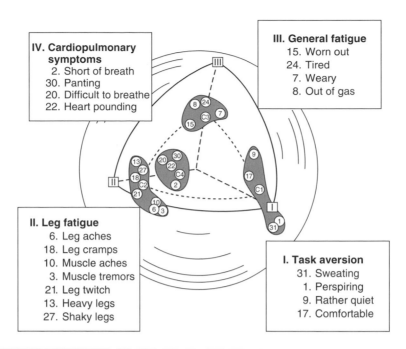

Figure 13.12 Spherical analysis diagram of four clusters at end of ride.

Adapted, by permission, from P.C. Weiser, R.A. Kinsman, and D.A. Stamper, 1973, "Task-specific symptomatology changes resulting from prolonged submaximal bicycle riding," *Medicine and Science in Sports and Exercise* 5 (2): 83.

Type A Behavior

When the Type A behavior pattern (TABP) was developed in the 1970s as a possible risk factor for developing heart disease, evidence suggested that Type A men were so motivated to accomplish more and more in less and less time that they suppressed perceptions of pain and fatigue. They might ignore chest pains or delay seeking medical treatment. There also was concern that Type A men would overexert during exercise and underrate perceived exertion. That view has persisted today, without good evidence to support it. Studies showing an association between TABP and RPE or a self-rating of fatigue did a poor job of measuring TABP or exercise intensity. The studies did not control for relative oxygen consumption or training history to ensure that Type A and Type B subjects had similar fitness levels, or did not use a valid measure of perceived exertion, or used a self-report measure of TABP rather than the structured interview, which is the "gold standard" measure of TABP (Dishman et al. 1991). More recent research using better methods has shown that there is no difference in RPE during standard exercise testing between men classified as Type A or Type B by the structured interview (Dishman, Graham, et al. 2001). It is still possible that people who show Type A behaviors might overexert or suppress perceived exertion during physical activities that foster competition, but this has not been shown in a scientific study.

Context and Perceived Exertion

Social, cultural, and contextual factors also can influence perceived exertion, but such influences are poorly understood (Acevedo et al. 1999; Boutcher et al. 1988; Hardy, Hall, and Presholdt 1986; Rejeski 1981). The attitudes people have toward physical activity are shaped by their culture, and these attitudes might affect how a person rates effort during exercise, especially when exercising for prolonged periods at a fairly constant intensity. A person who has learned that exercise is enjoyable may have a different perception of exertion than a person who has learned to expect that exercise is painful or boring. The setting where exercise occurs can also influence ratings. For example, the RPE of an exerciser could be influenced by characteristics of the scale administrator, such as gender, demeanor, or attractiveness. The preference of an individual for a particular mode of exercise is another potential influence on perceived exertion. If a person views a particular activity as distasteful (task aversion), the individual might rate that activity as more effortful than he or she would rate another activity of equal intensity. The influence of psychological factors may be on a conscious or subconscious level, and people may or may not be aware of the effect of these factors on RPEs. Therefore, it is important that the scale administrator be aware of the potential psychological and social-cultural influences on perceived exertion and attempt to create a neutral environment to promote accurate responding. In addition, the administrator must stress that honest responses are desired and that there are no right or wrong answers.

Though psychological and social-cultural factors likely influence perceived exertion and RPE, they haven't been adequately studied. The early line of research on the influence of personality traits and mood on RPE has not been pursued and verified. Also, such studies have relied mainly on correlational, not experimental, evidence based on absolute work rate without controlling for different levels of physiological strain among people having different levels of fitness or training. Hence, despite their seeming importance, the relative contri-

butions of psychological and social-cultural influences on perceived exertion remain unknown.

Perceived Exertion: The Final Common Pathway

How are the sensations during physical activity filtered and evaluated to yield an RPE? The hierarchical model for understanding fatigue illustrated in figure 13.13 proposes four levels of sensory processing of the physiological responses (*physiological substrata*) in bicycling exercise. The level *of discrete symptoms* refers to the specific sensations that originate from the physiological responses. At the *subordinate level*, discrete symptoms are organized into clusters representing differentiated symptoms that are specific to the type (i.e., mode) of exercise. At the *ordinate level*, these clusters are combined to produce a primary symptom that is specific to the type of exercise (e.g., bicycling fatigue). Task aversion and motivation clusters also emerge at this level. The final level is the *superordinate level*, which

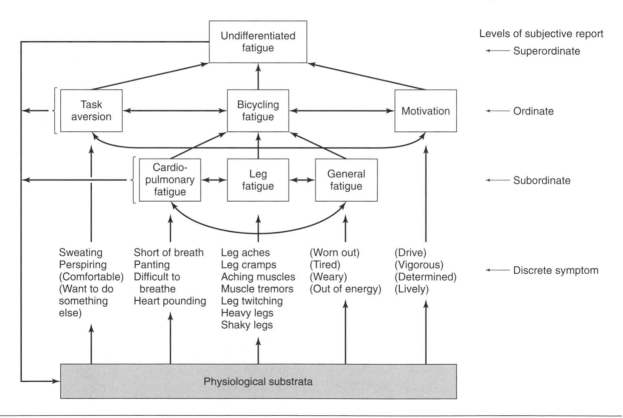

Figure 13.13 Pyramidal schema for subjective symptomatology during exercise.

Reprinted, by permission, from P.C. Weiser and D.A. Stamper, 1977, Psychophysiological interactions leading to increased effort, leg fatigue, and respiratory distress during prolonged strenuous bicycle riding. In *Physical work and effort*, edited by G.A. Borg (New York: Pergamon Press), 401–416.

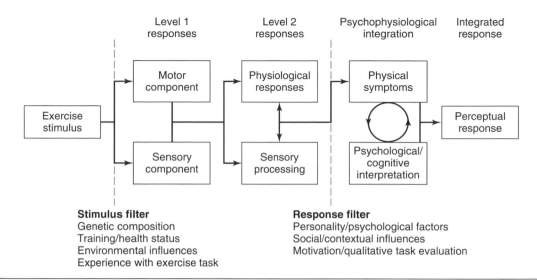

Figure 13.14 An integrated model of perceived exertion.
Provided by Heather O'Neal, the Exercise Psychology Laboratory, The University of Georgia.

represents an integration of symptoms to produce a global rating of fatigue.

Figure 13.14 presents a similar model for understanding RPE in which the exercise stimulus is influenced by individual differences that affect a person's physiological responses to exercise. For example, a person with a high level of fitness and acquired motor skills will have a different response to a physical task than someone who is untrained and unskilled in the activity. Level 1 responses refer to the activation of efferent and afferent pathways specific to the exercise stimulus. At level 2, discrete physiological responses (increased $\dot{V}O_2$, increased hydrogen ions) are processed in the sensory cortex and then filtered at a subconscious level to yield physical symptoms that are recognized by the individual (changes in breathing, sweating, etc.). An overall perceptual response results from the conscious interpretation of physical symptoms according to the unique psychological and cognitive characteristics of the individual.

Practical Use of Ratings of Perceived Exertion

Ratings of perceived exertion using Borg's RPE scales serve practical purposes in exercise testing, prescription, and monitoring of people's progress during training in preventive and rehabilitative medicine and in sport. The concept of perceived exertion is easily understood by most people over the age of 10 years (Bar-Or 2001), and about 9 of

10 adults are able to give accurate RPEs during most types of exercise (ACSM 2000). Assessments of RPE are time efficient, inexpensive, and easy to administer. However, it is important that the individual receive proper instructions. Some people might tend to focus on a single physiological, psychological, or environmental cue instead of rating their overall subjective feelings of exertion. Therefore, people must understand the scale instructions prior to rating perceived exertion, especially what the beginning and ending points on the scales mean concerning effort. Recent experience of a maximal effort is the best, but most people can remember or imagine what a maximal effort feels like based on past experiences.

Exercise Testing

Ratings of perceived exertion can be used to estimate perceived muscular force during resistance exercise, but RPE is most frequently obtained during a graded exercise test (GXT) in clinical and research settings. A GXT uses progressive increments in exercise intensity in order to determine a person's maximal exercise capacity (usually not submaximal endurance) and usually lasts between 8 and 20 min. The most technical GXTs involve 12-lead electrocardiograms, blood sampling, and continuous sampling of oxygen consumption while the person walks or runs on a treadmill at increasing inclines and/or speeds, or pedals a cycle ergometer while power output is increased. Results from a GXT can be estimated from simple field tests, such as time to complete a standard distance walking, running, or swimming. Graded exercise tests are used to estimate maximal level of oxygen consumption per unit time ($\dot{V}O_2$peak), which is the most commonly used criterion measure of cardiorespiratory fitness; by how many minutes a person can endure the GXT before quitting; or by the level of HR increase during the test.

The way perceived exertion is used during a GXT depends on the test protocol, the group of people being tested, and the exercise setting. In a clinical setting, a GXT is often used to aid in the diagnosis of pathology and to monitor improvement with treatment. Although a GXT is used mainly to assess exercise tolerance and general functional capacity in patients with conditions that limit physical capacity, a GXT may be used for assessment of patients' ability to perform everyday tasks or for building patients' confidence levels about their ability to exercise safely. In a research setting, the primary uses of a GXT are to determine the $\dot{V}O_2$peak, evaluate the effect of an intervention, and assess physiological responses to exercise. A GXT is generally used in a sport setting to screen for participation, assess training progress, and predict performance capacity.

The use of RPE during exercise testing has several specific purposes. First, it provides an index of subjective strain, so it can aid the tester in making judgments about a person's progress during the GXT, while giving signs when a person is nearing the end of the test. In older adults and patients, it is recommended that preparations to end a maximal GXT begin when the person reports an RPE of 15 to 17 on the 6-20 scale. The use of RPE for monitoring is especially important in people who may not have a normal physiological response to exercise (i.e., cardiac patients, pulmonary patients). Perceived exertion is not sensitive to heart ischemia, so HR and rhythm, BP, and chest pain are still key signs of strain during exercise in heart patients. The close relationship between RPE and %HRmax reserve still holds in patients taking drugs that blunt HR (e.g., β-blockers), as long as the HR reserve is computed from the resting and maximal exercise HRs obtained from a GXT while the patient is medicated at the therapeutic dose.

A second use of RPE during exercise testing is as a subjective indicator of peak exercise intensity, and an RPE near the top of the scale is a good indicator that a person exerted a maximal effort. Third, a predetermined RPE can be used to monitor changes in power output following exercise training. For example, %$\dot{V}O_2$peak at an RPE of 15 after training can be compared with %$\dot{V}O_2$peak obtained before training. After training, most people will be able to exercise at a higher relative intensity without perceiving the exercise as harder. Fourth, the use of RPE during exercise testing can aid in the monitoring of individuals with health conditions that might lower their tolerance for exercise or put them at risk for circulation problems during a test. Finally, RPE can be used to detect risk for staleness from overtraining among athletes who must train heavily in order to be competitive in their sports.

In older adults and heart or lung patients, RPE between 15 and 17 on Borg's 6-20 scale is a good sign for the tester to be ready to stop a GXT. Perceived exertion is not sensitive to heart ischemia, so HR and rhythm, BP, and chest pain are still key signs of strain during exercise in heart patients.

People administering exercise tests should keep in mind a few factors that may influence the perceptual response. With activation of smaller muscle mass, RPE at an absolute workload is higher than with the activation of larger muscle mass. For example, RPE at a given workload or MET level should be lower during treadmill running than during leg cycling, though RPE should be similar at a given %$\dot{V}O_2$peak. Though RPE during arm cranking is higher than during leg cycling when exercise intensity is expressed relative to %$\dot{V}O_2$peak of maximal leg cycling, it will be perceived similarly when intensity is expressed relative to %$\dot{V}O_2$peak of maximal arm cranking (Ekblom and Goldbarg 1971). Additionally, small but possibly important differences have been reported between genders, in aging populations, and during pregnancy and in different phases of menstrual cycle. Hostile environmental conditions (e.g., temperature and humidity extremes) may also influence RPE.

Exercise Prescription and Monitoring

Prescription of exercise falls into four areas: type (mode), intensity, duration (time), and frequency (number of bouts per week). Intensity is most directly related to RPE, but duration also affects RPE. An exercise program is prescribed at an intensity based on the results of the GXT. The ACSM guidelines for exercise prescription recommend that healthy individuals exercise three to five days per week for 20 to 60 min at an intensity of 45% to 85% $\dot{V}O_2$peak (ACSM 2000) (see tables 13.2 and 13.3). Because direct measurement of $\dot{V}O_2$ is time consuming, expensive, and cumbersome, exercise intensity is typically prescribed using one of the following methods to estimate % $\dot{V}O_2$peak: HR, metabolic equivalents (METs), and/or RPE (see table 13.3).

Heart Rate. Because HR and $\dot{V}O_2$ have a linear relationship, exercise intensity has traditionally been prescribed using a percentage of HRmax or a percentage of HR reserve. For that purpose, it is usually assumed that 60% to 90% of HRmax is equal to 50% to 85% of $\dot{V}O_2$max or HR reserve.

However, a large study of male and female employees at NASA's Johnson Space Center in Houston, Texas, showed that a prescription based on %HRreserve underestimated %$\dot{V}O_2$peak by about 5% to 10% at intensities between 50% and 60% HRreserve, but overestimated %$\dot{V}O_2$peak by about 4% to 8% at intensities between 80% to 85%

Heart Rate Reserve

Heart rate reserve can be calculated by subtracting resting HR from HRmax, and this value can be used to calculate a target training HR range using the Karvonen formula (e.g., [(HRmax – resting HR) × .60] + resting HR = training HR at 60%).

HRreserve (Weir and Jackson 1992). Thus, %HRreserve represents an inaccurate index of relative exercise intensity at low and high exercise intensities for many people. Adjusting %$\dot{V}O_2$peak for resting $\dot{V}O_2$ (i.e., $\dot{V}O_2$peak reserve), just as with %HRreserve, corrects this mismatch and yields a linear relationship between %$\dot{V}O_2$peak reserve and %HRpeak reserve. But making this adjustment is not practical in many exercise settings, and most exercise prescriptions are still made without it.

There are other problems with the use of HR for prescribing and monitoring exercise intensity. Often, HRmax is estimated based on a person's age rather than measured. Even when influences on HR due to age, training status, and type of exercise are accounted for, the standard deviation of true

---

Table 13.2

Recommended Use of Rating of Perceived Exertion and Heart Rate Guidelines Found Successful in the Prescription of Exercise for Healthy Adults

Measure of exercise intensity following exercise		Exercise prescription
Heart rate	**RPE**	
< 70% of HRmax	11	*Increase* intensity, duration, or both.
70-80% of HRmax	12-14	*Okay.* Increase intensity once monthly, usually in 5 s increments for each 1/4 mile. Increase duration once weekly, usually one extra 1/4 mile lap for each increase.
85-90% of HRmax	15	*Beware.* Check heart rate. Make sure that subject is running at the assigned velocity.
> 90% of HRmax	> 15	*Decrease* intensity, duration, or both. Make sure that subject is running at the new (slower) rate.

RPE = rating of perceived exertion; HRmax = maximal heart rate.

Reprinted, by permission, from E.J. Burke and M.L. Collins, 1984, Using perceived exertion for the prescription of exercise in healthy adults. In *Clinical sports medicine* (Lexington, MA: Callamore Press), 102. Adapted from E.J. Burke and J. Humphreys, 1982, *Fit to exercise* (London: Pelham Books).

Table 13.3

Classification of Physical Activity Intensity Based on Physical Activity Lasting up to 60 Minutes

Intensity	Endurance-type activity							Resistance-type exercise
	Relative intensity			Absolute intensity (METs) in healthy adults (age in years)				Relative intensity*
	$\dot{V}O_2R$ (%) heart rate reserve (%)	Maximal heart rate (%)	RPE†	Young (20-39 years)	Middle-aged (40-64 years)	Old (65-79 years)	Very old (80+ years)	Maximal voluntary contraction (%)
Very light	< 20	< 35	< 10	< 2.4	< 2.0	< 1.6	1.0	< 30
Light	20-39	35-54	10-11	2.4-4.7	2.0-3.9	1.6-3.1	1.1-1.9	30-49
Moderate	40-59	55-69	12-13	4.8-7.1	4.0-5.9	3.2-4.7	2.0-2.9	50-69
Hard	60-84	70-89	14-16	7.2-10.1	6.0-8.4	4.8-6.7	3.0-4.25	70-84
Very hard	85	90	17-19	10.2	8.5	6.8	4.25	85
Maximal∞	100	100	20	12.0	10.0	8.0	5.0	100

*Based on 8-12 repetitions for persons under age 50-60 years and 10-15 repetitions for persons aged 50-60 years and older.

†Borg Rating of Perceived Exertion 6-20 scale (Borg 1982).

∞Maximal values are mean values achieved during maximal exercise by healthy adults. Absolute intensity (MET) values are approximate mean values for men. Mean values for women are approximately 1-2 METs lower than those for men; $\dot{V}O_2R$ = oxygen uptake reserve.

HRmax is about 11 beats per minute (bpm). Hence, errors of 11 bpm above or below a true maximum can be expected in about 30% of the adult population when HRmax is estimated but not measured. It is therefore not surprising that some people given age-predicted HR ranges complain that the exercise intensity is too easy or too hard. So, RPE can be used along with HR to provide a more appropriate range of exercise intensity.

METs. American College of Sports Medicine guidelines for exercise prescription recommend that an individual's total weekly energy expenditure from exercise approximate at least 1000 kcal, with an optimal energy expenditure of 2000 kcal per week. The energy cost of a given activity can be calculated using the following formula:

$$\text{kcal/min} = \text{METs} \times 3.5 \times \text{kg body weight}/200$$

Rating of Perceived Exertion as an Adjuvant to Heart Rate

On the basis of Borg's early studies, exercise physiologists thought a model in which RPE × 10 = HR could be effective, but clinical observations suggested that a correction factor of 20 to 30 bpm had to be added (i.e., RPE × 10 + 20 to 30 bpm = HR) for RPEs of 11 to 16 and HRs within typical training ranges of 130 to 160 bpm.

The energy cost in METs has been determined for various physical activities, and most exercise physiology textbooks include tables listing the metabolic cost of different types of physical activity. The prescription of exercise intensity based on the energy cost of the activity is also susceptible to error due to individual differences. An individual's training status and skill level can influence the metabolic cost of the activity. For example, an unskilled swimmer expends more energy than an experienced, more economical swimmer who is swimming the same distance. Also, the intensity of the activity may vary within a given exercise session. Hence, the use of RPE during exercise prescribed according to energy cost can help the individual maintain the appropriate exercise intensity.

Accuracy of Ratings of Perceived Exertion

Ratings of perceived exertion between 12 to 16 usually correspond with recommended exercise intensities between 45% and 85% of maximum METs (multiples of resting metabolic rate) or 45% to 85% of HRreserve during level walking/jogging. Nonetheless, RPE will fall outside that range in as many as one-third of adults during their first GXT (Whaley et al. 1997). Normally, exercise intensity is prescribed based on the results of the GXT. During the GXT the participant *estimates* RPE throughout the test. These estimates are then matched to a percentage of maximum. If RPE is used in an exercise setting, the participant is asked to *produce* that rating. A problem with this estimation-production method is that the RPE in a GXT is commonly associated with a steady state achieved only briefly (e.g., 2 min). Then the participant moves on to another stage in the GXT, which itself is brief (i.e., 8 to 20 min). Normally, exercise is maintained at about the same intensity for a much longer period. This makes matching the exercise intensity from the GXT with an exercise intensity during training difficult with use of RPE. Errors between desired training range and actual training range are increased, so it is important to administer a production-production protocol when possible.

In a production-production protocol, the participant should be asked to produce an RPE that was associated with a desired intensity (e.g., metabolic rate) for training during the GXT. As the exercise session progresses, the test administrator should monitor the metabolic rate at the RPE; if the rate is not in the desired range, the participant should be asked to produce a new, appropriate RPE. This process should continue until the desired metabolic rate matches well with the RPE. Three practice tri-

als performed on separated days is generally sufficient to reduce errors in production of exercise intensity using RPE (Dishman et al. 1987).

It is also expected that reproduction of an intensity will be more accurate if the estimation task is intramodal (i.e., the same activity mode is used for estimation and production, e.g., cycling-cycling) rather than intermodal (i.e., the estimation task is a different mode of activity than the production task, e.g., cycling-running). Studies have shown acceptable errors of HR, oxygen uptake, and ventilation when intramodal production of intensity has followed RPE estimation during grade-incremented treadmill testing. Errors of production from cycling or treadmill RPE estimation approximate 10% to 15% for HR. Group mean errors for power output approximate 10 to 50 W and for $\dot{V}O_2$ are less than 5%, though the errors for a single person may be as high as 20% (Dunbar et al. 1992). The just noticeable differences for grade-incremented treadmill or load-incremented cycling have not been clearly established, but reports suggest that they are about 20 W. Production of exercise intensity during field jogging/running from treadmill RPE yields equivalent HR, lactic acid, and velocity at an RPE that is about 2 units lower in the field setting.

Training Status Effects on Rating of Perceived Exertion

Perceived exertion is influenced by a person's level of physical training. A common indicator that a person has increased in fitness is the ability to perform at a faster pace (i.e., a higher absolute $\dot{V}O_2$) while exercising at the same percentage of his or her maximal capacity as before the increased training. Ventilatory and lactate thresholds, which are physiological predictors of fitness, occur at lower relative work rates (50%-60% $\dot{V}O_2$peak) in untrained people and higher relative work rates (65%-80% $\dot{V}O_2$peak) in trained people. After increased training, RPE at the ventilatory and lactate thresholds stays around 12 to 15, corresponding with subjective categories of "somewhat hard" to "hard" on Borg's 6-20 category scale, despite the fact that those thresholds are occurring at a higher percentage of $\dot{V}O_2$peak and at a higher absolute level of work (Demello et al. 1987; Hill et al. 1987). Thus, RPE is an accurate indicator of exercise training status (Boutcher et al. 1989; Seip et al. 1991).

The Power Law and Borg's Rating of Perceived Exertion Scales

A potential problem of using category RPE (i.e., Borg's 6-20 RPE scale) to prescribe exercise is the curvilinear growth of perceived exertion when it is measured with ratio-setting methods, such as magnitude estimation or Borg's CR-10 scale. This can especially be a problem if Borg's RPE scale is used because of its linear relationship with increasing exercise intensity. However, within the training range of 45% to 85% of %$\dot{V}O_2$ recommended by the ACSM, the relationship of RPE to %$\dot{V}O_2$peak or power output is virtually linear (figure 13.15). The exception occurs during high-intensity walking, which has a power exponent of about 3. Thus, in most instances in which an exercise program is initiated at moderate intensities (i.e., 45-85% of $\dot{V}O_2$peak), the person should be able to use the 6-20 category RPE in a way that is generally linear with increasing exercise intensity. That is, if someone can perceive the increase from 12 to 13, he or she should be able to perceive the increase from 15 to 16 similarly; this would permit production of a linear increase in relative exercise intensity. However, if there is a shift from walking as a mode of exercise to running as a mode, it would appear that a new learning experience using a production-production approach should be conducted for the new mode of exercise. Other shifts in the training mode (e.g., from running to cycling) should not require new learning because the power exponents of those modes of exercise are similar enough for practical uses of the RPE scale.

Clinical Production of Perceived Force

It is a common practice in physical rehabilitation medicine to ask patients to produce muscular forces relative to a perceived maximal effort. Clinical judgments about treatment and outcome are based on the forces produced by the patient. Studies from psychophysics indicate that people should be able perform such forces accurately. In the first modern-day study of perceived force, magnitude estimation and production tasks were used to establish that perceived force during handgrip contractions grew exponentially, with power exponents ranging from 1.7 to 2.0 (Stevens and Mack 1959). Since that early research there have been few psychophysical studies of force production, but these have confirmed that perceived force grows according to a power function with the exponent ranging from about 1.4 to 1.7 during thumb opposition, handgrip, and leg or arm cranking on a cycle ergometer (see Borg 1982). These studies indicate that the perception of increments in muscular force grows exponentially, consistent with Stevens' power law.

Borg's range principle, stating that perceptual intensities of force for different people are approximately set equal at a subjective maximum, can be extended to predict that people who have had common experiences with resistance forces should be able to produce forces that represent equal proportions of their imagined maximal force. Studies have shown that the growth of percent perceived effort versus percent maximal force of voluntary opposition of the thumb, static and dynamic extension of the knee, and horizontal adduction of the shoulders during bench-pressing exercise is linear, with an exponent approximating 1.0 for the log-log plot of perceived versus actual relative force. Thus, perceived percent force production during horizontal shoulder adduction is directly proportional across a range of 25% to 75% voluntary maximal force (Jackson and Dishman 2000). Though people can produce actual forces that are linearly related to the desired forces, some people make large errors. This means that most patients

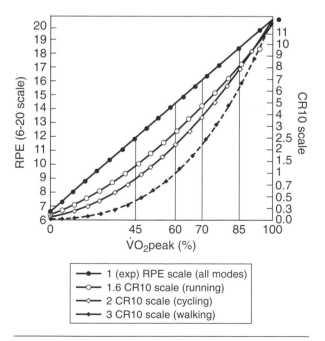

Figure 13.15 Category ratings of perceived exertion as they relate to physiological responses to different intensities and types of exercise.

Provided by J.B. Crabbe, the Exercise Psychology Laboratory, The University of Georgia.

asked to produce submaximal forces will perform at an acceptable level, but some will not. Those who overshoot the desired effort may increase their chance for a rehabilitation setback. Those who undershoot the desired effort may have their recovery rate decreased and recovery time increased.

Preferred Exertion

Prescribing exercise according to preferred exertion is a concept that may have important implications for increasing physical activity in the general public (Borg 1962). **Preferred exertion** is the level of exertion that is desirable to a person during exercise. Preferred intensity refers to the level of exercise a person chooses when he or she is allowed to "set the pace." Only a few studies of preferred exertion have been done, but reports on men indicate that they prefer to exercise at an intensity around 60% $\dot{V}O_2$peak corresponding to a category RPE of 13 ± 2, or "somewhat hard." Trained runners prefer a higher intensity of about 75% $\dot{V}O_2$peak and RPE of 9 to 12 (see Dishman 1994 for a review). So, it appears that most people prefer to exercise at an intensity around the thresholds for rapid onset of blood lactic acid and hyperventilation. For most individuals, this preferred intensity is adequate for improving cardiorespiratory fitness.

If people are allowed to exercise at an intensity that is preferable to them rather than at an intensity that is too easy or too hard, they may be more likely to continue to participate in exercise. A high level of strain during exercise may increase risks for musculoskeletal and orthopedic injuries that can lead to inactivity. If inactive people select, or are prescribed, an intensity that is perceived as very effortful, relative to their physiological responses, they may be less attracted to continued participation. Conversely, some individuals may prefer to exercise harder than recommended according to HR (King et al. 1991). Letting people exercise at their own pace could enhance comfort and enjoyment during exercise. However, it is not known what percentage of the population would prefer to exercise at an intensity too low for fitness (e.g., < 45-50% of capacity) or how many people who are at cardiovascular risk might prefer to exercise at a dangerously high intensity.

Exertional Symptoms

Compared with the evidence supporting the accuracy of RPE for estimating and producing exercise intensity, little is known about the usefulness of other subjective responses to exercise for prescribing and monitoring exercise intensity (Bayles et al. 1990). Though the use of self-report scales for angina pectoris and dyspnea is recommended by the ACSM (2000) and is common in exercise stress testing, the study and measurement of pain during and after exercise is an emerging area in exercise psychology (Borg 1998; Cook and Koltyn 2000; O'Connor and Cook 1999).

Summary

Gunnar Borg was the first to use a category rating scale that was valid for making interindividual comparisons of RPEs. This was based on the assumption of Borg's range principle, that all healthy people have the same perceptual range from which to make judgments of perceived exertion. Perceptions of exertion, when assessed using ratio scaling methods, follow a positively accelerating function as exercise intensity increases. Perceptions of exertion represent a gestalt, which is an integration of sensory signals from working muscles and noxious chemical stimulation plus respiratory/metabolic signals related to respiratory work and the relative metabolic strain of the exercise. In addition, psychological factors, such as our own memories and focus of attention, interact with these physiological signals, along with information from the external environment. It is only after the brain has integrated these signals that elaboration of the exercise occurs and a cognitive label can be provided to represent an overall feeling of exertion. The RPE scales can be used during exercise testing and prescription as a valid adjuvant to monitoring exercise intensity.

Suggested Readings

Borg, G.A. 1998. *Borg's perceived exertion and pain scales.* Champaign, IL: Human Kinetics.

Dishman, R.K. 1994. Prescribing exercise intensity for healthy adults using perceived exertion. *Medicine and Science in Sports and Exercise* 26 (9): 1087–1094.

Monahan, T. 1988. Perceived exertion: An old exercise tool finds new applications. *Physician and Sportsmedicine* 16: 174–179.

Noble, B.J., and R.J. Robertson. 1996. *Perceived exertion.* Champaign, IL: Human Kinetics.

Pandolf, K.B. 1983. Advances in the study and application of perceived exertion. *Exercise and Sport Sciences Reviews* 11: 118–158.

Snodgrass, J.G., G. Levy-Berger, and M. Hydon. 1985. *Human experimental psychology.* New York: Oxford University Press.

Web Sites

www.psych.yorku.ca/classics/Fechner/

www.semiophysics.com/menta10.htm

www.sosmath.com/algebra/logs/log4/log4.html

Glossary

5-HIAA—5-hydroxyindole acetic acid; a major metabolic breakdown product (metabolite) of serotonin (5-HT).

absolute intensity—Level of work expressed as a value that is the same for all people, for example, running at 6 mph.

accelerometer—Mechanical device that measures movement through use of transducers to record the acceleration of the body in one or more planes.

acetylcholine—Neurotransmitter substance at cholinergic synapses that causes cardiac inhibition, vasodilation, gastrointestinal peristalsis, and other parasympathetic effects; also acts in an excitatory manner between motor neurons and skeletal muscles.

actigraphy—Measurement of movement, acceleration, and deceleration in one plane.

active coping—Responses to perceived controllable stress that influence an outcome through mental or physical effort.

acute exercise—A single session of exercise; typically short, but can last for 4 h or more (e.g., a marathon).

adenosine—A purine nucleoside that has important roles in the reactions and regulation of metabolism and in the regulation of sleep in addition to inhibiting noradrenaline release from sympathetic nerve terminals and reducing adipose tissue sensitivity to noradrenaline.

adherence—Faithfully following a standard of behavior that has been established as part of a negotiated agreement; a person's continuation in an exercise program.

adrenal cortex—The outer covering of the adrenal gland, which is located adjacent to the kidney. Secretes glucocorticoid, mineralocorticoid, and sex hormones.

adrenal medulla—The inner core of the adrenal gland. Secretes epinephrine, norepinephrine, and enkephalins.

adrenaline—See *epinephrine*.

adrenergic—Relating to cells or fibers of the autonomic or central nervous system that use epinephrine as their neurotransmitter.

adrenocorticotropic hormone (ACTH)—A hormone released by the anterior lobe of the hypophysis (anterior pituitary); controls the production and release of hormones of the adrenal cortex.

aerobic fitness—The ability of the cardiorespiratory system to take up and use oxygen; the capacity to carry out activities that use large-muscle groups at moderate intensities, which permit the body to use oxygen for the production of energy and which can be sustained for more than a few minutes.

affect—Conscious expression of value given to a feeling state; general category including feelings, emotions, and mood as distinct from cognitions and behavior.

afferent—Referring to a neural axon that carries nerve impulses away from a sensory organ to the central nervous system.

allostasis—The ability to achieve stability through change, that is, adaptation to disruptions to homeostasis.

allostatic load—The long-term effects of the physiological response to stress, which include activation of the autonomic nervous system; the hypothalamic-pituitary-adrenal (HPA) axis; and the metabolic, cardiovascular, and immune systems.

alpha wave—Brain wave activity in the 8 to 12 Hz range, commonly described as relaxed wakefulness.

amygdala—A group of nuclei located in the limbic system; involved in the control of appropriate behavior for social situations, emotional memory, and the generation of anger and fear.

analogue model—A set of properties that represents the actual set of properties of an idea or event using transformation rules, such as in maps and graphs; for example, the study of normal behavior or psychological function as a proxy for the study of abnormal behavior or mental disorder.

antecedents—Events, whether internal (i.e., thoughts and affect) or external, that precede a target behavior; can be temporally close to the behavior (proximal) or can occur some time before the behavior (distal).

anxiety—An emotional response to perceived threat. Consists of feelings of tension, apprehension, and nervousness; unpleasant thoughts or worries; and physiological changes.

anxiety disorder—A mental illness characterized by apprehension or worry that is accompanied by restlessness, muscular tension, elevated heart rate, and breathlessness. Anxiety disorders include phobias, panic disorders, obsessive-compulsive disorders, and generalized anxiety disorder.

anxiolytic—Having the effect of decreasing anxiety.

arousal—A unidimensional state of physiological activation that runs on a continuum from sleep to extreme activation.

attitude— An evaluation of and reaction to an object, person, event, or idea; includes a cognitive, affective, and behavioral component.

augmenters—Individuals who consistently overestimate psychophysical stimuli while making judgments about size.

autonomic nervous system—Part of the peripheral nervous system that innervates smooth muscle, cardiac muscle, and glands; composed of the sympathetic, parasympathetic, and enteric divisions.

basal ganglia—Part of the telencephalon that consists of the corpus striatum and cell groups associated with the corpus striatum, such as the subthalamic nucleus and substantia nigra.

behavioral intention—What one aims to do or accomplish; intention is thought of in degrees (i.e., 90% likely that I will do something) rather than dichotomously (i.e., I will or I won't do something).

behavioral management—Intervention approach that targets changes in behavior through stimulus control, reinforcement control, contracting, and other strategies based on behaviorism and cognitive behaviorism.

behavioral neuroscience and comparative psychology—Subdisciplines of psychology that involve the study of perception and learning, neuroscience, cognitive psychology, and comparative psychology; the application of neural events to study of the brain and behavior.

behaviorism—A subdiscipline of psychology that developed out of learning theory to describe the associations between observable stimulus, response, and outcome as the basis for understanding behavior, with no role for personality or mental states for predicting and describing behavior.

beliefs—Expectations, convictions, or opinions.

beta-endorphin—Endogenous opioid peptide secreted by the anterior pituitary along with adrenocorticotropic hormone in response to stress.

bias—The systematic departure of results from the correct values as a consequence of errors in design or investigational technique; the effects of any factor that the researcher did not expect to influence the outcome (dependent variable).

biological psychology—Subdiscipline of psychology in which methods of natural science, such as those in physiology, endocrinology, pharmacology, and molecular biology, are applied to the study of the brain and behavior.

biopsychosocial model of disease—A model of disease introduced by George Engel in 1977 that proposes multicausal factors in health and disease, emphasizing the interaction of biological, psychological, and social factors.

brainstem—Continuous extension of the spinal cord upward into the cranial cavity; consists of the medulla, pons, and cerebellum (rhombencephalon) and midbrain (mesencephalon).

Cannon-Bard theory—Theory of emotion that describes a common physiological response, regardless of the type of emotion, involving sympathetic activation to prepare the body for flight or fight; when confronted with a stimulus, the brain decides the appropriate response to a stimulus, and the corresponding emotional response and the physiological activation occur simultaneously.

case-control design—Retrospective design in which healthy controls are matched with sick individuals ("cases"), often from the same setting, on age, gender, and race. Comparisons are made between the groups on past exposure to potential risk factors for the disease.

catecholamines—Class of synaptic transmitters that contain a single amine group (monoamines), including dopamine, norepinephrine, and epinephrine.

cerebellum—Portion of the brain that coordinates voluntary movement and adjusts the speed, force, and other factors involved during a period of muscular activity; organizes motor impulses before they are transferred to the muscles.

chronic exercise—Bouts of exercise that are repeated on a fairly regular basis over a period of time; exercise training or regular exercise that is defined by the type of activity, intensity, duration, frequency per week, and time period (e.g., weeks, months).

classical conditioning—Form of behavior modification in which the stimulus for a reflexive response (unconditioned stimulus) is paired repeatedly with a neutral stimulus until the neutral stimulus (now the conditioned stimulus) elicits the response in the absence of the unconditioned stimulus.

cognition—Mental process of knowing, including aspects such as awareness, perception, reasoning, and judgment.

cognitive behavior modification—Use of principles from learning theory to modify the cognitions and behaviors related to a behavior that is to be changed.

cognitive behaviorism—Theory of human behavior based on interactive dualism in that behavior is seen as an outcome of cognition, and changes in cognition are seen as determinants of behavior.

cognitive restructuring—Behavior change strategy based on cognitive behaviorism in which negative or faulty thoughts are modified or replaced with positive thoughts or thoughts that enable or enhance the behavior change process.

compliance—Following a prescribed standard of behavior, usually related to immediate and short-term health advice to alleviate symptoms, such as taking a specific regimen of medications; a sense of coercive obedience.

computerized axial tomogram (CAT scan, CT scan)—Method using X-ray absorption to examine brain structure in humans.

conditioned stimulus—A previously neutral stimulus that has been paired repeatedly with an unconditioned stimulus and now elicits the target conditioned response in the absence of the unconditioned stimulus.

confounder—An extraneous factor that is not a consequence of exposure or an experimental manipulation. A confounding variable exerts an effect on the outcome such that there is a distortion in a study's effects. Confounders are determinants or correlates of the outcome under study and are unequally distributed among the exposed and unexposed individuals, making it difficult or impossible to interpret the relations among the other variables.

consequence—Abstract or concrete event that follows a target behavior; temporally close (proximal) to or far (distal) from the behavior; can be reinforcing and thus increase the frequency of the target behavior, or punishing and thus decrease the frequency of the target behavior.

construct—An abstract idea that was developed (constructed) to describe the relationship among phenomena or for other research purposes; exists theoretically but is not directly observable.

contingency contract—Behavior change strategy in which an individual forms a contract with another person detailing rewards and punishments that are contingent (depend) on the performance or nonperformance of a target behavior.

control group—In experimental research, the group that does not experience, for the sake of comparison, the treatment the researcher is interested in studying.

convergent validity—Validity as indicated by the overlap between tests or instruments that are presumed to measure the same variable; related to concurrent validity, which is indicated by the correlation between one instrument and another instrument that measures the same construct and is assumed to be valid.

corpus striatum—Part of the basal ganglia that consists of the globus pallidus and the striatum, which is further divided into the caudate nucleus and the putamen.

corticotropin-releasing hormone (CRH)—Hormone released by the parvicellular area of the paraventricular nucleus of the anterior hypothalamus; controls the diurnal rhythms of adrenocorticotropic hormone release.

cortisol—A steroid hormone that is the major glucocorticoid secreted by the adrenal cortex; plays a primary role in the stress response and central nervous dysregulation associated with mood disorders; also involved in stimulation of formation and storage of glycogen and maintenance of blood glucose.

cosmology—Study of the physical universe considered as a totality of phenomena in time and space.

cranial nerves—Twelve pairs of sensory and motor nerves that are connected directly to the brain.

cross-sectional design—Research plan in which data from a single point in time are collected and participants are classified on predictor (independent) and outcome (dependent) variables.

cross-stressor adaptation hypothesis—The proposal that physiological adaptations to the repeated stress of exercise will result in adaptations to the physiological response to mental stress.

decisional balance—One of the three components of the transtheoretical model of behavior change (stages of change model) that are proposed to affect behavior change; the differences between the pros, or perceived benefits, of the target behavior and the cons, or the perceived costs.

dependent variable—The variable in a study whose values are predicted by the independent (predictor) variable, or that "depend" on another variable; outcome variable.

depletion hypothesis—See *monoamine depletion hypothesis.*

determinant—In exercise behavior research, a variable that has an established reproducible association or predictive relationship with an outcome variable.

diencephalon—The posterior part of the forebrain; major structures are the thalamus and the hypothalamus.

discipline—A branch of knowledge or teaching.

discriminative stimulus—A stimulus that is paired with a reinforcing stimulus during operant conditioning; provides information about the consequences of a response.

distal—Referring to an outcome or event that is temporally distant from the target behavior.

distraction hypothesis—Explanation for the beneficial psychological effects of exercise based on "time-out" from worrisome thoughts and daily stressors during exercise.

diurnal—Referring to a pattern that repeats once every 24 h.

divergent validity—The validity of a measure indicated by the lack of association with another measure that it should not be related to if it is valid; the mirror image of convergent validity.

dopamine—Biogenic amine and neurotransmitter that is the precursor for norepinephrine and epinephrine.

down-regulation—Development of a tolerance after repeated administration of a pharmacologically or physiologically active substance, or in response to excessively high levels of a substance; often characterized by an initial decrease in affinity of receptors for the substance and a subsequent decrease in the number of receptors.

dualism—The philosophical view that the world consists of or is explicable as two fundamental entities, such as mind and matter; the perspective that the mind and body function separately, without interchange.

dysregulation—Disruption in self-regulation.

dysthymia—Mild, chronic form of major depression.

ecological validity—A type of external validity that refers to how well the measurement taken in an experiment generalizes to non-laboratory conditions, or how well a finding from research with one group generalizes to another group.

effect size—Measure of an association or the strength of a relationship; the difference in the outcome for the average subject who received the treatment from that for the average subject who did not; broadly, any measure of association or strength of a relationship, often thought of as an indication of practical significance.

efferent—Referring to a neural axon that carries nerve impulses from the central nervous system to the muscles and glands.

effectiveness—The ability of an intervention or method to work in other settings, to be practically applied outside of a laboratory setting; level of ecological validity.

efficacy—The ability of an intervention or method to do what it was intended to do.

ego orientation—A motivational orientation in which success is seen through comparison of performance to that of others or in terms of an external standard.

electroencephalography (EEG)—The recording of gross electrical activity of the brain using large electrodes placed on the scalp in a standardized pattern.

electromyography (EMG)—The recording of the gross electrical activity of muscle contraction.

electrophysiology—Technique to measure neural activity in the brain; electrodes are positioned in the brain cortex or in specific regions of brain neurons to record electrical potentials during behavior or in response to stress.

emotion—An intense mental state that arises subjectively rather than through conscious effort and is accompanied by physiological changes related to autonomic activation; brief responses of negative or positive feelings.

empirical research—Data-based research that can be verified by observation or experience.

endocrine—Referring to glands that secrete hormones and other biochemicals to the interior of the body.

endogenous—Produced within the body.

endorphin—Endogenous opioid peptide that can act as a neurotransmitter, neuromodulator, and hormone.

endorphin hypothesis—Proposition that the mood enhancement associated with exercise is due to actions of endorphins, which are secreted during exercise.

enkephalin—One of three kinds of endogenous opioids, which are a class of compounds that exert an effect like that of opium, such as reduced pain sensitivity.

enteric system—The branch of the autonomic nervous system that regulates the intestines.

epidemiology—The study of the distribution and determinants of health-related states and events in a population and the application of this study to the control of health problems.

epinephrine (Epi)—Also known as adrenaline, a compound that acts as a hormone secreted by the adrenal medulla and as a neurotransmitter; post-ganglionic adrenergic mediator acting as a sympathomimetic substance; plays an important role in preparing for responding to stress.

exercise—A subset of physical activity consisting of planned, structured, repetitive bodily movements with the purpose of improving or maintaining one or more components of physical fitness or health.

exercise adoption—Behavioral and cognitive components of beginning regular, purposeful, structured physical activity; includes some degree of psychological commitment.

exercise prescription—Recommendation for a specific exercise mode, intensity, duration, and frequency per week to meet specific goals.

exercise psychology—The interdisciplinary field of study of the psychobiological, behavioral, and social factors in exercise and physical activity settings.

experimental design—The art of planning and executing an experiment in which the researcher has some control over the conditions in which the study takes place and the independent variable(s).

face validity—Logical or conceptual validity; according to experts, the extent to which the measurement instrument seems to make sense.

factor analysis—Statistical analysis used to determine whether the structure of a test seems consistent with the construct it purports to measure; analysis to find patterns in the variations among several variables to see if large numbers of variables can be grouped into "factors" that are conceptually or statistically related.

feeling—Subjective experience that can be overt or covert.

feeling state—Bodily sensations, cognitive appraisals, actual or potential instrumental responses, or some combination of these responses.

field theory—Post-Freudian theory of personality developed by Kurt Lewin proposing that behavior is determined by the person and his or her environment; takes into account contemporary interrelations and interconnections.

functional MRI (fMRI)—Method to determine brain activity that applies the magnetic resonance principle for the purpose of finding out which parts of the brain are activated by various types of physical sensations or motor activity.

galanin—Amino acid peptide neurotransmitter that hyperpolarizes noradrenergic neurons and inhibits locus coeruleus firing in vitro.

galvanic skin response—Change in the electrical resistance of the skin, or in its converse, conduction, through autonomic activation; measured by placing two electrodes on the skin and recording the changes in skin conductance/resistance in the tissue path between them.

gamma-aminobutyric acid (GABA)—Major inhibitory transmitter in the nervous system.

ganglion (plural: **ganglia**)—Aggregation of nerve cell bodies located in the peripheral nervous system.

general adaptation syndrome (GAS)—Hans Selye's theory that many diseases are "diseases of adaptation" and develop because of insufficient, excessive, or poorly regulated responses to environmental stressors; likewise, the GAS could be beneficially altered by experiences that could enhance resistance to psychosomatic and neurotic diseases.

generalized anxiety disorder (GAD)—Disorder characterized by excessive or pathologic worry about multiple concerns; exaggerated vigilance; and somatic symptoms of stress and anxiety, such as muscular tension.

genotype—The sum of all the genetic information in an organism.

gestalt—A configuration or pattern of elements so unified as a whole that its properties cannot be derived from a simple summation of its parts; the whole is more than the sum of its parts.

glucocorticoid—Class of hormones that affect carbohydrate metabolism; released by the adrenal cortex, for example, in response to stress.

glutamate (glutamic acid)—An amino acid that is a small-molecule, rapidly acting neurotransmitter—the major excitatory transmitter in the central nervous system.

goal setting—Process by which specific plans are established in order to achieve a desired outcome.

halo effect—An effect that occurs when the researcher ascribes certain characteristics to a subject based on other known characteristics, resulting in a bias on the part of the researcher (experimenter expectancy effect).

Hawthorne effect—Tendency for individuals in a research study to change simply because they are being studied.

health education—Programs and strategies based on a medical model that target behaviors related to the promotion of health; educational programs, mass media campaigns.

health psychology—The subdomain of psychology that is devoted to understanding the psychological influences on and consequences of health and illness, as well as the impact of health policy and health interventions.

health-related physical fitness—Components of physical fitness that have been empirically associated with overall health and ability to perform daily tasks and activities; components include cardiorespiratory fitness; body composition; flexibility; muscular strength and endurance; and metabolic variables, such as glucose tolerance.

heart rate variability—Variability described by the standard deviation of intervals between successive R waves of the cardiac cycle; provides index of modulation of heart rate by the autonomic nervous system.

hemispheric asymmetry—Differences in neural circuits between left and right hemispheres of the brain.

high-risk situation—Any situation that challenges confidence in one's ability to maintain a positive health behavior or to abstain from an unhealthy behavior.

hippocampus—Portion of the limbic system thought to be important in learning and memory.

homeostasis—The ability or tendency of an organism or a cell to maintain internal equilibrium by adjusting its physiological processes; the tendency for an internal environment to remain constant.

homologous—Referring to an animal model of disease that meets the standards of predictive validity and isomorphism and also has the same etiology as does the human disease.

hypothalamic-pituitary-adrenal axis (HPA axis)—The hypothalamus, pituitary, and the adrenal cortex.

hypothalamus—Part of the diencephalon; controls vegetative functions, regulates hormone balance, and plays a role in emotional behavior.

iconic model—Two- or three-dimensional model that looks similar to what it represents but is larger or smaller. Examples include pictures, sculptures, holograms, and virtual realities.

idealism—A philosophical theory contending that objective reality is actually perception and that it consists of ideas; that the essential nature of reality lies in consciousness.

immunocytochemistry—The study of cell components by immunologic methods, such as the use of fluorescent antibodies.

in situ—Referring to a technique to examine processes inside a cell or organism in its original, natural setting.

in situ hybridization histochemistry—A technique that uses a labeled, complementary single-strand of DNA to detect steady state levels of messenger RNA in a cell that is fixed in its natural position in a tissue.

in vitro—Occurring "in glass"; usually with reference to biological testing done outside the body, as in a laboratory dish.

in vivo—Within a living body, usually with reference to testing done with intact live subjects.

incidence—The number of new cases of a disease or condition divided by the number of people exposed over a specified period of time.

independent variable—A variable that is manipulated by the researcher with the idea that it will have an effect on another variable (dependent variable); variable that can be used to explain or predict the values of another variable.

indolamines—Class of biogenic amines that includes serotonin and melatonin.

intensity—The amount of work performed during exercise; expressed as an absolute quantity (e.g., watts), or relative to maximal capacity (e.g., 70% of maximal aerobic capacity), or as perception of effort (rating of perceived exertion of 13 on Borg scale).

intention—See *behavioral intention*.

isomorphic—Referring to an animal model of disease that evokes the same features as the human disease, which abate after administration of drugs that are clinically useful in humans; the features generated may not have the same etiology or course of development as in the human disease.

James-Lange theory—Theory of emotion proposing that emotions result from the evaluation of different physiological responses; different emotions have different constellations of physiological responses, and perception of these responses results in the corresponding emotion—thus bodily responses during emotion are the source of the emotional response.

just noticeable difference (j.n.d.)—Smallest amount of change in the intensity of a stimulus required for the change to be perceived.

latency—Length of time between the application of a stimulus and the response.

ligand—A molecule that binds to another, usually larger, molecule; examples include a hormone or neurotransmitter binding to a receptor.

Likert scaling—Questionnaire format in which respondents are given statements and are asked to respond to each statement by indicating how they relate to it by choosing among several different qualifiers anchored around a neutral point by two extreme responses (e.g., "strongly agree" and "strongly disagree"); most widely used type of attitude scale in the social sciences.

limbic system—Heterogeneous array of brain nuclei, located near the edge of the medial wall of the cerebral hemisphere, that innervate each other; includes the hippocampus, amygdala, and gyrus fornicatus; influences endocrine systems, as well as emotion and learning.

locus coeruleus (LC)—Located in the pons, the major nucleus for the production of norepinephrine; has a major role in inhibition of spontaneous firing in areas of the brain to which it projects.

magnetic resonance imaging (MRI)—Method to measure structural details of a living brain using radio waves and a strong magnetic field.

magnitude estimation—Presenting a standard stimulus (modulus), such as a 10 lb weight, to someone and asking him or her to label perception of sensation (e.g., heaviness or force) with any number; then asking the individual to assign a numerical value to differing stimuli (e.g., weights) presented in random order in reference to the rating assigned to the modulus.

magnitude production—Presenting a standard stimulus (modulus) to someone and asking him or her to produce a response or choose a stimulus that is proportional to a given magnitude (e.g., twice as heavy) of the stimulus.

maintenance—Sustaining a regular exercise program for a specific period of time, usually at least six months.

major depression—One of two major categories of mood disorders (the other being manic-depressive disorder) characterized by depressed mood or loss of interest or pleasure and other behavioral and psychological symptoms.

manic-depressive disorder—One of two major categories of mood disorders (the other being major depression) characterized by periods of depression alternating with periods of elevated mood and associated behavior.

mastery hypothesis—Explanation of enhanced mood, self-efficacy, and self-esteem based on the positive consequences of the successful completion of an important task, such as exercise.

materialism—The philosophical theory that material objects are the only reality, and that thoughts and feelings can be explained through states of and changes in matter and physical phenomena.

maximal aerobic capacity—The maximal amount of oxygen the body can take up and use.

mediated approach—Interventions that use some type of media or combinations of media (e.g., booklets).

mediator—Variable that transmits the effects of another variable (predictor) on the outcome.

medulla—Part of the brainstem that marks the transition from the spinal cord to the brainstem; contains motor and sensory nerves; dorsal surface of its upper half forms the floor of the fourth ventricle.

melatonin—Hormone that is released by the pineal gland in a true circadian rhythm; involved in the sleep-wake cycle.

messenger ribonucleic acid (mRNA)—Messenger or template RNA; RNA produced by transcription that reflects the exact nucleoside sequence of the genetically active DNA; carries the code for a particular protein from the nuclear DNA to a ribosome in the cytoplasm where protein is made in amino-acid sequences specified by the mRNA.

MET—Metabolic equivalent; ratio of energy expended in kilocalories divided by resting energy expenditure in kilocalories, either measured or estimated from body size; one MET is 3.5 ml/kg/min.

meta-analysis—Quantitative procedure for summarizing the effects of a number of research studies on a common topic.

method of adjustment—Technique in which a stimulus having a standard, objectively measured intensity is presented along with a comparison stimulus that is to be adjusted until it is perceived to be of the same intensity as the standard stimulus.

method of constant stimuli—Presentation of a standard stimulus and a comparison stimulus, with the task to determine whether the comparison stimulus is perceived and/or whether it is the same as or different from the standard stimulus.

method of limits—Technique used to determine the lower and upper thresholds for perception by recording judgments of magnitude of stimuli that are presented in a series across a range of intensities in ascending and descending orders.

MHPG—3-Methoxy-4-Hydroxyphenyglycol; the major metabolic breakdown product (metabolite) of norepinephrine that is secreted in the urine.

microdialysis—Method to determine extracellular levels of a substance through dialysis, which is the separation of molecules of different sizes through use of an artificial membrane that is permeable to only some molecules.

midbrain—Also known as the mesencephalon; forms the top of the brainstem and includes the reticular formation, substantia nigra, and red nucleus.

model—A generalized, simplifying representation of some aspect(s) of living and nonliving systems; models should be considered provisional and subject to change, improvement, and eventual replacement.

moderator—A variable that influences the relationship between two other variables; influences how an intervention or mediator affects the outcome.

monism—The philosophical view that material and immaterial matter are but different manifestations of one underlying phenomenon; mind exists only by the function of the body.

monoamine depletion hypothesis—Theory that depression is caused by a deficiency of norepinephrine at the central adrenergic receptors and/or a deficiency of serotonin, and that mania results from excessive norepinephrine.

monoamine dysregulation hypothesis—Theory that depression is the result of a disruption in the noradrenergic and serotonergic systems' self-regulating ability and overstimulation of neural centers such as the prefrontal cortex, amygdala, hippocampus, and periventricular gray; major proposed site of dysregulation is the locus coeruleus (LC).

mood—Type of affective state that is accompanied by anticipation, even unconscious, of pleasure or pain; moods can last less than a minute or for days.

motivated response distortion—See *social desirability responding*.

muscle dysmorphia—Pathological preoccupation with muscularity that can be found in both men and women.

muscle sense—Sensations arising from muscles and related structures as a result of changes in posture and locomotion.

negative feedback—Output that inhibits the activity of an initial input.

neocortex—The relatively recently evolved portion of the cerebral cortex that is composed of layers of nerve cells arranged in six layers; characterized by elaborate folding of tissue.

neurobiology—The study of the biological processes of the brain; areas of study include anatomy, physiology, and pathology of the nervous system.

neuroimaging—Methods to measure brain activity using techniques such as X-ray and computer technology (e.g., CATs, MRI).

neuropeptide Y (NPY)—Amino acid peptide that inhibits the locus coeruleus from firing in vitro, providing feedback inhibition to locus coeruleus neurons.

neurotransmitter—Any specific chemical agent that is released by the presynaptic cell, upon excitation, and crosses the synapse to stimulate, inhibit, or modify the postsynaptic cell; serves as the basis of communication between neurons.

noradrenergic—Relating to cells or fibers of the autonomic or central nervous system that use norepinephrine as their neurotransmitter.

norepinephrine (NE)—A neurotransmitter, also known as noradrenaline, that is the post-ganglionic adrenergic mediator. It is also produced in the adrenal medulla and centrally in the locus coeruleus; principal effects are excitatory.

nucleus (plural: **nuclei**)—A collection of neural cell bodies located within the brain.

obsessive-compulsive disorder (OCD)—Recurrent and persistent unwanted idea, thought, or impulse to carry out an unwanted act that the individual cannot voluntarily suppress; typified by repetitive acts or rituals to relieve anxiety.

ontology—The branch of philosophy that deals with the nature of being.

operant conditioning—A type of behavior modification in which a reinforcing or punishing event is paired with a voluntary behavior to change the frequency with which the behavior occurs; the goal is to change the rate of responding.

orthogonal—Referring to variables that are uncorrelated, or unrelated to each other.

outcome expectation—The anticipated results of an event or of engaging in a specific behavior.

outcome value—The reinforcement or incentive value of an expected outcome; can be something individuals want to obtain or avoid.

panic disorder—Repeated episodes of intense fear that strike abruptly and without obvious cause. Predominant symptoms include heart palpitations, breathing distress, tingling sensations, and fear of dying.

parasympathetic nervous system—One of three divisions of the autonomic nervous system; arises from the cranial nerves and the sacral portions of the spinal cord; primarily involved in energy conservation.

perceived behavioral control—The degree to which an individual believes he or she is able to have an effect on a specific outcome; ranges on a continuum from no control to total control.

perceived exertion—The subjective judgment of strain or effort during physical activity; a perception of quantity more than of quality of sensations.

phenomenology—The study of the expression of subjective experience by individuals; concern with the description of experience.

phobia—An obsessive, persistent, and unrealistic fear of an external situation or object that is out of proportion of the actual threat or danger.

physical activity—"Any bodily movement produced by skeletal muscles that results in energy expenditure" (Caspersen, Powell, and Christenson, 1985).

physical fitness—The capacity to meet successfully the present and potential physical challenges of life; a set of attributes that people have or achieve that relate to the ability to perform physical activity, such as muscular strength, cardiorespiratory capacity, and agility.

placebo—A treatment given to a control group in experimental research that is meant to have no effect; used in comparison to the treatment, or independent variable, that is being tested.

placebo effect—Changes that can not be attributed to a treatment, that are due instead to subjects' erroneous beliefs that they received an effective treatment.

polysomnography—Simultaneous measurement of multiple physiological indicators of sleep stages, such as brain waves, respiration, and muscle and chin movements to detect rapid eye movement.

pons—A part of the brainstem that wraps around the base of the cerebellum; contains the locus coeruleus, the major nuclei in the brain producing norepinephrine.

positron emission tomography (PET)—Method using radioactive chemicals to measure the dynamic activity of a living brain by detecting positrons emitted by radioactive glucose or other metabolic analog.

posttraumatic stress disorder—Anxiety and behavioral disturbances that develop within the first month after exposure to an extreme trauma.

predictive design—Research plan whose goal is to explain the values of a variable (e.g., disease) by using the values of one or more other variables; disease-free subjects are grouped according to exposure to variable(s) suspected to influence disease occurrence and are then evaluated over time to determine disease in exposed and unexposed groups.

predictive model—An animal model that includes specific signs or behaviors that can be reliably changed by drugs known to have clinical efficacy in humans.

preferred exertion—The level of exertion that someone is motivated to endure.

prevalence—The number of existing cases of a disease or condition divided by the total population at a point in time. Prevalence is used to measure the burden of the disease and to plan for the implementation of services.

processes of change—One of the three components of the transtheoretical model of behavior change that is said to explain behavior change; consists of 10 covert and overt activities that are used to change thinking, affect, behavior, or relationships.

proopiomelanocorticotropin (POMC)—Precursor peptide found predominately in the anterior pituitary from which the endogenous opioid β-endorphin and adrenocorticotropic hormone (ACTH) are derived.

prostaglandin—Physiologically active substance present in many tissues, with effects such as vasodilation, vasoconstriction, stimulation of intestinal or bronchial smooth muscle, uterine stimulation, and antagonism to hormones influencing lipid metabolism.

proximal—Referring to an outcome or event that is temporally close to the target behavior.

psychology—A scientific discipline concerned with the study and application of principles of behavior and mental processes in humans and other animals in their interaction with the environment; areas of study include processes of sense perception, thinking, learning, cognition, emotions and motivations, personality, abnormal behavior, interactions between individuals, and interactions with the environment.

psychometrics—The psychological theory and measurement of psychological variables; includes the design, administration, and interpretation of quantitative tests for the measurement of psychological variables.

psychophysics—The study of psychological judgments (sensations and perceptions) of physical stimuli using standardized methods to manipulate physical stimuli and to measure the perceptual response to the stimuli; the measurement of judgments people make about their physical environment.

punishment—Consequences of a specific behavior that decrease the frequency of the behavior.

randomized controlled trial—Research with large populations to test the associations between variables found in epidemiological or small laboratory experiments; includes representative population and treatment and control groups matched with respect to characteristics thought to affect outcome.

raphe nuclei—The major nuclei for the production of serotonin; located in the center line of the brainstem.

rapid eye movement (REM) sleep—Portion of sleep cycle characterized by dreaming, rapid eye movement, and alert EEG pattern; predominates during last one-third of the night's sleep.

receptor—A structural protein molecule, usually on the cell surface or within the cytoplasm, that combines with a specific factor, such as a hormone or neurotransmitter; the interaction of the factor and the receptor results in a change in cell function.

reciprocal determinism—Construct that is the central concept of causation for social cognitive theory; describes the bidirectional interacting influence of determinants of behavior; a mutually influencing relationship among two or more variables.

reducers—Individuals who consistently underestimate stimuli while making judgments.

referred appraisal—External standard we apply to ourselves that is based on how we think significant others perceive us.

reinforcement—Consequences of a target behavior that increase the frequency of the behavior.

reinforcement control—Behavior change strategy that manipulates the consequences of the target behavior to increase the frequency of the behavior.

reinforcing stimulus—Stimulus that is capable of eliciting a reflexive response (e.g., the smell of bread baking can be a reinforcing stimulus that will elicit salivation).

relapse prevention—Set of strategies designed to help keep people from returning to undesired behavior after successful behavior modification.

relative intensity—The work rate expressed in relation to maximal intensity, aerobic capacity, or workload.

relative risk—The ratio of the rates of occurrence of disease in two groups.

reliability—Characteristic of a measure that includes precision, accuracy, and stability across time; freedom from measurement or random error.

REM sleep—See *rapid eye movement sleep.*

reticular formation—Network of nerves that extends from the medulla through the thalamus; involved in the sleep-wake cycle and forebrain arousal.

RNA—Ribonucleic acid; nucleic acids that are associated with the control of cellular chemical activities.

Rosenthal effect—Also known as the self-fulfilling prophecy or the Pygmalion effect; participant is motivated to meet the expectations that the investigator has communicated about the participant's attributes or abilities.

scaling—The assignment of objects to numbers according to a rule; the development of an instrument to assign objects or statements to a response scale (numbers) according to specific rules; creating a scale by grouping items into a logical sequence.

Schachter's theory of emotion—Proposes that emotions are the result of the interaction between physiological activation and cognitive interpretation of a nonspecific arousal; cognitive interpretation (appraisal) of the context and intensity of the autonomic response leads to the subjective experience of a particular emotion.

self-concept—Organized configuration of perceptions about one's attributes and qualities that are within conscious awareness.

self-efficacy—Perception of one's ability to carry out behavior with known outcome; expectations of personal mastery regarding initiation and persistence of behavior.

self-enhancement hypothesis—View that behavioral choices are made based on evaluation of outcome expectations with respect to potential for enhanced feelings of competence and esteem.

self-esteem—Evaluation of the self-concept and feelings associated with that evaluation.

self-monitoring—Actions taken by the individual to assess the antecedents, consequences, and characteristics of attempts to engage in or avoid a target behavior.

self-motivation—Internal factor that arouses, directs, and integrates a person's behavior; energizing condition that causes a person to internalize an evaluation of his or her own performance and then to seek to meet these standards; behavioral tendency to persevere independent of situational reinforcements.

self-reflection—Ability to symbolize that enables individuals to anticipate and plan for future events and actions.

self-regulation—Ways in which people modify their own behavior; based on the assumption that behavior is under the direct control of the individual and is guided by internalized standards whose achievement will elicit positive self-evaluation.

self-schemata—Cognitive structure of the self and personal attributes that serves to guide selection, retrieval, and storage of information about the self.

sensitivity—The ability of a test to detect a disease or attribute; a test with high sensitivity will not miss the disease or condition if it is present.

serotonin—Also known as 5-HT, a synaptic transmitter classified as an indolamine that is produced and secreted by the raphe nuclei; general suppressor of neural gain.

skill-related physical fitness—Components of physical fitness that are related to the ability to take part in various activities and sports.

slow-wave sleep (SWS)—Sleep stages 3 and 4 combined; characterized by delta waves; stage when people are hardest to awaken; occurs during about 20% of a night's sleep and predominates during first one-third of a night's sleep.

social cognitive theory—Theory of human behavior, evolved from social learning theory, in which behavior is a function of social cognitions; key concept is triadic reciprocality.

social desirability responding—Tendency for people to respond in ways they perceive to conform to socially desirable images of themselves.

social psychology—Subdiscipline of psychology concerned with the effects of various social environments on the individual; includes the study of attitude measurement and change, group dynamics, social learning and personality, social cognition, aggression, and self-perception.

specificity—The ability of a test to discriminate; a test with high specificity will not incorrectly indicate the presence of the disease or condition if it is not present.

spinal cord—Part of the central nervous system containing neural circuits that control reflexive function, bring sensory information from the periphery to the brain, and carry motor signals to the periphery.

spinal nerves—Sensory and motor pathways in 31 pairs that join the spinal cord at regularly spaced intervals. Sensory information is carried from the periphery to the spinal cord, and motor impulses are transmitted from the spinal cord to muscles.

state anxiety—The immediate response to a conscious or unconscious threat; has somatic and cognitive symptoms that include elevated heart rate, muscle tension, and visceral motility, as well as transient feelings of lack of control, low confidence, and uncertainty.

stimulus control—Strategies to change the frequency of a target behavior by modifying the antecedents of the behavior.

strain—The deformation, distortion, or tension in an object as a result of stress.

stress—The way in which load impinges on a physical object; an imbalance in physiological systems that activates physiological and behavioral responses to restore balance, or homeostasis.

stressor—A force that acts on a biological system to cause stress, an imbalance, or disruption in homeostasis.

striatum—Area of the brain around the lateral ventricle that includes the caudate nucleus and putamen; striatum and the globus pallidus or pallidum form the corpus striatum.

sympathetic medullary system—System consisting of the sympathetic nervous system and the adrenal medulla; actions are associated with the stress response.

sympathetic nervous system—One of three divisions of the autonomic nervous system; arises from the thoracic and lumbar portions of the spinal cord; primarily involved in activities that require energy expenditure.

task orientation—A motivational orientation in which success is seen in terms of personal mastery and self-improvement.

telencephalon—Part of the forebrain; major structures are the neocortex, basal ganglia, and the limbic system.

temperament—Mainly stable, core component of personality that predisposes individuals to varying degrees of emotional responsiveness and changing moods.

thalamus—Located in the diencephalon; composed of sensory relay nuclei with bidirectional connections with many areas in the cerebral cortex.

theory—Formulation of underlying principles of certain observed phenomena that have been verified to some degree and are used to explain and predict; symbolic model used to guide the design, execution, and interpretation of research.

thermogenic hypothesis—Perspective that attributes the enhanced mood associated with exercise to increased body temperature.

thyroid-stimulating hormone—Secreted by the anterior hypothalamus; causes the anterior pituitary to release thyrotropic hormone, which stimulates the thyroid gland to secrete thyroxin.

trait—The tendency to respond to an internal or external event with a particular mood state; traits are relatively consistent over time, but changes in traits are also possible.

trait anxiety—Chronically generalized anxiety that predisposes someone to appraise events as threatening.

transcription—Transfer of genetic code information from one kind of nucleic acid to another; process by which mRNA forms bases that are complementary to a strand of DNA.

translation—Process directed by messenger RNA (mRNA) in which amino acids are linked together to form a protein molecule; the specificity of the synthesis is controlled by the base sequences of the mRNA.

transtheoretical model of behavior change—A dynamic model of intentional behavior change that is based on the stages and processes individuals go through to bring about long-term behavior change; also know as *stage of change model*.

triadic reciprocality—A key element of social cognitive theory, the concept that characteristics of the person, environment, and behavior are mutually influencing.

unconditioned stimulus—A stimulus that automatically elicits a response that is typically reflexive.

vagal tone—Baseline level of parasympathetic activation of the vagus nerve.

Bibliography

Aarts, H., T. Paulussen, and H. Schaalma. 1997. Physical exercise habit: On the conceptualization and formation of habitual health behaviors. *Health Education Research* 12: 363–374.

Acevedo, B.O., D.A. Dzewaltowski, K.A. Kubitz, and R.R. Kraemer. 1999. Effects of a proposed challenge on effort sense and cardiorespiratory responses during exercise. *Medicine and Science in Sports and Exercise* 31: 1460–1465.

Ainsworth, B.E., W.L. Haskell, A.S. Leon, D.R. Jacobs, Jr., H.J. Montoye, J.F. Sallis, and R.S. Paffenbarger, Jr. 1993. Compendium of physical activities: Classification of energy costs of human physical activities. *Medicine and Science in Sports and Exercise* 25 (1): 71–80.

Ajzen, I. 1988. *Attitudes, personality and behavior.* Chicago: Dorsey Press.

Ajzen, I., and M. Fishbein. 1974. Factors influencing intentions and the intention-behavior relation. *Human Relations* 27 (1): 1–15.

Allen, M.T., and M.D. Crowell. 1989. Patterns of autonomic response during laboratory stressors. *Psychophysiology* 26: 603–614.

Alpert, B., T.M. Field, S. Goldstein, and S. Perry. 1990. Aerobics enhances cardiovascular fitness and agility in preschoolers. *Health Psychology* 9 (1): 48–56.

American College of Sports Medicine. 1998. American College of Sports Medicine Position Stand. Exercise and physical activity for older adults. *Medicine and Science in Sports and Exercise* 30 (June): 992–1008.

———. 2000. *Guidelines for exercise testing and prescription.* 6th ed. Baltimore: Lippincott Williams & Wilkins.

American Psychiatric Association. 1994. *Diagnostic and statistical manual of mental disorders: DSM-IV.* 4th ed. Washington, DC: American Psychiatric Association.

———. 2000. Practice guidelines for the treatment of patients with major depressive disorders (revision). *American Journal of Psychiatry* 157 (4 suppl.): 1–45.

American Sleep Disorders Association. 1997. *Sleep hygiene. Behaviors that help promote better sleep.* Rochester, MN: American Sleep Disorders Association.

Andersen, L.B. 1996. Tracking of risk factors for coronary heart disease from adolescence to young adulthood with special emphasis on physical activity and fitness: A longitudinal study. *Danish Medical Bulletin* 43 (December): 407–418.

Anderson, D.F., and C.M. Cychosz. 1995. Exploration of the relationship between exercise behavior and exercise identity. *Journal of Sport Behavior* 18 (3): 159–166.

Anshel, M.H., D. Muller, and V.L. Owens. 1986. Effect of a sports camp experience on the multidimensional self-concepts of boys. *Perceptual and Motor Skills* 63 (2, pt. 1): 363–366.

Aşçii, F.H. 2002. The effects of step dance on physical self-perception of female and male university students. *International Journal of Sport Psychology* 33. In press.

Auweele, Y.A., R. Rzewnicki, and V. Van Mele. 1997. Reasons for not exercising and exercise intentions: A study of middle-aged sedentary adults. *Journal of Sports Sciences* 15: 151–165.

Averill, J.R., G.L. Clore, J.E. LeDoux, J. Panksepp, D. Watson, L.A. Clark, P. Ekman, and R.J. Davidson. 1994. What influences the subjective experience of emotion? In *The nature of emotion: Fundamental questions*, ed. P. Ekman and R.J. Davidson. New York: Oxford University Press.

Babyak, M., J.A. Blumenthal, S. Herman, P. Khatri, M. Doraiswamy, K. Moore, W.E. Craighead, T.T. Baldewicz, and K.R. Krishnan. 2000. Exercise treatment for major depression: Maintenance of therapeutic benefit at 10 months. *Psychosomatic Medicine* 62 (5): 633–638.

Baekeland, F. 1970. Exercise deprivation: Sleep and psychological reactions. *Archives of General Psychiatry* 22: 365–369.

Bahrke, M., and W.P. Morgan. 1978. Anxiety reduction following exercise and meditation. *Cognitive Therapy and Research* 2 (4): 323–333.

Bandura, A. 1977. *Social learning theory.* Englewood Cliffs, NJ: Prentice Hall.

Bandura, A. 1986. *Social foundations of thought and action.* Englewood Cliffs, NJ: Prentice-Hall.

Bandura, A. 1997a. Editorial: The anatomy of stages of change. *American Journal of Health Promotion* 12 (1): 8–10.

Bandura, A. 1997b. *Self-efficacy: The exercise of control.* New York: Freeman.

Baranowski, T., C. Anderson, and C. Carmack. 1998. Mediating variable framework in physical activity interventions: How are we doing? How might we do better? *American Journal of Preventive Medicine* 15: 266–297.

Barkley, R.A. 1998. *Attention-deficit hyperactivity disorder: A handbook for diagnosis and treatment.* 2nd ed. New York: Guilford Press.

Baron, R.M., and D.A. Kenny. 1986. The moderator-mediator variable distinction in social psychological research: Conceptual, strategic, and statistical considerations. *Journal of Personality and Social Psychology* 51: 1173–1182.

Bar-Or, O. 2001. Exertional perception in children and adolescents with a disease or a physical disability: Assessment and interpretation. *International Journal of Sport Psychology* 32: 127–136.

Bartholomew, J.B., and D.E. Linder. 1998. State anxiety following resistance exercise: The role of gender and exercise intensity. *Journal of Behavioral Medicine* 21 (2): 205–219.

Bartlett, M.S., J.C. Hager, P. Ekman, and T.J. Sejnowski. 1999. Measuring facial expressions by computer image analysis. *Psychophysiology* 36: 253–263.

Bartlewski, P.P., J.L. Van Raalte, and B.W. Brewer. 1996. Effects of aerobic exercise on the social physique anxiety and body esteem of female college students. *Women in Sport and Physical Activity Journal* 5 (2): 49–61.

Batson, C.D., L.L. Shaw, and K.C. Oleson. 1992. Differentiating affect, mood, and emotion: Toward functionally based conceptual distinctions. In *Emotion*, ed. M.S. Clark. Newberry Park, CA: Sage.

Baumeister, R.F. 1993. *Self-esteem: The puzzle of low self-regard.* New York: Plenum Press.

Bayles, C.M., K.F. Metz, R. Robertson, F.L. Gross, J. Cosgrove, and D. McBurney. 1990. Perceptual regulation of prescribed exercise. *Journal of Cardiopulmonary Rehabilitation* 10: 25–31.

Beckett, M.B., and J.A. Hodgdon. 1991. Psychological predictors of physical performance and fitness in U.S. Navy personnel. *Military Psychology* 3 (2): 73–87.

Berger, B.G., and R.W. Motl. 2000. Exercise and mood: A selective review and synthesis of research employing the profile of mood states. *Journal of Applied Sport Psychology* 12: 69–92.

Berger, B.G., D.R. Owen, R.W. Motl, and L. Parks. 1998. Relationship between expectancy of psychological benefits and mood alteration in joggers. *International Journal of Sport Psychology* 29 (1): 1–16.

Bernard, C.L. 1867. *Rapport sur les progres et la marche de la physiologie generale.* Paris: Balliere.

Berntson, G.G., J.T. Cacioppo, and K.S. Quigley. 1991. Autonomic determinism: The modes of autonomic control, the doctrine of autonomic space, and the laws of autonomic constraint. *Psychological Review* 98 (October): 459–487.

Berntson, G.G., J.T. Cacioppo, and K.S. Quigley. 1993. Cardiac psychophysiology and autonomic space in humans: Empirical perspectives and conceptual implications. *Psychological Bulletin* 114 (2): 296–322.

Berntson, G.G., J.T. Cacioppo, K.S. Quigley, and V.T. Fabro. 1994. Autonomic space and psychophysiological response. *Psychophysiology* 31 (1): 44–61.

Beunen, G., and M. Thomis. 1999. Genetic determinants of sports participation and daily physical activity. *International Journal of Obesity and Related Metabolic Disorders* 23 (suppl. 3) (April): S55–S63.

Biddle, S.J.H. 1997. Cognitive theories of motivation and the physical self. In *The physical self: From motivation to well-being*, ed. K.R. Fox. Champaign, IL: Human Kinetics.

Biddle, S.J.H., D. Akande, N. Armstrong, M. Ashcroft, R. Brooke, and M. Goudas. 1996. The Self-Motivation Inventory modified for children: Evidense on psychometric properties and its use in physical exercise. *International Journal of Sport Psychology* 27: 237–250.

Biddle, S.J.H., and C.R. Nigg. 2000. Theories of exercise behavior. *International Journal of Sport Psychology* 31 (2): 290–304.

Blair, S.N., M. Booth, I. Gyarfas, H. Iwane, B. Marti, V. Matsudo, M.S. Morrow, T. Noakes, and R. Shephard. 1996. Development of public policy and physical activity initiatives internationally. *Sports Medicine* 21 (3): 157–163.

Blamey, A., N. Mutrie, and T. Aitchison. 1995. Health promotion by encouraged use of stairs. *British Medical Journal* 311: 289–290.

Blaney, J., M. Sothmann, H. Raff, B. Hart, and T. Horn. 1990. Impact of exercise training on plasma adrenocorticotropin response to a well-learned vigilance task. *Psychoneuroendocrinology* 15: 453–462.

Blascovich, J., and J. Tomaka. 1991. Measures of self-esteem. In *Measures of personality and social psychological attitudes*, ed. J.P. Robinson, P.R. Shaver, and L.S. Wrightsman. San Diego: Academic Press.

Blumenthal, J.A., M.A. Babyak, K.A. Moore, W.E. Craighead, S. Herman, P. Khatri, R. Waugh, M.A. Napolitano, L.M. Forman, M. Appelbaum, P.M. Doraiswamy, and K.R. Krishnan. 1999. Effects of exercise training on older patients with major depression. *Archives of Internal Medicine* 159 (October 25): 2349–2356.

Blumenthal, J.A., S. Herman, P. Khatri, M. Doraiswamy, K. Moore, W.E. Craighead, T.T. Baldewicz, and K.R. Krishnan. 2000. Exercise treatment for major depression: Maintenance of therapeutic benefit at 10 months. *Psychosomatic Medicine* 62 (5): 633–638.

Blumenthal, J.A., S. Rose, and J.L. Chang. 1985. Anorexia nervosa and exercise. Implications from recent findings. *Sports Medicine* 2 (July-August): 237–247.

Bock, B.C., B.H. Marcus, T.K. King, B. Borrelli, and M.R. Roberts. 1999. Exercise effects on withdrawal and mood among women attempting smoking cessation. *Addictive Behaviors* 24 (3): 399–410.

Bollen, K.A. 1989. *Structural equations with latent variables.* New York: Wiley.

Bonnet, M., M.M. Bradley, P.J. Lang, and J. Requin. 1995. Modulation of spinal reflexes: Arousal, pleasure, action. *Psychophysiology* 32 (4): 367–372.

Booth, M.L., N. Owen, A. Bauman, O. Clavisi, and E. Leslie. 2000. Social-cognitive and perceived environmental influences associated with physical activity in older Australians. *Preventive Medicine* 31: 15–22.

Borg, G.A. 1961. Interindividual scaling and perception of muscular force. *Kungliga Fysiografiska Sällskapets I Lund Förhandlinger* 12 (31): 117–125.

———. 1962. *Physical performance and perceived exertion*. Vol. XI, *Studia Psychologica et Paedagogica. Seris altera*. Lund, Sweden: Gleerup.

———. 1970. Perceived exertion as an indicator of somatic stress. *Scandinavian Journal of Rehabilitative Medicine* 23: 92–98.

———. 1972. *The Basic "Noise Constant" in the Psychophysical Function of Perceived Exertion*. Reports from the Institute of Applied Psychology, no. 33. Stockholm: University of Stockholm.

———. 1982. Psychophysical bases of perceived exertion. *Medicine and Science in Sports and Exercise* 14: 377–381.

———. 1998. *Borg's perceived exertion and pain scales*. Champaign, IL: Human Kinetics.

Bouchard, C., and T. Rankinen. 2001. Individual differences in response to regular physical activity. *Medicine and Science in Sports and Exercise* 33: (6, Suppl.), S446–451.

Bouchard, C., R. Shephard, and T. Stephens. 1994. *Physical activity, fitness, and health: International proceedings and consensus statement*. Champaign, IL: Human Kinetics.

Boutcher, S.H., L.A. Fleischer-Curtian, and S.D. Gines. 1988. The effects of self-presentation on perceived exertion. *Journal of Sport & Exercise Psychology* 10 (3): 270–280.

Boutcher, S.H., F.W. Nugent, P.F. McLaren, and A.L. Weltman. 1998. Heart period variability of trained and untrained men at rest and during mental challenge. *Psychophysiology* 35 (January): 16–22.

Boutcher, S.H., R.L. Seip, R.K. Hetzler, E.F. Pierce, D. Snead, and A. Weltman. 1989. The effects of specificity of training on rating of perceived exertion at the lactate threshold. *European Journal of Applied Physiology* 59: 365–369.

Boyd, K.R., and D.W. Hrycaiko. 1997. The effect of a physical activity intervention package on the self-esteem of pre-adolescent and adolescent females. *Adolescence* 32 (Fall): 693–708.

Bozoian, S., W.J. Rejeski, and E. McAuley. 1994. Self-efficacy influences feeling states associated with acute exercise. *Journal of Sport & Exercise Psychology* 16 (3): 326–333.

Breus, M.J., and P.J. O'Connor. 1998. Exercise-induced anxiolysis: A test of the "time out" hypothesis in high anxious females. *Medicine and Science in Sports and Exercise* 30 (7): 1107–1112.

Breus, M.J., P.J. O'Connor, and S.T. Ragan. 2000. Muscle pain induced by novel eccentric exercise does not disturb the sleep of normal young men. *Journal of Pain* 1 (1): 67–76.

Broocks, A., B. Bandelow, G. Pekrun, A. George, T. Meyer, U. Bartmann, U. Hillmer-Vogel, and E. Ruther. 1998. Comparison of aerobic exercise, clomipramine, and placebo in the treatment of panic disorder [see comments]. *American Journal of Psychiatry* 155 (May): 603–609.

Broocks, A., T.F. Meyer, B. Bandelow, A. George, U. Bartmann, E. Ruther, and U. Hillmer-Vogel. 1997. Exercise avoidance and impaired endurance capacity in patients with panic disorder. *Neuropsychobiology* 36: 182–187.

Brown, R.D., and J.M. Harrison. 1986. The effects of a strength training program on the strength and self-concept of two female age groups. *Research Quarterly for Exercise and Sport* 57: 315–320.

Brownell, K., A.J. Stunkard, and J. Albaum. 1980. Evaluation and modification of exercise patterns in the natural environment. *American Journal of Psychiatry* 136: 1540–1545.

Bryan, R.J. 1990. Cerebral blood flow and energy metabolism during stress. *American Journal of Physiology* 259 (August): H269–H280.

Bryne, A., and D.G. Bryne. 1993. The effect of exercise on depression, anxiety and other mood states: A review. *Journal of Psychosomatic Research* 17: 565–574.

Brynteson, P., and T.M.I. Adams. 1993. The effects of conceptually based physical education programs on attitudes and exercise habits of college alumni after 2 to 11 years of follow-up. *Research Quarterly for Exercise and Sport* 64: 208–212.

Buckworth, J. 2000. Exercise determinants and interventions. *International Journal of Sport Psychology* 31 (2): 305–320.

Buckworth, J.B., V. Convertino, K.J. Cureton, and R.K. Dishman. 1997. Increased finger arterial blood pressure after exercise detraining in women with parental hypertension: Autonomic tasks. *Acta Physiologica Scandinavica* 160: 29–41.

Buckworth, J.B., R.K. Dishman, and K.J. Cureton. 1994. Autonomic responses by women with parental hypertension: Effects of $\dot{V}O_2$peak and physical activity. *Hypertension* 24: 576–584.

Bulbulian, R., and B.L. Darabos. 1986. Motor neuron excitability: The Hoffmann reflex following exercise of low and high intensity. *Medicine and Science in Sports and Exercise* 18 (December): 697–702.

Bull, F.C., K. Jamrozik, and B.A. Blanksby. 1998. Tailoring advice on exercise: Does it make a difference? *American Journal of Preventive Medicine* 16 (3): 230–239.

Burgess, M.L., J.M. Davis, T.K. Borg, and J. Buggy. 1991. Intracranial self-stimulation motivates treadmill running in rats. *Journal of Applied Physiology* 71 (October): 1593–1597.

Burke, E.J., and M.L. Collins. 1984. Using perceived exertion for the prescription of exercise in healthy adults. In *Clinical sports medicine*. Lexington, MA: Callamore Press.

Burton, R. 1632. *The anatomy of melancholy*. Oxford: Printed by Ion Lichfield for Henry Cripps.

Cacioppo, J.T., D.J. Klein, G.G. Berntson, and E. Hatfield. 1993. The psychophysiology of emotion. In *Handbook of emotions*, ed. M. Lewis and J.M. Haviland. New York: Guilford Press.

Cacioppo, J.T., R.E. Petty, M.E. Losch, and H.S. Kim. 1986. Electromyographic activity over facial muscle regions can differentiate the valence and intensity of affective reactions. *Journal of Personality and Social Psychology* 50: 260–268.

Cafarelli, E., and B. Bigland-Ritchie. 1979. Sensation of static force in muscles of different length. *Experimental Neurology* 65: 511–525.

Cafarelli, E., W.S. Cain, and J.C. Stevens. 1977. Effort of dynamic exercise: Influence of load, duration, and task. *Ergonomics* 20 (2): 147–158.

Cain, W.S., and J.C. Stevens. 1971. Effort in sustained and phasic handgrip contractions. *American Journal of Psychology* 84: 51–65.

Calfas, K.J., B.J. Long, J.F. Sallis, W. Wooten, M. Pratt, and K. Patrick. 1996. A controlled trial of physician counseling to promote the adoption of physical activity. *Preventive Medicine* 25 (3): 225–233.

Calfas, K.J., J.F. Sallis, B. Oldenburg, and M. French. 1997. Mediators of change in physical activity following an intervention in primary care: PACE. *Preventive Medicine* 26: 297–304.

Camacho, T.C., R.E. Roberts, N.B. Lazarus, G.A. Kaplan, and R.D. Cohen. 1991. Physical activity and depression: Evidence from the Alameda County Study. *American Journal of Epidemiology* 134: 220–231.

Campbell, D.D., and J.E. Davis. 1939-1940. Report of research and experimentation in exercise and recreational therapy. *American Journal of Psychiatry* 96: 915–933.

Campbell, D.T., and D.W. Fiske. 1959. Convergent and discriminant validation by the multitrait-multimethod matrix. *Psychological Bulletin* 56: 81–105.

Cannon, W.B. 1929. Organization for physiological homeostasis. *Physiological Review* 9: 399–431.

Cardinal, B.J. 1999. Extended stage model of physical activity behavior. *Journal of Human Movement Studies* 37: 37–54.

Carlson, N.R. 1994. *Physiology of behavior.* 5th ed. Boston: Allyn and Bacon.

Carlson, N.R. 1998. *Physiology of behavior.* 6th ed. Boston: Allyn and Bacon.

Carlson, N.R. 2001. *Physiology of behavior.* 7th ed. Boston: Allyn and Bacon.

Carron, A.V., H.A. Hausenblas, and D. Mack. 1996. Social influence and exercise: A meta-analysis. *Journal of Sport & Exercise Psychology* 18: 1–16.

Carskadon, M.A., and W.C. Dement. 1989. Normal human sleep: An overview. In *Principles and practice of sleep medicine*, ed. M.H. Kryger, T. Roth, and W.C. Dement. Philadelphia: Saunders.

Caruso, C.M., and D.L. Gill. 1992. Strengthening physical self-perceptions through exercise. *Journal of Sports Medicine and Physical Fitness* 32: 416–427.

Casper, R.C. 1993. Exercise and mood. *World Review of Nutrition and Dietetics* 71: 115–143.

Caspersen, C.J. 1989. Physical activity epidemiology: Concepts, methods, and applications to exercise science. *Exercise and Sport Sciences Reviews* 17: 423–473.

Caspersen, C.J., M.A. Pereira, and K.M. Curran. 2000. Changes in physical activity patterns in the United States, by sex and cross-sectional age. *Medicine and Science in Sports and Exercise* 32 (9): 1601–1609.

Caspersen, C.J., K.E. Powell, and G.M. Christenson. 1985.

Physical activity, exercise, and physical fitness: Definitions and distinctions for health-related research. *Public Health Reports* 100: 126–131.

Castro, C., J.F. Sallis, S.A. Hickmann, R.E. Lee, and A.H. Chen. 1999. A prospective study of psychosocial correlates of physical activity for ethnic minority women. *Psychology & Health* 14 (2): 277–293.

Centers for Disease Control and Prevention. 1998. Self-reported physical inactivity by degree of urbanization–United States, 1996. *Morbidity and Mortality Weekly Report* 47 (50): 1097–1100.

———. 2000. Fact Sheet: Youth Risk Behavior Trends From CDC's 1991, 1993, 1995, 1997, and 1999 Youth Risk Behavior Surveys.

———. 2001. Physical activity trend—United States, 1990-1998. *Morbidity and Mortality Weekly Report* 50: 166–169.

Chaouloff, F. 1997. Effects of acute physical exercise on central serotonergic systems. *Medicine and Science in Sports and Exercise* 29 (January): 58–62.

Charney, D.S., S.W. Woods, W.K. Goodman, and G.R. Heninger. 1987. Serotonin function in anxiety. II. Effects of the serotonin agonist MCPP in panic disorder patients and healthy subjects. *Psychopharmacology* 92: 14–24.

Charney, D.S., S.W. Woods, J.H. Krystal, L.M. Nagy, and G.R. Heninger. 1992. Noradrenergic neuronal dysregulation in panic disorder: The effects of intravenous yohimbine and clonidine in panic disorder patients. *Acta Psychiatrica Scandinavica* 86 (October): 273–282.

Chronicle of Higher Education. 2000. "Information Bank." www.chronicle.com.

Chrousos, G.P. 1998. Stressors, stress, and neuroendocrine integration of the adaptive response. The 1997 Hans Selye Memorial Lecture. *Annals of the New York Academy of Sciences* 851 (June 30): 311–335.

Chrousos, G.P., and P.W. Gold. 1998. A healthy body in a healthy mind—and vice versa—the damaging power of "uncontrollable" stress [editorial; comment]. *Journal of Clinical Endocrinology and Metabolism* 83 (June): 1842–1845.

Clore, G.L., N. Schwarz, and M. Conway. 1994. Affective causes and consequences of social information processing. In *Handbook of social cognition*, Vol. 1: *Basic processes*; Vol. 2: *Applications*, ed. R.S. Wyer, Jr., and T.K. Srull. 2nd ed. Hillsdale, NJ: Erlbaum.

Clutter, W., D. Bier, S. Shah, and P.E. Cryer. 1980. Epinephrine: Plasma metabolic clearance rates and physiologic thresholds for metabolic and hemodynamic actions in man. *Journal of Clinical Investigation* 66: 94–101.

Cockerill, I.M., and M.E. Riddington. 1996. Exercise dependence and associated disorders: A review. *Counseling Psychology Quarterly* 9 (2): 119–129.

Cohen, M.S., and S.Y. Bookheimer. 1994. Localization of brain function using magnetic resonance imaging. *Trends in Neurosciences* 17 (July): 268–277.

Cook, D.B., and K.F. Koltyn. 2000. Pain and exercise. *International Journal of Sport Psychology* 31 (2): 256–277.

Cooper-Patrick, L., D.E. Ford, L.A. Mead, P.P. Chang, and M.J. Klag. 1997. Exercise and depression in midlife: A prospective study. *American Journal of Public Health* 87: 670–673.

Coopersmith, S. 1967. *The antecedents of self-esteem.* San Francisco: Freeman.

———. 1975. *Coopersmith Self-Esteem Inventory, technical manual.* Palo Alto, CA: Consulting Psychologists Press.

Courneya, K.S., and T.M. Bobick. 2000. Integrating the theory of planned behavior with the processes and stages of change in the exercise domain. *Psychology of Sport and Exercise* 1: 41–56.

Courneya, K.S., and C.M. Friedenreich. 1999. Physical exercise and quality of life following cancer diagnosis: A literature review. *Annals of Behavioral Medicine* 21 (Spring): 171–179.

Courneya, K.S., and L.M. Hellsten. 1998. Personality correlates of exercise behavior, motives, barriers, and preferences: An application of the five-factor model. *Personality and Individual Differences* 24 (5): 625–633.

Courneya, K.S. and E. McAuley. 1994. Are there different determinants of the frequency, intensity, and duration of physical activity? *Behavioral Medicine* 20 (2): 84–90.

Courneya, K.S., and E. McAuley. 1995. Cognitive mediators of the social influence-exercise adherence relationship: A test of the Theory of Planned Behavior. *Journal of Behavioral Medicine* 18 (5): 499–515.

Crabbe, J.B., and R.K. Dishman. 2000. Exercise and brain electrocortical activity: a quantitative synthesis. *Medicine and Science in Sports and Exercise* 32 (suppl. 5): S43, S38.

Craft, L.L., and D.M. Landers. 1998. The effect of exercise on clinical depression and depression resulting from mental illness: A meta-analysis. *Journal of Sport and Exercise Psychology* 20: 339–357.

Crespo, C.J., E. Smit, R.E. Andersen, O. Carter-Pokras, and B.E. Ainsworth. 2000. Race/ethnicity, social class and their relation to physical inactivity during leisure time: Results from the third National Health and Nutrition Examination Survey, 1988-1994. *American Journal of Preventive Medicine* 18 (1): 46–53.

Crews, D.J., and D.M. Landers. 1987. A meta-analytic review of aerobic fitness and reactivity to psychosocial stressors. *Medicine and Science in Sports and Exercise* 19 (suppl. 5): S114–S120.

Crocker, P.R.E. 1997. A confirmatory factor analysis of the Positive Affect Negative Affect Schedule (PANAS) with a youth sport sample. *Journal of Sport & Exercise Psychology* 19 (1): 91–97.

Cronbach, L.J., and P.E. Meehl. 1955. Construct validity in psychological tests. *Psychological Bulletin* 52: 281–302.

Cuthbert, B.N., M.M. Bradley, and P.J. Lang. 1996. Probing picture perception: Activation and emotion. *Psychophysiology* 33 (2): 103–111.

Cuthbert, B.N., H.T. Schupp, M. Bradley, M. McManis, and P.J. Lang. 1998. Probing affective pictures: Attended startle and tone probes. *Psychophysiology* 35 (May): 344–347.

Damasio, H., T. Grabowski, R. Frank, A.M. Galaburda, and A.R. Damasio. 1994. The return of Phineas Gage: Clues about the brain from the skull of a famous patient [published erratum appears in *Science* 1994 (August 26), 265: 1159]. *Science* 264 (May 20): 1102–1105.

Darwin, C. 1872. *The expression of the emotions in man and animals.* London: J. Murray.

Davidson, R.J. 1992. Anterior cerebral asymmetry and the nature of emotion. *Brain and Cognition* 20: 125–151.

———. 1998a. Affective style and affective disorders: Perspectives from affective neuroscience. *Cognition & Emotion* 12 (3): 307–330.

———. 1998b. Anterior electrophysiological asymmetries, emotion, and depression: Conceptual and methodological conundrums. *Psychophysiology* 35 (5): 607–614.

———. 2000. Cognitive neuroscience needs affective neuroscience (and vice versa). *Brain and Cognition* 42 (February): 89–92.

Davidson, R.J., P. Ekman, C.D. Saron, J.A. Senulius, and W.V. Friesen. 1990. Approach-withdrawal and cerebral asymmetry: Emotional expression and brain physiology I. *Journal of Personality and Social Psychology* 58: 330–341.

Davidson, R.J., and W. Irwin. 1999. The functional neuroanatomy of emotion and affective style. *Trends in Cognitive Sciences* 3 (1): 11–21.

Davis, C. 1997. Body image, exercise, and eating disorders. In *The physical self: From motivation to well-being,* ed. K.R. Fox. Champaign, IL: Human Kinetics.

———. 2000. Exercise abuse. *International Journal of Sport Psychology* 31: 278–289.

Davis, C., G. Claridge, and H. Brewer. 1996. The two faces of narcissism: Personality dynamics of body esteem. *Journal of Social and Clinical Psychology* 15 (2): 153–166.

Davis, C., and K.R. Fox. 1993. Excessive exercise and weight preoccupation in women. *Addictive Behaviors* 18: 201–211.

Davis, H.P., M.R. Rosenzweig, L.A. Becker, and K.J. Sather. 1988. Biological psychology's relationships to psychology and neuroscience. *American Psychologist* 43: 359–371.

Davis, M. 1997. The neurolophysiological basis of acoustic startle modulation: Research on fear motivation and sensory gating. In *Attention and orienting: Sensory and motivational processes,* ed. P.J. Lang, R.F. Simons, and M. Balaban. Mahwah, NJ: Erlbaum.

Davis, M., W.A. Falls, S. Campeau, and M. Kim. 1993. Fear-potentiated startle: A neural and pharmacological analysis. *Behavioural Brain Research* 58 (1-2): 175–198.

Deci, E.L., and R.M. Ryan. 1980. Self-determination theory: When mind mediates behavior. *Journal of Mind & Behavior* 1 (1): 33–43.

Deci, E.L., R.J. Vallerand, L.G. Pelletier, and R.M. Ryan. 1991. Motivation and education: The self-determination perspective. *Educational Psychologist* 26 (3–4): 325–346.

Demeersman, R.E. 1993. Heart rate variability and aerobic fitness. *American Heart Journal* 125: 726–731.

Demello, J.J., K.J. Cureton, R.E. Boineau, and M.M. Singh. 1987. Ratings of perceived exertion at the lactate threshold in trained and untrained men and women. *Medicine and Science in Sports and Exercise* 19 (August): 354–362.

Descartes, R. 1972. *Treatise of man.* Translated by T.S. Hall. Cambridge, MA: Harvard University Press.

Desharnais, R., J. Jobin, C. Cote, L. Levesque, and G. Godin. 1993. Aerobic exercise and the placebo effect: A controlled study. *Psychosomatic Medicine* 55: 149–154.

deVries, H.A., and G.M. Adams. 1972. Electromyographic comparisons of single doses of exercise and meprobamate as to effects on muscular relaxation. *American Journal of Physical Medicine* 51: 130-141.

deVries, H.A., C.P. Simard, R.A. Wiswell, E. Heckathorne, and V. Carabetta. 1982. Fusimotor system involvement in the tranquilizer effect of exercise. *American Journal of Physical Medicine* 61 (June): 111–122.

deVries, H.A., R.A. Wiswell, R. Bulbulian, and T. Moritani. 1981. Tranquilizer effect of exercise. Acute effects of moderate aerobic exercise on spinal reflex activation level. *American Journal of Physical Medicine* 60 (April): 57–66.

Dietz, W.H. 1996. The role of lifestyle in health: The epidemiology and consequences of inactivity. *Proceedings of the Nutrition Society* 55: 829–840.

DiLorenzo, T.M., E.P. Bargman, R. Stucky-Ropp, G.S. Brassington, P.A. Frensch, and T. LaFontaine. 1999. Long-term effects of aerobic exercise on psychological outcomes. *Preventive Medicine* 28 (1): 75–85.

Dishman, R.K. 1982. Compliance/adherence in health-related exercise. *Health Psychology* 1 (3): 237–267.

———. 1985. Medical psychology in exercise and sport. *Medical Clinics of North America* 69 (January): 123–143.

———. 1986. Exercise compliance: A new view for public health. *Physician and Sportsmedicine* 14 (5): 127–145.

———. 1991. Increasing and maintaining exercise and physical activity. *Behavior Therapy* 22: 345–378.

———. 1992. Physiological and psychological effects of overtraining. In *Eating, body weight, and performance in athletes: Disorders of modern society*, ed. K. Brownell, and J. Rodin Philadelphia: Lea & Febiger.

———. 1994a. The measurement conundrum in exercise adherence research. *Medicine and Science in Sports and Exercise* 26 (11): 1382–1390.

———. 1994b. Prescribing exercise intensity for healthy adults using perceived exertion. *Medicine and Science in Sports and Exercise* 26 (9): 1087–1094.

———. 1997. Brain monoamines, exercise, and behavioral stress: Animal models. *Medicine and Science in Sports and Exercise* 29 (January): 63–74.

———. 1998. Physical activity and mental health. In *Encyclopedia of mental health*, ed. H.S. Friedman. Vol. 3. San Diego: Academic Press.

———. 2000. Introduction. *International Journal of Sport Psychology* 31: 103–109.

Dishman, R.K., and J. Buckworth. 1996a. Adherence to physical activity. In *Physical activity and mental health*, ed. W.P. Morgan. Washington: Taylor & Francis.

———. 1996b. Increasing physical activity: A quantitative synthesis. *Medicine and Science in Sports and Exercise* 28 (6): 706–719.

Dishman, R.K., A.L. Dunn, S.D. Youngstedt, J.M. Davis, M.L. Burgess, S.P. Wilson, and M.A. Wilson. 1996. Increased open field locomotion and decreased striatal $GABA_A$ binding after activity wheel running. *Physiology and Behavior* 60: 699–705.

Dishman, R.K., R.P. Farquhar, and K.J. Cureton. 1994. Responses to preferred intensities of exertion in men differing in activity levels. *Medicine and Science in Sports and Exercise* 26 (June): 783–790.

Dishman, R.K., R.E. Graham, J. Buckworth, and J.E. White-Welkley. 2001. Perceived exertion during incremental cycling is not influenced by the Type A behavior pattern. *International Journal of Sports Medicine* 22: 209–214.

Dishman, R.K., R.E. Graham, R.G. Holly, and J.G. Tieman. 1991. Estimates of Type A behavior do not predict perceived exertion during graded exercise. *Medicine and Science in Sports and Exercise* 23 (11): 1276–1282.

Dishman, R.K., S. Hong, J. Soares, G.L. Edwards, B.N. Bunnell, L. Jaso-Friedmann, and D.L. Evans. 2000. Activity-wheel running blunts suppression of splenic natural killer cell cytotoxicity after sympathectomy and footshock. *Physiology and Behavior* 71: 297–304

Dishman, R.K., and E.M. Jackson. 2000. Exercise, fitness, and stress. *International Journal of Sport Psychology* 31 (2): 175–203.

Dishman, R.K., E.M. Jackson, Y. Nakamura. 2002. Influence of fitness and gender on blood pressure responses during active or passive stress. *Psychophysiology* 39: 568-576.

Dishman, R.K., R.W. Motl, R. Saunders, M. Dowda, G. Felton, D. Ward, and R.R. Pate. 2001. Factorial invariance and latent mean structure of questionnaires measuring social-cognitive determinants of physical activity among black and white adolescent girls. *Preventive Medicine* 33. In press.

Dishman, R.K., B. Oldenburg, H. O'Neal, and R. Shephard. 1998. Worksite physical activity interventions. *American Journal of Preventive Medicine* 15 (4): 344–361.

Dishman, R.K., Y. Nakamura, M.E. Garcia, R.W. Thompson, A.L. Dunn, and S.N. Blair. 2000. Heart rate variability, trait anxiety, and perceived stress among physically fit men and women. *International Journal of Psychophysiology* 37 (August): 121–133.

Dishman, R.K., R.W. Patton, J. Smith, R. Weinberg, and A. Jackson. 1987. Using perceived exertion to prescribe and monitor exercise training heart rate. *International Journal of Sports Medicine* 8 (June): 208–213.

Dishman, R.K., K.J. Renner, J.E. White-Welkley, K.A. Burke, and B.N. Bunnell. 2000. Treadmill exercise training augments brain norepinephrine response to familiar and novel stress. *Brain Research Bulletin* 52 (July 15): 337–342.

Dishman, R.K., K.J. Renner, S.D. Youngstedt, T.G. Reigle, B.N. Bunnell, K.A. Burke, H.S. Yoo, E.H. Mougey, and J.L. Meyerhoff. 1997. Activity wheel running reduces escape latency and alters brain monoamine levels after footshock. *Brain Research Bulletin* 42: 399–406.

Dishman, R.K., and J.F. Sallis. 1994. Determinants and interventions for physical activity and exercise. In *Physical activity, fitness and health: International proceedings and consensus statement*, ed. C. Bouchard and R.J. Shephard. Champaign, IL: Human Kinetics.

Dishman, R.K., J.M. Warren, S.D. Youngstedt, H. Yoo, B.N. Bunnell, E.H. Mougey, J.L. Meyerhoff, L. Jaso-Friedmann, and D.L. Evans. 1995. Activity-wheel running attenuates suppression of natural killer cell activity after footshock. *Journal of Applied Physiology* 78 (April): 1547–1554.

Dorow, R. 1987. FG 7142 and its anxiety-inducing effects in humans. *British Journal of Clinical Pharmacology* 23 (June): 781–782.

Douglas, K.A., J.L. Collins, C.W. Warren, L. Kann, R. Gold, S. Clayton, J.G. Ross, and L.J. Kolbe. 1997. Results from the 1995 National College Health Risk Behavior Survey. *Journal of American College Health* 46: 55–66.

Doyne, E.J., D.J. Ossip-Klein, E.D. Bowman, K.M. Osborn, I.B. McDougall-Wilson, and R.A. Neimeyer. 1987. Running versus weight lifting in the treatment of depression. *Journal of Consulting and Clinical Psychology* 555: 748–754.

Drevets, W.C. 1998. Functional neuroimaging studies of depression: The anatomy of melancholia. *Annual Review of Medicine* 49: 341–361.

Driver, H.S., and S.R. Taylor. 2000. Exercise and sleep. *Sleep Medicine Reviews* 4: 387–402.

Driver, S., and S.R. Taylor. 1996. Sleep disturbances and exercise. *Sports Medicine* 21 (January): 1–6.

Dunbar, C.C., R.J. Robertson, R. Baun, M.F. Blandin, K. Metz, R. Burdett, and F.L. Goss. 1992. The validity of regulating exercise intensity by ratings of perceived exertion. *Medicine and Science in Sports and Exercise* 24 (January): 94–99.

Duncan, T.E., S.C. Duncan, and E. McAuley. 1993. The role of domain and gender-specific provisions of social relations in adherence to a prescribed exercise regimen. *Journal of Sport and Exercise Psychology* 15 (2): 220–231.

Dunn, A.L., R.E. Andersen, and J.M. Jakicic. 1998. Lifestyle physical activity interventions. History, short- and long-term effects, and recommendations. *American Journal of Preventive Medicine* 15: 398–412.

Dunn, A.L., and R.K. Dishman. 1991. Exercise and the neurobiology of depression. *Exercise and Sport Sciences Reviews* 19: 41–98.

Dunn, A.L., B.H. Marcus, J.B. Kampert, M.E. Garcia, H.W. Kohl, and S.N. Blair. 1997. Reduction in cardiovascular disease risk factors: Six-month results from Project Active. *Preventive Medicine* 26 (6): 883–892.

Dunn, A.L., B.H. Marcus, J.B. Kampert, M.E. Garcia, H.W. Kohl, and S.N. Blair. 1999. Comparison of lifestyle and structured interventions to increase physical activity and cardiorespiratory fitness: A randomized trial. *Journal of the American Medical Association* 281 (4): 327–334.

Dunn, A.L., T.G. Reigle, S.Y. Youngstedt, R.B. Armstrong, and R.K. Dishman. 1996. Brain norepinephrine and metabolites after treadmill training and wheel running in rats. *Medicine and Science in Sports and Exercise* 28: 204–209.

DuPont, R.L., D.P. Rice, L.S. Miller, S.S. Shiraki, C.R. Rowland, and H.J. Harwood. 1996. Economic cost of anxiety disorders. *Anxiety* 2: 167–172.

Durante, R., and B.E. Ainsworth. 1996. The recall of physical activity: Using a cognitive model of the question-answering process. *Medicine and Science in Sports and Exercise* 28 (10): 1282–1291.

Dykens, E.M., and D.J. Cohen. 1996. Effects of Special Olympics International on social competence in persons with mental retardation. *Journal of the American Academy of Child and Adolescent Psychiatry* 35 (February): 223–229.

Dykens, E.M., B.A. Rosner, and G. Butterbaugh. 1998. Exercise and sports in children and adolescents with developmental disabilities: Positive physical and psychosocial effects. *Child & Adolescent Psychiatric Clinics of North America* 7 (4): 757–771.

Dzewaltowski, D.A. 1994. Physical activity determinants: A social cognitive approach. *Medicine and Science in Sports and Exercise* 26: 1395–1399.

Ehrenberg, M.F., D.N. Cox, and R.F. Koopman. 1991. The relationship between self-efficacy and depression in adolescents. *Adolescence* 26: 361–374.

Einerson, J., A. Ward, and P. Hanson. 1988. Exercise responses in females with anorexia nervosa. *International Journal of Eating Disorders* 7: 253–260.

Ekblom, B., and A.N. Goldbarg. 1971. The influence of physical training and other factors on the subjective rating of perceived exertion. *Acta Physiologica Scandinavica* 83: 399–406.

Ekkekakis, P., and S.J. Petruzzello. 1999. Acute aerobic exercise and affect: Current status, problems and prospects regarding dose-response. *Sports Medicine* 28 (November): 337–374.

———. 2000. Analysis of the affect measurement conundrum in exercise psychology. *Psychology of Sport and Exercise* 1: 71–88.

Ekman, P. 1989. The argument and evidence about universals in facial expressions of emotions. In *Handbook of psychophysiology: The biological psychology of emotions and social processes*, ed. H. Wagner and A. Manstead. London: Wiley.

———. 1992. Are there basic emotions? *Psychological Review* 99: 550–553.

———. 1994. Moods, emotions, and traits. In *The nature of emotion: Fundamental questions*, ed. P. Ekman and R.J. Davidson. New York: Oxford University Press.

Ekman, P., R.J. Davidson, and W.V. Friesen. 1990. The Duchenne smile: Emotional expression and brain physiology II. *Journal of Personality and Social Psychology* 582: 342–353.

Ekman, P., and W.V. Friesen. 1971. Constants across cultures in the face and emotion. *Journal of Personality and Social Psychology* 17: 124–129.

———. 1976. Measuring facial movement. *Journal of Environmental Psychology and Nonverbal Behavior* 11: 56–75.

Engel, G.L. 1977. The need for a new medical model: A challenge for biomedicine. *Science* 196 (4286): 129–136.

Epstein, L.H. 1998. Integrating theoretical approaches to promote physical activity. *American Journal of Preventive Medicine* 15 (4): 257–265.

Epstein, L.H., B.E. Saelens, M.D. Myers, and D. Vito. 1997. Effects of decreasing sedentary behaviors on activity choice in obese children. *Health Psychology* 16: 107–113.

Ernst, E., J.I. Rand, and C. Stevinson. 1998. Complementary therapies for depression: An overview. *Archives of General Psychiatry* 55 (November): 1026–1032.

Espiritu, R.C., D.F. Kripke, S. Ancoli-Israel, M.A. Mowen, W.J. Mason, R.L. Fell, M.R. Klauber, and O.J. Kaplan. 1994. Low illumination by San Diego adults: Association with atypical depressive symptoms. *Biological Psychiatry* 35: 403–407.

Estabrooks, P.A. 2000. Sustaining exercise participation through group cohesion. *Exercise and Sport Sciences Reviews* 28 (April): 63–67.

Faigenbaum, A., L.D. Zaichkowsky, W.L. Wescott, C.J. Long, R. LaRosa-Loud, L.J. Micheli, and A.R. Outerbridge. 1997. Psychological effects of strength training on children. *Journal of Sport Behavior* 20 (2): 164–175.

Farmer, M.E., B.Z. Locke, E.K. Moscicki, A.L. Dannenberg, D.B. Larson, and L.S. Radloff. 1988. Physical activity and depressive symptoms: The NHANES I epidemiologic follow-up study. *American Journal of Epidemiology* 128: 1340–1351.

Fillingim, R.B., D.L. Roth, and E.W. Cook. 1992. The effects of aerobic exercise on cardiovascular, facial EMG, and self-report responses to emotional imagery. *Psychosomatic Medicine* 54 (1): 109–120.

Fitts, W.H. 1965. *Tennessee Self-Concept Scale: Manual.* Los Angeles: Western Psychological Services.

Fleming, J.S., and B.E. Courtney. 1984. The dimensionality of self-esteem: II. Hierarchical facet model for revised measurement scales. *Journal of Personality and Social Psychology* 46 (2): 404–421.

Fleming, J.S., and W.A. Watts. 1980. The dimensionality of self-esteem: Some results of a college sample. *Journal of Personality and Social Psychology* 39 (5): 921–929.

Flora, J.A., E.W. Maibach, and N. Maccoby. 1989. The role of media across four levels of health promotion intervention. *Annual Review of Public Health* 10: 181–201.

Focht, B.C., and K.F. Koltyn. 1999. Influences of resistance exercise of different intensities on state anxiety and blood pressure. *Medicine and Science in Sports and Exercise* 31 (3): 456–463.

Ford, D.H., and H.B. Urban. 1998. *Contemporary models of psychotherapy: A comparative analysis.* New York: Wiley.

Fotheringham, M.J., R.L. Wonnacott, and N. Owen. 2000. Computer use and physical inactivity in young adults: Public health perils and potentials of new information technologies. *Annals of Behavioral Medicine* 22: 269–275.

Fox, K.R. 1990. *The Physical Self Perception Profile manual.* DeKalb, IL: Office for Health Promotion, Northern Illinois University.

———. 1997. The physical self and processes in self-esteem development. In *The physical self: From motivation to well-being,* ed. K.R. Fox. Champaign, IL: Human Kinetics.

———. 1998. Advances in the measurement of the physical self. In *Advances in sport and exercise psychology measurement,* ed. J.L. Duda. Morgantown, WV: Fitness Information Technology.

———. 2000. Self-esteem, self-perceptions and exercise. *International Journal of Sport Psychology* 31 (2): 228–240.

Fox, K.R., and C.B. Corbin. 1989. The Physical Self-Perception Profile: Development and preliminary validation. *Journal of Sport & Exercise Psychology* 11 (4): 408–430.

Frankenhaeuser, M. 1971. Behavior and circulating catecholamines. *Brain Research* 31 (August 20): 241–262.

Franklin, B.A. 1988. Program factors that influence exercise adherence: Practical adherence skills for the clinical staff. In *Exercise adherence,* ed. R.K. Dishman. Champaign, IL: Human Kinetics.

Franz, S.I., and G.V. Hamilton. 1905. The effects of exercise upon the retardation in conditions of depression. *American Journal of Insanity* 62: 239–256.

Franzoi, S.L., and S.A. Shields. 1984. The Body Esteem Scale: Multidimensional structure and sex differences in a college population. *Journal of Personality Assessment* 48 (2): 173–178.

Fremont, J., and L.W. Craighead. 1987. Aerobic exercise and cognitive therapy in the treatment of dysphoric moods. *Cognitive Therapy and Research* 112: 241–251.

Friedman, H.S., and S. Booth-Kewley. 1987. The "disease-prone personality". A meta-analytic view of the construct. *American Psychologist* 42 (June): 539–555.

Freud, S. 1959. *The justification from neurasthenia of a particular syndrome: The anxiety neurosis.* Vol. 1, *Collected papers.* New York: Basic Books.

Fridlund, A.J., and J.T. Cacioppo. 1986. Guidelines for human electromyographic research. *Psychophysiology* 23: 567–589.

Fullerton, G.S., and J.M. Cattell. 1892. *On the perception of small differences.* Philadelphia: University of Pennsylvania Press.

Gandevia, S.C. 1982. The perception of motor commands on effort during muscular paralysis. *Brain* 105: 151–159.

Garcia, A.W., and A.C. King. 1991. Predicting long-term adherence to aerobic exercise: A comparison of two models. *Journal of Sport and Exercise Psychology* 13: 394–410.

Garvin, A.W., K.F. Koltyn, and W.P. Morgan. 1997. Influence of acute physical activity and relaxation on state anxiety and blood lactate in untrained college males. *International Journal of Sports Medicine* 18 (August): 470–476.

Gauvin, L., and W.J. Rejeski. 1993. The Exercise-Induced Feeling Inventory: Development and initial validation. *Journal of Sport & Exercise Psychology* 15 (4): 403–423.

Gauvin, L., W.J. Rejeski, and B.A. Reboussin. 2000. Contributions of acute bouts of vigorous physical activity to explaining diurnal variations in feeling states in active, middle-aged women. *Health Psychology* 19 (4): 365–375.

Gauvin, L., and J.C. Spence. 1998. Measurement of exercise-induced changes in feeling states, affect, mood, and emotions. In *Advances in sport and exercise psychology measurement,* ed. J.L. Duda. Morgantown, WV: Fitness Information Technology.

Gleser, J., and H. Mendelberg. 1990. Exercise and sport in mental health: a review of the literature. *Israel Journal of Psychiatry and Related Sciences* 27: 99–112.

Goddard, A.W., and D.S. Charney. 1997. Toward an integrated neurobiology of panic disorder. *Journal of Clinical Psychiatry* 58 (suppl. 2): 4–11.

———. 1998. SSRIs in the treatment of panic disorder. *Depression and Anxiety* 8 (suppl. 1): 114–120.

Godin, G. 1994. Social-cognitive models. In *Advances in exercise adherence,* ed. R.K. Dishman. 2nd ed. Champaign, IL: Human Kinetics.

Gold, P.W., and G.P. Chrousos. 1999. The endocrinology of melancholic and atypical depression: Relation to neurocircuitry and somatic consequences. *Proceedings of the Association of American Physicians* 111 (1): 22–34.

Goode, K.T., and D.L. Roth. 1993. Factor analysis of cognitions during running: Association with mood change. *Journal of Sport & Exercise Psychology* 15 (4): 375–389.

Gordon-Larsen, P., R.G. McMurray, and B.M. Popkin. 1999. Adolescent physical activity and inactivity vary by ethnicity: The National Longitudinal Study of Adolescent Health. *Journal of Pediatrics* 135: 301–306.

Gorman, J.M., and L.K. Gorman. 1987. Drug treatment of social phobia. *Journal of Affective Disorders* 13 (September-October): 183–192.

Graham, R.E., A. Zeichner, L.J. Peacock, and R.K. Dishman. 1996. Bradycardia during baroreflex stimulation and active or passive stressor tasks: Cardiorespiratory fitness and hostility. *Psychophysiology* 33: 566–575.

Greenberg, P.E., T. Sisitsky, R.C. Kessler, S.N. Finkelstein, E.R. Berndt, J.R. Davidson, J.C. Ballenger, and A.J. Fyer. 1999. The economic burden of anxiety disorders in the 1990s. *Journal of Clinical Psychiatry* 60 (July): 427–435.

Greenberg, P.E., L.E. Stiglin, S.N. Finkelstein, and E.R. Berndt. 1993. The economic burden of depression in 1990. *Journal of Clinical Psychiatry* 54: 405–418.

Greenwald, M.K., E.W. Cook III, and P.J. Lang. 1989. Affective judgment and psychophysiological response: Dimensional covariation in the evaluation of pictorial stimuli. *Journal of Psychophysiology* 3: 51–64.

Greist, J.H., M.H. Klein, R.R. Eischens, J. Faris, A.S. Gurman, and W.P. Morgan. 1979. Running as treatment for depression. *Comprehensive Psychiatry* 20 (January-February): 41–54.

Gross, P.M., M.L. Marcus, and D.D. Heistad. 1980. Regional distribution of cerebral blood flow during exercise in dogs. *Journal of Applied Physiology* 48 (February): 213–217.

Grosz, H.J., and B.B. Farmer. 1972. Pitts' and McClure's lactate-anxiety study revisited. *British Journal of Psychiatry* 120: 415–418.

Gruber, A.J., and H.J. Pope. 2000. Psychiatric and medical effects of anabolic-androgenic steroid use in women. *Psychotherapy and Psychosomatics* 69: 19–26.

Gruber, J.J. 1986. Physical activity and self-esteem development in children: A meta-analysis. In *Effects of physical activity on children*, ed. G.A. Stull and E.M. Eckert. *The Academy Papers* 19: 330–348.

Guardiola-Lemaitre, B. 1997. Toxicology of melatonin. *Journal of Biological Rhythms* 12: 697–706.

Guilleminault, C., A. Clerk, J. Black, M. Labanowski, R. Pelayo, and D. Claman. 1995. Nondrug treatment trials in psychophysiologic insomnia. *Annals of Internal Medicine* 155: 838–844.

Guttman, L. 1950. The basis for scalogram analysis. In *Measurement and prediction*, ed. S.A. Stouffer. Princeton, NJ: Princeton University Press.

Hardy, C.J., E.G. Hall, and P.H. Presholdt. 1986. The mediational role of social influence in the perception of exertion. *Journal of Sport and Exercise Psychology* 8: 88–104.

Hardy, C.J., and W.J. Rejeski. 1989. Not what, but how one feels: The measurement of affect during exercise. *Journal of Sport & Exercise Psychology* 11 (3): 304–317.

Harlow, J.M. 1868. Recovery from the passage of an iron bar through the head. *Publications of the Massachusetts Medical Society* 2: 327–347.

Harris, S.S., C.J. Caspersen, G.H. DeFriese, and E.J. Estes. 1989. Physical activity counseling for healthy adults as a primary preventive intervention in the clinical setting. Report for the U.S. Preventive Services Task Force [published erratum appears in *Journal of the American Medical Association* 1989 (October 20), 262 (15): 2094] [see comments]. *Journal of the American Medical Association* 261 (June 23-30): 3588–3598.

Harter, S. 1982. The Perceived Competence Scale for Children. *Child Development* 53 (1): 87–97.

———. 1985. Competence as a dimension of self-evaluation: Toward a comprehensive model of self-worth. In *The development of the self*, ed. R.H. Leahy. New York: Academic Press.

———. 1986. Cognitive-developmental processes in the integration of concepts about emotions and the self. *Social Cognition* 4 (2): 119–151.

———. 1996. Historical roots of contemporary issues involving self-concept. In *Handbook of self-concept: Developmental, social, and clinical considerations*, ed. B.A. Bracken. New York: Wiley.

Hartman, F.A., K.A. Brownell, and J.E. Lockwood. 1932. Cortin as a general tissue hormone. *American Journal of Physiology* 101: 50.

Hatfield, B.D., A.H. Goldfarb, G.A. Sforzo, and M.G. Flynn. 1987. Serum beta-endorphin and affective responses to graded exercise in young and elderly men. *Journal of Gerontology* 42: 429–431.

Hatfield, B.D., and D.M. Landers. 1987. Psychophysiology in exercise and sport research: An overview. *Exercise and Sport Sciences Review* 15: 351–387.

Hausenblas, H.A., A.V. Carron, and D.E. Mack. 1997. Application of the theories of reasoned action and planned behavior to exercise behavior: A meta-analysis. *Journal of Sport and Exercise Psychology* 19: 36–51.

Hayes, S.D., P.R.E. Crocker, and K.C. Kowalski. 1999. Gender differences in physical self-perceptions, global self-esteem and physical activity: Evaluation of the physical self-perception profile model. *Journal of Sport Behavior* 22 (1): 1–14.

Henriques, G.R., and L.G. Calhoun. 1991. Gender and ethnic differences in the relationship between body esteem and self-esteem. *Journal of Psychology* 133 (4): 357–368.

Hensley, L.D. 2000. State of required physical education in colleges and universities. *Research Quarterly for Exercise and Sport* 71: A-71–A-72.

Hetta, J., M. Almqvist, H. Agren, G. Hambert, B. Liljenberg, and B.A. Roos. 1985. Prevalence of sleep disturbances and related symptoms in a middle-aged Swedish population. In *Sleep '84*, ed. W.P. Koella, E. Ruther, and H. Schulz. Stuttgart, New York: Gustav Fischer Verlag.

Hilgard, E.R. 1989. *Psychology in America: A historical survey*. New York: Harcourt Brace Jovanovich.

Hill, D.W., K.J. Cureton, S.C. Grisham, and M.A. Collins. 1987. Effect of training on the rating of perceived exertion at the ventilatory threshold. *European Journal of Applied Physiology and Occupational Physiology* 56: 206–211.

Hirsch, B., and D.T. Lykken. 1993. Age and the self-perception of ability: A twin study analysis. *Psychology and Aging* 8 (1): 72–80.

Hirschfeld, R.M., M.B. Keller, S. Panico, B.S. Arons, D. Barlow, F. Davidoff, J. Endicott, J. Froom, M. Goldstein, J.M. Gorman, R.G. Marek, T.A. Maurer, R. Meyer, K. Phillips, J. Ross, T.L. Schwenk, S.S. Sharfstein, M.E. Thase, and R.J. Wyatt. 1997. The National Depressive and Manic-Depressive Association consensus statement on the undertreatment of depression. *Journal of the American Medical Association* 277 (January 22-29): 333–340.

Holets, V.R., T. Hokfelt, A. Rokaeus, L. Terenius, and M. Goldstein. 1988. Locus coeruleus neurons in the rat containing neuropeptide Y, tyrosine hydroxylase or galanin and their efferent projections to the spinal cord, cerebral cortex and hypothalamus. *Neuroscience* 24: 893–906.

Hollmann, W., H.G. Fischer, K. De Meirleir, H. Herzog, K. Herzog, and L-E. Feinendegen. 1994. The brain—regional cerebral blood flow, metabolism, and psyche during ergometer exercise. In *Physical activity, fitness and health: International proceedings and consensus statement*, ed. C. Bouchard, R. Shephard, and T. Stephens. Champaign, IL: Human Kinetics.

Horne, J.A., and V.J. Moore. 1985. Sleep EEG effects of exercise with and without additional body cooling. *Electroencephalography and Clinical Neurophysiology* 60: 33–38.

Horne, J.A., and B.S. Shackell. 1987. Slow wave sleep elevations after body heating: Proximity to sleep and effects of aspirin. *Sleep* 10: 383–392.

Horne, J.A., and L.H.E. Staff. 1983. Exercise and sleep: Body heating effects. *Sleep* 6: 36–46.

Horowitz, A.L. 1995. *MRI physics for radiologists: A visual approach*. 3rd ed. New York: Springer-Verlag.

Hsiao, E.T., and R.E. Thayer. 1998. Exercising for mood regulation: The importance of experience. *Personality and Individual Differences* 24 (6): 829–836.

Hughes, C.F., C. Uhlmann, and J.W. Pennebaker. 1994. The body's response to processing emotional trauma: Linking verbal text with autonomic activity. *Journal of Personality* 62 (December): 565–585.

Irwin, W., R.J. Davidson, M.J. Lowe, B.J. Mock, J.A. Sorenson, and P.A. Turski. 1996. Human amygdala activation detected with echo-planar functional magnetic resonance imaging. *Neuroreport* 711: 1765–1769.

Jackson, A.W., and R.K. Dishman. 2000. Perceived submaximal force production in young men and women. *Medicine and Science in Sports and Exercise* 32: 448–451.

Jackson, A., R.K. Dishman, C.S. La Croix, R. Patton, and R. Weinberg. 1981. The heart rate, perceived exertion, and pace of the 1.5 mile run. *Medicine and Science in Sports and Exercise* 13: 224–228.

Jackson, E.M., and R.K. Dishman. 2002. The effects of cardiorespiratory fitness on physiological responses during

stress: A quantitative synthesis. Unpublished manuscript, The University of Georgia.

Jakicic, J.M., C. Winters, W. Lang, and R.R. Wing. 1999. Effects of intermittent exercise and use of home exercise equipment on adherence, weight loss, and fitness in overweight women. *Journal of the American Medical Association* 282: 1554–1560.

James, W. 1884. What is an emotion? *Mind* 9: 188–205.

———. 1890. *The principles of psychology.* 2 vols. New York: H. Holt.

———. 1899. *Talks to teachers on psychology: And to students on some of life's ideals.* New York: H. Holt.

Janis, I.L., and L. Mann. 1977. *Decision making: A psychological analysis of conflict, choice, and commitment.* New York: Free Press.

Janis, I.L., and P.B. Field. 1959. A behavioral assessment of personality: Consistency of individual differences. In *Personality and Persuasibility*, ed. C.I. Jovland and I.L. Janis. New Haven, CT: Yale University Press.

Janson, C., T. Gislason, W. De Backer, P. Plaschke, E. Bjoarnsson, J. Hetta, H. Kristbjarnason, P. Vermeire, and G. Boman. 1995. Insomnia and sleep: Prevalence of sleep disturbances among young adults in three European countries. *Sleep* 18: 589–597.

Jonas, B.S., P. Franks, and D.D. Ingram. 1997. Are symptoms of anxiety and depression risk factors for hypertension? Longitudinal evidence from the National Health and Nutrition Examination Survey I Epidemiologic Follow-up Study. *Archives of Family Medicine* 6 (January-February): 43–49.

Kandel, E.R. 1998. A new intellectual framework for psychiatry. *American Journal of Psychiatry* 155: 457–469.

Kann, L., S.A. Kinchen, B.I. Williams, J.G. Ross, R. Lowry, J.A. Grunbaum, and L.J. Kolbe. 2000. Youth Risk Behavior Surveillance–United States 1999. *Morbidity and Mortality Weekly Reports* 49 (SS-5): 1–96.

Kann, L., S.A. Kinchen, B.I. Williams, J.G. Ross, R. Lowry, C.V. Hill, J.A. Grunbaum, P.S. Blumson, J.L. Collins, and L.J. Kolbe. 1998. CDC Surveillance Summaries: Youth Risk Behavior Survey–United States 1997. *Morbidity and Mortality Weekly Reports* 47 (SS-3): 1–89.

Kann, L., C.W. Warren, W.A. Harris, J.L. Collins, B.I. Williams, J.G. Ross, and L.J. Kolbe. 1996. Youth risk behavior surveillance–United States, 1995. *Morbidity and Mortality Weekly Report* 45 (SS-4): 1–83.

Kaplan, G.A., W.J. Strawbridge, R.D. Cohen, and L.R. Hungerford. 1996. Natural history of leisure-time physical activity and its correlates: Associations with mortality from all causes and cardiovascular disease over 28 years. *American Journal of Epidemiology* 144 (8): 793–797.

Kavussanu, M., and E. McAuley. 1995. Exercise and optimism: Are highly active individuals more optimistic? *Journal of Sport & Exercise Psychology* 17 (246): 258.

Kendzierski, D. 1994. Schema theory: An information processing focus. *Advances in exercise adherence*, 137–159.

Kerlinger, F.N. 1973. *Foundations of behavioral research.* 2nd ed. New York: Holt, Rinehart & Winston.

Kessler, R.C., K.A. McGonagle, S. Zhao, C.B. Nelson, M. Hughes, S. Eshleman, H. Wittchen, and K. Kendler.

1994. Lifetime and 12-month prevalence of DSM-III-R psychiatric disorders in the United States: Results from the National Comorbidity Survey. *Archives of General Psychiatry* 51: 8–19.

Killian, K.J. 1987. Limitations of exercise by dyspnea. *Canadian Journal of Sport Science* 12 (suppl. 1): 53S–60S.

Kimiecik, J. 1992. Predicting vigorous physical activity of corporate employees: Comparing the theories of reasoned action and planned behavior. *Journal of Sport and Exercise Psychology* 14: 192–206.

King, A.C., C. Castro, S. Wilcox, A.A. Eyler, J.F. Sallis, and R.S. Brownson. 2000. Personal and environmental factors associated with physical inactivity among different racial-ethnic groups of U.S. middle-aged and older-aged women. *Health Psychology* 19: 354–364.

King, A.C., W.L. Haskell, H.C. Taylor, and R.F. DeBusk. 1991. Group- vs. home-based exercise training in healthy older men and women. *Journal of the American Medical Association* 266: 1535–1542.

King, A.C., and J.E. Martin. 1993. Exercise adherence and maintenance. In *Resource manual for guidelines for exercise testing and prescription*, ed. J.L. Durstine, A.C. King, P.L. Painter, J.L. Roitman, and L.D. Zwiren. Philadelphia: Lea & Febiger.

King, A.C., R.F. Oman, G.S. Brassington, D.L. Bliwise, and W.L. Haskell. 1997. Moderate-intensity exercise and self-rated quality of sleep in older adults. A randomized controlled trial. *Journal of the American Medical Association* 277: 32–37.

King, A.C., C.B. Taylor, and W.L. Haskell. 1993. Effects of differing intensities and formats of 12 months of exercise training on psychological outcomes in older adults. *Health Psychology* 124: 292–300.

Klink, M., and S.F. Quan. 1987. Prevalence of reported sleep disturbances in a general adult population and their relationship to obstructive airways diseases. *Chest* 91: 540–546.

Knapp, D.N. 1988. Behavioral management techniques and exercise promotion. In *Exercise adherence*, ed. R.K. Dishman. Champaign, IL: Human Kinetics.

Kohl, H.W., and W. Hobbs. 1998. Development of physical activity behavior among children and adolescents. *Pediatrics* 101 (suppl. 5): 549–554.

Kollesch, J. 1989. Knidos as the center of the early scientific medicine in ancient Greece. *Gesnerus* 46 (1–2): 11–28.

Koltyn, K.F., N.A. Lynch, and D.W. Hill. 1998. Psychological responses to brief exhaustive cycling exercise in the morning and evening. *International Journal of Sport Psychology* 29: 145–156.

Koltyn, K.F., and W.P. Morgan. 1992. Influence of underwater exercise on anxiety and body temperature. *Scandinavian Journal of Medicine and Science in Sports* 2: 249–253.

Konorski, J. 1967. *Integrative activity of the brain: An interdisciplinary approach*. Chicago: University of Chicago Press.

Kostka, C.E., and E. Cafarelli. 1982. Effect of pH on sensation and vastus lateralis electromyogram during cycling exercise. *Journal of Applied Physiology* S2: 1181–1185.

Kovacs, K.J. 1998. c-Fos as a transcription factor: A stressful (re)view from a functional map. *Neurochemistry International* 33 (October): 287–297.

Kripke, D.F. 1999. Chronic hypnotic use: Deadly risks, doubtful benefit. *Sleep Medicine Reviews*. In press.

Kripke, D.F., M.R. Klauber, D.L. Wingard, R.I. Fell, J.D. Assmus, and L. Garfinkel. 1998. Mortality hazard associated with prescription hypnotics. Biological Psychiatry 43: 687–693.

Kriska, A.M., and C. Caspersen. 1997. Introduction to a collection of physical activity questionnaires. *Medicine and Science in Sports and Exercise* 29 (S6): S5–S9.

Kubitz, K.A., and A.A. Mott. 1996. EEG power spectral densities during and after cycle ergometer exercise. *Research Quarterly for Exercise and Sport* 67: 91–96.

Kugler, J., H. Seelbach, and G.M. Kruskemper. 1994. Effects of rehabilitation exercise programmes on anxiety and depression in coronary patients: A meta-analysis. *British Journal of Clinical Psychology* 33 (pt. 3) (September): 401–410.

Kyllo, L.B., and D.M. Landers. 1995. Goal setting in sport and exercise: A research synthesis to resolve the controversy. *Journal of Sport and Exercise Psychology* 17: 117–137.

LaBar, K.S., J.C. Gatenby, J.C. Gore, J.E. Ledoux, and E.A. Phelps. 1998. Human amygdala activation during conditioned fear acquisition and extinction: A mixed-trial fMRI study. *Neuron* 205: 937–945.

Landers, D.M., and S.J. Petruzzello. 1994. Physical activity, fitness, and anxiety. In *Physical activity, fitness, and health: International proceedings and consensus statement*, ed. C. Bouchard, R. Shephard, and J.C. Stevens. Champaign, IL: Human Kinetics.

Landolt, H.P., Meier, V., Burgess, H.J., Finelli, L., Cattelin, F., and Borbely, A.A. 1998. SR 46349B, a selective 5-HT2 receptor antagonist, enhances delta activity and reduces sigma activity in nonREM sleep in humans. *Sleep*, 21S: 85.

Lang, P.J. 1995. The emotion probe: Studies of motivation and attention. *American Psychologist* 50 (5): 372–385.

———. 2000. Emotion and motivation: Attention, perception, and action. *Journal of Sport & Exercise Psychology* 20: S122–S140.

Lang, P.J., M.M. Bradley, and B.N. Cuthbert. 1998. Emotion, motivation, and anxiety: Brain mechanisms and psychophysiology. *Biological Psychiatry* 44 (December 15): 1248–1263.

Lang, P.J., M.M. Bradley, and B.N. Cuthbert 1999. *International affective pictures system (IAPSI): Instruction manual and affective ratings*. Technical Report A-4, The Center for Research in Psychophysiology University of Florida.

LaPorte, R.E., H.J. Montoye, and C.J. Caspersen. 1985. Assessment of physical activity in epidemiologic research: Problems and prospects. *Public Health Reports* 100 (March-April): 131–146.

Lawlor, D.A., and S.W. Hopker. 2001. The effectiveness of exercise as an intervention in the management of depression: Systematic review and meta-regression analysis of randomised controlled trials. *British Medical Journal* 322: 1–8.

Layman, E.M. 1960. Contributions of exercise and sports to mental health and social adjustment. In *Science and Medicine of Exercise and Sports*, ed. W.R. Johnson. New York: Harper.

Lazarus, A.A. 2000. Will reason prevail? From classical psychoanalysis to New Age therapy. *American Journal of Psychotherapy* 54 (2): 152–155.

Lazarus, R.S. 1991. Emotion theory and psychotherapy. In *Emotion, psychotherapy, and change*, ed. J.D. Safran and L.S. Greenberg. New York: Guilford Press.

———. 1993. From psychological stress to the emotions: A history of changing outlooks. *Annual Review of Psychology* 44: 1–21.

Le Bihan, D., moderator. 1995. NIH conference: Functional magnetic resonance imaging of the brain. *Annals of Internal Medicine* 122: 296–303.

LeDoux, J.E. 1994. Emotion, memory, and the brain. *Scientific American* 271 (6): 50–57.

Lee, C. 1993. Attitudes, knowledge, and stages of change: A survey of exercise patterns in older Australian women. *Health Psychology* 12 (6): 476–480.

Lee, Y., D.E. Lopez, E.G. Meloni, and M. Davis. 1996. A primary acoustic startle pathway: Obligatory role of cochlear root neurons and the nucleus reticularis pontis caudalis. *Journal of Neuroscience* 16 (June 1): 3775–3789.

Lehtinen, V., and M. Joukamaa. 1994. Epidemiology of depression: Prevalence, risk factors and treatment situation. *Acta Psychiatrica Scandinavica* suppl. 377: 7–10.

Leibenluft, E. 1998. Why are so many women depressed? *Scientific American Presents* 9 (2): 52–60.

Leonard, F.E., and G.B. Affleck. 1947. *A guide to the history of physical education*. Philadelphia: Lea & Febiger.

Leslie, E., M.J. Fotheringham, J. Veitch, and N. Owen. 2000. A university campus physical activity promotion program. *Health Promotion Journal of Australia* 10: 51–54.

Leslie, E., N. Owen, J. Salmon, A. Bauman, J.F. Sallis, and S.K. Lo. 1999. Insufficiently-active Australian college students: Perceived personal, social and environmental influences. *Preventive Medicine* 28: 20–27.

Leslie, E., P.B. Sparling, and N. Owen. 2001. University campus settings and the promotion of physical activity in young adults: Lessons from research in Australia and the USA. *Health Education* 3: 116–125.

LeUnes, A., and J. Burger. 1998. Bibliography on the Profile of Mood States in sport and exercise psychology research, 1971-1998. *Journal of Sport Behavior* 21 (1): 53–70.

Lief, A., ed. 1948. *The commonsense psychiatry of Dr. Adolf Meyer*. New York: McGraw-Hill.

Likert, R. 1932. The method of constructing an attitude scale. *Archives of Psychology* 140: 44–53.

Lindsley, D.B. 1952. Psychological phenomena and the electroencephalogram. *Electroencephalography and Clinical Neurophysiology* 4: 443–456.

Lirgg, C.D. 1991. Gender differences in self-confidence in physical activity: A meta-analysis of recent studies. *Journal of Sport & Exercise Psychology* 13 (3): 294–310.

Littre, E. 1842. *Oeuvres d'Hippocrate*. Bruxelles: Société encyclographique des sciences médicales.

Lombard, D.N., T.N. Lombard, and R.A. Winett. 1995. Walking to meet health guidelines: The effects of prompting frequency and prompt structure. *Health Psychology* 14 (2): 164–170.

Lox, C.L., E. McAuley, and R.S. Tucker. 1995. Exercise as an intervention for enhancing subjective well-being in an HIV-1 population. *Journal of Sport & Exercise Psychology* 17 (4): 345–362.

Luepker, R.V., D.M. Murray, D.R. Jacobs, M.B. Mittelmark, N. Bracht, R. Carlaw, R. Crow, P. Elmer, J.R. Finnegan, A.R. Folsom, R.H.J. Grimm, P.J. Hannan, R.W. Jeffery, H. Lando, P. McGovern, R. Mullis, C.L. Perry, T. Pechacek, P. Pirie, J.M. Sprafka, R. Weisbrod, and H. Blackburn. 1994. Community education for cardiovascular disease prevention: Risk factor changes in the Minnesota Heart Health Program. *American Journal of Public Health* 84: 1383–1393.

Luepker, R.V., C.L. Perry, S.M. McKinlay, P.R. Nader, G.S. Parcel, E.J. Stone, L.S. Webber, J.P. Elder, H.A. Feldman, and C.C. Johnson. 1996. Outcomes of a field trial to improve children's dietary patterns and physical activity. The Child and Adolescent Trial for Cardiovascular Health. CATCH collaborative group. *Journal of the American Medical Association* 275 (March 13): 768–776.

Maas, J.W. 1979. Biochemistry of the affective disorders. *Hospital Practice* 14 (May): 113–120.

Macera, C.A., K.L. Jackson, G.W. Hagenmaier, J.J. Kronenfeld, H.W. Kohl, and S.N. Blair. 1989. Age, physical activity, physical fitness, body composition, and incidence of orthopedic problems. *Research Quarterly for Exercise and Sport* 60 (3): 225–233.

Macmillan, M.B. 2000a. *An odd kind of fame: Stories of Phineas Gage*. Cambridge, MA: MIT Press.

Macmillan, M.B. 2000b. Restoring Phineas Gage. *Journal of the History of Neurosciences* 9: 42–62.

Maddock, R.J., C.S. Carter, and D.W. Gietzen. 1991. Elevated serum lactate associated with panic attacks induced by hyperventilation. *Psychiatry Research* 38 (September): 301–311.

Maimonides, M. [1199] 1990. *Three treatises on health*. Translated by F. Rosner with bibliographies by J.I. Dienstage. Haifa, Isreal: Maimonides Research Institute.

Marcus, B.H., C.A. Eaton, J.S. Rossi, and L.L. Harlow. 1994. Self-efficacy, decision-making and the stages of change: An integrative model of physical exercise. *Journal of Applied Social Psychology* 24: 489–508.

Marcus, B.H., N. Owen, L.H. Forsyth, N.A. Cavill, and F. Fridinger. 1998. Physical activity interventions using mass media, print media, and information technology. *American Journal of Preventive Medicine* 15 (November): 362–378.

Marcus, B.H., V.C. Selby, R.S. Niaura, and J.S. Rossi. 1992. Self-efficacy and the stages of exercise behavior change. *Research Quarterly for Exercise and Sport* 63 (1): 60–66.

Marcus, B.H., and L.R. Simkin. 1993. The stages of exercise behavior. *Journal of Sports Medicine and Physical Fitness* 33: 83–88.

Marcus, B.H., and A.L. Stanton. 1993. Evaluation of relapse prevention and reinforcement interventions to promote exercise adherence in sedentary females. *Research Quarterly for Exercise and Sport* 64: 447–452.

Markland, D., and L. Hardy. 1993. The exercise motivation inventory: Preliminary development and validity of a measure of individuals' reasons for participation in regular physical exercise. *Personality and Individual Differences* 15 (3): 289–296.

Marlatt, G.A., and J.R. Gordon. 1985. *Relapse prevention: Maintenance strategies in addictive behavior change.* New York: Guilford Press.

Marsh, H.W. 1990. The structure of academic self-concept: The Marsh/Shavelson model. *Journal of Educational Psychology* 82 (4): 623–636.

———. 1993. Physical fitness self-concept: Relations of physical fitness to field and technical indicators for boys and girls aged 9-25. *Journal of Sport & Exercise Psychology* 15 (2): 184–206.

———. 1997. The measurement of physical self-concept: A construct validation approach. In *The physical self: From motivation to well-being*, ed. K.R. Fox, 27–58. Champaign, IL: Human Kinetics.

———. 1998. Age and gender effects in physical self-concepts for adolescent elite athletes and nonathletes: A multicohort-multioccasion design. *Journal of Sport & Exercise Psychology* 20 (3): 237–259.

———. 1999. Cognitive discrepancy models: Actual, ideal, potential, and future self-perspectives of body image. *Social Cognition* 17 (1): 46–75.

Marsh, H.W., J. Hey, L.A. Roche, and C. Perry. 1997. Structure of physical self-concept: Elite athletes and physical education students. *Journal of Educational Psychology* 89 (2): 369–380.

Marsh, H.W., and R. O'Neill. 1984. Self Description Questionnaire III: The construct validity of multidimensional self-concept ratings by late adolescents. *Journal of Educational Measurement* 21 (2): 153–174.

Marsh, H.W., J. Parker, and J. Barnes. 1985. Multidimensional adolescent self-concepts: Their relationship to age, sex, and academic measures. *American Educational Research Journal* 22 (3): 422–444.

Marsh, H.W., and N.D. Peart. 1988. Competitive and cooperative physical fitness training programs for girls: Effects on physical fitness and multidimensional self-concepts. *Journal of Sport & Exercise Psychology* 10 (4): 390–407.

Marsh, H.W., G.E. Richards, S. Johnson, and L. Roche. 1994. Physical Self-Description Questionnaire: Psychometric properties and a multitrait-multimethod analysis of relations to existing instruments. *Journal of Sport & Exercise Psychology* 16 (3): 270–305.

Marsh, H.W., I.D. Smith, and J. Barnes. 1983. Multitrait-multimethod analyses of the Self-Description Questionnaire: Student-teacher agreement on multidimensional ratings of student self-concept. *American Educational Research Journal* 20 (3): 333–357.

Martinsen, E.W. 1990. Physical fitness, anxiety and depression. *British Journal of Hospital Medicine* 43 (March): 194, 196, 199.

———. 1993. Therapeutic implications of exercise for clinically anxious and depressed patients. *International Journal of Sport Psychology* 24 (2): 185–199.

———. 1994. Physical activity and depression: Clinical experience. *Acta Psychiatrica Scandinavica* (Supplementum) 377: 23–27.

Martinsen, E.W., A. Hoffart, and O. Solberg. 1989. Comparing aerobic with nonaerobic forms of exercise in the treatment of clinical depression: A randomized trial. *Comprehensive Psychiatry* 30 (July-August): 324–331.

Martinsen, E.W., A. Medhus, and L. Sandvik. 1985. Effects of aerobic exercise on depression: A controlled study. *British Medical Journal (Clinical Research Edition)* 291 (July 13): 109.

Martinsen, E.W., L. Sandvik, and O.B. Kolbjornsrud. 1989. Aerobic exercise in the treatment of nonpsychotic mental disorders: An exploratory study. *Nordisk Psykiatrisk Tidsskrift* 43 (6): 521–529.

Martinsen, E.W., J. Strand, G. Paulsson, and J. Kaggestad. 1989. Physical fitness level in patients with anxiety and depressive disorders. *International Journal of Sports Medicine* 10 (February): 58–61.

Mason, J.W., J.T. Maher, L.H. Hartley, E.H. Mougey, M.J. Perlow, and L.G. Jones. 1976. Selectivity of corticosteroid and catecholamine response to various natural stimuli. In *Psychopathology of Human Adaptation*, ed. G. Serban. New York: Plenum.

Mausner, J.S., and S. Kramer. 1985. *Epidemiology: An introductory text.* 2nd ed. Philadelphia: Saunders.

McAuley, E. 1994. Physical activity and psychosocial outcomes. In *Physical activity, fitness, and health: International proceedings and consensus statement*, ed. C. Bouchard and R.J. Shephard. Champaign, IL: Human Kinetics.

McAuley, E., S.M. Bane, D.L. Rudolph, and C.L. Lox. 1995. Physique anxiety and exercise in middle-aged adults. *Journals of Gerontology: Series B: Psychological Sciences and Social Sciences* 50 (5): 229–235.

McAuley, E., and B. Blissmer. 2000. Self-efficacy determinants and consequences of physical activity. *Exercise and Sport Sciences Reviews* 28: 85–88.

McAuley, E., and K.S. Courneya. 1994. The Subjective Exercise Experiences Scale (SEES): Development and preliminary validation. *Journal of Sport & Exercise Psychology* 16 (2): 163–177.

McAuley, E., K.S. Courneya, D.L. Rudolph, and C.L. Lox. 1994. Enhancing exercise adherence in middle-aged males and females. *Preventive Medicine* 23: 498–506.

McAuley, E., C.L. Lox, and S.C. Duncan. 1993. Long-term maintenance of exercise, self-efficacy, and physiological change in older adults. *Journal of Gerontology* 48 (4): 218–224.

McAuley, E., and S.L. Mihalko. 1998. Measuring exercise-related self-efficacy. In *Advances in sport and exercise psychology measurement*, ed. J.L. Duda. Morgantown, WV: Fitness Information Technology.

McAuley, E., S.L Mihalko, and S.M. Bane. 1996. Acute exercise and anxiety reduction: Does the environment matter? *Journal of Sport & Exercise Psychology* 18: 408–419.

McAuley, E., S.L. Mihalko, and S.M. Bane. 1997. Exercise and self-esteem in middle-aged adults: Multidimensional relationships and physical fitness and self-efficacy influences. *Journal of Behavioral Medicine* 20 (February): 67–83.

McCabe, P.M., J.F. Sheridan, J.M. Weiss, J.P. Kaplan, B.H. Natelson, and W.P. Pare. 2000. Animal models of disease. *Physiology and Behavior* 68 (February): 501–507.

McCulloch, T.L., and J.S. Bruner. 1939. The effect of electric shock upon subsequent learning in the rat. *Journal of Psychology* 7: 333–336.

McDonald, D.G., and J.A. Hodgdon. 1991. *The psychological effects of aerobic fitness training: Research and theory*. New York: Springer-Verlag.

McEwen, B.S. 1998. Protective and damaging effects of stress mediators. *New England Journal of Medicine* 338: 171–179.

McGinty, D., and R. Szymusiak. 1990. Keeping cool: A hypothesis about the mechanisms and functions of slow wave sleep. *Trends in Neurosciences* 13: 480–487.

McNair, D.M., M. Lorr, and L.F. Droppleman. 1981. *Manual for the Profile of Mood States*. San Diego: Educational and Industrial Testing Service.

McNally, R.J., E.B. Foa, and C.D. Donnell. 1989. Memory bias for anxiety information in patients with panic disorder. *Cognition & Emotion* 3 (1): 27–44.

McNeil, J.K., E.M. LeBlanc, and M. Joyner. 1991. The effect of exercise on depressive symptoms in the moderately depressed elderly. *Psychology and Aging* 6 (3): 487–488.

McSherry, J.A. 1984. The diagnostic challenge of anorexia nervosa. *American Family Physician* 29 (February): 141–145.

Meeusen, R., I. Smolders, S. Sarre, K. De Meirleir, H. Keizer, M. Serneels, G. Ebinger, and Y. Michotte. 1997. Endurance training effects on neurotransmitter release in rat striatum: An in vivo microdialysis study. *Acta Psychiatrica Scandinavica* 159 (April): 335–341.

Meichenbaum, D. 1977. *Cognitive-behavior modification: An integrative approach*. New York: Plenum.

Meichenbaum, D., and R. Cameron. 1974. The clinical potential of modifying what clients say to themselves. *Psychotherapy: Theory, Research and Practice* 11 (2): 103–117.

Meichenbaum, D.H., and J. Goodman. 1971. Training impulsive children to talk to themselves: A means of developing self-control. *Journal of Abnormal Psychology* 77 (2): 115–126.

Mellinger, G.D., M.B. Balter, and E.H. Uhlenhuth. 1985. Insomnia and its treatment. Prevalence and correlates. *Archives of General Psychiatry* 42: 225–232.

Meloni, E.G., and M. Davis. 1999. Enhancement of the acoustic startle response in rats by the dopamine D-sub-1 receptor agonist SKF 82958. *Psychopharmacology* 144 (4): 373–380.

Menard, J., and D. Treit. 1999. Effects of centrally administered anxiolytic compounds in animal models of anxiety. *Neuroscience and Biobehavioral Reviews* 23 (March): 591–613.

Messick, S. 1989. Validity. In *Educational measurement*, ed. R.L. Linn. 3rd ed. New York: Macmillan.

Michael, E.D. 1957. Stress adaptations through exercise. *American Association for Health, Physical Education, and Recreation: Research Quarterly* 28: 50–54.

Miller, A. 1999. Millennial mind-set. *American Demographics*, January, 61–65.

Miller, G.A. 1956. The magical number seven, plus or minus two: Some limits on our capacity for processing information. *Psychological Review* 63: 81–97.

Mitchell, J.H., and P.B. Raven. 1994. Cardiovascular adaptation to physical activity. In *Physical activity, fitness, and health: International proceedings and consensus statement*, ed. C. Bouchard, R.J. Shephard, and T. Stephens. Champaign, IL: Human Kinetics.

Mobility, K.E., L.M. Rubenstein, J.H. Lenke, M.W. O'Hara, and R.B. Wallace. 1996. Walking and depression in a cohort of older adults: The Iowa 65+ rural health study. *Journal of Aging and Physical Activity* 4: 119–135.

Mogenson, G.J. 1987. Limbic-motor integration. *Progress in Psychobiology and Physiological Psychology* 12: 117–170.

Monahan, T. 1988. Perceived exertion: An old exercise tool finds new applications. *Physician and Sportsmedicine* 16: 174–179.

Mondin, G.W., W.P. Morgan, P.N. Piering, and A.J. Stegner. 1996. Psychological consequences of exercise deprivation in habitual exercisers. *Medicine and Science in Sports and Exercise* 28 (9): 1199–1203.

Montoye, H.J., H.C.G. Kemper, W.H.M. Saris, and R.A. Washburn. 1996. *Measuring physical activity and energy expenditure*. Champaign, IL: Human Kinetics.

Morgan, W.P. 1968. Selected physiological and psychomotor correlates of depression in psychiatric patients. *Research Quarterly* 39 (December): 1037–1043.

———. 1969. A pilot investigation of physical working capacity in depressed and nondepressed psychiatric males. *Research Quarterly* 40 (December): 859–861.

———. 1970. Physical working capacity in depressed and non-depressed psychiatric females: A preliminary study. *American Corrective Therapy Journal* 24 (January-February): 14–16.

———. 1973. Influence of acute physical activity on state anxiety. In *Proceedings, Annual Meeting of the College Physical Education Association for Men*, ed. C.E. Mueller. Minneapolis: University of Minnesota.

———. 1977. Involvement in vigorous physical activity with special reference to adherence. In *Proceedings of the National College Physical Education Association*, ed. L.I. Gedvilas and M.W. Kneer. Chicago: University of Illinois-Chicago Publications Service.

———. 1979a. Anxiety reduction following acute physical activity. *Psychiatric Annals* 9 (3): 36–45.

———. 1979b. Negative addiction in runners. *Physician and Sportsmedicine* 7: 57–70.

———. 1981. Psychophysiology of self-awareness during vigorous physical activity. *Research Quarterly for Exercise and Sport* 52: 385–427.

———. 1986. Presidential message. *American Psychological*

Association Newsletter, Division 47, Exercise and Sport Psychology 1 (1): 1–2.

———. 1994a. 40 years of progress: Sport psychology in exercise science and sports medicine. In *40th anniversary lectures*. Indianapolis: American College of Sports Medicine.

———. 1994b. Physical activity, fitness, and depression. In *Physical activity, fitness, and health: International proceedings and consensus statement*, ed. C. Bouchard, R.J. Shephard, and T. Stephens. Champaign, IL: Human Kinetics.

———. 1997. Methodological considerations. In *Physical activity and mental health*, ed. W.P. Morgan. *The series in psychology and behavioral medicine*. Washington, DC: Taylor & Francis.

Morgan, W.P., D.R. Brown, J.S. Raglin, P.J. O'Connor, and K.A. Ellickson. 1987. Psychological monitoring of overtraining and staleness. *British Journal of Sports Medicine* 21: 107–114.

Morgan, W.P., D.L. Costill, M.G. Flynn, and J.S. Raglin. 1988. Mood disturbance following increased training in swimmers. *Medicine and Science in Sports and Exercise* 20 (4): 408–414.

Morgan, W.P., and S.E. Goldston. 1987. *Exercise and mental health*. Washington, DC: Hemisphere.

Morgan, W.P., K. Hirota, G.A. Weitz, and B. Balke. 1976. Hypnotic perturbation of perceived exertion: Ventilatory consequences. *American Journal of Clinical Hypnosis* 18 (3): 182–190.

Morgan, W.P., P.B. Raven, B.L. Drinkwater, and S.M. Horvath. 1973. Perceptual and metabolic responsivity to standard bicycle ergometry following various hypnotic suggestions. *International Journal of Clinical and Experimental Hypnosis* 21 (2): 86–101.

Morgan, W.P., J.A. Roberts, F.R. Brand, and A.D. Feinerman. 1970. Psychological effect of chronic physical activity. *Medicine and Science in Sports and Exercise* 2 (Winter): 213–217.

Morgan, W.P., J.A. Roberts, and A.D. Feinerman. 1971. Psychologic effect of acute physical activity. *Archives of Physical Medicine and Rehabilitation* 52 (September): 422–425.

Motl, R.W., R.K. Dishman, R. Saunders, M. Dowda, G. Felton, and R.R. Pate. 2001. Measuring enjoyment of physical activity in adolescent girls. *American Journal of Preventive Medicine* 21: 110–117.

Motl, R.W., R.K. Dishman, R. Saunders, M. Dowda, G. Felton, D. Ward, and R.R. Pate. 2002. Examining social-cognitive determinants of intention and physical activity in adolescent girls using structural equation modeling. *Health Psychology* 21: 459–467.

Motl, R.W., R.K. Dishman, S.G. Trost, R. Saunders, M. Dowda, G. Felton, D. Ward, and R.R. Pate. 2000. Factorial validity and invariance of questionnaires measuring social-cognitive determinants of physical activity among adolescent girls. *Preventive Medicine* 31: 584–594.

Murray, C.L., and Lopez, A.D. 1996. The global burden of disease. A comprehensive assessment of mortality and disability from diseases, injuries, and risk factors in 1990 and projected to 2020. World Health Organization, World Bank, Harvard University.

Mutrie, N. 1997. The therapeutic effects of exercise on the self. In *The physical self: From motivation to well-being*, ed. K.R. Fox. Champaign, IL: Human Kinetics.

Nauta, W.J.H., and M. Feirtag. 1979. *The organization of the brain*. San Francisco: Freeman.

Nemeroff, C.B. 1998. The neurobiology of depression. *Scientific American* 278 (6): 42–47.

Newbold, R.F. 1990. Patterns of anxiety in Sallust, Suetonius and Procopius. *Ancient History Bulletin* 4 (2): 44–50.

Nieman, D.C., W.F. Custer, D.E. Butterworth, A.C. Utter, and D.A. Henson. 2000. Psychological response to exercise training and/or energy restriction in obese women. *Journal of Psychosomatic Research* 48 (1): 23–29.

Noble, B.J., G.A. Borg, I. Jacobs, and P. Kaiser. 1983. A category-ratio perceived exertion scale: Relationship to blood and muscle lactates and heart rate. *Medicine and Science in Sports and Exercise* 15: 523–528.

Noble, B.J., and R.J. Robertson. 1996. *Perceived exertion*. Champaign, IL: Human Kinetics.

North, T.C., P. McCullagh, and Z. Vu Tran. 1990. Effect of exercise on depression. *Exercise and Sport Sciences Reviews* 18: 379–415.

Nunnally, J.C., and I.H. Bernstein. 1994. *Psychometric theory*. 3rd ed. New York: McGraw-Hill.

O'Connor, P.J., L.E. Aenchbacher, and R.K. Dishman. 1993. Physical activity and depression in the elderly. *Journal of Aging and Physical Activity* 1: 34–58.

O'Connor, P.J., M.J. Breus, and S.D. Youngstedt. 1998. Exercise-induced increase in core temperature does not disrupt a behavioral measure of sleep. *Physiology and Behavior* 64: 213–217.

O'Connor, P.J., C.X. Bryant, J.P. Veltri, and S.M. Gebhardt. 1993. State anxiety and ambulatory blood pressure following resistance exercise in females. *Medicine and Science in Sports and Exercise* 25 (April): 516–521.

O'Connor, P.J., R.D. Carda, and B.K. Graf. 1991. Anxiety and intense running exercise in the presence and absence of interpersonal competition. *International Journal of Sports Medicine* 12: 423–426.

O'Connor, P.J., and D.B. Cook. 1999. Exercise and pain: The neurobiology, measurement, and laboratory study of pain in relation to exercise in humans. *Exercise and Sport Sciences Reviews* 27: 119–166.

O'Connor, P.J., and J.C. Davis. 1992. Psychobiologic responses to exercise at different times of the day. *Medicine and Science in Sports and Exercise* 24: 714–719.

O'Connor, P.J., S.J. Petruzzello, K.A. Kubitz, and T.L. Robinson. 1995. Anxiety responses to maximal exercise testing. *British Journal of Sports Medicine* 29: 97–102.

O'Connor, P.J., J.S. Raglin, and E.W. Martinsen. 2000. Physical activity, anxiety and anxiety disorders. *International Journal of Sport Psychology* 31 (2): 136–155.

O'Connor, P.J., and J.C. Smith. 1999. Physical activity and eating disorders. In *Lifestyle medicine*, ed. J.M. Rippe. Cambridge, MA: Blackwell Science.

O'Connor, P.J., J.C. Smith, and W.P. Morgan. 2000. Physical activity does not provoke panic attacks in patients with panic disorder: A review of the evidence. *Anxiety, Stress, and Coping* 13: 333–353.

O'Connor, P.J., and S.D. Youngstedt. 1995. Influence of exercise on human sleep. In *Exercise and Sport Sciences Reviews*, ed. J.O. Holloszy. Baltimore: Williams & Wilkins.

Ohayon, M.M., M. Caulet, and C. Guilleminault. 1998. How a general population perceives its sleep and how this relates to the complaint of insomnia. *Sleep* 20: 715–723.

Olivardia, R., H.J. Pope, and J.I. Hudson. 2000. Muscle dysmorphia in male weightlifters: A case-control study. *American Journal of Psychiatry* 157 (August): 1291–1296.

Oman, R.F., and A.C. King. 1998. Predicting the adoption and maintenance of exercise participation using self-efficacy and previous exercise participation rates. *American Journal of Health Promotion* 12: 154–161.

O'Neal, H., and R.K. Dishman. 2002. Physical activity and depression: A quantitative synthesis. Unpublished manuscript, The University of Georgia, Athens.

O'Neal, H.A., A.L. Dunn, and E.W. Martinsen. 2000. Depression and exercise. *International Journal of Sport Psychology* 31 (2): 110–135.

O'Neal, H., J.D. Van Hoomissen, P.V. Holmes, and R.K. Dishman. 2001. Preprogalanin messenger RNA levels are increased in rat locus coeruleus after exercise training. *Neuroscience Letters* 299: 69–72.

Orwin, A. 1974. Treatment of a situational phobia—a case for running. *British Journal of Psychiatry* 125: 96–98.

Osgood, C.E., G.J. Suci, and P.H. Tannenbaum. 1957. *The measurement of meaning*. Urbana: University of Illinois Press.

Ossip-Klein, D.J., E.J. Doyne, E.D. Bowman, K.M. Osborn, I.B. McDougall-Wilson, and R.A. Neimeyer. 1989. Effects of running or weight lifting on self-concept in clinically depressed women. *Journal of Consulting and Clinical Psychology* 57: 158–161.

Owen, N., E. Leslie, J. Salmon, and M.J. Fotheringham. 2000. Environmental determinants of physical activity and sedentary behavior. *Exercise and Sport Sciences Reviews* 28: 153–158.

Paffenbarger, R.S., S.N. Blair, I.M. Lee, and R.T. Hyde. 1993. Measurement of physical activity to assess health effects in free-living populations. *Medicine and Science in Sports and Exercise* 25 (January): 60–70.

Paffenbarger, R.S., I.M. Lee, and R. Leung. 1994. Physical activity and personal characteristics associated with depression and suicide in American college men. *Acta Psychiatrica Scandinavia* suppl. 377: 16–22.

Pagliari, R., and L. Peyrin. 1995. Norepinephrine release in the rat frontal cortex under treadmill exercise: A study with microdialysis. *Journal of Applied Physiology* 78 (June): 2121–2130.

Pagliari, R., and L. Peyrin. 1995b. Physical conditioning in rats influences the central and peripheral catecholamine responses to sustained exercise. *European Journal of Applied Physiology* 71: 41-52.

Palinkas, L.A., L.K. Palmer, K. Michiels, and B. Thigpen. 1995. Depressive symptoms in overweight and obese older adults: A test of the "jolly fat" hypothesis. *Journal of Psychosomatic Research* 40: 59–66.

Palkovitz, M., and M.J. Brownstein. 1988. *Maps and guide to microdissection of the rat brain*. New York: Elsevier.

Palmer, L.K. 1995. Effects of a walking program on attributional style, depression, and self-esteem in women. *Perceptual and Motor Skills* 81 (3, pt. 1): 891–898.

Pandolf, K.B. 1982. Differentiated ratings of perceived exertion during physical exercise. *Medicine and Science in Sports and Exercise* 14: 397–405.

———. 1983. Advances in the study and application of perceived exertion. *Exercise and Sport Sciences Reviews* 11: 118–158.

Papez, J.W. 1937. A proposed mechanism of emotion. *Archives of Neurology & Psychiatry* 38: 725–743.

Partonen, T., S. Leppaemaeki, J. Hurme, and J. Loennqvist. 1998. Randomized trial of physical exercise alone or combined with bright light on mood and health-related quality of life. *Psychological Medicine* 28 (6): 1359–1364.

Pate, R.R., G.W. Heath, M. Dowda, and S.G. Trost. 1996. Associations between physical activity and other health behaviors in a representative sample of US adolescents. *American Journal of Public Health* 86 (11): 1577–1581.

Pate, R.R., M. Pratt, S.N. Blair, W.L. Haskell, C.A. Macera, C. Bouchard, D. Buchner, W. Ettinger, G. Heath, A.C. King, A.M. Kriska, A.S. Leon, B.H. Marcus, J. Morris, Jr., R.S. Paffenbarger, K. Patrick, M.L. Pollock, J.M. Rippe, J.F. Sallis, and J.H. Wilmore. 1995. Physical activity and public health: A recommendation from the Centers for Disease Control and Prevention and the American College of Sports Medicine. *Journal of the American Medical Association* 273 (5): 402–407.

Pate, R.R., M.L. Small, J.G. Ross, J.C. Young, K.H. Flint, and C.W. Warren. 1995. School physical education. *Journal of School Health* 65 (October): 312–318.

Paulhus, D.L. 1984. Two-component models of socially desirable responding. *Journal of Personality and Social Psychology* 46 (3): 598–609.

Pearman, S.N., R.F. Valois, R.G. Sargent, R.P. Saunders, J.W. Drane, and C.A. Macera. 1997. The impact of a required college health and physical education course on the health status of alumni. *Journal of American College Health* 4: 77–85.

Petronis, K.R., J.F. Samuels, E.K. Moscicki, and J.C. Anthony. 1990. An epidemiologic investigation of potential risk factors for suicide attempts. *Social Psychiatry and Psychiatric Epidemiology* 25 (July): 193–199.

Petruzzello, S.J., and D.M. Landers. 1994. State anxiety reduction and exercise: Does hemispheric activation reflect such changes? *Medicine and Science in Sports and Exercise* 26 (8): 1028–1035.

Petruzzello, S.J., D.M. Landers, B.D. Hatfield, K.A. Kubitz, and W. Salazar. 1991. A meta-analysis on the anxiety-reducing effects of acute and chronic exercise. Outcomes and mechanisms. *Sports Medicine* 11 (March): 143–182.

Petruzzello, S.J., and A.K. Tate. 1997. Brain activation, affect, and aerobic exercise: An examination of both state-independent and state-dependent relationships. *Psychophysiology* 34 (5): 527–533.

Phillips, E.D. 1994, *Greek medicine: Philosophy and medicine from Alcmaeon to the Alexandrians*. London.

Phillips, K.A., R.L. O'Sullivan, and H.J. Pope. 1997. Muscle dysmorphia [letter]. *Journal of Clinical Psychiatry* 58 (August): 361.

Pinto, B.M., H. Lynn, B.H. Marcus, J. DePue, and M.G. Goldstein. 2001. Physician-based activity counseling: Intervention effects on mediators of motivational readiness for physical activity. *Annals of Behavioral Medicine* 23: 2–10.

Pitts, F.J., and J.J. McClure. 1967. Lactate metabolism in anxiety neurosis. *New England Journal of Medicine* 277 (December 21): 1329–1336.

Plutchik, R. 1994. *The psychology and biology of emotion.* New York: HarperCollins College.

Plutchik, R. 2001. The nature of emotions. *American Scientist* 89 (4): 344–350.

Pollock, M.L., J.F. Carroll, J.E. Graves, S.H. Leggett, R.W. Braith, M. Limacher, and J.M. Hagberg. 1991. Injuries and adherence to walk/jog and resistance training programs in the elderly. *Medicine and Science in Sports and Exercise* 23 (10): 1194–1200.

Pope, H.J., A.J. Gruber, P. Choi, R. Olivardia, and K.A. Phillips. 1997. Muscle dysmorphia. An underrecognized form of body dysmorphic disorder. *Psychosomatics* 38 (November-December): 548–557.

Pope, H.J., A.J. Gruber, B. Mangweth, B. Bureau, C. deCol, R. Jounent, and J.I. Hudson. 2000. Body perception among men in three countries. *American Journal of Psychiatry* 157: 1297–1231.

Porkka-Heiskanen, T., R.E. Strecker, M. Thakkar, A.A. Bjorkum, R.W. Greene, and R.W. McCarley. 1997. Adenosine: A mediator of the sleep-inducing effects of prolonged wakefulness. *Science* 276: 1265–1268.

Prochaska, J.O. 1979. *Systems of psychotherapy: A transtheoretical analysis.* Homewood, IL: Dorsey Press.

Prochaska, J.O., and C.C. DiClemente. 1982. Transtheoretical therapy: Toward a more integrative model of change. *Psychotherapy: Theory, Research and Practice* 20: 161–173.

———. 1983. Stages and processes of self-change of smoking: Toward an integrative model of change. *Journal of Consulting and Clinical Psychology* 51 (3): 390–395.

Prochaska, J.O., and B.H. Marcus. 1994. The transtheoretical model: Applications to exercise. In *Advances in exercise adherence*, ed. R.K. Dishman. Champaign, IL: Human Kinetics.

Prochaska, J.O., W.F. Velicer, J.S. Rossi, M.G. Goldstein, B.H. Marcus, W. Rakowski, C. Fiore, L.L. Harlow, C.A. Redding, D. Rosenblum, and S.R. Rossi. 1994. Stages of change and decisional balance for 12 problem behaviors. *Health Psychology* 13 (1): 39–46.

Radegran, G., and Y. Hellsten. 2000. Adenosine and nitric oxide in exercise-induced human skeletal muscle vasodilatation. *Acta Physiologica Scandinavica* 168 (April): 575–591.

Raglin, J.S. 1997. Anxiolytic effects of physical activity. In *Physical activity and mental health*, ed. W.P. Morgan. Washington, DC: Taylor & Francis.

Raglin, J.S., and L. Moger. 1999. Adverse consequences of physical activity: When more is too much. In *Lifestyle medicine*, ed. J.M. Rippe. Malden, MA: Blackwell Science.

Raglin, J.S., P.E. Turner, and F. Eksten. 1993. State anxiety and blood pressure following 30 min of leg ergometry or weight training. *Medicine and Science in Sports and Exercise* 25 (9): 1044–1048.

Raglin, J.S., and G.S. Wilson. 2000. Overtraining in athletes. In *Emotions in sport*, ed. Y. Hanin. Champaign, IL: Human Kinetics.

Raglin, J.S., and M. Wilson. 1996. State anxiety following 20 minutes of bicycle ergometer exercise at selected intensities. *International Journal of Sports Medicine* 17 (August): 467–471.

Rajala, U. A. Uusimaki, S. Keinanen-Kiukaanniemi, and S.L. Kivela. 1994. Prevalence of depression in a 55-year-old Finnish population. *Society of Psychiatry and Psychiatric Epidemiology* 29: 126–130.

Rasch, G. 1960. *Studies in mathematical psychology: I. Probabilistic models for some intelligence and attainment tests.* Copenhagen: Nielsen & Lydiche.

Rasmussen, K., D.A. Morilak, and B.L. Jacobs. 1986. Single unit activity of locus coeruleus neurons in the freely moving cat. I. During naturalistic behaviors and in response to simple and complex stimuli. *Brain Research* 371 (April 23): 324–334.

Raynor, D.A., K.J. Coleman, and L.H. Epstein. 1998. Effects of proximity on the choice to be physically active or sedentary. *Research Quarterly for Exercise and Sport* 69: 99–103.

Rector, N.A., and D. Roger. 1997. The stress buffering effects of self-esteem. *Personality and Individual Differences* 23 (5): 799–808.

Reed, G.R., W.F. Velicer, J.O. Prochaska, J.S. Rossi, and B.H. Marcus. 1997. What makes a good staging algorithm: Examples from regular exercise. *American Journal of Health Promotion* 12 (1): 57–66.

Reiman, E.M. 1997. The application of positron emission tomography to the study of normal and pathologic emotions. *Journal of Clinical Psychiatry* 58 (suppl. 16): 4–12.

Rejeski, W.J. 1981. Perception of exertion: A social psychophysiological integration. *Journal of Sport Psychology* 3: 305–320.

———. 1994. Dose-response issues from a psychological perspective. In *Physical activity, fitness and health: International proceedings and consensus statement*, ed. Bouchard, C., R. Shephard, and T. Stephens. Champaign, IL: Human Kinetics.

Research Quarterly for Exercise and Sport. 2000. Proceedings from the 9th Measurement and Evaluation Symposium of the Measurement and Evaluation Council of the American Association of Active Lifestyle and Fitness. 71 (2 Suppl).

Reuter, I., M. Engelhardt, K. Stecker, and H. Baas. 1999. Therapeutic value of exercise training in Parkinson's disease. *Medicine and Science in Sports and Exercise* 31 (11): 1544–1549.

Rice, D.P., and L.S. Miller. 1998. Health implications and cost implications of anxiety and other mental disorders in the United States. *British Journal of Psychiatry* 34 (suppl.): 4–9.

Richter, E.A., and J.R. Sutton. 1994. Hormonal adaptations to physical activity. In *Physical activity, fitness and health: International proceedings and consensus statement*, ed. C. Bouchard, R. Shephard, and T. Stephens. Champaign, IL: Human Kinetics.

Robertson, R.J., J.E. Falkel, A.L. Drash, A.M. Swank, K.F. Metz, S.A. Spungen, and J.R. LeBoeuf. 1986. Effect of blood pH on peripheral and central signals of perceived exertion. *Medicine and Science in Sports and Exercise* 18 (February): 114–122.

Robertson, R.J., R.L. Gillespie, E. Hiatt, and K.D. Rose. 1977. Perceived exertion and stimulus intensity modulation. *Perceptual and Motor Skills* 45: 211–218.

Robertson, R.J., and B.J. Noble. 1997. Perception of physical exertion: Methods, mediators, and applications. *Exercise and Sport Sciences Reviews* 25: 407–452.

Robinson, T.N. 1998. Does television cause childhood obesity? *Journal of the American Medical Association* 279: 959–960.

Roid, G.H., and W.H. Fitts. 1994. *Tennessee Self-Concept Scale [revised manual]*. Los Angeles: Western Psychological Services.

Ronis, D.L., J.F. Yates, and J.P. Kirscht. 1989. Attitudes, decisions, and habits as determinants of repeated behavior. In *Attitude structure and function*, ed. A.R. Pratkanis, S.J. Breckler, and A.G. Greenwald. Hillsdale, NJ: Erlbaum.

Rosen, C.S. 2000. Is the sequencing of change processes by stage consistent across health problems? A meta-analysis. *Health Psychology* 19 (6): 593–604.

Rosenberg, M. 1965. *Society and the adolescent self-image*. Princeton, NJ: Princeton University Press.

Rosenzweig, M.R., A.L. Leiman, and S.M. Breedlove. 1999a. *Biological psychology: An introduction to behavioral, cognitive, and clinical neuroscience*. 2nd ed. Sunderland, MA: Sinauer Associates.

Rosenzweig, M.R., A.L. Leiman, and S.M. Breedlove. 1999b. Emotions, aggression, and stress. In *Biological psychology: An introduction to behavioral, cognitive, and clinical neuroscience*, ed. M.R. Rosenzweig, A.L. Leiman, and S.M. Breedlove. 2nd ed. Sunderland, MA: Sinauer Associates.

Rowe, D.A., J. Benson, and T.A. Baumgartner. 1999. Development of the Body Self-Image Questionnaire. *Measurement in Physical Education and Exercise Science* 3 (4): 223–248.

Rowell, L.B. 1993. *Human cardiovascular control*. New York: Oxford University Press.

Rowland, T.W. 1998. The biological basis of physical activity. *Medicine and Science in Sports and Exercise* 30 (3): 392–399.

Rudolph, D.L., and J.G. Kim. 1996. Mood responses to recreational sport and exercise in a Korean sample. *Journal of Social Behavior and Personality* 11 (4): 841–849.

Russell, J.A. 1980. A circumplex model of affect. *Journal of Personality and Social Psychology* 39: 1161–1178.

Russell, J.A., M. Lewicka, and T. Niit. 1989. A cross-cultural study of a circumplex model of affect. *Journal of Personality and Social Psychology* 57 (5): 848–856.

Russell, J.A., A. Weiss, and G.A. Mendelsohn. 1989. Affect

Grid: A single-item scale of pleasure and arousal. *Journal of Personality and Social Psychology* 57 (3): 493–502.

Sacks, M.H., and M.L. Sachs. 1981. *Psychology of running*. Champaign, IL: Human Kinetics.

Sallis, J.F. 1993. Epidemiology of physical activity and fitness in children and adolescents. *Critical Reviews in Food Science and Nutrition* 33: 405–408.

Sallis, J.F., K.J. Calfas, J.F. Nichols, J.A. Sarkin, M.F. Johnson, S. Caparosa, S. Thompson, and J.E. Alcaraz. 1999. Evaluation of a university course to promote physical activity: Project GRAD. *Research Quarterly for Exercise and Sport* 70 (1): 1–10.

Sallis, J.F., W.L. Haskell, S.P. Fortmann, K.M. Vranizan, C.B. Taylor, and D.S. Solomon. 1986. Predictions of adoption and maintenance of physical activity in a community sample. *Preventive Medicine* 15: 331–341.

Sallis, J.F., and M.F. Hovell. 1990. Determinants of exercise behavior. *Exercise and Sport Sciences Reviews* 11: 307–330.

Sallis, J.F., M.F. Hovell, and C.R. Hofstetter. 1992. Predictors of adoption and maintenance of vigorous physical activity in men and women. *Preventive Medicine* 21: 237–251.

Sallis, J.F., and N. Owen. 1999. *Physical activity and behavioral medicine*. Thousand Oaks, CA: Sage.

Sallis, J.F., R.B. Pinski, R.M. Grossman, T.L. Patterson, and P.R. Nader. 1988. The development of self-efficacy scales for health-related diet and exercise behaviors. *Health Education Research* 3 (3): 283–292.

Sallis, J.F., J.J. Prochaska, and W.C. Taylor. 2000. A review of correlates of physical activity of children and adolescents. *Medicine and Science in Sports and Exercise* 32: 963–975.

Sallis, J.F., B.G. Simons-Morton, E.J. Stone, C.B. Corbin, L.H. Epstein, N. Faucette, R.J. Iannotti, J.D. Killen, R.C. Klesges, C.K. Petray, T.W. Rowland, and W.C. Taylor. 1992. Determinants of physical activity and interventions in youth. *Medicine and Science in Sports and Exercise* 24 (6): S248–S257.

Sapolsky, R.M. 1994. *Why zebras don't get ulcers—a guide to stress, stress-related diseases, and coping*. New York: Freeman.

Sarter, M., and J.P. Bruno. 1999. Abnormal regulation of corticopetal cholinergic neurons and impaired information processing in neuropsychiatric disorders. *Trends in Neurosciences* 22 (February): 67–74.

Schappert, S.M. 1998. Ambulatory care visits to physician offices, hospital outpatient departments, and emergency departments: United States, 1996, National Center for Health Statistics. *Vital Health Statistics* 13 (134).

Schlicht, W. 1994. Does physical exercise reduce anxious emotions? A meta-analysis. *Anxiety, Stress, and Coping* 6 (4): 275–288.

Schmitz, K., S.A. French, and R.W. Jeffery. 1997. Correlates of changes in leisure time physical activity over 2 years: The Healthy Worker Project. *Preventive Medicine* 26: 570–579.

Schneirla, T. 1959. An evolutionary and developmental theory of biphasic processes underlying approach and withdrawal. In *Nebraska Symposium on Motivation*, ed. M. Jones. Lincoln: University of Nebraska Press.

Secord, P.F., and S.M. Jourard. 1953. The appraisal of body-cathexis: Body-cathexis and the self. *Journal of Consulting Psychology* 17: 343–347.

Segar, M.L., V.L. Katch, R.S. Roth, A.W. Garcia, T.I. Portner, S.G. Glickman, S. Haslanger, and E.G. Wilkins. 1998. The effect of aerobic exercise on self-esteem and depressive and anxiety symptoms among breast cancer survivors [see comments]. *Oncology Nursing Forum* 25 (January-February): 107–113.

Sehested, J., G. Reinicke, K. Ishino, R. Hetzer, S. Schifter, E. Schmitzer, and V. Regitz. 1995. Blunted humoral responses to mental stress and physical exercise in cardiac transplant recipients. *European Heart Journal* 166: 852–858.

Seip, R.L., D. Snead, E.F. Pierce, P. Stein, and A. Weltman. 1991. Perceptual responses and blood lactate concentration: Effect of training state. *Medicine and Science in Sports and Exercise* 23 (January): 80–87.

Selye, H. 1936. A syndrome produced by diverse nocuous agents. *Nature* 138: 32.

Selye, H. 1950. *Stress*. Montreal: Acta.

Seraganian, P. 1993. *Exercise psychology: The influence of physical exercise on psychological processes*. New York: Wiley.

Sexton, H., A. Maere, and N.H. Dahl. 1989. Exercise intensity and reduction in neurotic symptoms: A controlled follow-up study. *Acta Psychiatrica Scandinavica* 80 (3): 231–235.

Shapiro, D., L.D. Jamner, J.D. Lane, K.C. Light, M. Myrteck, Y. Sawadea, and A. Steptoe. 1996. Blood pressure publication guidelines. *Psychophysiology* 33: 1–12.

Shapiro P.A., R.P. Sloan, E. Bagiella, J.T. Bigger, Jr., and J.M. Gorman. 1996. Heart rate reactivity and heart period variability throughout the first year after heart transplantation. *Psychophysiology* 331: 54–62.

Shapiro, P.A., R.P. Sloan, J.T. Bigger, Jr., E. Bagiella, and J.M. Gorman. 1994. Cardiac denervation and cardiovascular reactivity to psychological stress. *American Journal of Psychiatry* 1518: 1140–1147.

Shapiro, S. 1984. Utilization of health and mental health services: Three Epidemiologic Catchment Area sites. *Archives of General Psychiatry* 41 (10): 971–978.

Shavelson, R.J., J.J. Hubner, and G.C. Stanton. 1976. Self-concept: Validation of construct interpretations. *Review of Educational Research* 46 (3): 407–441.

Shaver, P., J. Schwartz, D. Kirson, and C. O'Connor. 1987. Emotion knowledge: Further exploration of a prototype approach. *Journal of Personality and Social Psychology* 52 (June): 1061–1086.

Shephard, R.J. 1991. Benefits of sport and physical activity for the disabled: Implications for the individual and for society. *Scandinavian Journal of Rehabilitation Medicine* 23: 51–59.

Sherrill, D.L., K. Kotchou, and S.F. Quan. 1998. Association of physical activity and human sleep disorders. *Archives of Internal Medicine* 158: 1894–1898.

Siegel, J.M. 2000. Brainstem mechanisms generating REM sleep. In *Principles and practice of sleep medicine*, 2nd ed., ed. M.K. Kryger, T. Roth, and W.O. Dement. New York: Saunders.

Silverberg, A.B., S.D. Shah, M.W. Haymond, and P.E. Cryer. 1978. Norepinephrine: Hormone and neurotransmitter in man. *American Journal of Physiology* 234: E252–E256.

Simkin, L.R., and A.M. Gross. 1994. Assessment of coping with high-risk situations for exercise relapse among healthy women. *Health Psychology* 13 (3): 274–277.

Singh, N.A., K.M. Clements, and M.A. Fiatarone. 1997. A randomized controlled trial of the effect of exercise on sleep. *Sleep* 20: 95–101.

Sinyor, D., S.G. Schwartz, F. Peronnet, G. Brisson, and P. Seraganian. 1983. Aerobic fitness level and reactivity to psychosocial stress: Physiological, biochemical, and subjective measures. *Psychosomatic Medicine* 45 (June): 205–217.

Skinner, B.F. 1938. *The behavior of organisms*. New York: Appleton-Century-Crofts.

Skrinar, G.S., S.P. Ingram, and K.B. Pandolf. 1983. Effect of endurance training on perceived exertion and stress hormones in women. *Perceptual and Motor Skills* 57 (December): 1239–1250.

Smith, J.C., and J.B. Crabbe. 2000. Emotion and exercise. *International Journal of Sport Psychology* 31 (2): 156–174.

Smith, J.C., P.J. O'Connor, J.B. Crabbe, and R.K. Dishman. 2002. Startle and corrugator supercilii responses after low and moderate intensity exercise and seated rest. *Medicine and Science in Sports and Exercise* 34: 1158-1167.

Snodgrass, J.G., G. Levy-Berger, and M. Hydon. 1985. *Human experimental psychology*. New York: Oxford University Press.

Soares, J., P.V. Holmes, K.J. Renner, G.L. Edwards, B.N. Bunnell, and R.K. Dishman. 1999. Brain noradrenergic responses to footshock after chronic activity-wheel running. *Behavioral Neuroscience* 113 (June): 558–566.

Sonstroem, R.J. 1978. Physical estimation and attraction scales: Rationale and research. *Medicine and Science in Sports* 10 (Summer): 97–102.

———. 1988. Psychological models. In *Exercise adherence: Its impact on public health*, ed. R.K. Dishman. Champaign, IL: Human Kinetics.

———. 1998. Physical self-concept: Assessment and external validity. *Exercise and Sport Sciences Reviews* 26: 133–164.

Sonstroem, R.J., L.L. Harlow, and L. Josephs. 1994. Exercise and self-esteem: Validity of model expansion and exercise associations. *Journal of Sport & Exercise Psychology* 16 (1): 29–42.

Sonstroem, R.J., and W.P. Morgan. 1989. Exercise and self-esteem: Rationale and model. *Medicine and Science in Sports and Exercise* 21 (3): 329–337.

Sonstroem, R.J., and S.A. Potts. 1996. Life adjustment correlates of physical self-concept. *Medicine and Science in Sports and Exercise* 28 (5): 619-625.

Sonstroem, R.J., E.D. Speliotis, and J.L. Fava. 1992. Perceived physical competence in adults: An examination of the Physical Self-Perception Profile. *Journal of Sport & Exercise Psychology* 14 (2): 207–221.

Sothmann, M.S., J. Buckworth, R.P. Claytor, R.H. Cox, J.E. White-Welkley, and R.K. Dishman. 1996. Exercise training and the cross-stressor adaptation hypothesis. *Exercise and Sport Sciences Reviews* 24: 267–287.

Sothmann, M.S., A.B. Gustafson, T.L. Garthwaite, T.S. Horn, and B.A. Hart. 1988. Cardiovascular fitness and selected adrenal hormone responses to cognitive stress. *Endocrine Research* 14: 59–69.

Spalding, T.W., L.S. Jeffers, S.W. Porges, and B.D. Hatfield. 2000. Vagal and cardiac reactivity to psychological stressors in trained and untrained men. *Medicine and Science in Sports and Exercise* 32: 581–591.

Sparks, A.C. 1997. Reflections on the socially constructed physical self. In *The physical self: From motivation to wellbeing*, ed. K.R. Fox. Champaign, IL: Human Kinetics.

Sparling, P.B., T.K. Snow, and B. Beavers. 1999. Serum cholesterol levels in college students: Opportunities for education and intervention. *Journal of American College Health Association* 48: 123–127.

Spielberger, C.D. 1983. *Manual for the State-Trait Anxiety Inventory*. Palo Alto, CA: Consulting Psychologists Press.

Ståhl, T., A. Rutten, D. Nutbeam, A. Bauman, L. Kannas, T. Abel, G. Luschen, D.J. Rodriquez, J. Vinck, and J. van der Zee. 2001. The importance of the social environment for physically active lifestyle—results from an international study. *Social Science and Medicine* 52: 1–10.

Stein, P.N., and R.W. Motta. 1992. Effects of aerobic and nonaerobic exercise on depression and self-concept. *Perceptual and Motor Skills* 74 (1): 79–89.

Steinberg, H., B.R. Nicholls, E.A. Sykes, N. LeBoutillier, N. Ramlakhan, T.P. Moss, and A. Dewey. 1998. Weekly exercise consistently reinstates positive mood. *European Psychologist* 3 (4): 271–280.

Steinhardt, M., and R.K. Dishman. 1989. Reliability and validity of expected outcomes and barriers for habitual physical activity. *Journal of Occupational Medicine* 31 (6): 536–546.

Stephens, T. 1988. Physical activity and mental health in the United States and Canada: Evidence from four population surveys. *Preventive Medicine* 17: 35–47.

Steptoe, A., J. Wardle, R. Fuller, A. Holte, J. Justo, R. Sanderman, and L. Wichstrom. 1997. Leisure-time physical exercise: Prevalence, attitudinal correlates, and behavioral correlates among young Europeans from 21 countries. *Preventive Medicine* 26 (6): 845–854.

Stevens, J.C., and J.D. Mack. 1959. Scales of apparent force. *Journal of Experimental Psychology* 58: 405–413.

Stevens, S.S. 1957. On the psychophysical law. *Psychological Review* 64 (3): 153–181.

Stevens, S.S., and E.H. Galanter. 1957. Ratio scales and category scales for a dozen perceptual continua. *Journal of Experimental Psychology* 54: 377–411.

Stewart, A.L., K.M. Mills, P.G. Sepsis, A.C. King, B.Y. McLellan, K. Roitz, and P.L. Ritter. 1997. Evaluation of CHAMPS, a physical activity promotion program for older adults. *Annals of Behavioral Medicine* 19 (4): 353–361.

Stone, E.J., T.L. McKenzie, G.J. Welk, and M. Booth. 1998. Effects of physical activity interventions in youth: Review and synthesis. *American Journal of Preventive Medicine* 15 (4): 298–315.

Sundgot-Borgen, J. 1994. Risk and trigger factors for the development of eating disorders in female elite athletes. *Medicine and Science in Sports and Exercise* 26 (April): 414–419.

Tancer, M.E., M.B. Stein, and T.W. Uhde. 1993. Growth hormone response to intravenous clonidine in social phobia: Comparison to patients with panic disorder and healthy volunteers. *Biological Psychiatry* 34 (November 1): 591–595.

Tantillo, M., C. Kesick, G. Kind, and R.K. Dishman. 2002. The effects of exercise on children with attention-deficit hyperactivity disorder. *Medicine and Science in Sports and Exercise* 34: 203-212.

Task Force of the European Society of Cardiology and the North American Society of Pacing and Electrophysiology. 1996. Heart rate variability: Standards of measurement, physiological interpretation and clinical use. *Circulation* 93: 1043–1065.

Tellegen, A. 1985. Structures of mood and personality and their relevance to assessing anxiety, with an emphasis on self-report. In *Anxiety and the anxiety disorders*, ed. A.H. Tuma and J. Maser. Hillsdale, NJ: Erlbaum.

Tenenbaum, G. 1999. The implementation of Thurstone's and Guttman's measurement ideas in Rasch analysis. *International Journal of Sport Psychology* 30: 3–16.

Thayer, J.F., B.H. Friedman, and T.D. Borkovec. 1996. Autonomic characteristics of generalized anxiety disorder and worry. *Biological Psychiatry* 39 (February 15): 255–266.

Thayer, R.E. 1987. Energy, tiredness, and tension effects as a function of a sugar snack vs. moderate exercise. *Journal of Personality and Social Psychology* 52: 119–125.

———. 1989. *The biopsychology of mood and arousal*. New York: Oxford University Press.

Thayer, R.E., J.R. Newman, and T.M. McClain. 1994. Self-regulation of mood: Strategies for changing a bad mood, raising energy, and reducing tension. *Journal of Personality and Social Psychology* 67 (November): 910–925.

Thomas, S.N., T. Schroeder, N.H. Secher, and J.H. Mitchell. 1989. Cerebral blood flow during submaximal and maximal dynamic exercise in humans. *Journal of Applied Physiology* 67 (August): 744–748.

Thorndike, E.L. 1904. *An introduction to the theory of mental and social measurements*. New York: The Science Press.

Thurstone, L.L. 1926. The scoring of individual performance. *Journal of Educational Psychology* 17: 446–457.

———. 1927. A law of comparative judgment. *Psychological Review* 34: 273–286.

———. 1928. *Attitudes can be measured*. Vol. 33. Chicago: University of Chicago Press.

———. 1931. The measurement of social attitudes. *Journal of Abnormal and Social Psychology* 26: 249–269.

Thurstone, L.L., and E.J. Chave. 1929. *The measurement of attitude*. Chicago: University of Chicago Press.

Tieman, J.G., L.J. Peacock, K.J. Cureton, and R.K. Dishman. 2001. Acoustic startle eyeblink response after acute exercise. *International Journal of Neuroscience* 106: 21–33.

Tieman, J.G., L.J. Peacock, K.J. Cureton, and R.K. Dishman. 2002. The influence of exercise intensity and physical activity history on state anxiety after exercise. *International Journal of Sport Psychology* 33: 155-166.

Troped, P.J., and R.P. Saunders. 1998. Gender differences in social influence on physical activity at different stages of exercise adoption. *American Journal of Health Promotion* 13: 112–115.

Tsuji, H., M.G. Larson, F.J.J. Venditti, E.S. Manders, J.C. Evans, C.L. Feldman, and D. Levy. 1996. Impact of reduced heart rate variability on risk for cardiac events: The Framingham Study. *Circulation* 94: 2850–2855.

Tsutsumi, T., B.M. Don, L.D. Zaichkowsky, K. Takenaka, K. Oka, and T. Ohno. 1998. Comparison of high and moderate intensity of strength training on mood and anxiety in older adults. *Perceptual and Motor Skills* 87 (pt. 1): 1003–1011.

Tucker, L.A. 1983. Effect of weight training on self-concept: A profile of those influenced most. *Research Quarterly for Exercise and Sport* 54 (4): 389–397.

Uhlenhuth, E.H., M.B. Balter, G.D. Mellinger, I.H. Cisin, and J. Clinthorne. 1983. Symptom checklist syndromes in the general population: Correlations with psychotherapeutic drug use. *Archives of General Psychiatry* 40: 1167–1173.

U.S. Congress and U.S. Department of Health and Human Services. 1994. National Commission on Sleep Disorders Research. 1994. *Wake up America: A national sleep alert.* Vol. 2: Working Reports. Washington, D.C.: U.S. Government Printing Office.

United States Department of Health and Human Services. 1996. *Physical activity and health: A report of the Surgeon General.* Report DHHS publication no. (PH5) 017-023-00196-5. Atlanta: U.S. Department of Health and Human Services, Centers for Disease Control and Prevention, National Center for Chronic Disease Prevention and Health Promotion.

———. 1999. *Mental health: A report of the Surgeon General.* Atlanta: U.S. Department of Health and Human Services, Centers for Disease Control and Prevention, National Center for Chronic Disease Prevention and Health Promotion.

United States Public Health Services. 1990. *Promoting health/preventing disease: Year 2000 objectives for the nation.* Washington, DC: U.S. Government Printing Office.

Van Hoomissen, J.D., H. O'Neal, J.E. Dishman, P.V. Holmes, and R.K. Dishman. 2002. Serotonin transporter mRNA in dorsal raphe is unchanged by treadmill exercise training. Manuscript submitted for publication.

Van Reeth, O., J. Sturis, M.M. Byrne, J.D. Blackman, M. L'Hermite-Baleriaux, R. Leproult, R. Oliner, S. Refetoff, F.W. Turek, and E. Van Cauter. 1994. Nocturnal exercise phase delays circadian rhythms of melatonin and thyrotropin secretion in normal men. *American Journal of Physiology* 266: E964–E974.

Vaux, C.L. 1926. A discussion of physical exercise and recreation. *Occupational Therapy and Rehabilitation* 5: 329–333.

Veasey, S.C., C.A. Fornal, C.W. Metzler, and B.L. Jacobs. 1995. Response of serotonergic caudal raphe neurons in relation to specific motor activities in freely moving cats. *Journal of Neuroscience* 15 (July): 5346–5359.

Vuori, I., H. Urponen, J. Hasan, and M. Partinen. 1988. Epidemiology of exercise effects on sleep. *Acta Physiologica Scandinavica* 574: 3–7.

Wadden, T.A., R.A. Vogt, R.E. Andersen, and S.J. Bartlett. 1997. Exercise in the treatment of obesity: Effects of four

interventions on body composition, resting energy expenditure, appetite, and mood. *Journal of Consulting and Clinical Psychology* 65 (2): 269–277.

Wallace, L.S., J. Buckworth, T.E. Kirby, and W.M. Sherman. 2000. Characteristics of exercise behavior among college students: Application of social cognitive theory to predicting stage of change. *Preventive Medicine* 31 (5): 494–505.

Walters, S.T., and J.E. Martin. 2000. Does aerobic exercise really enhance self-esteem in children? A prospective evaluation in 3rd–5th graders. *Journal of Sport Behavior* 23 (1): 51–60.

Wang, G.J., N.D. Volkow, J.S. Fowler, D. Franceschi, J. Logan, N.R. Pappas, C.T. Wong, and N. Netusil. 2000. PET studies of the effects of aerobic exercise on human striatal dopamine release. *Journal of Nuclear Medicine* 41 (August): 1352–1356.

Wankel, L.M., and J.M. Sefton. 1989. A season-long investigation of fun in youth sports. *Journal of Sport & Exercise Psychology* 11 (4): 355–366.

Watson, D., and L.A. Clark. 1994. The vicissitudes of mood: A schematic model. In *The nature of emotion: Fundamental questions,* ed. P. Ekman and R.J. Davidson. New York: Oxford University Press.

Watson, D., L.A. Clark, and A. Tellegen. 1988. Development and validation of brief measures of positive and negative affect: The PANAS scales. *Journal of Personality and Social Psychology* 54 (6): 1063–1070.

Watson, D., and A. Tollegen. 1985. Toward a consensual structure of mood. *Psychological Bulletin* 98: 219–235.

Watson, J.B. 1919. *Psychology from the standpoint of a behaviorist.* Philadelphia: Lippincott.

Weinstein, N.D., A.J. Rothman, and S.R. Sutton. 1998. Stage theories of health behavior: Conceptual and methodological issues. *Health Psychology* 17 (3): 290–299.

Weir, L.T., and A.S. Jackson. 1992. %$\dot{V}O_2$max and %HRmax reserve are not equal methods of assessing exercise intensity. *Medicine and Science in Sports and Exercise* 24 (5 suppl.): 1057.

Weiser, P.C., R.A. Kinsman, and D.A. Stamper. 1973. Task-specific symptomatology changes resulting from prolonged submaximal bicycle riding. *Medicine and Science in Sports and Exercise* 5: 79–85.

Weiser, P.C., and D.A. Stamper. 1977. Psychophysiological interactions leading to increased effort, leg fatigue, and respiratory distress during prolonged strenuous bicycle riding. In *Physical work and effort,* ed. G.A. Borg. New York: Pergamon Press.

Weissman, M.M., R.C. Bland, G.J. Canino, C. Faravelli, S. Greenwald, H.G. Hwu, P.R. Joyce, E.G. Karam, C.K. Lee, J. Lellouch, J.P. Lepine, S.C. Newman, M.A. Oakley-Browne, M. Rubio-Stipec, J.E. Wells, P.J. Wickramaratne, H.U. Wittchen, and E.K. Yeh. 1997. The cross-national epidemiology of panic disorder. *Archives of General Psychiatry* 54 (April): 305–309.

Weissman, M.M., R.C. Bland, G.J. Canino, C. Faravelli, S. Greenwald, H.G. Hwu, P.R. Joyce, E.G. Karam, C.K. Lee, J. Lellouch, J.P. Lepine, S.C. Newman, M. Rubio-Stipec, J.E. Wells, P.J. Wickramaratne, H. Wittchen, and E.K. Yeh. 1996. Cross-national epidemiology of major depression and bipolar disorder. *Journal of the American Medical Association* 276: 293–299.

Weissman, M.M., J.S. Markowitz, R. Ouellette, S. Greenwald, and J.P. Kahn. 1990. Panic disorder and cardiovascular/cerebrovascular problems: Results from a community survey. *American Journal of Psychiatry* 147: 1504–1508.

Weyerer, S. 1992. Physical inactivity and depression in the community: Evidence from the Upper Bavarian Field Study. *International Journal of Sports Medicine* 136: 492–496.

Whaley, M.H., P.H. Brubaker, L.A. Kaminsky, and C.R. Miller. 1997. Validity of rating of perceived exertion during graded exercise testing in apparently healthy adults and cardiac patients. *Journal of Cardiopulmonary Research* 17 (July-August): 261–267.

White-Welkley, J.E., B.N. Bunnell, E.H. Mougey, J.L. Meyerhoff, and R.K. Dishman. 1995. Treadmill training and estradiol moderate hypothalamic-pituitary-adrenal cortical responses to acute running and immobilization. *Physiology and Behavior* 57: 533–540.

White-Welkley, J.E., G.L. Warren, B.N. Bunnell, E.H. Mougey, J.L. Meyerhoff, and R.K. Dishman. 1996. Treadmill exercise training and estradiol increase plasma ACTH and prolactin after novel footshock. *Journal of Applied Physiology* 80 (March): 931–939.

Whybrow, P.C., H.S. Akiskal, and W.T. McKinney. 1984. *Mood disorders: Toward a new psychobiology.* New York: Plenum Press.

Wilfley, D., and J. Kunce. 1986. Differential physical and psychological effects of exercise. *Journal of Counseling Psychology* 33: 337–342.

Williams, J.W. Jr, C.D. Mulrow, E. Chiquette, P.H. Noel, C. Aguilar, and J. Cornell. 2000. A systematic review of newer pharmacotherapies for depression in adults: Evidence report summary. *Annals of Internal Medicine* 132: 743–756.

Willner, P. 1995. Animal models of depression: Validity and applications. In *Depression and mania: From neurobiology to treatment*, ed. G. Gessa, W. Fratta, L. Pani, and G. Serra. New York: Raven Press.

Wilmore, J.H., and D.L. Costill. 1994. *Physiology of sport and exercise.* Champaign, IL: Human Kinetics.

Wilmore, J.H., A.S. Leon, D.C. Rao, J.S. Skinner, J. Gagnon, and C. Bouchard. 1997. Genetics, response to exercise, and risk factors: The HERITAGE Family Study. *World Review of Nutrition and Dietetics* 81: 72–83.

Wilson, C.A., J.R. Pearson, A.J. Hunter, P.A. Tuohy, and A.P. Payne. 1986. The effect of neonatal manipulation of hypothalamic serotonin levels on sexual activity in the adult rat. *Pharmacology, Biochemistry, and Behavior* 24 (May): 1175–1183.

Winters, E., ed. 1951. *The collected works of Adolf Meyer.* Baltimore: Johns Hopkins Press.

World Health Organization. 1999. The "newly defined" burden of mental problems, Fact Sheet No. 217. World Health Organization [Online], April. Available: www.who.int/inf-fs/en/fact217.html [August 10, 2001].

Wozniak, R.H. 1992. *Mind and body: Rene Descartes to William James.* Bethesda, MD, and Washington, DC: National Library of Medicine and American Psychological Association.

Wylie, R.C. 1989. *Measures of self-concept.* Lincoln, NE: University of Nebraska Press.

Yates, A., K. Leehey, and C.M. Shisslak. 1983. Running—an analogue of anorexia? *New England Journal of Medicine* 308 (February 3): 251–255.

Yeung, R.R. 1996. The acute effects of exercise on mood state. *Journal of Psychosomatic Research* 40 (February): 123–141.

Yoo, H., H.A. O'Neal, S. Hong, R.L. Tackett, and R.K. Dishman. 1999. Brain β-adrenergic responses to footshock after wheel running. *Medicine and Science in Sports and Exercise* 31 (5) (suppl.): S289.

Yoo, H.S., R.L. Tackett, B.N. Bunnell, J.B. Crabbe, and R.K. Dishman. 2000. Antidepressant-like effects of physical activity vs. imipramine: Neonatal clomipramine model. *Psychobiology* 28: 540–549.

Yorio, J.M., R.K. Dishman, W.R. Forbus, and K.J. Cureton. 1992. Breathlessness predicts perceived exertion in young women with mild asthma. *Medicine and Science in Sports and Exercise* 24 (8): 860–867.

Young, D.R., W.L. Haskell, C.B. Taylor, and S.P. Fortmann. 1996. Effect of community health education on physical activity knowledge, attitudes, and behavior. *American Journal of Epidemiology* 144: 264–274.

Youngstedt, S.D. 1997. Does exercise truly enhance sleep? *Physician and Sportsmedicine* 25 (10): 73–82.

———. 2000. The exercise-sleep mystery. *International Journal of Sport Psychology* 31 (2): 241–255.

Youngstedt, S.D., R.K. Dishman, K.J. Cureton, and L.J. Peacock. 1993. Does body temperature mediate anxiolytic effects of acute exercise? *Journal of Applied Physiology* 74 (February): 825–831.

Youngstedt, S.D., D.F. Kripke, and J.A. Elliott. 1999. Is sleep disturbed by vigorous late-night exercise? *Medicine and Science in Sports and Exercise* 31 (June): 864–869.

Youngstedt, S.D., P.J. O'Connor, J.B. Crabbe, and R.K. Dishman. 1998. Acute exercise reduces caffeine-induced anxiogenesis. *Medicine and Science in Sports and Exercise* 30 (5): 740–745.

Youngstedt, S.D., P.J. O'Connor, J.B. Crabbe, and R.K. Dishman. 2000. The influence of acute exercise on sleep following high caffeine intake. *Physiology and Behavior* 68 (February): 563–570.

Youngstedt, S.D., P.J. O'Connor, and R.K. Dishman. 1997. The effects of acute exercise on sleep: A quantitative synthesis. *Sleep* 20 (March): 203–214.

Zhao, G., X. Zhang, X. Xu, M. Ochoa, and T.H. Hintze. 1997. Short-term exercise training enhances reflex cholinergic nitric oxide-dependent coronary vasodilation in conscious dogs. *Circulation Research* 80 (June): 868–876.

Index

Note: The italicized *f* and *t* following page numbers refer to figures and tables, respectively.

A

absolute intensity, of exercise 83
abstinence violation, relapse and 224-225, 249
abstraction, of subjective experience 20
accelerometers, in activity measurement 31*t*, 32-33
accessibility, as exercise determinant 194*t*, 205-206, 206*f*
accuracy, of psychological constructs 22, 25-28
acetylcholine, as neurotransmitter 45*f*, 48, 50-51
    in sleep activity 179-180
    in stress response 84, 86*f*
acidosis, impact of 119, 271-272
acoustic startle eye-blink response (ASER)
    in exercise studies 107*f*, 108-109, 124
    neuroanatomy of 100-101, 100*f*-101*f*
actigraphy, of sleep 181
action stage
    of behavior change 220*f*, 221, 222*f*
    intervention based on 231-232, 232*t*
activation, in affect and emotion 22, 92, 92*f*, 94, 98
activity. *See* physical activity
activity history. *See* exercise experience
activity type. *See* exercise mode
acute exercise 12, 28, 106
    anxiety impact of 120-121, 124, 129
adaptation, to stress and stressors 76-77, 77*f*, 85
addiction(s)
    chemical. *See* substance abuse
    to exercise 58, 113-114, 174
adenosine, sleep disturbances and 188
adenosine triphosphate (ATP), in brain signals 59, 60*f*
adenylate cyclase, in brain signals 59, 60*f*
adherence, to activity behavior. *See* exercise adherence/adoption
adrenal cortex
    in depression 147-148, 149*f*, 151
    in endocrine system 52-53, 52*f*
adrenal gland, functional anatomy of 47, 52, 52*f*
    in stress response 76-78, 83*f*, 85, 86*f*, 88
adrenaline. *See* epinephrine
adrenal medulla, in endocrine system 52, 52*f*
adrenergic receptors
    in depression 146-147, 150
    molecular biology of 59, 59*f*
    neurotransmitter role of 48, 50, 56, 56*f*
adrenocorticotropic hormone (ACTH)
    in depression 148, 149*f*, 151
    in endocrine system 52-53, 52*f*, 58
    in perceived exertion 272
    in stress response 83*f*, 85-86, 86*f*
aerobic capacity 29-30, 83
aerobic exercise
    affect and mood impact of 106-107, 112
    anxiety impact of 119-122, 125
    depression impact of 137, 138*f*-140*f*, 139-140
    intensity of 34, 34*t*, 263

    as lifestyle physical activity 241*t*, 242
    physiological response to 28-30, 83
    self-esteem and 167-171, 170*f*
    sleep disturbances and 184, 184*f*, 186
    as stress reduction 79, 86-88
aerobic fitness 29-30, 83
affect and affective disorders 91-114
    circumplex model of 92-93, 92*f*
    contemporary views of 98-99
    dimensions of 22, 92, 92*f*, 94
    exercise impact on
        behavioral assessment of 107-111, 111*f*
        factors influencing 102-104, 106
        measurement considerations 104-106
        mechanisms of 91-92, 112-114
        training studies 106-107
    in mental responses 73, 126, 132-133, 133*t*
    neuroanatomy of 99-102, 99*f*
        hemispheric asymmetry 101-102, 102*f*
        startle eye-blink response 100, 100*f*-101*f*, 107*f*, 108-109
    psychophysiological research on 104-107
        limitations of 111-112
        methods for 107-111, 107*f*, 110*f*-111*f*
    Web sites on 114
Affect Grid 104-105
affective style, neuroimaging of 99, 102
afferent nerves, functional anatomy of 42, 42*f*-43*f*, 44, 46-47
    in heart rate variability 51, 51*f*, 82*f*
    in perceived exertion 266, 267*f*, 271
age
    as exercise determinant x, 134, 152, 193*t*, 197-199, 198*f*, 206-209
    self-esteem and 158-160, 165, 167-170
agoraphobia 116, 122
Alameda County Study 135-136
aldosterone 52, 83*f*
all-or-none thinking 79
allostasis 77, 77*f*
allostatic load 77-78, 77*f*, 85
α-adrenergic receptors
    in depression 146-147
    neurotransmitter role of 48, 50, 56, 56*f*
alpha wave activity, in sleep-cycle 179, 179*f*
American Association of Active Lifestyle and Fitness 33
American College of Sports Medicine
    fitness recommendations of 141, 255-256, 280
    physical activity guidelines of 13, 221, 241-242, 241*t*
American Psychological Association ix, 9-11
amygdala, functional anatomy of 46, 48, 48*f*
    in mental responses 80, 99*f*, 100, 126
anabolic steroids, muscle dysmorphia and 173-174
anaesthesias, in emotion theory 97-98
analgesia, exercise-induced 152
analogue models, as theory 211, 212*t*
Andrews, H.L. 67
angina 283

animal behavior models, for psychological constructs 63-64
anorexia, self-esteem and 172-173, 173*t*
antecedents
    in behaviorism 212-214, 215*t*
    in emotion theory 99
    in interventions 243-245
    of relapse 224-225, 249
anterolateral system, in perceived exertion 266, 267*f*
antibodies, in brain gene regulation 62
anticipation, as mood component 93
antidepressants 136, 140, 140*f*, 144, 146, 147*t*, 150
anxiety and anxiety disorders 115-130
    animal behavior models for 64
    common types of 116-118
    emotion theory and 97, 100, 102, 113
    exercise impact on 11-12, 28, 115, 124-125
        cognitive mechanisms of 125-126, 129
        lactate association with 118-119
        neurobiological mechanisms of 126-129, 127*f*, 129*f*
        research issues of 122-124
        state *vs.* trait 119-121, 119*f*
        training programs and 120-122
    neuroscience of 51-52, 57
    physiological research on 123-124, 123*f*
    prevalence of 73-74, 115-116, 115*f*, 122
    sleep disturbances with 181*f*, 187
    social impact of 115-116, 171
    trait-state conception of 36, 117-118, 117*f*
    Web sites on 130
anxiolytics 120, 123-124, 126-127, 127*f*, 129, 178
appetite, in emotion theory 98-99, 107
approach-withdrawal model, of affect 98
Aristotle 5
arousal
    of affect 92-93, 92*f*, 103-104
    anxiety *vs.* 117, 125, 128
    of emotion 22, 98, 101, 108, 111
ARTEC (Active Recreation on Tertiary Education Campuses) 236
associations, in psychological constructs 18, 36
assumptions, in behavior change theory 212
attention 52, 144, 145*f*
attention-deficit hyperactivity disorder (ADHD) 109
attitudes
    as activity foundation 8, 223, 233, 275
    in structural equation modeling 27, 27*f*
atypical depression 132-133, 133*t*
augmentation, of perceived exertion 273
autonomic nervous system (ANS), functional anatomy of 42, 42*f*, 48-50, 49*f*
    in affect, mood, and emotion 99-101, 99*f*, 107-108
    heart rate variability and 50-52, 51*f*
    in stress response 81-86, 81*t*, 84*t*, 88
avoidance, in emotion theory 98, 107

B

Bandura, Albert 216, 218-219, 219f, 222
baroreflexes, in stress response 81-82, 82f
barriers, perceived, as exercise determinant 194t, 201-202
Bartley, S. Howard 274
basal ganglia, functional anatomy of 44f, 47, 47f-48f
Beck Depression Inventory 138f, 139
bedtime, exercise timing and 186
behavior
    brain relationship to. See behavioral neuroscience
    changing. See behavior change
    emotions and 94, 94t, 96-98, 107-112
    in exercise psychology ix-x, 8-9
    physical. See physical activity behavior
    in social cognitive theory 216-218, 216t, 217f, 222
behavioral attributes/skills
    in affect, mood, and emotion 94, 94t, 96-98
        limitations of 111-112
        methods for 107-111, 107f, 110f-111f
    as exercise determinant 193t-194t, 202-203
    intervention based on 238-239, 238t
    for self-enhancement 158, 159t, 252
behavioral contracts, as intervention 245, 246f
behavioral control, perceived, in behavior change 223-224
behavioral intention
    as exercise determinant 191, 201, 201f, 208
    in structural equation modeling 27, 27f
behavioral management, as intervention 9, 243-245, 244t
behavioral neuroscience 41-72
    animal models in 63-64
    brain activity in 17-18, 18f
        measurement of 9, 63-71
    brain biology in 58-63
    definition of 10, 18, 18f, 41
    in exercise psychology x, 1, 3, 7, 9, 41-42
    neural network in 42-55, 55f
    neurotransmitters in 53-58
    Web sites on 72
behavior change 211-227
    ability for 14-15
    interventions for
        context-based 230-239, 232t, 238t-239t
        effectiveness mediators of 251-253, 252f
        goal of 229-230
        specific strategies 14, 29, 239-251, 241t, 244t, 248t
    reasoned, testing of 27-28, 27f, 191, 223, 226
    self-efficacy relationship to 222, 224, 252, 252f
    stages of 219-221, 220f
    theories of 211-227, 212t
        application issues 225-226
        behavioral 213-216, 213f-214f, 215t, 223-224
        cognitive 212, 215-216, 219f, 222, 245-250
        miscellaneous 27-28, 27f, 191, 223-225
    Web sites on 227, 253
behaviorism
    antecedents and consequences in 212, 214-215, 215t
    cognitive 215-216
    conditioning theories of 213-214, 213f-241f
    as learning theory 8-9, 213-215
behavior therapy 9, 243-245, 244t
beliefs, in behavior change 8, 224, 233
Bell, Charles 265
benefits, of exercise, costs vs. 245
benzodiazepines 100-101, 129, 129f, 178
Berger, Hans 66-67
Bernard, Claude 75
β-adrenergic receptors
    in anxiety response 128

in depression 146-147, 150
molecular biology of 59, 59f
neurotransmitter role of 48, 50, 56, 56f
β-endorphin, as neurotransmitters 52, 58
    in mental responses 85, 86f, 112, 148, 152
    in physical activity response 28, 34, 272
beta wave activity, in sleep-cycle 179, 179f
between network validity, of self-esteem 163
bias
    in mental responses 93-94, 123, 125
    in research 34, 38
bicycling. See cycling
bioelectrical impedance analysis (BIA), of fitness 30t
biofeedback, in perceived exertion 269
biogenic amines, as neurotransmitters 54-57
biological psychology
    of affect, mood, and emotions 112
    of exercise ix-x, 6-7, 9, 193t, 200
biopsychosocial model of disease 7, 9, 18, 48, 74
bipolar depressive disorders 105, 132-133, 132f, 145
blood-brain barrier, depression and 145, 151-152
blood flow, in stress response 28, 81
blood pressure (BP)
    exercise impact on 28, 106, 123
    in perceived exertion 269-270, 271t
    in stress response 81-82, 84, 88-89
body, dualism vs. monism of 4-5
Body Cathexis Scale 164-165
body composition, as fitness component 29, 30t
Body Esteem Scale 164
body fat, as fitness indicator 29, 29f, 30t, 33
body heating hypothesis, of sleep 185, 185f-186f, 188
body image, in self-esteem 160-162, 168
    exercise impact on 172-174, 173t, 202
    measurement of 164, 164f, 168
body language, emotions and 94t, 95f, 96
body mass index (BMI), as fitness indicator 30t
Body Self-Image Questionnaire (BSIQ) 164, 166
body temperature 28, 112
    regulation of, in perceived exertion 269, 272
    sleep impact of 185, 185f-186f, 188
Borg, Gunnar 10f, 11, 256, 262
Borg's range principle, of perceived exertion 262-265, 263f, 270-271, 271f, 281-282
    rating scales in. See category-ratio (CR) scale
brain and brain activity
    in affect and emotion 99-102, 99f, 102f, 110-111
    in anxiety response 126, 127f
    behavior relationship to 17-18, 18f, 63-64
    in depression 145-152, 149f-150f
    dualism vs. monism of 4-6
    functional anatomy of 42f-45f, 43-48, 47f-48f
    gene expression in 44, 58-61, 63
    immunocytochemistry of 58, 62-63
    measurement of
        electroencephalography for 66-68, 67f, 181
        electrophysiology for 65
        microdialysis for 65-66, 65f-66f
        neuroimaging methods for 68-71, 68f-71f, 99, 102, 111
    molecular biology of 58-63, 59f-60f, 62f
    per mental states 66-67, 67f
    with physical activity 28
    signal transmission in 58-59, 59f-60f
    in situ hybridization histochemistry of 58, 61, 62f
    during sleep 179-181, 179f-180f
    in stress response 80-86, 83f, 86f
brainstem, functional anatomy of 45-46, 45f, 48
    in stress response 80, 85, 86f
breathing 28

in perceived exertion 268, 269t, 270, 272, 274, 281, 283
bright light exposure 144, 182-184, 187-188
Brodmann's areas, of brain, in perceived exertion 266, 266f
building codes, for exercise 250

C

calcium channels, for brain signals 57, 59, 60f
calorimetry, for activity measurement x, 31t, 34t
Canada Fitness Survey 121, 135, 141
Canada Home Fitness Test 30t
Cannon, Walter 76, 98
Cannon-Bard theory, of emotion 98
carbon dioxide, perceived exertion and 270-271
cardiac cycle, autonomic balance of 51, 51f
cardiac-vagal tone, in stress response 81-85, 82f-83f, 84t, 88
cardiorespiratory fitness
    as activity measure 29, 30t, 141
    neuroscience of 45, 50-52, 51f, 58
    in perceived exertion 274, 275f-276f, 276-278
cardiovascular response, to stress 80t, 81-85, 82f-83f, 84t
    research limitations on 87-89
case-control design, for research 36-37
catastrophic thinking 79
catecholamines, as neurotransmitters 54-56
    in perceived exertion 272-273
    in physical activity response 28, 34, 152
    in stress response 83, 88-89
category-ratio (CR) scale, of perceived exertion 262-264, 263f-265f
    mediators impact on 270-272, 271f
    rating issues 281-282, 282f
Caton, Richard 66
Cattell, McKeen 256
causality, in research 36
cause-and-effect, in behaviorism 212
Centers for Disease Control and Prevention 13, 221, 237-238, 241-242, 241t
central gray region, of brain 46
central nervous system, anatomy of 42-46, 42f, 44f. See also specific component
    in mental disorder etiologies 43-44
cerebellum, functional anatomy of 44f-45f, 46, 47f
cerebrum, functional anatomy of 44f-45f, 46, 57
change, process and stage of
    in behavior change 220f, 221-223, 222f, 226
    as exercise determinant 79, 193t, 202
    intervention based on 231-234, 232t, 245
Child and Adolescent Trial for Cardiovascular Health (CATCH) 235
χ-square, in confirmatory factor analysis 26
chronic exercise 12, 28, 121
    affect and mood impact of 106, 109, 110f
    depression impact of 136-137, 138f, 140f, 150-151
cigarette smoking
    as exercise determinant 192, 194t, 203
    smoking cessation programs for 107, 220-221, 236
cingulate cortex, in mental responses 99f, 100, 126
cingulate gyrus, functional anatomy of 48, 48f
circadian rhythms. See sleep-wake cycle
Circuit of Papez, for affect and emotion 99, 99f
circumplex model, of affect 92-93, 92f
cis-elements, in brain gene expression 61
clarity, in exploratory factor analysis 23, 25
classical conditioning, in behaviorism 213, 213f
clomipramine 64, 122
clonidine 128
coefficient α, of psychological constructs 22
cognitive behaviorism 8-9, 215-216
cognitive behavior modification, as intervention 215-216, 245-250, 248t
cognitive function
    anxiety and 125-126, 129

cognitive function *(continued)*
    in behavior change theories 212, 215-216,
        219*f*, 222, 226, 245
    depression and 138*f*, 140, 144
    emotion and 98, 102
    exercise determinants and 192, 193*t*-194*t*,
        195, 196*f*, 200-202
    in exercise psychology ix-xi, 7-8
    intervention based on 233-234, 245-250, 248*t*
    self-esteem and 160-161
    social. *See* social cognitive theory
cohort studies, for research 37
comfort, perceived exertion and 274, 275*f*
common-factor variance, in exploratory factor
    analysis 24
communalities, in exploratory factor analysis
    23-24
communities, as intervention setting 236-238,
    240-241, 250-251
Community Healthy Activities Model Program
    for Seniors (CHAMPS) 170
comorbidity studies 117, 117*f*, 131, 132*f*
comparative psychology 10
compliance. *See* exercise adherence/adoption
compulsive exercise 113
computerized tomography (CT) scans, of brain
    activity 68
computer-mediated programs, as intervention
    250-251
computer use, as exercise determinant 203, 235
concurrent validity, of psychological constructs 19
conditioning
    in adaptation to stress 76-77, 77*f*
    in behaviorism 213-214, 213*f*-214*f*
conditioning programs. *See* training programs
confirmatory factor analysis (CFA) 19, 25-27,
    26*f*, 36
confounder, in research 34
connotative meaning, three dimensions of 22-23
conscience, dualism *vs.* monism of 5
consciousness, exercise and 7, 9-10, 18
consequences, in behaviorism 212-214, 215*t*
construct validity, of psychological constructs 19
contemplation stage
    of behavior change 220*f*, 221-222, 222*f*, 226
    intervention based on 231, 232*t*
content validity, of psychological constructs 19
context, in exercise psychology 103, 275-276
contingency contracts, as intervention 245, 246*f*
control, personal, depression and 144, 145*f*
control groups, for research 37
convergent validity, of psychological constructs
    19, 162
Coopersmith's Self-Esteem Inventory (SEI) 166
coping
    active *vs.* passive 78-79
    as exercise determinant 194*t*, 201-202, 249
correlation, in factor analysis 22, 25-26, 26*f*
correlation matrix, in exploratory factor analysis
    23-25, 24*f*-25*f*
corrugator muscles, emotion and 109
corticotropin-releasing hormone (CRH)
    in depression 147-148, 149*f*, 151
    in endocrine system 52-53, 52*f*
    in stress response 85-86, 86*f*
cortisol
    in depression 148, 149*f*
    neural regulation of 52-53, 52*f*
    in physical activity response 28, 53, 272
    in stress response 76-78, 83*f*, 85, 86*f*
cosmological assumptions, of behavior change 212
costs
    of exercise, benefits *vs.* 245
    of mental illness 73, 116, 131-132
    of sleep disturbances 177-178
covariance modeling, of psychological
    constructs 25-26
cranial nerves 42, 43*f*. *See also* autonomic
    nervous system
criterion validity, of psychological constructs 19
cross-sectional designs, for research 36

cross-stressor adaptation hypothesis, of exercise
    76-77, 77*f*, 85
cues. *See* antecedents
cultural factors. *See* social psychology
cumulative scales, for subjective experience 22
curare experiments, in muscle recruitment 272
3'5'-cyclic adenosine monophosphate (cAMP),
    in brain signals 59, 60*f*
cycling
    energy and 32, 276, 282
    mental effects of 120, 203, 237-238
cyclothymia 132

D

Darwin, Charles 7*f*, 8, 124
Decade of the Behavior (2000s) ix, 9
Decade of the Brain (1990s) ix, 9
decibel (dB) scale, of sound perception 260
decisional balance 222, 222*f*, 245
degrees of freedom, in confirmatory factor
    analysis 26
demographics
    as exercise determinant 192, 193*t*-194*t*, 196-
        200, 196*f*, 198*f*, 205-206, 207*t*
    intervention based on 232-233, 232*f*, 238*t*,
        239
    in self-esteem 158-159, 167-169
Department of Health and Human Services,
    U.S. x, 9, 238
depletion hypothesis, of depression 144-147,
    146*t*-147*t*, 149*f*
depression 131-153
    animal behavior models for 64
    anxiety with 126
    bright light exposure for 144, 187
    clinical description of 132-133
    drug treatment for 136, 140, 140*f*, 144,
        146-147, 147*t*, 150
    etiologies of 131-133, 135, 144, 146-147
    exercise impact on 11-12, 28-29, 133-134
        ideal quantity of 141-142, 141*f*-142*f*
        meta-analyses of 136-137, 137*t*, 138*f*
        as prevention 134-136, 134*f*-135*f*
        relapse relation to 140-141, 140*f*, 142*f*
        supervision recommendations 142-143
        as treatment 14, 106, 134, 136
    neurobiology of 44, 48, 53, 144-145, 145*f*
        hypothalamic-pituitary-adrenal axis
            model 147-148, 149*f*
        hypothalamic-pituitary-adrenal cortical
            axis hypothesis 151
        monoamine depletion hypothesis 144-
            147, 146*t*-147*t*, 149*f*
        monoamine dysregulation hypothesis
            146-151, 150*f*-151*f*
    prevalence of 73-74, 131-132, 132*f*
    self-esteem and 171, 171*f*
    Web sites on 153
Descartes, René 4, 4*f*
developmental disabilities, self-esteem and 170
*Diagnostic and Statistical Manual of Mental
    Disorders-IV (DSM-IV)*, criteria in
    118, 118*f*, 133, 173-174
diencephalon 44*f*-45*f*, 46
dietary habits, as exercise determinant 135, 160,
    172, 193*t*, 199, 202-203
disciplines, of exercise psychology ix, 3, 9-10, 34
discrepancy model, of self-esteem 160-161
discrete emotions 94, 94*t*
discrete symptoms, in perceived exertion 276-
    277, 276*f*
discriminant validity, of psychological constructs
    19
discriminative stimulus, in behaviorism 214
disease(s)
    activity for prevention of 13-14, 74, 140, 242
    biopsychosocial model of 9, 74, 132
    as exercise determinant 193*t*, 201
    exercise impact on x, 9, 107, 170, 235
    psychological. *See* mental illness
distortion, motivated response 38

distraction hypothesis, of mental responses 113,
    119-120, 125, 144, 145*f*
distress 76, 76*f*, 78
diurnal variation, in feeling states 103
divergent validity, of self-esteem 162
DNA (deoxyribonucleic acid), in brain gene
    expression 60-61
dopamine (DA), as neurotransmitter 45*f*, 47,
    47*f*, 54
    activity measurement with 66, 108
    mental health and 54, 58, 108-109, 126,
        147, 151
    synthesis of 54-55, 55*f*
dorsal column medial lemniscal system, in
    perceived exertion 266, 267*f*
dorsal nerve roots, of spinal cord 44, 45*f*
"dose response" gradient, of physical activity
    28, 36, 141, 208
doubly-labeled water, in activity measurement
    31*t*, 32-33
down-regulation, in mental responses 59, 63,
    146, 150
dreaming, brain activity with 179
drop out rate, for exercise programs 14, 229, 251
drug treatment. *See also specific classification or drug*
    for depression 136, 140, 140*f*, 144, 146-
        147, 147*t*, 150
    for mental illness 12-13
    research designs for 63-64
dualism, of mind and body 4-5, 8, 93, 215
dynamometers, for fitness measurement 30*t*
dysmorphic disorder, muscular 173-174
dysregulation hypothesis, of depression 146-
    151, 150*f*-151*f*
dysthymia 132, 132*f*, 139

E

eating disorders, self-esteem and 172-173, 173*t*
ecological validity, of research 111, 122
education
    as exercise determinant 193*t*, 197-199, 198*f*
    intervention based on 235-236
effectiveness, in research 35
effect size, in research 34-35, 34*f*
efferent nerves, for motor function 42*f*, 44, 46,
    54, 57
efficacy
    in research 35
    of self. *See* self-efficacy
effort, constant, maintenance of 274
ego orientation, in exercise interventions 234
electroencephalography (EEG)
    electrode sites and nomenclature for 66, 67*f*
    frequency bandwidths in 66-68
    mental state recordings of 66-68, 67*f*
        applications of 102, 123, 181
        of emotions and exercise 109-111, 111*f*
electrolyte channels, for neurotransmitter
    reception 57, 59, 60*f*
electromyography (EMG)
    in emotion studies
        acoustic startle eye-blink response 100-
            101, 100*f*-101*f*, 107*f*, 108-109
        exercise impact 108-109, 110*f*
    of sleep 181
    in stress reduction studies 80
electrophysiology, of brain activity 65. *See also*
    electroencephalography
elite athletes 162
e-mail, as intervention strategy 250-251
emotional stress
    behavioral response to 76, 76*f*, 107-111, 111*f*
    physiological response to
        hypothalamic-pituitary-adrenal cortex
            system in 77, 83*f*, 85-86, 86*f*
        sympatho-vagal component 80-85, 81*t*,
            82*f*-83*f*, 84*t*
emotion families 94, 94*t*
emotion-related expressions 94
emotions and emotional response 91-114
    affective dimensions of 22, 92, 92*f*, 94

biological dimensions of 93, 99-101, 99f
in cognitive behaviorism 215
components of 94-96, 94t, 95f
conceptualizations of 94, 94t
contemporary views of 98-99
as exercise determinants 200-202
exercise impact on 91-92, 109, 110f
    measurement of 22, 107f, 108-111, 110f-111f
    mechanisms of 112-114
expressions of 94-96, 95f
historical views of 6-8, 7f, 10, 96-98
mood impact on 94, 103, 110
neuroimaging of 99, 102, 111
neuroscience of 46, 48, 99-102, 99f
perception and 96-98
psychophysiological research on
    limitations of 111-112
    methods for 107-111, 107f, 110f-111f
stress impact on. See emotional stress
encephalon. See brain
endocrine system, functional anatomy of 52-53, 52f
in anxiety response 126, 127f
in stress response 80-81, 83f
endocytosis, in brain signals 59
energy, affect activation and 92
energy conservation, parasympathetic nerves in 50
energy expenditure. See also exercise intensity
as activity measure 31-33, 209, 280
depression and 141, 141f
as exercise determinant 193t, 200, 209
quantification of 28-29, 209, 280
sympathetic nerves in 49-50
energy level, exercise impact on 92
Engel, George L. 9
enjoyment, as exercise determinant 58, 64, 201, 208, 250
enkephalins, as neurotransmitters 58, 152
enteric nervous system, functional anatomy of 42f, 48-50, 49f
environment(s)
as exercise determinant ix, 192, 194t, 195, 195f-196f, 203-206
intervention based on 237-239, 238t-239t, 250-251
in mental responses 96, 102-103, 124, 257
in social cognitive theory 216, 217f, 218, 222
epidemiology, in research designs 35-37
epinephrine (Epi), as neurotransmitter 48, 52, 52f, 54, 56, 56f
in mental responses 76, 78, 83f, 128
equal interval scales, for subjective experience 20-21
ergopsychology ix, 82, 82f
errors, in factor analysis 24, 26
escape-deficit model, of depression 64
estimation, in confirmatory factor analysis 26
estimation-production protocol, for ratings of perceived exertion 281
ethnicity
as exercise determinant 193t, 197-199, 202
intervention based on 232-233
self-esteem and 161, 169
euphoria, exercise impact on 112-113
eustress 76, 76f, 78
evaluation, in connotative meaning 22-23
evidence, in psychological constructs 19
excitation, brain waves during 66-67, 67f
exercise. See also specific type
acute vs. chronic 12, 28
cross-stressor adaptation hypothesis of 76-77, 77f, 85
goal setting for x, 229-230, 234
measurement of 29-30, 30t
mental health effects of x, 1, 3, 5, 11-14, 92
physical activity vs. 1, 12, 28
as stress reduction 79-80
exercise abuse 113-114, 174
exercise adherence/adoption
behavior change in 14, 29, 215, 224-225, 249

measurement of 15, 30, 37
variables of. See exercise determinants
Exercise and Self-Esteem Model 157-158, 158f, 166
exercise dependence 113-114, 174
exercise determinants 191-209
classification of 192-208, 195f-196f
    activity associations with 192, 193t-194t, 195, 195f
    environment as 194t, 203-206, 207t
    personal characteristics as 193t-194t, 196-203, 207t
    physical activity characteristics as 194t, 206, 208
research on
    benefits of 191-192, 229
    issues of 208-209
    review of x, 15, 91, 191
variables of 192, 195, 199, 204-205
Web sites on 209
exercise duration
anxiety impact of 123f, 124
depression impact of 136, 138f, 141, 141f
as exercise determinant 31, 103, 206, 208
in perceived exertion 278-279, 279t-280t
sleep impact of 183, 185-186
exercise experience. See also subjective experience
in affect, mood, and emotion 103-104
as exercise determinant 191-192, 193t, 202
exercise frequency
as activity measure 31, 33
as exercise determinant 206, 208
in perceived exertion 278-279, 279t
Exercise-Induced Feeling Inventory 104-105
exercise intensity. See also energy expenditure
anxiety impact of 120-121
classification based on activity duration 279, 280t
depression impact of 138f, 141, 141f, 144
emotions and 109, 112
as exercise determinant 192, 194t, 195, 206, 208-209
in perceived exertion 265, 268-276, 281
    prescription and monitoring of 255, 278-279, 279t-280t
preferred exertion and 283
scope and impact of 28-29, 31-34
stress response and 83-84
exercise intervention(s) 229-253
context-based
    level as 237-239, 238t-239t
    personal characteristics 231-234, 232f, 232t
    setting as 234-237
effectiveness mediators of 251-253, 252f
goal of 229-230
meta-analysis of 239-240, 251
specific strategies 14, 29, 239-251, 241t, 244t, 248t
Web sites on 253
exercise mode 31, 103. See also specific activity
exercise prescriptions
of American College of Sports Medicine 13, 221, 241
as intervention 241-242, 241t
perceived exertion in 255, 278-281, 279t-280t
exercise programs
for conditioning. See training programs
drop out rate for 14, 229, 251
maintenance of. See exercise adherence/adoption
strategies for. See behavior change; exercise intervention(s)
exercise psychology
contemporary 10-11
definition of ix, 17, 19
historical views of ix, 1, 3-11
as interdisciplinary field of study ix, 3, 9-10, 19, 34
sports psychology vs. ix, 1, 11

Web sites on 15
exercise stimulus
in activity measurement 33-34
control of, as intervention 243-244
in perceived exertion 257-259, 261, 264, 276-277, 277f
exercise stress, physiological response to
hypothalamic-pituitary-adrenal cortex system in 77, 83f, 85-86, 86f
sympatho-vagal component 80-85, 81t, 82f-83f, 84t
exercise testing 247, 255, 257
perceived exertion and 257, 264, 277-278
exertion
in activity measurement 33, 256
perceived. See perceived exertion
preferred 283
exertional symptoms 283
expectations
in affect, mood, and emotion 93, 103
depression and 144, 145f
as exercise determinant 38, 201
experience, with exercise. See exercise experience
experimental design, for research 36
exploratory factor analysis (EFA) 19, 23-25, 24f-25f, 24t
extraction, in exploratory factor analysis 23
extraversion, perceived exertion and 273-274
eye-blink response. See acoustic startle eye-blink response
Eysenck, Hans 273

F
face validity 19, 162
facial expressions, emotions and 93-94, 95f, 96, 108
factor(s)
in exploratory factor analysis 23-25, 24f-25f, 24t
in structural equation modeling 27, 27f
factor analysis, of psychological constructs 19, 23-27
variables of
    confirmatory 25-26, 26f
    exploratory 23-25, 24f-25f, 24t
factorial validity, of psychological constructs 19
factor loadings, in exploratory factor analysis 24-25, 25t
family influence, as exercise determinant 194t, 204-205
fatalistic thinking 79
fatigue, perceived exertion and 274-277, 275f-276f
Fatness Evaluation, in self-image 164, 166
fear
anxiety vs. 116
neuroscience of 48, 50, 64, 76, 100
Fechner, Gustav 4-5, 5f
Fechner-Weber law, of human perception 258-259, 259f
feedback regulation
of brain signals 59
in depression 147-148, 149f
of endocrine system 52-53, 52f
feedforward-feedback mechanism, of muscle recruitment 271-272, 271f
feelings 92, 103
depression and 144, 145f
emotions vs. 94, 112
scales for 104-105, 166
feeling state 92, 103
Ferrier, David 101
field theory, in behavior change 219
"fight-or-flight" response 50, 52, 52f, 77f, 81-82, 88
fit indices
in confirmatory factor analysis 26-27
in structural equation modeling 27-28
fitness
aerobic 29-30, 83
cardiorespiratory. See cardiorespiratory fitness
physical. See physical fitness

flexibility, as fitness component 29, 30t, 34t, 141
foot shock 64, 66, 66f, 86, 151
force
    constant, maintenance of 274
    perceived 282-283
forebrain, functional anatomy of 44, 44f, 46
    in sleep activity 179-180, 180f
fornix, functional anatomy of 48, 48f
Fos transcription factors, in brain gene
    regulation 63
Frankenhaeuser, Marianne 78
free fatty acids, in anxiety response 128
Freud, Sigmund 7, 116
frontal cortex, in emotional response 110-111,
    128

G
Gage, Phineas 101-102, 102f
galanin (GAL), as neurotransmitter 58, 61
galvanic skin response 107-108
gamma-aminobutyric acid (GABA), as
    neurotransmitter 53-54, 57
    in anxiety response 126-127, 129, 129f
ganglions, functional anatomy of 46
gender
    as exercise determinant 192, 193t, 197-199,
        198f, 202, 204, 206, 208
    exercise impact based on 3, 8, 108-109, 120,
        125, 131-134, 152
    intervention based on 232-233, 232f
    in self-esteem 158-159, 167-169
        body image distortion and 172-174, 173t
gene expression, in brain 44, 58-61, 63
general adaptation syndrome (GAS) 76-77
generalizability, of research 111, 122
generalized anxiety disorder (GAD) 117-118,
    117f-118f, 122, 124
genotype, as exercise determinant 193t, 200
Gestalt psychology 9, 255, 255f, 265
gigantocellular nucleus, of reticular formation 45f
Gilman, Alfred G. 59
"Global Burden of Disease" study 73-74
global self-esteem 12, 156f-158f, 163-164, 166
    exercise impact on 167-169, 168f-169f, 171
glucocorticoids, as neurotransmitters 53, 57
    in depression 147-148, 149f
    in stress response 76-78, 83f
glucose metabolism, in depression 149f, 152
glutamate, as neurotransmitter 53-54, 57
goal setting
    in behavior change 215, 225, 240
    as intervention 234, 240, 242, 245, 247
    for physical activity x, 229-230
    in self-efficacy theory 218-219
goniometers, for fitness measurement 30t
goodness of fit 26-28
G-proteins, for neurotransmitters 53, 57, 59, 60f
graded exercise test (GXT), in perceived
    exertion 277-279, 281
GRAD (Graduate Ready for Activity Daily)
    Project 236
group-based programs, as intervention 238t-
    239t, 242-243
group cohesion, as exercise determinant 194t,
    204-205
guanosine diphosphate (GDP), in brain signals 59
guanosine triphosphate (GTP), in brain signals 59
Guttman scale, of subjective experience 22
gymnastics, health and 3, 14, 22, 172

H
habit theory, of behavior change 225
halo effect, in research 38
Harvard alumni study 136, 141
Hawthorne effect, in research 38
health, psychological. See mental health
health belief model, of behavior change 224
health care facilities, as intervention setting
    234-235
health education, as intervention 240-241
health insurance regulation, as intervention 250
health psychology 10

health-related physical fitness 29, 30t
    interventions for. See exercise
        intervention(s)
health risk appraisals, as intervention 240
health screenings, as intervention 240
Healthy People 2010 (U.S. DHHS) x
heart rate
    as activity measure 31-33, 31t
    in perceived exertion 269-270, 271t, 274
        exercise monitoring and 278-281, 279t-
            280t, 283
    in stress response 82, 82f, 87-89
    target zone for 235, 279-280, 279t
heart rate maximum, in exercise monitoring
    279-280, 279t-280t
heart rate reserve, in exercise monitoring 279-
    280, 280t
heart rate variability (HRV), autonomic balance
    of 50-52, 51f, 84t
hedonic tone, of affect 92, 92f, 102-103
Helmholtz, Hermann von 4-5, 5f, 7
helplessness, depression and 144, 145f
hemispheric asymmetry, of brain 101-102, 102f
Herodicus 3
5-HIAA, in anxiety response 128
hierarchical model, of self-concept 156f, 163,
    165-166
high-performance liquid chromatography 65
high-risk groups, activity behavior change for 192
high-risk situations, relapse and 224-225, 249-
    250
hindbrain, functional anatomy of 44, 44f
hippocampus, functional anatomy of 46, 48, 48f
    in affect and emotion 99-100, 99f
    in depression 148, 149f
    in mental responses 80, 126
Hippocrates ix, 3, 6, 93, 124, 133
histochemistry, in situ hybridization, of brain
    gene regulation 58, 61, 62f
Hobbes, Thomas 5
home-based exercise programs 234
homeostasis 61, 76, 85
    in perceived exertion 274, 275f
homologous model, for research 64
homunculus, sensory cortex control function of
    266, 268f
Hooke, Robert 75
hopelessness, depression and 144, 145f
hormones
    emotions and 94, 94t
    neural regulation of 47, 58. See also
        neurotransmitters
    in physical activity response 28, 34, 85, 103
    in stress response 82, 83f, 84-85
H-reflex, exercise impact on 109, 110f
human environment. See social environment;
    social support
hydrogen ions, in physical activity response 28
5-hydroxytryptamine. See serotonin
hypnotic suggestion, in perceived exertion 274
hypothalamic-pituitary-adrenal axis (HPA),
    functional anatomy of 47, 52, 52f
    in depression 147-148, 149f, 151
    in stress response 77, 83f, 85-86, 86f
hypothalamus, functional anatomy of 44f, 46-
    47, 48f
    in anxiety response 126, 127f
    in depression 147-148, 149f, 151
    in endocrine system 52-53, 52f
    in sleep activity 180, 185
    in stress response 80, 85-86, 86f

I
iconic models, as theory 211, 212t
idealism, in cognitive psychology 212
illness. See disease(s); mental illness
illness avoidance model, of behavior change 224
imbalance, stress from 75
immobilization stress 85-86. See also foot shock
immune system, in stress response 85, 86f
immunocytochemistry, of brain gene regulation
    58, 62-63

importance, perceived 158, 159f, 162, 165
incentive value
    in self-efficacy theory 218, 219f, 238-239, 238t
    in social cognitive theory 216t, 217-218
incidence, in research 35
income, as exercise determinant 192, 193t, 199,
    239t
indolamines, as neurotransmitters 56-57
inference, in psychological constructs 18, 23, 63
information processing
    neural network for 42, 42f-43f, 44, 45f
    neurotransmitter role in 53-54, 53f
injury, as exercise determinant 208, 239
insomnia
    common types of 180-181
    exercise impact on 177, 181f, 184
    prevalence and impact of 177-179
intensity
    in affect and emotion 92, 92f, 98-99, 102
    of physical activity. See exercise intensity
intention
    for behavior. See behavioral intention
    in behavior change 221, 223
    in social cognitive theory 216, 216t
interest, as exercise determinant 201
interference, in activity measurement 32
internal environment, maintenance of 75-76
Internet. See also Web sites
    as intervention strategy 250-251
interpretation, in exploratory factor analysis 25,
    25t
interval scales
    of perceived exertion 261-263
    for subjective experience 19-20
intervention, for behavior change. See exercise
    intervention(s)
intraclass correlation, in psychometrics 22
introversion, perceived exertion and 273
invariance, of subjective experience 20
in vitro environment, gene regulation in 61
in vivo environment, gene regulation in 61
ion channels, for brain signals 57, 59, 60f
ionotropic receptors, for neurotransmitters 57,
    59, 60f
iproniazid, depression and 145
isokinetic machines, for fitness measurement 30t
isomorphic model, for research 64

J
James, William ix, 5-9, 7f, 14, 41, 91, 96, 124
James-Lange theory, of emotion 7, 96-98
Jasper, H.H. 67
job classification. See occupational work
jogging. See running
judgment(s)
    in perceived exertion 257, 265, 273
    in self-esteem 156, 160-161
    social, measurement of 18-20
just noticeable difference (j.n.d.), in perceived
    exertion 257-258, 260

K
K complexes, in sleep-cycle 179, 179f
kilocalories, expenditure of. See energy
    expenditure
kinesthetic figural aftereffect 273
Kleitman, Nathaniel 178
knowledge, as exercise determinant 193t, 197-
    199, 198f, 233-236
Kraepelin, Emil 7

L
lactate (lactic acid)
    anxiety association with 118-119
    perceived exertion and 268, 270-272, 271t,
        281, 283
Lang, Peter 101
latency, in behaviorism 214
latent means, in confirmatory factor analysis 27
learned helplessness 64
learning theory
    behavioral. See behaviorism

physiological 48, 52
social 9, 216, 224
legislation, to promote exercise 238-239, 238t-239t, 250-251
Leibniz, Gottfried von 4
leisure-time physical activity
effects and trends of x, 135, 141
as measurement tool 32, 206, 207t
Lewin, Kurt 8
life events, major, as stressful 78-79
lifestyle physical activity, recommendations for 241-242, 241t
ligands, for brain signals 57, 63
light treatment. See bright light exposure
Likert scale, of subjective experience 20-21, 163
limbic system, functional anatomy of 46-48, 48f, 55
in affect and emotion 99, 99f
in anxiety response 126, 129
in stress response 80, 83f
linearity, of subjective experience 20
linear regression, of psychological constructs 25
locomotion, neuroscience of 46, 57, 64
anxiety-associated 126, 127f, 129
depression and 151-152
locus coeruleus (LC), functional anatomy of 45-46, 45f, 48f, 55, 58
in anxiety response 126, 128
in depression 146-147, 151
in molecular brain studies 61, 62f
in stress response 80, 86f
locus of control, as exercise determinant 202
logical validity, of psychological constructs 18-19

M
magnetic resonance imaging (MRI), of brain activity 68-69
with emotions 99, 102
functional 68-70, 68f-69f
magnitude estimation, in perceived exertion 261-262
magnitude production, in perceived exertion 261
maintenance, of activity behavior. See exercise adherence/adoption
maintenance stage
of behavior change 220f, 221-222, 222f
intervention based on 232, 232t, 234
major depression 132-133, 132f-133f, 133t, 137, 140, 140f
manic-depressive disorders 132, 132f
mass media, as intervention strategy 233, 240-241, 250-251
mastery accomplishments, in self-efficacy enhancement 219, 247-248, 248t
mastery hypothesis, of mood 113
materialism, in behaviorism 212
maximal oxygen uptake ($\dot{V}O_2$max)
in depression and exercise 137
as fitness indicator 29, 30t
with lifestyle physical activity 241t, 242
quantitative semantics of 263-264, 264f
measurement. See also scales and scaling
of activity. See physical activity
of affect and mood 104-106
of anxiety 122-123
of brain activity. See brain and brain activity
of emotions 22, 104-106, 107f, 108-111, 110f-111f
of exercise determinants 197-198, 203, 208-209
perceived exertion and 256-257, 261
of physical fitness 29-30, 87
of psychological constructs 18-20, 22-25, 33
of self-esteem 162-166, 164f
mechanoreceptors, in stress response 82, 82f
media campaigns, as intervention strategy 233, 240-241, 250-251
medial lemniscal system, dorsal column, in perceived exertion 266, 267f
mediators, in research 35
of exercise interventions 251-253, 252f
of perceived exertion 265

peripheral 270-273, 271f
physiological 265-266, 267f, 268-273, 269t, 270f, 282f
psychological 265, 273-276, 275f
respiratory-metabolic 268-270, 269t, 271f
meditation, anxiety and 119-120, 119f
medulla, functional anatomy of 44f-45f, 45
in sleep activity 180, 180f
in stress response 82-83, 82f-83f
Meichenbaum, Donald 215
melancholia 132-133, 133t
melatonin 56, 178, 187
memory, neuroscience of 52-53
menopause, self-esteem and 160, 170
menstrual cycle 103, 170, 278
mental health
exercise impact on x, 1, 3, 5, 11-14, 92
self-esteem and 171, 172f
stress impact on 76, 76f
Surgeon General's conclusions on 12, 13f, 73, 118, 134
mental illness. See also specific diagnosis
animal models of 63-64
exercise and
relapse of 140-141, 140f, 142f
as treatment for 12-14, 74
global perspectives of 73-74
historical views of 7
as medical illness risk factor 73-74, 132
neuroscience of 44, 48, 53-54
mesencephalon. See midbrain
meta-analyses, in research 35
on depression 136-137, 137t, 138f
on exercise interventions 239-240, 251
on self-esteem 167-168, 167f
on sleep 183, 183t-184t
metabolism and metabolic rate
in depression 149f, 151-152
emotional response and 111, 119
as exercise determinant 53, 200
multiples of resting. See multiples of resting metabolic rate
in stress response 81-82, 84-85, 119
metaboreceptors, in stress response 82, 82f
metathetic continuum, of perception 256
metencephalon 44f
method of adjustment, in perceived exertion 257
method of constant stimuli, in perceived exertion 257
method of limits, in perceived exertion 257
3-methoxy-4-hydroxyphenylglycol (MHPG), in mental response 128-129, 145-146, 149
Meyer, Adolf 7
microdialysis, of brain activity 65-66, 65f-66f
midbrain 45-46, 45f, 126
Miller's Number 21
mind, dualism vs. monism of 4-5, 9
Minnesota Heart Health Project 237
minute ventilation (V_E), in perceived exertion 268, 269t, 270
Mischel, Walter 216
mixed models, as theory 212t
models, as theory 211, 212t
moderator, in research 35
molecular biology, of brain
key concepts of 58-61, 59f-60f, 63
techniques for 58, 61-63, 62f
monism, of mind and body 5, 7
monoamine oxidase (MAO), in depression 145
monoamine oxidase inhibitors (MAOIs) 147t
monoamines, as neurotransmitters 54-57
in depression
depletion hypothesis of 144-147, 146t-147t, 149f
dysregulation hypothesis of 146-151, 150f-151f
mood and mood disorders 91-114
biological component of 93
depression-related 132, 136
emotions and 94, 103, 110

exercise impact on 74, 91-92
acute vs. chronic 106-107
behavioral assessment of 107-111, 111f
mechanisms of 112-114
factors influencing 74, 93, 103
neuroscience of 44, 53-54, 58
in perceived exertion 273-274
psychophysiological research on
limitations of 111-112
methods for 107-111, 107f, 110f-111f
Web sites on 114
morality, dualism vs. monism of 5
Morgan, William P. ix, 10-11, 10f, 273
motion sensors, for sleep estimation 181
motivated response distortion, in research 38
motivation
as exercise determinant 14-15, 29, 201, 224
in mental responses 98-99, 161
neuroscience of 48, 52, 54
as research variable 37-38
motor function, neuroscience of 42f, 44, 46, 54, 57
multiples of resting metabolic rate (METs)
as activity measure 28, 31-32
in perceived exertion 280-281, 280t
multitasking, impact of 113
muscarinic cholinergic receptors, for neurotransmitters 48
muscle fiber, recruitment of
in perceived exertion 256, 265, 270-272, 271f
in perceived force 282-283
with physical activity 28
in stress response 80-81, 82f, 83
muscles
anxiety and 123, 128
dysmorphia of, self-esteem and 173-174
emotions and 94, 94t, 96, 108-109
muscle sense 256, 265
muscular endurance, as fitness component 29-30, 30t
muscular strength, as fitness component 29-30, 30t, 34t
myelencephalon 44f

N
National Health Interview Survey 197
National Longitudinal Study of Adolescent Health 199
natural selection attention 99
natural selection theory 7f, 8
near-infrared optical image scanning (iOIS), of brain activity 70-71, 71f
negative feedback, for brain signals 59, 147
neocortex, functional anatomy of 44f, 47
nerve roots, of spinal cord 44, 45f, 109
nerves. See also specific type or nerve
sensory vs. motor 42, 42f-43f, 44
nervous system. See also specific divisions
divisions of 42, 42f
dualism of 4-5, 8-9, 93
in exercise research 37-38
motor 42f, 44, 46, 54, 57
sensory
hierarchical model of 276-277, 276f-277f
in perceived exertion 265-268, 266f-268f
neurobiology 41
of anxiety 126-129, 127f, 129f
neurohormones. See neurotransmitters
neuroimaging
of affect and emotion 99, 102, 111
of brain activity 68-71, 68f-71f, 99
neurons
in autonomic nervous system 48-50, 49f
chemical synapse between 53-54, 53f
in sleep activity 179, 180f
neuropeptides, as neurotransmitters 57-58
neurophysiology, behavior relationship to. See behavioral neuroscience
neurotransmitters (NT), functional role of 45-46, 45f
in affect, mood, and emotion 108
in anxiety response 126-129, 127f, 129f

neurotransmitters (NT), functional role of
  (*continued*)
    biogenic amines as 54-57
    in depression 64, 144-152, 147*t*, 149*f*-151*f*
    excitatory *vs.* inhibitory 53-54
    microdialysis measurement of 65*f*, 66
    nervous system role in 48, 53-54, 53*f*
    neuropeptides as 57-58
    presynaptic *vs.* postsynaptic release of 53-55
    in sleep activity 179-180, 180*f*
nicotinic cholinergic receptors, for
    neurotransmitters 48
nighttime, exercise and 183, 186
nociceptive signals 44, 271. *See also* pain
nominal scales, of perceived exertion 261
nonreactivity, in activity measurement 32
noradrenergic receptors 128, 146
norepinephrine (NE), as neurotransmitter 45*f*,
    46, 48, 50-51, 54
    adrenergic receptors for 56, 56*f*, 59, 59*f*
    in anxiety response 128-129
    in depression 145-150, 146*t*, 151*f*
    in endocrine system 52, 52*f*, 56
    in stress response 78, 80-81, 83, 83*f*, 88
    synthesis and distribution of 54-56
nuclei, functional anatomy of 45-46, 45*f*, 48
nucleus accumbens, in affect 100
nucleus reticularis pontis oralis/caudalis (RPO/
    RPC), sleep and 179, 180*f*
nutrition. *See* dietary habits

O
obesity
    activity programs for 14, 107, 160, 233,
        236, 242
    as exercise determinant x, 193*t*, 200, 250
observation, in activity measurement 31*t*
obsessive-compulsive disorder 116
occupational work
    as exercise determinant 192, 193*t*, 197, 199
    in exercise psychology ix, 32, 236, 238*t*
ontological assumptions, of behavior change 212
operant conditioning, in behaviorism 213, 214*f*
opioid receptors 46, 58, 152
opposite emotions, paired 94, 94*t*
ordinal scales, of perceived exertion 261
ordinate symptoms, in perceived exertion 276-
    277, 276*f*
orthogonal rotation, in exploratory factor
    analysis 25
Osgood, Charles E. 22-23
osteoporosis, activity guidelines for 14
outcome expectancies
    relapse and 249
    in self-efficacy theory 218, 219*f*
    in social cognitive theory 216*t*, 217-218
outcome value
    in self-efficacy theory 218, 219*f*
    in social cognitive theory 216*t*, 217-218
outcome variables
    in activity measurement 33, 37-38
    of exercise interventions 252, 252*f*
overtraining, impact of 113-114, 174
oxygen uptake (V̇O₂)
    maximal. *See* maximal oxygen uptake
    peak. *See* peak oxygen uptake
    in perceived exertion 268-271, 269*t*, 277-
        279, 280*t*, 281-283
    in stress response 81, 87, 109

P
PACE (Physician-Based Assessment and
        Counseling for Exercise) Project
        234, 237
pain
    in exercise psychology xi, 283
    neuroscience of 44, 46, 54, 58
panic disorder 116, 126, 128
    emotion theory and 97-98
    exercise impact on 115, 118-119, 122
parasympathetic nervous system (PNS), functional
        anatomy of 42*f*, 48-50, 49*f*

heart rate variability and 51-52, 51*f*
parks, for exercise 238-239, 238*t*-239*t*, 250
paths, foot and bike, as intervention 238-239,
    238*t*, 250-251
Pavlov, Ivan 273
peak oxygen uptake (V̇O₂peak)
    in mental responses 87, 109, 120, 172
    in perceived exertion 268-271, 269*t*, 278,
        281-283, 282*f*
pedometers, in activity measurement 31*t*
peer pressure, as exercise determinant 191-192,
    194*t*, 198-199
perceived barriers, as exercise determinant 194*t*,
    201-202
perceived behavioral control, in behavior change
    223-224
perceived exertion 255-284
    Borg's 6-20 categories of 263-264, 263*f*,
        271, 281
    definition of 255-257, 255*f*
    as exercise determinant 194*t*, 255
    exercise prescriptions and 255, 278-281,
        279*t*-280*t*
    exercise testing and 257, 264, 277-278
    final common pathway of 276-277, 276*f*-277*f*
    history of 256-257
    lactate impact on 268, 270-272, 271*t*, 281,
        283
    mediators of 265
        peripheral 270-273, 271*f*
        physiological 265-266, 267*f*, 268-273,
            269*t*, 270*f*
        psychological 265, 273-276, 275*f*
        respiratory-metabolic 268-270, 269*t*, 271*f*
    rating of 256, 263*f*, 266, 267*f*
        people comparisons in 262-265
        practical use of 277-283
    signals to
        muscular sense 256, 265
        sensory nervous 265-268, 266*f*-268*f*
    Web sites on 284
perceived force, production of 282-283
perceived importance 158, 159*f*, 162, 165
perception 256
    in behavior change 223-224, 245
    emotion and 96-98
    in psychophysics 7, 10, 257, 260-261, 274
    in self-esteem 158-162, 159*f*, 165
    stress response and 51-53, 58, 77*f*, 82, 83*f*
performance
    in self-efficacy theory 218-219
    stress impact on 76, 76*f*
periaqueductal gray (PAG) area, of brain 58
    anxiety and 127, 127*f*, 129
peripheral mediators, of perceived exertion
    270-273, 271*f*
peripheral nervous system 42, 42*f*
    in stress response 80-81
personal characteristics
    in affect, mood, and emotion 102-103
    as exercise determinants 193*t*-194*t*, 196-203
    intervention based on 231-234, 232*f*, 232*t*,
        238-239, 238*t*-239*t*
        lifestyle-based 241-242, 241*t*
    in self-efficacy theory 218-219, 219*f*
    in social cognitive theory 216-218, 216*t*, 217*f*
personal control, depression and 144, 145*f*
personality
    as exercise determinant 202, 213
    in perceived exertion 273-276
    in trait anxiety 117-118
Petrie, Asenath 273
phenomenology, in psychological constructs 18
philosophy, in exercise psychology 3-6
phobias 100, 116, 122, 124, 128
phosphorylation, in brain signals 59
physical activity
    in connotative meaning 22-23
    effectiveness mediators of 251-253, 252*f*
    as exercise determinant 192, 193*t*-194*t*,
        195, 195*f*-196*f*, 206-209

exercise *vs.* 1, 12, 28
features of 28-29, 37-38
goals of x, 229-230, 234
legislation to promote 250
leisure-time x, 32, 135, 141, 206, 207*t*
lifestyle recommendations for 241-242, 241*t*
measurement of 29-34
    desirable instruments for 32
    dimensions of 30-31, 256
    free-living methods for 31-33, 31*t*
    markers of 31*t*, 33-34, 34*t*
mental health effects of x, 8, 11-14, 74, 91-92
professional guidelines for 13, 221
Surgeon General's conclusions on 12, 13*f*,
    73, 118, 134
U.S. population trends of x, 135, 141, 229,
    251
physical activity behavior, psychology of 189-192
    changing. *See* behavior change
    determinants in. *See* exercise determinants
physical body, in self-esteem 160-161, 164, 164*f*
    correlational evidence of 168, 168*f*
    distorted images and exercise 172-174, 173*t*
physical education, strategies for 235-236
physical environment
    as exercise determinant 194*t*, 196*f*, 205-
        206, 206*f*
    intervention based on 238-239, 238*t*-239*t*,
        250
Physical Estimation and Attraction Scales
    (PEAS) 166
physical fitness
    measurement of 29-30, 87, 120, 185
    types of 29, 30*t*, 160
physical inactivity
    determinants of. *See* exercise determinants
    factors associated with x, 14, 206
physical self-concept
    exercise impact on 12, 167-169, 168*f*-169*f*
    measurement of 165-166
Physical Self-Perception Profile (PSPP) 158,
    159*f*, 163, 165, 168
physical self-worth, in self-esteem 157-158,
    157*f*-159*f*
physical working capacity (PWC), as fitness
    measurement 30*t*
physicians, views on physical activity 3-4, 234,
    237
physiological mediators
    of perceived exertion 265-266, 267*f*, 268-
        273, 269*t*, 270*f*, 282*f*
    in self-efficacy enhancement 219, 247-248,
        248*t*
physiology
    in exercise psychology. *See* behavioral
        neuroscience
    of physical activity response 28-29, 37-38.
        See also brain and brain activity
    psychology *vs.* 18
physique anxiety 169
pituitary gland, functional anatomy of 47, 48*f*
    in depression 147-148, 149*f*, 151
    in endocrine system 52-53, 52*f*
    in stress response 83*f*, 85, 86*f*
placebo 172
placebo effect, in exercise impact 119, 171, 172*f*
planned behavior, in behavior change 223-224,
    226
Plato 4, 5
pleasure. *See* enjoyment
"point-of-decision" prompts, as intervention 244
polysomnography, of sleep 181, 182*f*
pons, functional anatomy of 44*f*-45*f*, 45-46
    in sleep activity 180, 180*f*
Positive Affect and Negative Affect Scales
    (PANAS) 104-105, 111
positron emission tomography (PET)
    of brain activity 68-70, 70*f*-71*f*
    of emotions 99, 102
postganglionic neurons 48-50, 49*f*
postsynaptic neurons, neurotransmitters and
    53-55, 57

posttranslational regulation, of brain gene expression 63
posttraumatic stress disorder 116, 126
potency, in connotative meaning 22-23
power law, Stevens', of human perception 259-262, 282, 282f
practicality, in activity measurement 32
precision, of psychological constructs 22
precontemplation stage
  of behavior change 220f, 221-222, 222f, 226
  intervention based on 231, 232t
predictive designs, for research 37, 63-64
preferred exertion 283
prefrontal cortex, in behavioral neuroscience 48f, 54, 55f, 100
  affect and emotion and 99-100, 99f, 102
  anxiety response and 126
preganglionic neurons 48-50, 49f
pregnancy, self-esteem and 159, 170
preparation stage
  of behavior change 220f, 221-222, 222f
  intervention based on 231, 232t
presynaptic neurons, neurotransmitters and 53-57
prevalence studies 35-36, 73-74
principal-axis-factor extraction, in exploratory factor analysis 23
processes of change
  as exercise determinant 193t, 202, 245
  in stage theory of behavior 222-223, 222f, 226
production-production protocol, for ratings of perceived exertion 281-282
Profile of Mood States (POMS) 104-106, 113, 122
Project Active 242
Project GRAD (Graduate Ready for Activity Daily) 236
Project PACE (Physician-Based Assessment and Counseling for Exercise) 234, 237
proopiomelanocorticotropin (POMC), in stress response 85
prostaglandins, sleep disturbances and 188
protein expression, in brain gene regulation 62-63
prothetic continuum, of perception 256
psychiatrists, views on physical activity ix, 5-7
psychoanalysis 8-9
psychobiology 7, 9, 18, 48, 74
psychological constructs 18-19, 22
  animal behavior models for 63-64
  covariance modeling of 25-28
  research design for 22, 36-38
  scales for
    multidimensional 22-25
    single dimension 19-22
  in stage theory of behavior 221-222, 222f
"psychological distance," between words 22
psychological factors
  as exercise determinants 191-192, 193t, 200-202, 201f
  of perceived exertion 265, 273-276, 275f
  of self-esteem 161-162
psychology. See also specific disciplines
  subdisciplines of ix-x, 9-10
  subjective constructs of 10, 18-22
psychometrics 18-19, 22
  animal behavior models for 63-64
  covariance modeling in 25-28
  research design for 22, 36-38, 171
  scales in 18-22
psychophysics 18
  classical 257-259, 262
  comparison of people with 262-265
  hierarchical model of 276-277, 276f-277f
  logarithm vs. power function in 260-261
  modern 259, 260f
  of perceived exertion 256-262
  power law in 261-262, 282, 282f
  scales in 261
psychophysiological integration
  of affect, mood, and emotion
    assessment methods for 107-111, 107f, 110f-111f

limitations of 111-112
  of perceived exertion 276-277, 276f-277f, 282, 282f
psychosocial theory. See social psychology
psychotherapy, contemporary 9, 12
  for depression 136, 138f, 139-140, 140f
public health, exercise impact on x, 114, 122
punishment, reinforcement vs. 244-245, 244t
Pygmalion effect, in research 38

Q
qualification, of subjective experience 19-20
quality of life, exercise impact on x, 16, 170
quantification, in research 35
  semantics of, in perceived exertion 263-265, 264f
  on subjective experience 19-20
questionnaires. See self-reports

R
race. See ethnicity
randomized controlled trials, for research 37
range principle. See Borg's range principle
raphe nuclei, functional anatomy of 45-46, 45f, 48f
  in mental responses 80, 86f, 127
rapid eye movement (REM) sleep
  brain activity during 179, 179f-180f
  exercise impact on 180, 183, 183t-184t
  neuroscience of 46, 64, 80, 178-179
Rasch, Georg 23
rating of perceived exertion (RPE) 256, 281
  category scale issues with 270-272, 271f, 282, 282f
  heart rate monitoring and 279t-280t, 280
  mediators of 266, 267f
    peripheral 270-273, 271f
    physiological 265-266, 267f, 268-273, 269t, 270f, 282f
    psychological 265, 273-276, 275f
    respiratory-metabolic 268-270, 269t, 271f
  people comparisons in 262-265
  practical use of 277-283
rational thinking, as stress management 79
ratio scales
  of perceived exertion 262. See also category-ratio (CR) scale
  for subjective experience 19-20
reasoned action, in behavior change 191, 223, 226
  structural equation modeling of 27-28, 27f
receptor-effectors, for brain signals 58-59, 59f.
    See also specific receptor
reciprocal control, in autonomic nervous system 50
reciprocal determinism, of exercise 195, 196f
reciprocality, triadic, in social cognitive theory 217f, 218
recreational facilities
  as exercise determinant 205-206
  as intervention 236-238, 250
recreational therapy 3
reduction, of perceived exertion 273
referred appraisal, in self-esteem 161-162
reflex(es) 4, 9, 109. See also specific reflex
reinforcement control, as intervention 243-245, 244t
reinforcement value
  in self-efficacy theory 218, 219f
  in social cognitive theory 216t, 217-218
reinforcing stimulus, in behaviorism 214
relapse
  of mental illness, exercise impact on 140-141, 140f, 142f
  of physical inactivity 229, 232, 237
    high-risk situations for 224-225, 249-250
relapse prevention
  as behavior change model 224-225, 232
  exercise intervention for 249-250
relative intensity, of exercise 83
relative risk, in research 35
relaxation
  brain wave patterns during 66-67, 67f

exercise impact on 115, 122-123
relaxation chair 5, 6f
reliability
  in activity measurement 32-33
  of psychological constructs 22, 24, 37, 163
repetitive patterns, neuroscience of 54, 55f
reproductive hormones, exercise impact on 85
research
  common terms in 34-35
  design descriptions for 36-38, 240
  experimental artifacts in 37-38
  review and issues of. See specific topic
reserpine, depression from 144-145
resistance exercise
  depression impact of 136-137, 139, 141
  perceived exertion and 280t, 282
respiratory-metabolic mediators, of perceived exertion 268-270, 269t, 271f
response
  in behaviorism 212-213, 215
  in perceived exertion 276-277, 277f
response interpretation, in self-efficacy enhancement 219, 247-248, 248t
response scales, for subjective experience 19-21, 23
reticular activating system 46
reticular formation, functional anatomy of 45-46, 45f, 48
reward pathway, neuroscience of 54, 55f
rewards, for exercise 244-245
  as relapse prevention 249-250
RNA (ribonucleic acid)
  in brain gene expression 60-61
  messenger, molecular studies of brain 58, 61-62, 62f, 150
Roberts, Robert Jeffries 189
Robertson, Bob 273
Rodbell, Martin 59
Rosenberg's Self-Esteem Scale 166, 170-171
Rosenthal effect, in research 38
rotation, in exploratory factor analysis 25
"runner's high" 58
running. See also treadmill exercise
  behavior change and 174, 214, 216-217
  energy expended by 32, 283
  mental effects of 13, 111-113, 120, 140f, 172, 174
run/walk test, for fitness 30t
Rush, Benjamin 5-6, 6f

S
safety
  as exercise determinant 205-206
  intervention based on 237-239, 238t-239t
sample-free calibration 20
sample selection, for research 37
sample size, for research 37
satisfaction, measurement of 20-21
scales and scaling, of psychological constructs 19. See also measurement; specific type
  multidimensional 22-25
  single dimension 18-22
Schachter, Stanley 98
schools, as intervention setting 235-236
scripture, physical activity per 3
second messengers, for brain signals 58-59, 60f
sedentary lifestyle
  depression and 131, 135, 141, 144
  as exercise determinant 192, 193t, 195, 202-203, 250
  health risks of x, 3, 8, 12, 182, 235
  interventions for 235, 241-242
selective serotonin reuptake inhibitors (SSRIs) 127, 127f, 147t, 150
self
  as complex system 155-158, 156f-157f
  internal vs. external standards for 161-162
  variable measurements of 162-166
Self Assessment Manikin (SAM) 111
self-concept
  multidimensional model of 156f, 163, 165-166

self-concept (continued)
  physical 12, 165-169, 168f-169f
  in self-esteem 157-161, 158f
    measurement of 162-166, 168, 170
    social environment and 161-162, 174
self-deception, as research variable 37-38
Self-Description Questionnaire (SDQ) 165
self-determination, in self-esteem 161
self-efficacy
  in affect, mood, and emotion 103, 107, 113
  Bandura's theory of 218-219, 219f
  in behavior change models 222, 224, 252, 252f
  enhancement strategies of 158, 159t, 168,
    247-248, 248t, 252
  as exercise determinant 191, 200-201, 201f,
    208
  intervention based on 233-234, 238t, 239,
    247-248
  self-esteem and 157, 171
  in social cognitive theory 216-217, 216t
  sources of 215t-216t, 217-219, 247, 248t
self-efficacy expectancy 218-219, 219f
self-enhancement 157-158, 159t, 168, 247-248,
    248t, 252
self-esteem 155-175
  in affect, mood, and emotion 103, 155
  definition of 155-157, 156f-157f, 161
  exercise impact on 11-12, 30, 155, 166-167,
    174-175
    correlational evidence of 168, 168f
    distorted body image and 172-174, 173t
    longitudinal studies of 168-169, 169f
    mechanisms of 171-172, 171f-172f
    meta-analyses of 167-168, 167f
    in special populations 159-160, 170-
      171, 170f
  factors influencing 158-162, 159f, 159t
  global vs. physical 12, 156f-158f, 163-169,
    168f-169f
  measurement of 22, 155, 162-164, 166,
    170-171
  psychosocial theory of 159t, 161-162, 171
  as research variable 37-38
  Web sites on 175
self-image, depression and 144, 145f
self-management, of exercise programs 234, 236
self-monitoring, as intervention 215, 245
self-motivation, for exercise 14-15, 201, 234
self-perception
  exercise impact on 167-170
  measurement of 162-165, 164f, 167
  in self-esteem 158-162, 159f
self re-evaluation, of behavior 222
self-regulation
  in exercise programs 234, 236, 238t, 239
  in social cognitive theory 216, 217f
self-reports, in exercise research
  for activity measurement 31t, 32-33
  on affect 104-106, 111, 113-114
  on anxiety 120-124
  on depression 135-137, 140, 140ft, 144
  on exercise determinants 197-198, 203,
    208-209
  on perceived exertion 276-277, 276f-277f, 283
  in psychological constructs 37-38, 63
  on self-esteem 163-166, 164f
  on sleep 181-185
  on stress reduction 79-80
self-schemata 156, 201, 239t
self-worth 157-158, 157f-159f, 165
Selye, Hans 76
semantic differential, in multidimensional scales
    22-23
sensation, in psychophysics 257, 260-261, 265,
    270
  pyramidal schema for 274, 275f-277f, 276
sensitivity, in research 35
sensory cortex, control function of 266, 268f
sensory nervous system. See also afferent nerves
  hierarchical model for 276-277, 276f-277f
  in perceived exertion 265-268, 266f-268f

serotonin (5-HT), as neurotransmitter 45-46,
    54, 56-57, 66
  in anxiety response 127-128, 127f
  in depression 145-146, 146t-147t, 148-151,
    150f
  in stress response 80-81, 86f
serotonin transporter (SERT), in depression
    150, 150f
7-Day Physical Activity Recall 236
Sherrington, Charles Scott 265
shift work, sleep disturbances with 187-188
signaling proteins, for neurotransmitters 53, 57,
    59, 60f
signal transmissions, in brain 58-59, 59f-60f
simple phobia 116, 124
single-photon emission computed tomography
    (SPECT), of brain activity 70, 71f
situational factors, in exercise psychology 103,
    275-276
skill-related physical fitness 29
skinfold analysis, as fitness measurement 29f, 30t
Skinner, B.F. 213
skin temperature, in perceived exertion 272
sleep 177-188
  components of 179-180, 179f
  depression and 64
  exercise impact on 177, 181-182, 181f
    epidemiological studies on 182-183, 182f
    mechanisms of 186-188
    meta-analysis of 183, 183t-184t
    research issues of 185-186, 185f-186f
    training programs and 183-184, 184f,
      184t
  measurement of 181, 182f
  research review of 178-179
  Web sites on 188
sleep apnea 181, 188
sleep disturbances 180-181
  bright light exposure and 182-184, 187-188
  prevalence and impact of 177-179
sleep hygiene, recommendations for 177
sleepiness, daytime 177-178, 182-183
sleep onset latency (SOL) 180, 184, 184t
sleep-wake cycle 103, 178
  neuroscience of 46, 54-55, 57
    brain wave patterns in 66-67, 67f, 179f
    stages in 179-180, 179f
  phase-shifting effects on 187-188
slow-wave sleep (SWS)
  brain activity during 179-180, 179f
  exercise impact on 183-185, 183t-184t,
    185f, 188
smoking cessation programs 107, 220-221
social cognitive theory
  assumptions of 216-217, 217f
  central concept of 218, 222, 240
  depression and 144
  of exercise determinants 192, 193t-194t,
    195, 196f, 203-205
  key variables in 216, 216t
  in research design 36, 63
social comparisons, in self-esteem 161-162
social desirability responding 38, 163
social environment
  intervention based on 238-239, 238t-239t,
    250
  in mental responses 103, 144, 145f, 161-162
  perceived exertion and 257, 275-276
social isolation, depression and 144, 145f
social judgments, measurement of 18-20
social learning theory 9, 216, 224
social mediators, of perceived exertion 265,
    273-276, 275f
social modeling, in self-efficacy enhancement
    215t, 217, 219, 247-248, 248t
social norms
  as exercise determinant 191-192, 194t, 198-
    199, 203-205, 226
  in structural equation modeling 27, 27f
social phobia 116, 124, 128. See also anxiety and
    anxiety disorders

social psychology, in exercise research ix-x, 8-9,
    18
  on affect, mood, and emotions 112-113
  on depression 144, 145f
  on perceived exertion 265, 273-276, 275f
  on self-esteem 159t, 161-162, 171, 174
social support
  in behavior change 224, 238-239, 238t
  depression and 144, 145f
  as exercise determinant 192, 194t, 199, 203-
    205
socioeconomic status (SES), exercise and 134,
    152, 192, 193t, 199
sodium DL-lactate infusions 119
soleus muscles, emotion and 109, 110f
somatic nervous system 42, 42f-43f
soul, dualism vs. monism of 4-5, 9
Spearman, Charles 23, 25
Special Olympics 170
special populations
  activity behavior change for 192
  self-esteem in 159-160, 170-171, 170f
specificity, in research 32, 35
specific variance, in exploratory factor analysis 24
Spencer, Herbert 8
spinal cord, functional anatomy of 44, 44f-45f
spinal nerves 42, 43f, 44, 45f, 109
sports psychology, exercise psychology vs. ix, 1, 11
stage of change
  in behavior change 219-223, 220f, 222f, 226
  as exercise determinant 193t, 202
  intervention based on 231-232, 232t, 234
staleness, as syndrome 113-114
Stanford Five-City Project 236-237
startle eye-blink response. See acoustic startle
    eye-blink response
state anxiety 117-122, 117f, 119f, 125
Stevens' power law, of human perception 259-
    262, 282, 282f
stimuli
  in activity measurement 33-34
  in behaviorism 212-215
  control of, as intervention 243-244
  in emotion theory 97-98
  in perceived exertion 257-259, 261, 264,
    276-277, 277f
strain
  relative, as fitness indicator 29
  stress vs. 75, 79
strategy, in behavior change theory 222, 222f.
    See also exercise intervention(s)
strength of excitement (SE), in perceived
    exertion 273
strength training
  mental effects of 104, 120, 139, 168, 171, 214
  sleep impact of 184, 184f
stress 75-89. See also specific type
  acute vs. chronic 48, 50, 78-89
  contemporary views on 86-88
  coping with 76-79, 77f, 85
  definition of 48, 50, 76, 76f, 78-79
  emotional vs. exercise 81-86, 82f-83f, 84t, 86f
  exercise for reduction of 79-80
  historical views of 76-78
  Web sites on 89
stress management 79-80
stressors 75
  cross adaptation hypothesis of 76-77, 77f
  dimensions of 78-79
  research limitations on 87-88
stress response
  common features of 80, 81t, 88
  "fight-or-flight" as 50, 52, 52f, 77f, 81-82, 88
  physiology of 77-78, 80
    acute vs. chronic 48, 50, 78-79
    autonomic nervous system in 81-86,
      81t, 84t
    emotional vs. exercise 81-86
    endocrine system in 80-81
    hypothalamic-pituitary-adrenal cortex
      system in 77, 83f, 85-86, 86f

perceived 51-53, 58, 77*f*, 82, 83*f*
  research limitations on 86-88
  sympatho-vagal component 81-85, 82*f*-83*f*, 84*t*
striatum 46
  in affect and emotion 100, 108-109
  in anxiety response 126, 129
structural equation modeling (SEM), of psychological constructs 27-28, 27*f*
subjective experience
  measurement of 19-22, 104-106
  psychological constructs of ix, 18-19
subordinate symptoms, in perceived exertion 276-277, 276*f*
substance abuse
  as exercise determinant 192, 194*t*, 203
  in muscle dysmorphia 173-174
  sleep disturbances with 181*f*, 182
substance-induced mental disorders 115, 132
substantia nigra, functional anatomy of 45*f*, 46-47, 47*f*
Suci, G. 22-23
suicide, depression as risk for 132, 133*f*
summated scales, for subjective experience 20-21, 27
superordinate symptoms, in perceived exertion 276-277, 276*f*
supervision, as exercise determinant 193*t*-194*t*, 195, 202, 205
Surgeon General, U.S.
  major conclusions from 12, 13*f*, 73, 118, 134
  reports of x, 9, 12
surveys. *See* self-reports
survival of the fittest 8, 124
swimming 32, 114, 120, 281
symbolic models, as theory 211-212, 212*t*
sympathetic nervous system (SNS), functional anatomy of 42*f*, 48-50, 49*f*
  in endocrine system 52, 52*f*, 55
  heart rate variability and 51-52, 51*f*
  in mental responses 107-108, 128
  in stress response 87-89
sympatho-vagal component, of stress response 81-85, 82*f*-83*f*, 84*t*
synapses, of neurons 53-54, 53*f*, 265

T
Tannenbaum, Percy 22-23
target behavior
  exercise characteristics as 229-230
  in self-efficacy theory 218, 219*f*
  in social cognitive theory 216*t*, 217-218
  in stage theories 220-221
task aversion, in perceived exertion 274, 275*f*-276*f*
task orientation, in interventions 234
tax incentives, as intervention 250
telencephalon 44*f*, 46
television viewing, as exercise determinant 203, 250
temperament 93, 103, 273
  emotion *vs.* 94, 102, 112
  in trait anxiety 117-118
temperature regulation. *See* body temperature
temporal dimension, of behavior change 36, 219, 239
tension, affect activation and 92
termination stage, of behavior change 221
test-free measurement 20
tests and testing, of psychological constructs 18, 20
  exercise applications of. *See* exercise testing

thalamus 44*f*, 46, 48*f*, 126
theory, symbolic models as 211-212, 212*t*
thermogenic hypothesis, of mood 112
Thoughts During Exercise Scale 113
threat(s), as stressful 78-79, 117, 125
  physiological response to 80-82, 83*f*
Thurstone scale, of subjective experience 20
thyroid-stimulating hormone 52
time element
  as exercise determinant 201-202, 239, 239*t*
  in perceived exertion 274
time-out hypothesis, of anxiety 119-120, 125
time zone travel, sleep disturbances with 187-188
total sleep time (TST), exercise impact on 180, 183, 183*t*-184*t*
trails, as intervention 238-239, 238*t*
training programs
  affect and mood effects of 106-109, 112
  anxiety effects of 120-122, 124, 128-129
  depression reduction with 137, 139-143, 139*f*-140*f*
  perceived exertion in 278, 281
  perceived force in 282-283
  self-esteem effects of 167-169, 171, 171*f*-172*f*
  sleep effects of 183-184, 184*f*, 184*t*
  stress reduction with 83, 85-86
trait anxiety 36, 117-118, 117*f*, 121
traits, definition of 93, 95*f*, 103
transcription, gene, in brain 58-61, 63
translation, gene, in brain 58-61
transtheoretical model, of behavior change 191, 218, 220-223, 220*f*, 226
travel, sleep disturbances with 187-188
treadmill exercise. *See also* running; walking
  affect and mood impact of 85-86, 108-109, 113
  depression impact of 150, 151*f*
  perceived exertion in 278, 281
  timing of, for fitness measurement 30*t*
triadic reciprocality, in social cognitive theory 217*f*, 218
tricyclic antidepressants (TCAs) 147*t*
tryptophan 57, 128, 150, 150*f*
type A behavior pattern (TABP), perceived exertion and 275
tyrosine, as neurotransmitter source 54-55, 58

U
unidimensionality, of subjective experience 20
unipolar affective disorders 104-105, 133, 133*t*, 136
units of movement, as activity measure 31
Upper Bavarian field study 135, 135*f*
up-regulation hypothesis, of depression 146-147
urbanization, as exercise determinant 192, 195*f*, 205-206, 207*t*
U.S. population
  national health goals for x, 12, 13*f*, 72, 118, 134
  physical activity trends of x, 135, 141, 229, 251

V
vagus nerve
  in heart rate variability 51, 84*t*
  in stress response 81-85, 82*f*-83*f*, 84*t*, 88
valence
  of affect 92-93, 92*f*, 99, 102-103
  of emotion 98-99
validity and validation
  in activity measurement 32-33

ecological, of research 111, 122
  of psychological constructs 18-19, 22, 37, 63
  of self-esteem 162-163, 165
values, as activity foundation 8, 224, 233
variables
  in activity measurement 30-34, 37-38
  in affect, mood, and emotion 102-103
  in behaviorism 213-214
  in factor analysis
    confirmatory 25-26, 26*f*
    exploratory 23-25, 24*f*-25*f*, 24*t*
  in structural equation modeling 27-28, 27*f*
variance
  in factor analysis 24-26, 26*f*
  in structural equation modeling 28
variance-covariance matrix
  in confirmatory factor analysis 25-26
  in structural equation modeling 27-28, 27*f*
ventilation, in perceived exertion 269, 272, 274, 281, 283
  minute 268, 269*t*, 270
ventral tegmental area (VTA) 46
  in anxiety response 126, 127*f*
  in depression 147, 151
  reward pathway of 54, 55*f*
verbal persuasion, in self-efficacy enhancement 219, 247-248, 248*t*
volunteers, for research 37

W
wakefulness, during night sleep 183
walking. *See also* treadmill exercise
  mental effects of 13, 107, 111-112, 144, 151
  strategies to increase 32, 237-238
Walk-to-School Day 238
Walter, W.G. 67
Watson, John B. 213
Weber's law, of human perception 258
Web sites
  on affect, mood and emotion 114
  on anxiety 130
  on behavioral neuroscience 72
  on behavior change 227, 253
  on depression 153
  on exercise determinants 209
  for exercise interventions 253
  on exercise psychology theory 15
  on perceived exertion 284
  on self-esteem 175
  on sleep 188
  on stress 89
weight bearing, as activity marker 34*t*
weightlifting. *See* strength training
weight loss, programs for 14, 107, 160, 233, 236, 242
well-being, psychological. *See* mental health
withdrawal, in emotion theory 98
within network validity, of self-esteem 163
work psychology. *See* occupational work
work site, as intervention setting 236, 238*t*
World Health Organization 73
worship places, intervention associated with 236, 250
Wundt, Wilhelm ix, 5-7, 6*f*, 92

Y
YMCA/YWCA, as intervention setting 236
yohimbine 128
Youth Risk Behavior Survey 197-198, 203

About the Authors

Janet Buckworth, PhD, is an assistant professor of sport and exercise science at The Ohio State University in Columbus. She has written and presented extensively on exercise psychology and behavior change.

Dr. Buckworth is a member of the Society of Behavioral Medicine and the American Alliance for Health, Physical Education, Recreation and Dance. She is also an American College of Sports Medicine fellow.

She resides in Columbus, Ohio, and enjoys jogging, canoeing, and reading science fiction.

Rod K. Dishman, PhD, is a professor of exercise science and the director of the Exercise Psychology Laboratory at The University of Georgia at Athens. He has served as a consultant on exercise to government agencies in the United States, Canada, and Europe.

Dr. Dishman is an American College of Sports Medicine fellow and a member of the jury for selection of the Olympic Prize in Sport Science awarded biannually by the Medical Commission of the International Olympic Committee.

He resides in Athens, Georgia, and enjoys running and resistance exercise.